THE
WISDEN
GUIDE TO
CRICKET GROUNDS

THE
WISDEN
GUIDE TO
CRICKET GROUNDS
William Powell

Stanley Paul

London

In memory of my grandmother Jessie May Graveney Powell

Stanley Paul & Co. Ltd

An imprint of Random Century Group Ltd
20 Vauxhall Bridge Road, London SW1V 2SA

Random Century Australia (Pty) Ltd
20 Alfred Street, Milsons Point, Sydney, NSW 2061, Australia

Random Century New Zealand Ltd
PO Box 40–086, Glenfield, Auckland, 10 New Zealand

Random Century South Africa (pty) Ltd
PO Box 337, Bergvlei, 2012, South Africa

© William A. Powell 1992

Phototypeset by Raven Typesetters, Ellesmere Port
Printed and bound in Great Britain by
Butler & Tanner Ltd, Frome, Somerset

British Library Cataloguing in Publication Data
Powell, William A.
  Wisden guide to cricket grounds
    1. England. Cricket grounds
    I. Title

ISBN 0 09 177188 9

Contents

Foreword

I am pleased to be asked to write a foreword to the second edition of the Wisden Guide To Cricket Grounds. This most useful publication will assume even greater importance in 1992 with the introduction of Durham C C C as the eighteenth First Class County. I suspect that many players and spectators making the trip to the north for the first time will need all the navigational assistance they can get.

How I wish there had been a Wisden Guide in 1983 when, despite being injured, I was forced to play in a Sunday League match against Surrey because two of my Northamptonshire team-mates got totally lost trying to find the ground at East Molesey!

The guide might also have been useful to the two young Middlesex cricketers who, when travelling from Lord's to an Under 25 match at Blackheath, got as far as a sign saying 'Dover 7' before they realised they might just have overshot their target! One of the players, incidentally, went on to play for England.

The guide is a must for any County cricketer's glove compartment as well as being an important point of reference on the TCCB bookshelves. I congratulate the author and am sure that in time this revised and updated second edition to the Wisden library will become as much a cricketing bible as the Almanack itself.

Tim Lamb

TIM LAMB
Cricket Secretary,
Test and County
Cricket Board
January 1992

TCCB

FOREWORD to First Edition

With all the cricketing blood flowing through the Powell family, it is hardly surprising that William – with suitable domestic encouragement – has produced such an excellent guide to our cricket grounds.

This work could have been achieved only by meticulous attention to detail and the support of so many dedicated county officials, without whom our game could not survive.

I congratulate the Powells, as well as my long-standing friend and critic Alex Bannister, and I hope that the book receives the acclaim it deserves. It is another important part of our cricketing history which both present and future lovers of the game will enjoy.

RAMAN SUBBA ROW
Chairman, Test and
County Cricket Board
March 1989

Acknowledgements

I am grateful to Alex Bannister for allowing me to include in this second edition the original short historial studies of the seventeen first-class counties, which I have revised and up-dated in this edition. I also extend my thanks to my father Peter W.G. Powell FRIBA, FRTPI, who has again contributed the sketch plans of all the grounds included in this edition together with the revision of the plans which appeared in the first edition.

I would also like thank the following who have assisted in a variety of ways in the preparation of the first and second editions of the guide book:

M. Aaronson, P.A.B. Abbott, C.T. Adamson, N.C. Allison, P.J. Andrews, R. Appleyard, D.J.M. Armstrong, M. Atkinson, P.G.M. August, Mr and Mrs S.P. Austin, A.G. Avery, A.D.P. Baird, A.F. Baker, R.W. Barclay, R.S. Barker, C.J. Bartlett, Miss R. Batra, M. Beaty, L. Beaumont, R.A. Beck, W. Bell, N. Bett, the late T. Billson, A.J. Birch, N.H. Birch, C. Bracey, J.M. Brearley, D.J.W. Bridge, R.W. Brooke, A. Brown, Mrs C. Byatt, G.C. Capper, A. Cheyne, Dr S.J. Cohen, S.P. Coverdale, D. Cracknell, C.M.S. Crombie, R. Cropper, J. Davies, S. Davies, B.T. Denning, J.B. Dixon, B. Doe, B. Dobson, D.S. Dredge, C.F. Driver, Miss A. Dunmayne, Miss D. Edgeley, Miss T. Edwards, P.J. Edwards, W. Edwards, G.R. Evans, H.S. Evans, F.J. Farmer, M.J. Fatkin, Miss R. Fitzgibbon, D.G. Fleetwood, W.R. Ford, J. Fox, A. Francis, W. Fuller, K.W. Gardiner, N. Garnham, M.E. Gear, R.A.N. Gillett, P.W. Gooden, Dr G. Gorski, S.E.A. Green, P. Griffiths, D. Guest, L.W. Hancock, J. Hardstaff, J.L.F. Harris, R. Harrison, C.D. Hassell, L.W. Hatton, P.W. Haynes, Rev. Canon H.F. Heal, D.M.W. Heath, Dr A.K. Hignell, M.F. Hill, C.E. Holland, Dr G. Holland, R.H. Holland, E. Howard, J.W.G. Howells, B. Hunt, B.H. Hurst, the late J. Iley, R.V. and V.H. Isaacs, C. James, P.J. James, D. Jenkins, D.E. Jones, W.D. Jones, L.V. Kelly, T.M. Lamb, R.J. Lark, E.I. Lester, K. Lewis, Mr and Mrs V.J. Lewis, the late J. Lister, D. Littlewood, Miss V. Lloyd, J.R. Lodge, E.E. Lomas, Rev. M.G. Lorimer, A. Lowe, J.D. Mace, G. McKiddie, N. Malik, N.A. Malik, S. Malik, T.J. Maple, Z.B. Marolia, H. Marsden, C.F.V. Martin, M.F. Martin, W.O. Matthews, R. Mawer, R. May, B. Maylen, T.D. Meneer, H.W.R. Milner, H.R. Milton, K. Montgomery, L.T. Newell, the late L.F. Newnham, C.F. Niker, C. Oakley, H.A. Osborne, D. Paul, F.G. Peach, A.J. Pearce, D. Pearce, B. Perkins, J.B. Pickup, P. Pigott, I.W. Plant, M. Pope, Dr S.R. Porter, M. Powell, D.P. Price, M. Pritchard, D. Pyne, D.E. Radcliffe, A. Rees, M. Robinson, Mr and Mrs M. Robertson, A.J. Robertson, P. Robins, P. Robinson, P.J. Robinson, B. Robson, D.M. Ryder, D. Scott, P.L. Scowcroft, D.G. Seward, C. Sexton, H.P.H. Sharp, Miss D. Shead, C.R. Sheppard, S.J. Skinner, K. Slaney, A.C. Smith, A.T. Smith, J.E.O. Smith, the late P.W. Smith, E.E. Snow, E. Solomon, M. Stanger, L. Stapleton, D.V. Stephen, E.J.H. Stephens, J.A. Stephens, Lt. Col. J.R. Stephenson, M. Stones, J. Stroud, R. Subba Row, P. Sykes, S.W. Tacey, M. Tarr, C.H. Taylor, J.J. Taylor, R. Thomas, R. Thurston, S.J. Tomlin, F.M. Turner, the late K.C. Turner, Rev M.G. Vockins, S.J. Wade, J. Warham, R. Whitworth, D.K. Wild, R.D. Wilkinson, G. Williams, R.J. Williams, W. Williams, A.J. Whinham, C.F. Woodhouse, D.H. Wright, L. Wynne, P. Wynne-Thomas, J.H.D. Young.
Many of the plans of grounds have in part been derived from Ordnance Survey material with the sanction of the Controller of Her Majesty's Stationery Office (Crown copyright reserved).

The Ground Plans

All ground plans are diagrammatic and are to an approximate scale
of 1:2000. Every attempt has been made to include as much
information as possible bearing in mind the size of the plans.

When defining seating areas, covered seating has taken preference
over open seating in those areas where open seating is banked above
covered seating as found at the major Test Match grounds. Executive
boxes and similar restricted covered areas have also been defined as
covered seating.

Toilets situated in separate buildings have been defined on the
plans, but additional toilets are to be found within most of the areas
of tiered seating and in other permanent buildings. Similarly, the
refreshment and restaurant facilities are usually to be found in the
existing permanent buildings or in temporary accommodation
specially provided on match days.

The areas available to the general public and to club members are
clearly defined at all the county grounds, but at local club grounds
and other venues only used on a single or a few days each year
arrangements may vary from match to match and from year to year.
Special arrangements apply at the six Test Match grounds and at any
other grounds where reserved numbered seat tickets and car park
tickets are sold in advance.

Key

◀	ENTRANCE		PITCH
	PAVILION		EXTENT OF PLAYING AREA
	COVERED SEATING		MARQUEES ANI TENTS
	OPEN SEATING		WALL OR FEN'
SB	SCOREBOARD		HEDGE
T	TOILETS		TREES
	OTHER BUILDINGS		BANF

Key to Ground Records and Scores

(PC)	Prudential Cup
(PT)	Prudential Trophy
(TT)	Texaco Trophy
(GC)	Gillette Cup
(NWBT)	National Westminster Bank Trophy
(BHC)	Benson & Hedges Cup
(JPL)	John Player Sunday League
(RAL)	Refuge Assurance Sunday League
(RAC)	Refuge Assurance Cup
(FT)	Fenner Trophy
(Asda)	Asda Challenge Trophy
(SFT)	Scarborough Festival Trophy
(JTFT)	Joshua Tetley Festival Trophy
(TTC)	Tilcon Trophy Competition
(ST)	Seeboard Trophy
(BC)	The Bass Cup
(SWE)	South Wales Electricity
(EE)	English Estates Knockout Cup
(Friendly)	Friendly Match
(Tour)	Tourists Match

Notes on Where to Stay and How to Get There

If you are planning a longer stay or require further details on where to eat en route, special bargain stays and local facilities/places of interest, contact the local Tourist Information Centre for city/town which you are visiting. Telephone numbers and addresses of Tourist Information Centres are available from Directory Enquiries.

If you plan to use public transport or your own – whether by bus, car, rail or air – refer to your local Bus Station, AA, RAC, British Rail Travel Centre/Station or travel agent for specific details.

N

DURHAM
HOUGHTON-LE-SPRING

YORKSHIRE
LEEDS (BASS HEADINGLEY)

LANCASHIRE
MANCHESTER
(OLD TRAFFORD)

NOTTINGHAMSHIRE
NOTTINGHAM (TRENT BRIDGE)

DERBYSHIRE
DERBY

LEICESTERSHIRE
LEICESTER

WARWICKSHIRE
BIRMINGHAM (EDGBASTON)

NORTHAMPTONSHIRE
NORTHAMPTON

WORCESTERSHIRE
WORCESTER

ESSEX
CHELMSFORD

MCC/MIDDLESEX
LONDON (LORD'S)

GLAMORGAN
CARDIFF

SURREY
LONDON
(THE FOSTER'S
OVAL)

SOMERSET
TAUNTON

KENT
CANTERBURY

SUSSEX
HOVE

HAMPSHIRE
SOUTHAMPTON

GLOUCESTERSHIRE
BRISTOL

Map of the Grounds in UK and Ireland

Introduction

In this second edition of the guide I have revised all existing sections to up-date information, facts generally and statistics. I have also included the newly appointed eighteenth first-class county Durham C C C, as well as the Minor Counties Cricket Association, Scotland, Ireland, League Cricket Conference and the Don Valley Stadium, which were not included in the first edition.

The grounds used regularly for county cricket now number about one hundred in all and vary from Lord's to the simplest of small club grounds, and from the established stadia that can accommodate some 28,000 spectators with facilities of every type, including covered seating and executive boxes, to simple local recreation grounds used for cricket (and other sports) with a modest clubhouse, a scoreboard and space for no more than 2,000 spectators on temporary seats.

Despite the contrasting nature of these grounds, all now provide the opportunity for the playing and watching of county cricket. This arises in part from the willingness of the County Clubs to travel from their home base – the County Ground – and, in the case of Derbyshire, Durham, Glamorgan, Gloucestershire, Northamptonshire and Nottinghamshire, to travel into adjoining counties which have no first-class cricket. All this requires dedicated work, not only from the county officials but also from the officials and members of the local clubs concerned. This work involves the provision of many hundreds of temporary seats, the construction of temporary tiered seating, the erection of tents and marquees for refreshments and hospitality, accommodation for officials (even players), temporary toilets, first-aid facilities, souvenir shops, press areas and the designation of suitable car parking areas. In this manner, therefore, nearly eighty grounds which otherwise attract only a few local club spectators and have only a single permanent building – a pavilion or clubhouse - and a carefully nurtured cricket square are transformed into venues for first-class county cricket attracting perhaps 5,000 or more spectators on a single day.

In addition to the familiar county cricket grounds (which include the ever more familiar – thanks to television coverage – six Test Match Grounds), first-class cricket is played at a variety of venues including private clubs, recreation grounds, universities, public schools and even grounds which form part of factory premises.

I have continued to communicate regularly with all club secretaries and other representatives, and with very few execptions each ground has been visited personally in order to record in detail its features and to check on the information supplied. Facts have been assembled on the establishment of the clubs and their general history and the cricket that has taken place since the inception of each ground. I am particularly grateful to all those clubs which have provided detailed plans of their grounds and the layout of facilities during a county match. However, improvements and changes are constantly being made at most grounds. At the smaller grounds, which only provide county cricket on a single day per year, the layout of facilities may vary as they are set out differently from year to year. This particularly applies to areas restricted to members and sponsors.

Some of the grounds included will be unfamiliar to many regular cricket followers and it is hoped that this volume will continue to be an indispensable guide for all those interested in cricket, whether they are players, officials or spectators who are intending to visit one of the grounds or simply watch on the television or listen to the radio. My visits to the grounds and my discussions and correspondence with those involved have been extensive in an attempt to be as accurate as possible, but there will still be omissions and no doubt errors. I trust that readers will keep the author informed of any discrepancies and changes so that future editions of the guide may be as thorough and up-to-date as possible. I would like to take this opportunity to thank all those readers who took the trouble to draw my attention to errors in the first edition.

This introduction cannot be concluded without my thanking, firstly, Tim Lamb, the Cricket Secretary of the Test and County Cricket Board, for kindly writing the foreword to this second edition and, secondly, the many people who have assisted me with this work. I have tried to record all those who have made some contribution in the Acknowledgements.

WILLIAM A. POWELL
Hemel Hempstead, Hertfordshire
January 1992

OTHER PUBLICATIONS BY THE AUTHOR

TRENT BRIDGE

CRICKET PAVILIONS
by William A. Powell
A series of 20 cards

Compiled by the author, this high quality set of full colour cards contains each major county cricket pavilion plus Oxford, Cambridge and Arundel. Each card has potted historical information printed on the reverse side.

The Pavilion at the Racecourse Ground, Durham City, Co. Durham.

DURHAM COUNTY CRICKET CLUB
Inaugural 1st class season

A fine series of postcards in full colour depicting the seven grounds to be used by Durham C.C.C. during the 1992 season. Brief historical notes on the reverse of each card by William A. Powell. Supplied with presentation envelope printed with the County crest.

Available from **County Print Services,**
28 Shakespeare Square, Hainault, Ilford, Essex IG6 2RU

MARYLEBONE CRICKET CLUB

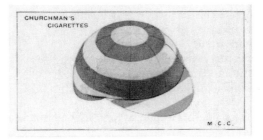

LONDON – LORD'S

Marylebone Cricket Club

Founded 1787
Colours Red and yellow
Crest The letters 'MCC'
Patron Her Majesty The Queen
President M.E.L. Melluish
Treasurer G.H.G. Doggart
Chairman of Finance D.L. Hudd
Secretary Lt. Col. J.R. Stephenson OBE
Assistant secretary administration J.R. Smith
Assistant secretary cricket J.A. Jameson
Assistant secretary finance M.R. Blow
Curator S.E.A. Green
Head coach C.T. Radley
Captain (selected on a match by match basis)
Groundsman M.J. Hunt
Ground Administrator A.W.P. Fleming
ICC administrator Miss S.A. Lawrence
Scorer/statistician E. Solomon
Computer Scoreboard Miss P. Whitehorn
Newsletter *MCC From Lord's*
Address Lord's Cricket Ground, St John's Wood Road, London NW8
8QN.
Telephone 071 289 1611/5 (pavilion reception)
071 289 8979 (club office)
071 289 3649 (indoor school)
071 289 1757 (shop)
071 289 8011 (prospects of play)
071 266 3825 (Gestetner tour of Lord's office)
Facsimile 071 289 9100
Rapid Cricketline County Scores 0891 567500
Test Match Commentaries Rapid Cricketline 0891 567567
Test Match Updates Rapid Cricketline 0891 567555

GROUND

London (Lord's Cricket Ground, St John's Wood Road).
No other grounds have been used since 1814.

SECOND XI (MCC YOUNG CRICKETERS)
In addition to the above mentioned ground the following are used for
Second XI matches: Birkbeck College (University of London), Birkbeck
Avenue, Oldfield Lane, Greenford. Telephone: 081 578 1930; National
Westminster Bank Sports Ground, Turle Road, Norbury, Surrey.
Telephone: (pavilion) 081 764 1170, (office) 081 679 5638.

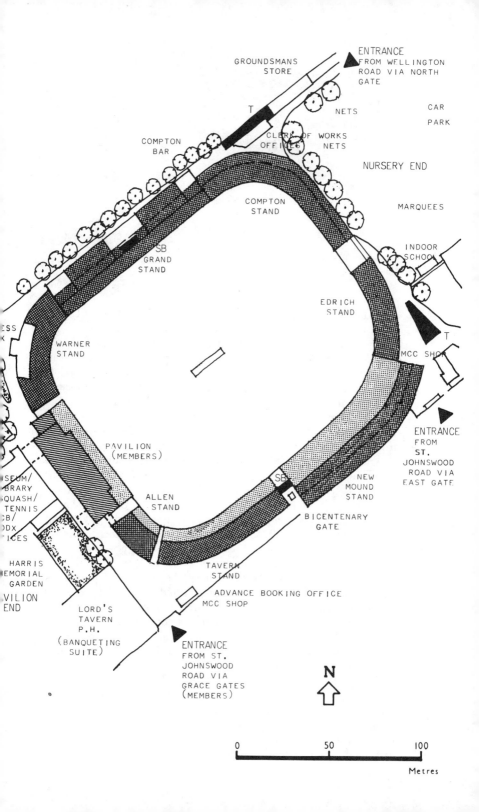

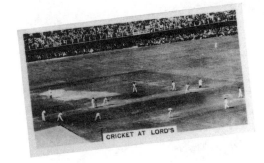

CRICKET AT LORD'S

WILLS'S CIGARETTES

THE KING AT A TEST MATCH, LORDS

The Marylebone Cricket Club was founded in 1787 and its early history relates directly to the development of Lord's cricket ground itself. Thomas Lord, a Yorkshireman born in Thirsk in 1755, had by 1780 found his way to London where he took employment at the recreation ground at White Conduit Fields, Islington. Here he met members of the White Conduit Cricket Club, founded in 1782, who were not satisfied with the cricket ground in Islington and suggested to Lord that he should find them a more exclusive ground for their use. This he found at Dorset Fields (Dorset Square now forms part of this area) and leased the ground from the Portman Estates. In 1787 the first match was played on this ground between Middlesex and Essex and the Marylebone Cricket Club was founded by Thomas Lord's patrons from the White Conduit Club head by Lord Winchilsea.

Thomas Lord and the cricket ground prospered as the ground became the principal cricket venue in London, which then had a population of little more than 750,000. Marylebone Cricket Club inherited from the Hambledon Cricket Club the responsibility for the government of the game throughout the country and two hundred years later still retains power to make the Laws of Cricket. It was, however, not too long before the expansion of the built-up area of London forced Lord and the Marylebone Cricket Club to move in 1810 to another ground in the area south of the present Lodge Road. This did not prove a popular ground and in 1812 the decision to construct the Regents Canal forced Lord to make a second move, taking with him on each occasion, it is said, the turf from the original pitch.

The first match on this ground at St. John's Wood was played between MCC and Hertfordshire C C C on 22 June 1814 and it was here that the M.C.C. found its permanent home. In 1825 Lord had visions of developing much of the ground area for housing as the district of St John's Wood was being developed at this time. This was probably prevented by the action of William Ward, a member of the club who

LORD'S

CHURCHMAN'S CIGARETTES

M.C.C.

bought out Lord. Later in 1835 Ward handed over to James Dark, under whose control the ground remained until 1864 when he sold the lease of the ground to the Club. To this day the former sweet shop, now souvenir clothing outlet, below the New Mound Stand still retains the name Dark's Shop. In 1860 the club had missed the opportunity to purchase the freehold but finally six years later paid Mr Moses £18,000 for the freehold of the ground as it then existed. This precipitated the improvement and extension of the pavilion and a new grandstand for the public. The first full-time groundsman was also employed. It was about this time that the then secretary, R.A. Fitzgerald, introduced the now familiar red and yellow colours of the club in place of the original blue and white.

In 1877 the club came to an agreement with Middlesex C C C to provide a home for the County Club and this arrangement has continued ever since. While the Australians were to meet MCC in a one-day match on their first tour of England in 1878, it was not until 1884 that England met Australia in a Test Match at Lord's, The Kennington Oval having led the way in staging Test cricket in the capital.

In 1887 the centenary of MCC was celebrated with a dinner in the Long Room and during this period the membership, then just over 5,000 was constantly increasing. While the then grandstand had two stories of covered seating, it was realized that the pavilion would have to be replaced. A new pavilion was built in 1889–90 designed by architect Thomas Verity (who had worked on details of the Royal Albert Hall), which stands to this day with little alteration to its external appearance; the only extensions being the professionals' changing rooms and the press box adjoining the north end which have since been converted to a members' bar and the MCC offices. Shortly afterwards the Club purchased a nursery garden at the eastern end of the ground, but no sooner had this been done than the Manchester and Sheffield Railway Company attempted to purchase the area for the development of the railway line from Marylebone Station. After due consideration the Club relinquished the freehold of the strip of land bordering Wellington Road currently the members' car park area and received in exchange the site of the Clergy Orphan School to the south, where the MCC Indoor Cricket School and main MCC Souvenir Shop are now sited.

It has been said that certain of the excavations from the tunnels below the Wellington Road side of the ground were used as banking for the original Mound Stand built in 1898–99 on the area which was previously the old tennis and racket courts, and which were rebuilt at the rear of the pavilion. Already critics were likening the ground to an amphitheatre and suggesting that Thomas Lord would 'turn in his grave' at the transformation.

Expansion continued apace with the advent of the twentieth century and the club was to acquire new responsibilities. In 1898 the Board of Control was set up under the chairmanship of the President of MCC to organize Test cricket in England. In 1904 the Advisory County Cricket Committee was founded and in 1909 England, Australia and South Africa founded the Imperial Cricket Conference. In 1903 the MCC also took over from various sponsors the responsibility of arranging and financing official England tours overseas. All these bodies had their headquarters at Lord's and still do to this day, although re-formed and completely separated administratively from the MCC in the form of the Test & County Cricket Board and the International Cricket Conference.

The new grandstand was built on the north side of the ground to the designs of architect Sir Herbert Baker, who had been responsible for many public buildings including the Bank of England and India House. He also presented to the MCC the now famous 'Father Time' weather vane which was to become an internationally known Lord's landmark.

In 1923 the Grace Gates were erected at the entrance on St John's Wood Road and in 1934 the garden was developed in memory of Lord Harris. It has since become traditional for team photographs to be taken in this garden. The 'Q' Stand was also built at the same time and all were the work of Sir Herbert Baker. The Stands at the nursery end were also erected and the car park developed beyond the nursery ground, and care was taken to retain the tree screen dividing the main ground from the nursery. 1937 saw the celebration of the Club's 150th anniversary. The Second World War gave the 66-year-old Sir Pelham Warner the opportunity to take charge at Lord's as acting Secretary while Col. R.S. Rait-Kerr was on war service. While the nursery ground became a barrage balloon site and Father Time was pulled down by a balloon cable, Lord's stayed open and 13,000 spectators watched a match on 10 August 1940. Lord's escaped serious damage and in 1945 international cricket recommenced, with matches against the Australians, in the 'Victory' Test and later against the Dominions.

In 1945 the MCC appointed its first curator and this led to the establishment of the Memorial Gallery which was opened in 1953. Further development took place in 1958 with the building of the Warner Stand with its two levels, snack bars and press box on the site of the single storey 'A' enclosure between the Pavilion and the grandstand. In

1968 the tavern and the adjoining buildings were demolished and replaced by the New Tavern Stand and the Lord's Tavern was itself re-sited adjoining the Grace Gates and the new banqueting suite. By 1969 the Club's direct control of first-class professional cricket in the United Kingdom had been relinquished to the Test & County Cricket Board (TCCB), in 1968 the National Cricket Association had taken over the responsibilities for amateur cricket and in the same year all professional cricket in the United Kingdom became the responsibility of the TCCB, leaving the MCC with the responsibility only for the Laws of Cricket. The Cricket Council was also established in 1968, composed of representatives of all cricketing authorities in the United Kingdom. The National Club Cricket Championship final has been staged at Lord's since 1969 and the National Village Championship final since 1972.

While so much of the Club's public duty has been transferred to other bodies, the MCC remains a large private club of some 18,000 members (and a substantial waiting list), with a magnificent ground, and is to most cricket lovers worldwide still the spiritual home of the great game. In 1987 the Club celebrated its bicentenary and marked this by the complete re-development of the Mound Stand and the erection of the Bicentenary Gates on the St John's Wood Road side of the ground. During 1989–91 the stands at the Nursery End were re-constructed following their naming in 1989 as the Compton and Edrich stands. The new stands were opened on 27 May 1991 by Denis Compton and Justin Edrich (son of Bill Edrich) during the luncheon interval of the third Texaco Trophy one-day international between England and the West Indies. The well-publicized delays to this construction did not prevent the re-construction winning the building category of the Concrete Society's award for 1991. The architects were Michael Hopkins & Partners, who were also responsible for the New Mound Stand. The ground is now truly closer to the amphitheatre which had first been a criticism in 1903.

In 1989 the 'Q' Stand was renamed the Sir George Allen Stand and this now includes at the lower level an enclosed MCC/Middlesex C C C members' room, from which cricket can be viewed and refreshments taken. This room is available to Middlesex members only during Middlesex matches. There is a display of Middlesex C C C memorabilia in cabinets and photographs on the walls. The MCC celebrated its bicentenary in 1987 with a match against the Rest of the World XI. Since 1989 the MCC has played the Champion County in the opening match of the season, which has been played for the Bass Trophy/Shield. The MCC versus Tourists match is played for the Bass Cup. In 1992 the MCC versus Champion County Essex has been classed as an England 'A' team and not an MCC XI.

London – Lord's

DESCRIPTION OF GROUND AND FACILITIES

The main entrance to the ground is from St. John's Wood Road through the Grace Gates, and is used by members and their guests. The public gain entrance through the North Entrance turnstiles and the North Gate for members and guests. The North Gate is also the entrance to the members' car park from Wellington Road which is restricted to MCC and Middlesex C C C members only. An entrance through the East Gate and adjoining turnstiles in St John's Wood Road is also available for the public.

All the buildings in the ground are permanent. The pavilion is the centre-piece and includes the famous 'Long Room'. The members and their guests also have exclusive use of the Warner Stand, the upper and lower Tavern Stand and the Sir George Allen Stand, although the upper part is only available to MCC members. The New Mound Stand constructed in 1986–87 by Higgs and Hill Construction has a floor level of executive boxes, an upper level of debenture holders' seats and covered and open seating at the lower level which is partly covered for public spectators. The Nursery End includes the Compton and Edrich Stands comprising of an upper and lower tier and is available to the public. Part of this stand is for MCC members only. The grandstand, balcony and lower tier are also available to the public, this building also includes a number of private boxes at each end and adjoining the main scoreboard which is a traditional manually operated unit. The official scorers and computer scoreboard operator sit above this scoreboard and just below Father Time at the top of the grandstand. Under the grandstand there are a number of refreshment areas, the Compton Bar and the scorecard printers' office, where fully printed-up completed match cards can be obtained twenty minutes after close of play on big match days. The Warner Stand includes a refreshment area at ground level and at first floor level the Warner Stand Bar and above it the press box and TV commentary box positions. The computerized scoreboard installed in 1988 is situated between the Tavern Stand and the New Mound Stand and is operated from the scorers' box.

At the rear of the pavilion are the Memorial Gallery and Museum together with the MCC library, squash and real tennis courts. At the back of this building is the TCCB headquarters and National Cricket Association office. To the south are the Lord Harris Memorial garden and the Middlesex C C C office and club shop. To the rear of the Warner Stand is the Coronation Garden, where members picnic during luncheon intervals of popular matches.

The Lord's Tavern is now situated next to the Grace Gates and adjoining the Lord's Banqueting Suite. There are two MCC souvenir shops on the ground, a large temporary building close to the Grace Gates and the main shop adjoining the East Gate. For popular matches there are also three other smaller outlets situated around the ground which include a tent close to the players' nets at the Nursery End. At the Nursery End in addition to the members' car park and nursery practice area where players take nets and the Cross Arrows Cricket Club play during September there is the MCC Indoor Cricket School and MCC School cricket shop where cricket coaching and equipment can be obtained throughout the year. All toilets are permanent and all individual stands include appropriate facilities for spectators. All the stands have covered accommodation and refreshments can be obtained at a number of points around the ground. Lunches can be taken in the Banqueting Suite where booking is advised and in the Tavern itself.

The playing area is 166 metres by 133 metres within which the actual playing area is defined by a rope stretching to the appropriate dimensions depending on the position of the wicket being used. There are facilities for disabled spectators adjoining the pavilion, and in public areas a special enclosure is situated in front of the Warner Stand and between the Sir George Allen Stand and the pavilion. The TV camera position is sited on the first floor balcony of the pavilion with an additional camera position on a gantry high above the sightscreen at the Nursery End between the Compton and Edrich Stands. The radio commentary box is located above the visiting players' dressing room and committee dining room at the top of the pavilion.

The current ground capacity after improvements in 1989–91 is now set at 28,000 and this has been achieved for all the popular matches staged in 1991 which included the Texaco Trophy, Cornhill Test, Benson & Hedges Cup Final and National Westminster Bank Trophy Final. The stands are numbered A to Q from the Warner Stand round to the Sir George Allen Stand and for the popular matches spectators are advised to book seats in advance as all seats are reserved and numbered. Ticket applications can be made to Lord's direct during the winter months. Middlesex C C C matches rarely attract a full house except when the county progress in one of the limited-overs knockout competitions or have an attractive match with one of the tourists. For Middlesex C C C matches spectators can choose to sit wherever they like in the public areas. During Middlesex matches the lower part of the Sir George Allen Stand known as the Middlesex Room is only available to Middlesex C C C members. This room is used by MCC members only for Test Matches and one-day finals and has been used by the TCCB for guests at certain matches.

Lord's cricket ground is the Mecca of cricket and has surely the best facilities of all the grounds included within this guide book. Throughout the year the public can visit Lord's by joining one of the many daily Gestetner Tours of Lord's, details of which can be obtained from the MCC office.

ADDRESS Marylebone Cricket Club, Lord's Cricket Ground, St John's Wood Road, St John's Wood, London NW8 8QN.
TELEPHONE NUMBER PROSPECTS OF PLAY 071 286 8011

GROUND RECORDS AND SCORES

TEST MATCHES
Highest innings total for England: 653 for 4 dec. *v*. India 1990
Highest innings total against England: 729 for 6 dec. by Australia 1930
Lowest innings total for England: 53 *v*. Australia 1888
Lowest innings total against England: 42 by India 1974
Highest individual innings for England: 333 G.A. Gooch *v*. India 1990
Highest individual innings against England: 254 D.G. Bradman for Australia 1930

Best bowling performance in an innings for England: 8 for 34 I.T. Botham *v.* Pakistan 1978

Best bowling performance in an innings against England: 8 for 53 R.A.L. Massie for Australia 1972

Best bowling performance in a match for England: 15 for 104 H. Verity *v.* Australia 1934

Best bowling performance in a match against England: 16 for 137 R.A.L. Massie for Australia 1972

LIMITED-OVERS INTERNATIONALS

Highest innings total: 334 for 4 by England *v.* India (PC) 1975

Lowest innings total: 132 for 3 by India *v.* England (PC) 1975

Highest individual innings: 138 I.V.A. Richards for West Indies *v.* England (PC) 1979

Best bowling performance: 5 for 38 J. Garner for West Indies *v.* England (PC) 1979

LIMITED-OVERS FINALS (GC/NWBT)

Highest innings total: 317 for 4 by Yorkshire *v.* Surrey (GC) 1969

Lowest innings total: 118 by Lancashire *v.* Kent (GC) 1974

Highest individual innings: 146 G. Boycott for Yorkshire *v.* Surrey (GC) 1969

Best bowling performance: 6 for 29 J. Garner for Somerset *v.* Northamptonshire (GC) 1979

LIMITED-OVERS FINALS (BHC)

Highest innings total: 290 for 6 by Essex *v.* Surrey 1979

Lowest innings total: 117 by Derbyshire *v.* Hampshire 1988

Highest individual innings: 132 n.o. I.V.A. Richards for Somerset *v.* Surrey 1981

Best bowling performance: 5 for 13 S.J. Jefferies for Hampshire *v.* Derbyshire 1988

FIRST-CLASS MATCHES

Highest innings total for MCC: 607 *v.* Cambridge University 1902

Highest innings total against MCC: 609 for 8 dec. by Cambridge University 1902

Lowest innings total for MCC: 15 *v.* Surrey 1839

Lowest innings total against MCC: 18 by Australians 1896

Highest individual innings for MCC: 278 W. Ward *v.* Norfolk 1820

Highest individual innings against MCC: 281 n.o. W.H. Ponsford for Australians 1934

Best bowling performance in an innings for MCC: 10 for 73 A. Shaw *v.* North 1874

Best bowling performance in an innings against MCC: 9 for 29 J. Lillywhite (Junior) for Sussex 1862

Best bowling performance in a match for MCC: 16 for 60 W.G. Grace *v.* Nottinghamshire 1885

Best bowling performance in a match against MCC: 16 for 93 C.D.B. Marsham for Gentlemen 1855

Best attendance: 137,915 England *v.* Australia 1953 (5 Days)

LIMITED-OVERS (BC)
Highest innings total for MCC: 224 for 4 *v.* New Zealanders 1990
Highest innings total against MCC: 309 for 4 by Australians 1989
Lowest innings total for MCC: 208 *v.* Australians 1989
Lowest innings total against MCC: 222 for 8 by New Zealanders 1990
Highest individual innings for MCC: 97 D.I.Gower *v.* New Zealanders 1990
Highest individual innings against MCC: 166 D.C. Boon for Australians 1989
Best bowling performance for MCC: 4 for 60 C.S. Cowdrey *v.* Australians 1989
Best bowling performance against MCC: 3 for 28 M.C. Snedden for New Zealanders 1990

MINOR COUNTIES C.A. KNOCKOUT FINAL LIMITED-OVERS FOR THE HOLT CUP
Highest innings total: 241 for 6 by Staffordshire *v.* Devon 1991
Lowest innings total: 188 for 7 by Hertfordshire *v.* Cumberland 1989
Highest individual innings: 108 n.o. S. Sharp for Cumberland *v.* Hertfordshire 1989
Best bowling performance: 4 for 44 D. Halliwell for Cumberland *v.* Hertfordshire 1989

NATIONAL VILLAGE CHAMPIONSHIP FINAL LIMITED-OVERS
Highest innings total: 267 for 5 by Goatacre *v.* Dunstall 1990
Lowest innings total: 82 for 9 by Longparish *v.* Marchwiel 1980
Highest individual innings: 123 K.M. Iles for Goatacre *v.* Dunstall 1990
Best bowling performance: 6 for 24 R. Coulson for Cookley *v.* Lindal Moor 1977.

For Middlesex C C C ground records and scores at Lord's, see Middlesex Section.

HOW TO GET THERE

Rail St John's Wood Underground Station (Jubilee Line), 0.5 mile.
Bus LRT 6, 8, 13, 16, 16A, 46, 74, 82, 113, 159 and 274 pass the ground. Also London Country Coaches 719, 757, 768 and 797 from home counties pass near ground. (Telephone: 071 222 1234).
Car From north: M1 to motorway terminal roundabout at Brent Cross, then follow North Circular Road, East A406, then branch left and follow signs West End, take A41 signposted Swiss Cottage and follow Finchley Road to St John's Wood, follow signs Lord's Cricket Ground and A5205 for St John's Wood Road and main Grace Gates entrance. The ground is situated opposite St John's Wood Church bounded by Wellington Road, Wellington Place, St John's Wood Road and Grove End Road, or follow A1 via Hendon and A41 signposted West End, then as above. From east: From Holloway district follow signs West End A503, then at Camden Town follow

signs Regent's Park A4201, enter Regent's Park at Gloucester Gate and use outer circle signposted London Zoo. After passing London Regent's Park Mosque, take immediate right into Hanover Gate and at T-junction take right into Park Road A41 for St John's Wood, keep left for St John's Wood Road A5205 at roundabout for Lord's Cricket Ground. From west: A40(M)/M41 follow signs Central London, then follow signs Paddington and A4206 in Bishop's Bridge Road, follow one-way system signposted Euston and follow A5 Edgware Road, then take right into St John's Wood Road A5202 for Lord's Cricket Ground. From south: From Hyde Park Corner follow signs Ring Road, Oxford into Park Lane A4202, then at Marble Arch follow signs Oxford Circus into Oxford Street A40, then at second traffic lights take A41 Portman Street, follow through Portman Square and Gloucester Place, follow signs A41 Aylesbury and the North, at John's Wood roundabout take left into St John's Wood Road A5205 for Lord's Cricket Ground.

No street parking, though limited areas available on meters and on Sundays. Car parking available for members only entrance from Cavendish Road and Wellington Road. During major matches local car parking is arranged by MCC for members on local school grounds. Public car parking in central London national car parks or near Regent's Park Zoo.

WHERE TO STAY AND OTHER INFORMATION

The Hilton International Regents Park Hotel (071 722 7722) opposite ground plus many other hotels in central or north-west London.

Disabled Areas   Special sections in front of Warner Stand and between Sir George Allen Stand and pavilion.
Local Radio Station(s)   Greater London Radio (94.9 MHz FM/1488 KHz MW), Capital Radio (95.8 MHz FM/1548 KHz MW), LBC (97.3 MHz FM/1152 KHz MW).
Local Newspaper(s)   Evening Standard.

DERBYSHIRE

DERBY

CHESTERFIELD

HEANOR

ILKESTON

CHEADLE

CHECKLEY

KNYPERSLEY

LEEK

REPTON

Derbyshire

Founded 4 November 1870
Colours Chocolate, Cambridge blue and amber
Crest Rose and imperial crown
President Rear Admiral Sir David Haslam KBE, CB, FRICS
Chairman of committee C.N. Middleton
Chairman of cricket committee B. Holling
Chief executive R.J. Lark
Administrative secretary H. Bakhda
County coach P.E. Russell
Cricket development officer A. Hill
Captain K.J. Barnett
Groundsman S. Birks
Scorer 1st XI S.W. Tacey
Scorer 2nd XI A. Aulton/M.R. Spencer
Statistician F. G. Peach
Sponsors Bass Carling Black Label
Newsletter *Derbyshire Members News*
Address County Cricket Ground, Nottingham Road, Derby, Derbyshire DE2 6DA
Telephone 0332 383211
Derbyshire Rapid Cricketline 0891 567501

ACHIEVEMENTS

County Championship Champions (1) 1936
Gillette Cup Finalists (1) 1969
National Westminster Bank Trophy Winners (1) 1981
Benson & Hedges Cup Finalists (2) 1978 and 1988
John Player Sunday League 3rd 1970
Refuge Assurance Sunday League Champions (1) 1990
Refuge Assurance Cup Finalists (1) 1990
Asda Trophy Winners (2) 1982 and 1985
Tilcon Trophy Finalists (1) 1977

GROUNDS

Derby (County Cricket Ground, Nottingham Road) Chesterfield (Queen's Park, Boythorpe Road) Heanor (Town Ground, Mayfield Road) Checkley (Uttoexter Road, Checkley) Knypersley (Victoria and Knypersley Social Welfare Centre, Tunstall Road) Leek (Highfield, Macclesfield Road) Ilkeston (Rutland Recreation Ground, West End Drive) Cheadle (Tean Road Sports Ground, Tean Road) and Repton (Repton School Ground, Repton).

Other grounds that have been used since 1969 are: Burton-upon-Trent (Ind-Coope Brewery Ground, Belevedere Road) (Allied Brewery

Sports Ground) Long Eaton (Trent College, Derby Road) Darley Dale (Station Road) and Buxton (The Park, Park Road).

SECOND XI GROUNDS
In addition to the above mentioned grounds the following are used for second XI matches: Belper Meadows C C, The Meadows, opposite Christchurch, Belper, Derbyshire. Telephone: 0773 826901; Shipley Hall C.C., Shipley Park, Shipley, Ilkeston, Derbyshire. Telephone: Directory Enquiries. Abbotsholme School, Rocester. Telephone: Directory Enquiries.

Derbyshire's reputation as a bowling force took root in their first first-class match at Manchester in 1871 when Lancashire, the only opponents deigning to meet them on equal terms, were routed for 25. To this day it is their lowest total in county cricket. Two years on Nottinghamshire, apparently succumbing to the lavish hospitality of a wine merchant at Wirksworth, staggered to 14 all out, an ignominy redressed in the course of time at Trent Bridge with Derbyshire dismissed for 16.

In 1874 Derbyshire, having won three and drawn one, were hailed as champions as the title at the time went to the side with the fewest defeats. A second opinion prevailed, however, that with only four matches played by Derbyshire it was an unfair situation and Gloucestershire were declared winners.

Inevitably the early years were an uphill climb and results were so bad that Derbyshire lost their first-class status for seven years. Money was tight, and the fraudulent enterprises of an assistant secretary were unmasked by none other than the legendary Australian fast bowler, F.R. ('Demon') Spofforth, who briefly played for the county after marrying a local girl. The miscreant bolted and was next heard of in Madrid where he became tailor to the King of Spain.

While he was qualifying Yorkshire, with generous imprudence, allowed Spofforth to play against them and he responded with a 15-wicket demonstration of his genius.

There was a bleak period up to and after the First World War culminating in the disaster of 1920 when 17 defeats were suffered in 18 matches. The other was washed out without a ball bowled, which suggests in a more typical summer they might have got off a little lighter! Drastic remedies were sought, and included the appointment of a 40-year-old captain in G.M. Buckston, and the re-engagement of the 45-year old fast bowler, Bestwick, who had been sacked for intemperance. Bestwick must have dryly pondered how many glasses were raised to him to salute his 147-wicket haul, including all ten for 40 at Cardiff.

Derbyshire moved up four places and gradually the foundation was laid for the summit achievement of 1936. It took an exceptional side to wrest the honours from Yorkshire in the 'thirties. Derbyshire had proved their strength with successive positions of 3rd and 2nd, and, true to tradition, their strength rested much on bowling. Only Worthington, Townsend and Denis Smith reached the comparatively modest batting

K. J. BARNETT

DERBY

average of between 30 and 35, while Copson, Alf Pope, Townsend and the leg spinner, Mitchell, took wickets at a cost from 12 to 20. They also carried the burden of the absence of George Pope, who completed only five overs before retiring for the season with cartilage problems.

The country's pride has been in its strain of pace bowlers, and a remarkable line of long-serving wicket-keepers: W. Storer, Humphries, H. Elliott, Dawkes and Taylor, whose 1,648 victims is a record. The boast was that a shout down a pit shaft produced a hostile bowler. But times change. Now it is more likely to be a phone call to the Caribbean to recruit a Holding or a Bishop. Who would have thought a West Indian and a Dane, Ole Mortensen, would be the new-ball successors to the Pope brothers, Rhodes, Jackson, Gladwin, Bestwick, Hendrick and Co.

In the 'fifties the shortage of runs provoked the captain, Guy Willatt, to compare Derbyshire batsmen to sailors in the Spanish Armada – subordinate and consigned to a secondary role. Not much was expected of them, and not much was forthcoming, but his successor, Donald Carr, later a top administrator at Lord's, lifted standards with graceful efficiency. He had few batting peers in the country.

Other shining examples include Worthington, the first Derbyshire player to score a Test century, Denis Smith, Hamer, Bolus and Barnett. Overseas blood, Wright and Kirsten, considerably enriched the stream, and the importation of Barlow, the combative South African all-rounder, was as wise an investment as the county ever made. As captain he left his mark with his infectious zeal and high fitness levels.

Derbyshire's contrasting fortunes were mirrored by the events of 1981. During the season the chairman, chief executive, the captain Miller, and the scorer resigned. Wood, formerly of Lancashire, took over the captaincy hours before a county match on 25 July, and on 5 September, accepted the NatWest Trophy after the closest of all finals at Lord's. With the scores level, Derbyshire beat Northamptonshire by virtue of losing fewer wickets. Derbyshire reached their second Benson and Hedges final in 1988 and were again beaten by a southern county in

T. B. Mitchell, 68

T. S. WORTHINGTON

MR. C. A. OLLIVIERRE,
DERBYSHIRE.

this competition. A decade before they had gone down to Kent. By now they were splendidly led by Barnett, who gained Test recognition, but then joined the rebel South African Tour captained by Gatting.

Derbyshire continued their climb up the championship table to 6th in 1989 and in 1990 Derbyshire won the Refuge Assurance Sunday League title for the first time, winning twelve matches in the process. In 1991 Mohammad Azharuddin, their overseas player, scored 1,773 runs with a highest score of 212 against Leicestershire at Grace Road and Derbyshire finished 3rd, winning nine matches, behind Warwickshire and Essex.

Derby

The ground occupies part of the former Derby racecourse and was known as the Racecourse Ground until officials became anxious that it be termed the County Cricket Ground. For racing Derby boasted a straight mile and a grandstand complete with a copper-domed viewing cupola and stables. All these still exist today (except for the straight mile) as the ground is now enclosed from the rest of the former racecourse, which now provides recreational facilities for people of the city. The grandstand was built in 1911 as is defined on a stone tablet below the county crest.

The cricket pitch used to be located in the centre of the racecourse but in 1939 when racing creased due to poor crowds and lack of finance, the ground moved to its present position. In 1970, the year of the club's centenary, there was talk of closing the ground altogether due to its poor facilities and wicket. Not until 1982 when the Lund Pavilion was built, was there truly a cricket pavilion on the ground, the players used to change in the old jockeys' quarters.

The ground now occupies an area of 17 acres and in 1982 a lease of 125 years was purchased from the owners, Derby City Council, thanks to a generous loan from the local authority. Since 1982 much building has taken place: in addition to the pavilion and sponsors' suites, a new scoreboard, the Butterley and the Steetley stands, the Derbyshire Heatseal Supporters' Club room, Tea Room and Derbyshire C C C Souvenir Shop have been erected.

The ground was for many years called the Charter Land as it was a portion of land given to the city by Queen Mary Tudor in her Charter of 1554. Once considered one of the least attractive of county cricket grounds, it has been much improved in recent years. New road construction has considerably altered the approach to the ground from the large Pentagon Roundabout.

Derbyshire county matches were played on the Racecourse Ground from 1884–1954. In 1955 the wicket was moved to its present position. Derby County Football Club played some matches at the Racecourse Ground before moving across the city to the Baseball Ground in 1891; the ground even staged one FA Cup Final replay and five semi-finals. The ground was first used in 1863, fifteen years after the establishment of the racecourse by South Derbyshire Cricket Club. It was on this ground that South Derbyshire C C played and defeated the Australian Aborigines, the first touring side in 1868. Following the formation of the Derbyshire C C C in November 1870 at the Guildhall, the first county match was staged in 1871.

Between 1871 and 1991 a total of 585 first-class matches have been staged by Derbyshire C C C at the Derby ground. The County Ground was used for one Prudential Cup match staged in 1983 when New Zealand played Sri Lanka.

Crowds of 4,500 are usual for weekend matches. The largest ever attendance was 14,500 against the Australians in 1948. Some 7,500 attended the Refuge Assurance League match against Essex in August 1990 when Derbyshire made sure of winning the Refuge Assurance Sunday League Trophy for the first time.

The 1991 season saw the opening of discussions in the long-awaited development at the County Ground which is to include offices, a sports complex and a hotel, which will be undertaken by Birch PLC.

Ground records at Derby include highest individual innings by T.S. Worthington and E.G. Hayes both n.o. Wickets have been taken with great effect by G. Davidson, J. Briggs, G. Porter and G. Giffen. In the limited-overs game Derbyshire made their highest innings total against Cornwall including a 153 by Alan Hill. Rob Bailey's 125 n.o. for Northamptonshire is the highest individual score against the home side. Best bowling achievements have been accomplished by the Dane Ole Mortensen and Robin Jackman.

ADDRESS County Cricket Ground, Nottingham Road, Derby, Derbyshire DE2 6DA.
TELEPHONE PROSPECTS OF PLAY 0332 383211

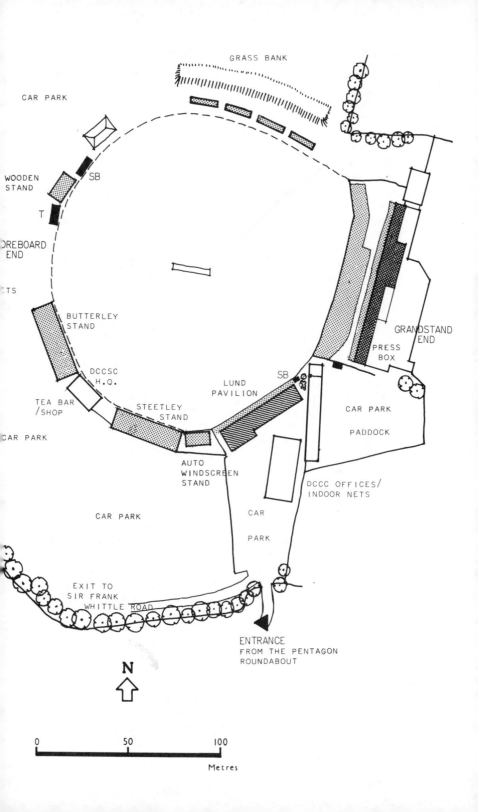

GRASS BANK

CAR PARK

WOODEN
STAND

SB

T

OREBOARD
END

CTS

BUTTERLEY
STAND

DCCSC
H.Q.

TEA BAR
/SHOP

CAR PARK

STEETLEY
STAND

LUND
PAVILION

SB

GRANDSTAND
END

PRESS
BOX

CAR PARK

PADDOCK

AUTO
WINDSCREEN
STAND

DCCC OFFICES/
INDOOR NETS

CAR PARK

CAR

PARK

EXIT TO
SIR FRANK
WHITTLE ROAD

ENTRANCE
FROM THE PENTAGON
ROUNDABOUT

N

0   50   100

Metres

DESCRIPTION OF GROUND AND FACILITIES

The main entrance to the ground is from the Pentagon roundabout at the junction with Nottingham Road. The main permanent buildings on the ground are the remains of the racecourse grandstand and the new Lund Pavilion and sponsors' suites which are both on the east side of the ground; on the south side of the playing area there are new tiered seating stands, the South Stand and an area for disabled spectators and their vehicles by the sightscreen. A new scoreboard has been erected on the west side opposite the grandstand. The old scoreboard building is now used as the radio commentary box. The north side of the playing area consists of a grassy bank which is sufficiently above the playing area to offer a good view of the play but some distance from the middle. It is possible to park and view the cricket from your car in this area or in front of the bank.

There is a good number of seats for members at the front of the old grandstand area. This together with the Lund Pavilion and adjoining stand are restricted to use by members' only. The public seats are on the south and west side of the playing area and these have been increased in recent years. The playing area is large, extending to 152 metres by 167 metres; although the playing area is restricted on the north and west sides by a boundary rope inside the pale fencing which encloses the ground, the boundary can still be as much as 78 metres from the square.

All refreshment facilities, including the Grandstand public house, are available to the public with the exception of the members' bar. Toilets are provided in the grandstand, pavilion and on the ground floor of the old scorebox. Sponsors' tents are usually sited in the north-west corner between the new scoreboard and the grassy bank. The club shop is situated near the Derbyshire C C Supporters' Club headquarters and Tea room with a secondhand Supporters' Club shop at the rear of the pavilion. The scorers' sit in the Old Finish Post building and the press box is situated within the grandstand at the pavilion end. The Derbyshire C C C offices and Indoor Cricket School adjoin the entrance and car parking area to the rear of the Lund Pavilion.

The TV camera/commentary box is positioned at the Scoreboard End when required. This is a large spacious ground with a capacity of some 9,500 and the facility to shelter in the grandstand in the event of rain. There are good tree backcloths to the north and recent planting following new road alignments has much improved the west and south sides of the ground.

GROUND RECORDS AND SCORES

FIRST-CLASS MATCHES
Highest innings total for County: 645 *v.* Hampshire 1898
Highest innings total against County: 661 by Nottinghamshire 1901
Lowest innings total for County: 26 *v.* Yorkshire 1880
Lowest innings total against County: 28 by Warwickshire 1928
Highest individual innings for County: 238 n.o. T.S. Worthington *v.* Sussex 1937

Highest individual innings against County: 273 n.o. E.G. Hayes for Surrey 1904

Best bowling performance in an innings for County: 9 for 39 G. Davidson *v.* Warwickshire 1895

Best bowling performance in an innings against County: 9 for 29 J. Briggs for Lancashire 1885

Best bowling performance in a match for County: 14 for 100 G. Porter *v.* Hampshire 1895

Best bowling performance in a match against County: 16 for 101 G. Giffen for Australians 1886

Best attendance: 14,500 *v.* Australians 1948

LIMITED-OVERS MATCHES

Highest innings total for County: 365 for 3 *v.* Cornwall (NWBT) 1986

Highest innings total against County: 300 by Northamptonshire (BHC) 1987

Lowest innings total for County: 70 *v.* Surrey (JPL) 1972

Lowest innings total against County: 61 by Sussex (JPL) 1978

Highest individual innings for County: 153 A. Hill *v.* Cornwall (NWBT) 1986

Highest individual innings against County: 125 n.o. R.J. Bailey for Northamptonshire (RAL) 1987

Best bowling performance for County: 6 for 14 O.H. Mortensen *v.* Ireland (NWBT) 1989

Best bowling performance against County: 6 for 34 R.D. Jackman for Surrey (JPL) 1972

Best attendance: 7,500 *v.* Essex (RAL) 1990

HOW TO GET THERE

Rail Derby Midland (BR) 1.25 miles.

Bus Trent 29 from BR Derby Midland Station to ground. Derby City 42–47 from BR Station to Bus Station, thence numerous services pass near ground (Telephone: 0332 754433).

Car From north: M1 junction 28 follow signs Derby A38 or A6 to Pentagon roundabout (island), ground adjoining Sir Frank Whittle Road and Nottingham Road, ground on north side of roundabout. From east: M1 junction 25, follow signs Derby A52 and A61 to Pentagon roundabout, then as north. From south: M1 junction 24 follow signs Derby A6, then A52 ring road to Spondon, then A61 to Pentagon roundabout, then as north. From west: A52, A38 and A5111 to ring road then A61 to Pentagon Roundabout, then as north.

WHERE TO STAY AND OTHER INFORMATION

Midland Hotel (0332 45894), Clarenden Hotel (0332 365235) Post House Hotel, Sandiacre (0602 397800).

Disabled Areas Next to boundary fence near the South Stand with space for 6–8 cars together with ample space outside the perimeter of the playing area. Access to the Grandstand is difficult as only steps are available.

Local Radio Station(s) BBC Radio Derby (104.5 MHz FM/1116 KHz MW) Radio Trent (96.2 MHz FM/999 KHz MW).

Local Newspaper(s) Derby Evening Telegraph, Derbyshire Times, Derby Trader.

Chesterfield

Queen's Park was laid out in 1897 to celebrate Queen Victoria's Diamond Jubilee and has remained a recreational area for the people of Chesterfield ever since. Derbyshire C C C first used the ground in 1898 when Yorkshire were the visitors and the initial first-class match was with Surrey. The county club have staged fixtures annually since including cricket weeks in May and August. Limited-overs matches and even matches with touring sides have been played at Chesterfield rather than the county headquarters in Derby. Between 1898 and 1991 some 379 first-class matches were staged there.

Queen's Park, Chesterfield is probably one of the most picturesque grounds in the country and is owned and maintained by Chesterfield Borough Council. It is also the home of Chesterfield Cricket Club who play in the Derbyshire County and Bassetlaw Cricket Leagues. The ground is circular and was once surrounded by a banked cycle track. The pavilion, which is half timbered, was built in 1897 and with the scoreboard and press box is the only permanent building on the ground. There is a marked slope from south, the Pavilion End, to the north, the Lake End (as it is known to locals). The famous twisted spire of All Saints' Church, some 238 feet high, looks down upon Queen's Park where so much cricket history has been made. For a public park there are ample facilities and crowds have been known to be large for popular matches. Probably the 14,000 attendance for the match with Yorkshire in 1948 was the best. Nowadays crowds of 4,000–5,000 are to be expected. The present ground capacity is set at 7,500.

The ground has one unusual feature, a boating lake which is situated behind the sightscreen at the Boythorpe Road end of the ground furthest from the pavilion. The lake is well populated by ducks and it has been known for the birds to find their way onto the square. This has provided the press with plenty of stories over the years.

Queen's Park was the ground where C.A. Ollivierre, the first West Indian to play county cricket, scored 229 against Essex in 1904. P.A. Perrin replied with 343 n.o. for the visitors, an Essex record and this match still stands out as possibly the most famous ever staged at Chesterfield. Ken Graveney of Gloucestershire took 10 for 66 in Derbyshire's second innings here in 1949 to set up victory by 184 runs. Chesterfield is one of the few grounds in the north of the county to have been used by the County Club, the others being Buxton (last used in 1988) and Darley Dale in 1975 for a single match.

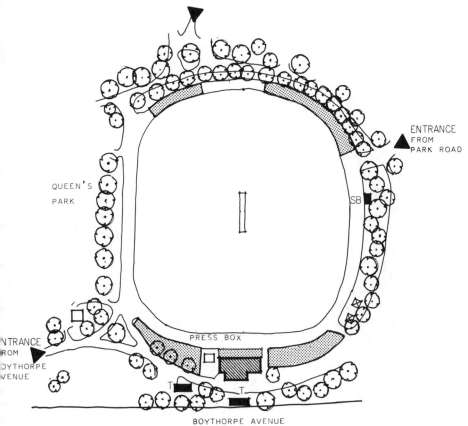

LAKE END
ENTRANCE FROM BOYTHORPE ROAD

ENTRANCE
FROM
PARK ROAD

QUEEN'S
PARK

SB

ENTRANCE
FROM
BOYTHORPE
AVENUE

PRESS BOX

T   T

BOYTHORPE AVENUE

PAVILION END

N

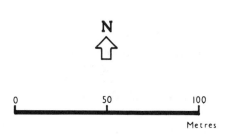

0   50   100

Metres

The 1990 Refuge Assurance Sunday League match with Kent provided a healthy crowd with a high-scoring match. Derbyshire won by 6 wickets to improve their position at the top of the table – a competition they were to win that season. Kim Barnett scored 127 out of a total of 277 for 4 with Kent scoring 276 for 4 in 40 overs.

Newcomers Durham C C C will play Derbyshire at Chesterfield in early June 1992.

ADDRESS Chesterfield Cricket Club, The Pavilion, Queen's Park, Boythorpe Avenue, Chesterfield, Derbyshire.
TELEPHONE PROSPECTS OF PLAY   0246 273090

DESCRIPTION OF GROUND AND FACILITIES

The ground is entered from Boythorpe Avenue or Park Road, where there are a number of entrances including one over the bridge from the town centre. The only permanent buildings are the pavilion and press box at the southern end and a scorebox on the east side under the trees. To the east and west of the pavilion are permanent terraces for members' with green bench seats. Elsewhere permanent timber seating areas are provided, as well as benches on the tarmac track surrounding the playing area.

Seating is provided for about 55 per cent of the normal attendance and for limited-overs matches spectators are advised to bring their own seats. Refreshments are available in the pavilion and in a kiosk to the west of the playing area.

Queen's Park is possibly the most scenic ground played on by Derbyshire C C C and both players and spectators enjoy their visits to this out ground. The ground is on a marked slope towards the boating lake end and is very pleasantly situated within the trees and shrubs of the beautiful Chesterfield park. Limited car parking is available within the ground to the west of the playing area near the sportscentre complex together with street parking and multi-storey car parks a short walk away in the town centre.

The playing area is 127 metres by 117 metres and is defined by a rope and advertising boards. The scorers' box is situated to the east of the pavilion within the terraced seating area in a shed. The Derbyshire C.C.C. souvenir shop and supporters' table is located to the west of the playing area near the bank. The position when required, for TV cameras/commentary boxes is on the pavilion balcony.

GROUND RECORDS AND SCORES

FIRST-CLASS MATCHES
Highest innings total for County: 552 *v.* Essex 1928
Highest innings total against County: 662 by Yorkshire 1898
Lowest innings total for County: 30 *v.* Nottinghamshire 1913
Lowest innings total against County: 29 by Middlesex 1957
Highest individual innings for County: 229 C.A. Ollivierre *v.* Essex 1904

Highest individual innings against County: 343 n.o. P.A. Perrin for Essex 1904

Best bowling performance in an innings for County: 8 for 21 E. Smith *v*. Worcestershire 1951

Best bowling performance in an innings against County: 10 for 66 J.K.R. Graveney for Gloucestershire 1949

Best bowling performance in a match for County: 14 for 48 A.G. Slater *v*. Somerset 1930

Best bowling performance in a match against County: 13 for 108 T.W. Cartwright for Somerset 1972

Best attendance: 14,000 *v*. Yorkshire 1948

LIMITED-OVERS MATCHES

Highest innings total for County: 277 for 4 *v*. Kent (RAL) 1990

Highest innings total against County: 276 for 4 by Kent (RAL) 1990

Lowest innings total for County: 92 *v*. Sussex (GC) 1973/Kent (JPL) 1979

Lowest innings total against County: 49 by Sussex (GC) 1969

Highest individual innings for County: 127 K.J. Barnett *v*. Kent (RAL) 1990

Highest individual innings against County: 109 B.W. Reidy for Lancashire (BHC) 1980

Best bowling performance for County: 6 for 18 T.J.P. Eyre *v*. Sussex (GC) 1969

Best bowling performance against County: 6 for 9 R.A. Woolmer for Kent (JPL) 1979

Best attendance: 7,500 *v*. Sussex (GC) 1969

HOW TO GET THERE

Rail   Chesterfield (BR) 0.75 mile.

Bus   Chesterfield Transport 1 from BR Chesterfield Station to within 0.25 mile of ground also Trent Buses and South Yorkshire Traction services from surrounding areas to Chesterfield Bus Station thence 200m from ground (Telephone: 0246 76666).

Car   From north: M1 junction 30 then follow signs Chesterfield A619, then follows signs to Buxton A619 and A632 for Queen's Park. From east: A632 or A617 signposted Chesterfield, then as north for Queen's Park. From south: M1 junction 29, then A617 to Chesterfield, then as north for Queen's Park or A61 signposted Chesterfield then as north for Queen's Park. From west: A619 or A632 signposted Chesterfield, then as north for Queen's park.

WHERE TO STAY AND OTHER INFORMATION

Chesterfield Hotel (0246 71141), Portland Hotel (0246 34504).

Disabled Areas   Next to boundary fence at pavilion end with space for approximately 6–8 cars; also around the perimeter of the playing area on the former cycle track.

Local Radio Station(s) BBC Radio Sheffield (104.1 MHz FM/1035 KHz MW), BBC Radio Derby (104.5 MHz FM/1116 KHz MW), Radio Hallam (103.4 MHz FM/1548 KHz MW), Radio Trent (96.2 MHz FM/999 KHz MW).

Local Newspaper(s) Derby Evening Telegraph, Derbyshire Times, Chesterfield Gazette, Chesterfield Star, Sheffield Star.

Heanor

Situated off Mayfield Avenue this ground has been the home of Heanor Town Cricket Club since 1864. It is today shared with the Heanor Town Football Club and the floodlights can be seen as soon as you enter the east Derbyshire mining town. The ground is owned by Amber Valley District Council. Heanor Town C C is a member of the Derbyshire County Cricket League, formerly Nottinghamshire and Derbyshire Border Cricket League and field three XIs throughout the season.

The ground slopes from the football stand end of the ground towards the cricket pavilion and tennis courts. It has fairly short boundaries, 50 metres compared with 75 metres at the county headquarters in Derby. With such a small playing area high scoring totals are frequent. In the only championship match to be played at Heanor (*v*.Hampshire in 1987) Malcolm Marshall playing for the visitors, was requested by the umpires to stop bowling fast, as when the wicketkeeper missed the ball it was dangerous for spectators, so short are the boundaries at the Stainsby Avenue and Town Ends.

Derbyshire C C C made their first visit to Heanor in 1976 for a John Player Sunday League match with Somerset. The County played one Sunday League match each season until 1989 when the last match was staged with Glamorgan. The ground has not been used for matches for the last two seasons other than by the Second XI. In recent years benefit matches have been staged under floodlights for players from Derbyshire, Leicestershire and Nottinghamshire.

The ground is well maintained and has a very fast outfield and reasonably good facilities for an out ground. Advantage of this was taken in 1987 when Derbyshire C C C staged a County Championship match for the first time at the Town Ground. The pavilion houses the Heanor Town Sports and Social Club and events are staged there throughout the year.

Matches attract crowds of about 4,000 for limited-overs games. The capacity is 5,000 and the best crowd was 4,000 for the John Player Sunday League match with Hampshire in 1986.

Ground records include centuries by Bruce Roberts and David Turner now playing for Wiltshire C C C, and best bowling performances by Paul Newman and Rajesh Maru. In the limited-overs game centuries have been recorded by Kim Barnett and John Morris both 100 n.o. against Glamorgan in 1989, with the highest individual innings by an opponent 95 from Robin Smith. Wickets have been collected by Michael Holding and Cardigan Connor.

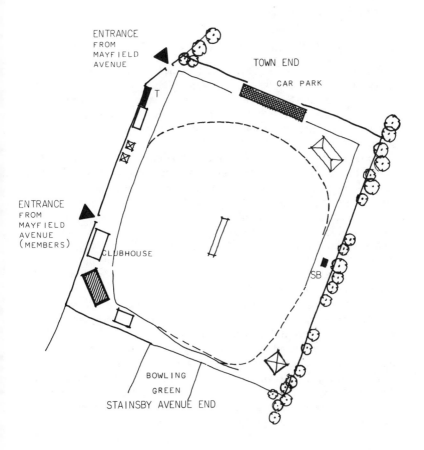

ENTRANCE
FROM
MAYFIELD
AVENUE

T

TOWN END

CAR PARK

ENTRANCE
FROM
MAYFIELD
AVENUE
(MEMBERS)

CLUBHOUSE

SB

BOWLING
GREEN
STAINSBY AVENUE END

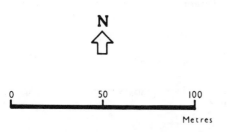

N

0   50   100

Metres

ADDRESS   Heanor Town Cricket Club, Heanor Town Sports and Social Club, Town Ground, Mayfield Avenue, Commonside, Heanor, Derbyshire DE7 7EN.
TELEPHONE PROSPECTS OF PLAY   0773 716703

DESCRIPTION OF GROUND AND FACILITIES

The ground is entered from Mayfield Avenue to the west. There are two entrances, one for members and players/officials close to the Heanor Town Football and Social Club and another for the public at the football ground end. Besides the social club, the only permanent cricket buildings on the ground are at the southern end – the pavilion and press room along with the members' enclosure.

To the east is the scoreboard and to the north the covered football stand, toilets and tea bar. Terracing and banking can be found at the football end. From this end there is a marked slope towards the tennis courts and bowling green. The sponsors' marquees are situated in the south-east corner of the ground near the members' enclosure. The rest of the ground is available to the public.

A refreshment tent is located on the football field and there are a number of mobile refreshment kiosks situated around the playing area. A Derbyshire C C C souvenir table and supporters' caravan can be found on the Mayfield Road side of the ground close to the radio commentary box. No car parking is available within the ground but ample space exists on the recreation ground to the north, with access from Wilmot Street and the Market Place.

The ground is owned by Amber Valley District Council who provide approximately 1,000 temporary seats for matches. Spectators are advised to bring their own seats to popular matches. The playing area is 118 metres by 106 metres, one of the smallest playing areas on the county circuit. All the seating is open and temporary except for the football stand and clubhouse.

GROUND RECORDS AND SCORES

FIRST-CLASS MATCH
Highest innings total for County: 314 for 7 dec. *v.* Hampshire 1987
Highest innings total against County: 349 for 2 dec. by Hampshire 1987
Lowest innings total for County: 298 for 6 *v.* Hampshire 1987
Lowest innings total against County: 261 for 6 dec. by Hampshire 1987
Highest individual innings for County: 106 B. Roberts *v.* Hampshire 1987
Highest individual innings against County: 104 n.o. D.R. Turner for Hampshire 1987
Best bowling performance in an innings for County: 3 for 92 P.G. Newman *v.* Hampshire 1987
Best bowling performance in an innings against County: 4 for 123 R.J. Maru for Hampshire 1987

Best bowling performance in a match for County: 4 for 171 P.G. Newman *v.* Hampshire 1987
Best bowling performance in a match against County: 7 for 213 R.J. Maru for Hampshire 1987
Best attendance: 3,000 *v.* Hampshire 1987

LIMITED-OVERS MATCHES
Highest innings total for County: 245 for 1 *v.* Glamorgan (RAL) 1989
Highest innings total against County: 258 for 8 by Gloucestershire (RAL) 1988
Lowest innings total for County: 184 *v.* Hampshire (JPL) 1986
Lowest innings total against County: 219 for 8 by Somerset (JPL) 1983
Highest individual innings for County: 100 n.o. K.J. Barnett *v.* Somerset (JPL) 1983/Glamorgan (RAL) 1989/J.E. Morris *v.* Glamorgan (RAL) 1989
Highest individual innings against County: 95 R.A. Smith for Hampshire (JPL) 1986
Best bowling performance for County: 3 for 29 M.A. Holding *v.* Hampshire (JPL) 1986
Best bowling performance against County: 4 for 25 C.A. Connor for Hampshire (JPL) 1986
Best attendance: 4,000 *v.* Hampshire (JPL) 1986

HOW TO GET THERE

Rail Langley Mill (BR) 1 mile.
Bus Trent Buses 120, 123, 124 and 125 from Derby pass BR Langley Mill Station and link with Heanor Market Place; also 132, 220, 231 and 330 from Nottingham Broadmarsh Centre close to BR Nottingham Midland Station link with Heanor Market Place five minutes from ground (Telephone: 0332 292200).
Car From north: M1 junction 27, then A608 signposted Heanor, ground situated in town centre near Market Place in Mayfield Avenue. From east: A610 or A608 signposted Heanor, then as north. From south: M1 junction 26, then A610 and A608 signposted Heanor, then as north. From west: A608 signposted Heanor, then as north.

WHERE TO STAY AND OTHER INFORMATION

Sun Inn, Eastwood (0773 712940).

Disabled Areas No special area, request suitable position. Car parking is available on the football field with entry from Mayfield Avenue.
Local Radio Station(s) BBC Radio Derby (104.5 MHz FM/1116 KHz MW), BBC Radio Nottingham (95.5 MHz FM/1548 KHz MW), Radio Trent (96.2 MHz FM/999 KHz MW).
Local Newspaper(s) Derby Evening Telegraph, Ripley and Heanor News, Derby Trader, Ilkeston and Heanor Shopper.

Ilkeston

Derbyshire C C C have visited the Rutland Recreation Ground, Ilkeston once a season and made their first visit in 1925 two months after the ground was re-opened. Nearby visitors Nottinghamshire were the opponents. The ground is the home of Ilkeston Rutland Cricket Club which was founded in 1829 and used to play at Market Street behind St. Mary's Church and Lawn Cottage until the Duke of Rutland allowed the club the use of a field in the Pimlico district of the town. Eight years later the ground was leased to the corporation on the understanding that it would be developed for recreational purposes.

When King George V visited the town in 1914 the ground was given to the corporation to commemorate his visit. Six years later the ground was extended. Derbyshire C C C have also staged limited- overs matches on the ground, the most recent being against Gloucestershire in the 1987 Refuge Assurance Sunday League. Some ninety first-class matches have been staged during the period 1925–80, the last first-class match was staged in August 1980 with Nottinghamshire. After a twelve year gap in August 1992 Derbyshire C C C will return to the Rutland Recreation Ground for a three day Britannic Assurance Championship match with Leicestershire.

A number of Ilkeston Rutland C C players have represented the county, including the Attenborough brothers, Tilson and Paxton. More recently there were Cliff Gladwin, Les Jackson, George Dawkes and G.M. Lee. The ground is now owned by Erewash District Council which maintains the whole area.

The ground is saucer-shaped and provides a natural banking around the arena extending to twenty acres. The only permanent buildings on the ground are the pavilion built after the 1914–18 War and the scoreboard/groundsman's store. There are also facilities for tennis, football, bowling and golf (putting). During the winter months the Ilkeston Ladies Vaders and Derby Ladies Hockey Clubs use the cricket club's facilities.

In 1979 a 150th anniversary match was staged between Frank Nicklin's XI and Ilkeston Rutland C C Crowds have been quite good over the years. Possibly the largest were 8,000 against Somerset for a Gillette Cup tie in 1977 and 10,000 against Nottinghamshire in 1948. The ground capacity is 7,000. A jubilee match was staged in 1977 between the Mayor's XI and Derbyshire C C C.

Ilkestonians refer to the ground, which forms part of the 2,000 acres former estate of the Duke of Rutland, as the 'Queen of the Erewash Valley', certainly a picturesque title for this splendid out ground which will be used for the first time in five years by the County Club.

Ground records include significant performances by Eddie Barlow, John Langridge, Alan Hill and Brian Rose with the bat and with the ball by A.G. Slater, Titch Freeman, George Pope, R. Harman, Alan Ward and 'Big Bird' Joel Garner.

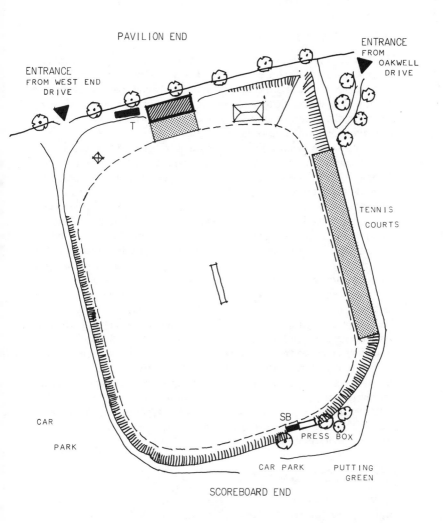

PAVILION END

ENTRANCE
FROM
OAKWELL
DRIVE

ENTRANCE
FROM WEST END
DRIVE

T

TENNIS
COURTS

CAR

PARK

SB

PRESS BOX

CAR PARK

PUTTING
GREEN

SCOREBOARD END

N

0   50   100

Metres

ADDRESS Ilkeston Rutland Cricket Club., The Pavilion, Rutland Recreation Ground, Oakwell Drive, Ilkeston, Derbyshire.
TELEPHONE PROSPECTS OF PLAY   0602 303036/440440 ext 353

DESCRIPTION OF GROUND AND FACILITIES

The Ilkeston ground is entered off West End Drive for members, players/officials and vehicles and from Oakwell Drive for the public and members on foot. Car parking is available for some eighty-five cars in a position to view the cricket and there is plenty of street parking close by and in the town centre car parks. Some cars can be parked to the west of the playing area on the football fields.

The only permanent buildings are the pavilion and the scoreboard/ groundsman's building which are situated at opposite ends of the playing area. To the west are the public enclosures and to the east a terrace with permanent seating. The north or West End Drive end of the ground includes a store/ equipment area, Derbyshire C C C souvenir tent and a refreshment tent which is situated within the members' enclosure and adjoining the pavilion. The south side includes a scoreboard and TV camera/commentary box positions when required. Both the press and radio commentary boxes are situated within the scorebox building. Ample toilet facilities can be found close to the bowling green on the Oakwell Drive side of the ground and at the rear of the pavilion.

The ground is situated in a bowl with ample banking from which to view the field. The playing area is 163 metres by 133 metres and is defined by a rope and advertising boards. Seating for only about 2,500 is provided so spectators are advised to bring their own seating for popular matches. Part of the terracing area is fitted with benches. Ample refreshment stalls exist but alcohol is sold only to members. Sponsors' marquees are situated on the west side of the ground. The surrounding trees and buildings are fairly close to the ground as are some busy traffic routes through the Derbyshire town.

GROUND RECORDS AND SCORES

FIRST-CLASS MATCHES
Highest innings total for County: 529 for 7 dec. *v.* Nottinghamshire 1952
Highest innings total against County: 443 by South Africans 1935
Lowest innings total for County: 62 *v.* Somerset 1936
Lowest innings total against County: 72 by Nottinghamshire 1958
Highest individual innings for County: 217 E.J. Barlow *v.* Surrey 1976
Highest individual innings against County: 234 n.o. John Langridge for Sussex 1949
Best bowling performance in an innings for County: 8 for 87 A.G. Slater *v.* Essex 1931
Best bowling performance in an innings against County: 9 for 50 A.P. Freeman for Kent 1930

Best bowling performance in a match for County: 12 for 101 G.H. Pope *v*. Nottinghamshire 1947
Best bowling performance in a match against County: 14 for 113 R. Harman for Surrey 1968
Best attendance: 10,000 *v*. Nottinghamshire 1948

LIMITED-OVERS MATCHES
Highest innings total for County: 222 for 5 *v*. Warwickshire (BHC) 1978
Highest innings total against County: 248 for 4 by Somerset (GC) 1977
Lowest innings total for County: 119 *v*. Essex (JPL) 1976
Lowest innings total against County: 105 for 8 by Glamorgan (JPL) 1972
Highest individual innings for County: 102 n.o. A. Hill *v*. Warwickshire (BHC) 1978
Highest individual innings against County: 128 B.C. Rose for Somerset (GC) 1977
Best bowling performance for County: 6 for 24 A. Ward *v*. Essex (JPL) 1976
Best bowling performance against County: 5 for 30 J. Garner for Somerset (GC) 1977
Best attendance: 8,000 *v*. Somerset (GC) 1977

HOW TO GET THERE

Rail   Langley Mill (BR), 4 miles; Nottingham Midland (BR), 9 miles.
Bus   Barton Buses 4, 18 and 51 from Nottingham Broadmarsh Centre, close to BR Nottingham Midland Station pass ground (Telephone: 0602 254881).
Car   From north: M1 junction 26, then A610 and A6096 signposted Ilkeston, ground situated in town centre off A6007 at rear of fire station. From east: A609, then as north. From south: M1 junction 25, then A52 to Stapleford, then A609 signposted Ilkeston, then as north. From west: A609 or A6096, then as north.

WHERE TO STAY AND OTHER INFORMATION

Rutland Arms Hotel, Bath Street (0602 323259) Post House Hotel, Sandiacre (0602 397800).

Disabled Areas   No special area although easy access is possible to all parts of the ground for disabled spectators, with the possible exception of the main pavilion terrace. Car parking is available within the ground at the Scoreboard End.
Local Radio Station(s)   BBC Radio Derby (104.5 MHz FM/1116 KHz MW), BBC Radio Nottingham (95.5 MHz FM/1584 KHz MW), Radio Trent (96.2 MHz FM/999 KHz MW).
Local Newspaper(s)   Derby Evening Telegraph, Nottingham Evening Post, Ilkeston Advertiser.

Cheadle

The ground of Cheadle Cricket Club has been the home headquarters of the town cricket club since 1922. The Cheadle Cricket Club play in the North Staffordshire and South Cheshire Cricket League and field three XIs throughout the season.

The club was founded sometime in the nineteenth century and has hosted limited-overs county matches since the first in 1973 when Derbyshire C C C visited Tean Road to play Minor Counties (North) in a Benson and Hedges Cup zonal group fixture. Derbyshire won the match by 5 wickets thanks to the bowling of Fred Rumsey, 4 for 19, and Indian Test spinner Venkataraghavan, 2 for 32.

Fifteen years later county cricket returned to Tean Road when Derbyshire C C C staged a home Refuge Assurance Sunday League match with Glamorgan.

The Derbyshire C C C have an agreement with Staffordshire County Council to stage three Sunday matches at different venues in Staffordshire on a basis of one in each district. The other grounds are Knypersley and Leek. The grounds are visited in alternate seasons: Cheadle C C is usually the year after Leek and before Knypersley. Cheadle C C was due for a match in 1991 but this was played instead at Checkley C C some 10 miles away – a ground which was used for the first time. Derbyshire C C C now play at four venues in Staffordshire.

The Cheadle ground is regularly used by Staffordshire C C C for Minor County Championship matches.

The current ground capacity is 4,000. Probably the largest crowd was between 1,500 and 2,000 for the Talbot Cup Final between Cheadle C C and Stone C C in 1981. A crowd of approximately 1,750 watched the match in 1973 and 2,000 in 1988. The ground is not to be confused with Cheadle C C in Cheshire, a mistake made by cricketers and spectators in the past !

Ground records include scores in the 40's by John Morris and Ravi Shastri with wickets being collected by Martin Jean-Jacques and Stephen Barwick.

ADDRESS   Cheadle Cricket Club., The Pavilion, Tean Road, Cheadle, Staffordshire.
TELEPHONE PROSPECTS OF PLAY   0538 75278

DESCRIPTION OF GROUND AND FACILITIES

The only access to the ground is from Tean Road where there are two entrances, one for members/officials and disabled spectators at the rear of the pavilion and a second for the public at the south-western corner of the ground close to the scorebox.

The pavilion is in the north-west corner with the members' enclosure in front. Sponsors' tents are at the north end of the ground. The Derbyshire C C C souvenir tent, supporters' caravan and temporary

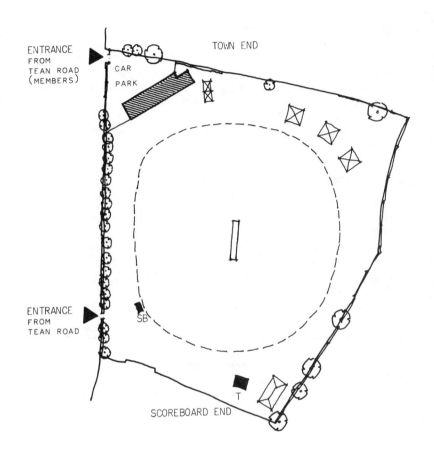

ENTRANCE
FROM
TEAN ROAD
(MEMBERS)

CAR
PARK

TOWN END

ENTRANCE
FROM
TEAN ROAD

SB

T

SCOREBOARD END

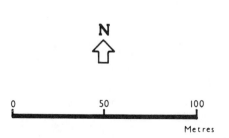

N

0   50   100

Metres

club office are situated close to the pavilion and at the southern perimeter of the playing area there are ample refreshment facilities, toilets and the groundsman's store. The playing area is 118 metres by 113 metres and is approximately circular in shape. It is defined by a rope and some advertising boards.

There is no car parking available within the ground but ample facilities are available 200 yards away at a nearby public car park or at the Master Potter public house in Tean Road. The only covered accommodation is in the pavilion and spectators are advised to bring their own seats to all matches as only 300 seats are provided.

When required, the T.V. camera/commentary box would be positioned at the Scoreboard End of the ground.

GROUND RECORDS AND SCORES

LIMITED-OVERS MATCH

Highest innings total for County: 176 for 9 v. Glamorgan (RAL) 1987
Highest innings total against County: 173 for 9 by Glamorgan (RAL) 1987
Highest individual innings for County: 49 J.E. Morris v. Glamorgan (RAL) 1987
Highest individual innings against County: 41 R.J. Shastri for Glamorgan (RAL) 1987
Best bowling performance for County: 3 for 38 M. Jean-Jacques v. Glamorgan (RAL) 1987
Best bowling performance against County: 3 for 25 S.R. Barwick for Glamorgan (RAL) 1987
Best attendance: 2,000 v. Glamorgan (RAL) 1987

HOW TO GET THERE

Rail   Blyth Bridge (BR) 4 miles, Stoke-0n-Trent (BR) 9 miles.
Bus   Potteries Motor Traction PMT X43, 247 links Hanley with Cheadle passing BR Blyth Bridge Station or 232, 236 links Stoke with Cheadle passing BR Stoke-on-Trent Station (Telephone: 0782 747000)
Car   8 miles east of Stoke-on-Trent M6 junctions 14 or 15. From north: A521 or A522 from A52, ground situated off A522. From east: A52 then A521 or A52, then B5032, then as north. From south: A522 from A50 then as north. From west: A521 from A50 then as north.

WHERE TO STAY AND OTHER INFORMATION
The Manor, High Street; The Wheatsheaf, High Street (0538 753174); or stay in Stoke-on-Trent.

Disabled Areas   Use members' and officials' entrance at rear of pavilion for access then request suitable position.

Local Radio Station(s) BBC Radio Stoke-on-Trent (94.6 MHz FM/ 1503 KHz MW), Radio Signal (102.6 MHz FM/1170 KHz MW), Radio Trent (96.2 MHz FM/999 KHz MW).
Local Newspaper(s) Derby Evening Telegraph, Cheadle and Tean Times, Cheadle Post and Times, Evening Sentinel.

Checkley

Checkley Cricket Club was founded in 1860 as Lower Tean C C and played on various grounds in the vicinity of the New Broom public house formerly the New Inn.

The Lower Tean C C was a member of the Blythe Bridge and District Cricket League between 1905 and 1914 and the club changed its name to Checkley C C in April 1909. An amalgamation with Tean C C in 1919 lasted for just one season and in that year Lt. Colonel H.B. Philips granted to the Checkley C C the use of their present ground situated at Four Trees and he encouraged the pursuit of cricket by providing the village cricket club with a pavilion and various equipment for a peppercorn rent of two ears of corn per annum. The Colonel was patron of the club until his death in 1951.

In accordance with his wishes the cricket ground and pavilion were purchased by the Checkley C C for £400 on 21 June 1951. Checkley C C did not play league cricket again until the 1966 season when admission was granted to the Stone and District League. Promotion was achieved from division four to division one in continuous seasons during the period 1970–74. In 1974 the club moved into the North Staffordshire District Cricket League which was a stronger standard and it took the club several seasons to establish themselves as a force at that level. The club fields three XIs throughout the season together with a midweek XI and a several junior teams. The club professional in 1990 was J.P. Taylor who played for Northamptonshire C C C during the 1991 season. Paul Taylor had previously represented Derbyshire 1983–87, Worcestershire 1989 and Staffordshire 1989–90. Gavin Carr who plays regularly for the club represented Staffordshire C C C minor county team during the 1989 season.

During the 1970s major ground improvements took place with the levelling of the playing area and the first phase of the pavilion reconstruction programme was completed in 1980. The second phase was completed in 1982 and this now provides a greatly improved social club area with bar and refreshment facilities. The pavilion was opened by the former Derbyshire C C C and England wicketkeeper R.W. 'Bob' Taylor MBE on 30 April 1982. The final stage of the pavilion extension saw new changing rooms and showers completed in September 1985 and was opened by Mr Pat McGarry on 4 June 1986.

Additional improvements to the ground included the installation of an artificial cricket wicket within the square and some practice cricket nets in 1989 together with a new permanent brick built scoreboard which was constructed in the winter of 1990–91.

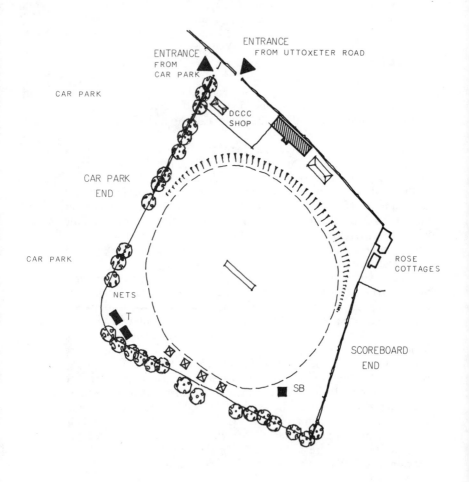

ENTRANCE FROM UTTOXETER ROAD

ENTRANCE FROM CAR PARK

CAR PARK

DCCC SHOP

CAR PARK END

CAR PARK

ROSE COTTAGES

NETS

T

SCOREBOARD END

SB

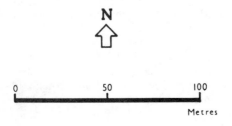

N

0   50   100

Metres

In 1991 Checkley C C were rewarded when Derbyshire C C C decided to stage a Refuge Assurance Sunday League match with Somerset on 16 June. This was switched to the County Ground, Derby as the outfield was waterlogged and it was not until later in the season that Checkley C C hosted a match with Glamorgan on 18 August in the same competition. Derbyshire won the match by 27 runs with Ewen McCray from Altrincham taking 4 for 49, despite Matthew Maynard scoring 101 on this small village ground.

ADDRESS Checkley Cricket Club, The Pavilion, Uttoxeter Road, Checkley, Staffordshire.
TELEPHONE PROSPECTS OF PLAY 0538 722666

DESCRIPTION OF GROUND AND FACILITIES

The ground is situated on the A522 between Blyth Bridge and Uttoexter, approximately ten miles east of Stoke-On-Trent. The single pedestrian access to the ground is direct from Uttoexter Road to the side of the pavilion. Ample car parking is available in the adjacent field through a separate entrance with an independent pedestrian access to the cricket ground. The ground is situated in a bowl and has a rather village cricket feel in a typically country location.

The pavilion stands on the northern side of the ground with the Derbyshire C C C caravan and office together with local radio commentary vans on the adjacent club car park. Public toilets are located in the south-west corner of the ground. The sponsors' courtesy marquees are sited along the southern side of the playing area. The members' enclosure is in front of the pavilion and on the northern banked area. A press/scorers' tent is situated near the scoreboard in the south-east corner.

Temporary seating is provided for only 600 so spectators would be well advised to bring their own seats to matches. Bar and refreshment facilities are available in the pavilion for players and officials only. A members' bar is available in a tent and a public refreshment tent is also available.

The playing area is 110 metres by 103 metres and is probably the smallest ground on the county circuit; it is defined only by advertising boards.

The ground capacity is 3,000 and some 2,500 attended the Glamorgan match staged on 18 August 1991.

GROUND RECORDS AND SCORES

LIMITED-OVERS MATCH
Highest innings total for County: 251 *v.* Glamorgan (RAL) 1991
Highest innings total against County: 222 for 9 by Glamorgan (RAL) 1991
Highest individual innings for County: 51 A.E. Warner *v.* Glamorgan (RAL) 1991

Highest individual innings against County: 101 M.P. Maynard for
Glamorgan (RAL) 1991
Best bowling performance for County: 4 for 49 E. McCray *v.*
Glamorgan (RAL) 1991
Best bowling performance against County: 3 for 30 D.J. Foster for
Glamorgan (RAL) 1991
Best attendance: 2,500 *v.* Glamorgan (RAL) 1991

HOW TO GET THERE

Rail Blyth Bridge (BR) Uttoexter (BR) both 6 miles.
Bus Potteries Motor Traction Company Hanley to Longton
Uttoexter service passes the ground hourly weekdays; and limited on
Sundays (Telephone: 0782 747000).
Car 12 miles east of Stoke-on-Trent M6 junction 15. From north:
M6 junction 15 then follow A500 for A50 and A52, follow signs
Checkley before reaching Uttoexter. From east: A516 then follow A50
for A52, follow signs Uttoexter then Checkley. From south: A34 to
A518 via Uttoexter then follow A522 for Checkley. From west: M6
junction 15, then follow A5035 signposted Trentham, then follow A50
and A52 signposted Uttoexter then follow signs Checkley.

WHERE TO STAY AND OTHER INFORMATION

White Hart Hotel, Carter Street, Uttoexter (05389 562437) The
Wheatsheaf, High Street, Cheadle (0538 753174) or stay in Stoke-on-
Trent.

Disabled Areas No special facilities, request suitable position.
Local Radio Station(s) BBC Radio Stoke-on-Trent 94.6 MHz FM/
1503 KHz MW), Radio Signal (102.6 MHz FM/1170 KHz MW), BBC
Radio Derby (104.5 MHz FM/1115 KHz MW).
Local Newspaper(s) Evening Sentinel, Cheadle and Tean Times,
Staffordshire Newsletter, Uttoexter Advertiser, Derby Evening
Telegraph.

Knypersley

The ground is located off the A527 trunk road between Congleton and
Stoke-on-Trent at Knypersley and forms part of the Victoria and
Knypersley Social Welfare Centre. The Knypersley Cricket Club was
founded in 1870 and cricket has been played on the ground since that
date, despite its geographical location in a basin.

The pavilion is of black and white timber and stands on a bank high
above the playing area and square at right angles to the wicket. The
Latin words *Floriat Knyperslium* are displayed on the pavilion above the
entrance doors. Knypersley Cricket Club play in the North Staffordshire
and South Cheshire Cricket League and field two XIs throughout the
season.

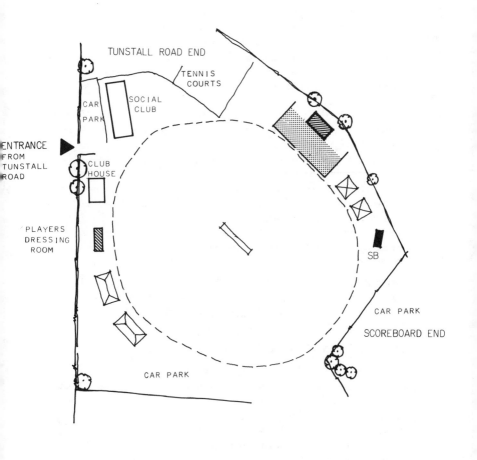

TUNSTALL ROAD END

TENNIS COURTS

CAR PARK

SOCIAL CLUB

ENTRANCE FROM TUNSTALL ROAD

CLUB HOUSE

PLAYERS DRESSING ROOM

SB

CAR PARK

SCOREBOARD END

CAR PARK

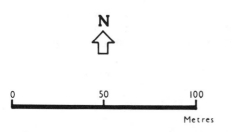

N

0   50   100

Metres

The ground is shared with the Social Welfare football team and there are fine facilities for bowling and tennis to the north of the playing area. The scoreboard and the old pavilion clubhouse are the only other permanent buildings on the ground. The Hall includes the bar/refreshment lounge and games room of the Social Welfare Centre.

The first match played here by Derbyshire C C C was in 1985 when a John Player Sunday League match was staged with Worcestershire. The county returned for a home fixture with the same opponents in 1988 for a Refuge Assurance Sunday League match and in 1990 the visitors were Leicestershire.

In 1985 Derbyshire hit 18 sixes here in an innings against Worcestershire. This still stands as a record in the Sunday League competition which has been running since 1969.

The ground is also used by Staffordshire C C C for Minor County Championship matches.

The three matches Derbyshire C C C have staged here have attracted crowds of 3,500–4,000. The current ground capacity is set at 5,000.

Ground records include highest individual innings by Bruce Roberts for the home side and Phil Neale of Worcestershire for the visitors. With the ball, the best performances have been achieved by Alan Warner and Steve McEwan who will be playing for Durham C C C in 1992.

ADDRESS Knypersley Cricket Club, Victoria and Knypersley Social Welfare Centre, Tunstall Road, Knypersley, Staffordshire.
TELEPHONE PROSPECTS OF PLAY 0782 513304

DESCRIPTION OF GROUND AND FACILITIES

Access to the ground is from Tunstall Road only for pedestrians and cars. The football ground area is used for car parking (about 100 spaces) as is the next field, if dry, and the local council car park is a short walk from the ground. The only permanent building is the pavilion which houses changing rooms, members' refreshment and bar facilities and toilets. The press are located in a tent near to the scorers' adjoining the scoreboard. The pavilion and seating within the fenced area are for members only; from where there is a fine view of the playing area down the slope at right angles to the wicket. On the south side of the playing area is the players' temporary changing facilities, toilets and the Derbyshire C C C souvenir tent. The other buildings close to the entrance are the old pavilion and the social club which includes bar, refreshment facilities and toilets.

The playing area is 142 metres by 120 metres and is oval in shape. In the region of 500 seats are provided for members in the pavilion area. This is a very pleasant ground and despite being close to a main road appears rather rural compared with other grounds used by Derbyshire C C C for home fixtures.

When required, the TV camera/commentary box would be positioned at the Tunstall Road End near the social club.

LIMITED-OVERS MATCHES
Highest innings total for County: 292 for 9 *v*. Worcestershire (JPL) 1985
Highest innings total against County: 280 for 9 by Worcestershire (RAL) 1988
Lowest innings total for County: 211 *v*. Worcestershire (RAL) 1988
Lowest innings total against County: 104 by Leicestershire (RAL) 1990
Highest individual innings for County: 77 B. Roberts *v*. Leicestershire (RAL) 1990
Highest individual innings against County: 91 P.A. Neale for Worcestershire (RAL) 1988
Best bowling performance for County: 5 for 39 A.E. Warner *v*. Worcestershire (JPL) 1985
Best bowling performance against County: 4 for 37 S.M. McEwan for Worcestershire (RAL) 1988
Best attendance: 3,500 *v*. Worcestershire (JPL) 1985

HOW TO GET THERE

Rail   Congleton (BR), Longport (BR) or Kidsgrove (BR); all 4 miles.
Bus   Crosville K87/88 from BR Congleton Station (Telephone: 0270 505350); PMT 6A/B from Hanley and 96, 98 from BR Longport Station pass ground (Telephone: 0782 747000).
Car   10 miles north of Stoke-on-Trent, M6 junctions 15 or 18. From north: M6 junction 18, then A54, A527 signposted Biddulph, ground situated off A527 at Knypersley. From east: A54 and A527 then as north. From south: M6 junction 15, then A500 and A527 then as north. From west: A53 to Stoke-0n-Trent, then A527 then as north.

WHERE TO STAY AND OTHER INFORMATION

Lion and Swan Hotel, Congleton (0270 273115).

Disabled Areas   No special area, request suitable position.
Local Radio Station(s)   BBC Radio Stoke-on-Trent (94.6 MHz FM/ 1503 KHz MW), Radio Signal (102.6 MHz FM/1170 KHz MW), Radio Trent (96.2 MHz FM/999 KHz MW).
Local Newspaper(s)   Derby Evening Telegraph, Evening Sentinel, Biddulph and Congleton Chronicle.

Leek

The ground is the home of Leek Town Cricket Club, which was founded in 1844. It has been the club's ground since 1919, when Leek Cricket Club and Leek Highfield Cricket Club amalgamated, mainly because so

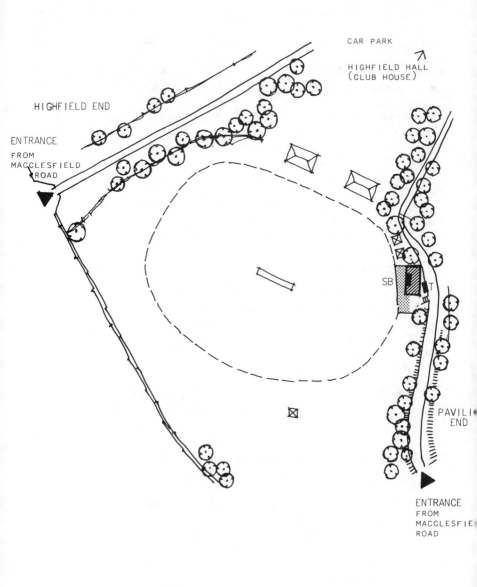

CAR PARK

HIGHFIELD HALL
(CLUB HOUSE)

HIGHFIELD END

ENTRANCE
FROM
MACCLESFIELD
ROAD

SB T

PAVILI
END

ENTRANCE
FROM
MACCLESFIE
ROAD

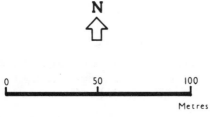

N

0   50   100

Metres

many members' had lost their lives in the Great War.

The ground is situated off the main A523 Leek to Macclesfield road and is on the edge of the town as you enter from the north. The cricket field occupies part of the grounds of Highfield Hall which now forms the main clubhouse. Leek C C has its own cricket pavilion located closer to the playing area with adjoining scoreboard.

Leek C C has staged a number of significant matches, including a match with All India in 1931 when Syd Barnes and C.J. Taylor, whose combined ages were 110 years, between them dismissed the All Indian team. Taylor took 7 for 51 and 3 for 50 (match figures of 10 for 101) and Barnes 2 for 56 and 3 for 29. The ground is used rent-free, thanks to the generosity of Mr. John Tatton who granted this facility in 1944.

Leek Town C C play in the North Staffordshire and South Cheshire Cricket League and field three XIs throughout the season.

The first Derbyshire C C C visit was in 1986 for a John Player Sunday League match with Warwickshire which proved a success. Derbyshire C C C returned to Leek Town C C in 1989 as part of the round-robin matches staged at four venues in Staffordshire against Lancashire who won by 23 runs. On the first Sunday of August in 1992 Derbyshire C C C will host Warwickshire for a Sunday League match at this pleasant out ground nestling in the Staffordshire countryside.

It is necessary to bring your own seats to matches as only 400 are provided. The ground capacity is 3,000–3,500. Some 2,500 spectators attended the Warwickshire match in 1986 and a similar crowd came when the racehorse Red Rum appeared at a donkey derby!

A benefit match was staged by the Leek C C in 1961 for John MacMahon when Keith Miller was a guest and some 3,500 locals attended. It was the best crowd ever seen on the ground. The most recent Test cricketer to have represented Leek Town C C was Athula Samarasekera, the Sri Lankan all-rounder in 1985.

The ground is also used for home Minor County Championship matches by the 1991 double champions Staffordshire C C C Two players who represented Staffordshire C C C last season play regularly for the Leek Town C C David Blank and David Cartledge.

Ground records include highest individual innings by Alan Hill and Mike Watkinson. No player has yet to record a 50 on this ground. Best bowling performances have been achieved by Ole Mortensen and Ian Austin.

ADDRESS Leek Town Cricket Club, The Clubhouse, Highfield Hall, Macclesfield Road, Leek, Staffordshire.

TELEPHONE PROSPECTS OF PLAY   0583 383693

DESCRIPTION OF GROUND AND FACILITIES

Entry to the ground is from Macclesfield Road A523 for pedestrians and cars. Car parking is available on the grass in front of Highfield Hall, the clubhouse. The pavilion includes a scoreboard facility and limited seating for members; there is also an adjacent fenced seating enclosure.

This is a small pleasant tree-enclosed ground with views of the surrounding fine countryside to the south. The north side of the ground is slightly sloping from the Highfield Hall down towards the cricket field where refreshment tents and temporary toilets are situated. Also on this side of the ground are the radio/press tents. On the Macclesfield Road side of the playing area is the Derbyshire C C C souvenir shop, supporters' caravan and some permanent timber bench seating.

Additional car parking is available at Leek Town Football Club and the hockey pitches within walking distance from the ground down the hill towards the town centre. The playing area is 140 metres by 103 metres and is defined by a rope and some advertising boards.

There is no covered accommodation except inside the pavilion or Highfield Hall which is some distance from the playing area.

When required, the TV camera/commentary box will be positioned at the Highfield End of the ground.

GROUND RECORDS AND SCORES

LIMITED-OVERS MATCHES
Highest innings total for County: 153 for 9 *v.* Lancashire (RAL) 1989
Highest innings total against County: 176 for 8 by Lancashire (RAL) 1989
Lowest innings total for County: 132 *v.* Warwickshire (JPL) 1986
Lowest innings total against County: 133 for 5 by Warwickshire (JPL) 1986
Highest individual innings for County: 43 A. Hill *v.* Warwickshire (JPL) 1986
Highest individual innings against County: 44 M. Watkinson for Lancashire (RAL) 1989
Best bowling performance for County: 2 for 19 O.H. Mortensen *v.* Lancashire (RAL) 1989
Best bowling performance against County: 4 for 28 I.P. Austin for Lancashire (RAL) 1989
Best attendance: 2,500 *v.* Warwickshire (JPL) 1986

HOW TO GET THERE

Rail   Congleton (BR), 8 miles.
Bus   PMT 218 links BR Stoke-on-Trent Station with Leek town centre, thence 1 mile walk to ground (Telephone: 0782 747000).
Car   10 miles north-east of Stoke-on-Trent M6 junctions 15 or 16. From north: A523 or A53 to Leek and town centre, ground situated off A523 on northern outskirts of town centre. From east: A523 and A52 then as north. From south: A523 or A520 then as north. From west: A53 then as north.

The Jester, Mill Street (0538 383997); Peak Weaver, King Street; Red Lion Hotel, Market Square.

Disabled Areas   Special area roped off for special matches, request suitable position.
Local Radio Station(s)   BBC Radio Stoke-on-Trent (94.6 MHz FM/ 1053 KHz MW), Radio Signal (102.6 MHz FM/1170 KHz MW), Radio Trent (96.2 MHz FM/999 KHz MW).
Local Newspaper(s)   Derby Evening Telegraph, Leek Post and Times, Evening Sentinel.

Repton

The ground is located within the remains of the twelfth century Augustinian Priory on the middle reaches of the River Trent, which today forms part of Repton School. The pitch is located close to the school buildings, where First XI matches are staged and bounded by Brook End (known as the Boot End because of the public house of that name) and Willington Road.

The priory was destroyed at the Reformation of the monasteries. The executors of Sir John Port paid £37 10s. for those buildings which survived, these now form the buildings of Repton School, which was founded in 1557. The former kitchen garden of the priory was converted in the nineteenth century to a splendid cricket ground.

It is a beautiful setting for cricket and only the second school ground to be used by Derbyshire C C C, (the first was Trent College, Long Eaton in the late 1970s). Derbyshire C C C first staged a Refuge Assurance Sunday League match at the ground in 1988 when Middlesex were the visitors and included in their side John D. Carr, a former pupil at the school. The inaugural match was witnessed by a crowd of 2,500 before the match was cut short by rain. The ground capacity is 4,000.

Repton School has plenty of cricketing history. Three previous Derbyshire C C C captains attended the school: D.B. Carr, D.J. Green and G.L. Willatt. Repton can justifiably claim to have produced one of the greatest schoolboy cricketers of all time, J.N. Crawford (1902–05) who subsequently played for Surrey C C C and England. An earlier Golden Age of Repton was represented by the play of C.B. Fry, often described as one of the most talented of all English athletes. Before World War One, Miles and John Howell maintained the line of outstanding Repton cricketers playing county cricket. John was killed in 1915 and the John Howell Room in the cricket pavilion commemorates him.

Other famous cricketers who played for the school are: R.A. Young, H.S. Altham the cricket author, A.T. Sharp, E.A. and W.T. Greswell, R. Sale, L.C.H. and R.C.N. Palairet, B.H. Valentine, R.H.C. Human and R.A. Hutton, not forgetting the brothers Ford, A.F.J., F.G.J. and W.J.

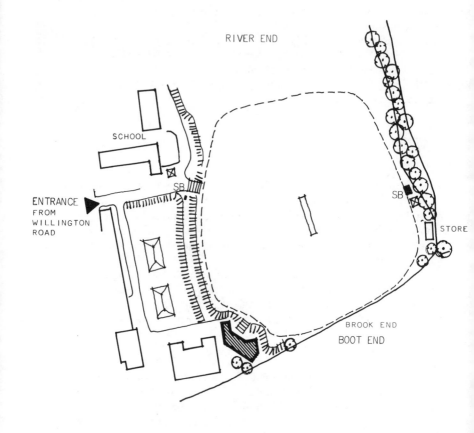

RIVER END

SCHOOL

SB

ENTRANCE
FROM
WILLINGTON
ROAD

SB

STORE

BROOK END
BOOT END

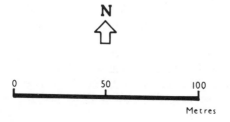

N

0   50   100

Metres

The current master in charge of cricket is Mr Mike Stones. Tours have been arranged to Barbados with the Old Boys' team, the Repton Pilgrims, in recent years.

Ground records in the only match staged at Repton include a single half century by Steve Goldsmith, 61, and 3 for 8 by Angus Fraser with the ball.

ADDRESS   Repton School, The Cricket Pavilion, School Grounds, Willington Road, Repton, Derbyshire DE6 6FH.
TELEPHONE PROSPECTS OF PLAY   0283 701921

DESCRIPTION OF GROUND AND FACILITIES

The only entrance to the Repton School ground is from Willington Road through the main gates near to St Wystan's Church. Limited car parking is available within the ground but only for players' and officials. A large car park is available at the rear of the chapel and main school buildings, a short walk from the cricket pitch. In the ground itself, the only permanent buildings are the pavilion with its thatched roof and the scoreboard on the east side of the playing area. The members' enclosure and refreshment tents are located on the steep bank close to the school buildings as are the Derbyshire C C C souvenir tent and supporters' caravan. The remainder of the ground is open to the public.

All spectators should bring their collapsible seats as no seats are provided whatsoever, except a few benches adjoining the front of the pavilion for the press and officials. There is no space for seating at the Brook End as the playing area is tight against the perimeter wall.

The north and east sides of the ground are lined with trees which with the school buildings, provide a fine scene for cricket. The playing area is 115 metres by 120 metres and is defined only by advertising boards.

GROUND RECORDS AND SCORES

LIMITED-OVERS MATCH
Highest innings total for County: 130 *v*. Middlesex (RAL) 1988
Highest innings total against County: 32 for 0 by Middlesex (RAL) 1988
Highest individual innings for County: 61 S.C. Goldsmith *v*. Middlesex (RAL) 1988
Highest individual innings against County: 15 n.o. J.D. Carr for Middlesex (RAL) 1988
Best bowling performance for County: 0 for 9 A.E. Warner *v*. Middlesex (RAL) 1988
Best bowling performance against County: 3 for 8 A.R.C. Fraser for Middlesex (RAL) 1988
Best attendance: 2,500 *v*. Middlesex (RAL) 1988

HOW TO GET THERE

Rail   Burton-upon-Trent (BR) 5 miles.
Bus   Trent Buses 103 and 104 link Derby Bus Station with Burton-upon-Trent, passing 0.5 mile from BR Burton-upon-Trent Station; also Derby City Buses 42–47 link BR Derby Station with Burton-upon-Trent Bus Station (Telephone: 0332 292200).
Car   5 miles north-east of Burton-upon-Trent. From north: A38 and A5008 to Repton, ground situated off Willington Road within Repton School grounds. From east: A50 and A5132 then B5008 then as north. From south: A38, A50 and B5008 then as north. From west: A50 or A5132 then A5008 then as north.

WHERE TO STAY AND OTHER INFORMATION

Bulls Head, High Street (0283 703297).

Disabled Areas   No special area request suitable position at River End.
Local Radio Station(s)   BBC Radio Derby (104.5 MHz FM/1116 KHz MW), Radio Trent (96.2 MHz FM/999 KHz MW).
Local Newspaper(s)   Derby Evening Telegraph, Burton Mail.

DURHAM

CHESTER-LE-STREET

DARLINGTON

DURHAM UNIVERSITY

GATESHEAD FELL

HARTLEPOOL

STOCKTON-ON-TEES

———————

JESMOND

Durham

Founded   10 May 1882
Colours   Maroon, Oxford blue and old gold
Crest   Coat of arms of County Durham
Patron   A.W. Austin
Overseas Patron   Sir D.G. Bradman AC
President   I.D. Caller
Chairman/Director   J.D. Robson
Directors   R.B. Caller, R. Jackson, H.W.M. Milner, I.D. Mills, T. Moffat MBE, N.A. Riddell, M. Roseberry and J. Sherrington
Chief executive   M.E. Gear
Director of cricket   G. Cook
Captain   D.A. Graveney
Ground administrator   J. Sherrington
Groundsman   T. Flintoft
Scorer/statistician   B. Hunt
Main Sponsor   Newcastle Breweries
Newsletter   Durham C C C *Newsletter*
Address   McEwans Indoor Cricket Centre, Mercantile Road, Rainton Bridge, Houghton-Le-Spring, Tyne and Wear DH4 5PH.
Telephone 091 512 0178
Facsimile 091 584 7525
Durham Rapid Cricketline   0891 567502

ACHIEVEMENTS

Minor County Championship   Champions (8) 1895, 1900, 1901, 1926, 1930, 1976, 1980 and 1981
Minor County Championship   Final Winners (1) 1984
Minor County English Estates Trophy Competition   Winners (1) 1985
County Championship   Initial season 1992
Benson & Hedges Cup   Initial season 1992
Gillette Cup   2nd Round 1973
National Westminster Bank Trophy   2nd Round 1985
Tilcon Trophy   Finalists (1) 1991
Joshua Tetley Festival Trophy   Semi-Finalists (1) 1991

GROUNDS

Darlington (Feethams Cricket Ground, South Terrace) Durham University (Racecourse Ground, Green Lane) Stockton-on-Tees, (Grangefield Road Ground) Hartlepool (Park Drive) Gateshead Fell (Eastwood Gardens, Low Fell) Chester-Le-Street (Ropery Lane) and Jesmond (Northumberland C C C Ground, Osborne Avenue, Newcastle-upon-Tyne).

Other grounds that have been used since 1969 are: Sunderland (Ashbrooke Cricket Ground) Durham City (Green Lane) South Shields (Westoe Ground, Dean Road), Bishop Auckland (King's Way) Wearmouth (Carley Hill) and Consett (Blackfyne Ground).

SECOND XI GROUNDS

In addition to the above mentioned grounds the following will be used for second XI matches: Norton C C, Station Road, Norton, Stockton-on-Tees, Co. Durham. Telephone: 0642 554031; Sunderland C C, Ashbrooke, Sunderland. Co. Durham. Telephone: 091 528 4536; Felling C C, Heworth Lane, Heworth, Felling, Co. Durham. Telephone: 091 469 3645; Philadelphia C C, Bunker Hill, Houghton-le-Spring, Tyne and Wear. Telephone: 091 584 1348; Boldon C C, Sunderland Road, East Boldon, Tyne and Wear. Telephone: 091 536 4180; Bishop Auckland C C, King's Way, Bishop Auckland. Telephone: 0388 603371; Shildon Railway C C, Hackworth Street, Shildon, Co. Durham. Telephone: 0388 772068; Durham City C C, The Pavilion, Green Lane, Durham City. Telephone: 091 386 9959; Eppleton C C, Church Road, Hetton-le-Hole, Tyne and Wear. Telephone: 091 526 1271; Durham School, Quarryhead Lane, Durham City. Telephone: 091 386 9959; Seaton Carew C C, The Pavilion, Hornby Park, Elizabeth Way, Seaton Carew, Hartlepool, Cleveland. Telephone: 0429 260945

It was on 23 May 1882 that a meeting took place at the Three Tuns Hotel in the City of Durham when representatives of eight clubs in the county decided to establish the Durham County Cricket Club. This proposal had been initiated by members of the South Shields Cricket Club.

The first match against neighbours Northumberland C C C was held at Chester Road, Sunderland, the ground of Sunderland Cricket Club on 12–13 June 1882 and on the evening of the first day the first committee meeting of the County Club was held at the Queen's Hotel, Sunderland. This was not the first county team, since a team calling themselves Durham County played as early as 1874 but that club did not survive. Following its foundation in 1882, Durham C C C found it difficult to arrange fixtures, the same reason that probably led to the demise of the earlier club. However, the foundation of the Second-Class Competition in 1895 (later to be renamed the Minor Counties Competition) led to renewed impetus; but this was not long lived as Durham C C C still continued to face difficulty in arranging fixtures – not least we must presume because the only means of travel from say Durham to Worcestershire or Oxfordshire was by train, probably via Birmingham. They therefore reverted to friendly games and several years passed of occasional appearances in the Second-Class Competition until 1899 when Durham C C C rejoined the competition, in which they remained continuously active until 1991, except for breaks during the two world wars.

The Pavilion at the Racecourse Ground, Durham City, Co. Durham.

The Pavilion at Park Drive, Hartlepool, Cleveland.

The Pavilion at Feethams Cricket Ground, Darlington, Co. Durham.

The Pavilion at Grangefield Road, Stockton-On-Tees, Cleveland.

The renewed enthusiasm coupled with some very able cricketers – the Whitwell brothers (William, Arthur and Joseph), Arthur Welch, Arthur Crosby, Dave Nichol, Fred Simpson, Tom Lambert, James Gregory, Edgar 'Tegger' Elliott, George Turnbull, Bob Bousfield and James 'Kellet' Kirtley – led to Durham C C C winning the Second-Class Championship in 1895, 1900 and 1907.

Durham C C C always endeavoured to field a strong team and between 1905 and 1914 their best bowler, Alf Morris from West Hartlepool C C, took 651 minor county wickets in 94 matches. However it was not until 1926 and 1930 that they were again to win the championship; these victories were in spite of the depression in the area causing many players to leave the north-east to seek employment elsewhere in the country. During the period 1920–39 the leading players included Charlie Adamson, Jack Carr, Thomas Dobson, Albert Howell, Maurice Nichol, Harry Gibbon, Stan Ellis and Arthur Austin who is now the patron of the County Club. After the Second World War leading players included R.B. 'Bill' Proud, Jack Keeler, Jack Watson, Norman Owen, Harry Bell, Russell Inglis, Alan Burridge, Stuart Young and Bobby Cole but it was not until 1976 that they again won the Minor Counties Championship. Since then Durham C C C have dominated the competition, being champions in 1980, 1981 and 1984 and runners-up in 1977, 1978 and 1979.

During this period they played 65 consecutive matches without defeat beating the Surrey second XI record of 44 set during the 1950s. The newly successful players included Neil Riddell, Steve Greensword, Steve Atkinson, Brian Lander, Stuart Wilkinson, Peter Birtwisle, Richard Mercer, John Johnston, Peter Kippax, Mohinder Amarnath (India), Lance Cairns (New Zealand), Wasim Raja (Pakistan) and Ashok Patel.

Durham C C C created Gillette Cup history in 1973 when as a minor county they beat Yorkshire a first-class county – the first occasion that this had happened since the competition commenced in 1963. Brian Lander received the Man-of-the-Match award for his 5 for 15 at St George's Cricket Ground, Harrogate. In 1985 this event was repeated when Durham C C C defeated Derbyshire at the County Cricket Ground, Derby in the 1st Round of the National Westminster Bank Trophy.

Over 100 players born in County Durham have played first-class cricket, including a number of Test players such as A.E. Stoddart (Middlesex), C.H. Parkin (Yorkshire and Lancashire), R.T. Spooner (Warwickshire), D.C.H. Townsend (Oxford University), J. McConnon (Glamorgan), C. Milburn (Northamptonshire and Western Australia), P. Willey (Northamptonshire, Leicestershire and Northumberland), R.G.D. Willis (Surrey and Warwickshire), R. Blunt (New Zealand) and J. Middleton (South Africa).

Durham C C C applied to the Test & County Cricket Board on 4 November 1990 for first-class status and this application was granted with effect from 1992. The former Durham C C C was dissolved at the Annual General Meeting in March 1991 and a Limited Company was established with officers and directors.

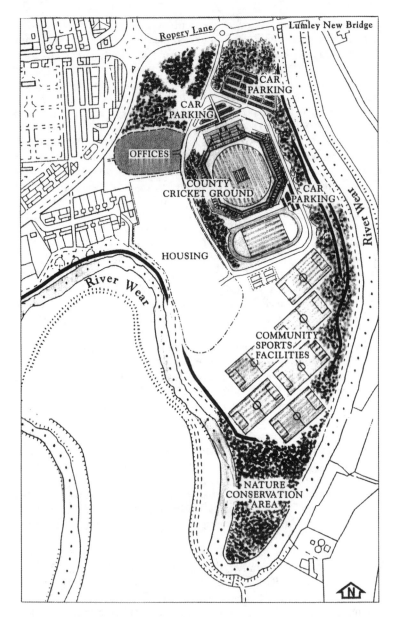

The proposed development of the County cricket ground at Chester-le-Street, reproduced by courtesy of Durham C C C

A number of players have been signed for the initial season in first-class cricket in 1992 under the director of cricket Geoff Cook and these include: David Graveney (Captain), Wayne Larkins, Ian Botham, Paul Parker, Steve McEwan, Simon Hughes, Ian Smith and Dean Jones (Victoria and Australia) as their one overseas player.

It has been agreed to establish a new County Cricket Ground at Chester-le-Street and it is proposed to create a new stadium at the picturesque Riverside Park site by 1995 in conjunction with the Chester-le-Street District Council. The area for the complex is approximately 43 hectares and this will include facilities for a County Cricket Ground, car parking, offices, community sports facilities and a nature conservation area near the River Wear as well as an area for housing. The cricket arena will therefore stand in a well landscaped recreational area which will itself enhance the Riverside area of Chester-le-Street. The site is south of Ropery Lane and only 0.5 mile from the existing Chester-le-Street C C ground which will be used in 1992 for a match with the tourists. Presently there is no County Cricket Ground so the headquarters of the Durham C C C is housed at the McEwans Indoor Cricket Centre in Houghton-le-Spring.

Chester-le-Street

The first Durham C C C minor county match to be staged at Ropery Lane, Chester-le-Street was on 3–4 August 1903 against Northumberland C C C

Chester-le-Street Cricket Club was established in 1834 and play in the Durham Senior Cricket League, fielding three XIs throughout the season. The club moved to their present ground in the late 1890s from the original ground which was ironically near the River Wear, where the new Durham C C C Headquarters Ground is due to be built during the next few years.

Chester-le-Street C C were Durham Senior Cricket League Champions in 1920, 1922, 1969, 1980, 1981 and 1983. The most successful season in the history of the club was in 1980 when as well as winning the Durham Senior Cricket League, the club also won the Vaux Tom Burn Cup, Exhibition Horner Cup and the Saunders Cup which is the most prestigious cricket knockout competition cup in the county. The club was also losing finalists in the Grangetown Bowl and the Armbrister Trophy. The 1980–81 teams included Norman Allison, Wasim Raja (Pakistan) and Diraj Prasana (India) the two club cricket professionals. Other notable club professionals have included the late Colin Milburn and Suresh Shastri (India).

Other fixtures staged at the Ropery Lane ground include four local cup finals namely the Exhibition Horner, George Coates Trophy, Vaux Tom Burn and Leyland Daf Invitation Trophy.

The first important match to be staged at Chester-le-Street by Durham C C C was against the touring New Zealanders on 18–19 June 1927. The New Zealand touring team won by 10 wickets thanks to 178 by C.S. Dempster and 5 for 66 by M. Henderson and 4 for 25 by W. Cunningham. J. Cook, the Durham number ten batsman, top scored with 106 n.o. and had a partnership with H. Brooks which took the total from 58 for 8 to 253 for 9 in their first innings.

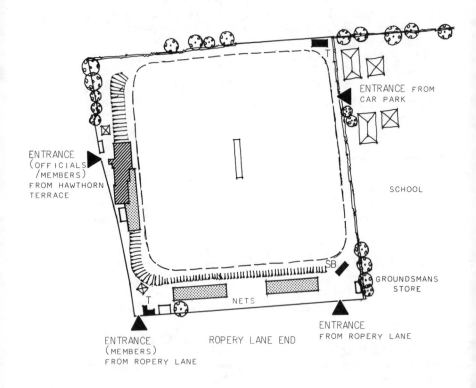

CHURCH END

ENTRANCE FROM
CAR PARK

ENTRANCE
(OFFICIALS
/MEMBERS)
FROM HAWTHORN
TERRACE

SCHOOL

SB

NETS

GROUNDSMANS
STORE

ENTRANCE
(MEMBERS)
FROM ROPERY LANE

ROPERY LANE END

ENTRANCE
FROM ROPERY LANE

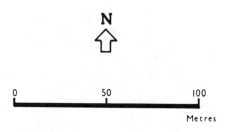

N

0   50   100

Metres

The Chester-le-Street C C have hosted several limited-overs matches against first-class counties in the Gillette Cup/National Westminster Bank Trophy for Durham C C C against Nottinghamshire (1967), Worcestershire (1968), Surrey (1972), Essex (1973), Yorkshire (1979) and Lancashire (1983). A single Benson & Hedges Cup zonal group match was staged between Minor Counties (North) and Yorkshire in 1973.

The only match at Ropery Lane in 1992 will be staged on 14–16 July with the touring Pakistanis. The only other occasion when Durham C C C have hosted the Pakistan tourists was in 1962 at Ashbrooke Ground, Sunderland when the match staged on 8–10 September was abandoned due to rain. Pakistan scored 282 and 15 for 0 with Durham replying with 222 for 7 dec. Scores of over fifty were recorded in the match by D.J. Ellis (100 n.o.) for Durham and Imtiaz Ahmed (65) and Javed Burki (53 n.o.) for Pakistan. Wasim Raja who played test cricket for Pakistan acted as Chester- le-Street C C cricket professional for a number of years and represented Durham C C C in Gillette Cup/ National Westminster Bank Trophy and Minor County Championship fixtures. Other players to have represented Chester-le-Street C C and Durham C C C are George March, John Tindall, John Wake and Russell Inglis.

The Ropery Lane ground is situated less than half a mile from the proposed new Riverside Stadium and Durham C C C County Cricket Ground development to the south of Ropery Lane near Lumley New Bridge. From the first floor of the pavilion you have a splendid view of the playing area and the Lumley Castle on the hillside opposite. The development proposals for the new County Cricket Ground at Chester-le-Street a total site of 43 hectares, are to include a 7-hectare cricket ground, 500 permanent car parking spaces for the cricket spectators of approximately 3 hectares, offices (1 hectare), Housing (7.5 hectares), Playing fields, athletic track, community sports facilities and additional car parking (14 hectares) together with an area of landscape and nature conservation of 10.5 hectares. The plans have been laid out and the project is likely to commence in the near future so that by the end of the century County Championship and possibly international cricket will be staged in County Durham. The joint aim of Durham C C C and Chester-le-Street District Council is to provide a superb new all seater cricket stadium with all necessary associated leisure facilities which will provide the north-east with a sound foundation for taking first-class cricket into the next century.

The present ground capacity is 5,000 and this has been achieved for Gillette Cup/National Westminster Bank Trophy matches with Surrey in 1972, Essex in 1973, Yorkshire in 1979 and for the Benson & Hedges Cup zonal Group match between Minor Counties (North) and Yorkshire in 1973.

Ground records at Ropery Lane include hundreds for the county by G. Turnbull and for the visitors by C.S. Dempster (New Zealand) in 1927 and G.V. Miller (Cambridgeshire) in 1984. With the ball A. Morris and

W.K. Laidlaw have achieved fine bowling spells for the county and J.M. Watson for the visitors.

In the limited-overs game both batting records were established in the 1972 Gillette Cup match staged against Surrey, with Micky Stewart the current England manager, recording the highest individual innings on the ground of 101. The best bowling performance is by S.P. Davis, 7 for 32 against Lancashire in the National Westminster Bank Trophy 1st round tie in 1983.

ADDRESS   Chester-le-Street Cricket Club., The Pavilion, Ropery Lane, Chester-le-Street, County Durham.

TELEPHONE NUMBER PROSPECTS OF PLAY   091 388 3684

DESCRIPTION OF GROUND AND FACILITIES

The ground is entered by members from Hawthorn Terrace to the rear of the pavilion and in Ropery Lane. A public entrance is also located in Ropery Lane and from the car park in the adjoining Chester-le-Street R C mixed and infant school to the east of the playing area.

Car parking is available for 1,000-plus vehicles within a few minutes walk of the ground in the adjoining school field entered from Eardulph Park. Car parking for players and officials is situated in Mains Park/ Hawthorn Terrace which is shut off during match days to through traffic.

The pavilion includes a members' bar and refreshment area together with a press room and radio commentary position on the upper floor level. The players' changing facilities are situated in the pavilion. There are a number of photographs and historic information about the club on view.

The members' enclosure is situated in front of the pavilion where the sky blue plastic seats are situated and to the south-east and north-east of the playing area on temporary seating. The rest of the ground is available to the public. Two plastic raised seating areas are situated on the bank at the Ropery Lane End either side of the sightscreen. The scoreboard is situated in the south-east corner of the ground and situated to the rear is the groundsman's store. The majority of facilities are temporary and these include refreshment tents, kiosks and bars together with a Durham C C C souvenir shop. Facilities for disabled spectators are available by arrangement in advance. Toilets are situated in the pavilion and to the south-east and north-west of the ground and in the adjoining field. Sponsors' tents are situated within the school grounds and cricket can be viewed from these tents.

The smooth playing area is 110 metres by 109 metres and is defined by a rope and advertising boards. The playing area falls slightly away from the pavilion towards the Lumley Castle side of the ground.

When required, the TV camera/commentary box will be positioned directly above and behind the sightscreen at the Ropery Lane End of the ground on a gantry.

The ground capacity is 5,000; permanent seating is available for 3,200 and in total 4,000 seats can be provided so spectators would be advised to bring their own seats to popular matches.

GROUND RECORDS AND SCORES

MINOR COUNTIES CHAMPIONSHIP/FIRST-CLASS MATCHES
Highest innings total for County: 467 *v*. Northumberland 1906
Highest innings total against County: 387 by Northumberland 1911
Lowest innings total for County: 60 *v*. Northumberland 1948
Lowest innings total against County: 37 by Northumberland 1937
Highest individual innings for County: 172 G. Turnbull *v*. Northumberland 1906
Highest individual innings against County: 178 C.S. Dempster for New Zealanders 1927
Best bowling performance in an innings for County: 9 for 51 A. Morris *v*. Northumberland 1909
Best bowling performance in an innings against County: 8 for 42 J.M. Watson for Northumberland 1953
Best bowling performance in a match for County: 12 for 65 W.K. Laidlaw *v*. Northumberland 1948
Best bowling performance in a match against County: 15 for 83 J.M. Watson for Northumberland 1953
Best attendance for a First-Class Match: 2,000 *v*. New Zealanders 1927

LIMITED-OVERS MATCHES
Highest innings total for County: 213 for 9 *v*. Yorkshire (GC) 1979
Highest innings total against County: 217 for 9 by Surrey (GC) 1972
Lowest innings total for County: 82 *v*. Worcestershire (GC) 1968
Lowest innings total against County: 98 by Worcestershire (GC) 1968
Highest individual innings for County: 78 J.G. March *v*. Surrey (GC) 1972
Highest individual innings against County: 101 M.J. Stewart for Surrey (GC) 1972
Best bowling performance for County: 7 for 32 S.P. Davis *v*. Lancashire (NWBT) 1983
Best bowling performance against County: 4 for 13 B.M. Brain for Worcestershire (GC) 1968
Best attendance: 5,000 *v*. Surrey (GC) 1972

HOW TO GET THERE

Rail Chester-le-Street (BR), 0.25 mile.
Bus X1, X2, X46, X69, 722, 723, 724 and 737 Go-Ahead Northern/Tees & District/United/OK Travel/Primrose Coaches/ Gardiners through Chester-le-Street 0.25 mile from ground (Telephone 091 386 4411 ext 2337).

Car   From north: A1(M) to Chester-le-Street junction, then follow Shields Road and Park Road North and Central following signs Durham A167, then at Ropery Lane roundabout turn right into Ropery Lane for ground and car parks. From east: as north. From west: A693 or A167 signposted Chester-le-Street, from town centre take Ropery Lane for ground. From south: A167 from Durham or A1(M) to Chester-le-Street junction, then as north.

WHERE TO STAY AND OTHER INFORMATION

Lumley Castle Hotel (091 389 1111) Lambton Arms Hotel (091 388 3265), The Lampton Worm (091 388 3386) or stay at one of several guest houses in Chester-le-Street.

Disabled Areas   No special area request suitable position, parking by prior arrangement.
Local Radio Station(s)   BBC Radio Newcastle (96.0 MHz FM/1458 KHz MW) BBC Radio Cleveland (95.0 MHz FM/1548 KHz MW), T.F.M. Radio (96.6 MHz FM/1170 KHz MW).
Local Newspaper(s)   Northern Echo, Evening Gazette.

Darlington

Darlington Cricket Club, established circa 1827 originally played on a ground in Park Street and the last match to be played there was in October 1866. The club moved to an area of ten acres of ground which they rented to the south of Feethams, the house where Mr. J. Pease lived. Late in 1866 a new cricket ground was levelled, with the turf being transferred from the previous Park Street ground.

The first Durham C C C Minor County Championship match staged at Feethams was on 24–25 June 1895 against Cheshire with the last match being against Staffordshire on 18–19 July 1990. No Minor County Championship match was staged at Darlington in 1991.

The Darlington Cricket and Athletic Club arranged some important early matches including in 1870 a three day match between an All England XI and twenty-two local players. In 1896 Darlington C C joined the North Yorkshire and South Durham Cricket League since renamed the Girobank NY&SDCL and won the league in their first season. In 1897 the club was told by its landlord that the ground was to be sold, but the club had first option to purchase it. After much effort the ground was purchased for £4,000 at a meeting in the Mechanics' Hall and transferred to a trust in 1903 and this still remains today. Darlington C C field three XIs throughout the season and play in the Kerridge, Banks, Saunders, Austin, Mathew Oswald, Smith Print, Haith, Robinson, James Bell, Ken Walsh, Thirds and Grainden County Cup knock-out competitions.

The new brick cricket pavilion was constructed in 1903 by Mr

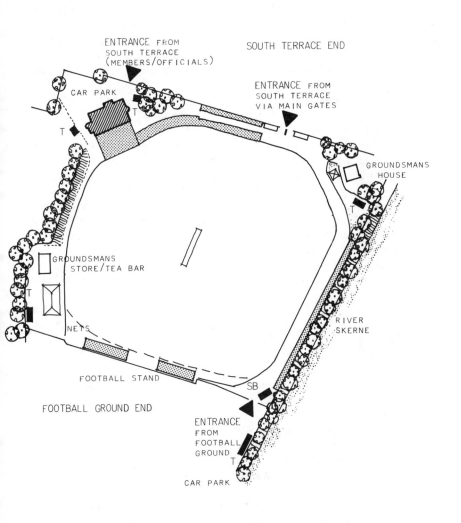

ENTRANCE FROM
SOUTH TERRACE
(MEMBERS/OFFICIALS)

SOUTH TERRACE END

CAR PARK

ENTRANCE FROM
SOUTH TERRACE
VIA MAIN GATES

T

GROUNDSMANS
HOUSE

T

GROUNDSMANS
STORE/TEA BAR

T

RIVER
SKERNE

NETS

FOOTBALL STAND

SB

FOOTBALL GROUND END

ENTRANCE
FROM
FOOTBALL
GROUND

T

CAR PARK

N

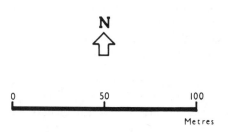

0   50   100

Metres

T. Boyd then principal building contractor of Darlington, at an estimated cost of £900 after the previous structure was demolished. The architect was Mr Fred W. Brookes. The pavilion was opened by Mr E.D. Walker and he remarked about bygone sports events staged on the ground in previous years including the Darlington Olympian Games. The pavilion was used by athletes, cricketers and footballers for changing and also by members for the three large club rooms could accommodate 320 people.

The ground was shared with the 'Quakers', Darlington Football Club who were formed in 1883 and turned professional in 1908. The cricket ground and football ground are now separated by the football stand at the Feethams End although the grounds are situated within the same complex and have the same entrance.

Darlington F C are currently in the Barclays League Division Three, but during the period 1988–89 were playing in the GMVC non-league as they were relegated from the Football League for one season; they were GMVC Champions in 1989. The only player to have represented Darlington cricket and football clubs (1950–56) to a high standard is Harry M. Clark, who also represented Sheffield Wednesday and Hartlepool Football Clubs (261 league matches scoring 63 goals).

Many famous players have played at Feethams Cricket Ground and these include Dr W.G. Grace, Learie Constantine, Len Hutton, Hedley Verity and Vivian Richards. In 1901 the touring South Africans played Durham and won by 446 runs thanks to 151 by A.V.C. Blisset and match bowling figures of 9 for 126 by J.H. Sinclair. On 10 July 1907 Dr. W.G. Grace played for a North Yorkshire and South Durham League XI against a North Durham XI and scored 51 runs. A copy of this scorecard is on display in the pavilion together with a number of photographs and cricket memorabilia relating to Feethams Ground and Darlington cricket.

On 17–19 September 1909 Sir E.D. Walkers's XI played Mr J. Bucknell's XI and included within these teams were W. Rhodes, S. Haigh, E. Drake, G. Hirst, E. Tyldesley and D. Denton.

In 1923 the West Indian tourists played Durham C C C on the ground winning by 180 runs and in 1991 the West Indians again visited Feethams when a two day match was staged by the Minor Counties Cricket Association. A number of limited-overs matches have been staged at Darlington and these have included Gillette Cup/National Westminster Bank Trophy matches hosted by Durham C C C against Hertfordshire 1964, Northamptonshire 1984, Middlesex 1987 and 1989, Somerset 1988 and Glamorgan 1991. Darlington also hosted one Benson & Hedges Cup zonal group match for Minor Counties against Northamptonshire in 1988 with Northamptonshire winning by 44 runs. Durham's National Westminster Bank Trophy 1st round tie against Glamorgan produced 630 runs in the match.

Darlington Borough Council contributed £20,000 in 1991 towards improving the facilities at Feethams to enable the ground to stage first-class cricket during the period 1992–95 during the development of the

Durham C C C new County Headquarters Ground at Chester-le-Street. The following improvements have been made for the 1992 season: lightweight covers, improved dressing room facilities, an upgraded scoreboard, larger sightscreen, an extension to the function room within the pavilion facing the pitch. These are amongst many other tasks which will be completed before March 1992.

Players to have represented Darlington C C and played first-class/minor county cricket include: Andy Fothergill, John Lister, Simon Daniels, Peter Barnes, John Johnston, Steve Malone, Neil Riddell, Simon Davis and Paul Romaines.

In 1992 the Feethams Cricket Ground will host eight days cricket commencing in early June with a three day Britannic Assurance Championship match with Somerset, followed in late August by a four-day championship match with Hampshire and a single limited-overs Sunday League match with Yorkshire.

The ground capacity is 5,000 and this has been achieved regularly for popular matches. Ground records include centuries by H.D. Bell and A.V.C. Blisset. Significant bowling performances have been achieved by K.D. Biddulph and T.H. Hirst. In the limited-overs game the highest individual scores have been recorded by John Glendenen and Matthew Maynard with best bowling returns by Stuart Young and Simon Hughes for his former county Middlesex.

ADDRESS Darlington Cricket and Athletic Club., Feethams Cricket Ground, South Terrace, Darlington, County Durham DL1 5JD.
TELEPHONE NUMBER PROSPECTS OF PLAY 0325 466415

DESCRIPTION OF GROUND AND FACILITIES

The spacious Feethams Ground lies on the southern edge of the town centre. The main entrance to the Feethams Cricket Ground is from South Terrace to the north of the playing area through the main gates and turnstiles. An entrance is also available at the rear of the pavilion for players, officials and members. Car parking for 120 cars is available in the ground for players, officials and senior stewards only and 400 car park spaces are available externally adjoining the ground. Other car parking is available nearby in the town centre car parks, and to the south of the ground street parking is available within the local neighbourhood.

The only permanent buildings are the main pavilion, terracing, groundsman's hut, scoreboard, bench seating and the groundsman's house. To the south of the playing area is the Darlington F C ground stands/floodlight pylons. The pavilion area is available to the players, officials, sponsors and members only. The members' enclosure is situated in the pavilion terraces and adjoining terracing to the north side of the ground at the Town End. A radio commentary position is situated on the pavilion balcony. The rest of the ground is available to the public. A disabled enclosure is sited to the left of the pavilion and disabled vehicles can be parked at the rear of the pavilion. Toilets are situated in the pavilion and in temporary facilities at both corners of the football stand. To the west of the playing area is the press box, sited in a temporary building on the bank with temporary raised plastic seating and the groundsman's hut which is located close to the refreshment/bar marquee, temporary toilets and cricket nets. At the Football Ground End are some small raised seating areas and in the south-east corner the refurbished scoreboard was donated by Press Construction in 1991. To the east of the playing area are new timber bench seats supplied by Jewsons and to the rear behind the tree backcloth is the River Skerne. Situated in front of the groundsman's house are some sponsors' tents, a temporary toilet and sited near the main entrance is a mobile Durham C C C souvenir shop.

The ground capacity is 5,000 with fixed permanent seating for 900 and approximately 2,200 folding temporary seats are installed for county matches. Refreshment facilities are available in the four corners of the ground in tents and kiosks. Spectators are advised to bring their own seats to one-day matches only.

The flat playing area is 124 metres by 133 metres and is defined by a rope and a white fence with some advertising boards. The square can accommodate twenty pitches and the ground has ample space for temporary facilities. Seating is available around the perimeter of the playing area on benches sited on the roadway/cycle track except at the Football Ground End.

When required the TV camera/commentary box would be positioned at the Football Ground End directly above and behind the sightscreen.

GROUND RECORDS AND SCORES

MINOR COUNTIES CHAMPIONSHIP/FIRST-CLASS MATCHES
Highest innings total for County: 457 for 9 dec. *v.* Cheshire 1909
Highest innings total against County: 502 for 9 dec. by South Africans 1901
Lowest innings total for County: 37 *v.* Yorkshire 2nd XI 1899
Lowest innings total against County: 49 by Yorkshire 2nd XI 1899
Highest individual innings for County: 186 H.D. Bell *v.* Lancashire 2nd XI 1960
Highest individual innings against County: 151 A.V.C. Blisset for South Africans 1901
Best bowling performance in an innings for County: 8 for 47 K.D. Biddulph *v.* Staffordshire 1964
Best bowling performance in an innings against County: 7 for 24 T.H. Hirst for Yorkshire 2nd XI 1899
Best bowling performance in a match for County: 13 for 94 K.D. Biddulph *v.* Staffordshire 1964
Best bowling performance in a match against County: 14 for 45 T.H. Hirst for Yorkshire 2nd XI 1899
Best attendance for a first-class match: 5,000 *v.* South Africans 1901/West Indians 1923

Highest innings total for County: 305 for 9 *v*. Glamorgan (NWBT) 1991

Highest innings total against County: 345 for 2 by Glamorgan (NWBT) 1991

Lowest innings total for County: 161 *v*. Middlesex (NWBT) 1989

Lowest innings total against County: 63 by Hertfordshire (GC) 1963

Highest individual innings for County: 109 J.D. Glendenen *v*. Glamorgan (NWBT) 1991

Highest individual innings against County: 151 n.o. M.P. Maynard for Glamorgan (NWBT) 1991

Best bowling performance for County: 4 for 13 S.H. Young *v*. Hertfordshire (GC) 1963

Best bowling performance against County: 4 for 20 S.P. Hughes for Middlesex (NWBT) 1989

Best attendance: 5,000 for M.C.C.A. *v*. West Indians 1990/Durham *v*. Middlesex (NWBT) 1987

HOW TO GET THERE

Rail   Darlington (BR), 0.25 mile.

Bus   Darlington Transport Company bus 2 links BR Darlington Station with ground also Darlington Transport Company and United buses 1, 1A, 3A, 3B, 4, 4A, 5, 6, 6A, 7, 11A, X13, X14, X35, X50, X51, X70, 68, 68A, 722 and 723 link Darlington Bus Station with surrounding areas. Bus Station 0.25 mile from ground (Telephone: 0325 488777 or 468771)

Car   From north: A1(M) then take A167 signposted Darlington and town centre, then follow signs Northallerton for Victoria Road, then after roundabout take left South Terrace for Feethams Ground. From east: A167 signposted Darlington and town centre, then as north. From west: A67 signposted Darlington and town centre, then at roundabout take third exit into Victoria Road, then as north. From south: A1(M) then A66(M) and A66 signposted Darlington and town centre, then at roundabout take fourth exit into Victoria Road, then as north.

WHERE TO STAY AND OTHER INFORMATION

Blackwell Grange Moat House (0325 380888) Coachman Hotel (0325 286116), Kings Head Swallow Hotel (0325 380222) Headlam Hall Hotel (0325 730238).

Disabled Areas   Special area situated to the left of the pavilion.

Local Radio Station(s)   BBC Radio Cleveland (95.0 MHz FM/1548 KHz MW) T.F.M. Radio (96.6 MHz FM/1170 KHz MW).

Local Newspaper(s)   Northern Echo, Evening Gazette, Darlington and Stockton Times, Darlington Journal.

Durham University

The first and only Durham C C C Minor County Championship match staged at the Durham University Racecourse Ground was on 19–20 August 1991 when Norfolk the visitors won by 1 wicket thanks to a splendid 101 n.o. by Roger Finney the former Derbyshire C C C player.

Later, on 16–20 September Durham C C C played two friendly matches with Victoria, the Sheffield Shield Champions of 1990–91 as part of the Australians' tour, preceding the Brittanic Assurance Challenge with the 1991 Britannic Assurance County Champions Essex at Chelmsford the following week. The first match was a limited-overs game which Victoria won by 75 runs and the second match, which lasted four days, was drawn. In April 1992 Durham C C C will play their inaugural home matches in the Sunday League against Lancashire, the Benson & Hedges Cup against Glamorgan and the initial first-class Britannic Assurance County Championship match with Leicestershire at the Racecourse Ground. In late July–early August seven days cricket will be played with Surrey and Yorkshire to include two championship matches and one Sunday League match. The Durham University C C ground will be used for a total of thirteen days cricket plus limited-overs knock-out matches subject to the county club qualifying for later rounds of various competitions.

The Racecourse Ground is situated between Green Lane and the River Wear in a large bowl with splendid views of the City of Durham, the Castle and the Cathedral towards the west and the Durham countryside to the north and east. To the east of the ground is the Durham City C C ground which will be used for a Second XI match with Leicestershire in June 1992. The Durham Rugby Union Football Ground, University rowing club boat house, swimming baths, squash courts and tennis courts as well as a bowling green are within a stone's throw of the Racecourse Ground. The ground takes its name from the former Durham Racecourse which was sited in this area. The ground is used by Durham University Cricket Club (which was established circa 1835) for University matches and games in the Commercial Union UAU Championship Senior and Junior sections. In 1990 Durham University beat Exeter University at Aigburth Cricket Ground, Liverpool to win the UAU Championship. The Durham University team included several players with first-class experience: Brian Evans, who has represented Hertfordshire C C C, Jon Longley, now of Kent C C C, Wasim Raja the former Pakistan Test player, and James Boiling, now of Surrey C C C Durham University have been finalists for the past seven consecutive years of UAU Championships and now without question are one of the leading universities for young cricketers.

The President of Durham University C C, geology lecturer Dr Grenville Holland, says that the Racecourse ground is one of England's leading cricket nurseries and has provided a number of first-class cricketers. Durham University has been associated with some fine

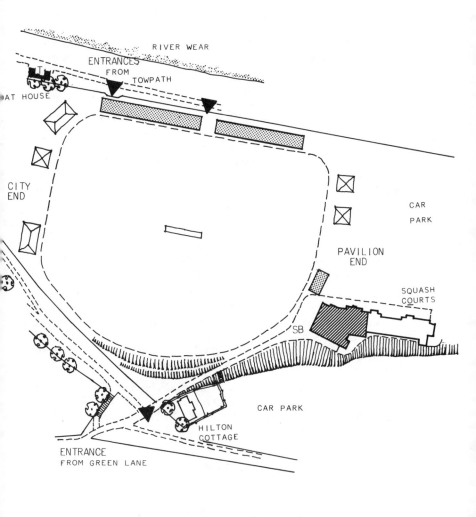

RIVER WEAR

ENTRANCES
FROM TOWPATH

AT HOUSE

CITY
END

CAR
PARK

PAVILION
END

SQUASH
COURTS

SB

CAR PARK

HILTON
COTTAGE

ENTRANCE
FROM GREEN LANE

N

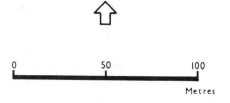

0   50   100

Metres

players in recent years who have graduated to the first-class game after leaving University. While the standard of Cambridge and Oxford University cricket has declined since the early 1970s Durham University's Racecourse Ground has certainly emerged as the setting for one of the new nurseries of county cricket. Five former old boys have already represented their country: Paul Allott and Graeme Fowler both of Lancashire C C C, Tim Curtis, the new captain of Worcestershire C C C, John Stephenson and Nasser Hussain, both of Essex C C C. A dozen other former students of Durham University C C have established themselves on the county circuit.

In 1989 for the first time Durham University students were selected for inclusion in the Combined Universities team for the Benson & Hedges Cup which had previously been selected from only students playing at Cambridge and Oxford. The Combined Universities team recorded zonal group victories over Surrey and Worcestershire and were beaten in the quarter-finals by Somerset at Taunton. The team which played in the quarter-final match included five Durham University students: James Boiling (Surrey C C C), Tim O'Gorman (Derbyshire C C C), Martin Speight (Sussex C C C), Jon Longley (Kent C C C) and Nasser Hussain (Essex C C C).

The ground capacity is 5,000 and the largest crowd to date was for the match with Victoria when 2,000 were present. Ground records include a single double century of 200 n.o. by John Glendenen against Victoria and centuries by S. Hutton (112 n.o.). against Norfolk and for the visitors Roger Finney (101 n.o.). and Dean Jones, 144 for Victoria against his new employer – for he will be Durham's overseas player in 1992. Match bowling performances have been achieved by Simon Brown for the county and by P.W. Jackson for the visitors.

ADDRESS Durham University Cricket Club, The Pavilion, The Racecourse Ground, Green Lane, Durham City, County Durham.
TELEPHONE NUMBER PROSPECTS OF PLAY Temporary line call Directory Enquiries.

DESCRIPTION OF GROUND AND FACILITIES

The main entry to the ground is from Green Lane, for members, players and officials, the public and cars. There are additional pedestrian entrances to the north and north-west of the playing area from the towpath of the nearby River Wear.

No car parking is available inside the ground but approximately 250 parking spaces are available on the adjacent football field to the south-east of the playing area to the rear of the pavilion and squash courts. There is also street parking close to the ground and within the city centre multi-storey car parks which are within easy walking distance.

The pavilion is situated to the south-east of the playing area with a small adjoining scoreboard, press tent and scorers' tent. The majority of seating which is limited to 1000-plus is of a temporary nature with small raised seating areas to the north of the playing area and also close to the pavilion. The members' enclosure includes the bank near Hilton Cottage and the pavilion to the north-west side of the ground. The sponsors' area includes a number of marquees and these are situated at the City End on the tennis courts. The rest of the ground is available to the public where temporary seating is provided. There are facilities for refreshments and snacks and bars to be found in a number of tents and kiosks around the ground, together with a Durham C C C souvenir shop. Facilities for disabled spectators are available by prior arrangement and parking is available within the ground for disabled vehicles. Permanent toilets are situated in the pavilion and squash courts building and near the bowling green with temporary facilities situated within the ground.

The playing area is superbly situated beside the River Wear and with Durham Cathedral and Castle as a backdrop is one of the most attractive venues to watch cricket on a fine day. The dimensions of the playing area are 148 metres by 118 metres, defined by a rope and advertising boards.

When required, the TV camera/commentary box will be positioned directly above and behind the sightscreen at the Pavilion End of the ground on a gantry.

The ground capacity is 5,000 and temporary seating is provided for 1000-plus, so spectators would be advised to bring their own seats to popular matches.

GROUND RECORDS AND SCORES

MINOR COUNTIES CHAMPIONSHIP/FIRST-CLASS MATCHES
Highest innings total for County: 354 for 3 dec. *v.* Victoria 1991
Highest innings total against County: 402 for 5 dec. by Victoria 1991
Lowest innings total for County: 172 for 8 *v.* Victoria 1991
Lowest innings total against County: 191 for 6 by Norfolk 1991
Highest individual innings for County: 200 n.o. J.D. Glendenen *v.* Victoria 1991
Highest individual innings against County: 144 D.M. Jones for Victoria 1991
Best bowling performance in an innings for County: 5 for 60 S.J.E. Brown *v.* Norfolk 1991
Best bowling performance in an innings against County: 6 for 53 P.W. Jackson for Victoria 1991
Best bowling performance in a match for County: 6 for 83 S.J.E. Brown *v.* Norfolk 1991
Best bowling performance in a match against County: 8 for 153 P.W. Jackson for Victoria 1991
Best attendance for a first-class match: 2,000 *v.* Victoria 1991

LIMITED-OVERS MATCHES
Highest innings total for County: 157 for 2 *v.* Victoria 1991
Highest innings total against County: 232 for 3 by Victoria 1991
Highest individual innings for County: 69 n.o. J.D. Glendenen *v.* Victoria 1991

Highest individual innings against County: 72 W.N. Phillips for Victoria 1991
Best bowling performance for County: 2 for 62 G.K. Brown *v.* Victoria 1991
Best bowling performance against County: 2 for 29 P.W. Jackson for Victoria 1991
Best attendance: 2,000 *v.* Victoria 1991

HOW TO GET THERE

Rail   Durham (BR), 1.25 mile.
Bus   20, 41, and 57 United/Gardiners/OK Travel buses pass 0.25 mile from ground. The No. 20 links BR Durham Station with Old Elvet leading to Green Lane and ground (Telephone 091 386 4411 ext 2337).
Car   From north: A1(M) to Durham City junction (north), then follow A690 for Durham and city centre, then take New Elvet Bridge and take left into Old Elvet for Green Lane and ground. From east: A690 for Durham and city centre then as north or A1(M) to Durham City junction (south), then follow A177 for Durham and city centre, then as north. From west: A167 then follow signs Durham and city centre, take Leazes Bridge and New Elvet Bridge, then as north. From south: A1(M) to Durham City junction (south), then follow A177 for Durham and city centre, then as north or A167 then as west and then as north.

WHERE TO STAY AND OTHER INFORMATION

Post House Hotel, Washington (091 416 2264) or stay at one of several guest houses in Durham.

Disabled Areas   Special position available near pavilion by prior arrangement and car parking area.
Local Radio Station(s)   T.F.M. (96.6 MHz FM/1170 KHz MW) BBC Radio Newcastle (96.0 MHz FM/1458 KHz MW), BBC Radio Cleveland (95.0 MHz FM/1548 KHz MW).
Local Newspaper(s)   Northern Echo, Journal, Evening Chronicle, Sunderland Echo, Durham Advertiser.

Gateshead Fell

Eastwood Gardens situated to the south of central Gateshead and the River Tyne, and within close proximity of the Gateshead International Sports Stadium is the home of Gateshead Fell Cricket Club established in 1878. Gateshead has the largest Metrocentre in Europe; there are many shops and leisure activities available in the huge complex and it is well worth a visit if play is washed out for the day.

The first Minor County Championship match staged at Gateshead Fell Cricket Club by Durham C C C was on 24–25 June 1959 against Staffordshire and the last match was staged on 4–5 August 1991 against neighbours Northumberland.

The Gateshead Fell C C moved to their present ground during 1880–81. The club used to play in the Tyneside Senior League until 1962 when the club applied for and was granted admission to the Durham Senior Cricket League. The club fields three XIs throughout the season in the Vaux Durham Senior League and the Churchill Investment League. The Eastwood Gardens ground has continued to be upgraded over the years but had a fire in 1966 which totally destroyed the club pavilion and players' changing facilities. These were replaced during the 1966–67 close season ready for the 1967 season. The clubhouse bar and lounge which is separate from the pavilion was extended in 1976, this is the building to the east of the pavilion with the club badge and year 1878 depicted in blue above the entrance.

It is said by locals that if you cannot see the spire of St John's Church from the pavilion then it is raining and if you can see it then it will be raining soon !

In 1992 Durham C C C will stage eight days cricket at Gateshead Fell C C, commencing in April with a Sunday League match with Leicestershire. This will be followed by Britannic Assurance County Championship matches with Kent in late June for three days and the final match of the season with Lancashire in mid-September for four days.

The only two current players to have represented Gateshead Fell C C and Durham C C C are Ian Robson, (son of Don Robson the National Cricket Association Chairman) who has also represented ESCA, NCA and Young England, and Iain Young. Other famous players to have represented the Gateshead Fell C C include Kenny Earle, Steve Greensword, Richie Richardson (the present West Indies Test Captain) and Damien Martyn from Western Australia, who captained the Young Australian team on their tour of England in 1991 and played for Leicestershire during the first part of the season.

The ground capacity is 4,500 and the largest attendance was for the English Estates match with Wiltshire in 1985 when some 1,450 attended.

Ground records include, with the bat, 156 n.o. by Russell Inglis against Northumberland in 1966 and 81 by Bernard Reidy the former Lancashire player for Cumberland in 1988. With the ball, wickets have been taken by C.W. Leach for the county and M.C. Fearnley for the

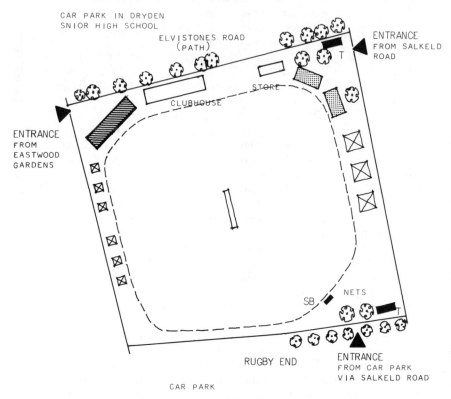

PAVILION END

CAR PARK IN DRYDEN
SNIOR HIGH SCHOOL

ELVISTONES ROAD
(PATH)

ENTRANCE
FROM SALKELD
ROAD

T

CLUBHOUSE

STORE

ENTRANCE
FROM
EASTWOOD
GARDENS

SB

NETS

T

RUGBY END

ENTRANCE
FROM CAR PARK
VIA SALKELD ROAD

CAR PARK

HEDLEY LAWSON PARK

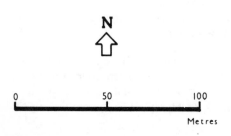

N

0   50   100

Metres

visitors. Only three limited-overs matches have been staged on the ground: one friendly, one English Estates knock-out match and one Holt Cup match which was abandoned without a ball being bowled in 1991. Northumberland C C C won by scoring 4–3 in a bowl out against a set of unguarded stumps. The highest individual innings in a limited-overs match is 95 by C.B. Lambert and the best bowling performance is by L. Beaumont 3 for 31.

ADDRESS Gateshead Fell Cricket Club, The Pavilion, Eastwood Gardens, Low Fell, Gateshead, Tyne and Wear NE9 5UB.
TELEPHONE NUMBER PROSPECTS OF PLAY 091 487 5746

DESCRIPTION OF GROUND AND FACILITIES

The ground is entered from Eastwood Gardens to the rear of the pavilion by players, officials and members and from Salkeld Road and Elvistones Road (path) by members and the public. An entrance from the rugby ground and Hedley Lawson Park is available for those using the car park.

Car parking is available for 30 cars within the ground for players and officials and to the south of the playing area in Hedley Lawson Park is a car park with over 500 spaces for members and the public; this is entered from Eastwood Gardens with an exit in Salkeld Road. Additional car parking is available in Dryden Annexe, which forms part of St Peter's School and Dryden Senior High School, for 400 cars and in neighbouring streets.

The only permanent buildings on the ground are the players' pavilion, members' clubhouse and groundsman's store which are all situated at the School End. To the south-east of the playing area is the main scoreboard. The majority of the facilities are temporary with a ground capacity of 4,500; only 400 permanent fixed seats are available and for county matches an additional 3,500 temporary seats are installed. These include two large raised plastic seating areas to the north-east of the playing area and a number of individual plastic seats. The east of the playing area is used for sponsors' marquees and to the west of the playing area are refreshment and beer tents together with a Durham C C C souvenir tent and temporary toilets in either corner of the ground. A disabled area is situated at the Rugby Ground End directly next to the sightscreen.

Some raised timber seating is available between the clubhouse and groundsman's store for members and the members' enclosure extends from the players' pavilion to the plastic raised seating in the north-east corner of the ground, therefore including the entire School End. A press tent and radio commentary position is situated at the Rugby Ground End.

The playing area is quite large, 120 metres by 126 metres, and is approximately circular in shape; it is defined by a rope and advertising boards. The playing area falls towards the Eastwood Gardens side of the ground. When required, the TV camera/commentary box would be positioned at the Rugby Ground End directly above and behind the sightscreen on a gantry. Some grass and artificial cricket nets are situated to the rear of the scoreboard.

GROUND RECORDS AND SCORES

MINOR COUNTIES CHAMPIONSHIP MATCHES
Highest innings total for County: 338 for 9 dec. *v.* Northumberland 1991
Highest innings total against County: 291 by Northumberland 1960
Lowest innings total for County: 51 *v.* Yorkshire 2nd XI 1963
Lowest innings total against County: 89 by Yorkshire 2nd XI 1963
Highest individual innings for County: 156 n.o. R. Inglis *v.* Northumberland 1966
Highest individual innings against County: 81 B.W. Reidy for Cumberland 1988
Best bowling performance in an innings for County: 6 for 9 C.W. Leach *v.* Staffordshire 1959
Best bowling performance in an innings against County: 6 for 29 M.C. Fearnley for Yorkshire 2nd XI 1963
Best bowling performance in a match for County: 12 for 49 C.W. Leach *v.* Staffordshire 1959
Best bowling performance in a match against County: 11 for 39 M.C. Fearnley for Yorkshire 2nd XI 1963
Best attendance: 1,400 *v.* Northumberland 1991

LIMITED-OVERS MATCHES
Highest innings total for County: 262 for 6 *v.* Wiltshire (EE) 1985
Highest innings total against County: 247 for 9 by Wiltshire (EE) 1985
Lowest innings total for county: 213 for 5 *v.* Lancashire (Friendly) 1990
Lowest innings total against county: 210 for 7 by Lancashire (Friendly) 1990
Highest individual innings for County: 95 C.B. Lambert *v.* Lancashire (Friendly) 1990
Highest individual innings against County: 63 n.o. S.P. Titchard for Lancashire (Friendly) 1990
Best bowling performance for County: 3 for 31 L. Beaumont *v.* Lancashire (Friendly) 1990
Best bowling performance against County: 3 for 74 R. Wilson for Wiltshire (EE) 1985
Best attendance: 1,450 *v.* Wiltshire (EE) 1985

HOW TO GET THERE

Rail   Newcastle-upon-Tyne Central (BR) 5 miles Gateshead Interchange (Tyne and Wear Metro: Green/Red/Yellow Lines), 2 miles.

Bus G2, G3, 27, 35 and 93 from Stand H Go-Ahead Northern/Tyne & Wear County bus service from Gateshead Interchange Metro to Low Fell, via Dryden Road for ground (Telephone: 091 222 0404). **Car** From north: A167 from Newcastle-upon-Tyne to Gateshead using Durham Road, then take Dryden Road for ground in Eastwood Gardens, follow signs county cricket. From east: A184 follow signs Gateshead and Felling, then follow signs county cricket for Dryden Road and Eastwood Gardens. From west: A692, A69, A6528 or A694 signposted Gateshead, then follow signs county cricket for Dryden Road and Eastwood Gardens. From south: A1(M) take A167 signposted Gateshead (South) prior to Gateshead College, then turn right into Valley Drive and at first junction turn right into Dryden Road and then take first left for Eastwood Gardens and car parking.

WHERE TO STAY AND OTHER INFORMATION

Springfield Hotel (091 477 4121) Swallow Hotel (091 477 1105), Post House Hotel (091 416 2264) Metropark Hotel (091 493 2233).

Disabled Areas Special position located at Rugby Ground End near sightscreen, car parking in ground by prior arrangement.
Local Radio Station(s) BBC Radio Newcastle (96.0 MHz FM/1458 KHz MW), TFM Radio (96.6 MHz FM/1170 KHz FM).
Local Newspaper(s) Newcastle Journal, Newcastle Evening Chronicle, Sunderland Echo, Northern Echo, Sunday Sun, South Shields Gazette.

Hartlepool

Hartlepool Cricket Club is set in parklands and is a most attractive ground situated on the west side of the town. The club has been at its present headquarters since 1912 after the move from the previous West Hartlepool C C ground at Clarence Road, where seven Minor County Championship matches were staged between 1897 and 1908. The first match at Clarence Road was against Cambridgeshire C C C and the last against Lincolnshire C C C. Hartlepool C C was originally formed in 1855. The first Durham C C C minor county match staged at Park Drive was on 11–12 June 1913 against Lincolnshire C C C.

The club was previously called the West Hartlepool Cricket Club and won the North Yorkshire and South Durham League in 1895, 1900, 1902 and 1905. Hartlepool C C compete in the North Yorkshire and South Durham Cricket League and in the Kerridge, McMillian, Robinson, Haith, Ken Welsh and Arthur Saunders knock-out cup competitions.

The Hartlepool club has hosted many minor county games and has been a member of the North Yorkshire and South Durham Cricket League since 1899; it fields three XIs throughout the season. Players

PARK DRIVE END

ENTRANCES FROM
PARK DRIVE

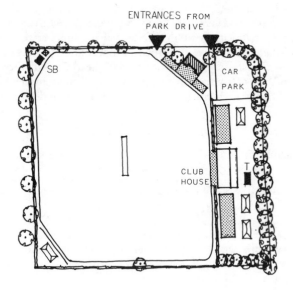

SB

CAR
PARK

CLUB
HOUSE

T

EGERTON ROAD END

N

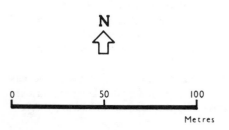

0   50   100

Metres

who have represented Hartlepool C C and Durham C C C include Peter Kippax and Askok Patel.

In 1991 a benefit match was staged on the ground during August for club cricket professional Clyde Butts, the West Indian player.

Also during the season the last Minor County Championship match, with Hertfordshire C C C and a friendly match with the touring Sri Lankans were staged on the ground.

The general facilities are what you would expect at a club ground and are being improved all the time. The ground capacity is 3,000-plus and the record attendance was 1,500 in 1991 when Durham C C C played the touring Sri Lankans in a one-day match.

In 1992 Durham C C C will stage eight days' cricket at Park Drive against the 1991 County Champions Essex in June and Glamorgan in August for one Britannic Assurance County Championship and one Sunday League match against each county.

Ground records at Park Drive include centuries by S.R. Atkinson 155 n.o. against Cheshire in 1982 and 130 by H. Wilson for Cheshire in 1924. Wickets have been taken by D.J. Halfyard and A. Coxon for Durham and for the visitors by H. Wilson and R. Collins. The Sri Lankans won the only limited-overs match to be staged on the ground by 72 runs in 1991. Roshan Mahanama top scored with 67 and S.T. Jayasuriya took 3 for 26.

ADDRESS   Hartlepool Cricket Club, The Pavilion, Park Drive, West Park, Hartlepool, Cleveland TS26 ODA.
TELEPHONE NUMBER PROSPECTS OF PLAY   0429 260875

DESCRIPTION OF GROUND AND FACILITIES

The ground is entered by all from Park Drive to the rear of the pavilion in the north-east corner of the ground. Car parking is available for 80 cars for players and officials only in the ground between the pavilion and clubhouse to the east of the playing area. Car parking for members and the public is available for 500 cars at the High Tunstall Comprehensive School off Elwick Road, plus ample street parking in the local neighbourhood. Additional car parking is also available for 500 cars at the English Martyrs R C Comprehensive School in Catecote Road, although this is some walking distance from the ground.

The tree-lined Park Drive ground can accommodate fourteen pitches which is surprising as the playing area is only 99 metres by 93 metres and is quite small by county standards. It is defined by a rope and advertising boards.

The pavilion and players' dressing rooms are situated in the north-east corner of the ground, and to the east of the playing area is the Hartlepool clubhouse which includes facilities for refreshments and bars. A number of photographs and items of cricket memorabilia can be found in this building. To the south-east corner of the playing area is a hospitality marquee for match sponsors together with a beer tent and some temporary plastic raised seating areas. A further plastic raised seating area is situated between the clubhouse and pavilion.

The scoreboard is situated in the north-west corner of the ground with a press tent within close proximity. Permanent toilets are available in the pavilion and clubhouse. A number of refreshment facilities and additional temporary toilets are available to the rear of the clubhouse. A Durham C C C souvenir shop is also available. A disabled spectators area is situated at the Egerton Road End of the ground near the refreshment tent.

The ground capacity is 3,000 and permanent seating of 1,000 is available and for county matches an additional 2,000 temporary seats are transported to the ground. A small temporary stand is available for Durham C C C and Hartlepool C C members only. The majority of temporary facilities are situated to the east of the playing area.

When required the TV camera/commentary box will be positioned directly above and behind the sightscreen at the Park Drive End situated on a gantry scaffold in the roadway. A radio commentary position is situated on the upper level of the pavilion.

GROUND RECORDS AND SCORES

MINOR COUNTIES CHAMPIONSHIP MATCHES
Highest innings total for County: 393 v. Yorkshire 2nd XI 1950
Highest innings total against County: 402 for 9 dec. by Cheshire 1924
Lowest innings total for County: 65 v. Cheshire 1927
Lowest innings total against County: 60 by Lancashire 2nd XI 1949
Highest individual innings for County: 155 n.o. S.R. Atkinson v. Cheshire 1982
Highest individual innings against County: 130 H. Wilson for Cheshire 1924
Best bowling performance in an innings for County: 9 for 23 D.J. Halfyard v. Staffordshire 1971
Best bowling performance in an innings against County: 8 for 26 H. Wilson for Cheshire 1927
Best bowling performance in a match for County: 15 for 86 A. Coxon v. Staffordshire 1952
Best bowling performance in a match against County: 10 for 142 R. Collins for Lancashire 2nd XI 1962
Best attendance: 500 v. Yorkshire 2nd XI 1950.

LIMITED-OVERS MATCH
Highest innings total for County: 149 v. Sri Lankans (Tour) 1991
Highest innings total against County: 221 for 9 by Sri Lankans (Tour) 1991
Highest individual innings for County: 62 P. Bainbridge v. Sri Lankans (Tour) 1991
Highest individual innings against County: 67 R.S. Mahanama for Sri Lankans (Tour) 1991
Best bowling performance for County: 2 for 31 J. Wood v. Sri Lankans (Tour) 1991

Best bowling performance against County: 3 for 26 S.T. Jayasuriya for Sri Lankans (Tour) 1991
Best attendance: 1,500 *v.* Sri Lankans (Tour) 1991

HOW TO GET THERE

Rail   Hartlepool (BR), 1.5 miles.
Bus   Hartlepool Bus Station, 1.5 miles; bus 15 stops close to ground 22, 241, 242 and 244 United/Favourite link Hartlepool with surrounding areas (Telephone 091 386 4411 ext 2337).
Car   From north: A19, then take Elwick Road signposted county cricket, for Park Drive; ground situated near Ward Jackson Park to the west of the town. From west: as north. From south: A19 then as north.

WHERE TO STAY AND OTHER INFORMATION

The Grand Hotel (0429 266345); Staincliffe Hotel (0429 264301); also smaller hotels and guesthouses.

Disabled Areas   Special area located at Egerton Road End of the ground, car parking available in the ground by prior arrangement.
Local Radio Station(s)   BBC Radio Cleveland (95.0 MHz FM/1548 KHz MW), T.F.M. Radio (96.6 MHz FM/1170 KHz MW).
Local Newspaper(s)   The Northern Echo, Hartlepool Mail, The Journal.

Stockton-on-Tees

The Stockton Cricket Club was established in 1816 and in 1847 an all England XI played Stockton C C in a two day, two innings game with the national side being victorious. Upwards of 3,000 spectators attended this match. Another six similar matches were staged between Stockton C C and England XIs up until the 1860 season. Other visiting teams during this period included Bradford C C, Harewood C C, Sheffield C C, Lascells Hall C C, Bedale C C, Sessay C C and Kelso C C. Stockton C C has four senior XIs and junior under-17, -15 and -13 teams.

The Stockton Club had several grounds over this period, but in 1891 they were told that their ground at that time was to be turned into a park and is known today as Ropner Park. The committee then found the present day ground in open fields and it was subsequently bought for £1537 2s 8d which included the costs of some levelling and drainage. On 4 June 1892 the first match was staged on the present ground and the hosts were victorious over a team from Constable Burton C C near Bedale.

In 1888 the Durham Challenge Cup competition was started and

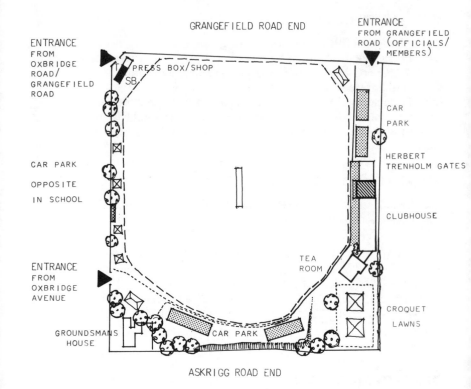

GRANGEFIELD ROAD END

ENTRANCE
FROM GRANGEFIELD
ROAD (OFFICIALS/
MEMBERS)

ENTRANCE
FROM
OXBRIDGE
ROAD/
GRANGEFIELD
ROAD

PRESS BOX/SHOP

SB

CAR
PARK

HERBERT
TRENHOLM GATES

CAR PARK

OPPOSITE

IN SCHOOL

CLUBHOUSE

TEA
ROOM

ENTRANCE
FROM
OXBRIDGE
AVENUE

CROQUET
LAWNS

GROUNDSMANS
HOUSE

CAR PARK

ASKRIGG ROAD END

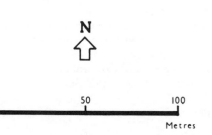

N

0   50   100

Metres

Stockton C C were runners-up to Philadelphia C C from Sunderland having beaten Norton C C and Durham City C C in earlier rounds. In 1890 Stockton C C won this competition, beating Bishop Auckland C C, Stanhope C C, West Hartlepool C C, Darlington C C and, finally, Whitburn C C in the final. Between 1891 and 1895 Stockton C C were in the Durham County Cricket League but found some places inconvenient to reach from the south of the county. So with Norton C C and Darlington C C, the Stockton club joined the North Yorkshire and South Durham Cricket League in 1896. They won this league in 1897 after a deciding match against Middlesbrough C C. It was not until 1948 that the club first XI again won the league; they repeated the feat in 1975. The leagues foremost cup competition, the Kerridge Cup was won in 1942 and three defeats in 1923, 1946 and 1953 are the clubs only other appearances in the final. The Stockton club has been more successful in the cup given by the former Tory M.P. for the town and Prime Minister Harold McMillan (later Lord Stockton), winning in 1945, 1951, 1955, 1966 and 1971. In 1900 the first cricket professional H. Page was engaged at £3 per week.

The first Durham C C C match was staged at Grangefield Road on 9–10 July 1947 against Staffordshire and the last Minor County Championship match to be played in the history of Durham C C C was staged on 21–22 August 1991 when Suffolk C C C were the defeated visitors by 48 runs. This is one of two venues to be used by Durham C C C during 1992 in the county of Cleveland, the other is Hartlepool C C at Park Drive. Durham C C C have to date staged twenty-seven matches on the Grangefield Road ground.

Durham C C C will make two visits to Stockton C C in 1992 against Northamptonshire in May and Gloucestershire in July for one Britannic Assurance Championship and one Sunday League match with each county. A total of eight days' cricket will be played on the ground.

The present patron of Durham C C C Mr. A.W. Austin was first XI captain from 1938 to 1959 except for the seasons 1945–46 and is life president of the Stockton Hockey Club which is part of the Cricket Club. Stockton C C is the only club with two officers of the Durham C C C: A.W. Austin and H.W.M. Milner. The club has had many cricket professionals over the years, including former Pakistan Test player Nasim-ul-Ghani for three seasons; West Indian Test player Irving Shillingford also stayed for three seasons whilst one Test man, Rakesh Shukla from India stayed for two seasons. The club professional in 1991 was New Zealander Paul Hodder. The present club professional is Pakistani Masood Anwar and the club also engages a full-time groundsman.

On 11 August 1952 a tablet was unveiled in the players' pavilion by the Rev. R.T. Heselton M.A. to commemorate the names of the four members who lost their lives in the Second World War.

The Grangefield Road ground has the benefit of seating all around the playing area, two areas of car parking and a very busy social club. Other active sections include Stockton Hockey Club with six teams, Stockton Ladies Hockey Club with two teams, a croquet section, table tennis, bowls and darts. The tea room facilities are second to none in the North Yorkshire and South Durham Cricket League and the Stockton club is certainly on solid foundations for the second century on the ground and the start of Durham C C Cs first-class status.

The pavilion was built in 1894–95 and the basement area of the pavilion/clubhouse was in fact used as a stable for the horses used for cutting the grass and rolling the pitch until the building was refurbished in 1950. The tea room and croquet pavilion were built at the turn of the century with extensions in 1950 to include a kitchen and toilets at a cost of £1,045 16s 11d. With the scoreboard, groundsman's house and store built in 1952 for £1,560 these are the only permanent structures on the ground. The club room was named the Chris Old Room in 1980, after the Yorkshire, Warwickshire and England bowler.

In 1991 Stockton C C celebrated 175 years of cricket and during the period 19–25 August a number of matches were staged including: Stockton C C Presidents XI v. Constable Burton XI, Durham C C C v. Suffolk C C C, T.F.M. Radio Allstars v. Radio Cleveland Allstars, Stockton C C v. Saltburn C C and Stockton Invitation XI v. An International XI.

The ground capacity is 5,000 and the record crowd to date is 4,000 for the 1947 Courage Cup Final between Stockton C C and Norton C C Ground records at Grangefield Road include centuries by Gary Brown, 106 n.o. against Norfolk and I.S. Lawrence 144 for Cambridgeshire in 1988. Ian Conn, S.P. Davis and K. Trotter for the home side and R.C. Green for the visitors have taken wickets. In the two limited-overs friendlies which have been staged on the ground, the highest individual innings was made by S.M. Brogan for Nottinghamshire second XI and the best bowling performance by A.C. Day of 4 for 39 against Yorkshire.

ADDRESS Stockton Cricket Club, The Pavilion/Clubhouse, The Grangefield Road Ground, Oxbridge Avenue, Stockton-on-Tees, Cleveland TS18 4JF.

TELEPHONE NUMBER PROSPECTS OF PLAY   0642 672835

DESCRIPTION OF GROUND AND FACILITIES

The ground is entered from Grangefield Road for members through Herbert Trenholm MBE Gates and the players and officials car park and from Oxbridge Road near the Groundsman's house for members and the public. There is also a new entrance at the rear of the new scoreboard/souvenir shop constructed during the winter 1991–92. Parking space for 62 cars is available within the ground for players', officials, press and disabled spectators only. However car parking is available in three locations close to the ground for 2,000 cars: Stockton Comprehensive School (during school holidays only) opposite, Stockton and Billingham Technical College in Oxbridge Avenue five minutes walk away, and Rudds Recreation Ground in Grangefield Road also five minutes walk away.

The pavilion and clubhouse includes a members' bar and refreshment area together with a radio commentary position and members'/players' dining area. There are a number of photographs of historic information on the club which can be viewed. The players' pavilion is adjoining as is the clubhouse and tea room where members can take refreshment and use bar facilities.

To the north-east of the playing area is the scoreboard, groundsman's store, refreshment area and Durham C C C souvenir shop. Some toilets are sited to the rear of this building with further facilities available in the pavilion/clubhouse and there are temporary facilities around the ground. The press room and scorers' room will be situated in the new scoreboard/shop structure at the Grangefield Road End.

The ground capacity is 5,000 and the fixed seating capacity is 880 in the small covered east stand and bench seating around the playing perimeter. The majority of the seating is temporary and 2,000 seats are provided so spectators will only be advised to bring their own seats to popular matches. Two plastic raised seating areas are situated at the Askrigg Road End either side of the sightscreen. Refreshments and bars are available in tents situated around the ground. The sponsors' marquees are situated at the Askrigg Road End of the ground and near the croquet lawns.

The playing area is flat and the dimensions are 137 metres by 122 metres, defined by a rope and advertising boards. The playing area falls slightly towards the pavilion side of the ground.

If required, the TV camera/commentary box will be positioned directly above and behind the sightscreen at the Askrigg Road End of the ground on a gantry.

GROUND RECORDS AND SCORES

MINOR COUNTIES CHAMPIONSHIP MATCHES
Highest innings total for County: 249 for 6 dec. *v.* Shropshire 1976
Highest innings total against County: 278 by Staffordshire 1947
Lowest innings total for County: 113 *v.* Suffolk 1983
Lowest innings total against County: 92 by Shropshire 1976
Highest individual innings for County: 106 n.o. G.K. Brown *v.* Norfolk 1989
Highest individual innings against County: 144 I.S. Lawrence for Cambridgeshire 1988
Best bowling performance in an innings for County: 6 for 37 I.E. Conn *v.* Cambridgeshire 1988
Best bowling performance in an innings against County: 7 for 69 R.C. Green for Suffolk 1983
Best bowling performance in a match for County: 8 for 106 S.P. Davis *v.* Suffolk 1983/K. Trotter *v.* Norfolk 1989
Best bowling performance in a match against County: 10 for 102 R.C. Green for Suffolk 1983
Best attendance: 1,750 *v.* Suffolk 1991

LIMITED-OVERS MATCHES

Highest innings total for County: 189 for 4 *v.* Yorkshire (Friendly) 1989

Highest innings total against County: 224 for 8 by Nottinghamshire 2nd XI (Friendly) 1991

Lowest innings total for County: 120 *v.* Nottinghamshire 2nd XI (Friendly) 1991

Lowest innings total against County: 186 for 7 by Yorkshire (Friendly) 1989

Highest individual innings for County: 73 G.K. Brown *v.* Yorkshire (Friendly) 1989

Highest individual innings against County: 86 S.M. Brogan for Nottinghamshire 2nd XI (Friendly) 1991

Best bowling performance for County: 4 for 39 A.C. Day *v.* Yorkshire (Friendly) 1989

Best bowling performance against County: 3 for 14 M.G. Field-Buss for Nottinghamshire 2nd XI (Friendly) 1991

Best attendance: 1,000 *v.* Yorkshire (Friendly) 1989

HOW TO GET THERE

Rail   Stockton (BR), 1 mile; connections from Darlington (BR) Inter City.

Bus   55A, 61, 163 and 235 OK Travel/United, alight at Grangefield Road and Grays Road close to ground (Telephone: 091 386 4411 ext 2337).

Car   From north: A19 or A689 to A19 turn off at Billingham/ Norton junction, then follow Stockton ring road A1027 to Oxbridge Road for Grangefield Road ground and car parking. From east: A178 to Stockton, then follow signs ring road for Grangefield Road ground and car parking or as north. From west: A177, A66 or A67 to Stockton, then follow signs ring road for Grangefield Road ground and car parking or as south. From south: A66 from Darlington to Middlesbrough, then take Eaglescliffe junction and approach ground via Darlington Road, Hartburn Avenue on to the ring road and Oxbridge Avenue for ground and car parking or A19 signposted Stockton and ring road for Grangefield Road ground.

WHERE TO STAY AND OTHER INFORMATION

Swallow Hotel (0642 679721), The Post House (0642 591213) Parkmore Hotel and Leisure Club (0642 786815).

Disabled Areas   No special area, please request position, car parking available within ground by prior arrangement.

Local Radio Station(s)   BBC Radio Cleveland (95.0 MHz FM/1548 KHz MW), T.F.M. Radio (96.6 MHz FM/1170 KHz MW).

Local Newspaper(s)   Northern Echo, Evening Gazette, Darlington and Stockton Times, Hartlepool Mail, Yorkshire Post, Journal, Sunday Sun.

Jesmond

Durham C C C will play their home Benson and Hedges Cup zonal fixture with Derbyshire at Jesmond on 5 May 1992. This will be the first time that Durham C C C has staged a home match at the Northumberland County Cricket Club's headquarters at Osborne Avenue, Jesmond, a district to the north of central Newcastle-upon-Tyne.

The ground was opened in 1887 and was known as the New Recreation Ground for the Newcastle Police Constabulary; it was situated behind All Saints' Cemetery and approached from Lovers' Lane. This was the first home for the County Club as previous matches had been staged at the South Northumberland C C, Burdon Terrace, Newcastle-upon-Tyne and Heaton Lane and Preston Lane, Tynemouth. The Northumberland C C C was founded in 1896. The Jesmond ground was acquired by the County Club in March 1897 and the first Northumberland C C C match staged at Jesmond was on 7–8 June 1897 against Durham C C C, with the visitors winning by 6 wickets. Mr F.G.H. Clayton, a committee member, took it upon himself to improve the county ground during the period from October 1897 to January 1898. This included building a terrace seating area at the Osborne Road End and terrace seating next to the Swiss chalet pavilion, which had been built for the Queen Victoria Jubilee Exhibition on the Town Moor in 1887 and was transferred to the ground to serve as a members' pavilion after the Exhibition ended. Further bench seating was constructed elsewhere in the ground during this period.

The Swiss chalet pavilion was demolished on 19 March 1962 and a new pavilion was constructed at a cost of £25,000 and was ready for next season. The new pavilion was opened on 3 June 1963 by Mr R.H. Houston during the Bank Holiday minor county match with Durham C C C.

On 27–28 July 1933 Northumberland C C C played the touring West Indians at Jesmond with the visitors out-playing their opponents from start to finish and winning easily by an innings and 183 runs. The West Indians scored 440 with Da Costa scoring 91 and in bowling the home side out for 129 and 128, Vin Valentine took match figures of 8 for 86.

The ground at Jesmond is the home of the Northumberland County Club who play in the Priory Northumberland County Cricket League and the Bellway Division. The club field three XIs throughout the season with a junior section. In addition to playing league cricket the County Club play in The Hunter Timber Trophy and Joyce McKay Cup knockout competitions. Since 1978 the County Club have won the following trophies: Priory League 1980, 1986 and 1987, Division 'C' Championship 1979, 1985 and 1986, Mallinson-Denny Cup 1979 and 1980 and Joyce McKay Cup 1987. Recent players to have represented the County Club and Northumberland C C C include Jonathan Benn, Paul Dutton and Martin Green.

Jesmond is the only ground used by Northumberland C C C for home fixtures in the Minor County Championship and knockout competi-

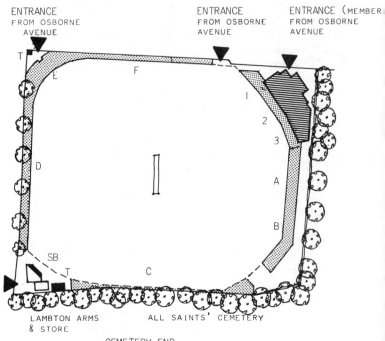

OSBORNE AVENUE END

ENTRANCE
FROM OSBORNE
AVENUE

ENTRANCE
FROM OSBORNE
AVENUE

ENTRANCE (MEMBER
FROM OSBORNE
AVENUE

T

E

F

I

2

3

D

A

B

SB

ENTRANCE
FROM
LOVERS'
LANE VIA
CLAYTON
ROAD

T

C

LAMBTON ARMS
& STORE

ALL SAINTS' CEMETERY

CEMETERY END

N

0   50   100

Metres

tions and in 1991 hosted matches with Bedfordshire, Lincolnshire, Cambridgeshire, Cumberland and Norfolk. The ground at Osborne Avenue has been used since 1981 for the Callers-Pegasus Cricket Festival and this includes two matches in early August each season. During the period 1981–84 the matches involved a Callers-Pegasus International XI playing two 55-over matches under Benson & Hedges Cup rules against a combined Northumberland and Durham XI. This ceased after the 1984 festival and since 1985 two limited-overs matches have been played by the Rest of the World XI and an England XI, and in 1991 the new festival sponsors were Yuill Heritage Homes.

Three previous Benson & Hedges Cup zonal group limited-overs matches have been staged at Osborne Avenue, in 1977, 1979 and 1989, by various Minor Counties C.A. teams (East and North) against Yorkshire. Yorkshire's three victories included one by 10 wickets; and the others were by 51 runs and 5 wickets respectively. Northumberland C C C have staged four National Westminster Bank Trophy matches at Jesmond: in 1985 Middlesex won by 85 runs and in 1986 Essex defeated the home team by 79 runs. Essex were again the visitors in 1987 and won by the margin of 176 runs. In 1989 Surrey were the opponents scoring 313 for 5 and winning by 68 runs.

The ground capacity is 3,500 and this is achieved for the majority of festival and limited-overs matches.

ADDRESS Northumberland County Cricket Club, The Pavilion, County Cricket Ground, Osborne Avenue, Jesmond, Newcastle-upon-Tyne NE2 1JS.
TELEPHONE NUMBER PROSPECTS OF PLAY   091 281 2738

DESCRIPTION OF GROUND AND FACILITIES

The ground is entered from three entrances in Osborne Road, to the rear of the pavilion for players, officials and members and through the other two entrances for the members and the public. A further entrance is situated to the south-west corner of the ground from Lovers' Lane to the rear of the scorebox.

There is no car parking available within this compact ground except for players' to the rear of the pavilion, but ample street parking is available to the north of the ground and in the main city centre multi-storey car parks within ten minutes' walk of the county ground. The ground is bounded to the north by Osborne Avenue and to the east and south by All Saints' Cemetery with a residential housing area to the north of the city centre. The ground is lined by trees to the west of the playing area, with shrubs and trees to the east and west behind the white walls of the Cemetery.

The only permanent buildings on the ground are the pavilion, which includes members' seating, refreshment, bars/restaurant at ground level and players' changing facilities, secretary's office, radio commentary position and press room at first floor/balcony level. To the south-west of the playing area is the scorebox/scorers' room with refreshment/tea room below, groundsman's stores and a permanent toilet. Toilets are also available within the pavilion and the north-west corner of the ground. The majority of seating is permanent and of a timber bench variety although in the pavilion terrace the seats are of a white plastic tip-up variety.

The pavilion enclosure is defined by areas 1, 2 and 3 and the seating areas are numbered alphabetically A to F, clockwise around the playing area from the pavilion. A total of 2,619 permanent bench seats are provided with a further 881 seats in the members' area, thereby providing the ground with a capacity of 3,500. Spectators are requested to bring their own seats to popular matches as these can be fitted in around the playing area in the south-east and south-west corners of the ground.

The playing area is rectangular in shape with dimensions of 117 metres by 140 metres and is defined by a rope, white fence and flower beds in front of the pavilion and advertising boards. When required, the TV camera/commentary box is positioned at the Cemetery End with additional cameras at the northern Osborne Avenue End and on the pavilion balcony.

GROUND RECORDS AND SCORES

LIMITED-OVERS MATCHES (BHC)
Highest innings total for Minor Counties: 179 for 6 by Minor Counties *v.* Yorkshire 1989
Highest innings total against Minor Counties: 218 for 9 by Yorkshire *v.* Minor Counties (East) 1977
Lowest innings total for Minor Counties: 85 by Minor Counties (North) *v.* Yorkshire 1979
Lowest innings total against Minor Counties: 86 for 0 by Yorkshire *v.* Minor Counties (North) 1979
Highest individual innings for Minor Counties: 61 N.A. Folland for Minor Counties *v.* Yorkshire 1989
Highest individual innings against Minor Counties: 73 G. Boycott for Yorkshire *v.* Minor Counties (East) 1977
Best bowling performance for Minor Counties: 3 for 27 I.E. Conn for Minor Counties *v.* Yorkshire 1989
Best bowling performance against Minor Counties: 3 for 11 C.M. Old for Yorkshire *v.* Minor Counties (North) 1979
Best attendance: 3,500 for Minor Counties (North) *v.* Yorkshire 1979

CALLERS–PEGASUS/YUILL HERITAGE HOMES INTERNATIONAL CRICKET FESTIVAL
(1981–84) NORTHUMBERLAND/DURHAM XI *v.* CALLERS PEGASUS XI
Highest innings total for Northumberland/Durham XI: 288 *v.* Callers–Pegasus XI 1982
Highest innings total for Callers–Pegasus XI: 406 *v.* Northumberland/Durham XI 1982

Lowest innings total for Northumberland/Durham XI: 151 for 4 *v*. Callers–Pegasus XI 1984
Lowest innings total for Callers–Pegasus XI: 176 for 7 *v*. Northumberland/Durham XI 1984
Highest individual innings for Northumberland/Durham XI: 114 S.R. Atkinson *v*. Callers–Pegasus XI 1983
Highest individual innings for Callers–Pegasus XI: 134 A.J. Lamb *v*. Northumberland/Durham XI 1982
Best bowling performance for Northumberland/Durham XI: 5 for 36 J.N. Graham *v*. Callers–Pegasus XI 1982
Best bowling performance for Callers–Pegasus XI: 4 for 72 B.L. D'Oliveria *v*. Northumberland/Durham XI 1982

(1985–91) ENGLAND XI *v*. REST OF THE WORLD XI
Highest innings total for England XI: 287 for 5 *v*. Rest of the World XI 1991
Highest innings total for Rest of the World XI: 300 for 6 *v*. England XI 1986
Lowest innings total for England XI: 179 *v*. Rest of the World XI 1990
Lowest innings total for Rest of the World XI: 183 for 0 *v*. England XI 1990
Highest individual innings for England XI: 127 n.o. M.W. Gatting *v*. Rest of the World XI 1985
Highest individual innings for Rest of the World XI: 115 n.o. M.J. Greatbatch *v*. England XI 1989
Best bowling performance for England XI: 4 for 35 P.J.W. Allott *v*. Rest of the World XI 1985
Best bowling performance for Rest of the World XI: 4 for 10 Javed Miandad *v*. England XI 1988

HOW TO GET THERE

Rail   Newcastle-upon-Tyne Central (BR), 2 miles; Jesmond Zone 26 (Tyne & Wear Metro: Green/Red/Yellow Lines), 0.50 mile.
Bus   4 Heaton-Gosforth and 33 Newcastle-Jesmond from city centre and BR Newcastle Central buses OK Travel/Newcastle Busways pass Jesmond via Osborne Avenue (Telephone: 091 222 0404).
Car   From north: A167, A69, A696 or A1 Great North Road, signposted Newcastle and city centre, then follow signs Jesmond and county cricket, take left into Clayton Road before reaching the North West Radial road for Osborne Road and Osborne Avenue. From east: A1058, B1307, A187 or A186, signposted Newcastle and city centre, then follow signs Jesmond and county cricket for Osborne Road and Osborne Avenue. From west: A187, A167, A186, B1311 or A695, signposted Newcastle and city centre, then follow signs Jesmond and county cricket, then as east. From south: A189, A1(M) then A1, B1307, A167, A184 or A19(M), signposted Newcastle and city centre, then follow signs Jesmond and county cricket for Osborne Road and Osborne Avenue.

WHERE TO STAY AND OTHER INFORMATION

Cairn Hotel (091 281 1358), Hospitality Inn (091 281 7881) Imperial
Swallow Hotel (091 281 5511), Northumberia Hotel (091 281 4961)
Swallow Hotel (091 232 5025), and various small hotels and
guesthouses.

Disabled Areas   Special area situated near main scoreboard and
groundsman's store at Cemetery End of the ground. No car parking is
available within the ground for disabled vehicles.
Local Radio Station(s)   BBC Radio Newcastle (96.0 MHz FM/1458
KHz MW).
Local Newspaper(s)   Newcastle Journal, Newcastle Evening
Chronicle, Northern Echo, Sunday Sun.

ESSEX

CHELMSFORD

COLCHESTER

ILFORD

SOUTHEND-ON-SEA

Essex

Founded   14 January 1876
Colours   Blue, gold and red
Crest   Three scimitars with word 'Essex' underneath
President   T.N. Pearce OBE, TD
Chairman   D.J. Insole CBE
Chairman cricket committee   G.J. Saville
Secretary/general manager   P.J. Edwards
Marketing manager   C. Blockley
Assistant secretary   M. Field
County coach   K.W.R. Fletcher OBE
Captain   G.A. Gooch OBE
Ground manager   B. Hughes
Groundsman   S. Kerrison
Scorer 1st XI   C.F. Driver
Scorer 2nd XI   R. Laws
Statistician   K. Montgomery
Sponsors   Access
Newsletter   *Essex News*
Address   County Cricket Ground, New Writtle Street, Chelmsford,
Essex CM2 0PG
Telephone 0245 252420
Essex Rapid Cricketline   0891 567503

ACHIEVEMENTS

County Championship   Champions (5) 1979, 1983, 1984, 1986 and
1991
Gillette Cup   Semi-finalists (1) 1978
National Westminster Bank Trophy   Winners (1) 1985
Benson & Hedges Cup Winners   (1) 1979; finalists (4) 1980, 1983,
1985 and 1989
John Player Sunday League   Champions (3) 1981, 1984 and 1985
Refuge Assurance Sunday League   3rd 1989
Refuge Assurance Cup   Winners (1) 1989
Fenner Trophy   Finalists (2) 1977 and 1981
Asda Trophy   Finalists (1) 1986
Ward Four Counties Knockout Competition   Winners (1) 1988;
finalists (1) 1989
Festival Trophy   Finalists (1) 1990
Joshua Tetley Festival Trophy   Finalists (1) 1991

GROUNDS

Chelmsford (County Cricket Ground, New Writtle Street), Colchester
(Castle Park, Sportsway off Catchpool Road), Ilford (Valentine's
Park, Cranbrook Road) and Southend-on-Sea (Southchurch Park).

Other grounds that have been used since 1969 are: Colchester (Garrison 'A' Ground, Napier Road) Brentwood (Old County Ground, Shenfield Road) Harlow (Sportscentre, Hammarskjold Road) Leyton (Leyton High Road Youth Sports Ground, High Road) Westcliff-on-Sea (Chalkwell Park) and Purfleet (Thames Board Mills Sports Ground).

SECOND XI GROUNDS
In addition to the above mentioned grounds the following are used for second XI matches: Brentwood C C, Old County Ground, Shenfield Road, Brentwood, Essex. Telephone: 0277 212580; Newbury Park C C, Newbury Park Sports Ground, Ford Sports and Social Club, Aldborough, Near Ilford, Essex. Telephone: 081 590 3797; Wickford C C, Patmore Memorial Ground, Runwell Road, Wickford, Essex. Telephone: 0268 763023; Orsett and Thurrock C C, School Lane, Orsett, Essex. Telephone: Directory Enquiries; Leigh-on-Sea C C, Chalkwell Park, London Road, Leigh-on-Sea, Essex. Telephone: 0702 76603; Maldon C C, The Promenade, Maldon High Street, Maldon, Essex. Telephone: Directory Enquiries; Aveley C C, Cricket Ground, Aveley, Essex. Telephone: Directory Enquiries; Romford C C, Gidea Park, Romford, Essex. Telephone: Directory Enquiries.

It took Essex 103 years to land their first championship, and less than a decade to confirm their status as arguably the best team, and the best led in the land. From the breakthrough season of 1979 until 1986 homely Essex, who had never won a first-class competition and were rarely in a challenging position, won the championship four times, the Benson & Hedges Cup, the NatWest Trophy and the John Player Sunday League three times. Twice they were beaten Benson & Hedges finalists by margins of 6 and 4 runs.

Fletcher, the wily campaigner, rightly acclaimed his rare tactical insight, became the first captain to carry off all four major competitions. Three of the championships were under him, the other under Gooch, and it is generally considered a folly that his captaincy of England was confined to the tour of India and Sri Lanka in 1981–82. A dozen or so years of far-seeing preparation produced the Fletcher team of class and adaptability, and he owed a lot to wise stewardship, a new and firm financial base, a permanent focal-point home at Chelmsford, a devoted following, and the enthusiasm of his predecessor, Taylor, who handed on playing quality and confidence.

Essex have always played with spirit and enterprise, and the modern attitude was born in the watershed 'sixties when the club was in such low financial water that the playing staff was reduced to twelve without the Test all-rounder Knight, who had moved to Leicestershire.

Historic events need a starting point, and the acquisition of the Chelmsford ground began the rise to glory. But for a chance remark by

CHELMSFORD

G. A. GOOCH

Trevor Bailey, a man of many parts in his 21-year association, at a dinner to celebrate Worcestershire's 1965 championship the opportunity to buy the land might have passed by. The happy sequel was an interest-free loan by the Warwickshire C C C Supporters' Association. Seldom has the chivalry between one club and another been better illustrated or more opportune.

Brentwood was the club's first home from 1876–85. The batting heroes were Perrin, whose record run aggregate for Essex was passed by Fletcher, and it is still said that Kortright was the fastest bowler ever known. Oddly, Perrin and Kortright, who clean bowled 226 of his 319 wickets between 1885 and 1898, never played for England. Just after the Second World War Kortright declared he would have been afraid to have bowled to the batsmen of the day. 'I'd have cut 'em in half,' he said.

Spinner Head, who played against Australia in 1899, was the first to take 100 wickets in a season for the county. J.W.H.T. ('Johnny Won't Hit Today') Douglas was one of the dominant personalities. A fine swing bowler and obdurate batsman he captained England in Australia and South Africa, and Essex from 1911 to 1928 – his highest place was 6th – and as a diversion from cricket won the middle-weight boxing title at the 1908 Olympics. He was drowned trying to rescue his father as their ship sank after a collision in thick fog.

Russell was the first England batsman to score a century in each innings in a Test match, against South Africa in 1922–23 at Durban – where Insole, another of the club's mainstays on and off the field, also hit a century for England 34 years later.

When Leyton was vacated in 1933 the team took to the road, and the circus trundled around nine different club grounds. There was no show like it on the county circuit. The equipment accompanying the team included hundreds of yards of seven-foot high screening with poles, marquees, tents, temporary stands, sundry seating, a press to print

D. J. INSOLE

P. A. PERRIN

ESSEX

J. W. H. T. DOUGLAS

scorecards, a heavy roller, a mobile office and two pensioned-off double decker buses serving as a scoreboard and ladies toilet.

Perhaps the constant change of wickets was a handicap, but Essex's reputation for inconsistency was long established. Perrin had the experience of scoring 343 not out, containing a record 68 fours, out of a total of 597 at Chesterfield in 1904 and finishing on the losing side by 9 wickets. On the same ground Peter Smith, who was considerably better than his allotted No. 11 position, and Vigar scored 218 in 140 minutes for the 10th wicket. Smith's contribution was 163.

A famous performance saw Yorkshire beaten by an innings before one o'clock on the second morning at Huddersfield in 1935. Nichols (4 for 17, Read 6 for 11) tumbled Yorkshire out for 31. In Essex's 334 Nichols hit 146 and proceeded to take 7 for 37 when Yorkshire were dismissed for 99 in their second innings. Nichols did the double in five successive seasons and was one of five pace bowlers of the time, including Farnes, England's choice in fifteen Tests. He lost his life in a flying accident in the war.

One of Essex's most impressive runs came in the late 'thirties, and but for Hitler's intervention they might have not had to wait so long to strike gold.

Essex played it hard but never so hard as not to have room for a laugh. 'I played frequently against them in those days of their progress to the unknown' wrote former Glamorgan captain Tony Lewis in *Wisden*. 'They had a quality which shone through even their worst performance – humour. They planned their one-day cricket like a war but played it like a party game.'

Pearce, an interested fielder during one of Compton's notorious running misadventures, observed Denis had three calls 'Yes', 'No', and 'Sorry', the first merely serving as a basis for negotiations. Canon F.H. Gillingham, a muscular batsman of the cloth, described his feeling after hitting a boundary off Yorkshire. 'I thought I was in Heaven,' he said and, after a pause, added, 'I just hope Heaven will last longer next time.'

At the burial of Walter Mead, the 'Essex treasure', who took almost 2,000 wickets with spin, the Minister intoned the hope that he would find perfect pitches to bowl on in the Elysium Field. There was a horrified silence from his old team-mates and a whispered, 'That's the *last* thing he wants.'

Even Douglas did not escape a leg pull. A flying ball on a dodgy pitch at Colchester brushed his gloves and went on to strike his head. He collapsed on to the ground and when he got to his feet was given out. He strode off without a word, but let vent his wrath in the dressing room. 'I've got a bump as big as a pigeon's head. How could I have been out?' he stormed. Perrin turned from watching the play and with a straight face said: 'Leg before.'

Pearce was a splendid influence in the re-building, and Fletcher, Gooch, Lever and Foster were among those who added to the long list of Essex players who served both their country and their county.

In 1989 Essex won the Refuge Assurance Cup beating Nottinghamshire at Edgbaston. The 1990 season saw fine batting from Graham Gooch and Mark Waugh, the Australian import. After a lapse of five seasons Essex again won the Britannic Assurance County Championship culminating with a thumping defeat of Middlesex at Chelmsford. Salim Malik, the Pakistani middle-order batsman, scored heavily and Neil Foster achieved over 100 wickets during the season.

Chelmsford

The County Ground, New Writtle Street has been the headquarters of Essex cricket since 1967 and the majority of the County Club's home matches are staged there. The ground had been used previously by Essex in 1925–39, 1946–48 and 1950–56 as Chelmsford C C rented the ground annually from the Wenley Trust. In those days the county headquarters was at Leyton a venue which is no longer used for staging first-class cricket. The initial first-class match to be staged at New Writtle Street was on 20, 22 and 23 June 1925 against Oxford University.

Other matches in Chelmsford have been staged at R H P Sports and Social Club in Rainsford Road, formerly the Hoffman's Athletic Ground in 1959 and 1961. The first match was with Lancashire and the last match was with South Africa Fezela.

The ground is situated barely half a mile from where the rivers Can and Chelmer meet and the River Can passes alongside the ground at the rear of the Tom Pearce Stand. In February 1964, assisted by a loan from the Warwickshire C C S C, Essex were able to purchase the ground for £15,000. Much development has taken place since then; about £750,000 has been spent to build a pavilion which was completed in 1970 and other stands. Most of the facilities are now permanent. The ground was

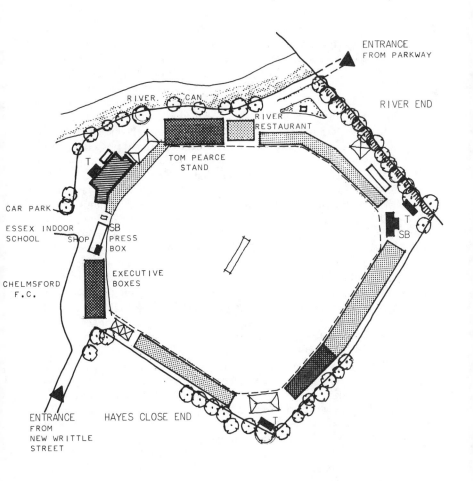

ENTRANCE
FROM PARKWAY

RIVER END

RIVER. CAN.

RIVER
RESTAURANT

TOM PEARCE
STAND

T

CAR PARK

ESSEX INDOOR
SCHOOL   SHOP

SB
PRESS
BOX

T
SB

CHELMSFORD
F.C.

EXECUTIVE
BOXES

ENTRANCE
FROM
NEW WRITTLE
STREET

HAYES CLOSE END

T

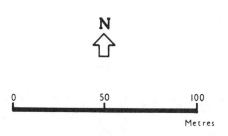

N

0   50   100

Metres

without a permanent scoreboard until 1981 when an attractive building was constructed including a groundsman store by Wimpey Construction.

Essex first staged a County Championship match here in 1926 against Somerset, at a time when most matches at home were still being staged at Leyton. It is a compact ground for a county headquarters, but much has been made of the limited space available. The ground slopes slightly from south-east to north-west and since the installation of a drainage system in 1982 is known as one of the best-drained grounds on the county circuit. Previously the ground was liable to flood because of the close proximity of the River Can and the high water table. The cricket field was for some time used as an emergency helicopter pad for the nearby hospital, until the casualty department was moved elsewhere in the town.

Many memorable performances have taken place here, including Graham Gooch's 275 against Kent in 1988 and Surrey's lowest innings of 14 in 1983. In first-class cricket in 1990 the highest innings total for and against the county were broken and in the limited-overs game Graham Gooch recorded the highest individual innings on the ground 144 against Hampshire (NWBT). In the same match Hampshire made the highest innings total to win a match batting second in the competition – a record.

The Chelmsford City Football Club ground is situated close to the ground and provides car parking for matches. 1990 saw the construction of the Memorial Gates at the New Writtle Street main entrance to the ground and the partial covering of the popular seats on the hospital side of the ground for the general public enclosure.

Additional improved car parking has also been introduced off New Writtle Street at a reasonable price. Crowds of 6,500–7,500 are usual and the ground capacity is set at 9,500. This is regularly attained for popular games as on the first day of the tour match with the West Indians and the Benson & Hedges semi-final tie with Worcestershire in 1991. The ground has hosted international cricket in 1983 when a Prudential Cup match was staged between Australia and India. A match was staged by Middlesex C C C against Somerset in the Schweppes County Championship at Chelmsford in 1977 as Lord's was being prepared for the Gillette Cup Final. In 1991 the ground was used for one of the Bull Test Matches between Young England and Young Australia and later in the season hosted the inaugural Britannic Assurance Challenge between Essex the 1991 County Champions and Victoria the Australian Sheffield Shield Winners of 1990–91.

ADDRESS   County Cricket Ground, New Writtle Street, Chelmsford, Essex CM2 OPG.
TELEPHONE PROSPECTS OF PLAY   0245 287921

DESCRIPTION OF GROUND AND FACILITIES

Entry to the ground for both pedestrians and members' cars is from New Writtle Street. There is another entrance for pedestrians only off

Parkway and under the bridge over the River Can. Main car parking is in the multi-storey car park on the north side of the River Can or in the new car park and temporary field parking areas off New Writtle Street. Street parking is also available a short walk from the ground to the south.

All the permanent buildings have been built over the past fifteen years and occupy the west and north sides of the ground, the areas of the ground allocated to members. The pavilion contains the players' changing accommodation and club offices on the first floor with a members' bar and lounge below where a number of items of cricket memorabilia relating to the county can be viewed. The Tom Pearce Stand and the adjoining River Restaurant Stand provide open seating at upper-floor level and provide the best view of the cricket; at ground-floor level covered seats are provided. There are two scoreboards on the ground; the main box is on the east side and a smaller secondary board is situated at high level next to the press box on the west side. To the west side of the playing area are executive boxes with suites for entertaining. All other seating is open, although part of the popular side is now covered, with most areas comprising of raised seating of the plastic tip-up variety. Some 6,500 seats are provided. The main Essex C C C souvenir shop is situated beneath the press box and there is a secondary smaller shop next to the bar and refreshment facilities at the River End of the ground. In the event of bad weather there is little cover, other than in the lower part of the Tom Pearce Stand, Pavilion or River Restaurant. Toilets are situated in various parts of the ground and facilities for disabled persons are to be found in the pavilion.

The Essex Cricket Library is situated at the rear of the pavilion opposite the Essex Indoor Cricket School in a temporary building and can be visited during breaks in play.

The playing area, which is defined by advertisement boards, is about 132 metres by 128 metres but is reduced on the north side in front of the Tom Pearce Stand due to the proximity of the nearby river. Chelmsford is a pleasant tree-surrounded ground on which much work has been done in recent years.

GROUND RECORDS AND SCORES

FIRST-CLASS MATCHES
Highest innings total for County: 761 for 6 dec. *v.* Leicestershire 1990
Highest innings total against County: 636 for 6 by Northamptonshire 1990
Lowest innings total for County: 65 *v.* Worcestershire 1947, and 1973
Lowest innings total against County: 14 by Surrey 1983
Highest individual innings for County: 275 G.A. Gooch *v.* Kent 1988
Highest individual innings against County: 244 W.R. Hammond for Gloucestershire 1928
Best bowling performance in an innings for County: 9 for 59 M.S. Nichols *v.* Hampshire 1927

Best bowling performance in an innings against County: 8 for 155 C.W.L. Parker for Gloucestershire 1928
Best bowling performance in a match for County: 13 for 117 J.K. Lever *v*. Leicestershire 1979
Best bowling performance in a match against County: 13 for 91 L.N. Constantine for West Indians 1939
Best attendance: 9,500 *v*. West Indians 1991

LIMITED-OVERS MATCHES
Highest innings total for County: 386 for 5 *v*. Wiltshire (NWBT) 1988
Highest innings total against County: 307 for 5 by Hampshire (NWBT) 1990
Lowest innings total for County: 99 *v*. Worcestershire (JPL) 1973
Lowest innings total against County: 58 by Somerset (JPL) 1971
Highest individual innings for County: 144 G.A. Gooch *v*. Hampshire (NWBT) 1990
Highest individual innings against County: 124 B.W. Luckhurst for Kent (JPL) 1973
Best bowling performance for County: 5 for 12 D.R. Pringle *v*. Oxfordshire (NWBT) 1985
Best bowling performance against County: 6 for 16 P.J. Hacker for Nottinghamshire (JPL) 1980
Best attendance: 9,500 *v*. Worcestershire (BHC) 1991

HOW TO GET THERE

Rail   Chelmsford (BR) 0.5 miles.
Bus   From surrounding areas to Bus Station, thence 0.5 mile walk.
Car   From north: M1 junction 8 then A120 and A130 to Chelmsford or M1 junction/M25 interchange to M25 junction 28 then A12 to Chelmsford, ground situated close to town centre, on the southern bank of the River Can, in New Writtle Street off Parkway A130. From east: A414 or A12 or A130 then as north. From south: M25 junction 28 then A12 to Chelmsford, then as north. From west: A414 or as from south, then as north.

WHERE TO STAY AND OTHER INFORMATION

County Hotel (0245 266911), Beechcroft Hotel (0245 352462) and South Lodge Hotel (0245 264564) – all within walking distance.

Disabled Areas   No restrictions – several suitable positions on hardstanding. Wheelchairs may be a problem on the popular side. Please request position in advance.
Local Radio Station(s)   Greater London Radio (94.9 MHz FM/1458 KHz MW), BBC Essex (103.5 MHz FM/765 KHz MW), Essex Radio (96.3 MHz FM/1431 KHz MW).
Local Newspaper(s)   Essex Chronicle, Chelmsford Weekly News, Yellow Advertiser.

Colchester

The Castle Park ground is the home of the Colchester and East Essex Cricket Club, which was founded in 1862 and fields two XI's throughout the season. The ground is located off Catchpool Road very close to the River Colne, which flows around the ground at the southern end. The pavilion was constructed in 1909 ready for the 1910 season. The initial first-class match staged at Castle Park was on 18–20 June 1914 against Worcestershire.

Castle Park is the second ground used by the county in Colchester. The Military Garrison 'A' ground was used from 1920 to 1931, in 1958 due to flooding at Castle Park, in 1966 and 1969–72. The first match at the Garrison 'A' ground was with Hampshire and the last game was with Somerset. A move to the Garrison ground was also made during the championship match with Derbyshire in 1966. This was to have been played at Castle Park, but after the first two days had been washed out, the final day's play was transferred to the Garrison ground. Wisden of the following year remarked 'though seventeen wickets fell for 246 runs, not even a first innings decision could be reached'. Castle Park is susceptible to flooding due to the high water table. The ground is near the Castle Mound from which parkland slopes away to the rich meadows of the valley and the cricket field. Castle Park also suffers from poor weather and this is well recorded in the club's history. In 1958 on the third day of a championship match with Leicestershire the ground was totally submerged in water; chairs and boundary boards floated across the playing area and the Colchester Secretary had to use waders to get about.

Essex first staged a championship match at Castle Park in 1914 when Worcestershire were the visitors. After a break of some years Essex returned in the period 1934–39 and then after World War Two, in 1946. Essex today take two championship matches and one limited-overs match to the ground usually in August for the Colchester Festival.

Colchester has one unique cricket record; it is the only ground on which a player has scored a double century in each innings of a match; this was achieved by Arthur Fagg for Kent in 1938. Castle Park was also a favourite ground of Doug Insole, who scored his only double century against Yorkshire in 1949. More recently Ken McEwan in four consecutive seasons scored over 500 runs on the ground, including 181 and 189 in one week. Ground records have included centuries before lunch by Gordon Barker and Arthur Fagg, a career best bowling performance by Peter Smith against Middlesex in 1947 and an aggregate of 600 runs in a John Player Sunday League match with Warwickshire in 1982.

ADDRESS Colchester and East Essex Cricket Club, Castle Park (Lower), Sportsway, off Catchpool Road, Colchester, Essex.
TELEPHONE PROSPECTS OF PLAY 0206 769071

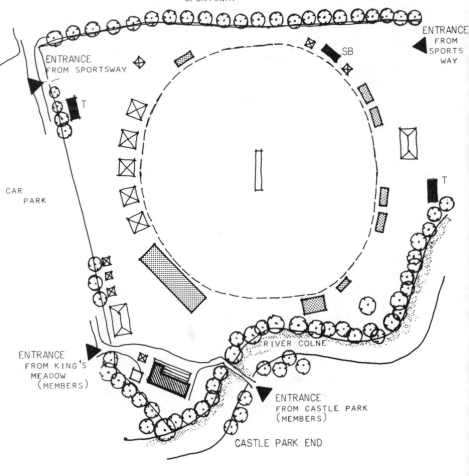

SPORTSWAY END

SPORTSWAY

ENTRANCE
FROM
SPORTS
WAY

ENTRANCE
FROM SPORTSWAY

SB

T

CAR
PARK

T

ENTRANCE
FROM KING'S
MEADOW
(MEMBERS)

RIVER COLNE

ENTRANCE
FROM CASTLE PARK
(MEMBERS)

CASTLE PARK END

N

0   50   100

Metres

DESCRIPTION OF GROUND AND FACILITIES

The main entry to the Castle Park ground is in the north-west corner off Catchpool Road. Ample car parking is available in Kings Meadow to the west and along Sportsway to the north-east, where there are further pedestrian entrances. There are also members' entrances near the pavilion from King's Meadow and Castle Park.

The River Colne forms the southern boundary of the ground. Adjoining the river in the south-west corner is the pavilion, the only permanent building, which is some 50 metres from the playing area. All other facilities are temporary and include tiered plastic seating for both members and the public. There is an Essex C C C souvenir shop situated in a tent close to the pavilion enclosure. Generally the west side of the ground is allocated to sponsors tents and entertainment areas while the public are allocated much of the east and north sides of the ground.

The playing area is approximately circular being 132 metres by 128 metres and is defined by advertisement boards. The scoreboard is the temporary travelling scorebox used by the county club for all matches away from Chelmsford. The capacity of the ground is 6,000 and sufficient temporary seating is provided. This is a pleasant park ground at which to watch cricket in good weather but can be unpleasant if the weather is poor. There are no special arrangements for disabled persons.

GROUND RECORDS AND SCORES

FIRST-CLASS MATCHES

Highest innings total for County: 588 for 9 dec. *v.* Northamptonshire 1937

Highest innings total against County: 487 by Kent 1946

Lowest innings total for County: 44 *v.* Nottinghamshire 1986

Lowest innings total against County: 56 by Sussex 1957

Highest individual innings for County: 219 n.o. D.J. Insole *v.* Yorkshire 1949

Highest individual innings against County: 244 A. Fagg for Kent 1938

Best bowling performance in an innings for County: 9 for 77 T.P.B. Smith *v.* Middlesex 1947

Best bowling performance in an innings against County: 8 for 57 C.W.L. Parker for Gloucestershire 1920

Best bowling performance in a match for County: 16 for 215 T.P.B. Smith *v.* Middlesex 1947

Best bowling performance in a match against County: 12 for 59 C.I.J. Smith for Middlesex 1936

Best attendance: 8,000 *v.* Middlesex 1947

LIMITED-OVER MATCHES

Highest innings total for County: 299 for 4 *v.* Warwickshire (JPL) 1982

Highest innings total against County: 301 for 6 by Warwickshire (JPL) 1982

Lowest innings total for County: 133 *v*. Yorkshire (JPL) 1979
Lowest innings total against County: 123 by Derbyshire (JPL) 1985
Highest individual innings for County: 156 n.o. K.S. McEwan *v*. Warwickshire (JPL) 1982
Highest individual innings against County: 114 D.R. Turner for Hampshire (JPL) 1984
Best bowling performance for County: 6 for 33 T.D. Topley *v*. Nottinghamshire (RAL) 1988
Best bowling performance against County: 4 for 22 D.P. Hughes for Lancashire (JPL) 1975
Best attendance: 9,000 *v*. Worcestershire (RAL) 1989

HOW TO GET THERE

Rail   Colchester (BR), 0.75 miles.
Bus   Eastern National and Colchester Corporation from surrounding areas to Bus Station, thence 0.75 miles walk to ground. Some buses from the north do pass closer to the ground.
Car   From north: A12 or A134 follow signs Colchester, Then Castle Park off A12 for County Cricket. From east: A120, A137 or A133 follow signs Colchester, then as north. From south: A12 to Colchester, then as north or B1025 or B1026 then as north. From west: A120 or A604 to Colchester, then as north or follow A12, then as north.

WHERE TO STAY AND OTHER INFORMATION

George Hotel (0206 578494) Marks Tey Hotel (0206 210001).

Disabled Areas   No restrictions, but there is no concrete hardstanding close to the playing area so wheelchairs may be a problem when weather is poor.
Local Radio Station(s)   Essex Radio (96.3 MHz FM/1431 Khz MW), Radio Orwell (97.1 MHz FM/1170 KHz MW).
Local Newspaper(s)   Colchester Leader, Essex County Standard, Evening Gazette, Yellow Advertiser.

Ilford

Valentine's Park is a public park and caters for many games; tennis courts and bowling greens are adjacent to the cricket field. It is one of the largest and most attractive parks in the east of Greater London. The park, which extends to 136 acres, used to surround the home of a Mrs Ingleby and it was from her that the Ilford C C obtained a lease in 1897 on roughly 8 acres to make the present ground. The only condition she demanded was that the pavilion should be built under the trees. Several years later she also insisted that the sightscreens be lowered so that they could not be seen from the windows of her home. In 1899 Ilford Council

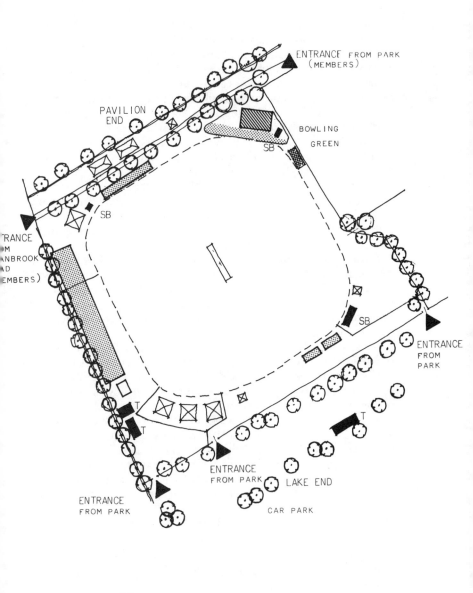

ENTRANCE FROM PARK
(MEMBERS)

PAVILION
END

BOWLING
GREEN

SB

SB

ENTRANCE
ROM
ANBROOK
AD
EMBERS)

SB

ENTRANCE
FROM
PARK

T

T

ENTRANCE
FROM PARK

LAKE END

ENTRANCE
FROM PARK

CAR PARK

N

0   50   100

Metres

purchased a large part of the parkland and lake. In 1906, when Mrs Ingleby died, they purchased the remainder of the park including her house.

The ground is the home of Ilford Cricket Club, founded in 1879 and is also used by Ilford and Woodford RAFA formerly RAFA (Ilford) established in 1951. Essex first played a match at Valentine's Park in 1923 when the West Indian touring team were the visitors. This first match against West Indians was also made conspicuous by the fact that the great Leary Constantine then only twenty-one, collected a pair! The ground lies on the west side of the park and today is the property of Redbridge Borough Council who maintain it. The cricket week is eagerly looked forward to by the local cricket fraternity. A good relationship exists between Ilford C C and Essex C C C in the organization of the annual Ilford Festival week in June. As the ground is such a pleasant venue for top-level cricket, it is not surprising that every first-class county and all the overseas touring countries except Pakistan and Sri Lanka have played on the ground. Essex have played on a number of club grounds and the Ilford C C ground in Valentine's Park will always rank as one of the most picturesque in the county.

Terracing along the Cranbrook Road side of the ground was built in 1949 in time for the visit of Glamorgan, the 1948 county champions. A crowd of 13,000 including members, were present on the Saturday and this is probably the largest crowd ever to watch a day's play at Valentine's Park. Crowds in recent years for limited-overs matches have been around 5,000–6,500.

Since World War Two the groundsman has kept the middle of the square entirely free from use until the county cricket week, so that the Ilford Festival week is usually held in the early part of the season. Today the county play two championship and one limited-overs match each season. Valentine's Park was the first ground to stage a championship match on a Sunday against Somerset in 1966. The first Sunday League match was against Middlesex in 1970 when some 8,000 attended. Two test players recently achieved highest individual innings for and against the county on the ground during the 1990s, namely Salim Malik and Desmond Haynes. Mark Waugh scored 204 n.o. against Gloucestershire in 1990 and Ken McEwan scored 186 against Northamptonshire in 1978.

Players who have represented Ilford C C and Essex C C C include G.M. Louden, J.K. Lever now club chairman, G.A. Gooch and N. Hussain.

ADDRESS Ilford Cricket Club, The Pavilion, Valentine's Park, Cranbrook Road, Ilford, Essex.
TELEPHONE PROSPECTS OF PLAY 081 518 2990

DESCRIPTION OF GROUND AND FACILITIES

Members enter the ground from Cranbrook Road while the public enter through the two entrances in Valentine's Park to the south. Car parking is available at the Lake End and in the adjoining streets. The only permanent structures are the pavilion, small scorebox and some grassed terracing on the Cranbrook Road side. All other facilities are temporary and these include tents, marquees, refreshments, seating and bars. Members' areas are to the north of the ground while the public are generally to the south.

The playing area is approximately circular and comparatively small, being only 124 metres by 122 metres. Sponsors' tents are sited in the south-west corner of the ground, as is the Essex C C C souvenir tent. A secondary shop is located near the players' dining tent and temporary club office at the Pavilion End.

GROUND RECORDS AND SCORES

FIRST-CLASS MATCHES

Highest innings total for County: 457 for 5 dec. v. Northamptonshire 1978
Highest innings total against County: 491 for 8 dec. by Lancashire 1938
Lowest innings total for County: 69 v. Somerset 1924
Lowest innings total against County: 64 by Worcestershire 1982
Highest individual innings for County: 215 Salim Malik v. Leicestershire 1991
Highest individual innings against County: 220 n.o. D.L. Haynes for Middlesex 1990
Best bowling performance in an innings for County: 8 for 30 R.E. East v. Northamptonshire 1977
Best bowling performance in an innings against County: 8 for 58 D.St.E. Atkinson for West Indians 1957
Best bowling performance in a match for County: 13 for 145 J.K. Lever v. Northamptonshire 1978
Best bowling performance in a match against County: 13 for 61 J.C. White for Somerset 1924
Best attendance: 13,000 v. Glamorgan 1948

LIMITED-OVERS MATCHES

Highest innings total for County: 256 for 5 v. Hampshire (JPL) 1986
Highest innings total against County: 257 for 4 by Hampshire (JPL) 1986
Lowest innings total for County: 127 for 9 v. Lancashire (JPL) 1979
Lowest innings total against County: 45 by Northamptonshire (JPL) 1971
Highest individual innings for County: 123 K.S. McEwan v. Warwickshire (JPL) 1976
Highest individual innings against County: 112 n.o. B.C. Rose for Somerset (JPL) 1980
Best bowling performance for County: 5 for 22 B.E.A. Edmeades v. Leicestershire (BHC) 1973
Best bowling performance against County: 5 for 32 W. Larkins for Northamptonshire (JPL) 1978
Best attendance: 8,000 v. Middlesex (JPL) 1970

HOW TO GET THERE

Rail Ilford (BR) or Gants Hill (London Underground Central Line), both 0.75 miles.

Bus LRT 123/9, 144, 150, 167, 179, 247 and 296 all pass BR Ilford Station and Gants Hill Underground Station (Telephone: 071 222 1234).

Car 10 miles north-east of Central London in the district of Redbridge. From north: M25 junction 27, then M11 and A12 to Gants Hill, then at roundabout follow Cranbrook Road, ground situated on your left off this road. From east: M25 junctions 28 or 29 then A12 or A126 to Ilford, ground situated close to A118, A1083 and A124 then as north. From south: A13 then A117 and A124 to Ilford, then as north. From West: A13 then A117 and A124 to Ilford, then as north.

WHERE TO STAY AND OTHER INFORMATION

Cranbrook Hotel (081 554 6544), Park Hotel (081 554 9616).

Disabled Areas No restrictions, preferably by the sightscreen or in front of the pavilion to the left on the hardstanding.

Local Radio Station(s) Greater London Radio (94.9 MHz FM/1458 KHz MW), Essex Radio (96.3 MHz FM/1431 KHz MW), Capital Road (95.8 MHz/1548 KHz MW), LBC (97.3 MHz FM/1152 KHz MW).

Local Newspaper(s) Ilford Independent, Ilford Recorder, Walthamstow Guardian Group, Yellow Advertiser.

Southend-on-Sea

Southend has two cricket grounds which have been used for first-class cricket by the County Club, Southchurch Park and Chalkwell Park at Westcliff-on-Sea. Southchurch Park has recently regained favour at the expense of Chalkwell Park because it can accommodate larger crowds and has plenty of space surrounding the playing area. However in 1989 the wicket at Southchurch Park was the first to be reported to the TCCB at Lord's as unfit for first-class cricket by the umpires during the Yorkshire Championship match which cost the home side 24 points and dashed their hopes of winning the championship.

Essex made their first visit to Southchurch Park in 1906 when the visitors were Leicestershire; a copy of the scorecard of this first match hangs in the pavilion today. Essex have played at Southchurch Park each season since 1914 except for 1959, 1962, 1965 and 1967–76. Since 1977 all matches staged by the county in the seaside resort have been played at Southchurch Park.

There are two pavilions at Southchurch Park, one is for the players and officials and the other belongs to the Southend Hockey Club who

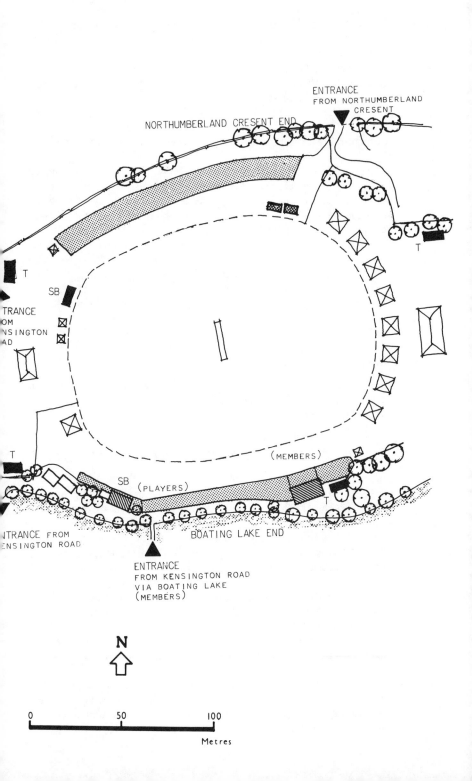

ENTRANCE
FROM NORTHUMBERLAND
CRESENT

NORTHUMBERLAND CRESENT END

T

SB

TRANCE
OM
NSINGTON
AD

T

(MEMBERS)

SB (PLAYERS)

T

NTRANCE FROM
ENSINGTON ROAD

BOATING LAKE END

ENTRANCE
FROM KENSINGTON ROAD
VIA BOATING LAKE
(MEMBERS)

N

0   50   100

Metres

play on the ground during the winter months. The ground is the home of Southend C C which was established in 1874. They have played here since 1895 and the cricket pavilion was built in 1929. Southend C C play in the Essex Cricket League and field four XIs on a Saturday and two XIs on a Sunday throughout the season. Southend C C won the Essex Cricket League in 1981. Southchurch Park is now owned and maintained by the local council. Incidently, it was in the ownership of the monks of Christ Church Canterbury from AD 823 and it was on the Southchurch foreshore that the cultivation of oysters is said to have begun.

The ground is sufficiently large to allow two club games to be played simultaneously. There are three separate cricket squares, of which the central one is used exclusively by the county for matches during the Southend Festival week which usually takes place annually in July. Essex now play two championship and one limited-overs match at Southend as Southchurch Park nearly always attracts a good crowd which in the past has been boosted by holiday makers. It is a quiet park, barely half a mile from the seafront, the crowded beach and a large boating lake. The largest crowd was 16,000 for the visit of the Australians in 1948, when the visitors amassed 721 in a single day. Don Bradman's 187 was scored in 125 minutes. Crowds today are usually around 5,000.

The most recent piece of history made on the ground was in 1983 when Essex managed 310 for 5 against Glamorgan with Graham Gooch hitting 176.

ADDRESS   Southend-on-Sea Cricket Club, The Pavilion, Southchurch Park, Northumberland Cresent, Southend-on-Sea, Essex.
TELEPHONE PROSPECTS OF PLAY   0702 61519

DESCRIPTION OF GROUND AND FACILITIES

Entry to Southchurch Park can be gained from Northumberland Cresent to the north and from Kensington Road to the west. The ground is situated north of the boating lake and the two pavilions are on the north side of the lake. The pavilion to the south-west is used by the players and that on the south-east by the members for refreshments. These, together with the terracing to the north and south of the ground, are the only permanent structures. Seating is provided for some 75 per cent of the capacity of 8,000. You are not encouraged to bring your own seats not least because there is no car parking available at the ground and it is necessary to find parking in the nearby streets or town centre. No provisions exist for disabled persons. The east side of the ground is allocated to sponsors' tents and the main refreshment areas for members. The north side is available to the public. There are temporary toilet facilities.

The playing area is usually 170 metres by 123 metres and defined by advertisement boards. This is a well-maintained, tree-enclosed recreation ground and a good view of the cricket may be obtained from all parts of the ground.

FIRST-CLASS MATCHES
Highest innings total for County: 503 *v.* Hampshire 1936
Highest innings total against County: 721 by Australians 1948
Lowest innings total for County: 56 *v.* West Indians 1963
Lowest innings total against County: 43 by Kent 1925
Highest individual innings for County: 205 M.S. Nichols *v.*
Hampshire 1936
Highest individual innings against County: 255 n.o. H. Sutcliffe for
Yorkshire 1924
Best bowling performance in an innings for County: 9 for 117 T.P.B.
Smith *v.* Nottinghamshire 1948
Best bowling performance in an innings against County: 10 for 53
A.P. Freeman for Kent 1930
Best bowling performance in a match for County: 12 for 131 G.M.
Louden *v.* Derbyshire 1920
Best bowling performance in a match against County: 16 for 94 A.P.
Freeman for Kent 1930
Best attendance: 16,000 *v.* Australians 1948

LIMITED-OVERS MATCHES
Highest innings total for County: 310 for 5 *v.* Glamorgan (JPL) 1983
Highest innings total against County: 254 for 4 by Glamorgan (JPL)
1983
Lowest innings total for County: 138 *v.* Leicestershire (GC) 1977
Lowest innings total against County: 153 for 6 by Lancashire (JPL)
1981
Highest individual innings for County: 176 G.A. Gooch *v.*
Glamorgan (JPL) 1983
Highest individual innings against County: 109 M. Newell for
Nottinghamshire (RAL) 1990
Best bowling performance for County: 5 for 41 D.R. Pringle *v.*
Gloucestershire (JPL) 1985
Best bowling performance against County: 5 for 19 J.F. Steele for
Leicestershire (GC) 1977
Best attendance: 5,000 *v.* Glamorgan (JPL) 1983

HOW TO GET THERE

Rail Southend East (BR), 0.5 mile.
Bus Eastern National No. 20 Shoeburyness-Hullbridge passing BR
Southend Central and Victoria Stations (Telephone: 0702 430534);
also Nos: 7, 8, 67 and 68 pass close to the ground.
Car From north and west: M25 junction 29 then A127 or A130,
follow signs Southend then to Southchurch and County Cricket,
ground situated 1.5 miles east of town centre.

WHERE TO STAY AND OTHER INFORMATION

Airport Moat House (0702 546344), Argyle Hotel (0702 339483), Balmoral Hotel (0702 342947), plus many other seaside hotels and guesthouses.

Disabled Areas   No restrictions, but request position on hardstanding at boating lake end.
Local Radio Station(s)   Essex Radio (96.3 MHz FM/1431 KHz MW).
Local Newspaper(s)   Evening Echo, Yellow Advertiser, Southend Standard, Southend District News, London Advertiser.

GLAMORGAN

CARDIFF

ABERGAVENNY

COLWYN BAY

NEATH

PONTYPRIDD

SWANSEA

ABERYSTWYTH

EBBW VALE

LLANELLI

MERTHYR TYDFIL

Glamorgan

Founded 6 July 1888
Colours Blue and gold
Crest Gold daffodil
Patron HRH The Prince of Wales
President W. Wooller
Chairman A.R. Lewis
Chairman cricket committee A.R. Lewis
Secretary G.R. Stone
Assistant secretary M.J. Fatkin
Commercial manager A.P. Dilloway
Marketing assistant Miss V.L. Snook
Captain A.R. Butcher
Senior county coach A. Jones MBE
Assistant coach D.J. Shepherd
Ground supervisor L.A. Smith
Scorer 1st XI B.T. Denning
Scorer 2nd XI G.N. Lewis
Statistician Dr A.K. Hignell
Sponsors ASW
Newsletter *Glamorgan Matters*
Address Sophia Gardens, Cardiff, Wales CF1 9XR.
Telephone 0222 343478
Glamorgan Rapid Cricketline 0891 567504

ACHIEVEMENTS

County Championship Champions (2) 1948 and 1969
Gillette Cup Finalists (1) 1977
National Westminster Bank Trophy Quarter-finalists (3) 1985, 1988 and 1990
Benson & Hedges Cup Semi-finalists (1) 1988
John Player Sunday League 8th 1977
Refuge Assurance Sunday League 6th 1988
Tilcon Trophy Winners (1) 198; finalists (1) 1987
Seven Trophy Finalists (1) 1987

GROUNDS

Cardiff (Sophia Gardens, Cathedral Road); Swansea (St Helen's Ground, Bryn Road); Neath (The Gnoll, Dyfed Road); Ebbw Vale (Eugene Cross Park, Newchurch Road); Abergavenny (Pen-y-Pound, Avenue Road); Merthyr Tydfil (Hoover Sports Ground, Merthyr Road); Llanelli (Stradey Park, Denham Avenue); Pontypridd (Ynysangharad Park, Ynysybwl Road); Aberystwyth (University College of Wales Sports Ground, Llanbadarn Road) and Colwyn Bay (Penrhyn Avenue, Rhos-on-Sea).

Other grounds that have been used since 1969 are: Newport (Athletic Club Sports Ground, Rodney Parade); Llandudno (The Oval, Gloddaeth Avenue) and BP Llandarcy (BP Oil Llandarcy Refinery Limited Sports Ground, Crymlyn Bog).

SECOND XI GROUNDS
In addition to the above mentioned grounds the following are used for second XI matches: Ammanford C C, Ammanford Park, Ammanford. Telephone: 0269 594988; Bridgend C C, New Bridge Fields, Bridgend. Telephone: 0656 663075; BP Llandarcy C C, BP Works Ground, Llandarcy. Telephone: 0792 813232; Panteg C C, Panteg House, Newport Road, Panteg. Telephone: 0495 756117; Pontarddulais C C, Pontarddulais Park, Pontarddulais. Telephone: 0792 882556; Pontymister C C, Cricket Ground, Pontymister. (No Telephone); Usk C C, Cricket Ground, Usk. Telephone: 0291 33754.

In 1921 Glamorgan, having met MCC's condition of finding eight clubs willing to guarantee home and away fixtures, became the 17th member of the first-class county community and began, in the words of John Clay, the 'rag time days'. Clay, a brilliant off spinner who bowled for England, was thought to be the author of an annual report which candidly admitted: 'In the first few seasons Glamorgan were like no other side; some will say it was not a side at all.' The same Clay at the age of 50 was to be a member of Wilfred Wooller's side of champions in 1948.

Glamorgan started with a financial burden carried over from their Minor Counties days, and too many of the players were past their prime. In the first season the bowling mainstays were Nash, aged 48, and Creber, 47, and often there were no specialist slip catchers and the elderly needed to be hidden in the field. The selection committee was thirty-two members strong including players.

According to Dai Davies, Glamorgan's first Welsh-born pro, the occasional amateur pressed into service didn't score a run, took nought for plenty, the only thing he caught in the field was sunstroke, he fell down the hotel stairs, left his luggage on the train and arrived home to find his wife had run away with his closest friend.

Reinforcements of the quality of Mercer from Sussex and the Irish-American spinner, Ryan, added potency to the attack, and, in due course, genuine Welsh talent was as welcome as spring daffodils.

The most significant arrival was Maurice Turnbull, a schoolboy from Downside. In 1930, having captained Cambridge, he took over the leadership, and a year later was appointed secretary. Glamorgan's second phase of development centred around his influence. At once he tackled the financial problems, and took Glamorgan to their highest position of 7th. In sixteen previous seasons only once, 8th in 1926, had Glamorgan escaped the lower half of the county table. Turnbull, the first from the county to score a century for England, also played rugby and

CARDIFF

D. J. SHEPHERD

hockey for Wales, and, alas, at the age of 33 fell to a sniper's bullet in Normandy.

Wooller, another Cambridge man and rugby international, succeeded Turnbull as the strong man captain-secretary, and, in 1948, shrewdly planned the fulfilment of an impossible dream. By the standards of other champions Glamorgan batted and bowled moderately, but the fielding and catching close to the wicket to support a leg stump attack was superb, at times miraculous. Wooller, Allan Watkins, whose all-round ability was appreciated by England, Clift and Dyson took 120 catches between them. Muncer, ex-Middlesex off-spinner, had 139 victims, but, fittingly, in the climax of victory at Bournemouth, Clay took six for 48, and Emrys Davies, another survivor of the difficult days, scored 74.

For weeks afterwards Clay said he felt as if he was floating in fairyland, and Cardiff station was packed to greet the homecoming heroes and rang to the sounds of a huge choir. Nothing like it had been seen since Cardiff City brought the English FA Cup back to Wales.

Twenty-one years later Tony Lewis, yet another Cambridge-trained leader, and soon to captain England, expertly guided Glamorgan to their second county title. Lewis had the further distinction of remaining unbeaten, a record no champions in the previous thirty-one seasons had managed. A decisive factor was a record bag of batting points which served to emphasize an excellent team's attitude. Again the crowds congregated in front of the pavilion, as they had done at Bournemouth, now at the new ground of Sophia Gardens.

Lewis was magnificently supported by Alan Jones, a worthy successor to the old batting favourites, Willie Jones and Parkhouse, Majid Khan, the exciting Pakistani, Nash's clever bowling, all-rounder Walker, as fine a close-in fielder as the game has known, and his first lieutenant Shepherd.

Like Clay and McConnon – considered good enough to be picked before Laker for Australia in 1954–55 – Shepherd was converted from pace to off spin. Born in a hamlet in the Gower peninsular Shepherd

M. J. TURNBULL

J. C. CLAY

GLAMORGANSHIRE

A. R. BUTCHER

became the first bowler of other than English birth to pass 2,000 wickets, and ended with 2,218, a record which will be hard to equal. An all-Welsh side may be an unrealistic dream, but Shepherd is one of many to demonstrate genuine cricket talent exists in Wales.

Glamorgan have shown prudent reality with the recruitment of overseas stars, the latest of which, no less than Vivian Richards, showed the club's initiative. Matthew Maynard also emerged as one of England's most exciting batting prospects, until he joined the rebel South African tour.

Glamorgan again finished bottom of the championship in 1989 but in 1990 the county, under the captaincy of Alan Butcher, climbed to 8th. Butcher scored 2,044 first-class runs with an average of 60.11. Hugh Morris was given an England call against the West Indies in 1991 after captaining the England 'B' winter tour in 1990–91.

Cardiff

The first matches staged by Glamorgan C C C at Sophia Gardens in 1967 were against the Indians and the first championship match was against Northamptonshire. This was after the club's removal from Cardiff Arms Park adjoining the National Stadium. The current ground is located close to the River Taff and takes its name from Sophia, the second wife of the second Marquess of Bute. The ground was originally part of the Bute Estate which stretched north from the city along both banks of the River Taff and close to Cardiff Castle. The Sophia Gardens were previously gardens where people of the city could promenade and listen to bands during the summer. There were ample outbuildings including the Sophia Gardens Pavilion, which was built in 1951 and which has held many events, including competitions in 1958 for the Commonwealth Games. The pavilion collapsed in 1982 and was

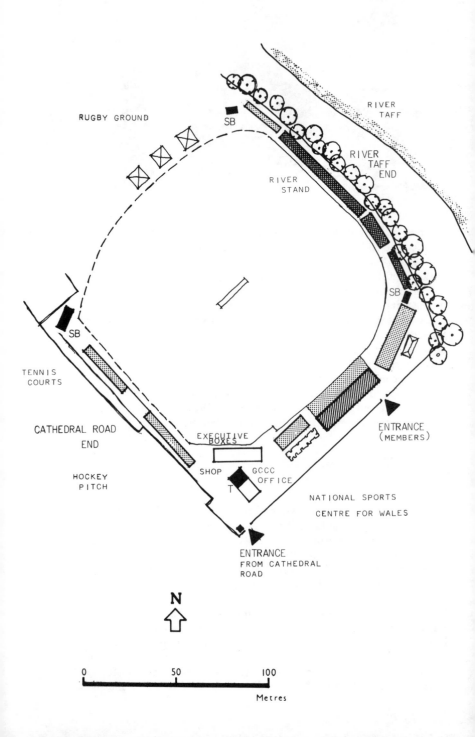

RUGBY GROUND

SB

RIVER
TAFF

RIVER
TAFF
END

RIVER
STAND

SB

TENNIS
COURTS

CATHEDRAL ROAD
END

EXECUTIVE
BOXES

ENTRANCE
(MEMBERS)

HOCKEY
PITCH

SHOP

T

GCCC
OFFICE

NATIONAL SPORTS

CENTRE FOR WALES

ENTRANCE
FROM CATHEDRAL
ROAD

N

0   50   100

Metres

demolished to make way for a car parking area.

Glamorgan C C C had requested use of the gardens during the 1950s but was turned down. In 1963 a scheme was put forward and agreed for the 23 acres of land at Gala Field to be developed to accommodate the Cardiff Athletic Club and the various sports sections which could no longer be housed at the Arms Park due to the redevelopment of the National Stadium. Cricket was included and Glamorgan moved to its present home in 1966–67 ready for the new season. Some 10.5 acres was used for cricket. The rest was taken in 1970–71 when the Cardiff Corporation offered land to the Sports Council so that the National Sportscentre for Wales could be constructed. The ground is also used by Cardiff Cricket Club, who first played at Sophia Gardens in 1966.

With a 99-year lease on the ground the Cardiff Athletic Club built a new pavilion, offices and a scoreboard in 1966–67, the latter thanks to a donation from a London Welsh sportsman Sir Edward Lewis. In 1967 Cardiff C C held a cricket week to celebrate the centenary of the club and the opening of the new ground. Matches were played with a number of sides, including MCC, the Glamorgan Nomads and the Forty 'XL' Club. The latter side including: Wilfred Wooller, Harold Gimblett, Dick Spooner, Bob Broadbent and Bob Appleyard. After the MCC match a civic reception was held at Cardiff Castle.

A pavilion built by E. Taylor and Company of Treforest houses all the facilities on the ground. At the River Taff End there is a covered stand and press/scorers' facilities and to the Cathedral Road End are ample open terraces and behind them hockey pitches and tennis courts. The ground is also used by Cardiff Rugby Football Club's second XV and facilities also exist for tennis, this being the home of the Cardiff Tennis Club. In 1987 the Glamorgan C C C offices moved from 6 High Street to the ground and these are now housed in the south-western corner of the ground with sponsors' facilities adjoining.

Some notable matches have been staged on the ground including that in 1969 when Glamorgan won the County Championship, beating neighbours Worcestershire. Some 16,000 people attended this match, still a record attendance for the ground. In 1976 Glamorgan deprived Somerset of the John Player Sunday League before 11,000 spectators; this was probably the largest crowd for a limited-overs match at the ground.

Wilfred Wooller has commented that Sophia Gardens is 'a quite delightful rural setting, spacious and well-treed but somehow it has never reproduced the cosy atmosphere at Cardiff Arms Park'. In 1985 Glamorgan lost so many days to poor weather that members suggested the ground's name should be changed to Sophia Lakes owing to the number of lakes forming on the outfield. Ground records have included one triple century of 313 n.o. by Jimmy Cook for Somerset in 1990, 252 by Wayne Larkins for Northamptonshire in 1983 and for Glamorgan 191 n.o. by Matthew Maynard against Gloucestershire in 1989. Records change nearly every season as only about 150 first-class matches have been staged on the ground. Glamorgan achieved their highest innings total on the ground when they declared at 543 for 8 against Somerset in 1988.

There is a proposal that the club should move to a new ground in Cardiff Docks where they will at last have sole responsibility for their own ground and future.

ADDRESS Cardiff Athletic Club, The Pavilion, Sophia Gardens, Cathedral Road, Cardiff, Wales CF1 9XR.
TELEPHONE NUMBER PROSPECTS OF PLAY 0222 43478/ 29956

DESCRIPTION OF GROUND AND FACILITIES

Sophia Gardens is situated just off the Cathedral Road, adjacent to the National Sports Centre for Wales and within a short distance of the River Taff. The ground is surrounded by trees and attractively landscaped areas. The pavilion which houses a small museum and library for use by members and the public by appointment, the club offices, press/scorers box, sponsors' suites, river stand and scoreboard are the only permanent covered buildings on the ground. The pavilion is to the south of the playing area, at right angles to the wicket and provides ample facilities for members. To the north side, opposite the pavilion, is a rugby field which is used by sponsors and during much of the season tents and large marquees can be found here. At the Cathedral Road End is the main computerised scoreboard; this is similar to the one at Abergavenny but larger. There are also two temporary, raised seating areas made of steel and timber. Behind the scoreboard are the hockey pitches which are both artificial and floodlit. The TV camera/ commentary box position is also at this end of the ground directly above and behind the sightscreen on a gantry.

There are two entrances to the ground, one for members which is directly behind the pavilion and another for the public which is at the rear of the club offices. The toilets and refreshments, the Glamorgan C C C souvenir caravan and areas of open seating, can be found near the public entrance at the rear of the Sportscentre.

The playing area is 142 metres by 146 metres and is defined by a rope and on two sides by a white pale fence with advertising boards. The seating capacity of the ground is 10,000 of which 50 per cent is provided permanently with additions made for popular matches as required. Spectators are advised not to bring their own seats to matches. Car parking within the ground is only for players/officials and committee members. Outside the ground car parking is available at the National Sportscentre, sometimes during festival weeks on the rugby field at the rear of the marquees and in Sophia Gardens car park south of the Sportscentre facilities.

GROUND RECORDS AND SCORES

FIRST-CLASS MATCHES
Highest innings total for County: 543 for 8 dec. *v.* Somerset 1988
Highest innings total against County: 535 for 2 dec. by Somerset 1990

Lowest innings total for County: 43 v. Leicestershire 1971
Lowest innings total against County: 52 by Hampshire 1968
Highest individual innings for County: 191 n.o. M.P. Maynard v. Gloucestershire 1989
Highest individual innings against County: 313 n.o. S.J. Cook for Somerset 1990
Best bowling performance in an innings for County: 8 for 63 A.W. Allin v. Sussex 1976
Best bowling performance in an innings against County: 9 for 57 P.I. Pocock for Surrey 1979
Best bowling performance in a match for County: 13 for 127 R.C. Ontong v. Nottinghamshire 1986
Best bowling performance in a match against County: 13 for 102 D.L. Underwood for Kent 1979
Best attendance: 16,000 v. Worcestershire 1969

LIMITED-OVERS MATCHES
Highest innings total for County: 318 for 4 v. Staffordshire (NWBT) 1989
Highest innings total against County: 330 for 4 by Somerset (GC) 1978
Lowest innings total for County: 76 v. Middlesex (JPL) 1975
Lowest innings total against County: 85 by Lancashire (BHC) 1976
Highest individual innings for County: 154 n.o. H. Morris v. Staffordshire (NWBT) 1989
Highest individual innings against County: 145 P.W. Denning for Somerset (GC) 1978
Best bowling performance for County: 5 for 17 J.G. Thomas v. Sussex (NWBT) 1985
Best bowling performance against County: 6 for 20 T.E. Jesty for Hampshire (JPL) 1975
Best attendance: 11,000 v. Somerset (JPL) 1976

HOW TO GET THERE

Rail Cardiff Central (BR), 1 mile.
Bus Cardiff Bus 32, 62 from BR Cardiff Central Station and also 21, 25 and 33 from city centre pass close to ground (Telephone: 0222 396521).
Car From north: A470 follow signs to Cardiff until junction with Cardiff bypass, then A48 Port Talbot and city centre, ground is situated off Cathedral Road A48 for Sophia Gardens. From east: M4 junction 29, then A48, then as north. From west: A4160 follow signs Cardiff, then A48, then as north.

WHERE TO STAY AND OTHER INFORMATION

Crest Hotel (0222 388681), Forte Post House (0222 731212), Park Hotel (0222 383471), Inn on the Avenue (0222 732520).

Disabled Areas   No special area, request suitable position; car parking available within ground by prior arrangement.
Local Radio Station(s)   BBC Radio Wales (882 KHz MW), Red Dragon Radio (97.4 MHz FM/1359 KHz MW).
Local Newspaper(s)   South Wales Evening Post, South Wales Echo, Western Mail, Cardiff Independent, Cardiff Post Series.

Abergavenny

Avenue Road is the home of Abergavenny Cricket Club, which was established in 1834 and is known to the locals as Pen-y-Pound. It is situated on the northern outskirts of the Gwent town, off Avenue Road and adjoining Avenue Crescent.

The 4.5 acre ground was opened in 1896 when a match was staged between a South Wales XI and an Abergavenny XI. There are ample facilities for hockey, bowls and tennis at the ground and the pavilion which was rebuilt in 1977 after a fire, has ample amenities. The clock over the entrance door survived the fire; its plaque notes that it was presented to the club by Mr and Mrs Lyons in 1921. The club during its early years moved from one ground to another until in 1895 an approach was made to the Marquess of Abergavenny, a keen follower of cricket and a one time President of Kent C C C, who leased the ground to the club. The ground took its name from the nearby lane Pen-y-Pound. The Marquess provided the original pavilion in 1915 after generously giving further land in 1910 and again in 1912.

As with Ebbw Vale C C, the ground was also used by Monmouthshire C C C for minor county matches. Glamorgan C C C first played second XI matches on the ground in 1948. The club has always shown an interest in staging benefit matches; these have included games for Dennis Brookes and George Tribe of Northamptonshire and Warwickshire players David Brown, Rohan Kanhai, Dennis Amiss and Neal Abberley. Abergavenny Cricket Club play in the Seven Counties Cricket League; the best-known player to have represented club and county was Malcolm Nash. Glamorgan C C C were so impressed with the Pen-y-Pound wicket and facilities that following several second XI, club and ground and benefit matches, they decided to play more cricket in Gwent.

The initial county match was with Worcestershire in the John Player Sunday League in 1981. Thanks to the work of the local groundstaff, the match went ahead despite torrential rain during the morning. As a result of this successful visit another Sunday League match was staged in 1982. In 1983 the initial first-class County Championship match was staged on the ground when Worcestershire were again the visitors. Championship cricket returned in 1985 when Worcestershire made their third visit. Subsequent visits have brought Derbyshire, Leicestershire and in 1988 Worcestershire, when Graeme Hick scored 159 setting up victory for the future champions. Since 1989 visits have been made by Middlesex, Worcestershire and Gloucestershire. In 1992 the visitors will be Somerset.

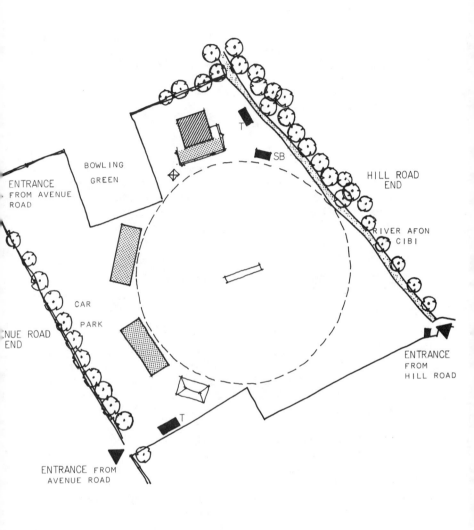

BOWLING
GREEN

ENTRANCE
FROM AVENUE
ROAD

T

SB

HILL ROAD
END

RIVER AFON
CIBI

CAR
PARK

NUE ROAD
END

ENTRANCE
FROM
HILL ROAD

T

ENTRANCE FROM
AVENUE ROAD

N

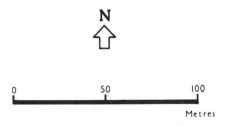

0   50   100

Metres

The ground has two scoreboards, one manual near the pavilion and another electronic scoreboard which has been used since 1985. The new scoreboard is in memory of Mr Bill McPherson who had been groundsman for many years. The ground is certainly one of the most beautiful in Wales and thanks to the organization from the local club visits are made very pleasant for players and spectators. Crowds at Abergavenny have been good when the weather has been kind and in 1988 some 5,000 attended the Worcestershire match. Crowds are usually around the 3,500–4,000 figure.

The ground is set at the foot of the Sugar Loaf Mountain, which is within the Brecon Beacons National Park and is known as the gateway to Wales. Abergavenny C C celebrated 150 years in 1984 and issued a booklet titled *Looking Back*, which no doubt will provide fond memories to all who have played or visited the ground. Glamorgan C C C usually play one single championship match at the ground each season. Ground records include highest innings totals for and against the county of 493 for 6 and 514 for 4 during the match with Worcestershire in 1990. Graeme Hick scored 252 n.o. in 1990 and averages over 200 on this ground.

ADDRESS Abergavenny Cricket Club, The Pavilion, Pen-y-Pound Cricket Ground, Avenue Road, Abergavenny, Gwent, Wales.
TELEPHONE NUMBER PROSPECTS OF PLAY 0873 852350

DESCRIPTION OF GROUND AND FACILITIES

The ground is surrounded by residential areas and has two entrances, one in Hill Road via Pen-y-Pound across the River Afron Cibi and a second in Avenue Road. The pavilion is situated to the north of the playing area, close to the bowling green and at right angles to the wicket. The members' enclosure is situated in front of the pavilion and the new electronic scoreboard. At the Avenue Road, western end of the ground there is a large, temporary, tiered area of seating. Behind this car parking and temporary facilities including toilets, bars and refreshment tents are available. Car parking is also available at the Abergavenny Football Ground, off Hill Road and in the surrounding streets. To the south of the playing area is a further area of temporary seating and some practice nets. A secretary's office in a caravan, the Glamorgan C C C souvenir caravan and press tents are situated close to the bowling green near the pavilion. The playing area is 117 metres by 118 metres and is circular in shape. It is defined by a rope and some advertising boards. The radio commentary box and TV camera/commentary box position is at the Avenue Road end of the ground at a high level situated directly behind and above the sightscreen on a gantry. The ground capacity is 5,000 and 60 per cent are provided with seating by the local council for matches. Spectators are advised to take their own seats only to popular matches.

Pen-y-Pound is certainly one of the most attractive grounds on the county circuit.

GROUND RECORDS AND SCORES

FIRST-CLASS MATCHES

Highest innings total for County: 493 for 6 *v.* Worcestershire 1990
Highest innings total against County: 514 for 4 dec. by Worcestershire 1990
Lowest innings total for County: 168 *v.* Derbyshire 1986
Lowest innings total against County: 143 for 7 dec. by Derbyshire 1986
Highest individual innings for County: 135 A.R. Butcher *v.* Leicestershire 1987
Highest individual innings against County: 252 n.o. G.A. Hick for Worcestershire 1990
Best bowling performance in an innings for County: 4 for 144 S.R. Barwick *v.* Middlesex 1989
Best bowling performance in an innings against County: 3 for 31 D.E. Malcolm for Derbyshire 1986
Best bowling performance in a match for County: 5 for 152 R.J. Shastri *v.* Leicestershire 1987
Best bowling performance in a match against County: 4 for 140 A.R.C. Fraser for Middlesex 1989
Best attendance: 5,000 *v.* Worcestershire 1988

LIMITED-OVERS MATCHES

Highest innings total for County: 229 for 7 *v.* Northamptonshire (JPL) 1982
Highest innings total against County: 170 for 7 by Worcestershire (JPL) 1981
Lowest innings total for County: 152 *v.* Worcestershire (JPL) 1981
Lowest innings total against County: 153 for 7 by Northamptonshire (JPL) 1982
Highest individual innings for County: 100 R.C. Ontong *v.* Northamptonshire (JPL) 1982
Highest individual innings against County: 43 E.J.O. Hemsley for Worcestershire (JPL) 1981
Best bowling performance for County: 2 for 21 M.A. Nash *v.* Northamptonshire (JPL) 1982
Best bowling performance against County: 3 for 17 J. Birkenshaw for Worcestershire (JPL) 1981
Best attendance: 3,000 *v.* Northamptonshire (JPL) 1982

HOW TO GET THERE

Rail   Abergavenny (BR), 2 miles.
Bus   National Welsh 20 Newport to Hereford; 21 Newport to Brecon. Alight at Bus Station, thence 1.5 mile walk to ground (Telephone: 0222 371331).
Car   From north: A465 or A40, follow signs Abergavenny, ground situated in Avenue Road off A40 Brecon Road. From east: A40 or A465, then as north. From west: A465 or A40, then as north. From south: M4 junction 26, then A4042 follow signs Abergavenny, then as north or A40, then as east.

WHERE TO STAY AND OTHER INFORMATION

Angel Hotel (0873 7121), Kings Arms, Nevill Street.

Disabled Areas   No special area, request suitable position. Car parking available within ground at Avenue Road End by prior arrangement.
Local Radio Station(s)   BBC Radio Wales (882 KHz MW), BBC Radio Cymru (93.1 MHz FM/882 KHz MW).
Local Newspaper(s)   South Wales Evening Post, Western Mail, Abergavenny Chronicle, Abergavenny Gazette, South Wales Argus.

Colwyn Bay

The Colwyn Bay Cricket Club was founded in 1924 and has played here at Penrhyn Avenue since that date. The first Glamorgan C C C fixture was played here on 27–30 August 1966 when Derbyshire were the visitors for a County Championship match at this attractive compact cricket ground offering facilities second to none in North Wales. However, at the initiative of Wilfred Wooller and Geoff Gadd, Glamorgan did make a visit to Colwyn Bay in 1947 when matches were staged with a North Wales XI and a Lancashire League XI which included Learie Constantine, George Tribe, Cec Pepper and Charlie Hallows. After 1966 further matches were staged with Worcestershire (1967), Cambridge University and Oxford University (1968), Leicestershire (1969), Pakistani Eaglets (1970), Gloucestershire (1971) and Sussex (1974). During the period 1972–73 two John Player Sunday League matches were staged with Worcestershire and Yorkshire.

Glamorgan C C C last played a championship match here in 1974 against Sussex and it was not until 1990 that the county travelled 180 miles from their Cardiff headquarters to again stage cricket at this ground located in Rhos-on-Sea when Lancashire were the visitors for a three-day championship match and a Refuge Assurance Sunday League match over a May Bank Holiday weekend. In 1991 Nottinghamshire were scheduled for a championship match but this was switched back to Cardiff. In 1992 Colwyn Bay will again host Lancashire on 12–15 June, when it is hoped that the weather will be as fine as in 1990 when crowds averaged 4,000 over the three days.

In 1929 Wales played the touring South Africans and in 1930 Wales played the Minor Counties C A at Colwyn Bay. The ground has been used by other teams in addition to Wales for Minor County Championship matches. During the period 1930–35 Denbighshire C C C used the ground. In 1984 the League Cricket Conference staged a two-day match with the West Indian touring team, West Indians scoring 401 and 275 for 2 declared, the Conference XI replying with 136 and 76 for 8. Richie Richardson top scored with 149 n.o. During 1955 a Colwyn Bay cricket festival was introduced and the following teams were represented: Glamorgan C C C, North Wales XI, R.W.V. Robin's XI, Vinoo

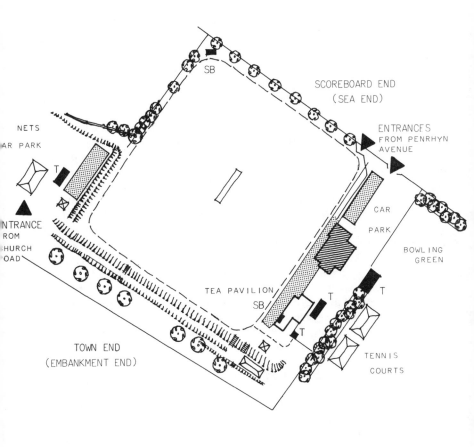

SCOREBOARD END
(SEA END)

ENTRANCES
FROM PENRHYN
AVENUE

NETS

AR PARK

T

NTRANCE
ROM
HURCH
OAD

CAR

PARK

BOWLING
GREEN

TEA PAVILION

SB

T   T

T

T

TOWN END
(EMBANKMENT END)

TENNIS

COURTS

SB

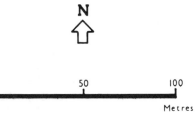

N

0   50   100

Metres

Mankad's Indian XI and R.H. Moore's XI. During one match Frank Worrell scored 194, which is still the highest individual score on the ground. It took just 112 minutes and included 5 sixes and 30 fours.

The pavilion is located to the south-east of the playing area with the main entrance to the ground off Penrhyn Avenue. The pavilion was built by voluntary subscriptions in recognition of those members who gave service to their country in World War Two and was opened by HRH The Duke of Gloucester on 8 June 1960. Some cricket memorabilia and photographs of old Colwyn Bay C C teams and some well-known players who have played on the ground are displayed on the walls of the bar and members' room. These include Sir Learie Constantine, the three W's – Worrell, Weekes and Walcott, Godfrey Evans, Syd Barnes, who lived in the town and played for the club, Wes Hall and George Headley.

Wilfred Wooller was brought up in Rhos-on-Sea and it is his presence which took county cricket to North Wales. Mr Wooller's grandfather had built the original pavilion which was opened by Lord Colwyn in May 1924. The ground was laid on the bed of the old Conway river, although locals say it was probably a swamp or large ditch. The ground is square in shape and little has changed since 1924 other than the introduction of some banking at the southern end of the ground which allows for some deck chairs on the terrace. Ground improvements in 1950 cost £4,000 and in 1969 the old pavilion was demolished and the existing structure was built. The pavilion offers excellent facilities and a glance at the records board will show that the club supported many charity raising events including a donation of £15,000 for the Prisoners of War Fund and the Liverpool Air Raid Disaster Fund. The Colwyn Bay C C have staged benefit matches for a number of players including: Haydn Davies, Willie Jones, Allan Watkins, Cyril Washbrook, Richard Pollard, Winston Place and Jack Ikin.

Colwyn Bay Cricket Club play in the North Wales Competition and field two XIs throughout the season together with a number of colts teams. The ground is shared with Colwyn Bay Hockey Club, and during the winter months Rhos United Football Club play on the adjoining field, which is used for car parking and refreshments during county matches.

ADDRESS Colwyn Bay Cricket Club, The Pavilion, 77 Penrhyn Avenue, Rhos-on-Sea, Colwyn Bay, Clwyd, North Wales LL28 4LR.
TELEPHONE NUMBER PROSPECTS OF PLAY 0492 44103

DESCRIPTION OF GROUND AND FACILITIES

The first thing you notice as you enter the main entrance from Penrhyn Avenue is the club's oak tree emblem on the side of the pavilion. The only other entrance is from Church Road via the car park. The ground is owned by the club and permanent facilities include the pavilion/clubhouse which contains changing rooms, toilets, two bars, refreshment areas, a games room and on the first floor level a balcony and groundsman's flat. Other facilities include the large tea pavilion and a two-storey scoreboard. The majority of seating is temporary and 2,000 seats are provided so spectators would be advised to bring their own seats to popular matches.

Car parking is available in an adjoining field off Church Road to the south-west of the playing area for members and the public. Car parking for players and officials is available at the rear of the pavilion. Street parking is also available in the local neighbourhood. The members' enclosure spans from the tea pavilion to the temporary covered stand near the main entrance at the Scoreboard/Sea End of the ground. The scoreboard is located in the northern corner of the ground and next to this is the press and scorers' tents. A temporary covered stand is available on the bank opposite the tea pavilion which is available for the public. To the rear of this structure are some cricket nets, refreshment marquees and temporary toilets. The TV camera/commentary box is located at the Embankment/Town End high above the playing area for it is located at the top of the bank. To the south-east corner of the ground are two refreshment tents located on the bank and a first-aid tent. Further temporary/permanent toilets are available at the rear of the tea pavilion, inside the main clubhouse and near the tennis courts and bowling green to the south-east of the ground. A Glamorgan C C C souvenir shop is located near the main entrance from Penrhyn Avenue. Sponsors' tents are located on the nearby tennis courts to the rear of the tea pavilion. In general the playing area is tight against the boundary walls and fences so during play it can become difficult to walk around the entire playing area.

The playing area is square in shape and falls slightly towards the Scoreboard/Sea End. The dimensions are 115 metres by 107 metres and the boundary is defined by a rope and some advertising boards. To the south of the ground the boundary is formed by the bottom of the embankment. The best views of the ground are offered from the Embankment End sitting at the top next to the concrete palisade fence. Generally Colwyn Bay is a splendid ground to view cricket at especially if the weather is fine.

GROUND RECORDS AND SCORES

FIRST-CLASS MATCHES
Highest innings total for County: 326 for 6 dec. *v.* Sussex 1974
Highest innings total against County: 399 for 7 dec. by Lancashire 1990
Lowest innings total for County: 183 *v.* Derbyshire 1966
Lowest innings total against County: 118 by Derbyshire 1966
Highest individual innings for County: 112 n.o. I. Smith *v.* Lancashire 1990
Highest individual innings against County: 121 n.o. M.G. Griffith for Sussex 1974
Best bowling performance in an innings for County: 9 for 49 A.E. Cordle *v.* Leicestershire 1969
Best bowling performance in an innings against County: 7 for 47 D.C. Morgan for Derbyshire 1966

Best bowling performance in a match for County: 13 for 110 A.E. Cordle *v.* Leicestershire 1969
Best bowling performance in a match against County: 9 for 82 D.C. Morgan for Derbyshire 1966
Best attendance: 6,000 *v.* Derbyshire 1966

LIMITED-OVERS MATCHES
Highest innings total for County: 242 for 6 *v.* Lancashire (RAL) 1990
Highest innings total against County: 246 for 6 by Lancashire (RAL) 1990
Lowest innings total for County: 175 for 8 *v.* Worcestershire (JPL) 1972
Lowest innings total against County: 177 for 7 by Worcestershire (JPL) 1972
Highest individual innings for County: 100 M.P. Maynard *v.* Lancashire (RAL) 1990
Highest individual innings against County: 104 n.o. G. Boycott for Yorkshire (JPL) 1973
Best bowling performance for County: 3 for 15 M.A. Nash *v.* Worcestershire (JPL) 1972
Best bowling performance against County: 3 for 26 V.A. Holder for Worcestershire (JPL) 1972
Best attendance: 5,500 *v.* Lancashire (RAL) 1990

HOW TO GET THERE

Rail Colwyn Bay (BR), 1.5 miles.
Bus Crosville Bus service M16 passes ground and links BR Colwyn Bay Station with Rhos-on-Sea (Telephone: Directory Enquiries).
Car From north: A470 or A546 signposted Rhos-on-Sea or as east. From east: A55 or A547 signposted Colwyn Bay, then follow A55 to junction signposted Rhos-on-Sea, then take exit and follow Llandudno Road for Church Road for car parking and Colwyn Bay C C. From west: A5 and A55 signposted Colwyn Bay, take junction signposted Rhos-on-Sea, then as east for ground. From south: A470 or B5106 or B5113 signposted Colwyn Bay, then follow A55 and signs Rhos-on-Sea for ground in Penrhyn Avenue.

WHERE TO STAY AND OTHER INFORMATION

Hotel Seventy Degrees (0492 534626), The Cedar Tree (0492 45867), Norfolk House Hotel (0492 531757).

Disabled Areas Special area provided on hardstanding path between scoreboard and pavilion at Penrhyn Avenue end of the ground, close to pedestrian entrance.
Local Radio Station(s) Radio Clwyd (657 KHz MW), Radio City (96.7 MHz FM/1548 KHz MW), BBC Radio Wales (882 KHz MW).
Local Newspaper(s) North Wales Weekly News, North Wales Pioneer.

Neath

The Gnoll Cricket Ground at Neath is the home of the Neath Cricket Club founded in 1848 and situated close to the better-known home of Neath Rugby Football Club. It is also the home of the Glamorgan C C C. Indoor Cricket School. Behind the pavilion, which is set at the foot of the Gnoll, is the high slope which rises behind like a timber curtain and on the top of which was once to be found Gnoll House, the former home of Sir Humphrey Mackworth who owned much of the land.

The Neath Cricket Club has been renowned for having fine cricketers. Those who have represented the club include: Tom Box, W.G. Grace, C.F. Walters, T.A. Whittington, A. Rees and A.R. Lewis. Bill Bestwick after leaving Glamorgan for Derbyshire, returned to the Gnoll to bowl out his old county. Bestwick's ball is mounted in the pavilion as is the bat with which W.G. Grace failed to score, and many other cricket photographs and items are to be found in the pavilion.

The first recorded mention of cricket in the town was in 1844 and the first games at the Gnoll were played in 1864. These included a match between Carmarthenshire C C C and Glamorganshire C C C. The Neath R F C was formed in 1871 and rugby football has been played on the ground since. Other sports played on the ground around that time were six-a-side football and bicycle racing. In 1908 Glamorgan C C C played Carmarthenshire C C C but not until 1934 did Glamorgan stage their initial first-class County Championship match on the ground, when Essex were the visitors. In 1923 the Gnoll House and estate was acquired by the Neath Corporation from the Evan Thomas family as a war memorial and to provide recreational and sporting facilities in the town. During World War Two the Gnoll sustained some damage and in 1947 the county club gave Neath Council £300 towards repairing the cricket arena. In 1948 cricket returned and in 1950 Glamorgan C C C decided to establish an indoor cricket school. The school was opened by R.E.S. Wyatt in 1954. More recently after modernization and refurbishment it was reopened by C.F. Walters in 1984.

Crowds at the Gnoll have been quite substantial; 12,000 watched the Warwickshire match in 1948 and 9,000 watched Somerset in 1963. Today crowds are usually 4,000–5,000. During the 1960s and 1970s the ground staged limited-overs matches in the John Player Sunday League and Benson & Hedges Cup competitions. In 1985 after an absence of eleven seasons Glamorgan C C C returned to the Gnoll thanks to sponsorship from the Neath Borough Council to stage the tour match with the Australians. This venture was so successful that championship matches have continued to be staged on the ground. The Australians again visited Neath in 1989 for a tour match in July. There are ample amenities and close by in the adjoining sportscentre are facilities for squash, weight-training and swimming. The visitors to Neath in 1992 will be Surrey between 3–6 July.

Ground records at Neath have included; 200 n.o. by Javed Miandad,

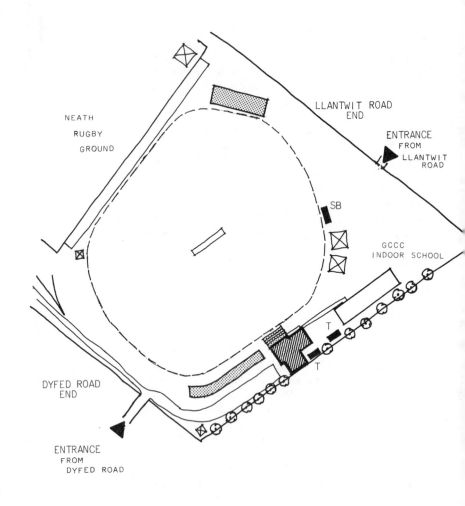

NEATH
RUGBY
GROUND

LLANTWIT ROAD
END

ENTRANCE
FROM
LLANTWIT
ROAD

SB

GCCC
INDOOR SCHOOL

T

T

DYFED ROAD
END

ENTRANCE
FROM
DYFED ROAD

N

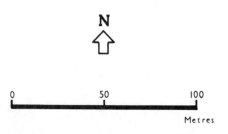

0   50   100

Metres

219 n.o. by Graeme Hick and wickets taken by Len Muncer, David Halfyard and Alan Moss. In limited-overs matches Somerset scored 360 for 4 in 40 overs in 1990 with Graham Rose hitting 148. This is a record innings total for the 40 overs competition. BBC TV commentator and Glamorgan chairman Tony Lewis once himself a Neath C C player holds the highest individual innings on the ground for Glamorgan. Wickets have been taken by Don Shepherd and Jack Flavell.

ADDRESS Neath Cricket Club, The Pavilion, The Gnoll Cricket Ground, Dyfed Road, Gnoll, Neath, West Glamorgan, Wales.
TELEPHONE NUMBER PROSPECTS OF PLAY 0639 3719

DESCRIPTION OF GROUND AND FACILITIES

The main entrance to the Gnoll is from Dyfed Road, through the entrance to the swimming baths and tennis club. This is for spectators and cars. However there are two further entrances, for pedestrians from Gnoll Park Road via the Neath Rugby Club and from Llantwit Road to the north-east of the ground. The pavilion and terracing and the Glamorgan C C C Indoor Cricket School are situated south of the playing area and at right angles to the wicket. A scoreboard and outdoor nets are situated close to the indoor school together with an area for sponsors' marquees. At the north-east end of the ground are two tiered, temporary, open seating areas and refreshment facilities, close to the football floodlight pylon. Terracing which is used by spectators for both rugby to the north and cricket to the south, is situated opposite the pavilion and also a press tent/box which also includes a radio commentary position. The pavilion houses a number of cricket photographs and a plaque commemorating W.G. Grace's 'pair' at the ground in 1868. At the south-west. Dyfed Road end there are two areas of temporary seating and a TV camera/commentary box position situated directly above and behind the sightscreen. Members' facilities can be found in the pavilion where there is a bar and refreshment area. There is also a temporary bar/refreshment tent near the tennis courts, toilets and a Glamorgan C C C souvenir caravan. Toilets can also be found in the pavilion and near the groundsman's stores.

The playing area is 133 metres by 115 metres and is defined by a rope and advertising boards. The ground capacity is 6,000 and with the exception of the pavilion terrace where seats are permanent, the Neath Council provide temporary seating but the number of seats depends on the particular game. Car parking within the ground is available for players and officials but the car parks in town are within five minutes walk of the ground and are recommended to spectators.

GROUND RECORDS AND SCORES

FIRST-CLASS MATCHES
Highest innings total for County: 409 for 3 dec. *v.* Australians 1985
Highest innings total against County: 373 for 4 dec. by Australians 1989

Lowest innings total for County: 43 *v*. Essex 1935
Lowest innings total against County: 57 by Surrey 1937
Highest individual innings for County: 200 n.o. Javed Miandad *v*. Australians 1985
Highest individual innings against County: 219 n.o. G.A. Hick for Worcestershire 1986
Best bowling performance in an innings for County: 8 for 48 B.L. Muncer *v*. Somerset 1949
Best bowling performance in an innings against County: 9 for 39 D.J. Halfyard for Kent 1957
Best bowling performance in a match for County: 12 for 94 B.L. Muncer *v*. Somerset 1949
Best bowling performance in a match against County: 13 for 51 A.E. Moss for Middlesex 1960
Best attendance: 12,000 *v*. Warwickshire 1948

LIMITED-OVERS MATCHES
Highest innings total for County: 208 for 9 *v*. Essex (GC) 1964
Highest innings total against County: 360 for 4 by Somerset (RAL) 1990
Lowest innings total for County: 90 *v*. Yorkshire (JPL) 1969
Lowest innings total against County: 97 by Leicestershire (JPL) 1971
Highest individual innings for County: 78 A.R. Lewis *v*. Worcestershire (GC) 1963
Highest individual innings against County: 148 G.D. Rose for Somerset (RAL) 1990
Best bowling performance for County: 4 for 20 D.J. Shepherd *v*. Leicestershire (JPL) 1971
Best bowling performance against County: 5 for 43 J.A. Flavell for Worcestershire (GC) 1963
Best attendance: 4,000 *v*. Somerset (RAL) 1990

HOW TO GET THERE

Rail   Neath (BR), 0.5 mile.
Bus   South Wales Transport from surrounding areas to Neath Bus Station, thence 0.25 mile.
Car   From north: A465 or A474 follow signs Neath, ground is situated north-west of town centre between River Neath and B4434 adjoining Neath Sportscentre and Neath R F C. From east and south: M4 junction 41, then follow A48 and A474 signposted Neath, then as north. From west: M4 junction 44, then follow A48 and A465 signposted Neath, then as north.

WHERE TO STAY AND OTHER INFORMATION

Cimla Court Hotel (0639 3771), Castle Hotel (where Welsh Rugby Union was founded).

Disabled Areas   No special area, request suitable position.
Local Radio Station(s)   BBC Radio Wales (882 KHz MW), BBC Radio
Cymru (93.1 MHz FM/882 KHz MW), Swansea Sound (96.4 MHz
FM/1170 KHz MW).
Local Newspaper(s)   South Wales Evening Post, South Wales Echo,
Western Mail, Neath Guardian Series.

Pontypridd

The Ynysangharad Park ground is the home of Pontypridd Cricket Club
which was formed in 1870 and plays in the Glamorgan Cricket League.
The ground is also the town's war memorial and is located on a flat area
of land on the eastern side of the River Taff between the river and the
main A470 trunk road. The parkland in which the ground now stands
was originally given to the town by the Lenox family as a memorial to
the soldiers and servicemen from the Welsh town who died in World
War One. The Park was opened in 1923 by Marshall Lord Allenby and
during the period 1924–30 facilities were also used by Pontypridd
Rugby Football Club until they moved to another ground in the town, at
Sardis Road during the late 1970s.

The first visit by Glamorgan C C C to the ground was in 1926 when
Derbyshire were the opposition, and during the late 1920s matches were
staged annually; these included a tour match with the South Africans in
1929. Over the years the ground has had problems with rain and the
majority of county matches so affected appear to be at Pontypridd. This
was commented upon by Webber and Arnott in the 1947 Glamorgan
C C C Review: 'Pontypridd appears to be Glamorgan's most unlucky
ground as rain interferes with the majority of matches played there.'

The county continued to play County Championship matches at
Pontypridd until 1971 when these were discontinued due to falling
attendances and unlucky weather. The last limited-overs matches were a
Benson & Hedges Cup zonal group game and a John Player Sunday
League match against Somerset and Essex in 1972. Not until 1988, as
part of the County Club's centenary celebrations, did Glamorgan return
to Ynysangharad Park. They played Lancashire in a Refuge Assurance
Sunday League fixture, only for the match to be ruined by rain – not for
the first time!

In 1989 the county staged a four-day County Championship match
with Worcestershire in September Glamorgan scoring 230 for 9 before
the weather had the last laugh yet again. In 1990 a four-day game in
September with Hampshire lasted three days with the visitors winning
by 8 wickets, Malcolm Marshall taking match figures of 11 for 92. In
1991 a single limited-overs Refuge Assurance League match was staged
with Essex; Glamorgan were 99 for 7 before the heavens opened and the
match was washed out. Derbyshire will be the visitors on 26 July 1992.

Crowds at Pontypridd average around 3,000–3,500. The largest
was in 1933 when 6,000 were attracted by the visit of neighbours
Gloucestershire.

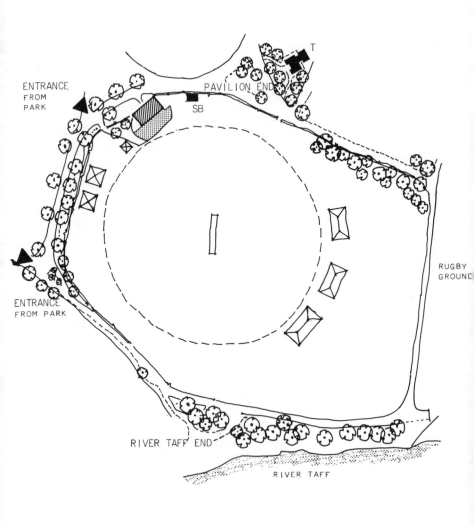

ENTRANCE
FROM
PARK

PAVILION END

SB

T

ENTRANCE
FROM PARK

RUGBY
GROUND

RIVER TAFF END

RIVER TAFF

N

0   50   100

Metres

A photograph of George Geary can be found in the pavilion showing just the stumps standing on the wicket, a worn strip known as Geary's Wicket, after he took 16 for 96 for Leicestershire in 1929. Jack Mercer holds the bowling records for Glamorgan and high scores have come from both James Pressdee and Charlie Barnett for Gloucestershire. In the limited-overs game records belong to Kevin Lyons, former first-class umpire and the present Worcestershire C C C coach, Keith Boyce, Stephen Barwick and Graham 'Burgie' Burgess.

ADDRESS Pontypridd Cricket Club, The Pavilion, Ynysangharad Park, Pontypridd, Mid Glamorgan, Wales.
TELEPHONE NUMBER PROSPECTS OF PLAY 0443 400785

DESCRIPTION OF GROUND AND FACILITIES

The ground is located within the Ynysangharad Park and is enclosed by a fence and well matured grounds from the rest of the park and the only permanent buildings are the pavilion, terrace and scoreboard. The members' enclosure is in front of the pavilion and on the adjoining terracing area. A radio commentary position and press tent is also found close to the pavilion as is the TV camera/commentary box position. The playing area is 120 metres by 114 metres and is defined by a line and advertising boards. The playing area is flat and there is ample space surrounding it for temporary facilities including seating, refreshment tents, temporary toilets and a Glamorgan C C C souvenir caravan. The east side of the ground is used primarily by sponsors for marquees. The ground capacity is 6,000 and seating is provided for 50 per cent. Spectators are advised to take their own seating to popular matches.

There is no car parking available within the ground for spectators, only for players and officials. Ample car parking is available a short distance away in the town centre car parks and there is also some street parking in the surrounding area.

GROUND RECORDS AND SCORES

FIRST-CLASS MATCHES
Highest innings total for County: 421 *v.* Warwickshire 1937
Highest innings total against County: 398 by Nottinghamshire 1929
Lowest innings total for County: 68 *v.* Leicestershire 1929
Lowest innings total against County: 53 by Somerset 1946
Highest individual innings for County: 150 n.o. J.S. Pressdee *v.* Cambridge University 1965
Highest individual innings against County: 154 C.J. Barnett for Gloucestershire 1933
Best bowling performance in an innings for County: 8 for 60 J. Mercer *v.* South Africans 1929
Best bowling performance in an innings against County: 10 for 18 G. Geary for Leicestershire 1929
Best bowling performance in a match for County: 14 for 119 J. Mercer *v.* South Africans 1929

Best bowling performance in a match against County: 16 for 96 G. Geary for Leicestershire 1929
Best attendance: 6,000 *v.* Gloucestershire 1933

LIMITED-OVERS MATCHES
Highest innings total for County: 163 for 9 *v.* Lancashire (RAL) 1988
Highest innings total against County: 193 for 7 by Essex (JPL) 1970
Lowest innings total for County: 99 for 7 *v.* Essex (RAL) 1991
Lowest innings total against County: 121 by Somerset (BHC) 1972
Highest individual innings for County: 40 K.J. Lyons *v.* Somerset (BHC) 1972
Highest individual innings against County: 58 n.o. K.D. Boyce for Essex (JPL) 1970
Best bowling performance for County: 3 for 8 S.R. Barwick *v.* Lancashire (RAL) 1988
Best bowling performance against County: 4 for 12 G.I. Burgess for Somerset (BHC) 1972
Best attendance: 3,000 *v.* Essex (JPL) 1970

HOW TO GET THERE

Rail   Pontypridd (BR), 0.25 mile.
Bus   Local bus to Ynysangharad Park via Ynysybwl Road from surrounding areas to Pontypridd Bus Station, thence 0.50 mile.
Car   From north: A470 follow signs Pontypridd, ground is situated off B4273 Ynysybwl Road adjoining Ynysangharad Park. From east and south: M4 junction 32, then follow A470 signs Pontypridd and town centre, then as north. From west: A4058 or A473, follow signs Pontypridd and town centre, then as north.

WHERE TO STAY AND OTHER INFORMATION

The Graig Hotel (0443 402844).

Disabled Areas   No special area, request suitable position. Car parking available within park by prior arrangement.
Local Radio Station(s)   BBC Radio Wales (882 KHz MW), Red Dragon Radio (97.4 MHz FM/1359 KHz MW).
Local Newspaper(s)   South Wales Evening Post, South Wales Echo, Western Mail, Pontypridd Observer.

Swansea

The second major ground at which Glamorgan C C C play is at St Helen's, Swansea, the home of the Swansea Cricket and Football Club. The ground is located to the west of the city centre off the Mumbles Road and enclosed by Bryn Road, Gorse Lane and Mumbles Road. The ground is shared and the majority of the terracing facilities are

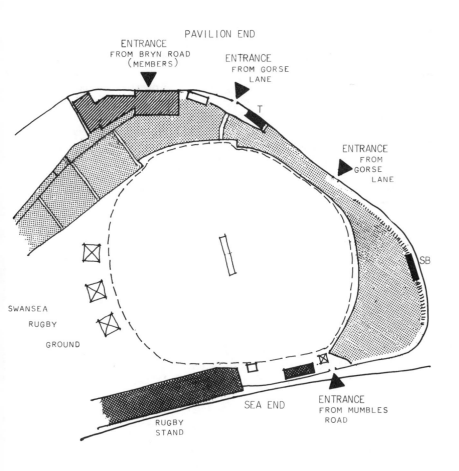

PAVILION END

ENTRANCE
FROM BRYN ROAD
(MEMBERS)

ENTRANCE
FROM GORSE
LANE

T

ENTRANCE
FROM
GORSE
LANE

SB

SWANSEA

RUGBY

GROUND

SEA END

ENTRANCE
FROM MUMBLES
ROAD

RUGBY
STAND

N

0   50   100

Metres

permanent and available for viewing both games. The pavilion was built in 1927 and has had various extensions, additions and refurbishment since; the most recent was in 1980 when a new eastern wing was constructed.

Glamorgan C C C first played at the ground in 1921 when Leicestershire were the visitors. Today four first-class matches are staged during a season plus at least three limited-overs matches. The ground was originally owned by an order of Augustinian nuns who built a convent dedicated to St Helen. Following the Dissolution of the Monasteries the ground and St Helen's Estate passed to Baron Herbert of Cardiff and Earl of Pembroke. They subsequently passed to Colonel Llewellyn Morgan and his family, who were major landowners in the city. Cricket has been played in Swansea since 1780, but the first formal games were in 1848 and 1850. In 1950 a Swansea Cricket Club was established and the first match was with Llanelli Cricket Club. In 1868 a match was staged with the Australian Aboriginal Team. Before their move to St Helen's in 1873 after £2,000 had been spent in levelling the ground, the club played at the Brunswick timber yard and Bryn-y-Mor. The new ground was known as New Cricket Field, St Helen's and was used for athletics and cricket. In 1874 Swansea Rugby Football Club and Swansea Cricket Club amalgamated to form the Swansea Cricket and Football Club and today still retains that same name.

International rugby matches were staged on the ground from 1882, when Wales played England, until shortly after World War Two. The ground has hosted many famous rugby matches and rugby and cricket memorabilia can be viewed in the pavilion and St Helen's Lounge. Other events staged on the ground have included hockey, rugby league football, jazz concerts and a programme in the 'It's a Knock-out' BBC TV series. Swansea can thank Sir John T.D. Llewellyn not only for donations but for being the County's first treasurer when Glamorgan C C C was founded at the Angel Hotel, Cardiff in 1888. In 1939 the ground was sold to the Swansea Town Corporation, now the City Corporation, which has remained the sole owner ever since. During World War Two the ground was used as a military training camp. Afterwards much building took place, including a new rugby grandstand, new terracing and pavilion facilities.

From the players' pavilion there used to be 67 steps down to the field. This could be a very long walk back for a batsman who had been dismissed first ball. Since building developments have taken place during the 1980s the distance has been reduced to 45 steps! In 1959 the Memorial Gates were installed opposite the Cricketers Inn in memory of past players who have represented Swansea Cricket and Football Clubs. The gates were donated by the Swansea and District R S C.

In 1964 140-feet high floodlight pylons were installed and they dominate the ground in each corner as do similar installations at the County Ground, Northampton. Much of the ground's facilities are used for both rugby and cricket, scoreboards for both can be found on the ground. Tourists usually play Glamorgan at Swansea and the county have defeated all Test nations here except West Indians and Sri Lankans.

Two international matches have been staged at St Helen's: in 1973 a Prudential Trophy match between England and New Zealand and in 1983 a Prudential Cup match between Pakistan and Sri Lanka.

Many of Glamorgan's finest hours have come at Swansea including in 1927 a victory over Nottinghamshire by an innings and 81 runs which deprived Nottinghamshire of the championship and in 1964 a victory over the Australians by 36 runs. The attendance at the latter match was 50,000 which remains a record today. Crowds for recent matches usually attract 5,000–6,000. However 10,000 attended in the England v. New Zealand Prudential Trophy match in 1973.

Three of the most significant cricket records took place here. In 1968, while batting for Nottinghamshire, Gary Sobers hit Malcolm Nash for 36 runs in a single six-ball over. (Frank Hayes of Lancashire hit 34 off one over from the same bowler in 1977.) Clive Lloyd hit 201 for the West Indians in two hours in 1976 and equalled Gilbert Jessop's record for the fastest ever double century in first-class cricket. In 1990 Tom Moody, playing for Warwickshire, scored the fastest century in first-class cricket, reaching his hundred off 36 balls in only 26 minutes to break the record of 37 minutes held jointly by P.G.H. Fender and S. O'Shaughnessy. Tom Moody hit 7 sixes and 11 fours but the bowling was tossed up by Matthew Maynard and Tony Cottey to obtain an early declaration.

Glamorgan C C C have staged matches in all competitions on this ground with over 375 first-class matches in all. Since 1988 Glamorgan have introduced an annual floodlit match with an International XI which usually takes place in early August. The ground is also used by Wales for Minor County Championship matches.

ADDRESS Swansea Cricket and Football Club, The Pavilion, St Helen's Cricket Ground, Bryn Road, Swansea, West Glamorgan, Wales. **TELEPHONE NUMBER PROSPECTS OF PLAY** 0792 466321

DESCRIPTION OF GROUND AND FACILITIES

St Helen's is the largest of Glamorgan's home grounds with a capacity of 25,000. Members' seating is permanent and spectators are advised to bring their own seats only to popular matches. Members' entry to the ground is from Bryn Road, to the rear of the pavilion. There are two public entrances in Gorse Lane and also one in Mumbles Road. Refreshments for members are in the pavilion and for the public in mobile outlets which are provided around the ground. Toilets can be found at various points around the playing area and there is a permanent scoreboard used for both cricket and rugby. The scorers' box and press box are high above the terracing close to the main pavilion and near the St Helen's Lounge. The TV camera/commentary box is positioned directly behind and above the sightscreen at the Sea End on a gantry. At this end of the ground close to the bar is a Glamorgan C C C souvenir caravan. The rugby pitch is used for sponsors' marquees and during the August festival period is heavily tented.

The playing area is 130 metres by 118 metres and is defined by a rope and advertising boards. The ground is dominated by the large floodlight pylons and huge areas of terracing. The members' enclosure is in front of the pavilion and owing to its steepness is not recommended for disabled spectators. No car parking is available in the ground except for players and officials, but space is easily found in Bryn Road, King Edward Road (close to the Cricketers' Hotel), St Helen's Avenue and the Mumbles car park area which is sited where the former seafront railway station was located. Should play be interrupted by rain or bad light then a visit to the Cricketers' Hotel opposite the ground may be of value. There are plenty of cricket items of interest here on the walls and meals are even served on place mats of old scorecards! Some photographs and historic items of cricket and rugby memorabilia can be viewed in the St Helen's Lounge.

GROUND RECORDS AND SCORES

FIRST-CLASS MATCHES

Highest innings total for County: 547 for 6 dec. *v.* Northamptonshire 1933
Highest innings total against County: 554 for 4 dec. by West Indians 1976
Lowest innings total for County: 36 *v.* Hampshire 1922
Lowest innings total against County: 40 by Somerset 1968
Highest individual innings for County: 233 M.J.A. Turnbull *v.* Worcestershire 1937
Highest individual innings against County: 257 A.H. Bakewell for Northamptonshire 1933
Best bowling performance in an innings for County: 9 for 43 J.S. Pressdee *v.* Yorkshire 1965
Best bowling performance in an innings against County: 9 for 60 H. Verity for Yorkshire 1930
Best bowling performance in a match for County: 17 for 212 J.C. Clay *v.* Worcestershire 1937
Best bowling performance in a match against County: 15 for 52 V.W.C. Jupp for Northamptonshire 1925
Best attendance: 50,000 *v.* Australians 1964

LIMITED-OVERS MATCHES

Highest innings total for County: 295 for 4 *v.* Dorset (NWBT) 1990
Highest innings total against County: 294 for 5 by Hampshire (NWBT) 1983
Lowest innings total for County: 42 *v.* Derbyshire (JPL) 1979
Lowest innings total against County: 76 by Minor Counties (BHC) 1985
Highest individual innings for County: 118 I.V.A. Richards *v.* Dorset (NWBT) 1990
Highest individual innings against County: 132 J.J. Whittaker for Leicestershire (JPL) 1984
Best bowling performance for County: 5 for 16 G.C. Holmes *v.* Yorkshire (JPL) 1985

Best bowling performance against County: 5 for 18 D.J. Brown for Warwickshire (GC) 1966
Best attendance: 6,000 *v.* Leicestershire (GC) 1977

INTERNATIONAL DAY/NIGHT MATCHES (SWE)
Highest innings total for County: 247 for 8 *v.* Invitation XI 1989
Highest innings total against County: 318 for 6 by Invitation XI 1989
Lowest innings total for County: 208 *v.* Invitation XI 1988
Lowest innings total against County: 237 for 5 by Invitation XI 1990
Highest individual innings for County: 66 M.P. Maynard *v.* Invitation XI 1990
Highest individual innings against County: 94 M. Greatbatch for Invitation XI 1988
Best bowling performance for County: 3 for 73 G. Holmes *v.* Invitation XI 1989
Best bowling performance against County: 4 for 51 M.D. Crowe for Invitation XI 1990

HOW TO GET THERE

Rail   Swansea (BR), 1.5 miles.
Bus   South Wales Transport 1, 2, 3 and 14 from Swansea Bus Station, 0.75 mile from BR Swansea Station – numerous services link BR Station with Bus Station which pass ground; also South Wales Transport to Mumbles, Sketty, Ostermouth and Brynmill pass close to ground (Telephone: 0792 485511).
Car   From north: A465, A4067 or A48, follow signs city centre, ground situated 1.5 miles west of city centre off Mumbles Road A4067 close to Gorse Lane and Bryn Road. Ground shared with Swansea R F C near seafront. From west: M4 junction 47, then follow A483 and A4216 to Mumbles Road, then as north. From east: M4 junction 44, then follow signs Swansea on A4217 and A4067 to Mumbles Road, then as north.

WHERE TO STAY AND OTHER INFORMATION

Dragon Hotel (0792 51074), Beaumont Hotel (0792 43044), Dolphin Hotel (0792 50011).

Disabled Areas   No special area, request suitable position. Pavilion enclosure not recommended due to steep steps. Ideal position at Sea End near sightscreen.
Local Radio Station(s)   BBC Radio Wales (882 KHz MW), BBC Radio Crmru (93.1 MHz FM/882 KHz MW), Swansea Sound (96.4 MHz FM/1170 KHz MW).
Local Newspaper(s)   South Wales Evening Post, Western Mail, South Wales Echo.

Aberystwyth

The Aberystwyth ground is one of the two in Dyfed at which Glamorgan C C C play; the other is at Stradey Park, Llanelli. The ground is the sports arena of the University College of Wales in the town and is located around half a mile from the town centre on the Llanbadarn Road and close to the main railway line east to Shrewsbury. The ground lies at the foot of the Penglais Hill and was previously known as Vicarage Field. This name arose because the land was formerly part of the vicarage and Llanbadarn Church prior to its destruction by the Vikings.

In 1906 the field was leased to the university for sports by Mr. David Davies, who was treasurer of the college at the time. It is used for all sports including athletics, soccer and rugby. Permanent buildings on the ground include a gymnasium built in 1908, a grandstand and changing facilities built between 1922 and 1927 and a cricket pavilion which is also used by tennis players. Cricket has only been played regularly since 1939. There has been much development since including the building of a swimming pool and athletics track.

Glamorgan C C C second XI have played matches on the ground since 1967 when a match was staged with the Welsh Universities. In 1977 as part of the town's 900th centenary celebrations a John Player Sunday League match was staged with Essex. This attracted TV coverage and a large crowd of 4,500. Essex won by 15 runs thanks to 80 runs and 2 for 28 by England skipper Graham Gooch. The West Indian Collis King scored 66 for Glamorgan but victory in their inaugural visit to Aberystwyth was not to be. Glamorgan C C C did not play again at the Vic as it is known to locals until 1989, after a lapse of twelve years, when a Refuge Assurance Sunday League match was played with Warwickshire. Warwickshire won by 6 wickets, replying to Glamorgan's 203 for 4, Warwickshire scored 207 for 4.

Cricket has been traced back to 1830 in Aberystwyth when the first matches were played at Gogerddan, home of the local MP Pryse Pryse.

ADDRESS The University College of Wales, The Pavilion, The University College of Wales Sports Ground, Llanbadarn Road, Aberystwyth, Dyfed, Wales.
TELEPHONE NUMBER PROSPECTS OF PLAY Temporary line – call Directory Enquiries

DESCRIPTION OF GROUND AND FACILITIES

The only entrance to the University College of Wales Sports Ground is from Llanbadarn Road which is on the outskirts of the town and some way from the main campus of the university. The permanent buildings are a pavilion which is used by players and officials, a members' enclosure in front of that; a gymnasium and a covered grandstand which provides seating for members and adjoins the cricket pavilion at the town end of the ground. There are also facilities for other sports

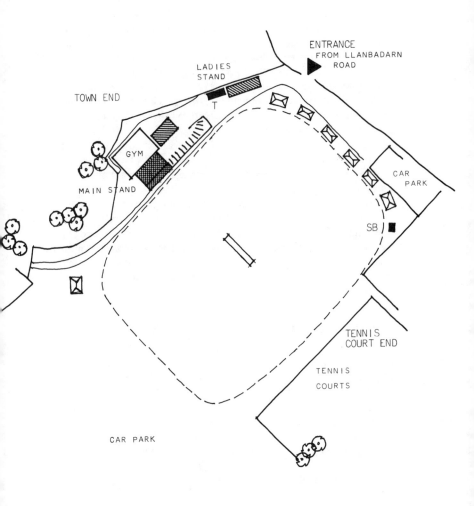

ENTRANCE
FROM LLANBADARN
ROAD

LADIES
STAND

TOWN END

T

GYM

MAIN STAND

CAR
PARK

SB

TENNIS
COURT END

TENNIS
COURTS

CAR PARK

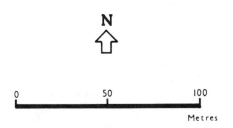

RUGBY CLUBHOUSE

N

0   50   100

Metres

including permanent pavilions for bowling and tennis. At the rear of the pavilion is St Padarn's Convent School and it is to this side of the ground that the majority of facilities are located. Toilet facilities can be found in the pavilion, gymnasium, and close to the ladies changing rooms. Temporary seating is provided around the perimeter of the playing area and tents with refreshment/bar areas are situated to the south-west and north-east of the playing area. Some sponsors' marquees are sited on the Llanbadarn Road side of the ground together with the committee tent and the scoreboard. The majority of seating is temporary and uncovered since the grandstand is only available for press and radio commentary as the structure is closed to the public, being a fire risk. A Glamorgan C C C souvenir shop is sited to the north-east of the playing area near the entrance from Llanbadarn Road. Car parking is available for players and officials to the rear of the committee tent off Llanbadarn Road and for members and the public to the south-west of the playing areas on an adjoining rugby field.

The ground capacity is 5,000 with seating provided for only 15 per cent. Spectators are well advised to bring their own collapsible seats to all matches. The playing are is 106 metres by 146 metres and is defined by a rope and several advertising boards. The TV camera/commentary box is positioned at the Tennis Courts End when required. The trees to the west of the ground provide a beautiful situation for this attractive Welsh venue.

GROUND RECORDS AND SCORES

LIMITED-OVERS MATCHES

Highest innings total for County: 219 for 7 *v*. Essex (JPL) 1977
Highest innings total against County: 234 for 7 by Essex (JPL) 1977
Lowest innings total for County: 203 for 4 *v*. Warwickshire (RAL) 1989
Lowest innings total against County: 207 for 4 by Warwickshire (RAL) 1989
Highest individual innings for County: 83 H. Morris *v*. Warwickshire (RAL) 1989
Highest individual innings against County: 80 G.A. Gooch for Essex (JPL) 1977
Best bowling performance for County: 3 for 42 G. Richards *v*. Essex (JPL) 1977
Best bowling performance against County: 2 for 28 G.A. Gooch for Essex (JPL) 1977
Best attendance: 4,500 *v*. Essex (JPL) 1977

HOW TO GET THERE

Rail Aberystwyth (BR), 0.5 mile.
Bus From surrounding areas to Bus Station adjoining BR Aberystwyth Station, then bus from Station to university campus and Llanbadarn farm for ground.

Car   From north: A487, follow signs Aberystwyth, ground situated at Llanbadarn off A44 east of town centre. From east: A44, follow signs Aberystwyth, then as north. From south: A487 or A4120 follow signs Aberystwyth, then as north.

WHERE TO STAY AND OTHER INFORMATION

Bay Hotel (0970 617356), Belle Vue Royal Hotel (0970 617558).

Disabled Areas   No special area, request suitable position. Car parking available within ground.
Local Radio Station(s)   BBC Radio Wales (882 KHz MW), BBC Radio Cymru (93.1 MHz FM/882 KHz MW).
Local Newspaper(s)   South Wales Echo, Western Mail, South Wales Evening Post.

Ebbw Vale

The first game of cricket in Ebbw Vale dates back to 1852 when a match was staged with Blaenau. The ground is located in the hollow-like valley of the Ebbw river between Beaufort Road and New Church Road. With an altitude of around 288 metres, the ground is amongst the highest cricket grounds in the country. It is know today as Eugene Cross Park and is the home of the Ebbw Vale Cricket Club and shared with the Ebbw Vale Rugby Football Club. The ground originally belonged to the Ebbw Vale Steel, Iron and Coal Company but in 1919 changed its name to the Ebbw Vale Welfare Association. At this time recreational facilities were available for football, rugby and cricket. The ground was known as the Welfare Association Sports Ground until in 1973 its name was changed to its present title, in honour of Sir Eugene Cross who had been the chairman of the welfare trustees. In 1981 a public trust was formed to take over the running and ownership of the ground.

Monmouthshire C C C have used the ground for matches since 1901 and with the later affiliation with Glamorgan C C C, second XI matches were staged on the ground. The initial first-class game with Worcestershire was staged in 1946 when some 5,000 spectators watched the first day's play. With the exception of 1955, matches were played each season until in 1967 when the wicket was reported by the umpires to Lord's as being unfit for first-class cricket. Not until 1969 did cricket return and then only a John Player Sunday League match. Since then, limited-overs matches have been staged annually and in 1983 Glamorgan C C C played one first-class match to gain experience of the quality of the wicket. In 1989 Glamorgan played a Refuge Assurance Sunday League match with Sussex, Glamorgan scoring 117 for 5 before rain ended play. In 1990 a three-day tourists match was staged and in 1991 a Refuge Assurance Sunday League match was staged with Hampshire who lost by 6 runs. In 1992 the visitors for a Sunday League match will be Yorkshire.

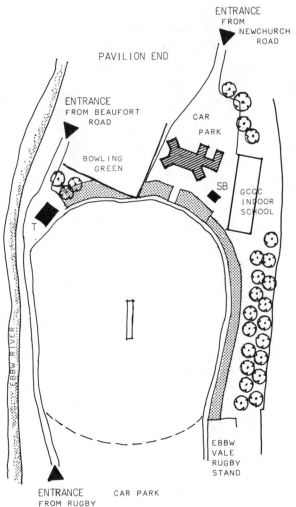

PAVILION END

ENTRANCE
FROM
NEWCHURCH
ROAD

ENTRANCE
FROM BEAUFORT
ROAD

CAR
PARK

BOWLING
GREEN

SB

GCCC
INDOOR
SCHOOL

T

EBBW RIVER

EBBW
VALE
RUGBY
STAND

ENTRANCE
FROM RUGBY
GROUND VIA
FOOTBRIDGE

CAR PARK

RUGBY GROUND END

N

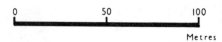

| 0 | | 50 | | 100 |

Metres

The pavilion and the majority of the facilities are to be found at the northern end of the ground and the rugby field to the south. There are ample facilities for bowls and tennis within the sports complex and badminton is also played in the Indoor Cricket School. Ebbw Vale C C was established in 1880 and plays in the Welsh Club Cricket Conference. The current secretary is the present Glamorgan C C C official scorer. Several famous cricketers have played for Ebbw Vale C C including: Percy Holmes, Harold Gimblett, George Macauley and Ted Whitfield. The most recent connection with Glamorgan C C C was Kim Norket who played for both club and county.

Some strange events have taken place on this ground including in 1948 against Gloucestershire, when *Wisden* commented, 'a mountain of mist enshrouded the ground for most of the day, but the strangest diversion of all was the appearance of a flock of sheep on the field'. While batting, Peter Walker commented that after pushing a ball straight down the wicket, he could hear tapping noises from beneath the wicket, which he guessed came from a coal miner just below ground! In 1948 a civic event was staged on the playing area when Field Marshall Montgomery of El Alamein visited the Welsh valleys. The ground is also used by Cardiff Blue Dragons who play rugby league football. A single tour match was staged on the ground in 1990 with the Sri Lankans, however rugby tourists have visited for matches with Ebbw Vale R F C on many occasions.

Crowds these days are around 2,500–3,500. The best crowds have been 12,000 *v.* Worcestershire in 1947 and 5,500 *v.* Derbyshire for a John Player Sunday League match in 1984. Ground records have included fine spells of bowling from both Ossie Wheatley and Ken Preston in the 1960s. In 1990 against the touring Sri Lankans, Glamorgan made their highest innings total on the ground and captain Hugh Morris scored the highest individual innings. The limited-overs game has seen centuries by Younis Ahmed, Alan Butcher and Nigel Briers with best bowling performances by G.C. Kingston and J.K. Lever.

ADDRESS Ebbw Vale Cricket Club, The Pavilion, Eugene Cross Park, Newchurch Road, Ebbw Vale, Gwent, Wales.
TELEPHONE NUMBER PROSPECTS OF PLAY 0495 305368

DESCRIPTION OF GROUND AND FACILITIES

Eugene Cross Park can be entered from both Newchurch Road and Beaufort Road and to the south from a footbridge via the Ebbw Vale Rugby Football Ground. The permanent buildings are located to the north of the playing area and are the pavilion, which includes a bar, together with an indoor cricket school building which provides refreshment, dining area and toilet facilities. To the north of the playing area is the scoreboard and scorer's/press area.

The members' area is in front of the pavilion and includes the adjacent terrace areas of seating. The west side of the ground is bounded by the Ebbw River and to the south are two raised seating areas. The radio commentary/TV camera/commentary box position is located directly behind and above the sightscreen at the Rugby Ground End on a gantry. To the east is a shallow terrace and plenty of trees. The playing area is 126 metres by 102 metres and is defined by a rope and a white railing except for the south perimeter adjoining the rugby ground. Temporary facilities and a Glamorgan C C C souvenir caravan are provided by the County Club. The ground capacity is 5,000 and seating is provided for about 50 per cent. Spectators will therefore only be required to bring their own seats to popular matches.

Car parking is available for players/officials at the rear of the pavilion and there is limited space on the rugby ground for members' cars. A large car park can be found at the Ebbw Vale Leisure Centre only a short walk from the ground and also in the town centre car parks.

GROUND RECORDS AND SCORES
FIRST-CLASS MATCHES
Highest innings total for County: 355 for 9 dec. *v.* Sri Lankans 1990
Highest innings total against County: 354 for 9 dec. by Essex 1954
Lowest innings total for County: 64 *v.* Essex 1962
Lowest innings total against County: 33 by Leicestershire 1965
Highest individual innings for County: 126 H. Morris *v.* Sri Lankans 1990
Highest individual innings against County: 132 H. Horton for Hampshire 1959
Best bowling performance in an innings for County: 9 for 60 O.S. Wheatley *v.* Sussex 1968
Best bowling performance in an innings against County: 6 for 29 K.C. Preston for Essex 1962
Best bowling performance in a match for County: 11 for 115 O.S. Wheatley *v.* Sussex 1968
Best bowling performance in a match against County: 10 for 97 K.C. Preston for Essex 1962
Best attendance: 12,000 *v.* Worcestershire 1947

LIMITED-OVERS MATCHES
Highest innings total for County: 277 for 6 *v.* Derbyshire (JPL) 1984
Highest innings total against County: 241 for 7 by Sussex (JPL) 1981
Lowest innings total for County: 92 *v.* Derbyshire (JPL) 1974
Lowest innings total against County: 96 by Derbyshire (JPL) 1969
Highest individual innings for County: 103 n.o. Younis Ahmed *v.* Derbyshire (JPL) 1984
Highest individual innings against County: 80 A.R. Butcher for Surrey (JPL) 1977/N.E. Briers for Leicestershire (JPL) 1980
Best bowling performance for County: 6 for 36 G.C. Kingston *v.* Derbyshire (JPL) 1969
Best bowling performance against County: 5 for 13 J.K. Lever for Essex (JPL) 1975
Best attendance: 5,500 *v.* Derbyshire (JPL) 1984

HOW TO GET THERE

Rail Rhymney (BR), 6 miles.
Bus Inter Valley Link 49 from close to BR Rhymney Station
(Telephone: 0222 851506), National Welsh X4, 444 from
Abergavenny 0.5 mile from BR Abergavenny Station and surrounding
areas, National Welsh 151 from BR Newport Station. All pass close
to ground (Telephone: 0222 371331).
Car From north and east: A465 and A4046, follow signs Ebbw
Vale, ground situated close to town centre adjoining Ebbw Vale
R F C ground off A4046. From west: A465 and A4046, follow signs
Ebbw Vale, then as north. From south: M4 junction 28, then follow
A467 and A4046 signposted Ebbw Vale, then as north.

WHERE TO STAY AND OTHER INFORMATION
County Hotel (0495 302418).

Disabled Areas No special area, request suitable position. Car
parking available at Rugby Ground End.
Local Radio Station(s) BBC Radio Wales (882 KHz FM), Radio
Gwent (95.9 MHz FM), Red Dragon Radio (97.4 MHz FM/1359
KHz MW).
Local Newspaper(s) South Wales Echo, Western Mail, South Wales
Evening Post, Newport Argus, Gwent Gazette.

Llanelli

The Stradey Park cricket ground is located on the northern side of the
famous Llanelli Rugby Football Club and the more famous 'Sospan
Fach'. Stradey Park, home of Llanelli Cricket Club, which was founded
in 1837, staged twenty-three first-class matches between the 1930s and
1960s. Llanelli C C has played at Stradey Park since 1874. Llanelli C C
play in the South Wales C A Cricket League. *Wisden* commented on the
first match: 'The match against Worcestershire at Llanelli proved a very
successful venture, for apart from the win by an innings, Carmarthenshire showed so much appreciation of being given the chance to see
first-class cricket that on the first day the attendance exceeded 4,000.'
   The ground used by Llanelli C C until their move to Stradey Park was
situated where the Llanelli Market is now situated, hence the Cricketers
public house in Murray Street. The name of the present ground is
believed to have been derived from the Welsh *ystrad* meaning broad
level area. The ground is part of the Stradey Recreational Complex
which once formed the grounds of Stradey Castle, the home of Mansel
Lewis in the seventeenth century. The ground has been used for matches
by Carmarthenshire C C C. In the early 1950s the ground was acquired
from the Stradey Estate at a cost of £4,000 by the Llanelli Athletic
Association in order to preserve for all time the playing area and to foster
and encourage sport and athletics in the town.

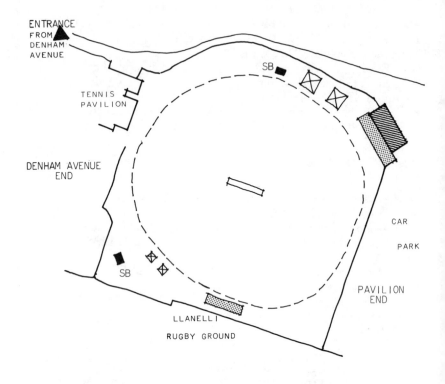

ENTRANCE
FROM
DENHAM
AVENUE

TENNIS
PAVILION

DENHAM AVENUE
END

SB

LLANELLI
RUGBY GROUND

SB

CAR

PARK

PAVILION
END

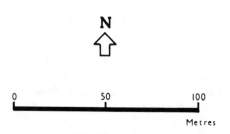

N

0   50   100

Metres

The ground once staged an international rugby fixture in 1887 between Wales and England when the adjoining rugby field was semi-frozen. The match was watched by a crowd of 8,000. Crowds for cricket have not been as good, the best being 7,500 for the visit of Surrey the county champions in 1952. Today, matches attract crowds of 3,000–4,000 for limited-overs fixtures in the Sunday League. County cricket ceased in 1965 (the last first-class match was with Essex) owing mainly to high costs, limited seating and poor catering facilities on the ground. In 1981 Llanelli C C took out a lease of sixty years on the ground and built a new pavilion costing £92,000 on the opposite side of the playing area to the old pavilion.

With the improvement in facilities Glamorgan C C C returned for a one-day friendly match with Somerset in 1986 for the Buckley's Brewery Challenge which Glamorgan won by 81 runs. With the success of this match further visits have included Refuge Assurance League matches with Leicestershire in 1988, which was restricted owwing to poor weather, to 13 overs a side. 1989 saw a visit by Nottinghamshire who won by 6 wickets and 1990 Kent who won by 2 wickets. No match was scheduled for 1991 but Surrey will be the visitors in July 1992.

Several professional players have appeared for Llanelli C C and also represented Glamorgan C C C. These include Roger Davis, Eifion Jones and Winston Davis.

The ground has seen some records including 161 by Gilbert Parkhouse and fine bowling from J.C. Clay and Robin Hobbs who achieved 12 for 94 and later captained Glamorgan. Peter Parfitt scored 118 for Middlesex in 1961 but Stradey Park will no doubt mean more to spectators of rugby football rather than cricket! A Rest of the World XI beat Glamorgan at Llanelli on 26 August 1991 by 8 runs.

ADDRESS   Llanelli Cricket Club, The Pavilion, Stradey Park, Denham Avenue, Sandy, Llanelli, Dyfed, Wales.
TELEPHONE NUMBER PROSPECTS OF PLAY   0554 773721

DESCRIPTION OF GROUND AND FACILITIES

The only entrance to Stradey Park for spectators and cars is from Denham Avenue, to the west of the ground. There are two pavilions on the ground, one for cricket (players/officials/members) and one for tennis, which is also used by members. The only other permanent buildings are the two scoreboards and groundsman's store. The majority of the facilities are temporary; there are marquees at the northern end, close to the pavilion and a members' enclosure, and to the south, backing onto the Llanelli R F C ground, a temporary stand of raised seats. Bar and refreshment facilities can be found in the pavilion and in the mobile outlets around the ground. The toilets are to be found in the pavilion, the temporary areas and the rugby clubhouse. The radio commentary position and Glamorgan C C C souvenir caravan are at the Rugby Ground End. The cricket ground is bounded by a fence and a wall to the west, north and east and by the rugby terracing to the south. There is also a rugby museum should rain or bad light stop play and many an hour could be spent examining the history of Stradey Park's 4.5 acre sports complex.

The playing are is 117 metres by 125 metres and is defined by a rope and advertising boards. The ground capacity is approximately 5,000 and 75 per cent are provided with seating, both permanent and temporary. Spectators are advised to bring seats to all popular matches. Car parking is available at the rear of the pavilion for players and officials and in the rugby car park for members. The TV camera/ commentary box is positioned at the Denham Avenue end of the ground when required.

GROUND RECORDS AND SCORES

FIRST-CLASS MATCHES
Highest innings total for County: 434 for 6 dec. *v*. Worcestershire 1933
Highest innings total against County: 298 by Sussex 1951
Lowest innings total for County: 96 *v*. Lancashire 1949
Lowest innings total against County: 71 by Worcestershire 1938
Highest individual innings for County: 161 W.G.A. Parkhouse *v*. Gloucestershire 1950
Highest individual innings against County: 118 P.H. Parfitt for Middlesex 1961
Best bowling performance in an innings for County: 9 for 54 J.C. Clay *v*. Northamptonshire 1935
Best bowling performance in an innings against County: 8 for 43 V.E. Jackson for Leicestershire 1956
Best bowling performance in a match for County: 15 for 86 J.C. Clay *v*. Northamptonshire 1935
Best bowling performance in a match against County: 12 for 94 R.N.S. Hobbs for Essex 1965
Best attendance: 7,500 *v*. Surrey 1952

LIMITED-OVERS MATCHES
Highest innings total for County: 221 for 5 *v*. Somerset (Buckley's Brewery Challenge) 1987
Highest innings total against County: 222 for 8 by Kent (RAL) 1990
Lowest innings total for County: 77 for 7 *v*. Leicestershire (RAL) 1988
Lowest innings total against County: 78 for 2 by Leicestershire (RAL) 1988
Highest individual innings for County: 91 A.R. Butcher *v*. Somerset (Buckley's Brewery Challenge) 1987
Highest individual innings against County: 76 n.o. R.T. Robinson for Nottinghamshire (RAL) 1989
Best bowling performance for County: 4 for 25 I. Smith *v*. Somerset (Buckley's Brewery Challenge) 1987
Best bowling performance against County: 3 for 9 G.J.F. Ferris for Leicestershire (RAL) 1988
Best attendance: 3,500 *v*. Somerset (Buckley's Brewery Challenge) 1987

HOW TO GET THERE

Rail Llanelli (BR), 1.5 miles.
Bus South Wales Transport 111, 112, 113 and 130 from town centre Bus Station and surrounding areas; also 181 and 182 link BR Llanelli Station and Llanelli Bus Station with ground (Telephone: 0792 475511).
Car From north: A476, follow signs Llanelli and town centre, ground is situated off Denham Avenue and Dyfed Road adjoining Llanelli Rugby Football Club ground at Stradey Park. From east: M4 junction 48, then follow A4138 signposted Llanelli and town centre, then as north. From west: A484 and B4309 to Llanelli, then as north. From south: A484 to Llanelli or as east.

WHERE TO STAY AND OTHER INFORMATION

Stradey Park (0554 758171), Diplomat Hotel (0554 756156).

Disabled Areas No special area, request suitable position. Car parking available within ground at Denham Avenue End of ground by prior arrangement.
Local Radio Station(s) BBC Radio Wales (882 MHz FM), Swansea Sound (96.4 MHz FM/1170 KHz MW).
Local Newspaper(s) South Wales Echo, Western Mail, South Wales Evening Post, Llanelli Star.

Merthyr Tydfil

The cricket ground is part of the Hoover PLC sports ground complex and is situated off the Merthyr Road (A470) adjoining the factory.

Glamorgan C C C visited Merthyr Tydfil for the first time in 1988 as part of their centenary celebrations to play a Refuge Assurance Sunday League match with Kent. The match was won by Kent by 5 wickets thanks to Chris Cowdrey, the former Kent skipper, who took 4 for 20 and a positive 62 from Neil Taylor. The event proved a great success with some 4,750 spectators attending and a further match was staged with Middlesex in the same competition in 1989. On this occasion the home side won by 37 runs thanks to 92 from Indian Test player Ravi Shastri and 3 for 32 from Rodney Ontong.

The record crowd before 1988 was for a visit from the Lord's Taverners XI in 1985 which attracted a crowd of 2,000. The ground is used by the Hoover PLC Sports C C, which is affiliated to the Welsh Cricket Association. There are facilities for bowling and tennis together with ample playing space for cricket and, in winter, rugby. The Hoover PLC factory in Merthyr opened on St. David's Day 1 March 1948 – the year Glamorgan C C C first won the County Championship. The factory covers some three-quarters of a million square feet and employs almost 2,000 staff. To help test their washing machines, Hoover wash

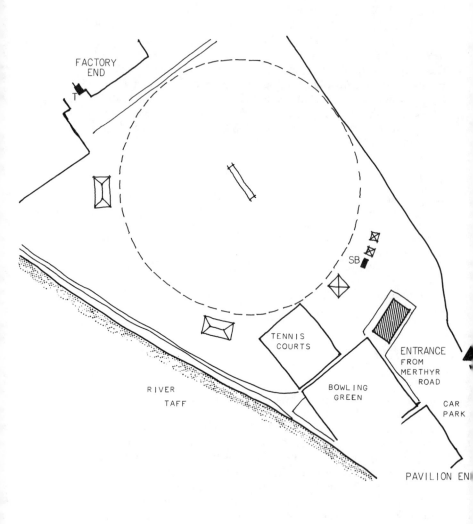

FACTORY
END

T

SB

TENNIS
COURTS

ENTRANCE
FROM
MERTHYR
ROAD

RIVER
TAFF

BOWLING
GREEN

CAR
PARK

PAVILION EN

N

0   50   100

Metres

the kits of local rugby and football clubs.

Merthyr Tydfil and Cheltenham (Dowty Arle Court) are the only two British grounds used for matches which are adjoining factory premises. Former factory grounds used include: Coventry (Courtaulds), Burton-on-Trent (Ind-Coope) and Yeovil (Westland's).

ADDRESS   Hoover Sports Cricket Club, Hoover PLC Sports Ground, Merthyr Road, Merthyr Tydfil, Mid Glamorgan, Wales.

TELEPHONE NUMBER PROSPECTS OF PLAY   0685 721222

DESCRIPTION OF GROUND AND FACILITIES

The ground is situated next to the Hoover factory and the entry adjoins the roundabout at the junction of the A470 and Merthyr Road. Car parking for 50 cars is available in the ground and there are several car parks within five minutes walk.

The playing area is 136 metres by 131 metres and is defined by a rope and advertising boards. The pavilion is the only permanent building for cricket and is also used by bowling and tennis players. Limited seating is provided for matches so spectators are well advised to bring their own collapsible seats to all matches. At the factory end of the ground there are refreshment facilities and mobile catering points. The ground capacity is 5,000 and seating is provided for about 10 per cent of this figure.

The radio commentary position and Glamorgan C C C souvenir caravan are to be found close to the pavilion, sponsors' tents are located on the north-west side of the playing area. The toilets are either temporary, in the pavilion or adjoining the factory canteen. The TV camera/commentary box position is at the factory end of the ground.

GROUND RECORDS AND SCORES

LIMITED-OVERS MATCHES

Highest innings total for County: 209 for 6 v. Middlesex (RAL) 1989

Highest innings total against County: 172 by Middlesex (RAL) 1989

Lowest innings total for County: 134 v. Kent (RAL) 1988

Lowest innings total against County: 135 for 5 by Kent (RAL) 1988

Highest individual innings for County: 92 R.J. Shastri v. Middlesex (RAL) 1989

Highest individual innings against County: 62 N.R. Taylor for Kent (RAL) 1988

Best bowling performance for County: 3 for 32 R.C. Ontong v. Middlesex (RAL) 1989

Best bowling performance against County: 4 for 20 C.S. Cowdrey for Kent (RAL) 1988

Best attendance: 4,750 v. Kent (RAL) 1988

HOW TO GET THERE

Rail   Pentre-Bach (BR), 300m; Troed-y-rhiw (BR), 1.25 miles.
Bus   Merthyr Tydfil Transport local services connect town centre with factory (Telephone: 0685 6161).
Car   Merthyr Tydfil is situated 26 miles north-west of Newport. From north: A470 or A465, follow signs Merthyr Tydfil, ground is situated off A470 near Pentre-Bach adjoining roundabout at Head of the Valley Road, south of central Merthyr Tydfil, for Hoover Sports Ground. From east: M4 junction 32, then follow A470 Head of the Valley Road to Pentre-Bach south of Merthyr Tydfil, for Hoover Sports Ground. From west: A465 or A470, then as north. From south: A470 or A4054 to Merthyr Tydfil, then as east.

WHERE TO STAY AND OTHER INFORMATION

Tregenna Hotel (0685 82055), Castle Hotel, Baverstocks (0685 2327).

Disabled Areas   No special area, request suitable position.
Local Radio Station(s)   BBC Radio Wales (882 KHz MW), BBC Radio Gwent (95.9 MHz FM), Red Dragon Radio (97.4 MHz FM/ 1359 KHz MW).
Local Newspaper(s)   South Wales Echo, Western Mail, South Wales Evening Post, Merthyr Express.

GLOUCESTERSHIRE

BRISTOL

CHELTENHAM (COLLEGE)

GLOUCESTER

CHELTENHAM (DOWTY ARLE COURT)

CHELTENHAM (TOWN)

LYDNEY

MORETON-IN-MARSH

SWINDON

TROWBRIDGE

Gloucestershire

Founded 1871
Colours Blue, green, gold, brown, sky-blue and red
Crest Coat of arms of the City and County of Bristol
Patron HRH The Princes of Wales
President F.J. Twisleton
Chairman R.W. Rossiter
Chairman cricket committee D.A. Allen
Secretary P.G.M. August
Assistant coach A.W. Stovold
Youth coach G.G.M. Wiltshire
Marketing manager A.J. Brassington
Captain A.J. Wright
Groundsman D. Brindle
1st XI Scorer B.H. Jenkins
2nd XI Scorer K.T. Gerrish
Statistician A.G. Avery
Sponsors AppleCentres West
Newsletter *Gloucestershire News*
Address Phoenix County Cricket Ground, Nevil Road, Bishopston, Bristol, Avon, BS7 9EJ
Telephone 0272 245216/246743/422503
Gloucestershire Rapid Cricketline 0891 567505

ACHIEVEMENTS

County Championship Champions (3) 1874, 1876 and 1877; joint champions (1) 1873
Gillette Cup Winners (1) 1973
National Westminster Bank Trophy Semi-finalists (1) 1987
Benson & Hedges Cup Winners (1) 1977
John Player Sunday League 6th 1969, 1973 and 1977
Refuge Assurance Sunday League 2nd 1988
Refuge Assurance Cup Semi-Finalists (1) 1988
Tilcon Trophy Winners (1) 1987; finalists (2) 1979 and 1982
Ward Four Counties Knockout Competition Semi-finalists (1) 1988
Seven Trophy Winners (1) 1987
Seeboard Trophy Finalists (1) 1991

GROUNDS

Bristol (Phoenix County Cricket Ground, Nevil Road); Cheltenham (College Ground, Thirlestaine Road); Gloucester (Winget Sports Ground, Tuffley Avenue); Cheltenham Town (Victoria Ground, Prince's Street); Cheltenham Dowty Arle Court (Dowty Arle Court C C, Sir George Dowty PLC Sports Ground); Lydney (Recreational Trust Ground, Swan Road); Moreton-in-Marsh (Moreton Cricket

Ground, Batsford Road); Swindon (County Ground, County Road) and Trowbridge (Trowbridge C C County Cricket Ground, Timbrell Street)

Other grounds that have been used since 1969 are: Stroud (Eriniod Ground) and Tewkesbury (Swilgate).

SECOND XI GROUNDS

In addition to the above mentioned grounds the following are used for second XI matches: Gloucester, Tuffley Park, Gloucester. Telephone: 0452 423011; King's School, School Grounds, Mercier Road, Gloucester. (No Telephone).

Gloucestershire is the county of cricket's immortals, Dr W.G. Grace and Walter Hammond, of Jessop, Barnett and Graveney, and, from the overseas treasure chest, Procter and Zaheer Abbas.

Grace was the sporting idol of Victorian England, whose genius and personality revolutionized and popularized the game. On pitches which today's players would dismiss as impossibly bad – even at Lord's there were small pebbles on the surface – he scored 54,896 runs and 126 first-class centuries, took 2,876 wickets and held 877 catches. Yet his true greatness was, in the words of Prince Ranjitsinjhi, to turn batting from an accomplishment into a science. He was the first to recognize forward and back play are of equal importance.

At the age of 47 he completed 1,000 runs between 9 and 30 May, and in August 1876 he had successive innings of 344 for MCC and 177 out of 262 for Gloucestershire against Nottinghamshire at Clifton College. On their way to Cheltenham for the next match Yorkshire's players met the departing visitors. 'What did the black bearded blighter do?' they asked. When told they were pleased, thinking Grace might have exhausted his run form.

The next day he made 318, which prompted one of the Yorkshiremen Tom Emmett to complain: 'We have grace before meat, grace after meat, and Grace all bloomin' day!'

There were five Grace brothers, and they played a major part in the club's formation and early successes of 3 titles, another bracketed first with Nottinghamshire, and 3 runner-up places in the 9 seasons between 1873 and 1881.

Three of the Graces, E.M., W.G. and G.F. were in the England side for the first home Test in 1880, with W.G. scoring 152 and sharing an opening stand of 91 with E.M., who suffered only by comparison with his brother. Sadly 6 weeks later Fred, only 29, caught a chill after sleeping between damp sheets and died. With his death Gloucester-shire's fortunes declined, and the Doctor, amid some acrimony, left to concentrate on managing London County.

Jessop's captaincy years, which relied heavily on his prowess as batsman, fast bowler and cover point, might have been better if Charles

BRISTOL

PLAYER'S CIGARETTES

T. W. GODDARD

Townsend, founder of Gloucestershire's dynasty of spin bowlers, had been available regularly. Jessop was not the slogger of popular imagination, but leaning low on his bat – hence 'The Croucher' – he accumulated runs at an extraordinary pace. His longest innings at Brighton in 1903 lasted 3 hours and produced 286 – an impossible rate facing today's defensive bowling, field placings and slow, by comparison, over rates. Jessop gained eternal fame, winning the Oval Test in 1902 with a memorable innings.

Hammond was born in Dover, spent his childhood in Malta, and, luckily for Gloucestershire, his family returned to Circencester. Magnificently and athletically built, Hammond excelled at any game he took up, and he had a majestic style on the cricket field whether cover driving, bowling or at slip, where he took the majority of his 819 catches. Nine of his 22 Test centuries were against Australia, and in his prime in the 1928–29 series he hit 905 runs and averaged 113. Australia's captain, Jack Ryder, said: 'My, how that man could hit a cricket ball. You'd need twenty fielders to stop him.'

For eight successive years Hammond headed the national batting averages, and, until Hutton broke it, he held the record individual Test score of 336 not out against New Zealand at Auckland in 1933. In all he scored 50,551 runs and 167 centuries.

To follow Grace as England and Gloucestershire captain Hammond was obliged by the conventions of the time to change his status from pro to amateur. The county were 3rd under him in 1939, but it is perhaps surprising that Hammond's brilliance could not bring the title south, short though they were of genuine speed. The irreverent Charlie Parker, quoted by David Foot in *Cricket's Unholy Trinity* had his own theory! 'There are only two weaknesses in our team – brewer's asthma and financial cramp, and, apart from the fact we ain't good enough.'

Parker's left arm spin brought 3,278 wickets. Dennett, before him, had 2,147 which meant a combined total of 5,425 with the one cap

PARKER

DR W.G. GRACE
Gloucestershire

WALTER HAMMOND

going to Parker between them. They were outstanding bowlers. Goddard, Allen, Mortimore and Cook were worthy successors.

The attack-minded Barnett, Graveney, with a touch as smooth as silk, and Emmett was extremely attractive, but Graveney left for Worcestershire in 1960 after the decision to depose him from the captaincy in favour of the amateur Tom Pugh. He not only enjoyed but flourished in his second career.

Milton, a double cricket and soccer international, the left-handed Crapp, were rightly called up by England, and under Tony Brown there was a consistency not achieved since the Graces. Though the title remained elusive – in four seasons since 1946 Gloucestershire were runners-up in tight finishes – the Gillette Cup was won in 1973, the first competitive victory for 96 years with the final a personal triumph for Brown.

The brilliant South African all-rounder Procter, a diamond ever sparkling, was also a decisive leader when the Benson & Hedges Cup was won and 3rd place was taken in the championship in 1977.

Pakistan's brilliant Zaheer Abbas achieved the unique distinction of scoring a double and a century in the same match on no less than four occasions, the victims being Surrey, Kent, Sussex and Somerset. Even more remarkably he was not dismissed once. He also scored two separate centuries in a match eight times. The next best was Hammond with seven, and Zaheer completed a career, comparable with the best in history, with 108 centuries.

After eight years as captain (1982–89), David Graveney left the club in 1990 and joined Somerset for the 1991 season. Tony 'Billy' Wright took over the captaincy in 1990 and under the coaching of Eddie Barlow, the former South African player, the county improved its standing in the championship. Jack Russell and David Lawrence were both on Test duty so the main achievers during 1991 were Bill Athey, Tony Wright and Dave Gilbert.

Bristol

The Phoenix County Ground at Bristol, as it has been known since it was purchased by the Phoenix Assurance Company in 1976, is situated in Ashley Down, on the northern outskirts of the city. The observant visitor will notice that the surrounding roads bear the names of other first-class and minor counties. The county's previous home ground was Clifton College.

The present ground, which was first used by Gloucestershire C C C in 1899 against Lancashire, was laid out to W.G. Grace's specification. Later, in 1916, it was sold to Fry's chocolate company to get the County Club out of debt and became known as Fry's Ground. The County Club repurchased the ground in 1932 after forming the Gloucestershire C C C Limited Company.

Since W.G. Grace first contemplated the development of the ground a century ago, many changes have taken place, but there still remains a sense of spaciousness about the area. The ground now houses facilities for indoor cricket nets, squash courts, tennis and even an outdoor golf driving range as well as football and hockey pitches during the winter months. The Gloucestershire C C C have played on three other grounds in the city, at Clifton College (1871–1932), Durdham Down (1870) and Greenbank (1922–28). Clifton was the last to be used when a match was staged with All India in August 1932.

From 1840 until the 1870s the ground was used by Muller's orphanage. The orphanage building still exists today and now forms part of the Bristol Polytechnic campus. The main entrance to the ground from Nevil Road is through the Grace Gates and the tablet was erected on the centenary of W.G.'s birth 18 July 1948, John Arlott wrote, 'in the public mind W.G. was Gloucestershire'; he scored many of his centuries at Bristol.

Ground improvements proposed for the future include a new indoor cricket school together with the replacement of wooden seating around the ground with the introduction of seats of the plastic tip-up variety. Some development has taken place since 1989 and currently other works are in hand, including the refurbishment of the pavilion. It is for this reason that a number of matches will be played away from Bristol, the county headquarters during the early part of the 1992 season.

The pavilion was built during the 1880s; other additions have been made in recent years. The Jessop Tavern which also houses the press box was built in 1958 and the nearby scoreboard was constructed in 1971. The Mound Stand was built during the 1960s. The Grace Room and Hammond Room now form the main restaurant for member' at the pavilion end.

Crowds at Bristol are usually around 5,000–6,000 for popular matches. The best crowds were around 15,000 for the visits of the touring Australians in 1930 and 1948. In the limited-overs game probably the 7,500 crowd for the 1987 National Westminster Bank Trophy semi-final with Nottinghamshire was the best in recent years. In

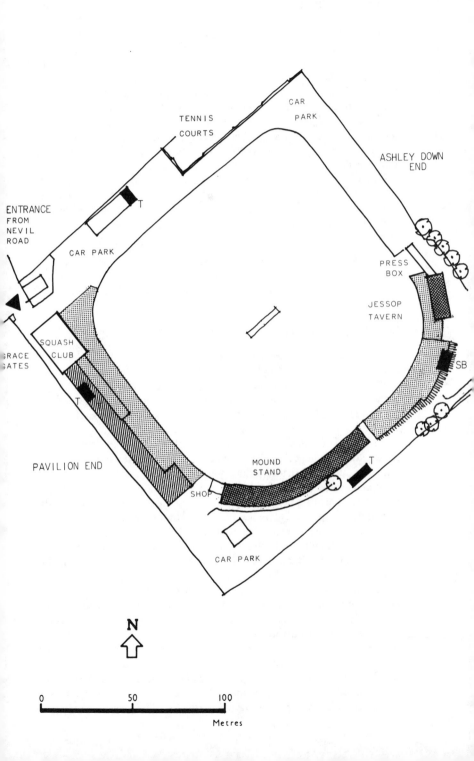

TENNIS
COURTS

CAR
PARK

ASHLEY DOWN
END

ENTRANCE
FROM
NEVIL
ROAD

CAR PARK

T

PRESS
BOX

JESSOP
TAVERN

GRACE
GATES

SQUASH
CLUB

SB

T

PAVILION END

MOUND
STAND

T

SHOP

CAR PARK

N

0   50   100

Metres

August 1930 Gloucestershire tied with the tourists and the city erupted with excitement. Gloucestershire were dismissed for 72 in their first innings and in their second Wally Hammond scored 89 before Tom Goddard and Charlie Parker tied up the match including Bradman and all.

Ground records include highest individual innings by Wally Hammond and Arthur Morris for the touring Australians together with wickets collected by E.G. Dennett, Tom Goddard, F.A. Tarrant and F.H. Parris. All but one of the limited-overs records on the ground belong to overseas players, two South Africans and two Pakistanis. Two overseas nations played at Bristol in 1983 when a Prudential Cup game was staged between New Zealand and Sri Lanka.

With Grace and Jessop, Dipper and Hammond, Sinfield and Barnett, Crapp and Emmett, Goddard and Parker, Graveney and Allen, Zaheer and Proctor, Russell and Walsh. . . few grounds can have a record to compare with Bristol's for nurturing some of the best players in the game.

ADDRESS   Phoenix County Cricket Ground, Nevil Road, Bishopston, Bristol, Avon BS7 9EJ.
TELEPHONE NUMBER PROSPECTS OF PLAY   0272 248461

DESCRIPTION OF GROUND AND FACILITIES

There are two entrances to the Phoenix County Ground, the main entrance from Nevil Road through the Grace Gates and a further entrance from the Ashley Down Road, behind the Jessop Tavern. Most of the permanent buildings are sited at the south and south-east side of the ground and include the pavilion, the county offices, changing facilities, scorers' box and dining areas together with members' seating enclosures. The squash courts, indoor cricket school, Hammond and Grace Rooms where refreshment/bar facilities are sited along with the clubroom and bar are also situated at the pavilion end.

There is some raised seating above the Hammond Room and ample ground level seating near to the playing area for members. The south-east side of the ground includes the Mound Stand, which is covered and a terrace of yellow, plastic seats situated in front of the main scoreboard. Public refreshment/bar facilities are available in the Jessop Tavern, in front of which further seats can be found. The press box is sited at this end above the groundsman's stores.

The north side of the ground includes car parking, a groundsman's store, toilets and some tennis courts. Also, during Bristol cricket festival week, a number of sponsors' marquees are sited at this side. There is the facility to bring in further seating of the raised temporary variety for popular matches and these are usually sited at the Ashley Down End and in front of the squash court building to the west of the playing area. The members' enclosure spans the pavilion end completely. The playing area is 154 metres by 156 metres and is defined by a rope and advertising boards completely surrounding the perimeter. The ground capacity is

8,000 and around 3,500 seats are provided but further seating is installed for popular matches. Spectators would however be advised to bring their own seats to these important matches. The TV camera/commentary box is positioned next to the press box above the Jessop Tavern and directly above and behind the sightscreen at the Ashley Down End.

The ground is surrounded by residential streets and to the south are the Bristol Polytechnic campus buildings, built of similar stone to that of the pavilion. Many photographs of old county teams and former players together with some history of the Gloucestershire C C C, can be found in the pavilion and bar areas.

GROUND RECORDS AND SCORES

FIRST-CLASS MATCHES
Highest innings total for County: 643 for 5 dec. *v.* Nottinghamshire 1946
Highest innings total against County: 774 for 7 dec. by Australians 1948
Lowest innings total for County: 22 *v.* Somerset 1920
Lowest innings total against County: 25 by Somerset 1947
Highest individual innings for County: 302 n.o. W.R. Hammond *v.* Glamorgan 1934
Highest individual innings against County: 290 A.R. Morris for Australians 1948
Best bowling performance in an innings for County: 10 for 40 E.G. Dennett *v.* Essex 1906
Best bowling performance in an innings against County: 9 for 41 F.A. Tarrant for Middlesex 1907
Best bowling performance in a match for County: 17 for 106 T.W. Goddard *v.* Kent 1938
Best bowling performance in a match against County: 15 for 98 F.H. Parris for Sussex 1894
Best attendance: 15,000 *v.* Australians 1930 and 1948

LIMITED-OVERS MATCHES
Highest innings total for County: 297 for 8 *v.* Scotland (NWBT) 1983
Highest innings total against County: 349 for 6 by Lancashire (NWBT) 1984
Lowest innings total for County: 49 *v.* Middlesex (JPL) 1978
Lowest innings total against County: 77 by Hampshire (JPL) 1970
Highest individual innings for County: 128 Sadiq Mohammad *v.* Minor Counties (BHC) 1974/Zaheer Abbas *v.* Worcestershire (GC) 1976
Highest individual innings against County: 138 n.o. I.T. Botham for Worcestershire (BHC) 1990
Best bowling performance for County: 6 for 20 D.V. Lawrence *v.* Combined Universities (BHC) 1991

Best bowling performance against County: 6 for 33 E.J. Barlow for Derbyshire (BHC) 1978
Best attendance: 7,500 *v*. Nottinghamshire (NWBT) 1987

HOW TO GET THERE

Rail   Montpelier (BR), 0.75 mile; Bristol Temple Meads (BR), 2.5 miles; Bristol Parkway (BR), 5 miles.
Bus   City Line 78 from BR Bristol Temple Meads Station Approach Road, 72 or 73 from BR Bristol Parkway Station and 71–78 from city centre pass close to the ground (Telephone: 0272 553231).
Car   From north: M5 junction 17, then follow signs Bristol A38 and city centre, then follow signs for county cricket in Nevil Road off Gloucester Road A38. From east: M4 junction 19, then follow M32 to junction 2, then follow signs to Bristol and city centre on A38, then as north. From south: A37 or A4 to Bristol city centre, then as west. From west: as north or A370, A369 or A38 to Bristol and city centre, then follow A38 Gloucester Road for Nevil Road and county cricket.

WHERE TO STAY AND OTHER INFORMATION

Grand Hotel (0272 291645) Holiday Inn (0272 294281), Clifton Hotel (0272 736882), Unicorn Hotel (0272 230333).

Disabled Areas   No special area, request suitable position. Car parking is available within the ground in a position to view the cricket.
Local Radio Station(s)   BBC Radio Bristol (95.5 MHz FM/1548 KHz MW), Great Western Radio (96.3 MHz FM/1260 KHz MW).
Local Newspaper(s)   Bristol Evening Post, Western Daily Press, Bristol Journal, Bristol Observer, Sunday Independent.

Cheltenham (College)

Gloucestershire C C C have staged a cricket festival at the Cheltenham College Ground since 1872. This usually takes place in August after the college term has ended. The initial match was with Surrey in July 1872 and the county have visited two other grounds in the town and in 1992 will play for the first time at Dowty Arle Court C C situated to the west of the town centre.

Gloucestershire today take three championship and two limited-overs Sunday League matches to the College ground. These are always well supported, crowds tend to be about 6,000 and the largest was 15,000 against Middlesex in 1947.

The first visits to Cheltenham College were organized by James Lillywhite, the former Sussex player. He died in 1882 and never knew the full success of the venture he had initiated. The festival is the longest

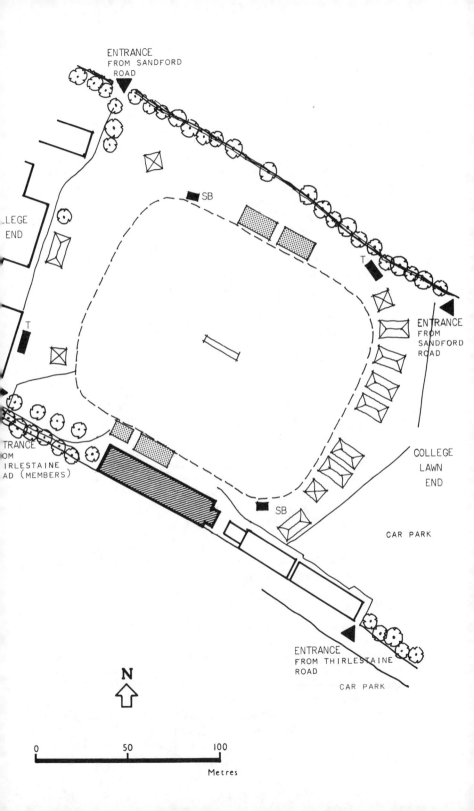

on the county circuit and spans at least eleven consecutive cricket days (weather permitting!). The 1992 festival will last from 17–28 July.

The main permanent building on the ground used by the county is the gymnasium with its twin steeples of yellow brick and its trellised balcony. This is used as a pavilion and stands on the Thirlestaine Road side of the ground. Other buildings on this side of the playing area are smaller pavilions for schoolboy cricket, used during term time only. The college chapel which overlooks the ground was built in 1893. It is possibly the most significant feature of the College Ground and appears in many photographs.

In 1969 the first limited-overs match was staged and after good attendances a second was added in 1975. The ground has seen many achievements over the years, including 318 n.o. from Dr W.G. Grace and match figures of 17 for 89. The county collapsed to 17 all out against the touring Australians in 1896 thanks to some fine bowling by the visitors – Trumble 6 for 8 and M'Kibbin 4 for 7. Other achievements include Jessop (born in Cheltenham) who hit 51 in 18 minutes against Yorkshire in 1895 and Hammond who, in 1928, in his first match on the famous ground scored 139 and 143 and while fielding took ten catches against Surrey. Tom Goddard and Charlie Parker, two great county bowlers, have both enjoyed matches here especially after rain and before wickets were covered.

Three overseas players have fond memories of Cheltenham College: Mike Proctor the South African all-rounder who in 1979 against Yorkshire repeated his own record of three lbws in a hat trick, (the previous was against Essex in 1972), Zaheer Abbas of Pakistan who scored 205 and 108 both n.o. against Sussex in 1977 and finally Glenn Turner the New Zealander who scored 181 for neighbours Worcestershire in 1974 during their championship winning season. Matches have been staged with touring teams here rather than at Bristol. In recent years limited-overs centuries have been scored by Bill Athey (113 against Surrey in 1990) and Richard Blakey (100 n.o. for Yorkshire in 1990, which equalled Richard Hadlee's 100 n.o. made for Nottinghamshire in 1982).

ADDRESS Cheltenham College, College Sports Ground, Thirlestaine Road, Cheltenham, Gloucestershire.

TELEPHONE NUMBER PROSPECTS OF PLAY   0242 522000

DESCRIPTION OF GROUND AND FACILITIES

There are three entrances to the College Ground, two in Thirlestaine Road and one in Sandford Road. Car parking is available within the ground at the College Lawn End, through the entrance to the south of the ground, which is also used by spectators. Car parking is also available in the adjacent college fields. The permanent buildings, sited to the south of the playing area, are the gymnasium which is used as a pavilion by players and members for refreshments and the pavilion and stores which are used for catering requirements.

Much of the south side is used as a members' enclosure and sponsors' marquees surround the college lawn end. The Sandford Road side has two large, temporary, open tiered seating areas as well as a temporary scoreboard, press/scorers' tent and Gloucestershire C C C supporters' club souvenir marquee and caravan. At the College End is the Gloucestershire C C C secretary's temporary office sited in a bus, telephones, several refreshment marquees and further sponsors' tents. In front of the gymnasium which serves as a pavilion are two large, raised plastic seating stands, a further permanent green scorebox and more refreshment facilities. Most of the seating is of a temporary nature and of bench, plastic or raised seating variety. The ground capacity is 8,000 and seating for about 65 per cent is provided. Spectators would be advised to bring their own seating to popular matches. The playing area is 120 metres by 150 metres and is defined by advertising boards and a rope around part of the playing area. When required, the TV camera/commentary box is positioned on a gantry at the College Lawn End.

The school buildings provide a beautiful backcloth to the cricket festival on this extremely pleasant out ground. A festival newsletter was introduced for the first time in 1991 for each day titled *The Cheltenham Spectator*, produced by Gerry and Deborah Wolstenholme.

GROUND RECORDS AND SCORES

FIRST-CLASS MATCHES

Highest innings total for County: 608 for 7 dec. *v.* Sussex 1934
Highest innings total against County: 607 for 6 dec. by Kent 1910
Lowest innings total for County: 17 *v.* Australians 1896
Lowest innings total against County: 27 by Surrey 1874
Highest individual innings for County: 318 n.o. W.G. Grace *v.* Yorkshire 1876
Highest individual innings against County: 181 G.M. Turner for Worcestershire 1974
Best bowling performance in an innings for County: 10 for 113 T.W. Goddard *v.* Worcestershire 1937
Best bowling performance in an innings against County: 10 for 66 A.A. Mailey for Australians 1921
Best bowling performance in a match for County: 17 for 89 W.G. Grace *v.* Nottinghamshire 1877
Best bowling performance in a match against County: 15 for 184 W.H. Lockwood for Surrey 1899
Best attendance: 15,000 *v.* Middlesex 1947

LIMITED-OVERS MATCHES

Highest innings total for County: 233 for 5 *v.* Yorkshire (JPL) 1983
Highest innings total against County: 283 for 6 by Essex (JPL) 1975
Lowest innings total for County: 122 *v.* Hampshire (JPL) 1978
Lowest innings total against County: 85 by Warwickshire (JPL) 1973
Highest individual innings for County: 113 C.W.J. Athey *v.* Surrey (RAL) 1990
Highest individual innings against County: 100 n.o. R.J. Hadlee for

Nottinghamshire (JPL) 1982/R.J. Blakey for Yorkshire (RAL) 1990
Best bowling performance for County: 5 for 20 J.H. Shackleton *v.*
Surrey (JPL) 1977
Best bowling performance against County: 4 for 18 D.L. Underwood
for Kent (JPL) 1975
Best attendance: 6,750 *v.* Essex (JPL) 1975

HOW TO GET THERE

Rail Cheltenham Spa (BR), 1 mile.
Bus Cheltenham and District L from town centre (F/G link BR
Cheltenham Spa Station with town centre) (Telephone: 0242
522021).
Car From north: M5 junction 10, then follow A4019 signposted
Cheltenham and town centre, ground is situated in Thirlestaine Road
adjoining Cheltenham College, or A435 to town centre. From east:
A436 or A40, then follow signs Charlton Kings and Cheltenham, to
town centre, then as north. From west: M5 junction 11, then follow
A40 Cheltenham and town centre, then as north or A46 or A435 to
town centre. From south: M4 junction 15, then A419, A417 and
B4070 or A435 to Cheltenham and town centre, then as north.

WHERE TO STAY AND OTHER INFORMATION

Queen's Hotel (0242 514724), George Hotel (0242 35751), Carlton
Hotel (0242 514453), Park Place Hotel (0242 525353).

Disabled Areas No special area, request suitable position.
Local Radio Station(s) BBC Radio Gloucestershire (104.7 MHz
FM/865 KHz MW), Seven Sound (102.4 MHz FM/774 KHz MW).
Local Newspaper(s) Gloucestershire Echo, Cheltenham News,
Gloucestershire County Gazette, The Source.

Gloucester

The first ground in the city used by Gloucestershire C C C was the Spa
Ground on 13–14 July 1882 against Somerset and the last match was on
30 May–1 June 1923 against Leicestershire. The Spa Ground is
presently used by Gloucester City C C. The move to Tuffley Avenue
came in 1923 when the first match staged on the ground was with
Lancashire on 2–5 June 1923. Since that initial visit the ground has had
various names, first it was known as the Gloucestershire Railway
Carriage and Wagon Company Ground until in 1962 it was taken over
after 102 years by the Gloucester Engineering Sports Club and then
shortly afterwards by the Babcocks and Wilcox Sports Club. The
ground today is called Winget Sports Ground and is used by Winget
Cricket Club.

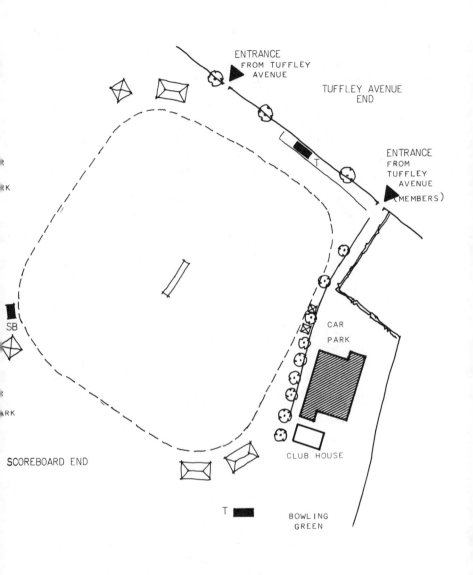

ENTRANCE
FROM TUFFLEY
AVENUE

TUFFLEY AVENUE
END

ENTRANCE
FROM
TUFFLEY
AVENUE
(MEMBERS)

T

SB

CAR
PARK

CLUB HOUSE

SCOREBOARD END

T

BOWLING
GREEN

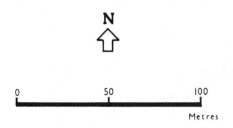

N

0   50   100

Metres

The ground was originally thirty-three acres or so and was bought by the railway carriage company from the executors of a Colonel Collett in 1917 under the provisions of the 1916 Finance Act for £4,005. Twenty acres were sold off for £525,000 in 1973 to a house builder; the remainder forms the ground, which is situated in residential Gloucester south of the city centre. There used to be twelve plane trees in front of the pavilion but upon the death of a prominent club member and cricketer one tree was felled.

The connection of railways with the ground is still prominent: the pavilion serving the nearby bowling green adjacent to the main cricket pavilion is an old railway carriage. It was built for the Central Argentine Railway – Ferro Carril Central Argentina El Pacifico – in 1914 and was shipped early in 1915. The ship was torpedoed, but two carriages were salvaged and brought back to Gloucester and placed on the ground. One is still used by bowls players and cricketers but the second was burnt down some years ago. The present scoreboard was sponsored by Gloucester City Council.

In recent years the ground has again changed hands and is now owned by the city council which acquired it for £75,000 – a nominal price for the thirteen remaining acres – and so saved the ground from being developed into a housing estate. The council's hope was that Gloucestershire C C C might make Gloucester, the county town, its permanent home. This was not to be and the county today takes three championship and at least one limited-overs match to the ground in June to make up the Gloucester cricket festival.

The ground has had many famous visitors including A.J. Paish, Dr W.G. Grace and G.L. Jessop who laid the ground out in 1917–18. The present groundsman also prepares the wicket for first-class matches at the Cheltenham College ground. Crowds have been good at Tuffley Avenue and the best was 9,000 for the visit of Surrey in 1959. In recent years matches have attracted crowds in the region of 4,000–5,500.

The ground has seen its fair share of records including 317 by Wally Hammond in 1936, 263 n.o. by H.T.W. Hardinge and fine bowling from Charlie Parker and M.S. Nichols. Other double centuries have been recorded by McCorkell for Hampshire and Dollery for Warwickshire.

Fast hundreds have included one from Tom Graveney against Combined Services. Limited-overs records have included centuries by players who have represented both Leicestershire and Gloucestershire during their careers: the Rhodesian Brian Davison and Barry Dudleston who is presently a first-class umpire. Mike Proctor's 5 for 8 against Middlesex and Gloucestershire's 325 for 4 against Lincolnshire in the National Westminster Bank Trophy 1st round match in 1990 are also significant ground records.

ADDRESS Winget Sports Cricket Club, The Pavilion, Winget Sports Ground, Tuffley Avenue, Gloucester, Gloucestershire GL1 5NS.

TELEPHONE NUMBER PROSPECTS OF PLAY 0452 423011

DESCRIPTION OF GROUND AND FACILITIES

The ground is entered from Tuffley Avenue where there are two entrances, one for players and officials and another for spectators and cars. The pavilion, clubhouse and all permanent buildings are sited to the east of the playing area with the press, scorer's and groundsman's tents under the trees. A number of sponsors' marquees and a bus are sited to the south near the tennis courts and bowling green. At this end is the TV camera/commentary box position and radio commentary point together with the main scoreboard. To the west is the large car parking area and, close to the main entrance, two large refreshment tents and a large marquee for public and members' bars.

There is also a first aid caravan and a Gloucestershire C C C souvenir supporters' shop sited in a caravan. A number of smaller refreshment and temporary toilets and a secondary smaller scoreboard is sited near the Tuffley Avenue boundary. There is no covered seating and all seating is of a temporary nature, comprising of plastic seats or benches two to three deep around the playing area. The playing area is defined by a rope and advertising boards and is 146 metres by 154 metres. It is roughly circular in shape. The ground capacity is 6,000 and 70 per cent are provided with seating. Spectators are only advised to bring seats to popular matches. The members' enclosure spans an area from the Tuffley Road End sightscreen towards the sightscreen at the Scoreboard End and in front of the pavilion. The south and west side of the ground is slightly banked and hence a good view of the play can be gained from this vantage point towards the flat playing area.

GROUND RECORDS AND SCORES

FIRST-CLASS MATCHES

Highest innings total for County: 529 *v*. Glamorgan 1933
Highest innings total against County: 553 by Essex 1938
Lowest innings total for County: 42 *v*. Yorkshire 1924
Lowest innings total against County: 34 by Cambridge University 1946
Highest individual innings for County: 317 W.R. Hammond *v*. Nottinghamshire 1936
Highest individual innings against County: 263 n.o. H.T.W. Hardinge for Kent 1928
Best bowling performance in an innings for County: 9 for 44 C.W.L. Parker *v*. Essex 1925
Best bowling performance in an innings against County: 9 for 37 M.S. Nichols for Essex 1938
Best bowling performance in a match for County: 17 for 56 C.W.L. Parker *v*. Essex 1925
Best bowling performance in a match against County: 15 for 165 M.S. Nichols for Essex 1938
Best attendance: 9,000 *v*. Surrey 1959

LIMITED-OVERS MATCHES

Highest innings total for County: 325 for 4 *v.* Lincolnshire (NWBT) 1990

Highest innings total against County: 272 for 4 by Derbyshire (JPL) 1984

Lowest innings total for County: 107 *v.* Kent (JPL) 1979

Lowest innings total against County: 86 by Middlesex (JPL) 1977

Highest individual innings for County: 103 B.F. Davison *v.* Yorkshire (JPL) 1985

Highest individual innings against County: 109 n.o. B. Dudleston for Leicestershire (JPL) 1974

Best bowling performance for County: 5 for 8 M.J. Proctor *v.* Middlesex (JPL) 1977

Best bowling performance against County: 4 for 17 V.A. Holder for Worcestershire (JPL) 1971

Best attendance: 7,000 *v.* Worcestershire (JPL) 1971

HOW TO GET THERE

Rail Gloucester Central (BR), 1.5 miles.

Bus City of Gloucester Bus Company 8, 20, 20A or 50 from city centre passing within 300m of BR Gloucester Central Station pass ground (Telephone: 0452 27516).

Car From north: M5 junction 11, then follow signs Gloucester A40 and A38 to Tuffley district 1.5 miles south of city centre, ground situated in Tuffley Avenue off A38. From east: A436, A417 to Gloucester, then follow ring road, then A38 to Tuffley district, then as north. From west: A417, A48 and B4215 follow signs Gloucester, then follow ring road, then A38 to Tuffley district, then as north. From south: M5 junction 12, then follow A38 to Tuffley district, then as north or A4173.

WHERE TO STAY AND OTHER INFORMATION

New County Hotel (0452 24977), Fleece Hotel (0452 22762), Bowden Hall (0452 64121), Crest Hotel (0452 63311).

Disabled Areas No special area request suitable position. Cars can be taken into the ground and parked at the Scoreboard End.

Local Radio Station(s) BBC Radio Gloucestershire (104.7 MHz FM/865 KHz MW), Seven Sound (102.4 MHz FM/774 KHz MW), BBC Radio Hereford and Worcester (94.7 MHz FM).

Local Newspaper(s) Gloucester Citizen, Gloucestershire Echo, Gloucester Express, Gloucester News, The Source.

Cheltenham (Dowty Arle Court)

Due to the refurbishment of the pavilion and facilities at the County Cricket Ground headquarters at Bristol, Gloucestershire C C C have had to arrange some home matches during the season at a number of out grounds in the county.

One such venue is the Dowty Arle Court Cricket Club which is situated to the south-west of Cheltenham town centre off the A40 Golden Valley Bypass and Gloucester Road, only one mile from the M5 motorway, junction 11.

This venue in Cheltenham will be the fourth venue to have been used by the county club to stage home matches, the other grounds which have been used are the East Gloucestershire C C ground in 1888 and 1903, Cheltenham Town C C between 1923 and 1937 with a single match in 1986 and, finally the most famous Cheltenham College ground between 1882 and 1914 and from 1918 to date.

The Dowty Arle Court C C is a factory sports field ground situated off Hatherley Lane next to the Sir George Dowty PLC, Dowty Defence and Air Systems Limited (Fuel Systems Division) factory. The Arle Court House, Sports and Social clubhouse/pavilion named the Sir George Dowty Memorial Clubhouse is situated within the factory complex to the south of Hatherley Brook and Redgrove Park.

The Dowty Arle Court C C was established in 1938 and the ground has been used for cricket, together with other factory social sports ever since. The ground has been used by Gloucestershire C C C for Second XI Championship matches since 1988 when Warwickshire were the visitors. Other matches have seen Worcestershire (1989), Warwickshire (1990), Essex and Warwickshire (1991).

The factory ground has also been used for benefit matches and the most recent was in 1991 to celebrate the 150th Anniversary of the Gloucestershire Police Constabulary which included a match between Gloucestershire Police XI and Gloucestershire C C C.

Two matches will be staged at Dowty Arle Court by Gloucestershire during April 1992 in the Benson and Hedges Cup zonal rounds against Leicestershire and the Minor Counties Cricket Association.

The ground capacity is approximately 4,000 which is dependent on temporary seating being installed by Gloucestershire C C C. The largest attendance was 6,000 for a company sports day in 1985.

Match scores from Second XI matches include amongst others: Gloucestershire 174 (R.D.O. Earl 9 for 70) and 173 for 4 dec. Warwickshire 109 for 5 dec. and 237 for 5, match drawn (1988); Gloucestershire 274 for 3 dec. (G.D. Hodgson 130) and 155 for 8 dec. Worcestershire 165 (M.W. Pooley 4 for 43) and 167 for 2, match drawn (1989). Gloucestershire 193 (G. Welch 5 for 42) and 279 E.T. Milburn 65 n.o.), Warwickshire 500 for 7 dec. (S.J. Green 122, G.W. Humpage 122 D.P. Ostler 103), won by an innings and 28 runs (1990).

ADDRESS   Dowty Arle Court Cricket Club, Sir George Dowty PLC

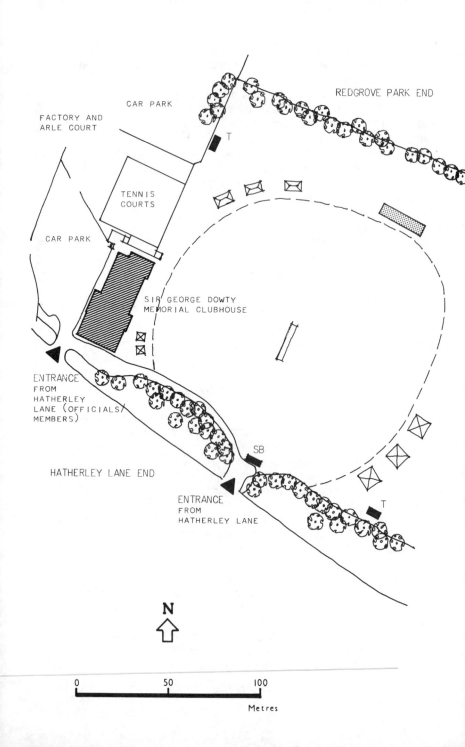

FACTORY AND
ARLE COURT

CAR PARK

REDGROVE PARK END

T

TENNIS
COURTS

CAR PARK

SIR GEORGE DOWTY
MEMORIAL CLUBHOUSE

ENTRANCE
FROM
HATHERLEY
LANE (OFFICIALS/
MEMBERS)

SB

HATHERLEY LANE END

ENTRANCE
FROM
HATHERLEY LANE

T

N

0   50   100

Metres

Sports and Social Society, Sir George Dowty Memorial Clubhouse, Hatherley Lane, Arle Court, Cheltenham, Gloucestershire GL51 OTP. **TELEPHONE NUMBER PROSPECTS OF PLAY** 0242 533231

DESCRIPTION OF GROUND AND FACILITIES

The ground is situated in part of the Arle Court estate and is in quite a picturesque setting bordered on two sides by various types of trees, with housing on one side, partially hidden by new tree planting and the Sir George Dowty Memorial clubhouse building, tennis courts, and a view of Arle Court House the remaining elevation.

The large cricket square comprises an area used for the club junior teams and the local associations for cup semi-finals and finals. The remainder of the playing area is utilized by the club's football and hockey teams during the winter months.

The Sir George Dowty Memorial Clubhouse, currently under modification, has a large bar and lounge, a skittle alley, two squash courts and three snooker tables. New facilities which will be provided once the building work has been completed will include a function room, conservatory and the current areas are being upgraded. The programme of work will not be fully completed until the end of 1992.

The ground is entered from Hatherley Lane by players, officials and members together with those spectators travelling by car. Car parking is available to the north-west of the playing area in a separate field towards the lake. Additional car parking is available within the Dowty Group company car park off Hatherley Lane near factory Unit No. 1A.

Once in the ground the only permanent buildings are the Sir George Dowty Memorial Clubhouse, the mobile scorebox and the toilets.

For county matches temporary seating will be installed by Gloucestershire C C C for approximately 50 per cent of the ground capacity of 4,000. The members' enclosure includes the clubhouse, where bar, refreshment and toilet facilities are available together with players' dressing rooms. The rest of the ground is available to the public who would be advised to bring their own seating to matches. Refreshment facilities are available in a number of tents to the south-east of the playing area opposite the clubhouse for the public. A press tent, scorers' tent and a Gloucestershire C C C souvenir caravan is situated on the ground.

There is no special area for disabled spectators, who may park cars in a position to view the cricket but are advised to request a suitable position in advance. Toilets are available in the clubhouse and in a couple of temporary facilities around the ground. The scorebox is situated at the Hatherley Lane End of the ground. A number of sponsors' marquees are situated on the football pitch at the Redgrove Park End of the ground.

The playing are is 150 metres by 140 metres and is approximately circular in shape. When required, the TV camera/commentary box would be positioned at the Hatherley Lane End on a gantry facility above the sightscreen.

GROUND RECORDS AND SCORES

No previous Gloucestershire C C C matches have been staged at this venue.

HOW TO GET THERE

Rail   Cheltenham Spa (BR), 1 mile.
Bus   Cheltenham & District F or G from BR Cheltenham Spa Station to Hatherley Lane; 97 or 98 from town centre to Hatherley Lane or 94 from town centre to Golden Valley, approximately 10 minutes walk (Telephone: 0242 522021).
Car   From north: M5 junction 11, then A40 Cheltenham and town centre, at first roundabout take right for Hatherley Lane, follow road for approximately 500 m, the ground is on the left hand side with a concealed entrance about the Dowty factory complex; or A4019 or A435 to town centre then as east. From east: A436 or A40, then follow signs Cheltenham and town centre, then A40 and Gloucester (M5 junction 11), then take left at roundabout for Hatherley Lane, then as north. From west: M5 junction 11, then as north; or A46 or A435 to town centre, then as east. From south: M4 junction 15, then A419, A417 and B4070 or A435 signposted Cheltenham and town centre, then as east.

WHERE TO STAY AND OTHER INFORMATION

Golden Valley Hotel (0242 232691), Queen's Hotel (0242 514724) George Hotel (0242 35751), Carlton Hotel (0242 514453), Park Place Hotel (0242 525353).

Disabled Areas   No special area, request suitable position, car parking available within ground.
Local Radio Station(s)   BBC Radio Gloucestershire (104.7 MHz FM/865 KHz MW), Seven Sound (102.4 MHz FM/774 KHz MW).
Local Newspaper(s)   Gloucestershire Echo, Cheltenham News, Gloucestershire County Gazette, The Source.

Cheltenham (Town)

Gloucestershire C C C first played a first-class match at the Cheltenham Victoria Ground on 27–29 June 1923 when the visitors were Glamorgan. The last first-class match with a county was on 23–24 June 1937 against Kent and the only other first-class match to have been staged on this ground since was a match staged on 10–12 May 1986 between Gloucestershire and the touring Indians.

The Victoria Ground is situated to the north-east of the Cheltenham town centre and is the home of the Cheltenham Town Cricket Club who field three XIs throughout the season and have a midweek XI and junior teams.

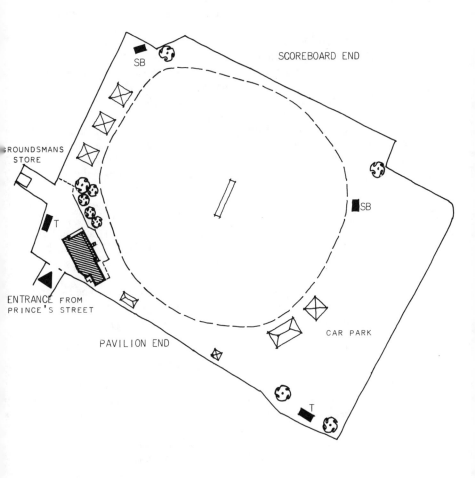

SCOREBOARD END

SB

GROUNDSMANS
STORE

SB

T

ENTRANCE FROM
PRINCE'S STREET

CAR PARK

PAVILION END

T

N

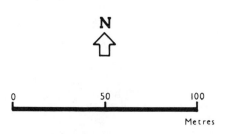

0   50   100

Metres

Cheltenham Town C C play in the Famous Grouse Western Cricket League and have won the league on three occasions (in 1976, 1979 and 1985). The club reached the National Club knockout final at Lord's in 1970 for the Derrick Robins Trophy and in 1978 for the John Haig Trophy. The club has also during the period from 1970 to date won the Seven Counties League, Gloucestershire County knockout Cup and the Gloucester Federation Indoor Sixes competition.

On 13 June 1986 the ground was used for an ICC World Cup qualifying match between Holland and Canada. The Midlands Club Cricket Conference have used the facilities at the Victoria Ground for matches with the MCC in previous years.

The ground is owned by Cheltenham Town C C and during the summer of 1991 an auction was arranged to raise funds for ground improvements by selling cricket memorabilia; the pavilion is to be enlarged and furnished with new changing rooms and a balcony. The improvement in standards should enable Gloucestershire C C C to return to this attractive and well maintained ground.

Ground records include an innings of 252 n.o. by A.G. Dipper and 166 by T. Cook for Sussex together with wickets by Tom Goddard, Charlie Parker and F. Ryan. The ground capacity is 4,500 and the best crowd was 4,750 for match with Glamorgan in 1923.

ADDRESS Cheltenham Town Cricket Club, The Pavilion, The Victoria Cricket Ground, Prince's Street, Cheltenham, Gloucestershire.

TELEPHONE NUMBER PROSPECTS OF PLAY   0242 523364

DESCRIPTION OF GROUND AND FACILITIES

The ground is entered from Prince's Street by players'/officials and all spectators. Limited car parking is available to the south-east of the playing area and in adjoining streets.

The only permanent buildings on the ground are the pavilion, toilets, groundsman's store and scoreboard. For county matches additional temporary seating is provided together with refreshment tents, bars, sponsors' marquees and a Gloucestershire C C C souvenir supporters' caravan. The press and scorers' tents are situated close to the pavilion next to the umpires cabin. The members' enclosure spans from in front of the pavilion to the south-east side of the playing area.

The playing area is approximately 127 metres by 134 metres and is circular in shape. The ground is bounded by residential housing on all four sides and there are a number of trees planted within the enclosed ground.

GROUND RECORDS AND SCORES

FIRST-CLASS MATCHES
Highest innings total for County: 481 *v*. Glamorgan 1923
Highest innings total against County: 406 by Sussex 1927

Lowest innings total for County: 112 *v*. Derbyshire 1931
Lowest innings total against County: 54 by Glamorgan 1924
Highest individual innings for County: 252 n.o. A.G. Dipper *v*.
Glamorgan 1923
Highest individual innings against County: 166 T. Cook for Sussex
1927
Best bowling performance in an innings for County: 9 for 21 T.W.
Goddard *v*. Cambridge University 1929
Best bowling performance in an innings against County: 7 for 40 F.
Ryan for Glamorgan 1926
Best bowling performance in a match for County: 16 for 109 C.W.L.
Parker *v*. Middlesex 1930
Best bowling performance in a match against County: 12 for 90 F.
Ryan for Glamorgan 1926
Best attendance: 4,750 *v*. Glamorgan 1923

HOW TO GET THERE

Rail   Cheltenham Spa (BR), 1 mile.
Bus   Cheltenham & District which link with BR Cheltenham Spa
Station and town centre Bus Station (Telephone: 0242 522021) pass
close to the ground.
Car   From north: M5 junction 10, then A4019 follow signs
Cheltenham and town centre, ground situated in Prince's Street off
King's Road and Hale's Road to the north-west of the town centre, or
A435 to town centre. From east: A436 or A40 then follow signs
Cheltenham and town centre, then as north. From west: M5 junction
11, then follow A40 Cheltenham and town centre, then as north.
From south: M4 junction 15, then follow A419, A417 and B4070 or
A435 to Cheltenham and town centre, then as north

WHERE TO STAY AND OTHER INFORMATION

Queen's Hotel (0242 514724), George Hotel (0242 35751), Carlton
Hotel (0242 514453) Park Place Hotel (0242 525353).

Disabled Areas   No special area, request suitable position; car
parking available within the ground.
Local Radio Station(s)   BBC Radio Gloucestershire (104.7 MHz
FM/865 KHz MW), Seven Sound (102.4 MHz FM/774 KHz MW).
Local Newspaper(s)   Gloucestershire Echo, Cheltenham News,
Gloucestershire County Gazette, The Source.

Lydney

Gloucestershire C C C made their first visit to Lydney on 24–27 August 1963 for a county championship match with Surrey. The first Limited-overs match was on 29 June 1969 against Sussex in the John Player Sunday League. The last first-class match was on 28 and 30 June 1969 against Sussex. Gloucestershire C C C played a total of eight John Player Sunday League matches at the Recreational Trust Ground off Swan Road between 1969 and 1975. A match was scheduled with Essex in 1977 but was transferred to Gloucester. Gloucestershire may again visit Lydney in 1992 for a Sunday League Match.

The first mention of cricket in Lydney was in 1862 when Charles Bathurst the first captain and club president staged a match at Lydney Park on the delightful ground owned by his family. The first ground was made available by the Squire of Lydney, the Rev. William Hiley Bathurst, the father of the club captain. When the Lydney Mansion was constructed in 1875 it was necessary for the ground to be moved to a new venue within the park. The wicket was exceptionally good and many famous players visited the ground, including E.M. Grace, G.L. Jessop, W.R. Hammond and C.W.L. Parker. The second ground was used until 1939 and the pavilion was taken down and reconstructed by the North Foreland School. After the Second World War the club moved to a third ground in Bathurst Park and soon afterwards in 1949 moved to their present home venue, the Lydney Recreation Trust Ground. The original pavilion was moved to the new ground. A tree is sited within the boundary, and the towering spire of St Mary's Church can be seen from the ground behind the trees and shrubs. The Lydney Rugby Football Club ground is also sited near the cricket ground.

During the early years of the club its official name was Lydney and Aylburton Cricket Club. A number of 'House' cricket matches were staged at Lydney and the following players made visits: J.H. Brain, W.H. Brain, E.A. Nepean, W.D. Llewellyn and V.T. Hill. E.M. Grace 'The Little Doctor' and later in life 'The Coroner', had a most memorable association with the club when not playing for the County Club. He scored 133 n.o. against Thornbury on 15 May 1888 at Alveston. In 1938 Reg Sinfield's XI staged a match with Lydney and included in the side were Charlie Parker, B.H. Lyon, Jack Crapp and Alec Kennedy. Other benefit matches have been staged for Charles Barnett, Monty Cranfield, Jack Crapp, Tom Graveney and Arthur Milton. The Tom Graveney Benefit match in 1969 attracted a crowd of 5,000.

Lydney C C field three XIs throughout the season and play in the Verderers' Cup competition and Three Counties League. The club play against both Gloucestershire and Welsh-based teams together with a number of clubs from other parts of the UK who maybe on tour in the Forest of Dean.

The wicket is traditionally good although in 1959 Bomber Wells described it as The Burma Road! Lydney is a proud club and the names of Bathurst, Jones, Jarrett and James stand out in the club annals.

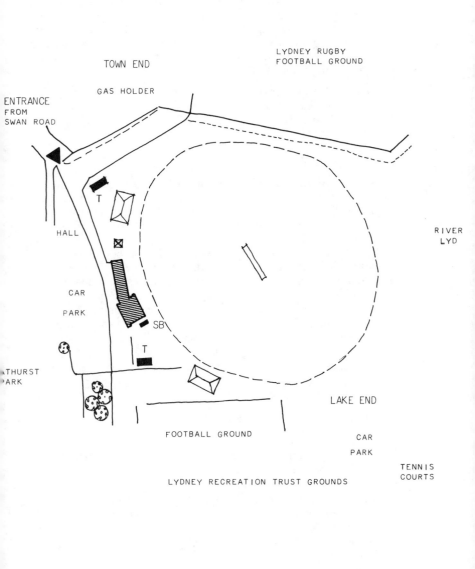

LYDNEY RUGBY
FOOTBALL GROUND

TOWN END

GAS HOLDER

ENTRANCE
FROM
SWAN ROAD

RIVER
LYD

HALL

T

CAR
PARK

SB

T

THURST
PARK

LAKE END

FOOTBALL GROUND

CAR
PARK

TENNIS
COURTS

LYDNEY RECREATION TRUST GROUNDS

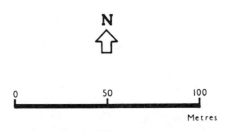

N

0   50   100

Metres

The club chairman is Mr Peter James and his son Stephen P. James has represented Lydney C C, Cambridge University C C and is currently on the staff with Glamorgan C C C. Only one player has represented club and county, that being Hugh Jones in 1914, who died on Armistice Day. Other notable players who have represented the club have included Graham 'Burgie' Burgess and Brian Rajadurai the Sri Lankan leg spinner who toured England in 1988.

ADDRESS Lydney Cricket Club, The Pavilion, Recreational Trust Ground, Swan Road, Lydney, Gloucestershire.
TELEPHONE NUMBER PROSPECTS OF PLAY Temporary line, call Directory Enquiries

DESCRIPTION OF GROUND AND FACILITIES

The ground is entered from Swan Road, off the High Street and some car parking is available to the south of the playing area and in Bathurst Park adjoining. The only permanent buildings on the ground are the single-storey pavilion and dining room, the scoreboard, groundsmans store and toilets.

The playing area is flat with a tree sited within the boundary and the dimensions of the playing area are 138 metres by 122 metres. The playing area is defined by a rope and some advertising boards. The majority of seating is temporary and this includes, in addition to benches which are provided, some plastic seats and raised seating areas.

Facilities include marquees and tents for the sponsors' enclosure, refreshments, beer and a Gloucestershire C C C souvenir supporters caravan. The ground capacity is 5,000 and seating is provided for 25 per cent so spectators would be advised to take their own collapsible seating to all matches.

GROUND RECORDS AND SCORES

FIRST-CLASS MATCHES
Highest innings total for County: 330 for 7 dec. *v*. Derbyshire 1964
Highest innings total against County: 320 by Derbyshire 1964
Lowest innings total for County: 87 *v*. Yorkshire 1965
Lowest innings total against County: 88 by Sussex 1969
Highest individual innings for County: 132 R.B. Nichols *v*. Derbyshire 1964
Highest individual innings against County: 103 n.o. P.M. Walker for Glamorgan 1967
Best bowling performance in an innings for County: 8 for 34 D.A. Allen *v*. Sussex 1969
Best bowling performance in an innings against County: 7 for 38 D. Lloyd for Lancashire 1966
Best bowling performance in a match for County: 10 for 47 D.A. Allen *v*. Sussex 1969
Best bowling performance in a match against County: 10 for 114 D. Lloyd for Lancashire 1966
Best attendance: 4,500 *v*. Lancashire 1966

LIMITED-OVERS MATCHES
Highest innings total for County: 185 for 6 *v*. Glamorgan (JPL) 1971
Highest innings total against County: 220 for 6 by Middlesex (JPL) 1970
Lowest innings total for County: 82 *v*. Hampshire (JPL) 1974
Lowest innings total against County: 48 by Middlesex (JPL) 1973
Highest individual innings for County: 73 R.B. Nichols *v*. Northamptonshire (JPL) 1970
Highest individual innings against County: 83 G.M. Turner for Worcestershire (JPL) 1972
Best bowling performance for County: 4 for 11 J. Davey *v*. Glamorgan (JPL) 1975
Best bowling performance against County: 5 for 13 D.A. Marriott for Middlesex (JPL) 1973
Best attendance: 4,000 *v*. Worcestershire (JPL) 1972

HOW TO GET THERE

Rail   Lydney (BR), 2 miles.
Bus   From surrounding areas to Lydney. Also buses link Lydney with Chepstow, Monmouth, Cinderford and Gloucester.
Car   From north: B4234 or A48, signposted Lydney and town centre, then follow Swan Road, off the High Street near Lydney Rugby Football Club Ground and Bathurst Park for the Recreational Trust Ground. From east: M4 junction 22, then follow A48 via Chepstow for Lydney and town centre, then as north. From west: B4231 or A48 signposted Lydney and town centre, then as north. From South: A48 signposted Lydney and town centre, then as north.

WHERE TO STAY AND OTHER INFORMATION

The Speech House, Forest of Dean (0594 822607), the George, Chepstow (0291 625363.

Disabled Areas   No special area, request suitable position; car parking available within ground.
Local Radio Station(s)   BBC Radio Wales (882 KHz MW), BBC Radio Cymru (93.1 MHz FM/882 KHz MW) BBC Radio Gloucestershire (104.7 Mhz FM/865 KHz MW) Severn Sound (102.4 MHz FM/774 KHz MW).
Local Newspaper(s)   Gloucestershire Echo.

Moreton-in-Marsh

Gloucestershire C C C travel once a season to the Cotswold village of Moreton-in-Marsh to play a limited-overs match. The first visit was made in 1884 when a first-class match was staged with Yorkshire. The county club also played at Batsford Road during the period 1885–88 and again in 1914 but not until the introduction of one-day cricket did Gloucestershire C C C return. The first limited-overs match at Moreton-in-Marsh was a Benson & Hedges Cup match with Hampshire in 1972. Since then one match has been staged each season in the Sunday League, usually in June or late August at this attractive village venue.

In 1991 the Refuge Assurance Sunday League match with North-amptonshire lasted for just one ball bowled by Alan Walker and must be the shortest match ever contested by these two teams. A freak thunderstorm hit the ground just after play commenced. It is hoped that on 12 July 1992 when Northamptonshire will again be the visitors to Batsford Road that the weather is better!

The ground is the home of the Moreton-in-Marsh Cricket Club which was founded in 1856. In that year, having no pavilion, members decided to purchase a tent to serve the purpose. The decision is recorded in the club's minute book which is still kept in the pavilion today. Although the club do not own their own ground they now have a fine pavilion and the fifteen acres of land on which the cricket pitch, hockey pitches and tennis courts are situated still costs the same annual fee that they have paid for as long as anyone can remember. There is a plaque on the pavilion which states 'To the memory of Stanley Frederick, chairman of this club 1952–69 by whose effort and industry this pavilion was built'. Originally the land was owned by Baron Redesdale, a farmer (a local hostelry in the High Street still bears his Coat of Arms) and at one time the ground was the property of the Freeman-Mitford family. Whoever owned the land, however, cricket still continued.

The Moreton-in-Marsh C C has spent money on improving the drainage system but after heavy rain the field tends to be waterlogged and boggy in places. At the rear of the pavilion is Queen Victoria's Garden. The only entrance to the ground is from Batsford Road past the Cricket Lodge House which overlooks the field of play. Crowds have been good at Moreton-in-Marsh, for locals tend to support matches well and 3,500–4,000 can be expected on a fine day. Moreton-in-Marsh draws many visitors as Gloucestershire C C C usually select northern or midlands opponents to visit Batsford Road and this improves greatly the attendance from these areas on what would be expected if the match was arranged at Bristol. Moreton-in-Marsh is closer to Edgbaston, Worcester and Northampton than the County's Bristol headquarters.

In the early years of Gloucestershire's visits to Moreton-in-Marsh there were some outstanding performances, including 227 n.o. by Arthur Shrewsbury for Nottinghamshire and 116 by H.V. Page against Somerset. Not until a hundred years later in 1985 did a Gloucestershire player score a century on the ground. This was in a John Player Sunday League match, when Bill Athey hit 121 n.o. against neighbours Worcestershire. In 1888 Lord Harris took his Kent side to Batsford Road and suffered the mortification of seeing them dismissed for 28 in an hour and a half when Woof (5 for 18) and Roberts (5 for 8) dismissed them. In their second innings Kent only managed 52. Gloucestershire won by an innings and 44 runs.

Ground records for limited-overs matches include Gloucestershire's

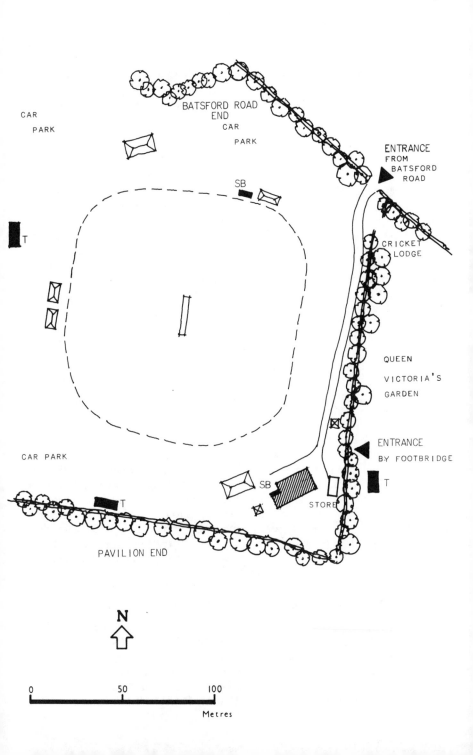

CAR PARK

BATSFORD ROAD END
CAR PARK

SB

T

ENTRANCE FROM BATSFORD ROAD

CRICKET LODGE

QUEEN VICTORIA'S GARDEN

ENTRANCE BY FOOTBRIDGE

T

CAR PARK

SB

STORE

T

PAVILION END

N

0   50   100
Metres

highest innings total of 269 for 8 made against Kent in 1988 and centuries recorded against the home county by Alvin Kallicharran and Wayne Larkins. Best bowling performances have been achieved by David Graveney and Peter Sainsbury who has acted as coach for Hampshire C C C in recent seasons.

ADDRESS   Moreton-in-Marsh Cricket Club, The Pavilion, Batsford Road, Moreton-in-Marsh, Gloucestershire GL56 OJD.
TELEPHONE NUMBER PROSPECTS OF PLAY   0608 50190/ 50178

DESCRIPTION OF GROUND AND FACILITIES

The main entrance to the ground for all pedestrians and vehicles is from Batsford Road. There is also a pedestrian entrance only via the footbridge from Queen Victoria's Garden near the pavilion. The only permanent building on the ground is the pavilion which comprises changing facilities for players and a dining area and bar/refreshment facilities for members. There is also a groundsman's store to the rear and a scoreboard built within the pavilion structure. The members' enclosure is in front of the pavilion and, as with all the seating around the ground, is at ground level. All the facilities are temporary including the toilets, an additional scoreboard and a Gloucestershire C C C souvenir supporters' tent and table. Refreshments for members and the public are also available in two large marquees near the tennis courts to the west of the playing area. The TV camera/commentary box and radio commentary van are located at the pavilion end close to the sightscreen. Both sightscreens are temporary as the club sightscreens are rather old and are not up to standard for county matches since the ground is surrounded by a number of trees and bushes. A press/scorers' tent is situated close to the temporary main scoreboard at the Batsford Road End of the ground near the entrance. Car parking is available within the ground and also surrounding the seats which are usually 2–3 deep around the playing area. Cricket can therefore be viewed from the car. Space is available for approximately 2,000 cars and the ground capacity is 6,000 but seating is provided for only 15 per cent. Spectators are advised strongly to take their own seats to all matches. Car parking is also available in the adjacent show field or off the High Street which is only a short walk away through Queen Victoria's Garden over the foot bridge. The playing area is circular in shape, 126 metres by 132 metres and is defined by a rope and several advertising boards.

GROUND RECORDS AND SCORES

FIRST-CLASS MATCHES
Highest innings total for County: 448 *v.* Somerset 1885
Highest innings total against County: 430 by Nottinghamshire 1886
Lowest innings total for County: 96 *v.* Worcestershire 1914
Lowest innings total against County: 28 by Kent 1888
Highest individual innings for County: 116 H.V. Page *v.* Somerset 1885

Highest individual innings against County: 227 n.o. A. Shrewsbury for Nottinghamshire 1887
Best bowling performance in an innings for County: 7 for 28 W.A. Woof *v.* Somerset 1885
Best bowling performance in an innings against County: 9 for 38 A.J. Conway for Worcestershire 1914
Best bowling performance in a match for County: 12 for 50 W.A. Woof *v.* Somerset 1885
Best bowling performance in a match against County: 15 for 87 A.J. Conway for Worcestershire 1914
Best attendance: 4,000 *v.* Worcestershire 1914

LIMITED-OVERS MATCHES
Highest innings total for County: 269 for 8 *v.* Kent (RAL) 1988
Highest innings total against County: 258 for 6 by Warwickshire (JPL) 1979
Lowest innings total for County: 70 *v.* Hampshire (BHC) 1972
Lowest innings total against County: 109 for 7 by Nottinghamshire (RAL) 1987
Highest individual innings for County: 121 n.o. C.W.J. Athey *v.* Worcestershire (JPL) 1985
Highest individual innings against County: 101 A.I. Kallicharran for Warwickshire (JPL) 1979/W. Larkins for Northamptonshire (RAL) 1989
Best bowling performance for County: 4 for 23 D.A. Graveney *v.* Worcestershire (JPL) 1976
Best bowling performance against County: 4 for 17 P.J. Sainsbury for Hampshire (BHC) 1972
Best attendance: 4,500 *v.* Worcestershire (JPL) 1979

HOW TO GET THERE

Rail   Moreton-in-Marsh (BR), 1.25 miles.
Bus   Pullhams Buses from surrounding areas to Terminal in village centre, then 5 minutes walk.
Car   From north: A429, follow signs Moreton-in-Marsh, ground situated north of main High Street off Batsford Road, turning into Batsford Road adjoining railway bridge at top end of High Street, on northern village outskirts. From east and west: A44 follow signs Moreton-in-Marsh, then as north. From south: A429 follow signs Moreton-in-Marsh, then as north.

WHERE TO STAY AND OTHER INFORMATION

Manor House Hotel (0608 50501), Redesdale Arms (0608 50308), White Hart Royal Hotel (0608 50731).

Disabled Areas   No special area, request suitable position. Car parking available within ground in a position from which the cricket may be viewed.

Local Radio Station(s)   BBC Radio Gloucestershire (104.7 MHz
FM/865 KHz MW) Severn Sound (102.4 MHz FM/774 KHz MW)
BBC Radio Oxford (95.2 MHz FM/1485 KHz MW).
Local Newspaper(s)   The Citizen, Gloucestershire County Gazette,
Gloucestershire Echo, Evesham Journal, Cotswold Standard.

Swindon

Proud tenant of a ground it fairly claims to be one of the best in the west
of England, Swindon Cricket Club was formed in 1844 when home and
away fixtures were played with Malmesbury. In 1990 Swindon C C
celebrated 100 seasons at their present home, the County Ground.

In 1844 the club's home ground was in the area where Upham Road
now is. It was in this era that one of the most famous cricketers ever to
represent Swindon C C, E.H. Budd, played, in 1848 at the age of 63 he
took 10 wickets in a match against Stroud C C. In the prime of his career
E.H. Budd played for the Gentlemen against the Players during the
period 1806–30. In 1849 the club moved to a ground in the Greywethers
Avenue area of the town; records indicate that during this period the
club had no pavilion and instead used tents. 1860 saw Swindon C C
merge with the Swindon Rangers Football Club; they played at a ground
called the Sands in the Goddard Avenue area. In the early 1890s a small
group of businessmen formed a company with a capital of £700 to
acquire and develop the club's 5.5-acre present headquarters at the
County Ground. It was at this time that the Great Western Railway C C
and Swindon C C combined to form Swindon C C as we know it today.
The new club moved to the present ground in 1895. In the first year
Bobby Reynolds scored 192 against Chippenham C C, to this day the
highest individual innings on the ground.

Another feat was that of Billy Overton who played regularly for
Wiltshire C C C and in 1903 was the first bowler to take 100 wickets in a
Minor Counties season. He helped Wiltshire to secure the Championship in 1902 and 1909, the last time they won it. Playing for the MCC
against the club in 1903 he took 6 for 3 as Swindon were dismissed for
just 10. Other Swindon players to have made significant contributions to
Minor Counties cricket were Ted Nash and Bert Lloyd. Ted Nash kept
wicket for the county and made almost 200 appearances, Bert Lloyd is
best remembered for his 196 against Surrey second XI at the Oval when
he is alleged to have tamed the Bedser twins.

In 1940 the County Ground was requisitioned by the War Department and became a temporary prisoner-of-war camp. The ground is
located at the rear of Swindon Town Football Club and was first used by
Gloucestershire C C C in 1970 when a John Player Sunday League
match was staged with Sussex. Not until fifteen years later in 1985 did
Gloucestershire C C C return, this time again for a Sunday League
match when the opponents were again Sussex. In 1986 Essex were the
visitors and on this occasion Allan Border the Australian captain, who

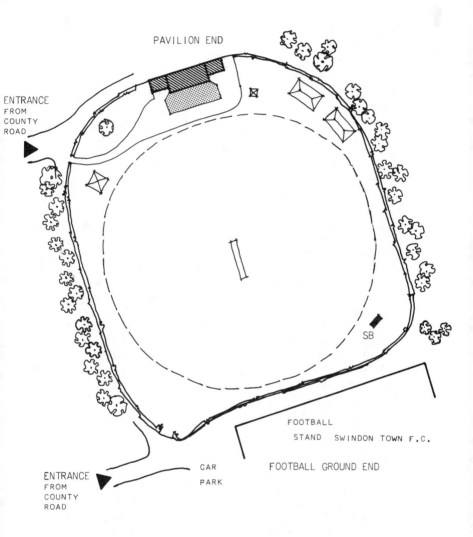

PAVILION END

ENTRANCE
FROM
COUNTY
ROAD

SB

FOOTBALL
STAND   SWINDON TOWN F.C.

FOOTBALL GROUND END

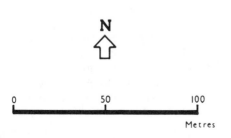

ENTRANCE
FROM
COUNTY
ROAD

CAR
PARK

N

0   50   100

Metres

was playing for Essex, opened the new scorebox. In 1987 Sussex made another visit, this time for a Refuge Assurance Sunday League match. In 1973 Swindon C C hosted a Minor Counties (South) Benson and Hedges Cup zonal match with Gloucestershire. Gloucestershire won by 7 wickets thanks to 43 by Sadiq Mohammad and 3 for 15 by John Mortimore.

In 1988 Warwickshire were due to visit and a Benson & Hedges Cup zonal fixture was also planned between Minor Counties C.A. and Worcestershire, but these two matches had to be rearranged at Bristol and Old Hill C C in the West Midlands because the pitch had been damaged by weedkiller. The ground is also used by Wiltshire C C C for Minor County Championship matches; in recent years National Westminster Bank Trophy 1st Round matches have been staged with Leicestershire and Northamptonshire. In 1967 the Minor Counties C.A. staged a match with the touring Pakistanis. This was the first important match at the County Ground.

The ground was not used again by Gloucestershire C C C until 1990 when the visitors for a Refuge Assurance Sunday League match were Sussex, their fourth visit to Swindon. In 1991 the opponents were neighbours Hampshire and Swindon played host to a match full of runs. Paul Terry scored 123, and half centuries were recorded by Richard Scott 77 against his former County, Bill Athey 85 and Tony Wright 60 n.o. On 14 June 1992 the visitors will be Kent for a Sunday League match.

Crowds at the County Ground have usually been 2,500–3,500. In 1984 3,500 people attended the Wiltshire C C C National Westminster Bank Trophy tie with Leicestershire and were rewarded by a knock of 155 by James Whittaker. The best Gloucestershire crowd was 3,000 against Hampshire in 1991.

ADDRESS Swindon Cricket Club, The Pavilion, The County Ground, County Road, Swindon, Wiltshire.
TELEPHONE NUMBER PROSPECTS OF PLAY 0793 23088

DESCRIPTION OF GROUND AND FACILITIES

The County Ground is entered from County Road where there are two entrances. The pavilion, which includes first floor seating for members as well as two large groundsman's stores, is situated at the northern end of the ground, close to the bowling club. The ground is over-shadowed by the back of the large Swindon Town Football Stand and tall floodlight pylons to the south of the playing area. The members' enclosure is in front of the players pavilion and close to the sponsors' marquees and members'/public beer tent and refreshment area. There are a number of temporary toilets and at least two or three rows of seats and benches surrounding the playing area which are transported for the day from Bristol. There is a new scoreboard in the south-east corner and the TV camera/commentary box is sited directly behind the bowler's arm at the Football Ground End. A press and scorers' tent is situated close to the pavilion near the Gloucestershire C C C secretary's caravan. A secondary scoreboard is sited in the pavilion for county matches. Car parking is available close to the pavilion for players and officials and to the west side of the football ground about 200 yards from the ground for members and the public.

The ground is sited close to the recreation ground and athletics track but is enclosed by trees and a hedge to the east and housing and hedges to the west and north. The playing area is 148 metres by 142 metres and is defined by a rope and some advertising boards.

GROUND RECORDS AND SCORES

LIMITED-OVERS MATCHES
Highest innings total for County: 281 for 2 *v*. Hampshire (RAL) 1991
Highest innings total against County: 255 for 6 by Hampshire (RAL) 1991
Lowest innings total for County: 115 for 5 *v*. Sussex (JPL) 1985
Lowest innings total against County: 128 for 1 by Sussex (JPL) 1985
Highest individual innings for County: 85 C.W.J. Athey *v*. Hampshire (RAL) 1991
Highest individual innings against County: 123 V.P. Terry for Hampshire (RAL) 1991
Best bowling performance for County: 3 for 25 M.J. Proctor *v*. Sussex (JPL) 1970
Best bowling performance against County: 3 for 11 Imran Khan for Sussex (JPL) 1985
Best attendance: 3,000 *v*. Hampshire (RAL) 1991

HOW TO GET THERE

Rail Swindon (BR), 0.75 mile.
Bus Thamesdown 7, 16, 17 or 18 from BR Swindon Station also Swindon TPT from surrounding areas to Bus Station thence 0.5 mile walk (Telephone: 0793 23700).
Car From north: A419, A361 or A420 to town centre, ground situated off County Road adjoining Swindon Town F C From east: A420 to town centre, then as north, or M4 junction 15, then follow A419 and A4253 to town centre, then as north. From west: M4 junction 16, then follow signs Swindon and town centre, then as north. From south: A361 or A345 to Swindon and town centre, then as north.

WHERE TO STAY AND OTHER INFORMATION

Goddard Arms (0793 692313), Wiltshire Hotel (0793 28282).

Disabled Areas No special area, request suitable position; car parking available within the ground.

Local Radio Station(s)   GWR Radio (96.3 MHz FM/1260 KHz MW).

Local Newspaper(s)   Swindon Evening Advertiser, Swindon Messenger, Wiltshire Star, Wiltshire Gazette and Herald, The Citizen, Gloucestershire Echo.

Trowbridge

The Trowbridge Cricket Club was established in 1840 and the first match at the present headquarters, the County Ground, was played against the Bath Association on 11 May 1895 when the Trowbridge Captain was F.W. Stancomb, whose name figures large in the club history.

Having played for Harrow School in 1879–80 he returned to Trowbridge and was elected captain for the 1882 season. There then followed a period which must be unique in cricket history in that F.W. Stancomb retained the captaincy of the club for fifty years. In addition to being one of the club's main benefactors F.W. Stancomb played for, and was later chairman, then president of the Wiltshire C C C His service to Trowbridge C C is commemorated by the club badge which is an amalgamation of the Coat of Arms of the Stancomb family and that of the old Trowbridge Urban District Council.

Trowbridge C C for some years played teams from Wiltshire, south Gloucestershire and north Somerset but not until the rise of league cricket did the club join the Wiltshire Cricket League. In 1981 the club became a founder member of the Wessex Cricket League and when it appeared that the league standard was poor the club also joined the improved County Alliance League. The club were first and second XI champions in 1985.

1981 saw the formation of the Trowbridge Cricket and Sports Club which incorporates the West Wiltshire Hockey Club and Trowbridge Ladies Hockey Club. During the 1980s major renovation work costing in excess of £40,000 was carried out on the pavilion together with improvements to the playing facilities. In 1986 an adjoining field was leased to provide a second ground and this serves as a car parking area for county/important matches.

The club fields three XIs throughout the season together with a popular youth section with over one hundred members. The club reached the Under-15 XI NCA Harry Secombe Cup National Finals in 1985.

The County Ground was first used for an important match in 1987 when Wiltshire staged a National Westminster Bank Trophy 1st round tie with Yorkshire. In 1988 the Minor Counties C A hosted a match with the touring West Indians which attracted a crowd of 3,500; Carl Hooper, who will be playing for Kent in 1992, scored 140 n.o. and little Gus Logie made 100. Thanks to the support and fine facilities the MCCA followed with a similar tour match with the 1989 Australians,

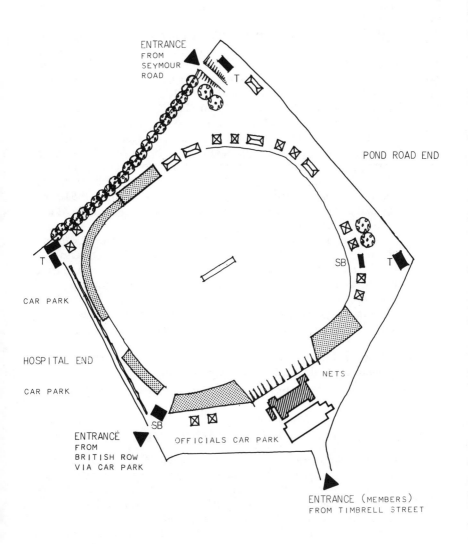

ENTRANCE
FROM
SEYMOUR
ROAD

T

POND ROAD END

CAR PARK

T

SB

T

HOSPITAL END

CAR PARK

NETS

ENTRANCE
FROM
BRITISH ROW
VIA CAR PARK

SB

OFFICIALS CAR PARK

ENTRANCE (MEMBERS)
FROM TIMBRELL STREET

N

0   50   100

Metres

Geoff Marsh scoring 110 and the Australians winning by 27 runs, which attracted the ground's best crowd of 4,000. Also in 1989 Gloucestershire C C C staged their first match on the ground, a Refuge Assurance Sunday League match with near neighbours Hampshire. Gloucestershire won by 21 runs.

1990 saw a Wiltshire National Westminster Bank Trophy 1st Round match with Surrey, who won by 9 wickets thanks to 93 n.o. by Chris Bullen and a three-day first-class MCCA match with the Indian tourists which was drawn. Centuries were recorded in this match by Gary Brown of Durham, brother of K.R. of Middlesex (103), Ravi Shastri (105) and Indian Test skipper Mohammad Azharuddin (105). In 1991 the ground was used by the MCCA for two Benson & Hedges Cup zonal group matches with Glamorgan and Hampshire. Glamorgan won by 17 runs with Ravi Shastri, again showing his liking for the wicket at Trowbridge, scoring 138 n.o. and Hampshire won by 8 wickets thanks to 78 n.o. by Chris Smith, now Marketing Manager for the Western Australian Cricket Association, and 70 n.o by Julian Wood. On 28 June 1991 a one day match was staged between the League Cricket Conference XI and the touring West Indians.

The ground capacity is 5,500 and the best crowd to date was against the Australians in 1989. The club celebrated its 150th anniversary in 1990. Trowbridge C C is certainly a splendid ground by out ground standards and in 1990 MCCA secretary Mr David Armstrong stated that 'the arrangements at Trowbridge have always been wholly admirable' and it is for that reason that important matches have been staged at this ground rather than at larger venues.

ADDRESS Trowbridge Cricket Club, The Pavilion, County Cricket Ground, Timbrell Street, Trowbridge, Wiltshire.

TELEPHONE NUMBER PROSPECTS OF PLAY   0225 752538

DESCRIPTION OF GROUND AND FACILITIES

The main entrance to the ground is from Timbrell Street to the rear of the pavilion for players, officials and members. There are two further entrances to the south-west of the playing area from British Row through the car park at the Hospital End and to the north-east of the ground from Seymour Road. The ground is bounded by tall poplar trees to the north and housing to the east with the Trowbridge Hospital situated close by at the western end of the ground.

Car parking is available for 400 cars at the Hospital End in an adjacent field. Local street parking is also available within close proximity of the ground. The only permanent buildings on the ground are the attractive two storey black and white pavilion situated to the south of the playing area at right angles to the wicket and a scoreboard situated close to the entrance from British Row.

For county matches approximately 3,750 temporary seats are provided together with one large plastic raised seating area. It is not necessary for members of the public to bring their own seating to matches. The members' enclosure is situated in front of the pavilion and the eastern Pond Road End of the ground is available for sponsors where a number of coloured marquees are located. Refreshment and bar facilities are available for members in the pavilion and in the two tents situated close to the secondary scoreboard near the cricket nets. Refreshments for the public are located in the north-west corner of the ground. Toilets are situated in the pavilion and in temporary facilities at three corners of the ground. A scorers' caravan and Gloucestershire C C C souvenir supporters' caravan are situated near the main scoreboard. The press box is situated within the pavilion as is the sponsors' and committee balcony which provides the best view of the play.

The playing area is 132 metres by 115 metres and the wicket is situated in a west-east disposition. The playing area is defined by a rope and advertising boards. A first aid tent is available near the pavilion and facilities for radio commentary are on the pavilion balcony. When required, the TV camera/commentary box is situated at the Hospital End of the ground.

GROUND RECORDS AND SCORES

LIMITED-OVERS MATCH
Highest innings total for County: 184 for 8 v. Hampshire (RAL) 1989
Highest innings total against County: 163 by Hampshire (RAL) 1989
Highest individual innings for County: 41 n.o. A.J. Wright v. Hampshire (RAL) 1989
Highest individual innings against County: 66 K.D. James for Hampshire (RAL) 1989
Best bowling performance for County: 3 for 38 P. Bainbridge v. Hampshire (RAL) 1989
Best bowling performance against County: 4 for 30 M.C.J. Nicholas for Hampshire (RAL) 1989
Best attendance: 3,500 v. Hampshire (RAL) 1989

HOW TO GET THERE

Rail Trowbridge (BR), 1 mile.
Bus Trowbridge Bus Station situated in Market Place 1 mile from ground services; 264 and 265 link Trowbridge town centre with Bath and pass close to ground.
Car From north: A363, signposted Trowbridge, ignore signs to Trowbridge which by-pass Bradford-on-Avon town centre, take right into Stancomb Avenue and left at 'T' junction then second right into Timbrell Street for Trowbridge C C From east: B3106 signposted Trowbridge and town centre, then follow signs Staverton/Holt and Canal Road Industrial Estate for ground in Timbrell Street. From west: A366 signposted Trowbridge and town centre, then as east. From south: A363 signposted Trowbridge and town centre, then as east.

WHERE TO STAY AND OTHER INFORMATION

Gordons Hotel (0225 752072), Hilbury Court Hotel (0225 752949), Polebarn Hotel (0225 777006), or stay in Bath.

Disabled Areas Special area situated in front of the pavilion, request suitable position.
Local Radio Station(s) GWR Radio (97.2 MHz FM/1161 KHz MW).
Local Newspaper(s) Wiltshire Times, Bath & West Evening Chronicle, Western Daily Press, Bristol Evening Post.

HAMPSHIRE

SOUTHAMPTON

BASINGSTOKE

BOURNEMOUTH

PORTSMOUTH

Hampshire

Founded 12 August 1863
Colours Blue, gold and white
Crest Tudor rose and crown
President W.J. Weld
Chairman D. Rich
Chairman cricket committee J.R. Gray
Chief executive A.F. Baker FCA
County coach T.M. Tremlett
Marketing manager M.N.S. Taylor
Captain M.C.J. Nicholas
Groundsman N. Gray
Scorer 1st XI V.H. Isaacs
Scorer 2nd XI A.E. Weld
Statisticians V.H. and R.V. Isaacs
Sponsors Brooking Knowles & Lawrence Chartered Accountants
Newsletter *Hampshire News*
Address County Cricket Ground, Northlands Road, Southampton, Hampshire SO9 2TY.
Telephone 0703 333788/333789
Facsimile 0703 330121
Hampshire Rapid Cricketline 0891 567506

ACHIEVEMENTS

County Championship Champions (2) 1961 and 1973
Gillette Cup Semi-Finalists (2) 1966 and 1976
National Westminster Bank Trophy Winners (1) 1991; semi-finalists (6) 1983, 1985, 1987, 1988, 1989 and 1990
Benson & Hedges Cup Winners (1) 1988; semi-finalists (2) 1975 and 1977
John Player Sunday League Champions (3) 1975, 1978 and 1986
Refuge Assurance Sunday League 5th 1990
Fenner Trophy Winners (3) 1975, 1976 and 1977; joint winners (1) 1980
Asda Trophy Winners (2) 1984 and 1986
Tilcon Trophy Winners (1) 1976
Ward Four Counties Knockout Competition Winners (1) 1990

GROUNDS

Southampton (County Cricket Ground, Northlands Road) Bournemouth (Dean Park, Cavendish Road) Basingstoke (May's Bounty, Bounty Road) and Portsmouth (United Services Officer's Sports Ground, St Michael's Road)
   No other grounds have been used since 1969.

No additional grounds are used for second XI matches.

Contrary to widely-held beliefs cricket's beginnings were in the Weald of Kent and Sussex, and not on Broadhalfpenny Down, but in the mid-1700s Hambledon's fame was unsurpassed. From John Nyren's writings, it would seem, the men of Hampshire enjoyed their cricket. 'The punch,' recorded Nyren, 'would make a cat speak. Sixpence a bottle. Ale that would flare like turpentine. Twopence per pint'.

By 1793 Hambledon had given way to a Hampshire County Club, and by 1895 Hampshire had first-class status. No serious impact was made until the arrival from The Oval of Philip Mead, all-rounder Newman, bowler Kennedy and the character and man of all parts George Brown, in turn batsman, opening bowler and wicket-keeper. All gave yeomen and brilliant service until the 'thirties. Another pre-First War acquisition was C.B. Fry, who had taken charge of the training ship *Mercury* in the Hamble.

Mead scored 48,892 of his career's 55,061 runs for Hampshire, and as he was the very devil to get out, his emergence from the pavilion is said to have provoked more unseemly language from fielders than any other batsman in history. For a batsman who scored 153 centuries, including four for England, in twenty-six innings, oddly he never overcame his nervousness in the 'nineties. But having completed a hundred he would turn to the wicket-keeper and say: 'That's another bag of coal for the winter.'

Life under the captaincy of the 3rd Baron Tennyson, captain from 1919 to 1933, was recalled by H.L.V. Day, rugby international and amateur batsman. He would cajole, harangue, curse or applaud as the fancy took him, and had a habit of sending telegrams to batsmen at the wicket couched in language less flowery than his grandfather's poetry. After being felled by a fast ball at Trent Bridge, Day recovered to read: 'What do you think your – bat's for – Lionel.' A young amateur had the message: 'For God's sake get out and let someone else take a hundred off this jam.'

An occasional amateur, having an unhappy experience fielding on the boundary of Portsmouth, painfully exposed his inexperience by calling to his captain at the end of an over: 'And where do you want me now, Lionel?' The answer arrived loud and clear – but he remained on the field!

Day was invited in 1922 to travel with his captain from Southampton to Birmingham, a journey interrupted by visits to several country houses and ending as dawn was breaking. The next morning Hampshire were bowled out for 15 (Mead 6 not out) and following on 208 behind, made 521 at the second attempt, and won by 155 runs.

Tennyson was undaunted by adversity or speed merchants, and he is best remembered for the way he stood up to Gregory and McDonald during Australia's triumphant 1921 tour. After a brave 74 not out in the

SOUTHAMPTON

M. D. MARSHALL

second Test Tennyson was appointed captain. A year before odds of 1,000 to one against such a happening had been offered and taken!

With the passing of the grand old guard Hampshire suffered lean seasons leading up to the Second World War. Arnold was the most consistent batsman, and joined the elite of double cricket and soccer internationals. Rogers was another fine opener, always on the edge of honours.

The path to the glory of Hampshire's first championship in 1961 – the first after sixty-six seasons – was laid by Desmond Eagar, a captain-secretary of utter devotion to his club's cause. During his years Shackleton from Todmorden was changed from a moderate spinner-batsman into one of the most dangerous bowlers in the country at medium pace. His career ended with 2,857 wickets at only 18.65 apiece, and his new ball partnership with Cannings was consistently successful.

The gods were kind to Colin Ingleby-Mackenzie, Eager's successor. He inherited mustard-keen fielders, and though Cannings had left, Shackleton bowled with as much guile as ever and his new partner, White, was genuinely fast. Batting was powerful, and headed by Marshall, who exhibited all the exciting freshness of a player bred on Barbadian pitches. Horton, Gray, Livingstone, the captain himself, and all-rounder Sainsbury were just right for an apostle of brighter cricket, who thrived on declarations. At the time there was an experiment disallowing the follow on, and the engaging Ingleby-Mackenzie was a past master at judging situations. He also hit the right note in his attitude to the players and, if his declared discipline – nothing more than to have the players assembled at breakfast – was a leg pull, he had the knack of leadership. He was not to taste the fruits of victory again, but at least left his mark on Yorkshire when Shackleton, White and Cottam between them dismissed Yorkshire on a lively pitch at Middlesbrough for 23, their lowest total ever.

Twelve years later Richard Gilliat, no less enterprising, led a side, originally rated as no better than a fifty to one prospect, to Hampshire's

C. P. MEAD

BROWN, G.

HAMPSHIRE

D. SHACKLETON

second county title. By then Barry Richards, the world's leading batsman from South Africa, and Gordon Greenidge, born in Barbados but a product of a Reading School, had been taken aboard. Later Andy Roberts, one of the breed of West Indies fast bowlers, spearheaded the attack, and, in due course, he was replaced by Malcolm Marshall.

As captain from 1971 to 1978 Gilliat had a championship, a second snatched from him by rain, and two victories in the Sunday League, to underscore Hampshire's strength. A third in the 40-over competition came to Mark Nicholas, who also broke the ice of Hampshire's failures to knock-out competitions by winning the Benson & Hedges Cup in 1988 – without the formidable assets of Greenidge and Marshall, who were otherwise engaged to the discomforture of England.

Not all Gilliat's triumphs were due to the presence of star quality. The championship was won with a supposedly weak attack. Taylor, Herman, Mottram and all-rounder Jesty made that prediction look silly. There was the evergreen Sainsbury, batsman Turner, and wicket-keeper Stephenson to emphasize the team spirit. Stephenson went on to the captaincy, and preserved the wicket-keeping tradition of McCorkell and Harrison, as did Parks, the latest in the line from the noted Sussex family of cricketers.

During the 1989 and 1990 seasons Malcolm Marshall took 64 and 72 wickets. David Gower joined Hampshire in 1990 and during his second season guided his new county to the National Westminster Bank Trophy against Surrey at Lord's in 1991. Mark Nicholas was unable to captain as he had broken a finger during an earlier match. Robin Smith was on Test duty for much of the season and in the absence of Marshall the overseas replacement was Aaqib Javed from Sheikhupura, Pakistan.

Southampton

The County Cricket Ground at Northlands Road, which was opened on 9 May 1885 by the Countess of Northesk, wife of the then president of the club, was the third ground to be played on in the city. The ground was leased for an annual payment of £160 with the condition that a pavilion be built. This was done and £2,000 was raised before the grand opening and a match between North and South Hampshire took place afterwards. The first county match was with Derbyshire in 1885 and the initial first-class match with the MCC in the same season. In 1893 the Hampshire County Ground Company was founded and purchased the freehold of the ground from Sir Edward Hulse for £5,400. A football stand used to be sited close to where the main pavilion and offices are located and in 1896/97 Southampton Football Club used the ground for home matches. With crowds of over 12,000 the facilities were inadequate and after a couple of seasons the club moved to their present ground at The Dell approximately 10 minutes walk away. In 1896 the present pavilion frontage was built, together with a ladies pavilion adjacent. Further building took place in 1900 and 1911, the football stand was redeveloped and a scoreboard was built opposite the members' pavilion. The ground has also been used for hockey and at the now City End of the ground, formerly the Bannister Park End, was Bannister Park Speedway Stadium. This has now been replaced by housing. Facilities for tennis and bowling are still available behind the indoor school which was built in 1958.

After World War Two donations were invited for ground improvements but the £10,927 raised was insufficient to carry out all the works envisaged. The 1960s saw the link between the two pavilions built and the present bell installed from the old Cunard liner *Athlone Castle*. There were no further major developments until in 1982 the Hampshire Squash and Sports Club was built, comprising squash courts, sauna, jacuzzi and solarium, and was opened in April 1983. The Desmond Eagar Room can be found on the first floor and is used for hospitality suites during county matches. The most recent addition in 1986 was the Philip Mead Stand which provides hospitality boxes close to the club offices and next to the cricket nets for executive members.

Hampshire have played over 550 matches on the ground and over 130 limited-overs matches since 1885. In 1985 they celebrated 100 years of County Cricket at Northlands Road. It is said the ground is worth over several million pounds and in the 1990s the county club will move from Northlands Road to a new greenfield site to the east of the city.

Ground records at Northlands Road have included double centuries from Philip Mead and L.C.H. Palairet. 1990 saw Hampshire's highest innings total on the ground against Sussex. In limited-overs matches, a total of 371 for 4 against Glamorgan in the Gillette Cup, including 177 by Gordon Greenidge in 1975, will be long remembered, as will Mike Proctor's spell of 6 for 13 for Gloucestershire to gain a Benson & Hedges final place at the expense of the home side in 1977. Other celebrations at

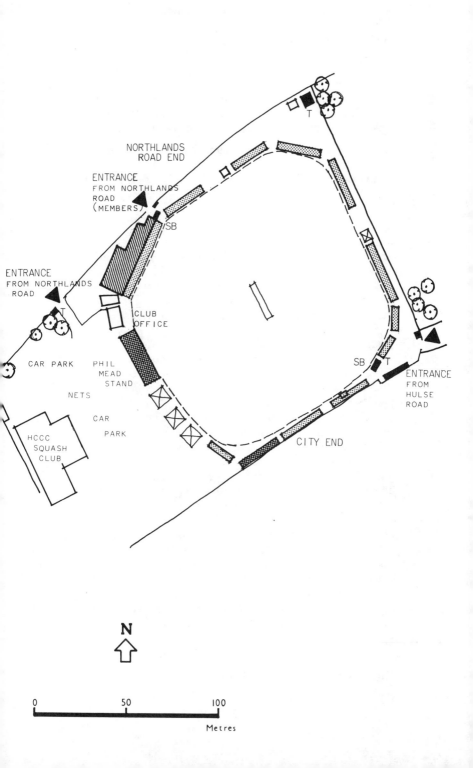

NORTHLANDS
ROAD END

ENTRANCE
FROM NORTHLANDS
ROAD
(MEMBERS)

SB

ENTRANCE
FROM NORTHLANDS
ROAD

T

CLUB
OFFICE

CAR PARK

PHIL
MEAD
STAND

NETS

CAR
PARK

HCCC
SQUASH
CLUB

SB

T

ENTRANCE
FROM
HULSE
ROAD

CITY END

N

0   50   100

Metres

Southampton were Hampshire's championship in 1973 and the Prudential Cup match in 1983 between Australia and Zimbabwe, the only international ever staged on the ground.

Crowds at the County Ground have been good; 5,000–6,000 is not unusual and limited-overs matches seem to attract the most; some 7,500 were present for the Gillette Cup semi-final with Northamptonshire in 1977 as was a similar crowd for the NatWest semi-final with Middlesex in 1989. The largest crowd recorded was 15,000 for the visit of the 1934 Australians. The present ground capacity is set at about 7,000.

ADDRESS   County Cricket Ground, Northlands Road, Southampton, Hampshire SO9 2TY.
TELEPHONE NUMBER PROSPECTS OF PLAY   0703 333788/ 333789

DESCRIPTION OF GROUND AND FACILITIES

The main access to the Southampton ground is on Northlands Road. There is a pedestrian entrance from Hulse Road. Car parking is available within the ground for members but in the main it is necessary to park in adjoining streets or on the nearby common. The main permanent buildings are the pavilion, the club offices and the new executive suite of boxes. There is tiered seating on the north-east and south of the ground, while the west side is used for entertainment and tents. The members' enclosures are those directly in front of the club offices and the pavilion. The main scoreboard is in the south-west corner of the ground with a smaller secondary scoreboard adjoining the pavilion. The scorers' and press boxes can be found on the first floor of the club offices. Hampshire C C C provide a caravan and souvenir table which is also taken to the other out grounds when matches are staged away from Southampton. While both the pavilion and the new canvas-roofed executive suite are attractive buildings, the old members' entrance gate adjoining the pavilion is also an important feature. Southampton is a small ground of about 130 metres by 128 metres defined by advertisement boards. The players' accommodation is modest and housed in a small two-storey building wedged between the pavilion and the club offices. The ground is now much overshadowed by residential housing and the flats on the east side appear at first sight to be part of the ground, so close are they to the boundary. You are advised to bring you own seats to important matches. Only one small public stand on the south side is roofed, allowing some cover if the weather is poor.

Ask club officials if you wish to see the items of historic interest, including various items of cricket memorabilia, that are displayed on the staircase of the club office.

GROUND RECORDS AND SCORES

FIRST-CLASS MATCHES
Highest innings total for County: 600 for 8 *v.* Sussex 1990

Highest innings total against County: 708 for 7 dec. by Australians 1921
Lowest innings total for County: 30 *v.* Nottinghamshire 1932
Lowest innings total against County: 32 by Kent 1952
Highest individual innings for County: 280 n.o. C.P. Mead *v.* Nottinghamshire 1921
Highest individual innings against County: 292 L.C.H. Palairet for Somerset 1896
Best bowling performance in an innings for County: 8 for 24 A.S. Kennedy *v.* Gloucestershire 1924
Best bowling performance in an innings against County: 9 for 40 W. Mead for Essex 1900
Best bowling performance in a match for County: 14 for 171 C.B. Llewellyn *v.* Worcestershire 1901
Best bowling performance in a match against County: 17 for 119 W. Mead for Essex 1900
Best attendance: 15,000 *v.* Australians 1935

LIMITED-OVERS MATCHES
Highest innings total for County: 371 for 4 *v.* Glamorgan (GC) 1975
Highest innings total against County: 319 for 2 by Somerset (BHC) 1987
Lowest innings total for County: 99 *v.* Kent (NWBT) 1984
Lowest innings total against County: 82 by Wiltshire (GC) 1973
Highest individual innings for County: 177 C.G. Greenidge *v.* Glamorgan (GC) 1975
Highest individual innings against County: 155 n.o. M.D. Crowe for Somerset (BHC) 1987
Best bowling performance for County: 7 for 30 P.J. Sainsbury *v.* Norfolk (GC) 1965
Best bowling performance against County: 6 for 13 M.J. Proctor for Gloucestershire (BHC) 1977
Best attendance: 7,500 *v.* Northamptonshire (GC) 1976

HOW TO GET THERE

Rail   Southampton Central (BR), 1 mile.
Bus   Hampshire Bus 47, 147 Southampton-Winchester and Solent Blue Line 48 Southampton-Eastleigh all pass within 0.25 mile of the ground (Telephone: 0962 52352).
Car   From north: M3 to junction 10, then follow A33 Southampton and city centre, ground situated in Northlands Road off The Avenue (A33), west of Southampton Common and 0.75 miles north of the city centre, or A3037 and A35 to city centre. From east: M27 junction 5, then follow signs Southampton and city centre, A35 and A33, then as north. From west: M27 junction 3 then M271, A35; or A3024 follow Southampton and city centre, then as north.

WHERE TO STAY AND OTHER INFORMATION

Northlands Hotel (0703 333871), Dolphin Hotel (0703 226178), The Polygon (0703 330055), Forte Post House Hotel (0703 330777).

Disabled Areas   No special area, request suitable position.
Local Radio Station(s)   BBC Radio Solent (96.1 MHz FM/1359 KHz MW), Radio Victory (95.0 MHz FM/1170 KHz MW).
Local Newspaper(s)   Evening Echo & Hampshire Chronicle, Southern Evening Echo, The News, Southampton Advertiser, Southampton Guardian, Portsmouth News.

Basingstoke

The May's Bounty Ground is the home of Basingstoke and North Hants Cricket Club founded, in 1865, member of both the Thames Valley and Hampshire cricket leagues. The club celebrated 125 years in 1990 and produced a splendid brochure and tie. Cricket has been played in Basingstoke since 1817, but the Folly or May's Bounty Ground was not used for cricket until 1855. The club was created by John May as president after the Gents of Basingstoke C C was disbanded in 1864, 24 years after it was formed. Cricket has been played at May's Bounty ever since. In 1880 John May purchased the land in order to prevent building taking place on the ground and in 1885 the Basingstoke Athletic Club was formed with cricket, football and cycling sections. This reflected poor support for cricket, but in 1893 cricket interest increased and the cricket club was reinstated. In 1901 the club's title was changed to its present name. The ground was purchased in 1950 for £450 freehold and the cricket club became the proprietor of one of the finest cricket grounds in the county for an absurdly low price.

The original pavilion was built in 1877 and was a single-storey thatched building. It was replaced in 1901 by the present building which had subsequent additions in 1965, in 1974 (two squash courts), in 1979 (a further club room and kitchen) and, in 1986 a third squash court, committee/snooker room and general club office.

The ground is also used by London Welsh and Odiham hockey clubs through the winter months. During the cricket season matches have been staged for Victoria C C, Basingstoke Total Abstinence C C, Queen Mary's School and the Hampshire Police. Hampshire C C C first staged a match at May's Bounty in 1906 when Warwickshire were the visitors. Over thirty-five visits have been made since then and over twenty limited-overs matches have been staged including a Gillette Cup match against Lincolnshire in 1967 and John Player Sunday League/Refuge Assurance Sunday League fixtures. Today Hampshire C C C take one championship and one limited-overs match to this, the most northerly ground in the county, usually in early June. John Arlott OBE, who was born in Basingstoke, witnessed his first cricket match at May's Bounty and in 1938 played his one and only game for the club. In 1974 Colin

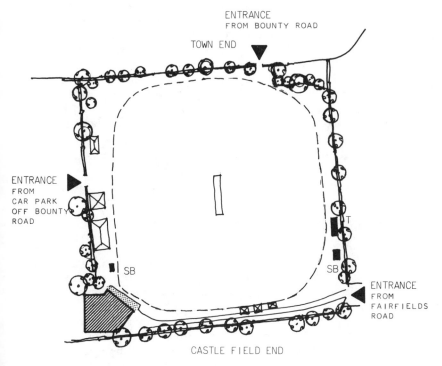

ENTRANCE
FROM BOUNTY ROAD

TOWN END

ENTRANCE
FROM
CAR PARK
OFF BOUNTY
ROAD

SB

T

SB

ENTRANCE
FROM
FAIRFIELDS
ROAD

CASTLE FIELD END

CAR PARK

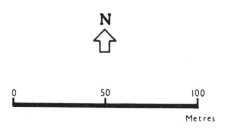

N

0   50   100

Metres

Cowdrey was hit while batting by West Indian fast bowler Andy Roberts, after he mistimed a hook. He fell onto his stumps and retired from the match. Another accident in 1990 saw Paul Downton the Middlesex wicket keeper suffer an eye injury from a flying bail and a season later he had to retire from the game due to this accident. At May's Bounty in 1991 after batting for Lancashire Graeme Fowler described the wicket as 'being constructed like shredded wheat'; the Basingstoke groundsman provided Fowler with a bowl of cereal the following morning after his comments in the press.

Crowds are good at May's Bounty, usually 3,500–4,500. The 4,300 crowd for the Warwickshire John Player Sunday League match in 1977 was one of the largest. Ground records have included 204 n.o. by Alan Jones for Glamorgan and a match winning bowling performance from another Welshman, Malcolm Nash.

ADDRESS Basingstoke and North Hants Cricket Club, May's Bounty, Bounty Road, Basingstoke, Hampshire.
TELEPHONE NUMBER PROSPECTS OF PLAY   0256 473646

DESCRIPTION OF GROUND AND FACILITIES

Closely hemmed in by housing and community buildings, this is a small ground to which access is gained either from Fairfields Road or through the car park in a playing field off Bounty Road. There is a small entrance on Bounty Road for pedestrians but as the road has no footpath it is not used by many spectators.

The only permanent building is the pavilion which has been extended in recent years. The members' area in front of the pavilion provides a small area of tiered seating. The ground contains some benches but the vast majority of the seating is temporary and you are advised to bring your own seats to important matches. There is a small scoreboard on the east side of the ground but all other facilities are temporary. These include refreshment tents of various kinds, a press tent, scorers' tent and a series of temporary toilets. At the Castle Field End is the Hampshire C C C souvenir shop situated close to the scorers and boundary rope.

This is a small club ground with a playing area of 120 metres by 115 metres and the space behind the boundary boards is very limited on the east and north sides. There is, however, good tree planting on three sides of the ground, making it a pleasant venue at which to watch cricket. Some old photographs are displayed in the pavilion, which is a two storey building with a balcony for players to view the cricket.

GROUND RECORDS AND SCORES
FIRST-CLASS MATCHES
Highest innings total for County: 401 for 5 dec. *v.* Surrey 1986
Highest innings total against County: 461 by Cambridge University 1937
Lowest innings total for County: 61 *v.* Nottinghamshire 1936

Lowest innings total against County: 64 by Surrey 1986
Highest individual innings for County: 172 J. Arnold *v.* Cambridge University 1937
Highest individual innings against County: 204 n.o. A. Jones for Glamorgan 1980
Best bowling performance in an innings for County: 8 for 67 A. Jaques *v.* Derbyshire 1914
Best bowling performance in an innings against County: 9 for 56 M.A. Nash for Glamorgan 1975
Best bowling performance in a match for County: 14 for 105 A. Jaques *v.* Derbyshire 1914
Best bowling performance in a match against County: 14 for 137 M.A. Nash for Glamorgan 1975
Best attendance: 5,000 *v.* Surrey 1986

LIMITED-OVERS MATCHES
Highest innings total for County: 251 *v.* Glamorgan (JPL) 1974
Highest innings total against County: 226 for 8 by Warwickshire (JPL) 1973
Lowest innings total for County: 43 *v.* Essex (JPL) 1972
Lowest innings total against County: 114 by Glamorgan (JPL) 1974
Highest individual innings for County: 123 B.A. Richards *v.* Glamorgan (JPL) 1974
Highest individual innings against County: 85 A.I. Kallicharran for Warwickshire (JPL) 1977
Best bowling performance for County: 5 for 31 M.D. Marshall *v.* Kent (JPL) 1982
Best bowling performance against County: 5 for 32 D.L. Williams for Glamorgan (JPL) 1974
Best attendance: 4,300 *v.* Warwickshire (JPL) 1977

HOW TO GET THERE

Rail Basingstoke (BR), 0.75 mile.
Bus Hampshire bus 322/3/4 from BR Basingstoke Station to within 0.25 mile of ground (Telephone: 0256 464501).
Car From north: M4 junction 11, then A33 follow signs Basingstoke or M4 junction 12, then A4 and A340 follow signs Basingstoke, the ground is situated 0.5 mile from the town centre south-west of the town off the A30 Winchester Road in Bounty Road. From east: M3 junction 6, then follow signs Basingstoke and A30 Winchester Road, then into Bounty Road, or A30. From west: M3 junction 7 then follow signs Basingstoke, then as north. From south: A339 or A32 and A30 to Basingstoke, then as north.

WHERE TO STAY AND OTHER INFORMATION

Crest Hotel (0256 468181), Red Lion Hotel (0256 28525).

Disabled Areas No special area, request suitable position.

Local Radio Station(s)   Radio 210 (97.0 MHz FM/1431 KHz MW), County Sound (96.4 MHz FM/1476 KHz MW).
Local Newspaper(s)   Southern Evening Echo, The News, Basingstoke and North Hants Gazette.

Bournemouth

The ground at Dean Park was laid out in 1869 and the first match took place in 1871. It was one of the oldest cricket grounds in the county but is now in Dorset. The first county match to be staged was with Somerset in 1882. In 1897 the initial first-class match took place with the touring Philadelphians. A year later Somerset were the adversaries in the first County Championship match. In all over 330 matches have been played on the ground and over 65 limited-overs matches by the County Club.

In 1927 the County Club formed a company to take over the lease of the Bournemouth ground from the Cooper-Dean family and in 1948 the ground was taken under the direct control of the Hampshire C C C. Colonel R.A.W. Binny was appointed to manage the club facilities. Formerly part of the Cooper-Dean family estate, Dean Park was one of the few privately-owned cricket grounds. It is now named the Bourne-mouth Sports Club. The family continues to support the club and in 1974 Miss A. Ellen Cooper-Dean presented a new scoreboard. This is situated opposite the pavilion which was itself built in 1902. The ground, which is located in the northern suburb of the town, extends to 4.5 acres and is enclosed by fine trees and residential properties. The entrances are from Cavendish Road which is not easily found by those who are strange to the area.

Bournemouth is one of the most pleasant of Hampshire grounds and the county today stage three championship and at least two limited-overs matches on the ground; a first visit in May and then a cricket festival week in August while the holiday makers are at the south coast seaside resort. Dean Park was the ground where the county won the championship for the first time in 1961 and also where in 1978 they defeated Middlesex to win the John Player Sunday League. No doubt, players and supporters have fond memories of matches staged at Dean Park. The ground has been used by Dorset C C C for Minor Counties Championship matches and home matches in the NatWest Bank Trophy 1st round. In 1992 Hampshire the NatWest Bank Trophy holders for 1991, will meet Dorset at Southampton. Dean Park should not be confused with Bournemouth C C who play at Kinsor Sports Ground in the Northbourne district of the town.

W.G. Grace played in the first Bournemouth Festival Week on the ground in 1902. Such events at Bournemouth, however, tended to be less successful than the others of the time at Hastings and Scarborough. Ground records include big scores from R.H. Moore and Len Hutton and some splendid bowling performances from J.A. Newman and Derek Shackleton.

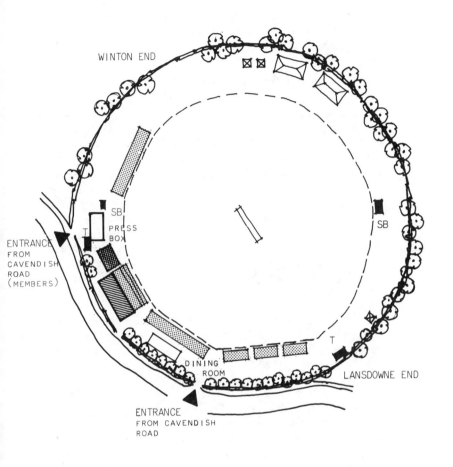

WINTON END

ENTRANCE
FROM
CAVENDISH
ROAD
(MEMBERS)

SB

T

PRESS
BOX

SB

T

DINING
ROOM

LANSDOWNE END

ENTRANCE
FROM CAVENDISH
ROAD

N

0   50   100

Metres

Bournemouth has seen good crowds with 5,000–6,000 expected for cricket weeks. The largest crowd was 15,000 for the first day of the Gloucestershire match in 1947.

ADDRESS Bournemouth Sports Club, The Pavilion, Dean Park, Cavendish Road, Bournemouth, Dorset.
TELEPHONE NUMBER PROSPECTS OF PLAY 0202 25872

DESCRIPTION OF GROUND AND FACILITIES

Main access to the Dean Park ground is from the western, Cavendish Road side of the ground where there are two entrances, one for members and cars and another for the public. The pavilion, adjoining covered stand, press/scorers' building and players' dining room are the only permanent buildings, together with a new scoreboard and enclosure of tiered benches adjoining the pavilion and groundsman's stores. The members' enclosure is on the west side in front of the pavilion and dining area. The remainder of the ground is open to the public. All the seating from the pavilion southwards towards the sightscreen at the Town End is permanent open raised timber seating. Refreshments are available in the pavilion on the ground floor for members and in temporary mobile facilities to the east close to the new scoreboard for the public. A further refreshment area, Hampshire C C C souvenir supporters caravan/table and sponsors' tents can be found at the northern Winton End of the ground.

The ground is enclosed by trees and the surrounding housing and is bounded by a tall hedge. The playing area is 140 metres by 135 metres roughly circular, and defined by a rope and advertising boards. Spectators are advised to bring their own seats to popular matches but members' seating is adequate for large crowds. Some 65 per cent of seating is supplied, of a ground capacity of 8,000. Toilets can be found in the pavilion and at the rear of the press building.

A fine view can be gained from the first floor of the pavilion next to the Hampshire secretary's office, one of the two areas of covered accommodation for spectators. Members can park inside the ground and there is plenty of street parking in the residential housing area close by.

GROUND RECORDS AND SCORES

FIRST-CLASS MATCHES
Highest innings total for County: 536 *v.* Warwickshire 1928
Highest innings total against County: 610 by Kent 1906
Lowest innings total for County: 31 *v.* Worcestershire 1965
Lowest innings total against County: 37 by Somerset 1956
Highest individual innings for County: 316 R.H. Moore *v.* Warwickshire 1937
Highest individual innings against County: 270 n.o. L. Hutton for Yorkshire 1947
Best bowling performance in an innings for County: 9 for 131 J.A. Newman *v.* Essex 1921

Best bowling performance in an innings against County: 9 for 93 S. Venkataraghavan for Indians 1971
Best bowling performance in a match for County: 14 for 99 D. Shackleton *v.* Warwickshire 1965
Best bowling performance in a match against County: 14 for 91 J.W.H.T. Douglas for Essex 1921
Best attendance: 15,000 *v.* Gloucestershire 1947

LIMITED-OVERS MATCHES
Highest innings total for County: 261 *v.* Yorkshire (GC) 1977
Highest innings total against County: 250 for 9 by Derbyshire (GC) 1963
Lowest innings total for County: 111 *v.* Derbyshire (JPL) 1978
Lowest innings total against County: 77 by Leicestershire (JPL) 1974
Highest individual innings for County: 132 n.o. B.A. Richards *v.* Kent (JPL) 1970
Highest individual innings against County: 119 n.o. N.E. Briers for Leicestershire (JPL) 1981
Best bowling performance for County: 5 for 32 T.E. Jesty *v.* Middlesex (JPL) 1978
Best bowling performance against County: 5 for 26 D.P. Hughes for Lancashire (JPL) 1970
Best attendance: 6,000 *v.* Middlesex (JPL) 1978

HOW TO GET THERE

Rail   Bournemouth (BR), 500m.
Bus   Numerous local services to with 0.25 mile of the ground.
Car   From north: M27 junction 1, then follow A31 and A338 follow signs County Cricket. Dean Park is situated 1 mile north of the seafront between the A347 Wimborne Road and B3064 Lansdowne Road. Dean Park is signposted from the A347 junction with the A338 or A348 and A341 to town centre, then Wimborne Road for County Cricket. From east: A35 to town centre then as north. From west: A31, A35, A350 or A341 to town centre, then as north.

WHERE TO STAY AND OTHER INFORMATION

Carlton Hotel (0202 22011), Beleveder Hotel (0202 21080), Pavilion Hotel (0202 291266), plus numerous small hotels and guest houses.

Disabled Areas   No special area, request suitable position.
Local Radio Station(s)   BBC Radio Solent (96.1 MHz FM/1359 KHz MW), Two Counties Radio (97.2 MHz FM/828 KHz MW), Ocean Sound (103.2 MHz FM/1557 KHz MW).
Local Newspaper(s)   Bournemouth Evening Echo, Southern Evening Echo, The News.

Portsmouth

The Burnaby Road Ground is the United Services Officers sports ground. It is used for services matches, including matches with touring sides, as it is now the only military ground used for first-class cricket. The ground is used by United Services Portsmouth Cricket Club established in 1880, who play in the Save and Prosper Southern Cricket League. The ground is shared with U S Portsmouth Rugby Football Club and there are facilities for tennis adjoining the club.

Hampshire's association with the United Services ground began in 1888 when they played Sussex. They did not use the ground again until they attained first-class status in 1895 when a solitary match was staged with Leicestershire. Since then matches have been played on the ground every year except 1975; some 300 first class matches have been staged by the county and over 40 limited-overs matches. Hampshire take two championship and one limited-overs match to the ground each year, usually in July for a Portsmouth Cricket Week. The first ever first-class match was staged in 1882 when the Australians played Cambridge Past and Present. In 1893 the Australians scored 843 against Cambridge and Oxford Past and Present; the innings lasted into a third day which was a record for first-class cricket at the time and still remains the highest ever score made by an Australian team in this country. The scorecard of this match is still displayed in the pavilion.

Behind the pavilion and across the road the railway runs between the Portsmouth & Southsea and Portsmouth Harbour Stations. Passing trains can be heard and seen from the ground. At the other end of the ground the Portsmouth Polytechnic buildings dominate the enclosed playing area, as does the U S club which was built in 1950 as a recreational and residential centre for services sport, principally for the Royal Navy.

Ground records for first-class matches include a number for Yorkshire, including Percy Holmes and Hedley Verity. Trevor Jesty hit 166 n.o. in a John Player Sunday League match against Surrey in 1983. Bobby Parks took 10 catches in a match against Derbyshire in 1981, who in 1990, the season they were to win the Refuge Assurance Sunday League, were dismissed for 61 in front of the Sky TV cameras. Derek Shackleton holds the record for the most wickets taken for Hampshire on the ground, both in a season and in a career.

Crowds today are usually around 5,000. The highest attendance was 10,000 for the championship match with Sussex in 1948.

ADDRESS   United Services Portsmouth Cricket Club, United Services Officers Sports Ground, Burnaby Road, Portsmouth, Hampshire.
TELEPHONE NUMBER PROSPECTS OF PLAY   0705 22351

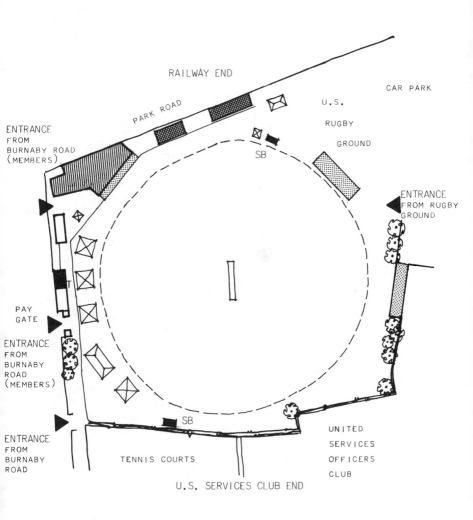

RAILWAY END

PARK ROAD

CAR PARK

U.S.

RUGBY

GROUND

ENTRANCE
FROM
BURNABY ROAD
(MEMBERS)

SB

ENTRANCE
FROM RUGBY
GROUND

T

PAY
GATE

ENTRANCE
FROM
BURNABY
ROAD
(MEMBERS)

ENTRANCE
FROM
BURNABY
ROAD

SB

TENNIS COURTS

UNITED

SERVICES

OFFICERS

CLUB

U.S. SERVICES CLUB END

N

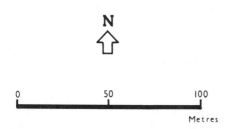

0	50	100

Metres

DESCRIPTION OF GROUND AND FACILITIES

Access to the ground is from Burnaby Road for members and through the King James Gate for the public, together with a pedestrian and car access point on the rugby ground. The King James Gate is one of the original city gates of Portsmouth. The main permanent buildings are the pavilion, club room/bar and the rugby club's two covered stands. There is some car parking on the rugby ground for members' but other car parking can be found in the city centre car parks and nearby adjoining streets. The Portsmouth Polytechnic car park can also be used if the building is closed out of term time.

The members' enclosure is on the north-west side of the ground in front of the pavilion and club room/bar area. The press box and Hampshire secretary's office can be found on the first floor of the club house. There are two scoreboards on the ground: the main one at the U S Officers Club End of the ground and a temporary secondary scoreboard next to the club shop on the rugby ground. There is temporary seating for about 2,500 so it is advisable to take your own seats to important matches. The scorers sit in a temporary caravan in front of the pavilion enclosure. The playing area is approximately circular and is 145 metres by 140 metres and is defined by advertising boards. The pitch is in a north-south position at an angle of 40 degrees to the pavilion. The toilets are in a permanent structure but all other facilities are temporary. There are no specific facilities for disabled persons, who are advised to ask for a suitable position on the ground, ideally near the pavilion. The Burnaby Road side of the ground is used for sponsors' tents and public seating. On the rugby ground there is a large open temporary raised seating area together with refreshment facilities and the Hampshire C C C souvenir caravan/table.

Portsmouth still boasts the heaviest of heavy rollers, weighing some 5.5 tons. The United Services Ground is a historic urban ground which is now overshadowed not only by the railway embankment to the Railway End but by the buildings of the Portsmouth Polytechnic and the central business district of the city.

GROUND RECORDS AND SCORES

FIRST-CLASS MATCHES
Highest innings total for County: 616 for 7 dec. *v.* Warwickshire 1920
Highest innings total against County: 585 for 3 dec. by Yorkshire 1920
Lowest innings total for County: 35 *v.* Middlesex 1922
Lowest innings total against County: 36 by Warwickshire 1927
Highest individual innings for County: 213 n.o. J.R. Gray *v.* Derbyshire 1962
Highest individual innings against County: 302 n.o. P. Holmes for Yorkshire 1920
Best bowling performance in an innings for County: 9 for 30 D. Shackleton *v.* Warwickshire 1960

Best bowling performance in an innings against County: 8 for 25 W. Andrews for Somerset 1947
Best bowling performance in a match for County: 13 for 86 M. Heath *v.* Sussex 1958
Best bowling performance in a match against County: 13 for 107 H. Verity for Yorkshire 1935
Best attendance: 10,000 *v.* Sussex 1948

LIMITED-OVERS MATCHES
Highest innings total for County: 292 for 1 *v.* Surrey (JPL) 1983
Highest innings total against County: 231 for 9 by Worcestershire (JPL) 1976
Lowest innings total for County: 113 *v.* Leicestershire (JPL) 1971
Lowest innings total against County: 61 by Derbyshire (RAL) 1990
Highest individual innings for County: 166 n.o. T.E. Jesty *v.* Surrey (JPL) 1983
Highest individual innings against County: 87 A. Kennedy for Lancashire (JPL) 1975
Best bowling performance for County: 5 for 13 M.D. Marshall *v.* Glamorgan (JPL) 1979
Best bowling performance against County: 6 for 22 R.R. Bailey for Northamptonshire (JPL) 1972
Best attendance: 5,000 *v.* Surrey (JPL) 1983

HOW TO GET THERE

Rail Portsmouth & Southsea (BR), 500m; Portsmouth Harbour (BR), 0.5 mile.
Bus From surrounding areas to The Hard Interchange, thence 0.5 mile.
Car From north: A3 or M3(M) follow signs Portsmouth and IOW Ferry Terminal, ground is situated in Old Portsmouth off the A3 London Road, close to the Guildhall and United Services' Sports Club. The ground is shared with USO Portsmouth Royal Navy. From east: A27 then A2030 signposted Portsmouth and Ferry Terminal. From west: M27 junction 12, then M275 follow signs Portsmouth harbour and Ferry Terminal, then as north.

WHERE TO STAY AND OTHER INFORMATION

Crest Hotel (0705 827651), Holiday Inn (0705 383151), Keppel's Head Hotel (0705 833231).

Disabled Areas No special area, request suitable position.
Local Radio Station(s) BBC Radio Solent (96.1 MHz FM/1359 KHz MW), Ocean Sound (103.2 MHz FM/1557 KHz MW).
Local Newspaper(s) Southern Evening Echo & Hampshire Chronicle, Portsmouth Evening News.

KENT

CHURCHMAN'S CIGARETTES

KENT.

CANTERBURY

DARTFORD

FOLKESTONE

MAIDSTONE

TUNBRIDGE WELLS

Kent

Founded   6 December 1870
Colours   Maroon and white
Crest   White horse on red background
Patron   HRH The Duke of Kent
President   D.S. Kemp
Chairman   P.H. Edgley
Chairman cricket committee   A.J.P. Woodhouse
Secretary   Brigadier S.T.W. Anderson OBE, MC.
Cricket administrator   B.W. Luckhurst
Commercial manager   P.J. Foster
Groundsman   B.A. Fitch
County coach   D.H. Foster
Captain   M.R. Benson
Scorer 1st XI   J. Foley
Scorer 2nd XI   C. Coultate
Statistician   H.R. Milton
Sponsors   Blue Circle
Newsletter   *Kent Calling*
Address   St Lawrence Cricket Ground, Old Dover Road,
Canterbury, Kent CT1 3NZ
Telephone 0227 456886
Facsimile 0227 762168
Kent Rapid Cricketline   0891 567507

ACHIEVEMENTS

County Championship   Champions (6) 1906, 1909, 1910, 1913,
1970 and 1978; Joint Champions (1) 1977
Gillette Cup Winners   (2) 1967 and 1974; finalists (1) 1971
National Westminster Bank Trophy   Finalists (2) 1983 and 1984
Benson & Hedges Cup   Winners (3) 1973 1976 and 1978; finalists
(2) 1977 and 1986
John Player Sunday League   Champions (3) 1972, 1973 and 1976
Refuge Assurance Sunday League   6th 1987
Fenner Trophy   Winners (2) 1971 and 1973
Tilcon Trophy   Finalists (1) 1980
Seeboard Trophy   Winners (1) 1990; finalists (1) 1989

GROUNDS

Canterbury (St Lawrence Cricket Ground, Old Dover Road)
Dartford (Hesketh Park, Pilgrims Way)   Folkestone (Folkestone
Sports Ground, Cheriton Road)   Maidstone (Mote Park, Willow
Way) and Tunbridge Wells (Nevill Cricket Ground, Warwick Park).

Other grounds that have been used since 1969 are: Blackheath

St Lawrence Cricket Ground from the air, reproduced by courtesy of the Kent Messenger

(Rectory Field, Charlton Road); Dover (Crabble Athletic Ground, Lewisham Road); Gillingham (Garrison Stadium, Marlborough Road); Gravesend (Bat and Ball Ground, Wrotham Road) and New Beckenham (Midland Bank Sports Ground, Lennard Road).

SECOND XI GROUNDS
In addition to the above mentioned grounds the following are used for second XI matches: Dover C C, Crabble Athletic Ground, Lewisham Road, Dover, Kent. Telephone: 0304 204452; Bowaters Sports Ground, Sittingbourne, Kent. Telephone: 0795 24411 Ext. 260; Orpington C C Sports Ground, Orpington, Kent. Telephone: 0689 34902; Gore Court C C, Sports Ground, Sittingbourne, Kent. Telephone: 0795 23813.

The story of Kent is the story of cricket. Long before the marriage of the Canterbury and Maidstone clubs produced the offspring of the county club in 1870, the famous Kent XI were hailed as the champions and the biggest attraction in the growing game. In 1744 Kent were powerful enough to take on All-England. Indeed three years later they played England three times and beat them three times. Kent were Hambledon's most serious rivals, and many were the epic struggles with Surrey.

The Canterbury festival, the father of all cricket weeks, began in 1842, and, on the present St Lawrence ground, in 1847. The beautiful game

CANTERBURY

FRANK WOOLLEY

with the beautiful name now had its most beautiful setting. A county's style and character is often the reflection of its environment, and, amid the marquees, tents and flowers of Canterbury, Maidstone, Tunbridge Wells and Dartford Kent have paraded a glittering host.

From Alfred Mynn, the first of cricket's heroes, Fuller Pilch and Felix, whose real name was Nicholas Wanostrocht, to J.R. Mason, A.P.F. Chapman, Frank Woolley, Leslie Ames, Doug Wright, Godfrey Evans, Colin Cowdrey, Derek Underwood, Alan Knott and the Pakistani Asif Iqbal, Kent have had actors to do honour to their stage.

For sixty years Kent was dominated by the powerful personality of the 4th Lord Harris, a formidable autocrat of the old school and a pillar of the establishment. He captained Kent from 1871 to 1889, England in the first home Test in 1880 and in Australia in 1878–79, was chairman, president and secretary of Kent, and president and honorary treasurer of MCC. Apart from spells as Governor of Bombay, Under-Secretary for India and Under-Secretary for War, his life was devoted to cricket. He ruled both amateur and professional, strictly but with impartiality, but only Lord Harris could have sent a dismissal notice to a wretched bowler half-way through an over in a county match!

A dependence on amateurs often led to erratic results as they were unable to make consistent appearances, and one of the most significant events – matched later only by the alliance of Ames and Cowdrey – was the setting-up of the Tonbridge nursery in 1897, which supplied a stream of high professional quality and more settled sides. The products included Woolley, 'Tich' Freeman, Humphries, Fielder, Seymour, Hubble the wicket-keeper – a position always in safe hands in Kent – and Fairservice. At last Kent were champions in 1906, Woolley's first season, and again in 1909, 1910 and 1913. In between they were twice 2nd and once 3rd.

Apart from Mason the bowling was professional, headed by Fielder, fast, and Blythe, classical slow left arm, and the batting mainly amateur and aggressive. Fielder's extra celebration in 1906 was to take all 10

L. Ames, 65

A. P. FREEMAN

H. T. W. HARDINGE

Gentlemen wickets, and in the following tour of Australia he had 25 wickets in the series.

In the sixteen seasons until he joined up in August 1914, never to return, Colin Blythe took 2,506 wickets, and in his last three seasons he headed the national averages. A violinist, he was of such a sensitive nature that he was forbidden by doctors to play in Test cricket after he had taken 100 wickets in 19 matches at only 18.63. A memorial to a much-loved cricketer stands at Canterbury.

With Blythe and Woolley together Kent enjoyed unrivalled spin. It is hard to credit that a batsman of such elegant flair to be compared with Australia's Victor Trumper and scorer of 58,969 and 145 centuries – an aggregate of runs exceeded only by Hobbs – was in the upper tier of slow left arm bowlers. Yet Woolley gave up bowling at the age of 35 with 2,068 wickets, twelve more than Wright – a statistic designed not to belittle Wright, an unlucky genius, but to underline Woolley's contributions. A cast-off line is his 1,018 catches, a comfortable record.

Bowlers of the class of Tate and Constantine confessed they could not bowl to the tall willowy figure, such was the range and invention of his strokes, nor curb his aggressive approach. On no fewer than thirty-five occasions he was out between ninety and ninety-five. 'I never gave a thought to the "nervous nineties"' he said on his retirement in 1938. 'We were never allowed to play for averages in Kent sides.'

Leslie Ames played in forty-seven Tests to Woolley's sixty-four, and maintained the fashion of wicket-keeper-batsman. In both departments Ames was remarkably successful, scoring 102 centuries and collecting 1,121 victims behind the stumps. The combination of Ames and Freeman, the 5ft 2ins leg spinner, whose aggregate was bettered only by Rhodes, was irresistible, but Kent owed as much to Ames the team-building secretary-manager as Ames the player.

Kent had often been in the hunt between the wars, but were too inconsistent to unseat Yorkshire, and from 1946 there were more disappointments than successes. The halcyon years seemed to belong to a long-distant past, but a new dawn broke in 1957 when the new captain Cowdrey linked with Ames the manager.

A brilliant era began with the winning of the Gillette Cup in 1967. That year and the next Kent were runners-up, and appropriately in 1970, their centenary year, the title justly went to Cowdrey – remarkably as they were bottom on 1 July. Kent were in the thick of all the competitions, sharing the title with Middlesex under the Pakistani Asif Iqbal in 1977, and in the following season Ealham, a superb fielder, who had taken over from Iqbal, then with Packer, did even better with the championship and the Benson & Hedges Cup for the third time.

Mike Denness, the Scot who captained England and formed an outstanding opening partnership with Luckhurst, had five years as Cowdrey's successor, twice winning both the Sunday League and the Benson & Hedges Cup in the same season. He also took the Sunday League and the 2nd position in the championship in 1972. Five other appearances in Lord's finals from 1971 to 1986 were further proof of the county's brilliant adoption of single innings cricket.

There have been few better batsmen than Cowdrey – at his best perhaps another Hammond – and he ended his distinguished career with a record 114 Tests, twenty-two centuries for England, and having rekindled Kent's pride. Moreover he saw his son, Christopher, carry the torch as captain of Kent and England.

Cowdrey, Wright, Evans, Knott, who added five Test centuries to his wicket-keeping prowess, and Underwood, with 2,465 wickets, including 297 for England, more than upheld the standards set by the Kent titans of bygone days. Having finished 2nd in the championship in 1988, Kent slumped to 15th in 1989 and 16th in 1990. With the introduction of Foster, the Western Australian coach, the position improved in 1991 to 6th. Mark Benson took over the captaincy from Chris Cowdrey in 1991. Steve Marsh scored a century and took eight catches in a match with Middlesex at Lord's in 1991 earning himself a place on the England 'B' tour of the West Indies. Alan Igglesden played one Test in 1989 at the Oval against the Australians.

Canterbury

The St Lawrence Cricket Ground in Old Dover Road was opened in 1847 and was known at that time as the Beverley cricket ground. This name came from the previous ground which was used by the club from 1841–46 and was situated beyond the cavalry barracks. The ground has been used for housing close to Vauxhall lakes and the nearby gravel quarry workings. The present name, the St Lawrence Cricket Ground, comes from the adjoining St Lawrence House which was originally the St Lawrence priory founded in 1137. The St Lawrence Ground is the only cricket ground in Kent that is owned by Kent C C C.

The pavilion was built in 1900 at a cost of £2,340 and was refurbished, enlarged and renamed on its existing site, the Stuart Chiesman Pavilion

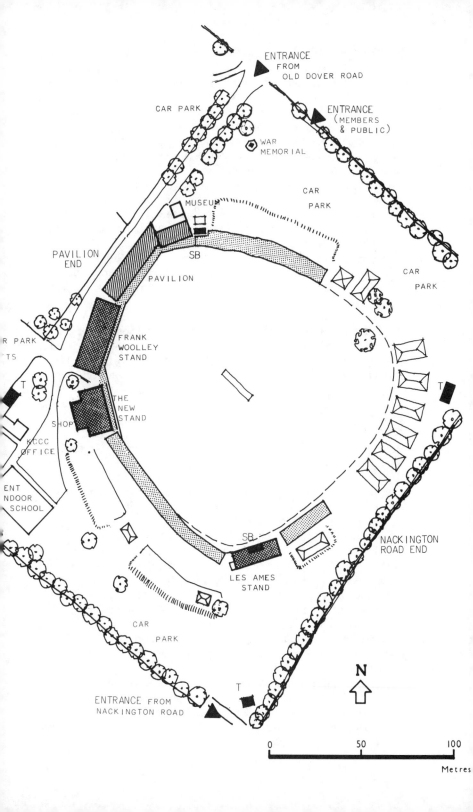

in 1970 as a result of the Club Centenary Appeal. The Iron Stand was constructed in 1897 and renamed the Leslie Ames Stand in 1973. It now accommodates sixteen private executive boxes and a new enlarged scoreboard. The concrete stand was built in 1926–27 and renamed the Frank Woolley Stand. The most recent addition is the New Stand which was built in 1986 at a cost of £600,000 and comprises two levels containing the Kent C C C souvenir shop and scorecards sales point at the rear with public bar and fast food restaurant on the ground floor. A dining room for members together with modern seating is also available and the top floor houses the Kent executive club and suite. Much of the funds to build the New Stand came from the Kent C C C Project '85 appeal. In 1990–91 the Howard Levett Kent Indoor Cricket School was demolished and during 1991–92 the Ames Levett Indoor Cricket School is being constructed by Abbott Construction, to include cricket nets, changing facilities and hospitality suites for use during county matches. A lime tree stands within the playing area on the Old Dover Road side of the ground and was once cleared by a hit from Learie Constantine, the only player to accomplish this feat.

Originally the ground formed part of the Winter's farm Estate, Nackington. It was bought from the landlord, Lord Sondes, for £4,500 in 1896. In addition to the games staged by Kent C C C the ground is also used by the Beverley C C, The St Lawrence & Highland Court C C formerly The St Lawrence C C established in 1864 with the specific purpose of making greater use of the ground and the 'F' Division of the Kent Police. The first match of importance staged on the ground was in early August; 1847 when Kent played England and won by 3 wickets. A Canterbury cricket festival is always staged in early August, the first was organized in 1848 and in recent years the Canterbury Festival has included two championship matches and two limited-overs matches together with a match against the tourists.

Crowds at Canterbury are usually 7,500–8,000. The ground capacity is now set at 14,000, which is usually reached for limited-overs matches of importance in whatever competition.

Ground records have included 344 by W.G. Grace for MCC in 1876, which was followed in matches against Nottinghamshire and Yorkshire with 177 and 318 n.o. respectively, a record 839 in three consecutive innings which still stands today. His younger brother E.M. took 10 for 92 and scored 192 n.o. for MCC against the Gentlemen of Kent in 1862. Frank Woolley hit the highest individual innings on the ground for Kent of 270 although in recent seasons Trevor Ward and Mark Benson have also recorded large double centuries. David Ward of Surrey made 263 in 1990 against the home county. 'Titch' Freeman, Doug Wright and in recent seasons Derek Underwood have also taken bowling records on their home ground. Limited-overs matches have seen significant performances by Chris Tavaré now the Somerset captain, Graeme Clinton, Derek Underwood and Don Wilson. In 1989 Kent made their highest innings total in limited-overs cricket on the ground when Dorset allowed the home side to accumulate 359 for 4 in 60 overs.

ADDRESS St Lawrence Cricket Ground, Old Dover Road, Canterbury, Kent CT1 3NZ.

TELEPHONE NUMBER PROSPECTS OF PLAY   0227 457323

DESCRIPTION OF GROUND AND FACILITIES

There are three entrances to the St Lawrence Cricket Ground, which are located in Nackington Road, with two in Old Dover Road for members, cars, and the public through the adjoining turnstiles. Ample car parking is available at most matches for members and the public although this depends on weather conditions. During Canterbury Festival week and Benson & Hedges or National Westminster Bank Trophy quarter and semi-finals space maybe limited to members only and there is an overflow car park off Nackington Road in the nearby school field. There is also limited street parking surrounding the ground and in city centre car parks approximately 15 minutes walk from the ground. Cricket can be viewed from your own car on the ring to the south but space is limited so you need to arrive early to take up these positions.

The Leslie Chiesman Pavilion, pavilion annexe, Leslie Ames enclosure, Frank Woolley Stand, ground floor and first floor of the New Stand are only available to members. The general public can sit anywhere else in the ground and can also pay a transfer charge at the ticket office for the day to enter the members' enclosures although this is restricted to certain matches only.

Disabled spectators have a special area reserved in the ground floor of the Frank Woolley Stand where an attendant and a number of wheelchairs is available. Special provision for invalid cars are available on prior request. Seating is provided with approximately 6,500 green plastic tip-up seats, so spectators can bring their own seats to matches if they wish. Bar and refreshment facilities including light snacks and hot meals, are available to members and the general public in the restaurant on the second floor of the New Stand and on the ground floor for fast food. Toilet facilities are available around the ground, including a disabled facility at the rear of the Frank Woolley and pavilion annexe stands. The supporters Kent C C C souvenir shop, scorecard sales point and the museum are also close at hand at the Pavilion End. The TV camera and commentary box is at the Nackington Road End and the radio Commentary box is on the top floor of the pavilion.

The playing area is 150 metres by 135 metres and is defined by a rope and advertising boards. During a break in play a visit to the Kent museum at the rear of the annexe and to the cabinets in the pavilion Long Room will bring back memories of the county's past glory years and performers. On the Old Dover Road side of the ground, close to the roped off area for press car parking is the war memorial of Colin Blythe, a former Kent C C C player.

The new Ames Levett Indoor Cricket School is currently being constructed close to the county offices at the top end of The Drive. The ground capacity is 14,000 and there is seating for 70 per cent available.

Additional facilities brought in for Festival week and popular matches include the traditional marquees for local clubs and organizations on the Old Dover Road side of the ground.

GROUND RECORDS AND SCORES

FIRST-CLASS MATCHES
Highest innings total for County: 568 *v*. Sussex 1906
Highest innings total against County: 676 by Australians 1921
Lowest innings total for County: 46 *v*. Surrey 1862
Lowest innings total against County: 37 by Philadelphians 1908
Highest individual innings for County: 270 F.E. Woolley *v*. Middlesex 1923
Highest individual innings against County: 344 W.G. Grace for MCC 1876
Best bowling performance in an innings for County: 9 for 35 J. Jackson *v*. England 1858
Best bowling performance in an innings against County: 10 for 92 W.G. Grace for MCC 1873
Best bowling performance in a match for County: 15 for 94 A.P. Freeman *v*. Somerset 1931
Best bowling performance in a match against County: 15 for 147 W.G. Grace for MCC 1873
Best attendance: 26,500 *v*. Australians 1948

LIMITED-OVERS MATCHES
Highest innings total for County: 359 for 4 *v*. Dorset (NWBT) 1989
Highest innings total against County: 293 for 8 by Surrey (NWBT) 1985
Lowest innings total for County: 73 *v*. Middlesex (BHC) 1979
Lowest innings total against County: 80 by Surrey (JPL) 1983
Highest individual innings for County: 136 n.o. C.J. Tavaré *v*. Gloucestershire (JPL) 1978
Highest individual innings against County: 146 G.S. Clinton for Surrey (NWBT) 1985
Best bowling performance for County: 5 for 14 D.L. Underwood *v*. Surrey (JPL) 1983
Best bowling performance against County: 6 for 18 D. Wilson for Yorkshire (JPL) 1969
Best attendance: 14,000 *v*. Somerset (GC) 1974

HOW TO GET THERE

Rail   Canterbury East (BR), 1 mile; Canterbury West (BR), 1.5 miles.
Bus   East Kent Buses 15–17 from Canterbury Bus Station–Folkestone pass ground also 339 from City Centre; C1/2/5 link BR Canterbury Stations with the Bus Station (Telephone: 0843 581333).
Car   From north: A290, A291 and A28 follow signs Canterbury and

city centre, ground is situated 0.5 mile south of city centre off Old Dover Road. From east: A257 to Canterbury, then as north. From west: M2 to junction 7, then A2 to bridge, turn off on Canterbury bypass, then A290 to Canterbury and Old Dover Road signposted county cricket for St Lawrence Cricket Ground. From south: A2, A28 and B2068 follow Canterbury signs, then Old Dover Road signposted county cricket.

WHERE TO STAY AND OTHER INFORMATION

County Hotel (0227 66266), The Chaucer Hotel (0227 464427).

Disabled Areas In Frank Woolley Stand and as requested elsewhere in the ground by arrangement.
Local Radio Station(s) BBC Radio Kent (104.2 MHz FM/1035 KHz MW), Invicta Radio (103.1 MHz FM/1242 KHz MW).
Local Newspaper(s) Evening Post, Kentish Gazette, Kent Messenger, Kent and Sussex Courier.

Dartford

Hesketh Park is the third ground to be used by Kent C C C for home matches in the town. The previous grounds were the 'Brent' at Brent Lane close to East Hill used from 1709–93 and the Bowman's Lodge near to Dartford Heath used in 1806. Dartford Cricket Club, founded in 1727, played at the 'Brent' until 1905 when, after the club had a lawsuit, the ground was sold for building development. Fortunately for the club Mr Everad Hesketh, a well-known local person, gave the Hesketh Park ground 'for the free use of the inhabitants of Dartford for ever'. More important Hesketh stipulated the main playing area must be retained as a cricket ground. The Dartford ground was named after him. The first match staged on the ground was in 1906 between the Daily Telegraph XI and the Riverside Mills XI. Hesketh bowled the first over on the ground.

Since 1906 Dartford Cricket Club has been the tenant and rents the ground from the Dartford Borough Council. The first Kent C C C match was staged in May 1956 when Essex were the visitors. Prior to the match a new pavilion was constructed to accommodate county members and of course provide players' changing and dining facilities. Hesketh Park is almost all that remains untouched by building development of the original 'Brent' ground which was covered by houses in Rochester, Bedford and Carlton Roads close to the ground.

Kent C C C second XI first used the ground in 1947 and limited-overs matches in the Benson & Hedges Cup have been staged with Essex in 1978 and 1981. The old pavilion still stands and is used as the press box for county matches. The playing area is flat and is rather enclosed despite being located close to the A2 trunk road and within a mile of the M25 and Dartford Tunnel and river crossing bridge recently constructed.

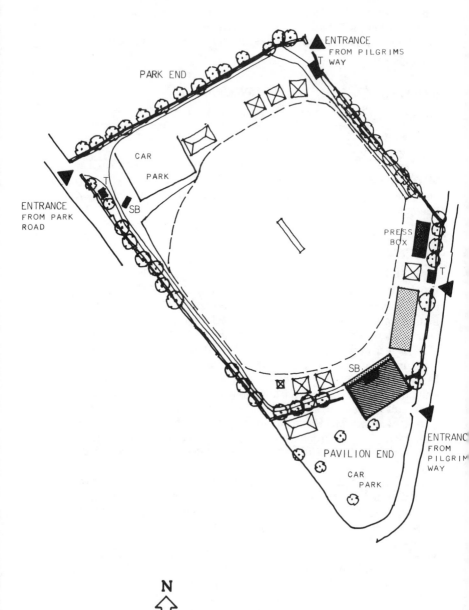

ENTRANCE
FROM PILGRIMS
WAY

PARK END

ENTRANCE
FROM PARK
ROAD

CAR
PARK

T

SB

PRESS
BOX

T

SB

ENTRANCE
FROM
PILGRIMS
WAY

PAVILION END

CAR
PARK

N

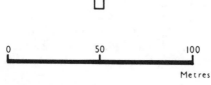

0   50   100

Metres

Dartford C C field three XIs throughout the season and plays in the Kent County Cricket League. The Hesketh Park ground is also used by Dartford Crackenfield Ladies, Woolwich and New Ash hockey clubs during the winter months. In recent seasons Kent C C C have usually played one championship match at Hesketh Park in May or July.

Cricketers to have played first-class cricket, who have graduated from Dartford C C include Alan Dixon, Derek Ufton, Neil Taylor and Graham Dilley. Crowds at Hesketh Park are usually 3,000–3,500; the largest for a single day was 3,750 against Essex in 1985 when a total of 10,000 watched the three days of the championship match. Ground records include a double hundred from Alan Ormrod for Worcestershire and fine bowling from Frederick Ridgway for Kent in 1960. Clive Lloyd hit the fastest hundred on the ground and then went on to score 163 in 140 minutes for Lancashire in 1970. Nottinghamshire the then county champions were dismissed for 65 in 1988. Championship cricket was not played in 1991, the last match being in 1990 against Leicestershire when Kent won by 7 wickets with Richard Davis and Minal Patel taking 10 wickets each in the match. The last occasion this happened for Kent was in 1912 when C. Blythe and F.E. Woolley took 11 and 9 wickets respectively bowling unchanged against Nottinghamshire.

ADDRESS Dartford Cricket Club, The Pavilion, Hesketh Park, Pilgrims Way, Dartford, Kent DA1 1ST.

TELEPHONE NUMBER PROSPECTS OF PLAY   0322 25152

DESCRIPTION OF GROUND AND FACILITIES

There are four entrances into Hesketh Park, from the south in Park Road and Pilgrims Way and two further entrances, one to the north of the playing area in Park Road and another off Watling Street. Car parking is available for players, officials, press and members to the rear of the pavilion, to the north on the tennis courts and at the rear of the marquees behind the sponsors' and Mayor's tents. Car parking is also available for 300 cars in the school field opposite the ground situated off Princes Road.

The main pavilion is used by members for refreshment and in addition to its use by players', also provides a Kent Secretary's office and toilet facilities. The scorers sit in the small room in the roof of the pavilion and above this room is the TV camera/commentary box position. Also, between the pavilion and the old pavilion, are two temporary raised seating areas and a cricket net. However, much of the temporary seating is of bench variety and at ground level. To the west of the pavilion is the Kent C C C souvenir tent, the scorecard printer's tents and two large public and members' refreshment areas. A scoreboard is located to the north-west corner, close to the tennis courts. A groundsman's tent is situated near the old pavilion and toilet facilities are available to the north and south of the playing area.

The members' enclosure is in front of the pavilion and is situated to the west of the pavilion, just to the east of the old pavilion. The playing area is 132 metres by 126 metres and is defined by a rope and advertising boards. Some 2,500 seats are provided so members of the public should bring their own seats. Some historic photographs of Dartford C C are on view in the pavilion and are well worth viewing during a break in play.

GROUND RECORDS AND SCORES

FIRST-CLASS MATCHES
Highest innings total for County: 476 for 9 *v.* Essex 1985
Highest innings total against County: 463 by Worcestershire 1973
Lowest innings total for County: 82 *v.* Essex 1966
Lowest innings total against County: 65 by Nottinghamshire 1988
Highest individual innings for County: 150 n.o. C.J. Tavaré *v.* Essex 1985
Highest individual innings against County: 204 n.o. J.A. Ormrod for Worcestershire 1973
Best bowling performance in an innings for County: 8 for 39 F. Ridgway *v.* Lancashire 1960
Best bowling performance in an innings against County: 8 for 84 Muhammad Munaf for Pakistan Eaglets 1963
Best bowling performance in a match for County: 12 for 101 F. Ridgway *v.* Lancashire 1960
Best bowling performance in a match against County: 10 for 89 R.G.M. Carter for Worcestershire 1964
Best attendance: 3,750 *v.* Essex 1985

LIMITED-OVERS MATCHES
Highest innings total for County: 226 for 4 *v.* Essex (BHC) 1978
Highest innings total against County: 222 for 6 by Essex (BHC) 1978
Lowest innings total for County: 162 for 2 *v.* Essex (BHC) 1981
Lowest innings total against County: 161 by Essex (BHC) 1981
Highest individual innings for County: 79 n.o. R.A. Woolmer *v.* Essex (BHC) 1981
Highest individual innings against County: 73 G.A. Gooch for Essex (BHC) 1978
Best bowling performance for County: 3 for 24 J.N. Shepherd *v.* Essex (BHC) 1978
Best bowling performance against County: 2 for 25 S. Turner for Essex (BHC) 1978
Best attendance: 2,750 *v.* Essex (BHC) 1978

HOW TO GET THERE

Rail   Dartford (BR), 1 mile.
Bus   Kentish Bus 1/3, 19 from BR Dartford Station (Telephone 0474 321300), also London Transport Buses 494, 499, 480, 486, 423 and 450 pass the ground.
Car   From north: M25 junction 2, then follow signs Dartford, A2

and A225 Princes Road, the ground is situated adjoining Park Road and Pilgrims Way 0.5 west of the M25 and 0.75 mile east of Dartford town centre. From east: A2, A296 follow signs Dartford for Princes Road, A225 for Park Road and Pilgrims Way. From west: A2, A296, A225 and A206 signposted Dartford and town centre, then as north. From south: M25 junction 2 then as north or B258 to Dartford, then A225 Princes Road for ground.

WHERE TO STAY AND OTHER INFORMATION
Royal Victoria and Bull (0322 24415), Crest Hotel (0322 526900) Princes Hotel (0322 20352).

Disabled Areas   No special area, request suitable position.
Local Radio Station(s)   BBC Radio Kent (104.2 MHz FM/1035 KHz MW), Invicta Radio (103.1 MHz FM/1242 KHz MW).
Local Newspaper(s)   Evening Post, Kentish Times, Dartford & Gravesend Reporter.

Folkestone

The first matches staged by Kent C C C in Folkestone were at the Sandgate Hill ground, the original home of the Folkestone Cricket Club in 1862–63. Folkestone C C was established in 1856 and after searching for a new ground at the turn of the century, they were given a piece of land, barely a mile from the town centre and close to the North Downs, which was originally a part of the Earl of Radnor's Broad Mead Farm in the Cheriton district. Once acquired, thanks to the benevolent Earl, the ground was levelled and prepared under the supervision of Alec Hearne, a former Kent player for the inaugural match in 1905 when a local side played a Kent Club and Ground XI. Lord Harris commented in his after-dinner speech at a reception given after the match that first-class cricket should be staged on the ground.

Nevertheless the initial first-class match was not staged until twenty years later in September 1925 when the Gentlemen played the Players. Following this match Kent C C C played the MCC and hence the Folkestone Festival week began. Matches were played intermittently from 1928 until, in 1961, the Folkestone week became a regular feature in late August. In recent years, however, only one championship and one limited-overs match has been staged in May. The home of a late-summer cricket festival during the period 1925–38, it has also been used by Kent C C C second XI since 1910.

The present pavilion and stands were built in 1926 at a cost of £1,000, the cash being advanced from Lord Radnor. The buildings were designed by architect R. Pope. The ground extends to some 30 acres, which includes the nearby Folkestone Town Football Club ground, tennis courts and bowling greens. The ground is also used for hockey and both Folkestone men and ladies clubs use the recreation area facilities during the winter months. The Cheriton Road ground is

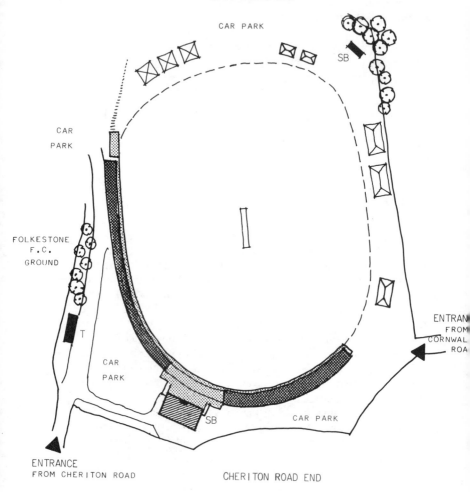

NORTH DOWNS END

CAR PARK

SB

CAR
PARK

FOLKESTONE
F.C.
GROUND

T

CAR
PARK

ENTRANCE
FROM
CORNWALL
ROAD

SB

CAR PARK

ENTRANCE
FROM CHERITON ROAD

CHERITON ROAD END

N

0   50   100
Metres

located very close to the Folkestone Channel Tunnel Terminal which is due for completion in mid-1993. The construction area can be seen from the ground and earth moving machinery and major items of plant can also be heard. The ground was originally called the Municipal Sports Ground but since being taken over by Folkestone and Shepway Council, has been known to locals as the Cheriton Road ground. Folkestone C C play in the Woolwich Kent County League and field two XIs throughout the season.

Crowds at Folkestone are usually 4,000–5,000; the best crowd was 7,500 for a John Player Sunday League match with Essex in 1976. Major performances on the ground have included double centuries from two England opening batsman, Les Ames and Herbert Sutcliffe. 'Titch' Freeman always enjoyed his visits to Cheriton Road as did Robin Marlar, who as a student, performed well with the ball for Cambridge University in 1953. Limited-overs records include a hundred from Chris Tavaré and 5 for 60 by John Jameson, now the assistant secretary (cricket) at Lord's while playing for Warwickshire in 1974, although he is remembered more as an opening batsman. In 1991 Essex scored 544 all out with Salim Malik the Pakistani hitting 173 against Kent.

ADDRESS   Folkestone Cricket Club, The Pavilion, Cheriton Road, Cheriton, Folkestone, Kent CT19 5JU
TELEPHONE NUMBER PROSPECTS OF PLAY   0303 53366

DESCRIPTION OF GROUND AND FACILITIES

From the south, entry to the ground is from Cheriton Road and from the east via Cornwallis Avenue. Car parking for members is available on the polo ground but spectators can also view cricket from their cars at the northern end of the ground. The majority of permanent buildings are situated south of the playing area and include the pavilion with scoreboard, and covered and open seating for members. There are also two covered stands on either side of the pavilion which surround the complete west and southern sides of the playing area. Toilets can be found in the pavilion and close to the car park at the rear of the pavilion. Entrance to this car park is from Cheriton Road or from Cherry Garden Avenue. Car parking is also available at the nearby Presto Supermarket store, but only on Sundays.

At the opposite end of the ground to the pavilion there is a public catering marquee together with a scorecard printers' tent and the Kent C C C souvenir tent. The main scoreboard is to the north-east of the ground and also has a store for the groundsmans equipment. The east side of the playing area is bounded by sponsers' marquees and entertainment areas. The TV camera and commentary box position is directly above and behind the sightscreen at the Cheriton Road End. The radio commentary box is situated on the roof of the pavilion adjoining the press box room.

The playing area is 134 metres by 170 metres and is defined by a rope and advertisement boards. The ground capacity is 8,000 and approximately 4,000 seats are provided so spectators are only advised to bring seats to popular matches. The members' enclosure is in front of the pavilion and in the adjoining covered stand to the west of the ground. The rest of the seating accommodation is available to both members and the public. A disabled area for vehicles is near the main scoreboard and sightscreen at the northern end of the ground.

GROUND RECORDS AND SCORES

FIRST-CLASS MATCHES
Highest innings total for County: 592 for 5 dec. *v.* Gloucestershire 1933
Highest innings total against County: 544 by Essex 1991
Lowest innings total for County: 61 *v.* Essex 1929
Lowest innings total against County: 65 by Warwickshire 1985
Highest individual innings for County: 295 L.E.G. Ames *v.* Gloucestershire 1933
Highest individual innings against County: 230 H. Sutcliffe for Yorkshire 1931
Best bowling performance in an innings for County: 9 for 61 A.P. Freeman *v.* Warwickshire 1932
Best bowling performance in an innings against County: 8 for 32 R.G. Marlar for Cambridge University 1953
Best bowling performance in a match for County: 17 for 92 A.P. Freeman *v.* Warwickshire 1932
Best bowling performance in a match against County: 13 for 90 R.G. Marlar for Cambridge University 1953
Best attendance: 5,000 *v.* Gloucestershire 1933

LIMITED-OVERS MATCHES
Highest innings total for County: 281 for 5 *v.* Warwickshire (JPL) 1983
Highest innings total against County: 225 by Middlesex (RAL) 1990
Lowest innings total for County: 84 *v.* Gloucestershire (JPL) 1969
Lowest innings total against County: 118 by Derbyshire (JPL) 1976
Highest individual innings for County: 122 n.o. C.J. Tavaré *v.* Warwickshire (JPL) 1983
Highest individual innings against County: 86 by R.T. Robinson for Nottinghamshire (JPL) 1984
Best bowling performance for County: 4 for 15 D.L. Underwood *v.* Gloucestershire (JPL) 1982
Best bowling performance against County: 5 for 60 J.A. Jameson for Warwickshire (JPL) 1974
Best attendance: 7,500 *v.* Essex (JPL) 1976

HOW TO GET THERE

Rail Folkestone Central (BR), 0.5 mile; Folkestone West (BR), 0.5 mile and Folkestone (TML), 0.75 mile (open mid-June 1993).
Bus From surrounding areas to Bus Station, thence 1 mile. East

Kent F1/3/6/9 link Bus Station and BR Folkestone Central Station with ground (Telephone: 0843 581333).

Car From north: A260 to Folkestone, then follow signs Cheriton, ground is situated 0.5 mile west of town centre off A20 Cheriton Road. From east: A20 to Folkestone, then west of town centre, then as north. From west: M20 junction 12, then A20 to Cheriton district, ground situated off A20 Cheriton Road.

WHERE TO STAY AND OTHER INFORMATION

Clifton Hotel (0303 41231), Burlington Hotel (0303 55301).

Disabled Areas Disabled area at Northern End of ground, near sightscreen, request suitable position.
Local Radio Station(s) BBC Radio Kent (104.2 MHz FM/1035 KHz MW), Invicta Radio (103.1 MHz FM/1242 KHz MW).
Local Newspaper(s) Evening Post, Folkestone & Dover People, Folkestone Hythe & Romney Marsh Herald.

Maidstone

This cricket ground is located in the loveliest of settings; Mote Park within the Mote Estate of some 558 acres to the east of the town centre of the county town, Maidstone. The ground dates back to the thirteenth century and situated within the park is the Mote House, a late eighteenth-century building which is now a Cheshire Home. The cricket ground dates back to the formation of the Mote Cricket Club in 1857 and is one of the oldest clubs in the county. Sir Marcus Sammel, later the First Viscount Bearstead, the last private owner of the Mote Estate was responsible in 1908 for levelling the playing area. It is now on three terraces. At that time the wicket was moved 90 degrees, to its present layout.

The main pavilion was constructed in 1909–10. The smaller pavilion, known as the Tabernacle, which is one of cricket's architectural curiosities, was originally Viscount Bearstead's private pavilion from which he viewed matches. The Tabernacle is used as an office by Kent C. C. C during the county festival week. After his death, the Second Viscount Bearstead sold the estate in 1928 to its present owner, the Maidstone Borough Council, but the cricket ground was reserved and presented to the Mote C. C after the sale.

The first Kent C. C. C match at Mote Park was in June 1859 when an MCC team were the visitors. Further visits were made in 1861–62 for matches with Surrey and Cambridgeshire, but it was not until 1870 that Kent C C C began to play regularly at Maidstone. A cricket festival week was granted in 1907 and has been a permanent feature since 1910. In recent years two championship and one limited-overs match have been staged, usually in early July. Matches with touring sides have occasionally been staged at Mote Park rather than at Canterbury and

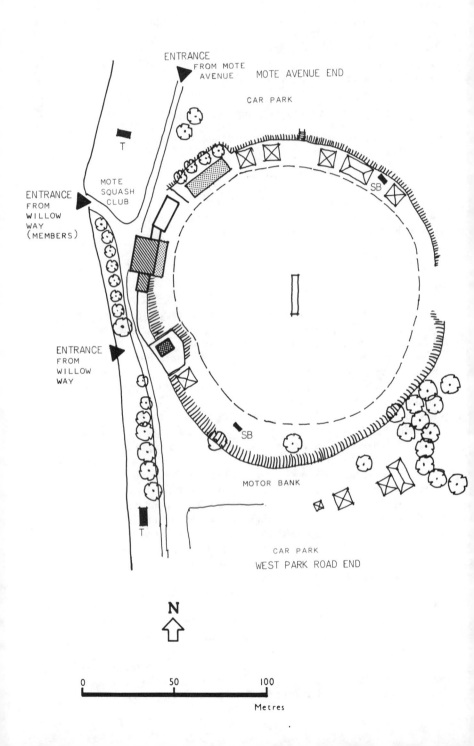

these have included the Australians in 1890, Philadelphians in 1897 and South Africans in 1912. Mote C C play in the Woolwich Kent County Cricket League and field four XIs on a Saturday and three XIs on a Sunday throughout the summer. The club also has one mid-week team and a colts section.

Crowds at Mote Park are usually 5,000–6,000; the best was 14,000 for a John Player Sunday League match against Lancashire in 1974 which resulted in Kent becoming Sunday League Champions for the first time that year. Ground performances have included double centuries from Percy Chapman against Lancashire and, in recent years, Graeme Fowler for the red rose county. 'Tich' Freeman, David Halfyard and Derek Underwood have all enjoyed fine bowling spells here for the home county. In limited-overs matches the highest individual innings on the ground was made by Gehan Mendis (121) while playing for his former county Sussex.

ADDRESS The Mote Cricket Club, The Pavilion, Mote Park, Willow Way, Maidstone, Kent ME15 7RN.
TELEPHONE NUMBER PROSPECTS OF PLAY 0622 54159/ 54545

DESCRIPTION OF GROUND AND FACILITIES

There are two entrances to the ground from Willow Way to the west of the ground and two areas for car parking: one to the north, down the bank and the other to the south, high above the playing area. The ground is on three levels and the cricket pitch is a flat, circular area. The pavilion, together with the Mote Squash Club and permanent raised seating, is situated on the west side of the ground. There is also a members' enclosure between the pavilion and the Tabernacle. Close to the Tabernacle is a small area for sponsors' tents and a small secondary scoreboard is located under the trees. Situated high above the bank at the West Park Avenue End, is the scorecard printer's tent, a Kent C C C Souvenir Shop in a large red and white striped tent and a large refreshment marquee and bar.

The TV camera position and commentary box is situated directly above and behind the sightscreen at the southern end. The radio commentary box is located within the pavilion area. The scorers' box is in the roof of the pavilion and the press box is situated in the pavilion at first floor level. All the seating to the south-east of the playing area, as far as the main scoreboard, is made of temporary benches which nestle close to the bank and under the trees. The northern end of the ground comprises at least ten tents and marquees of various sizes. This includes a Kent C C C supporters' club marquee amongst other organizations represented. Toilets are situated within the pavilion, at the rear, in a separate building and to the south of the ground. The members' enclosure is situated between the Tabernacle to the south-west and in front of the pavilion and ceases after the open raised seats to the north-west. There is no special disabled enclosure, but cricket can be viewed from vehicles at the south end of the ground. The playing area is 136 metres by 135 metres and is defined by a rope and some advertising boards. The ground capacity is 8,000 and seating for roughly 85 per cent is provided. Spectators are advised to bring their own seating to popular matches.

The Mote Park is probably one of the finest grounds in the south of England and the pavilion, which has two levels one of the most attractive at a county out ground.

GROUND RECORDS AND SCORES

FIRST-CLASS MATCHES

Highest innings total for County: 580 for 6 *v*. Essex 1947
Highest innings total against County: 502 by Essex 1947
Lowest innings total for County: 38 *v*. Lancashire 1881
Lowest innings total against County: 31 by Hampshire 1967
Highest individual innings for County: 260 A.P.F. Chapman *v*. Lancashire 1927
Highest individual innings against County: 226 G. Fowler for Lancashire 1984
Best bowling performance in an innings for County: 10 for 131 A.P. Freeman *v*. Lancashire 1929
Best bowling performance in an innings against County: 9 for 108 T.P.B. Smith for Essex 1948
Best bowling performance in a match for County: 15 for 117 D.J. Halfyard *v*. Worcestershire 1959
Best bowling performance in a match against County: 15 for 123 F.G. Roberts for Gloucestershire 1897
Best attendance: 8,000 *v*. Essex 1948

LIMITED-OVERS MATCHES

Highest innings total for County: 278 for 5 *v*. Gloucestershire (JPL) 1976
Highest innings total against County: 259 for 3 by Lancashire (RAL) 1990
Lowest innings total for County: 86 *v*. Somerset (JPL) 1978
Lowest innings total against County: 65 by Warwickshire (JPL) 1979
Highest individual innings for County: 106 Asif Iqbal *v*. Gloucestershire (JPL) 1976
Highest individual innings against County: 121 G.D. Mendis for Sussex (JPL) 1982
Best bowling performance for County: 5 for 19 D.L. Underwood *v*. Gloucestershire (JPL) 1972
Best bowling performance against County: 4 for 15 J. Birkenshaw for Leicestershire (JPL) 1977
Best attendance: 14,000 *v*. Lancashire (JPL) 1974

HOW TO GET THERE

Rail Maidstone East (BR), 1 mile; Maidstone West (BR), 1.25 miles.
Bus Boro' Line 85 from High Street 0.25 mile from both BR
Stations; also routes 5 and 12 pass the ground (Telephone: 0622
690060).
Car From north: M20 junctions 6 or 7, then either A229 or A249
to Maidstone town centre, ground situated off Ashford Road A20
through Square Hill Road and Mote Road for Mote Park. From east:
M20 junction 8, then A20 to town centre, then as north or A274 or
A229 to town centre then as north. From west: M20 junction 5 then
follow signs Maidstone and town centre, then as north. From south:
A26, A229 or A274 to Maidstone and town centre, then as north.

WHERE TO STAY AND OTHER INFORMATION

Great Danes, Hollingbourne (0622 30022) Royal Star Hotel (0622
55721), Larkfield Hotel (0732 846858).

Disabled Areas No special area, request suitable position.
Local Radio Station(s) BBC Radio Kent (104.2 MHz FM/1035 KHz
MW), Invicta Radio (103.1 MHz FM/1242 KHz MW).
Local Newspaper(s) Evening Post, Kentish Gazette, East Kent
Mercury, Maidstone Borough News.

Tunbridge Wells

The Nevill Cricket Ground is located at Nevill Gate and is the home of
Tunbridge Wells Cricket Club established in 1762 and Blue Mantles
Cricket Club established in 1895. Tunbridge Wells C C previously
played at the Higher Common Ground in Fir Tree Road between 1786
and 1884 until its move to Nevill Gate in 1895. Kent C C C also played
on the Common from 1845–1884 and other clubs who played there
included the Linden Park Cricket Club and the Madhatters Hockey
Club.

The Nevill Gate Ground was acquired on a lease of 99 years from the
Eridge Park Estate of the Marquess of Abergavenny (family name
Nevill) to the Tunbridge Wells Cricket, Football and Athletic Club. The
ground has been used for football, cycle racing, athletics, archery,
hockey and lawn tennis. Tennis courts border the ground on one side
and a notable tennis tournament is staged, usually in August each year.
The ground was opened in 1898 by the Marquess of Abergavenny and
the first Kent C C C match was in 1901 when Lancashire were the
visitors. The present pavilion and additional buildings were constructed
in 1903 at a cost of £1,200, but in 1913 when the suffragettes were
campaigning it suffered extensive fire damage and was rebuilt shortly
afterwards. After the 1914–18 War the ground became a picketing area
for the cavalry; several hundred horses tethered over the playing area did
little to improve the wickets! The ground is now owned by the

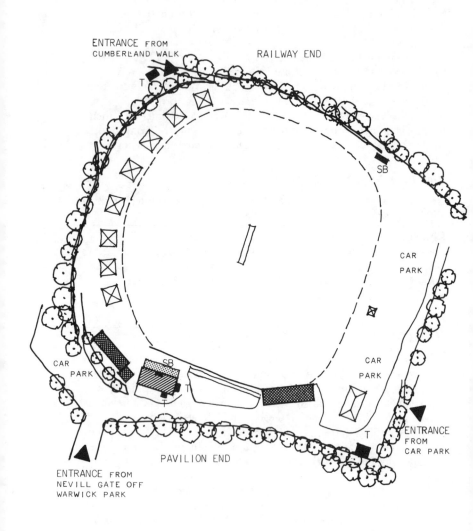

ENTRANCE FROM
CUMBERLAND WALK

RAILWAY END

T

SB

CAR
PARK

CAR
PARK

SB

T

T

CAR
PARK

ENTRANCE
FROM
CAR PARK

T

PAVILION END

ENTRANCE FROM
NEVILL GATE OFF
WARWICK PARK

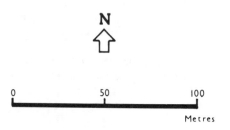

N

0   50   100

Metres

Tunbridge Wells Borough Council which took control in 1946 and looks after its upkeep.

The Nevill Ground is probably one of the most beautiful grounds on the county circuit, especially during Tunbridge Wells festival week, which is usually staged in early June when the giant purple blooms of the rhododendrons curving around the playing arena form a superb setting for county cricket. Tunbridge Wells C C plays in the Woolwich Kent County Cricket League and has three XIs most weekends throughout the season. The Blue Mantles C C play friendly matches throughout the season on weekdays and matches have been played with MCC and other established clubs in the past. In 1983 an international match was staged on the ground when the Prudential Cup fixture between India and Zimbabwe followed the traditional Kent and Sussex County Championship match during the festival. Kapil Dev hit a super 175 n.o. in that match, the highest individual innings in the history of the competition until beaten by Vivian Richards in Karachi during the 1987 Reliance World Cup.

Kent C C C usually play a week of cricket at Tunbridge Wells and this includes two championship and one limited-overs match. A celebrity match is also occasionally staged with county players during this week. Crowds at the Nevill Ground are usually 5,000–6,000, the largest was in 1950 when 10,000 attended the two days with Lancashire. Players who have represented Tunbridge Wells C C and played first-class cricket include: Mike Willard of Cambridge University, Peter Hearn and Bob Woolmer both of Kent. Ground records at the Nevill Ground have included hundreds from James Seymour and Wally Hammond and fine bowling from 'Tich' Freeman, V.W.C. Jupp and A.E. Lewis. Limited-overs centuries have been scored by Peter Richardson and Ken Suttle. Colin Blythe once bowled 12 overs here against Sussex and gave only one run away in an hour.

ADDRESS Tunbridge Wells Cricket Club, The Pavilion, Nevill Cricket Ground, Nevill Gate, Warwick Park, Tunbridge Wells, Kent TN2 5ES.
TELEPHONE NUMBER PROSPECTS OF PLAY 0892 20846

DESCRIPTION OF GROUND AND FACILITIES

Entrance to the Nevill Cricket Ground is from Nevill Gate off Warwick Park and to the north of the playing area from the Railway End. Two further entrances to the ground, for pedestrians only are from the path off Warwick Park and from the adjoining car park to the west of the playing area. Car parking is available within the ground for players, officials and some members near the hard tennis courts. There is also a four acre field available for parking adjoining the ground and more spaces in nearby streets.

All the permanent buildings are located at the Pavilion End, where the secondary small scoreboard and scorers' rooms are situated on the roof of the main pavilion with the small press box. There is seating for members in front of the pavilion and in the two other stands either side of the enclosure: the grandstand to the east and the covered enclosure, adjoining the Martlets C C private pavilion which is used as a players' enclosure to the west. To the west of the playing area, backing onto the tennis courts, is temporary seating plus a number of marquees which are sited around the playing area. The main scoreboard is situated in the north-east corner of the ground, on the east side of the playing area. There is an area for disabled spectators to the side of the main pavilion. The scorecard printer's tent and the Kent C C C souvenir shop housed in a large tent is located on the grass tennis courts with several small refreshment points.

There is also a large catering area for the public and members, who may also take refreshment in the pavilion. Toilets are available in the north-west corner, south-east corner and at the rear of the members' pavilion. The playing area which is 138 metres by 135 metres, is flat, situated in fine grounds of trees and shrubs and is defined by a rope and advertising boards. The ground capacity is 5,500 and only 2,500 seats are provided so spectators would be well advised to bring their own seats to all popular matches.

GROUND RECORDS AND SCORES

FIRST-CLASS MATCHES
Highest innings total for County: 519 for 6 *v.* Warwickshire 1928
Highest innings total against County: 563 by Gloucestershire 1934
Lowest innings total for County: 58 *v.* Leicestershire 1938
Lowest innings total against County: 25 by Worcestershire 1960
Highest individual innings for County: 214 J. Seymour *v.* Essex 1914
Highest individual innings against County: 290 W.R. Hammond for Gloucestershire 1934
Best bowling performance in an innings for County: 8 for 38 A.P. Freeman *v.* Northamptonshire 1932
Best bowling performance in an innings against County: 10 for 127 V.W.C. Jupp for Northamptonshire 1932
Best bowling performance in a match for County: 16 for 82 A.P. Freeman *v.* Northamptonshire 1932
Best bowling performance in a match against County: 14 for 141 A.E. Lewis for Somerset 1910
Best attendance: 10,000 *v.* Lancashire 1950

LIMITED-OVERS MATCHES
Highest innings total for County: 242 *v.* Sussex (GC) 1963
Highest innings total against County: 314 for 7 by Sussex (GC) 1963
Lowest innings total for County: 173 *v.* Sussex (BHC) 1972
Lowest innings total against County: 120 by Surrey (JPL) 1970
Highest individual innings for County: 127 P.E. Richardson *v.* Sussex (GC) 1963
Highest individual innings against County: 104 K.G. Suttle for Sussex (GC) 1963
Best bowling performance for County: 3 for 20 R.A. Woolmer *v.* Surrey (JPL) 1970

Best bowling performance against County: 2 for 22 D.L. Williams for Glamorgan (JPL) 1972
Best attendance: 6,000 *v*. Sussex (GC) 1963

HOW TO GET THERE

Rail   Tunbridge Wells (BR), 0.75 mile.
Bus   From surrounding areas to Frant Road End, routes 252, 254, 256, 280, 283 and 791; also via Hawkenbury End, route 285 (Telephone: 0622 690060).
Car   From north: A21, A26 or A227 to Tunbridge Wells, the ground is situated 0.5 mile south of the town centre off A267 Hastings Road, then into Roedean Road and Warwick Park. From east and west: A264 to Tunbridge Wells then as north. From south: A267 to Tunbridge Wells, then as north.

WHERE TO STAY AND OTHER INFORMATION

Calverley Hotel (0892 36801), Russell Hotel (0892 44833).

Disabled Areas   Available close to main pavilion, otherwise request suitable position.
Local Radio Station(s)   BBC Radio Kent (104.2 MHz FM/1035 KHz MW) Invicta Radio (103.1 MHz FM/1242 KHz MW).
Local Newspaper(s)   Evening Post, Kent and Sussex Courier.

LANCASHIRE

MANCHESTER – OLD TRAFFORD

BLACKPOOL

LIVERPOOL

LYTHAM

SOUTHPORT

Lancashire

Founded   12 January 1864
Colours   Red, green and blue
Crest   Red rose
Patron   HM The Queen
President   A.J. Leggat
Chairman   R. Bennett
Chief Executive   J.M. Bower
Secretary   Miss R.B. Fitzgibbon
Cricket Manager   J.A. Ormrod
Cricket Coach   J.S. Savage
Marketing Manager   J. Cumbes
Captain   N.H. Fairbrother
Ground Superintendent   P. McCabe
Groundsman   P. Marron
Physiotherapists   L. Brown and Sheena Storah
Scorer 1st XI   W. Davies and A. Lowe
Scorer 2nd XI   W. Lodge
Statistician/Librarian   Rev. M.G. Lorimer
Curator   K.A. Hayhurst
Sponsors   Bass North West
Newsletter   *Red Rose News*
Address   Old Trafford Cricket Ground, Talbot Road, Old Trafford, Manchester M16 OPX
Telephone 061 848 7021
Facsimile 061 848 9021
Lancashire Rapid Cricketline   0891 567508
Test Match Commentaries Rapid Cricketline   0891 567567
Test Match Updates Rapid Cricketline   0891 567555

ACHIEVEMENTS

County Championship   Champions (8) 1881, 1897, 1904, 1926, 1927, 1928, 1930 and 1934; joint Champions (4) 1879, 1882, 1889 and 1950
Gillette Cup Winners   (4) 1970, 1971, 1972 and 1975; finalists (2) 1974 and 1976
National Westminster Bank Trophy   Winners (1) 1990; finalists (1) 1986
Benson & Hedges Cup   Winners (2) 1984 and 1990; finalists (1) 1991
John Player Sunday League   Champions (2) 1969 and 1970
Refuge Assurance Sunday League   Champions (1) 1989
Refuge Assurance Cup   Winners (1) 1988; finalists (1) 1991; semi-finalists (2) 1989 and 1990
Fenner Trophy   Finalists (2) 1971 and 1972
Asda Trophy   Winners (1) 1983; finalists (3) 1982, 1985 and 1987

Old Trafford from the air, reproduced by courtesy of Jeffersons Air Photography

Ward Four Counties Knockout Competition Semi-finalists (1) 1988
Lambert & Butler Cup (TCCB 7-a-side Floodlit Competition) Winners (1) 1981

GROUNDS

Manchester (Old Trafford Cricket Ground, Talbot Road) Blackpool (Stanley Park, West Park Drive) Liverpool (Aigburth Cricket Ground, Aigburth Road) Lytham (Church Road, Lytham) and Southport (Trafalgar Road, Birkdale).

No other grounds have been used since 1969.

SECOND XI GROUNDS

In addition to the above mentioned grounds the following are used for second XI matches: Lancaster C C, Lune Road, Lancaster. Telephone: 0524 65087; Northern C C, Moor Park, Great Crosby, Liverpool. Telephone: 051 924 1594; Wigan C C, Bull Hey off Park Road, Wigan. Telephone: 0695 41581.

In his *History of Lancashire*, John Kay, the county's foremost authority, boldly nominated the best team of players from 1864 when it all began from the seed planted by Manchester Cricket Club. His choice was: A.G. MacLaren, C. Washbrook, J.T. Tyldesley, C.H. Lloyd, E. Tyldesley, F.M. Engineer, J. Briggs, C.H. Parkin, S.F. Barnes, E.A. McDonald, J.B. Statham. 12th man, E. Paynter.

No A.N. ('Monkey') Hornby, authoritative captain and leading batsman, no R.H. Spooner, the epitome of batting grace, nor A.G. Steel, accomplished batsman and slow bowler, the pro batting stalwarts Barlow, Hallows, Watson and Makepeace, or fast bowler Brearley.

There is, of course, no way to judge the merits of Washbrook against Barlow, Hornby's opening partner. He played in 17 Tests against Australia, including 3 tours in which he played in every fixture, and opened both batting and bowling for England. It is also possible to imagine Hutton, who regarded Washbrook as his favourite partner, saying: 'I can't think Barlow could have been better than Washbrook.'

Kay includes three 'foreigners' – Lloyd, the West Indies captain, McDonald, one of Australia's finest fast bowlers, and the Indian wicket-keeper, Engineer. Presumably Engineer's batting wins him preference over Duckworth, rated the best stumper of his day.

Lancashire have never been thin-skinned about the geography of their recruits, and at one stage the Bolton-born Barlow was the only Lancastrian in the side, a state of affairs which led to acrimonious cards being exchanged with Nottinghamshire. Nottinghamshire's response to cheeky Christmas card was a New Year's message which read:

LANCASHIRE COUNTY CRICKET

The only rules necessary for players in the County Eleven are that they shall neither have been born in, nor reside in, Lancashire. Sutton-in-Ashfield will have the preference.

Since Johnny Briggs, a major all-rounder, came from Sutton-in-Ashfield, less than 20 miles from Trent Bridge, Nottinghamshire had cause to feel touchy. Only 5ft 5ins tall Briggs bowled left arm at slow to medium pace with uncanny accuracy and invention, and was an able enough batsman to have scored a century at Melbourne in one of his six visits to Australia. At Cape Town in 1888–89, under the captaincy of C.A. Smith – to become Sir Aubrey the Hollywood film actor – Briggs had 15 wickets for 28. Briggs was a jovia character, and once answered Hornby's charge of drunkenness with an exhibition of trick cycling. Unhappily he died from a mental disorder at the age of 39.

Lancashire's early teams confortably established the county as one of the Big Six, joining Yorkshire, Nottinghamshire, Surrey, Gloucestershire and Middlesex. They were the sides which dominated the championship almost up to the liberating 'sixties. Lancashire's share of the prizes was 6 championships, including a hat-trick from 1926 to 1928, and 3 shared.

Archie MacLaren, as captain and batsman, mirrored the Golden Age.

He took 424 off Somerset at Taunton in 1895, still an English record, and there was batting of the highest class from J.T. Tyldesley, the elder brother by 16 years of Ernest, who more than upheld the family name. J.T.'s 31 Tests with 37,897 runs and 86 centuries stands beside Ernest's 14 Tests, 28,874 runs and 102 centuries: both pillars of strength.

Only once, in 1904, was MacLaren able to claim the championship, but Lancashire were invariably in contention, and his batting fired the imagination. His contribution to the romantic legends of the game was to take Sydney Barnes to Australia on the evidence of his bowling in the Old Trafford nets. Some contend there was never a better bowler, but Barnes had an estimation of his value which did not coincide with Lancashire's and he was lost to the Leagues.

Walter Brearley, like Barnes, would have been a godsend to today's media. After a dressing room dispute between the rival teams he fired a succession of high full tosses at Jessop. At Lord's he asked a luminary: 'Are you the manager of this 'ere bloomin' 'ipperdrome?' and, after being left out of a Test match, stationed himself below the box of Sir Henry Leveson Gower, chairman of selectors and began a commentary which included 'Brearley for England': 'I often get 6 wickets in an innings, and generally the leading batsmen', and 'I don't always trust the fieldsman so I clean bowl 'em.' The result was a gathering of curious spectators and a policeman arriving and telling Brearley to stop 'singing' as he was causing an obstruction!

The 'twenties saw a powerful side enriched by the dual purpose bowling of Parkin – another lost to the Leagues – Dick Tyldesley, a leg spinner of wide girth and dry humour ('he's no good to me' was his heartfelt summing up of Bradman during his 334 at Leeds in 1930), the magnificent McDonald, Duckworth and Ernest Tyldesley. All the diverse talents were welded into a team of champions by Leonard Green, a military man and firm believer in discipline and fairness. 'He gets on with his job and we get on with ours,' remarked Duckworth succinctly explaining the best of the old amateur captain-pro relationship.

Hallows hit 1,000 runs between 5 and 31 May in 1928, and the title returned to Old Trafford in 1930 and 1934. Though honours were shared with Surrey in 1950 Lancashire's standards fell below expectations after the war. Pride was abandoned when the club advertised in *The Times* for a captain. Yet in the course of time the evergreen Simmons, the hero of many a Cup tie, Statham and Bond demonstrated they knew all about the arts of captaincy. Simmons' achievements for Tasmania bordered on the miraculous, and Statham, a natural fast bowler if ever there was one, took 252 wickets in 70 Tests and formed a famous partnership with Trueman. In all Statham had 2,260 wickets.

Bond had modest recommendations as a batsman, but as a captain, inspired his teams on the principles of fitness, loyalty and enjoyment, he enjoyed a remarkable five-year triumph. He had the luck to be positively supported by chairman Cedric Rhodes, to be in at the start of single-innings cricket and to have players singularly equipped for the new format, from Clive Lloyd to the long-serving David Hughes. As Bond took the Sunday League in its first two seasons and a hat-trick of the

OLD TRAFFORD

PLAYER'S CIGARETTES

C. WASHBROOK

Gillette Cup from 1970 to 1972, there seemed to be a happy conspiracy between Bond and his two overseas stars, Clive Lloyd and Engineer, and his mainstays Simmons, Hughes, Wood, David Lloyd, Pilling, Peter Lever, Hayes and Sullivan.

The West Indies captain made a tremendous impact with his free hitting ('if I see it I hit it') and cover fielding, and both home and away Lancashire drew huge crowds. In the final game of the John Player Trophy against Yorkshire in 1970 the gates at Old Trafford were closed for the first time since 1948. When he retired *Wisden* said Bond 'managed' rather than led Lancashire from the depths of despair to the heights of success in one-day cricket. 'He created team spirit and guarded it jealously,' *Wisden* added. Sadly for Bond his wheel of fortune was to turn full circle.

David Lloyd, Bond's successor, again took the Cup, making four victories in five years, and in 1984 with John Abrahams in charge, Lancashire carried off the Benson & Hedges Cup, an achievement soured by a 16th position in the championship. For the first time in 110 years they had won only one game and, for the 9th successive year, they were in the bottom six. There was a brief glimpse of glory with a final place in the NatWest Trophy in 1986 when Clive Lloyd was one of Sussex bowler Reeves' four victims out for a duck. There were too many failures to stomach and at the season's end Lloyd was replaced by Hughes as captain and, while the playing staff was retained, manager Bond and coach Lever were dismissed.

A sad ending, but the days of Bond and Clive Lloyd will remain forever a saga of Old Trafford.

Since 1989 Lancashire have won the Refuge Assurance Sunday League and both the Benson & Hedges Cup and National Westminster Bank Trophy in the same year (1990) defeating Worcestershire and Northamptonshire at Lord's. In 1991 a repeat of the 1990 Benson & Hedges Cup Final was won by Worcestershire on the second day. The

J. BRIGGS
Lancashire

WILLS'S CIGARETTES.

MR. A. C. MACLAREN (LANCS.).

W. BREARLEY

OGDEN'S *Guinea Gold Cigarettes*
New Series

main contributors to Lancashire's success in the late 1980s and early 1990s have been David Hughes, Neil Fairbrother the new captain for 1992, Michael Atherton, Warren Hegg, Philip de Freitas and Pakistani Test star Wasim Akram.

Manchester – Old Trafford

Old Trafford has been the home of Lancashire cricket since 1857 when the new ground was opened. Lancashire C C C play most of their matches at Old Trafford and of course the ground also stages Test Matches and one day limited-overs internationals.

Old Trafford is the third ground to be used in Manchester for cricket. The first was at Moss Lane, Moss Side, Hulme. This ground was closed in 1847 and play moved to Chester Road, Stretford where matches were staged from 1848 to 1854 by the Manchester Cricket Club. After the final move to the present venue, the Stretford ground became the White City greyhound stadium.

Situated a short distance westwards, and still Sir Thomas de Trafford's land, was Old Trafford. The first match staged at Old Trafford was between Manchester C C and neighbours Liverpool C C The initial first-class match was between England and Another England XI in 1860. Lancashire C C C was formed in 1864 and the first Lancashire C C C match was staged with Middlesex in 1865. The first Test Match was staged in 1884 when England played Australia.

The 18 acre ground was owned by de Trafford until 1898 when Manchester C C purchased it from the de Trafford Estate for £24,082. The pavilion was built in 1894, four years earlier. The pavilion was used as a hospital during World War One and was bombed during the blitz of World War Two. Most of the buildings are located on the Talbot Road

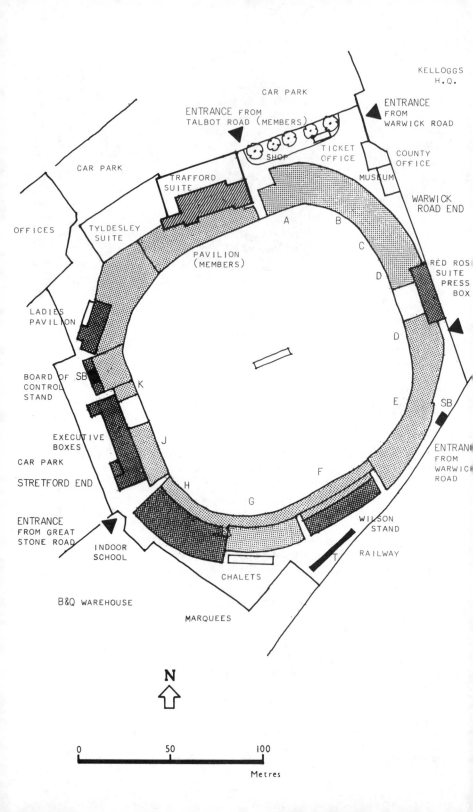

KELLOGGS
H.Q.

CAR PARK

ENTRANCE FROM
TALBOT ROAD (MEMBERS)

ENTRANCE
FROM
WARWICK ROAD

CAR PARK

SHOP

TICKET
OFFICE

COUNTY
OFFICE

OFFICES

TRAFFORD
SUITE

TYLDESLEY
SUITE

MUSEUM

WARWICK
ROAD END

A   B

C

D

RED ROS
SUITE
PRESS
BOX

PAVILION
(MEMBERS)

LADIES
PAVILION

BOARD OF SB
CONTROL
STAND

K

D

E   SB

ENTRAN
FROM
WARWIC
ROAD

EXECUTIVE
BOXES

CAR PARK

STRETFORD END

J

H

F

G

ENTRANCE
FROM GREAT
STONE ROAD

INDOOR
SCHOOL

WILSON
STAND

RAILWAY

T

B&Q WAREHOUSE

CHALETS

MARQUEES

N

0   50   100

Metres

side of the ground and all the seating is permanent and the majority is now of the blue plastic tip-up variety. In 1982 a ground development appeal raised £200,000 and in 1984 a further £47,000 was raised from a Test Centenary Appeal. Much development has taken place with this money, including some executive boxes and press/commentary facilities. Other additions have included a Lancashire C C C museum and a members' library in the pavilion. There are plenty of items of cricket interest in the pavilion, which was designed by A.T. Muirhead the same architect who designed the Oval pavilion. The 1984 season saw the centenary of Test Cricket at Old Trafford and in 1989 Lancashire celebrated their 125th anniversary.

The ground is also used by Manchester C C and the Lancashire second and Club and Ground XIs. Part of the ground at the Stretford End was leased to a DIY store and garden centre during the 1980s. All the nearby government office towers are named after famous former Lancashire C C C cricketers: Statham, MacLaren, Duckworth and Washbrook.

Crowds at Old Trafford have always been large. The record attendance was 78,617 for the Roses Match in 1926 with 46,000 attending the first day of the match. For limited-overs matches the record is 33,000 for the John Player Sunday League match in 1970 against Yorkshire. The current ground capacity is 20,000 and this is achieved regularly for Test Matches, one-day internationals and limited-overs matches. The ground has staged all major county competitions as well as Prudential Trophy, Prudential Cup and Texaco Trophy competitions.

Ground performances have included scores of 300 or more from Frank Watson and Bobby Simpson. Bowling achievements include Jim Laker's 19 Australian wickets in 1956 and fine bowling by Johnny Briggs, 'Titch' Freeman, Walter Brearley and George Giffen. In the limited-overs game West Indian players seem to hold all the records with the bat: Vivian Richards (189 n.o. in a Texaco Trophy match in 1984), Clive Lloyd and Gordon Greenidge. With the ball, Colin Croft and Keith Boyce are record holders. In 1990 Lancashire recorded their highest innings total at Old Trafford in limited-overs cricket: 372 for 5 against Gloucestershire in the NatWest Bank Trophy. The 1991 Refuge Assurance Cup final was staged at Old Trafford with Worcestershire beating Lancashire for the second time in a major final in the same season.

ADDRESS   Old Trafford Cricket Ground, Talbot Road, Manchester M16 OPX.
TELEPHONE NUMBER PROSPECTS OF PLAY   061 872 0261

DESCRIPTION OF GROUND AND FACILITIES

Situated in the Old Trafford district of Manchester, the ground is bounded by Talbot Road to the north, Warwick Road to the north-east, Great Stone Road to the west and to the south the Altrincham to

Manchester railway line. The main entrance is through the turnstiles and main gate next to the Lancashire C C C offices in Warwick Road and there is access for members' car parking from Talbot Road and for the public in Great Stone Road where car parking is available on the practice ground.

This area is not available for important matches as it is used for marquees and the corporate hospitality chalet village during Test matches. At weekends there is a car park in the government offices in Talbot Road. In the arena itself the members' enclosure stretches from the Ladies' Stand/Pavilion to the main pavilion and in front of these two buildings. The pavilion comprises the Trafford suite, Tyldesley suite, Lancaster Library and catering facilities as well as refreshments, toilets, bars and changing rooms for players and officials. The pavilion also provides seating, both covered and uncovered, inside and outside the building. The stands are numbered A to K, circle the ground and comprise plastic tip-up seats and blue timber bench seats which are covered under the Red Rose suite at the Warwick Road End, the Wilson Stand opposite the pavilion, which includes a rather unusual light meter and H Stand.

The executive suites together with TV camera/commentary box and radio commentary positions are sited on the roof at the Stretford End high above the playing area. Adjoining the executive suite is the Board of Control Stand with secondary scoreboard and TCCB boxes along with sponsor's seating. The Ladies' Pavilion includes the Jubilee Britannia suite and is only available to members. Since the 1990 season ladies have been allowed in the main members' pavilion, Lord's is now the only pavilion in the country where Ladies are refrained from entry. At the Stretford End is the indoor cricket school with an area for marquees to be erected during the Test Match. The main scoreboard is sited near the Warwick Road railway station, at the rear of the seating area in enclosure E. Toilet facilities are available throughout the ground as are bars, refreshment areas, an enlarged and improved Lancashire C C C souvenir shop which has several smaller outlets at popular matches and a Lancashire C C C cricket museum which is situated under the A and B enclosures near the main entrance.

The press box is known as The Sir Neville Cardus Gallery and was opened by John Arlott OBE on the eve of the First Cornhill Test Match between England and Pakistan on 3rd June 1987. Restaurants are available to members and sponsors throughout the season. Other buildings include the groundsman's house in the Talbot Road car park; the ticket office where transfers can be obtained adjoins the secretary's office/Lancashire C C C offices and groundsman's equipment stores. A first aid room, toilets for disabled spectators and several disabled areas are available in enclosures A and B, the Wilson Stand and in the special wheelchair enclosure adjoining the ringside seats to the east side of the E enclosure and Wilson Stand.

The ground capacity is 20,000 and seating is provided for all. The playing area is flat and defined by a rope and advertising boards mounted on a white metal fence. The playing area is 143 metres by 149 metres and is approximately circular in shape. Should poor weather end a match early or provide a lengthy break in play a visit to the Manchester United Football Club museum is recommended as it is only a short walk from the ground to the home of probably one of the finest and most famous clubs in the world.

GROUND RECORDS AND SCORES

TEST MATCHES
Highest innings total for England: 627 for 9 dec. *v.* Australia 1934
Highest innings total against England: 658 for 8 dec. by Australia 1964
Lowest innings total for England: 71 *v.* West Indies 1976
Lowest innings total against England: 58 by India 1952
Highest individual innings for England: 256 K.F. Barrington *v.* Australia 1964
Highest individual innings against England: 311 R.B. Simpson for Australia 1964
Best bowling performance in an innings for England: 10 for 53 J.C. Laker *v.* Australia 1956
Best bowling performance in an innings against England: 8 for 31 F. Laver for Australia 1909
Best bowling performance in a match for England: 19 for 90 J.C. Laker *v.* Australia 1956
Best bowling performance in a match against England: 11 for 157 L. Gibbs for West Indies 1963

LIMITED-OVERS INTERNATIONALS
Highest innings total: 295 by England *v.* Pakistan (PT) 1982
Lowest innings total: 45 by Canada *v.* England (PC) 1979
Highest individual innings: 189 n.o. I.V.A. Richards for West Indies *v.* England (TT) 1984
Best bowling performance: 4 for 8 C.M. Old for England *v.* Canada (PC) 1979

FIRST-CLASS MATCHES
Highest innings total for County: 676 for 7 dec. *v.* Hampshire 1911
Highest innings total against County: 597 by London County 1903
Lowest innings total for County: 25 *v.* Derbyshire 1871
Lowest innings total against County: 24 by Sussex 1890
Highest individual innings for County: 300 n.o. F. Watson *v.* Surrey 1928
Highest individual innings against County: 282 n.o. A. Sandham for Surrey 1928
Best bowling performance in an innings for County: 10 for 55 J. Briggs *v.* Worcestershire 1900
Best bowling performance in an innings against County: 10 for 79 A.P. Freeman for Kent 1931
Best bowling performance in a match for County: 17 for 137 W. Brearley *v.* Somerset 1905

Best bowling performance in a match against County: 16 for 65 G. Giffen for Australians 1886
Best attendance: 78,617 *v.* Yorkshire 1926

LIMITED-OVERS MATCHES
Highest innings total for County: 372 for 5 *v.* Gloucestershire (NWBT) 1990
Highest innings total against County: 314 for 5 by Worcestershire (BHC) 1980
Lowest innings total for County: 76 *v.* Somerset (JPL) 1972
Lowest innings total against County: 68 by Glamorgan (BHC) 1973
Highest individual innings for County: 134 n.o. C.H. Lloyd *v.* Somerset (JPL) 1970
Highest individual innings against County: 162 n.o. C.G. Greenidge for Hampshire (JPL) 1983
Best bowling performance for County: 6 for 10 C.E.H. Croft *v.* Scotland (BHC) 1982
Best bowling performance against County: 8 for 26 K.D. Boyce for Essex (JPL) 1971
Best attendance: 33,000 *v.* Yorkshire (JPL) 1970

REFUGE ASSURANCE CUP FINAL (RAC)
Highest innings total: 235 for 5 by Worcestershire *v.* Lancashire 1991
Lowest innings total: 228 by Lancashire *v.* Worcestershire 1991
Highest individual innings: 105 S.J. Rhodes for Worcestershire *v.* Lancashire 1991
Best bowling performance: 5 for 42 N.V. Radford for Worcestershire *v.* Lancashire 1991

HOW TO GET THERE

Rail   Warwick Road (Metro/Tram) adjacent from Manchester Piccadilly (BR).
Bus   GB Buses 112, 113, 115 and 720 from Piccadilly to ground (Telephone: 061 228 7811).
Car   From north: M61 then M63 junction 4, follow signs Manchester, A5081, then after 2.5 miles left into Warwick Road and right into Talbot Road for Old Trafford. The ground is situated 2.5 miles south-west of the city centre on the east side of the main A56 in the Old Trafford district of Manchester. From east: M62 junction 17, then A56 follow signs Manchester, Old Trafford is signposted on your right in Talbot Road. From west: M62 then M63 junction 4, then as north. From south: M6 junction 19, then follow signs Stockport A556, then Altrincham A56, from Altrincham follow signs County Cricket/Test match for Old Trafford and Manchester. Old Trafford is signposted on your right off Talbot Road.

WHERE TO STAY AND OTHER INFORMATION

Hotel Piccadilly (061 236 8414), Portland Thistle (061 228 3567),

The Grand Hotel (061 236 9559) Post House Hotel (061 998 7090) and many others.

Disabled Areas   E Stand enclosure for wheelchairs, and for members in special enclosure adjoining pavilion.
Local Radio Station(s)   Greater Manchester Radio (95.1 MHz FM/ KHz MW), Radio Piccadilly (103 MHz FM/1152 KHz MW), BBC Radio Lancashire (104.5 MHz FM/1557 KHz MW).
Local Newspaper(s)   Manchester Evening News, North West Times, Saturday and Sunday Sports Pink.

Blackpool

Cricket has been played in Blackpool since 1890 when there was a ground close to the Royal Palace Gardens. The present ground at Stanley Park, formerly Whitegate Park, was donated to the club in 1924 by Sir Lindsay Parkinson who required that the ground should be owned by Trustees comprising one member of the Blackpool Cricket Club and either himself or another member of his family. Another condition was that the club should erect a stand for spectators, the present pavilion was built in 1925 to satisfy this condition. The ground covers an area of five acres and is enclosed within the park. In 1957 an additional stand was built, costing £6,000, as well as a scoreboard and groundsman's store.

During late summer, Blackpool Cricket Club has staged festivals which comprised a county match, followed by a tourists' match and then club games. The club has staged four tourists' games with the Indians, South Africans and the West Indians. In 1961 when the Australians were unable to attend, a match was staged between XIs from the North and the South. The main Blackpool cricket festival was abandoned in 1961 and Lancashire ceased playing matches at Stanley Park in 1978. Not until ten years later in 1988 did county cricket return with a Refuge Assurance Sunday League match with Middlesex.

Blackpool Cricket Club was founded in 1888 and they play in the Northern Cricket League. In 1988 the club celebrated its centenary season and issued a super brochure. The initial first-class match was staged in 1905 when the North played the South. Lancashire C C C first staged a match on the present ground in 1904 against an England XI. In order to prolong the match the laws of cricket were not adhered to in the later stages of the game and the match was ruled not to be first-class. Lancashire C C C today play one County Championship match at Stanley Park, usually in August to attract the holidaymakers. In 1989 a Refuge Assurance Sunday League match was staged with Glamorgan. In 1990 and 1991 there were County Championship matches with Surrey and Worcestershire. Derbyshire are due to visit Stanley Park in May 1992 for a Britannic Assurance County Championship match. Many benefit matches have been staged on the ground including one for Geoffrey Boycott and Ian Botham in 1984.

Blackpool Cricket Club's Stanley Park ground is rather a long walk

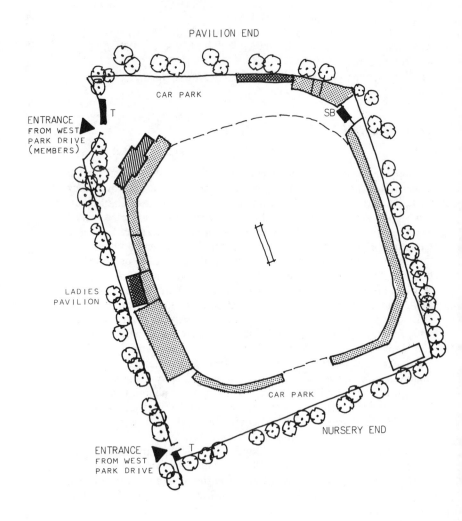

PAVILION END

CAR PARK

ENTRANCE
FROM WEST
PARK DRIVE
(MEMBERS)

T

SB

LADIES
PAVILION

CAR PARK

NURSERY END

ENTRANCE
FROM WEST
PARK DRIVE

T

N

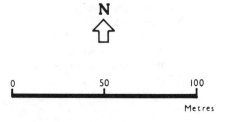

0   50   100

Metres

from the seafront and most holiday residential areas. As it is located within a large park there are ample facilities for other recreations including putting and tennis. The Blackpool club has a great tradition of having cricket professionals with Test Match status. These have included: E.A. McDonald, C.S. Dempster, H. Larwood, W.E. Alley, R.B. Kanhai, Hanif Mohammad, Collie Smith, J. Parks (Sen.), P. Roy, Mushtaq Mohammad, M. Singh and Jack Simmons. Bernard Reidy who represented Lancashire and Cumberland C C Cs plays regularly for the club.

Many of the permanent buildings on the ground have been dedicated to officials. These include members' seating adjoining the pavilion 'dedicated to Winnie and Fred Dawson for their lifetime work for the club', the scoreboard 'thanks to donations from Mr W.B. Corry' in 1954 and in 1979 in 'memory of past chairman Mr J. Holden – funds raised by ladies committee'.

Ground attendances are usually 5,500–6,000, but the best was 13,872 for the County Championship match with Glamorgan in 1950 and 12,000 for the limited-overs John Player Sunday League match with Sussex in 1976. Ground performances have included double hundreds from Ken Grieves and Peter Kirsten, the South African, while playing for Derbyshire. Bowling performances include those of R. Berry, T.B. Mitchell, C.H. Parkin and D.L. Underwood. In the limited-overs game Neil Fairbrother's 100 n.o. against Glamorgan in 1989 was achieved in 86 minutes from 71 balls with 4 sixes and 7 fours. Lancashire's highest total is 244 for 5 made in the same match and the lowest innings total against 110 by the visitors Glamorgan who were defeated by 134 runs.

ADDRESS Blackpool Cricket Club, The Pavilion, Stanley Park, West Park Drive, Blackpool, Lancashire.
TELEPHONE NUMBER PROSPECTS OF PLAY 0253 33347/ 301950

DESCRIPTION OF GROUND AND FACILITIES

There are two entrances for members to Stanley Park from West Park Drive through the main gates/turnstiles at the rear of the clubhouse/ pavilion and a further entrance for the public, to the south-west of the playing area. The pavilion, which is used by members for refreshments as well as seating, is situated to the north-west of the ground. The west side of the ground is the members' enclosure but the rest of the ground is for the public. The ladies' pavilion and open seating on the terrace, provides a fine view of the playing area for members.

South of the playing area there are deep concrete steps which are used for seating. At the top of the bank there is the facility for car parking and for people to view cricket from their vehicles. Further car parking is available in Stanley Park and in the surrounding streets. An area for disabled vehicles is available at the northern end of the ground by prior arrangement. Ample seating is available for about 75 per cent of the ground capacity of 9,000. Spectators are advised only to bring seats to very popular matches. There are both permanent and temporary refreshments and toilets are available around the ground for spectators' use. Other temporary facilities include a press tent and a Lancashire C C C Souvenir Shop situated in a small tent. The main scoreboard is sited to the north-east of the playing area and to the north there is more car parking as well as the groundsman's store and some additional seating which, although rather distant from the playing area, still provides a reasonable view. The ground is completely enclosed by a wall and trees on all four sides. The playing area is flat and is defined by a rope and some advertising boards. The playing area is 131 metres by 126 metres. The TV camera/commentary box is situated at the Nursery End of the ground, directly above and behind the sightscreen on a gantry.

Some historic photographs of Blackpool Cricket Club can be found in the pavilion bar and lounge area. Blackpool is an established ground with permanent facilities similar to Liverpool.

GROUND RECORDS AND SCORES

FIRST-CLASS MATCHES
Highest innings total for County: 494 *v*. Essex 1948
Highest innings total against County: 478 for 7 dec. by Essex 1948
Lowest innings total for County: 62 *v*. Kent 1966
Lowest innings total against County: 39 by Hampshire 1967
Highest individual innings for County: 202 n.o. K.J. Grieves *v*. Indians 1959
Highest individual innings against County: 204 n.o. P.N. Kirsten for Derbyshire 1981
Best bowling performance in an innings for County: 10 for 102 R. Berry *v*. Worcestershire 1953
Best bowling performance in an innings against County: 8 for 38 T.B. Mitchell for Derbyshire 1933
Best bowling performance in a match for County: 15 for 95 C.H. Parkin *v*. Glamorgan 1923
Best bowling performance in a match against County: 10 for 68 D.L. Underwood for Kent 1966
Best attendance: 13,782 *v*. Glamorgan 1950.

LIMITED-OVERS MATCHES
Highest innings total for County: 244 for 5 *v*. Glamorgan (RAL) 1989
Highest innings total against County: 155 by Middlesex (RAL) 1988
Lowest innings total for County: 155 for 1 *v*. Sussex (JPL) 1976
Lowest innings total against County: 110 by Glamorgan (RAL) 1989
Highest individual innings for County: 100 n.o. N.H. Fairbrother *v*. Glamorgan (RAL) 1989
Highest individual innings against County: 50 J.E. Emburey for Middlesex (RAL) 1988
Best bowling performance for County: 4 for 17 M. Watkinson *v*. Middlesex (RAL) 1988
Best bowling performance against County: 3 for 43 S.P. Hughes for Middlesex (RAL) 1988
Best attendance: 12,000 *v*. Sussex (JPL) 1976

HOW TO GET THERE

Rail Blackpool North (BR), 1 mile; Blackpool South (BR), 0.75 mile.
Bus Blackpool Transport 16 and 26 from Talbot Square adjacent to
BR Blackpool North Station to within 0.25 mile of ground (Telephone:
0523 23931).
Car From north: M6 junction 32, then follow M55 to junction 4
Blackpool and seafront; the ground is located off the A583 in West
Park Drive adjoining Stanley Park which is 0.5 mile south-east of the
town centre; or A584, A587, A586 to town centre then A583 as above.
From east: M6 junction 32, then follow M55 to junction 4 Blackpool
and Seafront, then as north. From south: A584, A583 or B5261 to
Blackpool town centre, then as north.

WHERE TO STAY AND OTHER INFORMATION

Imperial Hotel (0253 23971), Savoy Hotel (0253 52561), any of many
small hotels and guest houses.

Disabled Areas Special area at Pavilion End of ground with facility
for disabled vehicles by prior arrangement.
Local Radio Station(s) Red Rose Radio (97.3 MHz FM/999 KHz
MW), BBC Radio Lancashire (104.5 MHz FM/1557 KHz MW).
Local Newspaper(s) Lancashire Evening Telegraph, Lancashire
Evening Post, West Lancashire Gazette, Blackpool Evening Gazette.

Liverpool

In the Aigburth district of the city barely five miles from the Liver
Building is the Aigburth Cricket Ground. which as been the home of the
Liverpool Cricket Club since 1881. Liverpool C C was founded in 1807,
in the days of the Mosslake Cricket Society. Prior to this, cricket had
been played at Mersey Bowman's Archery Ground but no organized
cricket club existed until the Mosslake Society was formed in 1807.
Liverpool C C emerged from this club and moved to Wavertree Road,
Edgehill in 1829. This ground staged cricket between 1859 and 1872
including first-class matches between the Gentlemen of the North and
Gentlemen of the South. Three further moves took place due to housing
needs and in 1877 Liverpool C C was without a ground. The Earl of
Sefton rescued the club with an offer of a temporary ground at Croxteth
Park until their present move to Aigburth in 1881.

Liverpool first staged a Lancashire C C C match in 1881 when
Cambridge University were the visitors. Since then first-class and in
recent years limited-overs matches have been staged regularly. Aigburth
will not be used in 1992 for the first time in some years as it is Liverpool's
turn to miss a match since the county also take matches away from its
headquarters to Blackpool, Lytham and Southport. Liverpool is the
county's oldest home venue for matches outside Old Trafford.

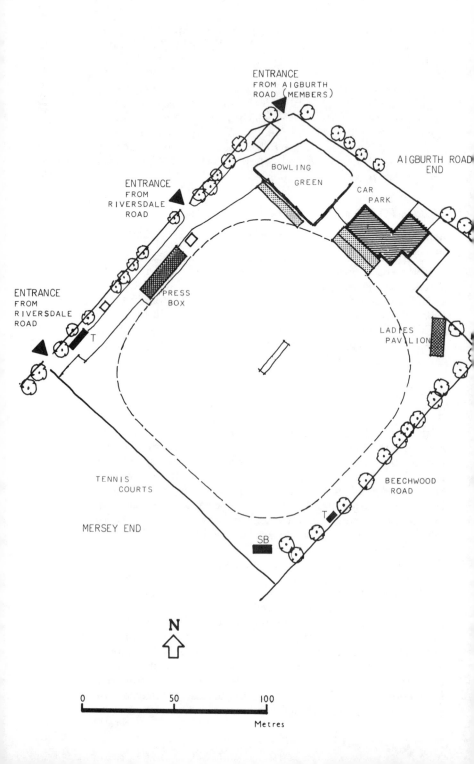

The ground is located on the corner of Aigburth Road and Riverside Road which leads down towards the River Mersey. The pavilion was constructed in 1880 by the building contractor Cubitts; it is located at the Aigburth Road End and is very grand for an out ground. During the 1880s when it was built, Liverpool was a thriving port and plenty of money was available thanks to generous support from members. There are facilities for tennis and bowling and in 1894 the Northern Lawn Tennis Tournament was staged on the ground. Hockey is played by Liverpool teams on the ground during the winter months.

Many famous players have represented Liverpool C C and Lancashire C C C including: A.G. Steel, D.Q. Steel, E.C. Hornby, R.E. Barlow and J. White. Many tour matches have been staged at Aigburth since the 1882 Australians visited the ground. Other tourists have been the South Africans, West Indians, Canadians, Philadelphians and the Parsees. Liverpool C C is a founder members of the Youngers Liverpool and District Competition and fields four XIs throughout the season. Lancashire C C C today play one County Championship and occasionally one limited-overs match at Aigburth, usually in the early part of the season.

Crowds at Aigburth regularly number around 5,000–5,500. The largest attendance was some 15,164 for the visit of Northamptonshire in 1948. The Aigburth pavilion boasts probably the largest players' dressing rooms on the county circuit, larger than at most Test venues.

During Lancashire C C C's long association with Liverpool C C there have been many memorable performances on the ground. In 1903 J.T. Tyldesley scored 248, and 29 years later Wally Hammond scored 264 for Gloucestershire, still the highest individual innings on the ground. Ground records for Lancashire include fine performances with the ball from H. Dean and for the visitors A.S. Kennedy and T.G. Wass. The majority of first-class records were made in the distant past and no doubt tax even the memories of older members. Notable performances at limited-overs matches have included 186 n.o. by Gordon Greenidge while batting for the West Indians in 1984 and effective bowling by Peter Lever and Richard Hadlee.

In 1983 while batting for his county Hampshire, Gordon Greenidge scored 104 and 100 n.o. in a championship match at Aigburth and during the Sunday League match at Old Trafford he hit 162 n.o., giving him an aggregate of 366 runs over four days.

ADDRESS Liverpool Cricket Club, The Pavilion, Aigburth Road, Grassendale, Liverpool, Merseyside L19 3QF.
TELEPHONE NUMBER PROSPECTS OF PLAY   051 427 2930

DESCRIPTION OF GROUND AND FACILITIES

Aigburth is entered from the corner of Aigburth Road and Riversdale Road. However, there are two additional pedestrian and vehicle entrances in Riversdale Road. The extensive Liverpool pavilion would be a credit to any county ground and provides first class facilities for players and members alike, with large bars, refreshment areas and ample permanent seating. The pavilion balcony, high above the playing area and directly behind the sightscreen at the pavilion end, is used as the radio commentary box and TV camera/commentary box. To the side of the pavilion is the ladies' pavilion which includes a restaurant and fine bar facilities.

The main scoreboard is situated in the south corner of the ground, and to the north-west is the covered stand with seats, groundsman's stores, toilets, bar and refreshment facilities. There is a small press box at ground level within this stand and this is known as the poorest press facility on any out ground by members of the cricketing press. The official scorers sit nearby on this side, below the level of the playing area, so it is difficult to view the play and is known by most first-class scorers as one of the worst grounds to score on. There is a special small area for disabled spectators where vehicles can be parked on the Riversdale Road side of the ground.

Temporary seating is provided and with permanent bench seats, around 7,000 seats in total which means about 80 per cent of the ground capacity can be accommodated on seats provided. The pavilion and the lawn in front of the ladies' pavilion is available to members only but the rest of the ground is open to the public. Temporary facilities for county matches include refreshment tents, a Lancashire C C C souvenir shop and an area for sponsors' marquees, all of which can be found at the Grassendale End of the ground, on the tennis courts. The flat playing area is 142 metres by 138 metres and is defined by a rope and advertising boards. Car parking is available within the ground for players' and officials only, but members may park on the lower ground adjoining the Merseyrail railway line, off Riversdale Road and Beechwood Road. Street parking is also available within a short walk from the ground.

GROUND RECORDS AND SCORES

FIRST-CLASS MATCHES
Highest innings total for County: 502 for 9 *v.* Leicestershire 1929
Highest innings total against County: 514 by Gloucestershire 1932
Lowest innings total for County: 28 *v.* Australians 1896
Lowest innings total against County: 22 by Glamorgan 1924
Highest individual innings for County: 248 J.T. Tyldesley *v.* Worcestershire 1903
Highest individual innings against County: 264 by W.R. Hammond for Gloucestershire 1932
Best bowling performance in an innings for County: 9 for 35 H. Dean *v.* Warwickshire 1909
Best bowling performance in an innings against County: 9 for 33 A.S. Kennedy for Hampshire 1920
Best bowling performance in a match for County: 17 for 91 H. Dean *v.* Yorkshire 1913
Best bowling performance in a match against County: 16 for 69 T.G. Wass for Nottinghamshire 1906

Best attendance: 15,164 v. Northamptonshire 1948

LIMITED-OVERS MATCHES

Highest innings total for County: 257 for 7 v. Derbyshire (BHC) 1988
Highest innings total against County: 297 for 6 West Indians (Tour) 1984
Lowest innings total for County: 173 v. Warwickshire (JPL) 1980
Lowest innings total against County: 162 for 4 by Derbyshire (BHC) 1975
Highest individual innings for County: 94 G. Fowler v. West Indians (Tour) 1984
Highest individual innings against County: 186 n.o. C.G. Greenidge for West Indians (Tour) 1984
Best bowling performance for County: 5 for 23 P. Lever v. Northamptonshire (JPL) 1970
Best bowling performance against County: 4 for 53 R.J. Hadlee for Nottinghamshire (BHC) 1986
Best attendance: 4,750 v. West Indians (Tour) 1984

HOW TO GET THERE

Rail   Aigburth (BR), 0.5 mile) Liverpool Lime Street (BR), 4 miles.
Bus   Merseybus 82, Crosville X5 and H25 from BR Liverpool Lime Street Station pass ground (Telephone: 051 236 7676).
Car   From north: M6 junction 28, then follow signs Liverpool on A48 and then A562 Aigburth; ground is situated south-east of the city centre in the Aigburth and Grassendale district. From east: M6 junction 21a, then M62 to junction 4, then follow signs Aigburth and County Cricket or B5180 and A561 to ground. From west: Mersey Tunnel into Liverpool city centre, then follow A562 to Grassendale and Aigburth for County Cricket and ground.

WHERE TO STAY AND OTHER INFORMATION

Holiday Inn (051 709 0181), Royal Garden (051 928 2332), St George's Hotel (051 709 7090).

Disabled Areas   Special small area sited on Riversdale Road side of the ground or where requested.
Local Radio Station(s)   BBC Radio Merseyside (95.8 MHz FM/1485 KHz MW) Radio City (96.7 MHz FM/1548 KHz MW).
Local Newspaper(s)   Liverpool Daily Post, Liverpool Echo, Liverpool Star.

Lytham

Church Road, Lytham receives one County Championship visit from Lancashire C C C each season usually in August and this is always well supported by the locals and people on summer holidays on the Fylde Coast. The venue should not be confused with Lytham St Anne's C C which is a different club.

The ground is the home of the Lytham Cricket and Sports Club and comprises a pleasant ground of some 11.25 acres nestling in trees close to the Preston-Blackpool South railway line. This passes through a cutting at the northern end of the ground. The facilities for cricket are ample and are shared with the Lytham Hockey Club, Lytham Tennis Club and Clifton Casuals Football Club. Lytham Cricket Club play in the Manchester Association Cricket League and also have teams represented in the Liverpool and District Competition.

Lancashire C C C made their initial visit to Church Road in 1985 for a County Championship fixture with Northamptonshire which was affected by rain. Since then visits have been made by Glamorgan, Sussex, Nottinghamshire, Essex and Northamptonshire. In 1992 Surrey are due to visit the seaside resort. A match was not staged in 1990 as several wickets within the square were being re-laid.

The only permanent buildings on the ground are the players' pavilion and clubhouse, located close to the parish hall, and St Cuthbert's Church. An interesting old scoreboard is located under the trees near the tennis courts. A smaller secondary scoreboard is located opposite. The clubhouse has a number of photographs and items of cricket interest including an aerial photograph of the first match staged in 1985. The majority of facilities for county matches are temporary and include raised open seating at the Church Road End.

Lytham C C has staged benefit matches for Lancashire C C C players, the most recent for Clive Lloyd in 1986. Crowds at Church Road are usually around 3,000–3,500. The largest for a single day was 3,500 against Glamorgan in 1986 and for three days 6,750 against Sussex in 1987.

Performances at Lytham have included one achievement from a number ten batsman: in 1985 against Northamptonshire David Makinson, now playing for minor county Cumberland C C C, hit 7 sixes off Richard Williams in his innings of 58 n.o. Lytham has also seen some fine bowling performances from Mike Watkinson, Dermot Reeve for his former county Sussex, Jack Simmons and Rodney Ontong for Glamorgan. With the bat, centuries have been recorded by Graham Lloyd for the home county and for the visitors by John Stephenson, Nasser Hussain, Allan Lamb and Neil Stanley. Lancashire made their highest and lowest innings total against Essex in the same match in 1989.

ADDRESS   Lytham C C, Lytham Cricket and Sports Club, Church Road, Lytham, Lancashire.
TELEPHONE NUMBER PROSPECTS OF PLAY   0253 734137

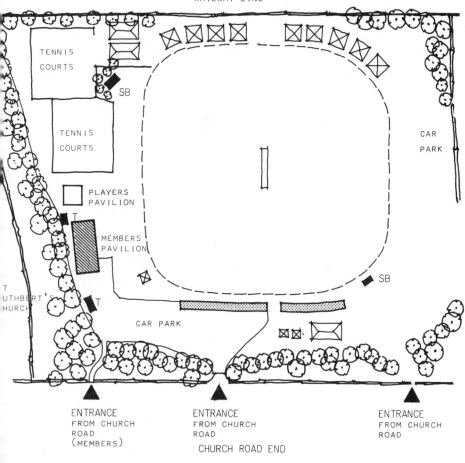

RAILWAY END

RAILWAY LINE

TENNIS
COURTS

SB

TENNIS
COURTS

CAR
PARK

PLAYERS
PAVILION

T

MEMBERS
PAVILION

ST
CUTHBERT'S
CHURCH

T

SB

CAR PARK

ENTRANCE
FROM CHURCH
ROAD
(MEMBERS)

ENTRANCE
FROM CHURCH
ROAD

CHURCH ROAD END

ENTRANCE
FROM CHURCH
ROAD

N

0   50   100

Metres

DESCRIPTION OF GROUND AND FACILITIES

The main entrance for spectators and vehicles is Church Road. There are additional pedestrian entrances off Church Road and for members' and sponsors' car parking, from Upper Westby Street. Car parking is also available in nearby streets and in a council car park only 250 yards from the main entrance. All the permanent buildings are to the west of the playing area and include a clubhouse and players' pavilion for members where there is a bar and refreshment area. The pavilion is used by players and officials only. The main scoreboard and groundsman's store are situated under the trees near to the tennis courts. Members' dining facilities and seats can be found to the west of the playing area and in a marquee at the Railway End of the ground. Hospitality marquees are also located at the Railway End and to the east of the playing area is the general temporary seating for the public, a secondary temporary scoreboard and some members' car parking. At the south Church Road End there are permanent open raised timber seating areas together with a large refreshment tent. There is no special area for disabled spectators. A press tent is sited near the clubhouse/players' pavilion and the scorers sit in the main scoreboard. The playing area is 136 metres by 131 metres and is defined by a rope and some advertising boards. A Lancashire C C C souvenir shop is also sited in a tent at the Church Road End. Permanent and temporary toilets are located around the ground. The ground capacity is 6,000 and 2,500 seats are provided so spectators are advised to bring their own seats to matches. A radio commentary position is located in the clubhouse and if required a TV camera/commentary position would be located at the Church Road End.

GROUND RECORDS AND SCORES

FIRST-CLASS MATCHES
Highest innings total for County: 381 *v*. Essex 1989
Highest innings total against County: 450 for 6 dec. by Northamptonshire 1991
Lowest innings total for County: 95 *v*. Essex 1989
Lowest innings total against County: 96 by Sussex 1987
Highest individual innings for County: 100 G.D. Lloyd *v*. Essex 1989
Highest individual innings against County: 171 J.P. Stephenson for Essex 1989
Best bowling performance in an innings for County: 7 for 25 M. Watkinson *v*. Sussex 1987
Best bowling performance in an innings against County: 7 for 37 D.A. Reeve for Sussex 1987
Best bowling performance in a match for County: 10 for 145 J. Simmons *v*. Glamorgan 1986
Best bowling performance in a match against County: 7 for 74 R.C. Ontong for Glamorgan 1986
Best attendance: 6,750 *v*. Sussex 1987

HOW TO GET THERE

Rail   Lytham (BR), 0.5 mile.

Bus   From surrounding areas to town centre, thence 0.5 mile. 11A to Lytham, 167 (St Anne's to Preston) and 193 (St Anne's to Kirkham) also pass the ground.

Car   From north: M6 junction 32, then follow M55 to junction 3, then A585 to Kirkham and B5259 signposted Lytham; ground is situated in Church Road 0.25 mile west of Lytham town centre and the seafront. From east: A583 and A584 to Lytham or as north.

WHERE TO STAY AND OTHER INFORMATION

Clifton Arms Hotel (0253 739898), Fernlea Hotel (0253 726726), St Ives Hotel (0253 720011); plus many other small hotels and guest houses. Also consider staying in Blackpool.

Disabled Areas   No special area, request suitable position.
Local Radio Station(s)   BBC Radio Lancashire (104.5 MHz FM/ 1557 KHz MW) Red Rose Radio (97.3 MHz FM/999 KHz MW).
Local Newspaper(s)   Lancashire Evening Telegraph, Lancashire Evening Post, Lancashire Evening Gazette, Lytham St Anne's Express.

Southport

The Trafalgar Road Cricket Ground is the home of the Southport and Birkdale Cricket Club which was founded in 1859. The ground was purchased in 1884, with agreement from the Weld-Blundell family and the Birkdale Park Land Company, when the Birkdale Cricket Ground Company was established. Originally the ground was largely an area of waste and sandhills to the south of the Southport to Liverpool railway line but in 1850 much development took place in the area thanks to a Mr. J. Aughton, an enterprising builder from Preston. In 1881 the present pavilion was erected for about £300 and this stood until 1965, when it was rebuilt as the facilities were no longer satisfactory, nor adequate for the annual county visit by Lancashire C C C Birkdale Cricket Club was founded in 1874 and the club merged with the Southport Cricket Club in 1901.

The new pavilion, built in 1965 cost £28,000 and was opened by Lord Derby in that year. The fixture with Derbyshire was staged in the same season and Lancashire disposed of the visitors in two days, which perhaps was just as well as it rained heavily on the third day. The Ladies' Pavilion was erected in 1958 along with a bowling green. The ground was used in 1957 by the Minor Counties Cricket Association and has been used for Southport Hockey Club, Lancashire County Police and the Australian Ladies Cricket Team, and has hosted schoolgirl hockey.

The first Lancashire C C C visit was in 1959 when Worcestershire were the visitors for a County Championship match, although there was

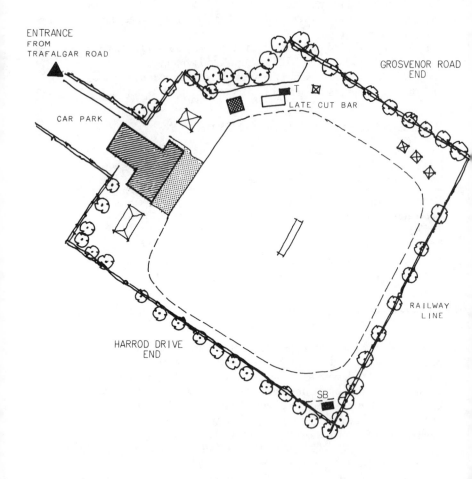

ENTRANCE
FROM
TRAFALGAR ROAD

GROSVENOR ROAD
END

CAR PARK

T

LATE CUT BAR

RAILWAY
LINE

HARROD DRIVE
END

SB

N

0   50   100

Metres

a previous visit for a Brian Statham benefit match. Since then, championship cricket has been played each summer, usually in June, and in 1969 the first limited-overs match was staged with Glamorgan in the John Player Sunday League. Other limited-overs matches have followed, the most recent was a Benson & Hedges Cup zonal group match with Scotland. The initial limited-overs match was televised and some 10,500 spectators attended. This is still a record attendance for a match on the ground. Crowds usually are 4,500–5,000 daily for championship matches.

Southport and Birkdale Cricket Club play in the Liverpool and District Cricket Competition and in recent years has spent considerable money on a new scoreboard and tiered terracing, which accommodates 2,000 spectators. The ground is entered from Trafalgar Road and the pavilion is close to the main entrance. The railway embankment runs along the far side of the ground. The Birkdale area is known more for golf than cricket, for Royal Birkdale Golf Club is only a short distance from the ground.

Ground performances at Southport have included 142 by Ken Grieves for Lancashire in the first county match, with highest individual innings on the ground of 180 by Gehan Mendis for Lancashire against Nottinghamshire in 1990, and 254, a career best by Geoff Humpage the former Warwickshire wicket-keeper during a record 470 run fourth-wicket partnership shared with Alvin Kallicharran who hit 234 n.o. Other notable performances with the bat have included Graeme Fowler who scored 126 and 128 n.o. in 1982 when batting in both innings with the aid of a runner. Bowling performances have included wickets from Ian Folley, Ken Palmer (now a first-class umpire), Jack Simmons and Eddie Hemmings. Lancashire made their highest innings total in 1990 of 452 against Nottinghamshire. In the limited-overs game the only century was scored by David Lloyd against Essex. Best bowling figures have included five wicket hauls by Barry Wood and Mike Hendrick.

ADDRESS Southport and Birkdale Cricket Club, The Pavilion, Trafalgar Road, Birkdale, Southport, Merseyside PR8 2HF.
TELEPHONE NUMBER PROSPECTS OF PLAY 0704 69951

DESCRIPTION OF GROUND AND FACILITIES

The only entrance to the ground is from Trafalgar Road to the north-west, as the ground is enclosed and surrounded by housing and on the east side is bounded by the railway line. The only permanent buildings on the ground are the pavilion, Ladies' Pavilion, 'Late-Cut' bar and a scoreboard, together with several out-buildings used as a groundsman's store and toilets. These are all located on the north-west side of the playing area, except for the scoreboard which is sited in the south-east corner, near the railway line. With the exception of the raised, permanent terrace seating in front of the scoreboard, all the seating is temporary and consists of plastic seats or benches. The members' enclosure is on the Trafalgar Road side and has a dining tent, refreshments, temporary toilets, Lancashire C C C souvenir tent and the secretary's office in addition to the permanent buildings.

At the Grosvenor Road End are the press tent, mobile tea cabin and some limited car parking for members. Public seating is available throughout the rest of the ground and is all uncovered. All seating is at ground level except the terrace area which is approximately eight feet above the playing area.

The ground is well tree-lined and rather confined compared with other Lancashire C C C home venues. Car parking for players' and officials and some members' is available in the main entrance car park at the rear of the pavilion off Trafalgar Road, and space is also available in Harrod Drive to the south of the ground and in the public car park at the Royal Birkdale Golf Club situated off the main A565 truck road some ten minutes walk from the ground. The radio commentary box and TV camera/commentary box positions are at the Harrod Drive End. The playing area is 121 metres by 126 metres and is defined by a rope and some advertising boards. The ground capacity is 6,000 and seating is provided for 75 per cent. Spectators need only take their own seats to popular matches.

GROUND RECORDS AND SCORES

FIRST-CLASS MATCHES
Highest innings total for County: 452 *v.* Nottinghamshire 1990
Highest innings total against County: 523 for 4 dec. by Warwickshire 1982
Lowest innings total for County: 70 *v.* Northamptonshire 1974
Lowest innings total against County: 70 by Essex 1978
Highest individual innings for County: 180 G.D. Mendis *v.* Nottinghamshire 1990
Highest individual innings against County: 254 G.W. Humpage for Warwickshire 1982
Best bowling performance in an innings for County: 7 for 15 I. Folley *v.* Warwickshire 1987
Best bowling performance in an innings against County: 7 for 56 K.E. Palmer for Somerset 1966
Best bowling performance in a match for County: 12 for 133 J. Simmons *v.* Gloucestershire 1983
Best bowling performance in a match against County: 10 for 175 E.E. Hemmings for Nottinghamshire 1986
Best attendance: 4,500 *v.* Worcestershire 1959

LIMITED-OVERS MATCHES
Highest innings total for County: 195 for 2 *v.* Essex (JPL) 1974
Highest innings total against County: 218 for 6 by Warwickshire (BHC) 1979
Lowest innings total for County: 162 for 9 *v.* Derbyshire (BHC) 1976
Lowest innings total against County: 110 by Derbyshire (BHC) 1976
Highest individual innings for County: 101 D. Lloyd *v.* Essex (JPL) 1974

Highest individual innings against County: 71 I.L. Phillip for Scotland (BHC) 1987
Best bowling performance for County: 5 for 12 B. Wood *v.* Derbyshire (BHC) 1976
Best bowling performance against County: 5 for 30 M. Hendrick for Derbyshire (BHC) 1976
Best attendance: 10,500 *v.* Glamorgan (JPL) 1969

HOW TO GET THERE

Rail   Birkdale Merseyrail (BR), Hillside Merseyrail (BR) both 0.5 mile.
Bus   Merseybus 16, 105, 284 from Southport Monument to within 0.25 mile of the ground; also 10 and 17 from surrounding area pass ground (Telephone: 051 236 7676).
Car   From north: A565 follow signs Southport, then Birkdale and Royal Birkdale Golf Club and County Cricket for Trafalgar Road, the ground is 1 mile south of Southport town centre and seafront. From east: M6 junction 26, then M58 and A570 to Southport, then as north. From south: A565 to Birkdale or as from east, then as from north.

WHERE TO STAY AND OTHER INFORMATION

Prince of Wales Hotel (0704 36688), Royal Clifton Hotel (0704 33771) plus many small hotels and guest houses.

Disabled Areas   No special area, request suitable position.
Local Radio Station(s) BBC Radio Merseyside (95.8 MHz FM/1485 KHz MW) Red Rose Radio (97.3 MHz FM/999 KHz MW), BBC Radio Lancashire (104.5 MHz FM/1557 KHz MW).
Local Newspaper(s)   Daily Post, Liverpool Echo, Southport Visitor.

LEICESTERSHIRE

CHURCHMAN'S CIGARETTES.

LEICESTERSHIRE.

LEICESTER

HINCKLEY

Leicestershire

Founded   25 March 1879
Colours   Dark green and scarlet
Crest   Gold running fox on green ground
President   C.H. Palmer CBE
Chairman   J.M. Josephs
Chairman cricket committee   P.R. Haywood
Chief Executive   F.M. Turner MA
Secretary   J.J. Stone
Administrative secretary   K.P. Hill
Commercial manager   M.J. Turner
Manager   J. Birkenshaw
Captain   N.E. Briers
Groundsman   L.A. Spencer
Scorer 1st XI   G.R. Blackburn
Scorer 2nd XI   S.G. Chamberlain
Curator   J. Barlow
Statisticians   G.R. Blackburn and D.A. Lambert
Sponsors   Carling Black Label
Newsletter   *Inside Edge*
Address   County Cricket Ground, Grace Road, Leicester,
Leicestershire LE2 8AD
Telephone 0533 831880
Facsimile 0533 832128
Leicestershire Rapid Cricketline   0891 567509

ACHIEVEMENTS

County Championship   Champions (1) 1975
Gillette Cup   Semi-finalists (1) 1977
National Westminster Bank Trophy   Semi-finalists (1) 1987
Benson & Hedges Cup   Winners (3) 1972, 1975 and 1985; finalists
(1) 1974
John Player Sunday League   Champions (2) 1974 and 1977
Refuge Assurance Sunday League   12th 1987
Fenner Trophy Winners (1) 1979
Tilcon Trophy   Winners (2) 1984 and 1986
Ward Four Counties Knockout Competition   Semi-finalists (1) 1989
**Lambert & Butler Cup (TCCB 7-a-side Floodlit
Competition)**   Finalists (1) 1981

GROUNDS

Leicester (County Cricket Ground, Grace Road) and Hinckley
(Hinckley C C, Sports Ground, Leicester Road).
    Other grounds that have been used since 1969 are: Coalville
(Snibston Colliery Ground, Owen Street) Loughborough (Park Road,
Loughborough) and Hinckley (Coventry Road).

SECOND XI GROUNDS
In addition to the above mentioned grounds the following are used
for second XI matches: Market Harborough C C, Cricket Ground,
Market Harborough. Telephone: Directory Enquiries; Uppingham
School, School Grounds, Uppingham, Rutland. (No Telephone);
Lutterworth C C, Church Street, Lutterworth. (No Telephone);
Kidworth C C, Cricket Ground, Kidworth. (No Telephone); Oakham
C C, Cricket Ground, Oakham. Telephone: Directory Enquiries;
Loughborough Grammar School, Loughborough. Telephone:
Directory Enquiries.

Cricket in Leicestershire can be traced back to 1744, and the present
club to 1879, but the hunting shire did not make its presence felt until the
best part of a century later with the arrival from Worcestershire of
Charles Palmer.

When Palmer was appointed secretary-captain in 1950 Grace Road
was still council property and, for the most part since first-class status
was gained in 1895, it was a struggle to keep pace with the pack. The
highest-ever position was 5th in 1905. The former schoolmaster's
formidable task was to rebuild and change the image of the club, and in
his third season Leicestershire were 6th, and 3rd in the next but, if
patchy results followed, a foundation was laid.

Palmer's own batting qualities – he twice went on MCC's tours – set
more ambitious standards and he was more than a useful bowler. When
Surrey were at their peak he took 8 for 7 against them when his intention
was to bowl an over to change his bowlers round. All 8 wickets were
taken without conceding a run, and the crowd urged him to take himself
over to ensure breaking Jim Laker's record of 8 for 2. By fate Laker was
next in, and he managed a boundary!

After seven years Palmer passed the captaincy to Yorkshire's Willie
Watson, who found a new lease of life, but it was another distinguished
import, Tony Lock, then also captaining Western Australia, who fired
Leicestershire to 8th and then on to equal 2nd with Kent.

An aura of confidence engulfed Grace Road, which now belonged to
the club. Mike Turner, a former player, who had been secretary since
1960, was appointed secretary-manager in 1969, and of his mountain of
achievements the Everest must have been the signing of Ray Illingworth,
who left Yorkshire after years of sterling service.

In the next decade the Turner-Illingworth partnership, a fusion of
enterprise and tactical skill, worked like a charm. The county's first-ever
title, the Benson & Hedges Cup, was won in 1972, and the Sunday
League taken in 1974 and 1977. Twice more the Benson & Hedges Cup
went to Grace Road, the 3rd time in 1985 under David Gower, but the
biggest fish of all was the championship in 1975. It was the culmination
of 96 years of endeavour. A double was the cause of double celebration,
and Illingworth rightly said it was a magnificent team effort. In the last
decisive match at Chesterfield Balderstone, another acquisition from
Yorkshire, scored an unusual century. At the end of the second day he

LEICESTER

MR.C.E.DE TRAFFORD,
LEICESTERSHIRE

was 51 not out, and at stumps was rushed to Doncaster to play in a Football League match. The next morning he completed his century.

One of Illingworth's gifts was to get his side working for him. He had two gifted overseas men in Graham McKenzie, Australia's fast bowler, and Davison, from Bulawayo, one of the most punishing batsmen anywhere. Higgs, Steele and McVicker were untiring bowlers, but it would have been a supreme test for the captain who brought the Ashes back from Australia to have made much of many of the older Leicestershire sides.

They did not lack fine individualists, but there weren't enough of them. C.E. ('Noisy') De Trafford, a noted hitter, led Leicestershire into first-class cricket and to a sensational victory over the champions, Surrey, in the first match. De Trafford was in charge for sixteen years both in second and first-class levels.

Bowling was the main strength in the early days with Woodcock, one of the fastest of his time, and Pougher, who topped the national averages. There was Knight, a devout lay preacher, who prayed before each innings, studied Greek and Latin and played for England, and C.J. Wood shared a record with W.C. Grace in carrying his bat seventeen times. At Bradford in 1907 he did it in both innings and put up such a stout defence that George Hirst said: 'Next time, Maister Wood, we'll bring a gun to get tha out!'

Ewart Astill was the first pro to be appointed the regular captain of any county in 1935, and the brilliant New Zealand batsman, C.S. Dempster, followed Astill. Alec Skelding, that irrepressible character, was distinctly sharp and became an umpire with remarks that have become part of the game.

Les Berry and Hallam were dependable and free-scoring openers, and the Australians, Jackson and Walsh, did much to put Leicestershire on the road to success. But George Geary and David Gower evoked the warmest local pride. Geary was fast-medium pace with an easy rhythm,

MR. W. W. ODELL,
LEICESTERSHIRE.

G. GEARY

J. J. WHITAKER

Leicestershire's mainstay. In 14 Tests he took 46 wickets and played a notable role in Australia and South Africa – on the mat he was compared to Sydney Barnes. At home he had 100 wickets in 11 seasons, and a useful batsman he notched 8 hundreds.

For natural talent Gower was one of the brightest discoveries of post-war cricket, and was an immediate success on every rung of the ladder to the top. But perhaps, like Cowdrey, he set himself too high a standard too soon and he gave the impression of being too relaxed and laid back. His sense of timing and stroke range makes batting look easy, but he surrendered both the Leicestershire and England captaincy, though in 1988 he regained the former.

Willey, from Northamptonshire succeeded him as captain in the late 1986 season, and was yet another player to find pastures new to his liking. Tolchard, also a nimble-footed batsman, was one of the county's best wicket-keepers.

Little has gone the way of Leicestershire since 1985 with the loss of de Freitas, Gower, Such and Lewis to new counties. The departure of Agnew to become BBC cricket correspondent and the retirement of Taylor, Benjamin and Willey have left gaps for youngsters to fill. Briers the senior pro has taken the captaincy with Whittaker as his deputy.

Leicester

Cricket in Leicester is said to have begun in about 1780 at Saint Margaret's Pasture, between the River Soar and the canal, but it was in 1877 that the Leicestershire Cricket Ground Company purchased some 16 acres of land bordered by Grace, Milligan and Hawkesbury Roads. It is from Grace Road that the ground takes its name, not the famous cricketer Dr W.G. Grace.

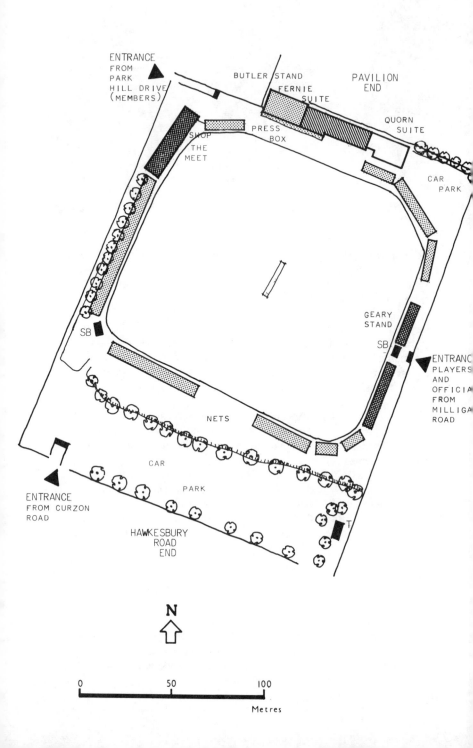

The greater part of this area was laid out and prepared for cricket and the first match took place in April 1878. The initial first-class match was with Yorkshire in 1894 and the first county match in 1895. The County Club used the ground from 1879 but after five years of County Championship cricket it was thought that in 1900 that a more accessible ground was needed closer to the city. The county club moved to Aylestone Road and in the same year the company sold most of its land.

County cricket continued at the Aylestone Road ground until 1939, but during World War Two the ground was damaged and partly used for industrial developments. Improvements in public transport suggested a return to Grace Road and once again the County Club moved to the ground they had left 46 years earlier. At this time the ground was owned by the local education authority and was the sports ground of the City of Leicester School. The County brought with them from Aylestone Road the pavilion known as the 'Meet' and a heavy roller. In 1966 the ground was finally purchased and later years have seen considerable development with the erection of a new pavilion, dressing rooms and the facilities in winter of an indoor cricket school. Situated about two miles south from the city centre, the ground remains rather inaccessible being closely surrounded by residential property. It is perhaps one of the best equipped grounds on the county circuit other than the Test match grounds.

Crowds at Grace Road in recent years have reached 12,000 which is the ground capacity for limited-overs semi-finals. The record attendance was 16,000 in 1948 when the visitors were the touring Australians.

A Prudential Cup match was staged in 1983 between India and Zimbabwe and Grace Road has been used for Young England Bull Test Matches in recent years. Outstanding batting performances have been achieved by David Gower, Keith Miller and Zaheer Abbas. Ken Higgs the former coach holds the record for the best bowling performance in a limited-overs match. In 1991 a Young England v. Young Australia Test match was staged at Grace Road, Leicester.

In 1992 the club was given an interest free loan of £100,000 by Mr Trevor Bennett, a club vice-president, towards the construction of a £450,000 indoor cricket complex to be built at the Hawkesbury Road end of the ground. On completion the intention is to re-name this the Bennett End.

ADDRESS   County Cricket Ground, Grace Road, Leicester, Leicestershire LE2 8AD.
TELEPHONE NUMBER PROSPECTS OF PLAY   0533 836236

DESCRIPTION OF GROUND AND FACILITIES

Access to the ground is via the Milligan and Curzon Road entrances, the latter being used by all entering the car park where there is space for some 500 cars. Members enter by a narrow roadway leading from Park

Hill Drive. Once inside, one quickly perceives the general spaciousness as the ground is only bounded by two-storey houses. Generally the northern end of the ground, including the pavilion, Butler Stand and the Fernie and Quorn suites and the tiered seating above, are reserved for members and visiting members, as is the Geary Stand on the east side. In the north-west corner is the Meet which, while looking like a barn with its barrel-vaulted roof, is now much changed since it was brought from Aylestone Road in 1946. It now provides refreshment facilities on the first floor for members and on the ground floor for the public. A good view of play can be obtained from the first floor of the Meet while taking refreshments. An improved Leicestershire supporters' souvenir shop has been built within the ground floor of the Meet.

A white boundary fence runs all round the perimeter of the playing area which measures some 151 metres by 133 metres. The pitch is disposed in a north-south direction providing a view from behind the wicket from the first floor of the pavilion. The Fox Bar in the pavilion displays a collection of many photographs as well as other items of cricket memorabilia including caps, ties and chinaware. More photographs and plaques can be found in the adjoining room and on the first floor of the Meet.

The main scoreboard is on the east side of the ground. In 1987 a memorial clock tower surmounted by a running fox weathervane was added to the building, as a result of a bequest in the will of Cecily Williams, widow of the late Bishop of Leicester.

The rest of the ground has permanent tiered seating and the south-east corner is also covered. Adequate toilets are available in the Meet, within the pavilion, and in a separate building in the car park area which has facilities for the disabled. Areas are set aside for handicapped spectators in the members' enclosure and at the Hawkesbury Road End of the ground. It is possible to view the cricket from a limited number of cars in the car park area if you get to the ground early, but the reflection of the sun off the windscreens can cause problems to players in the afternoon and you are advised to cover you windscreen if required. There is an excellent view from all parts of the ground. The main TV camera position is on the top of the pavilion roof as is the Radio commentary box at the northern end of the ground.

GROUND RECORDS AND SCORES

FIRST-CLASS MATCHES
Highest innings total for County: 609 for 8 dec. *v.* Sussex 1900
Highest innings total against County: 694 for 6 by Australians 1956
Lowest innings total for County: 28 *v.* Australians 1889
Lowest innings total against County: 24 by Glamorgan 1971
Highest individual innings for County: 228 D.I. Gower *v.* Glamorgan 1989
Highest individual innings against County: 281 n.o. K.R. Miller for Australians 1956

Best bowling performance in an innings for County: 9 for 29 J. Cotton *v*. Indians 1967
Best bowling performance in an innings against County: 9 for 68 G.G. Walker for Derbyshire 1895
Best bowling performance in a match for County: 15 for 136 A. Woodcock *v*. Nottinghamshire 1894
Best bowling performance in a match against County: 15 for 108 J.B. Statham for Lancashire 1964
Best attendance: 16,000 *v*. Australians 1948

LIMITED-OVERS MATCHES
Highest innings total for County: 326 for 6 *v*. Worcestershire (GC) 1979
Highest innings total against County: 314 for 4 for Gloucestershire (GC) 1975
Lowest innings total for County: 36 *v*. Sussex (JPL) 1973
Lowest innings total against County: 62 by Northamptonshire (GC) 1974
Highest individual innings for County: 156 D.I. Gower *v*. Derbyshire (NWBT) 1984
Highest individual innings against County: 158 Zaheer Abbas for Gloucestershire (NWBT) 1983
Best bowling performance for County: 6 for 17 K. Higgs *v*. Glamorgan (JPL) 1973
Best bowling performance against County: 6 for 22 M.K. Bore for Nottinghamshire (BHC) 1980
Best attendance: 8,000 *v*. Northamptonshire (NWBT) 1987

HOW TO GET THERE

Rail Leicester Midland (BR), 2 miles; South Wigston (BR) 2.25 miles.
Bus Midland Fox Nos: 68 and 73 from Belvoir Street, 0.25 miles from Leicester BR Station (Telephone: 0533 511411); also Leicester Corporation Bus No. 23 from city centre.
Car From north: M1 junction 22 or A46, A607 into city centre, follow signs to Rugby into Almond Road, then into Aylestone Road and follow signs County Cricket to Park Hill Drive for County Ground. From east: A47 into city centre, then as north. From west: M69 to junction with M1 or A50 to city centre then as north or south. From south: M1 junction 21 or M69, then A46 signposted Leicester city centre, A426, then Park Hill Drive for County Ground signposted County Cricket. The ground is located 1.5 miles south of the city centre south of the B582 which links the A426 and A50.

WHERE TO STAY AND OTHER INFORMATION

Grand Hotel (0533 555599), Forte Post House (0533 896688), Holiday Inn (0533 531161).

Disabled Areas No special area, request suitable position. A limited amount of space is set aside for disabled cars at the Hawkesbury Road End of the ground.

Local Radio Station(s)   BBC Radio Leicester (95.1 MHz FM/837 KHz MW), Leicester Sound (103.2 MHz FM/1260 KHz MW).
Local Newspaper(s)   Leicester Mercury, Leicester Mail, Leicester Trader and Saturday Sports Mercury.

Hinckley

Hinckley Town Cricket Club was formed in 1841 and their home ground has been a venue for county cricket since 1911. The present ground on the north side of Leicester Road is the third ground in the town to have been used for first-class cricket, the previous two venues being Ashby Road (1911–37) and Coventry Road (1951–64).

The current ground was formed from an area of farmland and adjoins the Hinckley Town Rugby Club with which it shares the clubhouse and parking facilities. It was opened in 1968 but not until in 1981 did Leicestershire return to the town for a championship match against neighbours Nottinghamshire. The county team now travel the 10 miles from the county headquarters at Grace Road, Leicester once a season for a single championship match at Hinckley. The ground is regularly used for Leicestershire second XI championship fixtures. Only one limited-overs Sunday League match has been staged at Leicester Road – against Essex in 1984.

Hinckley Town C C play in the Leicestershire County Cricket League and field three XIs throughout the season, together with a colts section. Players to have represented Hinckley Town C C and played first-class cricket include M.J.K. Smith (Warwickshire and England), K. Higgs (Lancashire, Leicestershire and England), L.B. Taylor (Leicestershire and England) and N.M.K. Smith, son of M.J.K., (Warwickshire).

Crowds at Hinckley have been in the region of 2,000–2,500 but for the return of county cricket to the town in 1981 some 3,000 attended. Outstanding performances at Leicester Road have included fine bowling by George Ferris and hundreds from James Whittaker, Brian Davison, Graham Gooch and Tony Cottey.

The ground is about two miles from the centre of Hinckley on the Leicester Road heading towards Earl Shilton.

ADDRESS   Hinckley Town Cricket Club, The Tavern, Leicester Road, Hinckley, Leicestershire.
TELEPHONE NUMBER PROSPECTS OF PLAY   0455 615062

DESCRIPTION OF GROUND AND FACILITIES

Approached through a single entrance off Leicester Road, the cricket ground is to the right and the rugby ground to the left. Between these areas are the two main permanent buildings on the site, the clubhouse and the Tavern Bar/pavilion. Car parking is available adjoining the entrance and on the rugby field, providing in all some 500 car spaces. The area available for members is around the clubhouse and the Tavern

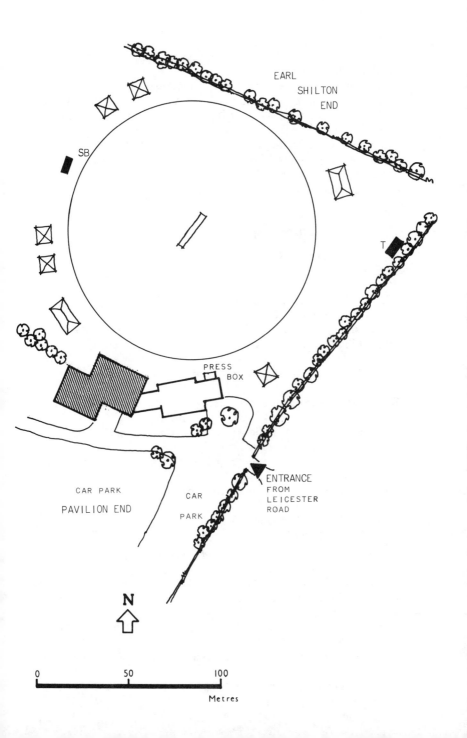

EARL
SHILTON
END

SB

T

PRESS
BOX

CAR PARK

PAVILION END

CAR
PARK

ENTRANCE
FROM
LEICESTER
ROAD

N

0   50   100
Metres

Bar/pavilion which also houses the press box and players' changing area/balcony. It extends westwards around the ground to the excellent new scoreboard that has been erected on the north-east boundary in recent years.

The playing area is circular approximately 136 metres in diameter, and is defined by a low white wooden fence. The pitch is situated in a north-east to south-west position.

Additional facilities provided for Leicestershire C C C matches include refreshment tents, Leicestershire C C C souvenir shop, sited in a small tent, sponsors' tents, as well as adequate temporary toilets. The ground capacity is set at 3,000 and members of the public are advised to bring their own seats as only 800 seats are set aside by the club for a championship match and 1,600 seats for a one-day limited-overs match. Space is available for handicapped persons and a suitable position should be requested.

GROUND RECORDS AND SCORES

FIRST-CLASS MATCHES
Highest innings total for County: 431 for 8 dec. *v*. Nottinghamshire 1981
Highest innings total against County: 354 by Nottinghamshire 1981
Lowest innings total for County: 233 *v*. Somerset 1988
Lowest innings total against County: 109 by Glamorgan 1983
Highest individual innings for County: 138 J.J. Whittaker *v*. Warwickshire 1989
Highest individual innings against County: 125 P.A. Cottey for Glamorgan 1990
Best bowling performance in an innings for County: 7 for 42 G.J.F. Ferris *v*. Glamorgan 1983
Best bowling performance in an innings against County: 6 for 64 R.C. Ontong for Glamorgan 1983
Best bowling performance in a match for County: 10 for 104 G.J.F. Ferris *v*. Glamorgan 1983
Best bowling performance in a match against County: 6 for 95 R.J. Doughty for Surrey 1986
Best attendance: 3,000 *v*. Nottinghamshire 1981

LIMITED-OVERS MATCH (JPL)
Highest innings total for County: 118 *v*. Essex 1984
Highest innings total against County: 148 for 7 by Essex 1984
Highest individual innings for County: 51 P. Willey *v*. Essex 1984
Highest individual innings against County: 51 G.A. Gooch for Essex 1984
Best bowling performance for County: 2 for 25 P. Willey *v*. Essex 1984
Best bowling performance against County: 2 for 5 J.K. Lever for Essex 1984
Best attendance: 2,000 *v*. Essex 1984

HOW TO GET THERE

Rail Hinckley (BR), 2.5 miles.
Bus Midland Fox Cub from The Borough, 600m from BR Hinckley Station (Telephone: 0533 511411).
Car From north: M1 junction 21, then M69 to junction 2, then A5070 signposted Hinckley; ground is situated off A47 Leicester Road between Hinckley and Earl Shilton; or A447 and A47 signposted Hinckley then as north. From east: B4069 or M69 junction 2, then as north. From south: M1 junction 18, then A5 signposted Hinckley, then as north; or M6 junction 2, then M69 junction 2, then as north.

WHERE TO STAY AND OTHER INFORMATION

Sketchley Grange Hotel (0455 634251).

Disabled Areas No special area, request suitable position.
Local Radio Station(s) BBC Radio Leicester (95.1 MHz FM/837 KHz MW), Leicester Sound (103.2 MHz FM/1260 KHz MW).
Local Newspaper(s) Leicester Mercury, The Hinckley Times.

MIDDLESEX

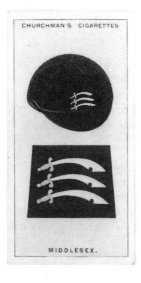

LONDON – LORD'S

UXBRIDGE

SOUTHGATE

Middlesex

Founded 2 February 1864
Colours Blue
Crest Three seaxes
Patron HRH The Prince Philip, Duke of Edinburgh KG, KT.
President D.C.S. Compton CBE
Chairman M.P. Murray
Chairman cricket committee R.A. Gale
Secretary J. Hardstaff MBE
County coach D. Bennett
Assistant coach I.J. Gould
Groundsmen M.J. Hunt (Lord's) and R. Ayling (Uxbridge)
Captain M.W. Gatting MBE
Scorer 1st XI H.P.H. Sharp
Scorer 2nd XI A.P. Jones
Statistician E. Solomon
Sponsors Smith Kline Beecham
Newsletter *Middlesex Matters*
Address Lord's Cricket Ground, St. John's Wood Road, London
NW8 8QN
Telephone 071 289 1300/1310
Middlesex Rapid Cricketline 0891 567510

ACHIEVEMENTS

County Championship Champions (10) 1866, 1903, 1920, 1921,
1947, 1976, 1980, 1982, 1985 and 1990; joint champions (2) 1949
and 1977
Gillette Cup Winners (2) 1977 and 1980; finalists (1) 1975
National Westminster Bank Trophy Winners (2) 1984 and 1988;
finalists (1) 1989
Benson & Hedges Cup Winners (2) 1983 and 1986; Finalists (1)
1975
John Player Sunday League 2nd 1982
Refuge Assurance Sunday League 3rd 1990
Refuge Assurance Cup Winners (1) 1990

GROUNDS

London (Lord's Cricket Ground, St John's Wood Road), Uxbridge
(Gatting Way, Park Road) and Southgate (The Walker Cricket
Ground, Waterfall Road).

Other grounds that have been used since 1969 are: Enfield (Lincoln
Road, Enfield) and Watford Town (Woodside, Garston).

SECOND XI GROUNDS
In addition to the above mentioned grounds the following are used
for second XI matches: Birkbeck College (University of London),

Birkbeck Avenue, Oldfield Lane, Greenford. Telephone: 081 578 1930; Ealing C C, Corfton Road, Ealing, London W5. Telephone: 081 997 1858; Enfield C C, Lincoln Road, Enfield, Middx. Telephone: 081 363 2841; Finchley C C, East End Road, Finchley, London N3. (adjoining Middlesex C C C Indoor Cricket School/ Squash Centre) Telephone: 081 346 1822; Harefield C C, Breakspear Road, North Harefield, Middx. Telephone: 0895 822225; Harrow C C, Wood End Road, Harrow, Middx. Telephone: 081 422 0932; Lensbury Club, Broom Road, Teddington, Middx. Telephone: 081 977 8821; Old Actonians C C, Gunnersbury Drive, Ealing, London W5. Telephone: 081 567 4556; Old Merchant Taylors C C, Durrants Sports Ground, Croxley Green, Rickmansworth. Telephone: 0923 773014; Potters Bar C C, The Walk, Potters Bar, Herts. Telephone: 0707 54801; R.A.F. Sports Ground, Vine Lane, Uxbridge, Middx. Telephone: 0895 37144; Richmond C C, Old Deer Park, Kew Road, Richmond, Surrey. Telephone: 081 940 2520; South Hampstead C C, Milverton Road, Hampstead, London NW6. Telephone: 081 459 2801; St. Albans C C, Clarence Park, Clarence Road, St. Albans, Herts. Telephone: 0727 50388; Watford Town C C, Woodside, Garston, Watford, Herts. Telephone: 0923 79589; Winchmore Hill C C, Ford's Grove, Winchmore Hill, London N21. Telephone: 081 360 1271.

A provisional committee circulated a letter to newspapers in 1863 which began with a challenge: 'Middlesex being the only cricketing county in England that has no county club . . .' Its birth, a year later, coincided with the acceptance of over-arm bowling, and the first edition of John Wisden's *Cricketers' Almanack*.

The Walker brothers of Southgate, all seven of them, were prime movers in the launch and long continued to be influential on and off the field. When the championship was won in 1920, Sir Plum Warner's last season, the president was R.D. Walker, who had been a member of the 1866 champions.

Several different grounds were used before Middlesex accepted an invitation by MCC in 1877 to play at Lord's. Middlesex have been identified with Lord's ever since, and it has proved, a century later, to be no disadvantage to take part in knock-out finals on their home ground. In eight finals they have won either the Gillette or the NatWest Trophy in four out of six attempts, and the Benson & Hedges Cup twice with one defeat.

Middlesex's early reputation was identified with the dashing amateur batsman. The Fords, Studds and Lytteltons set a fashion of family links which continued with the Manns, Comptons and the Robbins, father and son. The Hearne cousins from Bucks gave years of brilliant professional service. In one of his 12 Tests in 1899 at Leeds John Thomas performed the famous hat-trick dismissing Hill, Gregory and Noble, and John William ('Young Jack') bowled his googlies like an

WILLS'S CIGARETTES.

MR. P. F. WARNER (MIDDLESEX).

M. A. RAMPRAKASH

angel and formed with Elias ('Patsy') Hendren one of the most illustrious batting partnerships in county cricket. He scored 96 centuries, took 1,839 wickets, and played in 24 Tests.

Among the captains to score in the grand manner was A.E. Stoddart, who led England in two of his four tours of Australia. His approach was summed up in a single word when Aussie propaganda tried to persuade him Monty Noble's flight was a problem for England. 'Rats,' he snorted.

A wealth of talent was available up to 1914 including such names as Warner, Bosanquet, the inventor of the googly which he called the 'twisti-twosti,' A.J. Webbe, player, captain, honorary secretary and president over sixty-one years, Sir T.C. O'Brien, and the two Australian pros, Albert Trott and Frank Tarrant. Gregor MacGregor was regarded as the finest wicket-keeper of his, or maybe, any period.

Trott qualified after being omitted from his brother Harry's party to England in 1896, despite outstanding form against Stoddart's side in 1894–95. In his second and third seasons he had over 200 wickets and 1,000 runs, and in 1899 straight drove over the Lord's pavilion, a feat never accomplished before or since. In the end it did him no good as he often lost his wicket trying to repeat the shot.

His benefit in 1907 was ruined ending on the second day when he took 4 wickets with successive deliveries, and polished off the Somerset innings with a second hat-trick. 'I bowled myself into the workhouse,' he lamented. Brilliant though he was, there was a feeling that he could have been even better and his skipper MacGregor told him: 'If you had a head instead of a turnip, Alberto, you'd be the best bowler in the world.'

Tarrant, slow to medium left arm, averaged 100 wickets and 1,200 runs over a decade, and his ally J.W. Hearne provided Warner with a fine attack and runs. They did not reappear together after the First World War when Warner enriched his long career for England and county with Middlesex's 3rd championship. Warner was carried off the field in the last exciting match with Surrey.

PAT HENDREN

J. D. ROBERTSON

D. C. S. COMPTON

Warner's life was given to cricket and his beloved Lord's, and only Sir George Allen can match the length, fidelity and variation of his stewardship. Gentlemen *v*. Players, a fixture long before Test matches were thought of, was the love of his sporting life, because it represented the fabric of first-class cricket in England. 'I pray and believe it will never die,' wrote Warner. Fate decreed that he should die (in 1963), the year after the decision was taken to do away with the distinction between amateur and professional, which meant a traditional fixture, started in 1806, was no longer played.

F.T. Mann succeeded Warner in 1921 and led the championship race from starter's pistol to tape, but despite being able to call on the high talents of amateurs Allen, Stevens, Robins, Peebles, Haig, Enthoven, Killick and Owen-Smith, Middlesex had to wait until the Compton-Edrich run orgy of 1947 to taste victory again. The inability of the leading amateurs to play regularly, plus their absence on Test call, possibly cost Middlesex the honours, as they were 3rd in 1935, and runners-up in the four years up to 1939, a position retained in the first season after the war.

Hendren, with 170 centuries and 57,611 runs, and a splendid record in 51 Tests, was not merely a superb batsman and entertainer, but a personality who left a trail of warmth wherever he performed. Middlesex were singularly blessed when Compton and Edrich took over the mantle of Hendren and Hearne.

Compton, also an Arsenal footballer, collector of a Cup winners medal and a war-time international, was the most glamorous sportsman of his day. He batted as if it was fun and not a grim technical exercise, and few bowlers succeeded in shackling his genius. Mere figures seem intruders within the radius of his unique skills which had no affinity with the coaching manuals. But for a football injury he would have improved on his record of 123 centuries. Seventeen of these were for England, and a record 18, with 3,816 runs, came in the fabulous summer of 1947 when the visiting South Africans also felt the whiplash of his remarkable form. 'Far from feeling tired I wished it could have gone on forever with the season never ending,' Compton confessed. He served a demanding captain in Robins who asked for quick runs so as to leave time to bowl out his opponents twice. The first four in the Middlesex order – the thoroughbred Robertson, Brown, Edrich and Compton – responded with consistent brilliance. Centuries peeled from their bats, and remarkably Compton and Edrich augmented the bowling which included the high-class spin of Sims and Young. Middlesex have rarely had a more eventful season.

One of Middlesex's finest spinners, Titmus, collected 2,830 wickets with his off spin, and was a leading all-rounder in 53 Tests. Fast bowlers Moss, Warr, Price, Cowans and Daniel made a considerable impact as did the spinners, Emburey and Edmonds. Parfitt was invariably in the runs for both club and country, and Murray, 1,527 victims, Leslie Compton and Downton stand high in wicket-keeping ratings.

Brearley, a man of scholarship and understanding, was a captain of rare talent. As a batsman he was perhaps half a class short of Test match requirements, but he made useful scores, caught superbly at slip and was worth his weight in gold as a leader.

Gatting travelled the same road without the benefit of Brearley's apprenticeship of captaincy at Cambridge. He, too, returned from Australia a winning captain and was firmly established as England's No. 3, but his patience was over-taxed in Pakistan and he lost the captaincy. He was a victim of the pernicious practice of planting a microphone on the pitch and an altercation with an umpire was relayed to the world. Such are the pitfalls of modern international captaincy.

In 1989 Middlesex were defeated in the National Westminster Bank Trophy final at Lord's thanks to a lusty final blow from Neil Smith. A year later however, the men from St John's Wood tied up the championship and the Refuge Assurance Cup beating Derbyshire in the final at Edgbaston. Many of the achievements were thanks to the fine batting of Haynes and Gatting. The departure of Carr, Butcher, Hughes, Downton through injury and absence of Angus Fraser have left a gap but Middlesex will be looking to the future with the youngsters Ramprakash who has already played for England, Roseberry, Weekes, Hutchinson, Pooley, Keech, Headley, Farbrace and the left arm spinner Tufnell.

London – Lord's

For history and description of ground and facilities, see Marylebone Cricket Club section.

FIRST-CLASS MATCHES

Highest innings total for County: 612 for 8 dec. *v*. Nottinghamshire 1921

Highest innings total against County: 665 by West Indians 1939

Lowest innings total for County: 20 *v*. MCC 1864

Lowest innings total against County: 35 by Somerset 1899

Highest individual innings for County: 277 n.o. E.H. Hendren *v*. Kent 1922

Highest individual innings against County: 316 n.o. J.B. Hobbs for Surrey 1926

Best bowling performance in an innings for County: 10 for 40 G.O.B. Allen *v*. Lancashire 1929

Best bowling performance in an innings against County: 9 for 38 R.C. Robertson-Glasgow for Somerset 1924

Best bowling performance in a match for County: 15 for 47 F.A. Tarrant *v*. Hampshire 1913

Best bowling performance in a match against County: 15 for 122 A.P. Freeman for Kent 1933

Best attendance: 15,000 *v*. Derbyshire 1947

LIMITED-OVERS MATCHES

Highest innings total for County: 290 for 6 *v*. Worcestershire (RAL) 1990

Highest innings total against County: 272 for 4 by Gloucestershire (JPL) 1983

Lowest innings total for County: 73 *v*. Essex (BHC) 1985

Lowest innings total against County: 59 by Somerset (GC) 1977 (Reduced match)

Highest individual innings for County: 158 G.D. Barlow *v*. Lancashire (NWBT) 1984

Highest individual innings against County: 140 n.o. S.R. Waugh for Somerset (RAL) 1988

Best bowling performance for County: 7 for 22 J.R. Thomson *v*. Hampshire (BHC) 1981

Best bowling performance against County: 6 for 33 V.A. Holder for Worcestershire (JPL) 1972

Best attendance: 15,000 *v*. Somerset (NWBT) 1983

Uxbridge

Uxbridge Cricket Club, founded in 1789, claims to be the oldest club in Middlesex. Its ground at Park Road was only inaugurated in 1971, but cricket in the Uxbridge district is said to date from about 1730 and the previous grounds used were the Moor, Uxbridge Common, opposite the present ground and from 1858 the site in Cricketfield Road. The latter was vacated after 112 years use at the end of the 1970 season in order to

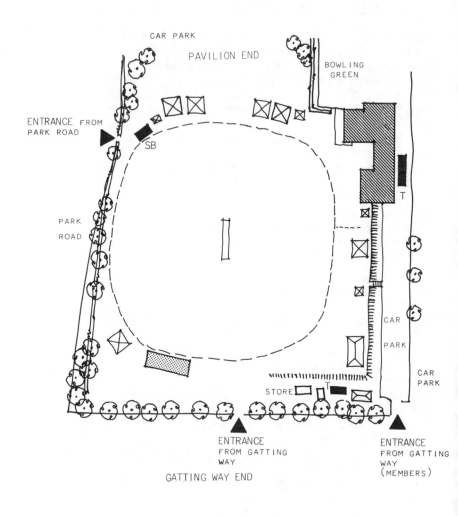

CAR PARK

PAVILION END

BOWLING GREEN

ENTRANCE FROM PARK ROAD

SB

PARK ROAD

T

STORE

T

CAR PARK

CAR PARK

ENTRANCE FROM GATTING WAY

ENTRANCE FROM GATTING WAY (MEMBERS)

GATTING WAY END

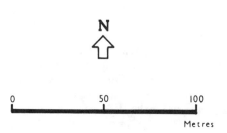

N

0   50   100

Metres

make way for the construction of the new Uxbridge Civic Centre close to the main shopping street in the town centre.

Middlesex C C C were approached to play a match at Uxbridge C C in 1979 by Club President Mr Tom Try and staged a one-day Prudential Cup warm-up match with the West Indians. This initial match only last 49 minutes before the heavens opened and the match was washed out. Middlesex C C C were not perturbed and returned the following season to play their initial first-class game at Uxbridge C C in August 1980 against Derbyshire who were defeated by 10 wickets. The venue was chosen primarily to free Lord's Cricket Ground to allow preparations to be made for the Centenary Test Match between England and Australia and the eighteenth and last Gillette Cup final which Middlesex won beating neighbours Surrey. Since 1981, Middlesex C C C have staged two first-class matches at Uxbridge each season as an Uxbridge Cricket Festival. There have been six limited-overs matches staged at Uxbridge: in the National Westminster Bank Trophy with Cumberland in 1985, Nottinghamshire 1987 and 1989 and Surrey 1990; in 1983 a Benson & Hedges Cup zonal match with Glamorgan was abandoned without a ball being bowled; in 1991 for the first time in the history of Sunday League cricket Middlesex staged two home matches away from Lord's at Southgate and with Leicestershire at Uxbridge, which was televised by Sky TV

The ground is part of a large sports complex providing facilities for squash, football, tennis and bowls as well as a swimming pool and a dry ski slope all with ample car parking adjoining. The pavilion has been extended since it was constructed in 1970–71 to include squash courts and an additional members' bar which is used as a players' dining area. The County Bar and viewing area was opened in 1981 by Phil Edmonds. As late as a month before the first club match in 1971 the outfield was still desolate, resembling a paddyfield. The first match was staged on 11 July 1971 when Colin Smith's XI played Uxbridge C C At that match with considerable foresight Freddie Brown the then president of MCC said that county cricket would be staged on the ground. Two first-class groundsmen assisted with the square in the club's early years Ted Swannell from Lord's and Chris Hawkins from Old Trafford. In 1991 Richard Ayling the present groundsman was presented with the TCCB Runners-up award for the best out ground of the season by Donald Carr.

Approaching the ground off Park Road through Gatting Way, the observant visitor will also notice Brearley Close in the neighbouring housing estate. Uxbridge Cricket Club field four XIs and one mid-week side throughout the season. Among players to have represented Uxbridge C C and Middlesex C C C are B.J.T. Bosanquet, Norman Cowans and Roland Butcher. The club play in the Thames Valley Cricket League and were founder members of the league. Uxbridge C C emerged as one of the leading club teams in Middlesex thanks to the sterling efforts of A.W.P. 'Tony' Fleming known to many as the grounds administrator at Lord's.

The ground capacity is 5,500 and to date the highest attendance for a

Middlesex match was 5,750 for the National Westminster bank Trophy match against Nottinghamshire in 1987. In 1991 an exhibition match between India and Pakistan attracted a crowd of 6,500 and had to be abandoned when the crowd invaded the pitch.

Ground records have included double centuries by Desmond Haynes 206 n.o. against Kent and in 1985 a career best 200 against Northamptonshire from Clive Radley, now the head coach at Lord's. For the visitors major innings have included 152 by Jimmy Cook for Somerset in 1990 and 148 by Chris Balderstone for Leicestershire in 1982. Best bowling performances on the ground for the home county have been achieved by Phil Edmonds and Vincent van der Bijl, the tall South African from Natal and for the visitors, from spinners Nick Cook and Keith Medlycott.

In the limited-overs game a high scoring match was staged with Surrey in the 2nd Round National Westminster Bank Trophy match in 1990. Batting records have been achieved by Mark Ramprakash and Tim Robinson while best bowling performances have been by Phil Edmonds and Andy Pick. In 1988 the touring Aboriginal Australian cricketers staged a match with a Gents of Uxbridge XI at Park Road.

The pavilion houses a number of cricket photographs and cricket memorabilia of Uxbridge C C In 1989 Uxbridge C C celebrated their bicentenary and many functions took place during the season including a club tour of Australia and Bangkok.

The ground is the only venue currently used for first-class matches by the county other than Lord's Cricket Ground. The ground has been used for second XI cricket since 1973 when the opposition was Warwickshire. Visitors in 1992 include Northamptonshire, Yorkshire and Worcestershire for Britannic Assurance Championship matches, with a possible 2nd round National Westminster Bank Trophy match between Middlesex and Durham, the eighteenth county, if both sides win their 1st round matches.

ADDRESS   Uxbridge Cricket Club, The Pavilion, Gatting Way, Park Road, Uxbridge, Middlesex.
TELEPHONE NUMBER PROSPECTS OF PLAY   0895 37571

DESCRIPTION OF GROUND AND FACILITIES

Although Park Road is one of the main access roads from Uxbridge town centre to the M40 motorway, the ground is screened from the road by high hedges and there is therefore little distraction to watching the cricket. The ground is approximately level and the playing area is near circular and 124 metres by 122 metres. The pitch is in a north-south disposition. Access to the ground is from Gatting Way for members and the public. There is an additional entrance off Park Road to the rear of the scoreboard and from car park No. 4 at the Pavilion End. There is sufficient car parking for members and the public in four large areas to the rear of the pavilion and adjoining the sports complex and swimming pool off Gatting Way (car parks Nos 1 to 3). A few cars are allowed into the ground and can be parked at the Gatting Way End from which the cricket can be viewed. This facility is sometimes withdrawn as the area is used for temporary facilities.

The pavilion/clubhouse, a good modern complex, is situated in the north-east corner of the ground furthest from the entrance, while the scoreboard is in the north-west corner. These are the only two permanent buildings on the ground other than a groundsman's store. For Middlesex C C C festival matches many additional temporary facilities are provided and these normally include raised plastic seating, a number of sponsor's marquees, members' refreshment tents and bars. These are positioned at the Pavilion End and to the east of the playing area. The members' enclosure usually extends from the clubhouse/players' balcony to the scoreboard. Other provisions include a Middlesex C C C office and souvenir tent close to the main entrance, a press tent and radio commentary area close to the pavilion and several temporary portable toilets. Some temporary tiered seating is also provided for the public at the Gatting Way End in the south-west corner close to the cricket nets. There is plenty of temporary seating in all areas so it is usually unnecessary to bring your own seats with you. The TV camera/commentary position is located directly above and behind the sightscreen at the Gatting Way End of the ground an a gantry. No special facilities exist for disabled spectators other than the provision of car parking close to the entrance at the Gatting Way End. It is advisable to ask for a suitable position.

GROUND RECORDS AND SCORES

FIRST-CLASS MATCHES
Highest innings total for County: 567 for 8 *v.* Northamptonshire 1985
Highest innings total against County: 445 for 6 dec. by Somerset 1990
Lowest innings total for County: 159 *v.* Surrey 1986
Lowest innings total against County: 121 by Hampshire 1983
Highest individual innings for County: 206 n.o. D.L. Haynes *v.* Kent 1989
Highest individual innings against County: 152 S.J. Cook for Somerset 1990
Best bowling performance in an innings for County: 6 for 48 P.H. Edmonds *v.* Hampshire 1982
Best bowling performance in an innings against County: 6 for 32 N.G.B. Cook for Leicestershire 1982
Best bowling performance in a match for County: 10 for 59 V.A.P. van der Bijl *v.* Derbyshire 1980
Best bowling performance in a match against County: 10 for 118 K.T. Medlycott for Surrey 1986
Best attendance: 3,500 *v.* Gloucestershire 1986

LIMITED-OVERS MATCHES
Highest innings total for County: 291 for 5 *v.* Surrey (NWBT) 1990

Highest innings total against County: 288 for 8 by Surrey (NWBT) 1990
Lowest innings total for County: 129 for 9 *v.* Leicestershire (RAL) 1991
Lowest innings total against County: 152 by Cumberland (NWBT) 1985
Highest individual innings for County: 104 M.R. Ramprakash *v.* Surrey (NWBT) 1990
Highest individual innings against County: 79 R.T. Robinson for Nottinghamshire (NWBT) 1987
Best bowling performance for County: 4 for 28 P.H. Edmonds *v.* Cumberland (NWBT) 1985
Best bowling performance against County: 3 for 39 R.A. Pick for Nottinghamshire (NWBT) 1987
Best attendance: 5,750 *v.* Nottinghamshire (NWBT) 1987

HOW TO GET THERE

Rail   Uxbridge Underground Station (Metropolitan/Piccadilly lines), 0.75 mile.
Bus   L.R.T. 223 from Uxbridge and West Ruslip Underground Stations pass ground; also from surrounding areas 128 and 129 (Telephone: 071 222 1234).
Car   From north: M25 junction 16, then M40 to junction 1, then follow A412 signposted Uxbridge and County Cricket, ground and car parks are situated off A412 Park Road in Gatting Way, 1 mile north of the town centre opposite Uxbridge Common. From east: A40 Western Avenue from Central London to junction 1 of M40, then A412 signposted Uxbridge and County Cricket from ground, then as north. From west: M40 junction 1, then follow signs Uxbridge and County Cricket, then as north. From south: M25 junction 6, then as north or M4 junction 4, then A412 signposted Uxbridge and County Cricket.

WHERE TO STAY AND OTHER INFORMATION

The Guest House (081 574 3977), Master Brewer Hotel (0895 51199), The Barn Hotel, Ruslip, or stay in Central London/Heathrow Airport hotels within 15 minutes drive.

Disabled Areas   Space available for vehicles in car park. No special area, request suitable position.
Local Radio Station(s)   Greater London Radio (94.9 MHz FM/1458 KHz MW), Capital Radio (95.8 MHz FM/1548 KHz MW), LBC (97.3 MHz FM/1152 KHz MW).
Local Newspaper(s)   Evening Standard.

Southgate

The Walker Cricket Ground is the home of Southgate Cricket Club founded in 1855. The Southgate C C have two picturesque cricket grounds together with a full time groundsman, and catering and bar staff. Many famous cricket personalities have been associated with Southgate C C including: Sir Cyril Hawker and T.N. 'Tom' Pearce.

Probably the most famous of Middlesex cricketing families played their cricket at Waterfall Road, Southgate – the Walker family lived close by at Cannon Hill and all seven brothers represented the local club. John Walker founded Southgate C C in 1855 and was responsible for levelling and returfing the ground. The Walker family single handedly raised a team entitled 'Middlesex' to play Kent at Southgate in 1859 and they were also responsible for founding Middlesex C C C in 1863–64 and producing a county team who first played at Lord's in 1877. Another brother Vyell Walker took ten wickets in an innings in three separate matches during his career. Vyell Walker was elected president of Middlesex C C C in 1891 and he was also a member of the MCC committee.

The ground was originally called Chapel Fields and many of the early matches staged on the ground involving United All England teams, MCC and Southgate C C attracted crowds of 10,000 or more. The ground was given the name 'The Walker Cricket Ground' by a deed of trust on 19 December 1907 when the document was duly signed by R.D. Walker who was the last surviving of the seven brothers.

There is also a thriving squash club with six courts. The ground has an electronic scoreboard, artificial pitch within the square and some grass cricket nets.

Southgate C C field four XIs on both Saturday and Sunday together with a mid-week team. Southgate C C were founder members of the Middlesex County Cricket League in 1972 and the club have won the league trophy twice in 1976 and 1977. The club play some of the best amateur cricket in the county and have since 1969 reached at least the quarter-final stages in eleven of the last nineteen years of the National Club Championship now called The Cockspur Cup. Southgate C C won the John Haig Trophy at Lord's in 1977, beating Bowden C C from Cheshire.

The ground facilities are shared with the Southgate Adelaide C C (1870), Southgate Hockey Club (1886), Southgate Adelaide Hockey Club (1926), Squash Rackets Club (1975), Oakwood Netball Club (1958), 6th Southgate Scout Group (1918), The Walker Association (1975) and The Weld Lawn Tennis Club (1924).

The Southgate Hockey Club compete in the Pizza Express National Hockey League and amongst others club members include Richard Dodds, the GB Captain and our internationally famous striker Sean Kerly.

Players to have represented Southgate C C and Middlesex C C C

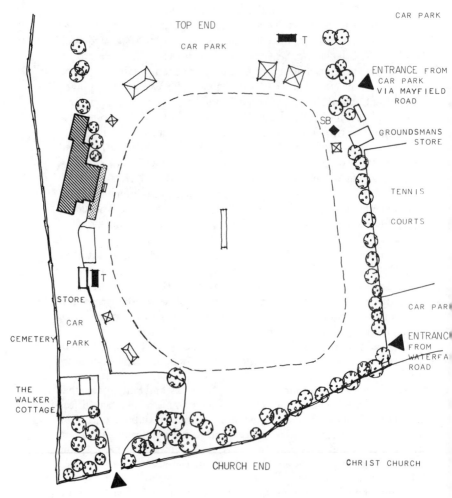

TOP END
CAR PARK

CAR PARK

T

ENTRANCE FROM
CAR PARK
VIA MAYFIELD
ROAD

SB

GROUNDSMANS
STORE

TENNIS

COURTS

CAR PARK

ENTRANCE
FROM
WATERFALL
ROAD

STORE

CAR
PARK

CEMETERY

THE
WALKER
COTTAGE

T

CHURCH END

CHRIST CHURCH

ENTRANCE
(MEMBERS)
FROM WATERFALL ROAD

N

0   50   100

Metres

include Alan Fairbairn, the late Wilf Slack and current Test spin bowler Phil Tufnell.

The current ground capacity is 7,000 and the record attendance was approximately 10,000 for the match with Kent in 1859. Last season the Refuge Assurance Sunday League match with Kent staged 132 years later attracted 4,000.

Ground records in the single first-class match involving Middlesex include achievements by John Wisden and Vyell Walker for the home county and for the visitors by W. Goodhew and G. Wigzell. In the first limited-overs match staged in 1991 against Kent fifties were recorded by Michael Roseberry and Mark Benson.

ADDRESS Southgate Cricket Club, The Walker Cricket Ground Trust, The Pavilion, The Waterfall Cricket Ground, Waterfall Road, Southgate, London N14 7JZ.

TELEPHONE NUMBER PROSPECTS OF PLAY   081 886 8381

DESCRIPTION OF GROUND AND FACILITIES

The ground is entered next to the cemetery from Waterfall Road for players/officials and members. There is also an entrance from the car park adjoining the tennis courts for members and the general public to the south-east of the playing area. A further entrance for car parking on the third XI ground is located in Mayfield Avenue off the High Street, where space is available for 500 cars. There is also plenty of street parking in the neighbouring housing areas close to the ground. The only permanent buildings on the ground are the pavilion/clubhouse including squash courts, electronic scoreboard, groundsman's house known as The Walker Cottage, and store.

For Middlesex C C C matches the majority of facilities are temporary and these include at the Top End sponsor's marquees, refreshment and bar tents, temporary toilets, cricket nets, press/scorers' tent and temporary plastic seating. To the east and south of the playing area are more temporary seats together with several refreshments kiosks, a first-aid tent and scorecard sales point. To the west of the playing area is the pavilion/ clubhouse and in front the members' enclosure. There are several small refreshment stalls, a small bar, temporary toilets and a Middlesex C C C office and Souvenir tent to the south-west of the playing area. A restaurant and refreshment area is also available inside the pavilion for members. The smooth playing area is 145 metres by 124 metres and falls towards the Church End to the south. There is no special area for disabled spectators although vehicles can be parked at the Church End. The TV camera/commentary box position would be situated at the Top End if required. The ground capacity is 7,000 and approximately 50 per cent of seating is provided so spectators would be advised to bring their own seating to popular matches.

Inside the pavilion can be found two old cricket bats used by the Walker brothers of Southgate together with a report which is titled

'Cricket in the time of the Walkers'. There is also a number of team photographs and a large display of the 1977 John Haig Cup final with Bowden and other Southgate memorabilia on display. During a break in play one can visit the library in the pavilion run by The Administrative Director of the Walker Cricket Ground Trust, Mr Christopher Sexton and also the gravestones of the Walker brothers in the nearby graveyard of Christ church in Waterfall Road.

GROUND RECORDS AND SCORES

FIRST-CLASS MATCH

Highest innings total for County: 160 *v*. Kent 1859
Highest innings total against County: 106 by Kent 1859
Lowest innings total for County: 71 *v*. Kent 1859
Lowest innings total against County: 47 by Kent 1859
Highest individual innings for County: 42 J. Wisden *v*. Kent 1859
Highest individual innings against County: 24 W. Goodhew (twice)/ W.S. Norton for Kent 1859
Best bowling performance in an innings for County: 6 for 31 V.E. Walker *v*. Kent 1859
Best bowling performance in an innings against County: 7 for 20 G. Wigzell for Kent 1859
Best bowling performance in a match for County: 7 for 68 V.E. Walker *v*. Kent 1859
Best bowling performance in a match against County: 11 for 50 G. Wigzell for Kent 1859
Best attendance: 10,000 *v*. Kent 1859

LIMITED-OVERS MATCH

Highest innings total for County: 255 for 9 *v*. Kent (RAL) 1991
Highest innings total against County: 276 for 6 by Kent (RAL) 1991
Highest individual innings for County: 79 M.A. Roseberry *v*. Kent (RAL) 1991
Highest individual innings against County: 78 M.R. Benson for Kent (RAL) 1991
Best bowling performance for County: 2 for 48 J.E. Emburey *v*. Kent (RAL) 1991
Best bowling performance against County: 2 for 37 A.P. Igglesden for Kent (RAL) 1991
Best attendance: 3,500 *v*. Kent (RAL) 1991

HOW TO GET THERE

Rail Southgate Underground Station (Piccadilly Line), 0.75 mile; New Southgate and Frien Barnet Station (BR), 1 mile.
Bus L.R.T. W9, 121, 125 and 298 pass near the ground (Telephone: 071 222 1234).
Car From north: M25 junction 24, then follow A111 signposted Cockfosters, until you reach Southgate Underground Station at

Southgate Circus, then take High Street A1004 to the Green, then take right into Waterfall Road A1003 for cricket ground opposite Christ church. From: east: M25 junction 24, then as notyh above; or North Circular Road A406 to A105 junction with Green Lanes, then take right into Green Lanes A105, then left into Alderman's Hill A1004 passing Palmer's Green and Southgate BR Station, then right into Cannon Hill A1004, then left at the Green take first left into Waterfall Road A1003 for cricket ground opposite Christ church. From west: M25 junction 24, then as north; or North Circular Road A406 to New Southgate then take A110 Bowes Road left, then right at New Southgate for A1003 Waterfall Road and cricket ground situated on left opposite Christ church. From south: as west or east or A105 from Wood Green district to Alderman's Hill, Palmer's Green, then as east.

WHERE TO STAY AND OTHER INFORMATION

Forte Post House Hampstead (071 794 8121), or stay in Central or North-west London.

Disabled Areas No special area, request suitable position. Parking of disabled vehicles at Church End.
Local Radio Station(s) Greater London Radio (94.9 MHz FM/1458 KHz MW), Capital Radio (95.8 MHz FM/1548 KHz MW) LBC (97.3 MHz FM/1152 KHz MW).
Local Newspaper(s) Evening Standard.

NORTHAMPTONSHIRE

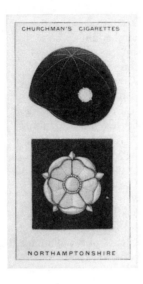

NORTHAMPTON

LUTON

WELLINGBOROUGH

FINEDON

TRING

Northamptonshire

Founded   31 July 1878
Colours   Maroon
Crest   Tudor rose
Patron   The Earl of Dalkeith
President   W.R.F. Chamberlain
Chairman   L.A. Wilson
Chairman cricket committee   A.P. Arnold
Chief executive   S.P. Coverdale MA., LLB.,
Director of cricket   M.J. Proctor
County coach   R.M. Carter
Cricket development officer   B.L. Reynolds
Captain   A.J. Lamb
Groundsman   R. Bailey
Scorer 1st XI   A. Kingston
Scorer 2nd XI   B.H. Clarke
Statistician   L.T. Newell
Sponsors   Carling Black Label
Newsletter   *Northamptonshire News*
Address   County Cricket Ground, Wantage Road, Northampton, Northamptonshire NN1 4NJ
Telephone 0604 32917
Facsimile 0604 232855
Northamptonshire Rapid Cricketline   0891 567511

ACHIEVEMENTS

County Championship   2nd (4) 1912, 1957, 1965 and 1976
Gillette Cup   Winners (1) 1976
National Westminster Bank Trophy   Finalists (3) 1981, 1987 and 1989
Benson & Hedges Cup   Winners (1) 1980; finalists (1) 1987
John Player Sunday League   4th 1974
Refuge Assurance Sunday League   3rd 1991
Refuge Assurance Cup   Semi-finalists (1) 1991
Fenner Trophy   Winners (1) 1978
Tilcon Trophy   Winners (2) 1982 and 1983; finalists (1) 1981

GROUNDS

Northampton (County Cricket Ground, Wantage Road) Luton (Wardown Park, Old Bedford Road) Wellingborough (Wellingborough School, Irthlingborough Road) Finedon (Dolben Cricket Ground, Avenue Road) and Tring (Pound Meadow, Station Road).

Other grounds that have been used since 1969 are: Peterborough (Baker Perkins Sports Ground); Peterborough Town C C (Bretton

Gate, Westwood); Kettering (Kettering C C, Northampton Road); Brackley (Brackley C C, off Buckingham Road); Bedford (Bedford School, Burnaby Road); Milton Keynes (Bletchley C C, Manor Fields, Bletchley) and Horton (Horton House C C, Horton).

SECOND XI GROUNDS
In addition to the above mentioned grounds the following are used for Second XI matches: Oundle School, School Ground, Oundle. (No Telephone); Bedford School, Burnaby Road, Bedford. Telephone: 0234 53435 (school hours only); Old Northamptonians C C, Cricket Ground, Northampton. Telephone: Directory Enquiries; Peterborough Town C C, Bretton Gate, Westwood, Peterborough, Cambs. Telephone: 0733 262202; Great Oakley C C, Cricket Ground, Great Oakley. (No Telephone); Bedford Modern School, School Grounds, Bedford. (No Telephone); Banbury Twenty Club., Daventry Road, Banbury, Oxon. Telephone: 0295 3757.

Promotion to first-class status in 1905 was gained on the persuasive talents of George Thompson, the first from Northamptonshire to be selected by England and regarded as the finest local-born cricketer. As *Wisden* observed at the time: 'Thompson, to a greater extent than all the other members of the side put together, rendered the promotion possible.' *Wisden* might not have done justice to William East, another medium pace bowler and able batsman, but the combined excellence of Thompson, who scored 125 against the Gentlemen while still in the Minor Counties and East, was impressive.

On the whole the new ranking was justified up to 1914, despite the county's small population and moderate standard of club cricket. The unpleasant experience of being dismissed for a record low total of 12 at Gloucester Spa in 1907 ('come home to mother' telegraphed the secretary) was banished in 1912 when, with a settled pool of only twelve, Northamptonshire were runners-up to Yorkshire. Nine of the side, captained by G.A.T. Vials, played in every match, including the Denton twins, S.G. Smith, a white West Indian and the first of the line of overseas players.

Wounded in the war, Thompson was never again the same force, the pre-war side crumbled, and the cold facts of the club's frugal resources caused financial embarrassment and a sharp decline in playing strength. As late as the 'fifties a committee minute was recorded that the life span of the club was no more than two years unless the situation improved.

In the twenty-four years between 1919 and 1948 Northamptonshire were bottom ten times, bottom-but-one in six others, and four seasons passed between May 1935 and May 1939 without a single champion-ship victory. When the ice was broken the crowd, such as it was, assembled in front of the pavilion in celebration.

The threadbare existence was punctuated by public appeals, and on more than one desperate occasion it was admitted there were simply not

NORTHAMPTON

R. J. BAILEY

the means to support first-class cricket. Many and varied were the fund-raising schemes. Sir Thomas Beecham took his orchestra to the town free of charge with the proceeds of the concert divided between the club and the local YMCA, and the Northamptonshire Regiment, serving in India, had a 'voluntary' collection familiar to most servicemen.

Fortunately there were two fairy godfathers: Albert Cockerill, who presented the ground in trust to the club – previously they had played on the old Racecourse – and Stephen Schilizzi. In post-war years the Herculean efforts of secretary Ken Turner turned the accounts from red to black and created facilities only dreamed of through football competitions, discos and rock concerts. Without him Northampton-shire would assuredly have gone to the wall.

Founded in 1878, when Northamptonshire won the Gillette Cup in 1976, their first ever success, it was with a side largely built on the profits from rock and disco. 'If only the crowds queuing to get into the ground for the concerts had been to watch cricket I would have been a happy man,' said Turner. The side also took 2nd place in the championship. Captained by Mushtaq Mohammad, and including his fellow Pakistani, Sarfraz Nawaz, and Bishen Bedi, the Indian captain and classic slow left arm bowler, this was by general consent Northamptonshire's strongest-ever team. Other captains, Brookes and Andrew, who also achieved runner-up positions, stand comparison, and Peter Watts added more distinction to a once-humble club with the Benson & Hedges Cup in 1980.

Northamptonshire had capable players in the dark days of the calibre of Vallance Jupp, wooed from Sussex as player-secretary, Timms, Bakewell, Brookes, Walden, Clark, and Claude Woolley, Frank's brother, but there was no in-depth strength. Clark and Capel followed Thompson as local-born Test players. Clark, fast left arm, had a firebrand reputation, and was one of the first cricketers to be used in a national advertising campaign. Shown in the eye-catching moment of

G. J. THOMPSON (NORTHAMPTON.).

15. V. W. C. JUPP

FRANK TYSON

delivering the ball, he was paid the princely sum of £100.

Clark had a lot to put up with. One morning after a second slip catch had been spilled he suddenly stopped on the way back to his bowling mark, looked at a skylark in full song overhead, and roared: 'What the — have you got to sing about?'

Both Bakewell and Milburn, two England batsmen, were tragically victims of car crashes at the peak of their careers. Bakewell, at 27, never played again while Milburn, one of the biggest crowd-pullers and most popular figures in the game, valiantly but briefly returned with only one eye.

Dennis Brookes, JP, a former chairman of the Northampton bench, scored 30,874 runs with 71 centuries, and served as batsman, captain, coach, assistant secretary and president with equal distinction. His ability deserved more than one cap and, typical of his tardy recognition, was to be told by the captain, Hammond, to get measured for his kit for the Australian tour of 1946–47 only to be passed over once again.

The escape from the post-war gloom dated from the inspired recruitment of F.R. Brown, who had virtually retired from first-class cricket. Never was there a better investment. Brown's direct and honest approach gave Northamptonshire new purpose and hope. England, too, had cause to be grateful for the resurrection of his career. What he did for his adopted county, he did for his country.

Tyson, and the immaculate wicket-keeper Andrew, seemingly unwanted by Lancashire, were the first of the county's pros to be selected for an Australian tour, and 'Typoon' Tyson's part in Hutton's triumph is history. Yet but for Northampton Brown and Tyson, such successes in Australia, might have faded out of first-class cricket.

Overseas stars have included Lamb, Kapil Dev, Harper, Davis and Dennis Lillee, and from a wide choice Turner rates Mushtaq and the Australian googly left arm bowler Tribe as the two most gifted. Raman Subba Row was another successful captain from Surrey, and the

Australian, Livingstone, was a heavy scorer and an invaluable link with the northern Leagues when Turner's recruitment drive was in full swing.

As assistant secretary Turner shrewdly assessed the needs of county cricket, and, as secretary from 1958, he put his ideas into practice. A backroom staff of Brookes, Mercer and Davis scoured the country for talent, and the policies were so successful that by his retirement no fewer than nine first-time Test caps had been won – Milburn, Larter, Prideaux, Larkins, Geoff Cook, Lamb, Steele, Willey and Subba Row. Many were coached by Brookes and Bailey, capped in 1988, was also taken on by Turner. Reynolds was also a first-rate coach.

Inevitably there were set-backs. The centenary season began with the building of a new £100,000 pavilion and ended with an injury-ridden side at the bottom, Bedi and a groundsman took the club to Industrial Courts alleging wrongful dismissal but lost their claims, and four Lord's finals, including two in 1987, ended in defeats. Yet it could be said in truth there was a time when Northamptonshire would have been wild outsiders to win anything but sympathy from the more fortunate clubs.

The club has been rebuilding since the departure of Geoff Cook, Wayne Larkins and Simon Brown to Durham, Robinson to Yorkshire and the retirement from county cricket of Davis, Wild and Thomas. The new overseas stars are Curran and Baptiste, although Ambrose is likely to return in 1992. Mike Proctor was appointed director of cricket and with the influx of Fordham, Stanley, Penberthy, Noon and Taylor the future looks bright.

Northampton

The ground was formed from land in the Abingdon district on the east side of Northampton and laid out by the Northampton County Cricket and Recreation Grounds Company Limited in 1885 for £2,000 under the guidance of H.H. Stephenson, an old Surrey cricketer who captained the first ever England team to visit Australia. The county club moved to this venue in 1886 having previously played at the Northampton Racecourse before being forcibly ejected. The ground is shared with Northampton Town Football Club and association football has been played on the ground since 1897, which restricts cricket games at the beginning and end of the season. The Old Pavilion was originally shared with the football and bowling clubs but is now in sole use of the cricket club and forms the members' main enclosure.

The initial first-class match staged at the County Ground, Northampton was on 5–7 June 1905 against local neighbours Leicestershire.

The members' old pavilion was refurbished in the winter of 1990–91 and now includes a bar and club room together with a sponsors' area and an enlarged open and covered area for members on a variety of coloured plastic tip-up seats. In 1979 a new players' pavilion was erected in place of the old ladies' pavilion. This now houses facilities for players, umpires and executive boxes at first floor level together with the club

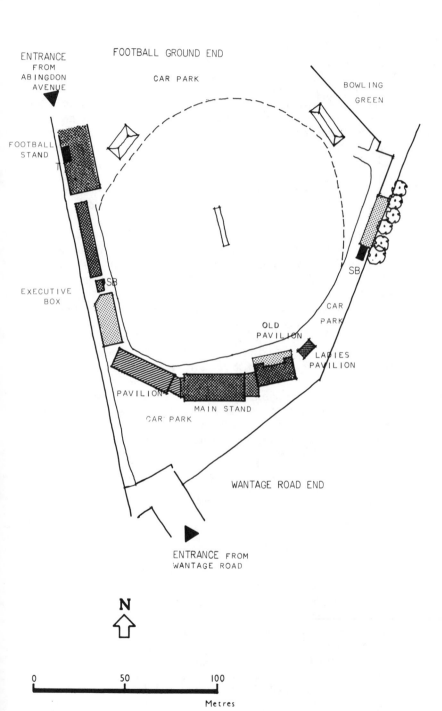

ENTRANCE
FROM
ABINGDON
AVENUE

FOOTBALL GROUND END

CAR PARK

BOWLING
GREEN

FOOTBALL
STAND

EXECUTIVE
BOX

SB

SB

OLD
PAVILION

CAR
PARK

LADIES
PAVILION

PAVILION

MAIN STAND

CAR PARK

WANTAGE ROAD END

ENTRANCE FROM
WANTAGE ROAD

N

0   50   100
Metres

offices. On the ground floor can be found the members' bar, members' room and the players' dining area. The new pavilion was added to in 1987 and 1988 and is now joined to the main stand, so increasing the size of the administration offices.

The ground has struggled for recognition and praise over the years; although it is now owned by the cricket club's trustees, major redevelopment has yet to take place. This is however likely to take place when the football club move to a new modern out of town multi-purpose stadium. Alfred Cockerill guaranteed the cricket club possession of the ground in perpetuity, something they could not have managed themselves, and in 1923 handed it over for a small rent for 1,000 years. The whole area of 8.5 acres is used jointly with the football club although the overlap between pitches is little more than twenty metres or so. Crowds of 4,500 are usual and popular limited-overs matches sometimes attract 6,500 spectators. The record crowd for a single day was 21,770 against the Australians in 1953 with a total of 31,000 for the three days. The present ground capacity is 4,000. In comparison, the record crowd for football was 24,523 against Fulham when Northampton Town were a Division One side in April 1966.

The pavilion includes the Colin Milburn Room which was opened in 1990 and there is a fine display of blazers and caps belonging to the former Northamptonshire and England player.

Ground records at Wantage Road include double centuries for Raman Subba Row and J.R. Freeman along with fine bowling spells from George Tribe, the Australian, for the home county and Colin Blythe for the visitors. The fastest century scored in first-class cricket by Tom Moody at Swansea in 1990 beat the record created by P.G.H. Fender of Surrey at Northampton in 1920. On that occasion this remarkably free scoring hitter not only scored his first century in first-class cricket, but it only took him 35 minutes. Another batting feat at the ground was in 1973 when Glenn Turner scored his 1,000th run in May, while with the touring New Zealanders, off the bowling of Bishen Bedi, the Indian Test spinner.

ADDRESS County Cricket Ground, Wantage Road, Northampton, Northamptonshire NN1 4NJ.
TELEPHONE NUMBER PROSPECTS OF PLAY 0604 37040

DESCRIPTION OF GROUND AND FACILITIES

The main entrance to the County Ground is from Wantage Road, off the Wellingborough Road, but there is also a pedestrian access from Abingdon Avenue through the football turnstile entrance. Car parking within the ground is limited to the football field and the area between the old pavilion and the main scoreboard. There is however ample street parking available within the local residential housing surrounding the ground. The main permanent buildings are the old pavilion, originally a timber structure, now refurbished, of which the upper part is now restricted to vice presidents of the club; and the Main Stand which provides a bar, refreshment facilities, toilets and the Northants C C C supporters' souvenir shop on the ground level, and on the first floor covered seating for members together with TV commentary, radio point, press box and scorers' room. The new pavilion provides an area where refreshment facilities can be obtained by members. These three buildings comprise the section of the ground that is primarily available for members only.

Seating is available on the east and west of the ground for the public and around 2,000 seats in all are provided. It is advisable to bring your own seats to popular matches for use at the football ground end. Disabled spectators are advised to request a suitable position to view the cricket in front of the main stand. Permanent toilets are available in the Main Stand, old pavilion, new pavilion and rear of the covered football terracing.

The playing area is approximately 133 metres by 132 metres and the northern part extends across the football field, where a number of cars are allowed to park in a position to enable viewing the cricket. This facility is withdrawn for popular matches and when temporary raised plastic seating is installed at the Football Ground End either side of the sightscreen. Cover during poor weather is limited to the Main Stand, which houses the indoor cricket school during winter months, and the new stand constructed on the west side of the ground. The TV camera position is usually sited on the first floor of the Main Stand adjoining the press box. There are two scoreboards on the ground; the main one houses the groundsman's equipment store on the ground floor and also offers a message board with computerized scoring which also activates the secondary scoreboard in front of the old scorebox and shop opposite.

Watching cricket at the County Cricket Ground, Wantage Road one feels that the future development of cricket will forever be overshadowed by the football stands and floodlight pylons. Northampton is the only cricket ground in the country shared with a professional football league club.

GROUND RECORDS AND SCORES

FIRST-CLASS MATCHES
Highest innings total for County: 592 for 6 dec. *v*. Essex 1990
Highest innings total against County: 631 for 4 dec. by Sussex 1938
Lowest innings total for County: 15 *v*. Yorkshire 1908
Lowest innings total against County: 33 by Lancashire 1977
Highest individual innings for County: 260 n.o. R. Subba Row *v*. Lancashire 1955
Highest individual innings against County: 286 J.R. Freeman for Essex 1921
Best bowling performance in an innings for County: 9 for 43 G.E. Tribe *v*. Worcestershire 1958
Best bowling performance in an innings against County: 10 for 30 C. Blythe for Kent 1907

Best bowling performance in a match for County: 15 for 31 G.E. Tribe *v.* Yorkshire 1958

Best bowling performance in a match against County: 17 for 48 C. Blythe for Kent 1907

Best attendance: 21,770 *v.* Australians 1953

LIMITED-OVERS MATCHES

Highest innings total for County: 360 for 2 *v.* Staffordshire (NWBT) 1990

Highest innings total against County: 303 for 7 by Middlesex (BHC) 1977

Lowest innings total for County: 41 *v.* Middlesex (JPL) 1972

Lowest innings total against County: 69 by Hertfordshire (GC) 1976

Highest individual innings for County: 134 R.J. Bailey *v.* Gloucestershire (BHC) 1987

Highest individual innings against County: 129 G.D. Barlow for Middlesex (BHC) 1977

Best bowling performance for County: 7 for 37 N.A. Mallender *v.* Worcestershire (NWBT) 1984

Best bowling performance against County: 6 for 22 C.E.B. Rice for Nottinghamshire (BHC) 1981

Best attendance: 7,000 *v.* Lancashire (NWBT) 1981

HOW TO GET THERE

Rail   Northampton (BR), 2 miles.

Bus   Northampton Transport 1 from Northampton BR Station to within 200m of ground (Telephone: 0604 51431); also Northampton Transport 6, 8 and 15 from town centre to within 200m of ground.

Car   From north: M1 junction 16, then A45 follow signs Northampton and town centre, then follow A43 signposted Kettering, then follow signs County Ground for County Cricket in Abingdon Road and main entrance in Wantage Road. From east: A45, A4500 or A428 signposted Northampton then follow signs County Ground, then as north. From west: A45 or A43 to town centre, then as north. From south: M1 junction 15, then follow signs Northampton A508, then A43 for Wellingborough Road and Wantage Road for County Ground, follow signs County Cricket.

WHERE TO STAY AND OTHER INFORMATION

Westone Moat House (0604 406262), Northampton Moat House Hotel (0604 22441), Grand Hotel (0604 34416), Stakis Country Court Hotel (0604 700666).

Disabled Areas   None specified, plenty of freedom of movement throughout the ground but advise a position on the hardstanding at the Pavilion End.

Local Radio Station(s)   BBC Radio Northampton (104.2 MHz FM/ 1107 KHz MW), Hereward Radio (96.6 MHz FM/1557 KHz MW), Chiltern Radio (96.9 MHz FM/792 KHz MW).

Local Newspaper(s)   Chronicle and Echo, Northampton Post, Sports Pink (Saturday only), Mercury & Herald, Northamptonshire Image.

Luton

Founded in 1906 Luton Town Cricket Club is probably one of the strongest club sides in the county and fields three XIs throughout the season. The club plays in the Bryan-Grasshopper Hertfordshire Cricket League. The ground was first used by Northamptonshire C C C in 1973 for a John Player Sunday League match with Nottinghamshire and each season thereafter for Sunday League matches. This one match was so successful that in 1986 the county club staged its initial first-class match at Wardown Park. The inaugural match was with Yorkshire, and now four days of the county's season is spent on this attractive and well maintained club ground in Bedfordshire.

The ground was formed from an area in the north of Wardown Park and the town gardens, the club has played here since its establishment. The ground has been used by Bedfordshire C C C for home Minor County Championship matches together with Gillette Cup and National Westminster Bank Trophy 1st round ties. In winter the Luton Nomads C C and Bedfordshire Eagles Hockey Club also use the fine facilities available.

Crowds of 4,000–5,000 are usual with good weather. The record attendance was for a Benefit Match in 1961 for Tom Clark of Surrey C C C when 6,000 were present. Photographs from this match can be viewed on the stairs of the pavilion. Northamptonshire's championship match with Middlesex in 1988 attracted 4,000 and the Sunday League match with Warwickshire in 1983 approximately 4,500.

Wardown Park was the place where Worcestershire's Tom Graveney attended one of his benefit matches on the rest day of the 1st England *v.* West Indies Test at Old Trafford, Manchester in 1969 and as a result lost his Test Match place.

Ground records at Wardown Park include a double century by Robert Bailey in the inaugural first-class match and a sparkling knock in the Sunday League and a career best by Wayne Larkins, now of Durham in 1983. In the 1989 Sunday League match Les Taylor took 5 for 20 as Leicestershire dismissed the home county for the lowest limited-overs total on the ground of 81.

The 1990 and 1991 Minor Counties Championship finals were staged at Wardown Park with Hertfordshire beating Berkshire in 1990 and Staffordshire beating Oxfordshire last year. In late June 1992 Northamptonshire will host four days cricket with Glamorgan and on 27 May the England Amateur XI will play the touring Pakistanis at Luton in a one-day match.

ADDRESS   Luton Town Cricket Club, Wardown Park, Old Bedford Road, Luton, Bedfordshire.
TELEPHONE NUMBER PROSPECTS OF PLAY   0582 27855

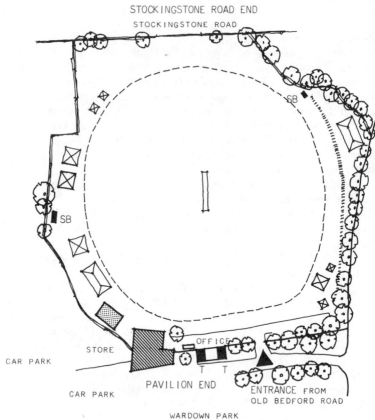

STOCKINGSTONE ROAD END

STOCKINGSTONE ROAD

SB

SB

CAR PARK

STORE

OFFICE

T T

CAR PARK

PAVILION END

ENTRANCE FROM
OLD BEDFORD ROAD

WARDOWN PARK
AND MUSEUM

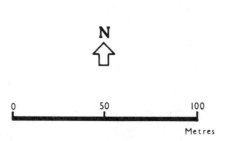

N

0   50   100

Metres

DESCRIPTION OF GROUND AND FACILITIES

Entry to the ground is from Wardown Park and pedestrians can approach from either Old Bedford Road or New Bedford Road through the park. All cars are required to enter Wardown Park from the New Bedford Road where parking is available on the grass. The pavilion is a new extension of an existing building, the latter still houses the players' changing rooms.

This is a very pleasant tree-enclosed ground which has been levelled so that a raised area exists to the east Old Bedford Road side of the ground, backed by trees and a timber fence. This provides a most advantageous position for the public to view the cricket. To the west of the ground is the main scoreboard now with electronic numbering, and an area given over for sponsors' tents. The members' enclosure is in front of the pavilion and to either side of the players' entrance and contains a small section of tiered seating. A good number of seats are provided so it is not always necessary to take your own, except to popular limited-overs matches. Toilets are situated at the Pavilion End to the rear of the sightscreen and secretary's portacabin office. The playing area is defined by a rope and advertising boards and is approximately circular in shape with dimensions of 131 metres by 132 metres.

Refreshment facilities and the Northants C C C souvenir shop are located to the east side near the cricket nets and are housed in tents. The main TV camera position is situated on a gantry high above the sightscreen at the Pavilion End. The press box and radio commentary positions are to be found on the first floor of the pavilion and balcony area.

In the event of bad weather, an hour or so can be spent visiting Wardown House Museum which is situated a short walk away in Wardown Park adjoining the players' and officials car park. Here one can learn the methods and history of hat-making in Luton and other historical information on the Bedfordshire town. A mini-golf course and facilities for tennis are available in the park.

GROUND RECORDS AND SCORES

FIRST-CLASS MATCHES
Highest innings total for County: 385 for 4 dec. *v.* Yorkshire 1986
Highest innings total against County: 314 for 6 dec. by Yorkshire 1986
Lowest innings total for County: 193 for 7 dec. *v.* Yorkshire 1986
Lowest innings total against County: 174 by Warwickshire 1987
Highest individual innings for County: 200 n.o. R.J. Bailey *v.* Yorkshire 1986
Highest individual innings against County: 151 A.A. Metcalfe for Yorkshire 1986
Best bowling performance in an innings for County: 5 for 38 N.G.B. Cook *v.* Somerset 1989

Best bowling performance in an innings against County: 4 for 58
A.R.C. Fraser for Middlesex 1988
Best bowling performance in a match for County: 5 for 38 N.G.B.
Cook *v.* Somerset 1989
Best bowling performance in a match against County: 4 for 76
A.R.C. Fraser for Middlesex 1988
Best attendance: 3,500 *v.* Yorkshire 1986

LIMITED-OVERS MATCHES
Highest innings total for County: 298 for 2 *v.* Warwickshire (JPL)
1983
Highest innings total against County: 264 for 8 by Warwickshire
(JPL) 1983
Lowest innings total for County: 81 *v.* Leicestershire (RAL) 1989
Lowest innings total against County: 126 for 8 by Somerset (RAL)
1991
Highest individual innings for County: 172 n.o. W. Larkins *v.*
Warwickshire (JPL) 1983
Highest individual innings against County: 105 n.o. M.W. Gatting
for Middlesex (RAL) 1988
Best bowling performance for County: 5 for 30 R.G. Williams *v.*
Warwickshire (JPL) 1983
Best bowling performance against County: 5 for 20 L.B. Taylor for
Leicestershire (RAL) 1989
Best attendance: 4,000 *v.* Middlesex (RAL) 1988

HOW TO GET THERE

Rail   Luton (BR) Midland and Thameslink, 1 mile.
Bus   Luton & District 26 from Mill Street (200m from Luton BR
Station) to ground (Telephone: 0582 404074); and 6 from Town
Centre to ground.
Car   From north: M1 junction 11, then follow signs Luton A505
into Dunstable Road for town centre, follow signs A6 from town
centre to New Bedford Road for Wardown Park and main car park.
The ground is situated 0.5 mile from the town centre. From east:
A505 signposted Luton, from town centre follow New Bedford Road
for Wardown Park. From west: A505 signposted Luton, then as
north. From south: M1 junction 10/10a, then follow signs Luton and
town centre, then signs A6 from town centre to New Bedford Road
for Wardown Park.

WHERE TO STAY AND OTHER INFORMATION

Fort Crest Hotel (0582 575911), Strathmore Thistle Hotel (0582
34199).

Disabled Areas   Within the members' enclosure and close to
sightscreen at Pavilion End.
Local Radio Station(s)   Chiltern Radio (96.9 MHz FM/792 KHz

MW), BBC Radio Bedfordshire (95.5 MHz FM/1161 KHz MW).
Local Newspaper(s) Luton News, The Luton Herald, Sports Pink (Saturday Only).

Wellingborough

This is the ground of Wellingborough School, which was founded in 1595 and has been used for first-class cricket since 1946 when Hampshire were the inaugural visitors. The first limited-overs match was in 1970 when Worcestershire were the opponents. The pavilion is an attractive thatched roofed building with a clock tower and was built in 1929. The steps of the pavilion include the stone that was once the threshold to the Downend home of Dr W.G. Grace in Bristol. The stone is inscribed 'Not of an age, but for all time' and was laid on 10 July 1940 by Henry Grierson, the founder of the Forty Club 'XL'. Beneath the pitch bottles have been buried for posterity on Halloween to record the names of every county player to appear at the school ground, including their signatures and a scorecard.

This is the second ground to be used in the town for county cricket, for in 1929 the County played a home championship match at the Town Ground for one season. Northamptonshire usually take four days of cricket to the School Ground in August, one championship and one limited-overs match, at a time when the county headquarters is undergoing changes for the start of the Northampton Town F C football league season. Crowds of 4,000 are usual. The largest crowd of recent years was 7,000 for the John Player Sunday League match with Somerset, when Ian Botham rewarded the spectators during a rain-interrupted game. The record attendance was 24,000 against Yorkshire in 1949 for a championship match over three days.

Wellingborough School is a small ground by first-class standards but nevertheless a historic ground. C.B. Fry's footprints were once to be found in concrete close to the school chapel. In recent years Ian Botham's innings of 175 n.o. in 1986 will be long remembered by those who saw it. Possibly the best known of Old Wellingburians was G.J. Thompson who played for the County Club and who represented England six times and MCC once. He also toured New Zealand with Lord Hawke's Team and West Indies with Brackley. Others were the Denton twins J.S. and W.H. brothers of A.D., Jack Timms, T.E. Manning, G.A.T. Vials, R.O. Raven, A.H. Bull and W.C. Brown. Northamptonshire C C C abandoned the wicket for one year in 1982 due to its poor condition but returned a year later.

Ground records include significant scores from Jock Livingston and Len Hutton. Bowling records belong to Frank Tyson and Bishen Bedi for the home county and Jack van Geloven and Derek Shackleton for the visitors. In 1990 David Capel scored 115 against Sussex in the Refuge Assurance Sunday League and a year later Nottinghamshire bowled

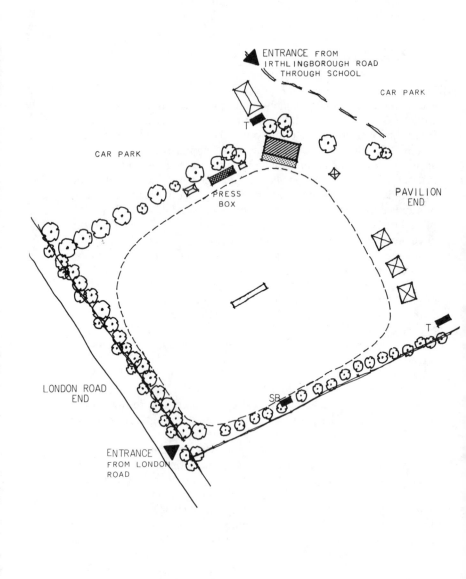

ENTRANCE FROM
IRTHLINGBOROUGH ROAD
THROUGH SCHOOL

CAR PARK

CAR PARK

T

PRESS
BOX

PAVILION
END

T

LONDON ROAD
END

SB

ENTRANCE
FROM LONDON
ROAD

N

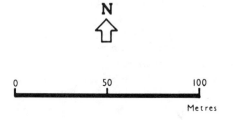

0   50   100

Metres

Northamptonshire out for 68 on the Saturday, the second day, to win by an innings.

ADDRESS Wellingborough School, The Pavilion, School Grounds, Irthlingborough Road, Wellingborough, Northamptonshire NN8 2BX. **TELEPHONE NUMBER PROSPECTS OF PLAY** 0933 223705/ 222427

DESCRIPTION OF GROUND AND FACILITIES

While pedestrians can enter the ground from London Road, it is necessary for all spectators entering by cars and other vehicles to enter from Irthlingborough Road through the school entrance. Car parking is permitted on the football fields to the north of the playing area and where permitted by the stewards.

The school cricket ground is to the south of the main school buildings and the only permanent structures are the pavilion to the north-east corner and a shed-like building to the north which is used by scorers' and members of the press. The main scoreboard is on the south side of the ground with a secondary board next to the press box. All other facilities are temporary and housed in tents or temporary buildings. Enclosed by trees and close to the London Road, the ground is quite small and the playing area is no more than 113 metres by 133 metres, defined by a rope with a number of advertising boards. The playing area falls towards the scoreboard side of the ground. Sponsors' tents are available to the south-east of the playing area at the Pavilion End. There is limited space for spectators to sit at the London Road End and to the south near the main scoreboard. The members' enclosure is on the north and east sides in the area from the pavilion, including the shed and space in front of the trees which separate the cricket and football fields to the north. The TV commentary position and cameras are positioned high above the sightscreen at the Pavilion End on a gantry. You are advised to bring your own seats to popular matches as only 1,200 seats are provided. Toilets are located in the pavilion, rear of the press box, in temporary accommodation and for ladies only in the school premises a short walk away.

This is a very pleasant school ground to watch cricket providing there is not too great a crowd. Wellingborough is one of the few school grounds being used for county cricket.

GROUND RECORDS AND SCORES

FIRST-CLASS MATCHES
Highest innings total for County: 395 v. Warwickshire 1976
Highest innings total against County: 523 for 8 by Yorkshire 1949
Lowest innings total for County: 68 v. Nottinghamshire 1991
Lowest innings total against County: 62 by Middlesex 1977
Highest individual innings for County: 172 n.o. L. Livingston v. Essex 1955

Highest individual innings against County: 269 n.o. L. Hutton for Yorkshire 1949

Best bowling performance in an innings for County: 7 for 46 F. Tyson *v*. Derbyshire 1956

Best bowling performance in an innings against County: 6 for 28 J. van Geloven for Leicestershire 1962

Best bowling performance in a match for County: 11 for 107 B.S. Bedi *v*. Middlesex 1977

Best bowling performance in a match against County: 11 for 104 D. Shackleton for Hampshire 1963

Best attendance: 24,000 *v*. Yorkshire 1949

LIMITED-OVERS MATCHES

Highest innings total for County: 234 for 1 *v*. Leicestershire (JPL) 1979

Highest innings total against County: 272 for 5 by Somerset (JPL) 1986

Lowest innings total for County: 114 *v*. Hampshire (JPL) 1980

Lowest innings total against County: 132 by Yorkshire (JPL) 1981

Highest individual innings for County: 115 D.J. Capel *v*. Sussex (RAL) 1990

Highest individual innings against County: 175 n.o. I.T. Botham for Somerset (JPL) 1986

Best bowling performance for County: 3 for 8 B. Crump *v*. Worcestershire (JPL) 1970

Best bowling performance against County: 4 for 24 T.M. Tremlett for Hampshire (JPL) 1980

Best attendance: 7,000 *v*. Somerset (JPL) 1986

HOW TO GET THERE

Rail   Wellingborough (BR), 1.25 miles.

Bus   United Counties 46 from Church Street (0.75 mile from Wellingborough BR Station) (Telephone: 0604 36681).

Car   From north: A509 signposted Wellingborough and town centre, then follow signs for London Road, Wellingborough School is situated off this road next to the Dog and Duck pub. The main entrance is off Irthlingborough Road. The school is situated south-east of the town centre. From east: A45 or A510 to Wellingborough, then as north. From west: A45 or A4500 signposted Wellingborough, then as north. From south: M1 junction 14, then follow A509 signposted Wellingborough, then as north.

WHERE TO STAY AND OTHER INFORMATION

Hind Hotel (0933 222827), High View Hotel (0933 78733)

Disabled Areas   No special area, request suitable position.

Local Radio Station(s)   BBC Radio Northampton (104.2 MHz FM/

1107 KHz MW), Hereward Radio (96.6 MHz FM/1557 KHz MW),
Chiltern Radio (96.9 MHz FM/792 KHz MW).
Local Newspaper(s) The Evening Telegraph, The Chronicle and
Echo, Sports Pink (Saturday Only).

Finedon

Founded in 1836, Finedon Dolben Cricket Club has always been an
active venue for cricket and over the years has produced some fine
players. Foremost of these was without doubt A.G. Henfrey who played
for Northamptonshire C C C from 1886 to 1889 and captained the
county club in 1894–95. Henfrey also represented England at international football on five occasions. Other Finedon cricketers who
reached first-class level were R.W. Clarke, who was also a top class
footballer, J. Minney and Rev. H.H. Gillet.

The fact that Finedon has always been a strong club, by local
standards, must to some extent be attributed to the fine club ground,
which is the home of the village club Dolben. For approximately a
century, minus the few years lost to ironstone excavation close to the
ground, cricket has been played at Avenue Road. The ironstone
workings are why the ground is some 15 feet below road level. In the
early 1920s the ground was purchased from the Ebbw Vale Mining
Company and in recent years a number of improvements have been
made. These have not gone unnoticed by the county club which has
staged a number of Second XI championship matches at the ground.

In 1986, to celebrate the 150th Anniversary of the Finedon Dolben
C C, a number of special fixtures were arranged on the ground. Visitors
included MCC, a Northamptonshire County Select League XI and Tring
Park C C from Hertfordshire, another club who host county matches for
the county club. The highlight of the celebrations was a limited-overs
John Player Sunday League match with Derbyshire which attracted a
good crowd of 4,400. With this show of support the county club
returned for Refuge Assurance Sunday League matches with Gloucestershire in 1987 which was rain-interrupted, Sussex in 1988 which
was subsequently transferred to the County Ground, Northampton
because the Dolben ground was waterlogged and Nottinghamshire in
1989, which was the last visit. The wicket was reported to be unfit for
county cricket after the match in 1989.

The club play in the Northamptonshire County Cricket League and
also has teams represented in the Higham and District Youth League
which is a source of raw material for the club's ongoing youth policy. A
benefit match was staged for Wayne Larkins in 1986 and was well
supported.

Ground records at Dolben include 97 by Allan Lamb the county
captain and 53 by Duncan Martindale for Nottinghamshire. Five-
wicket hauls have been taken by Duncan Wild for the home county and
Kevin Saxelby for Nottinghamshire the visitors.

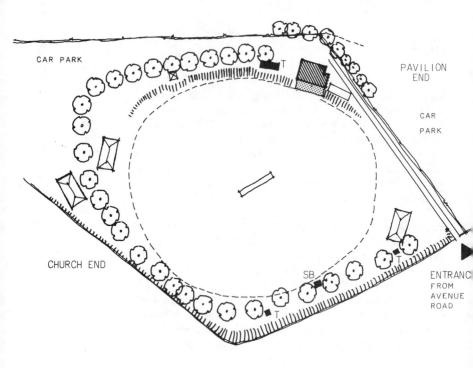

CAR PARK

T

PAVILION
END

CAR
PARK

CHURCH END

SB

T

T

ENTRANCE
FROM
AVENUE
ROAD

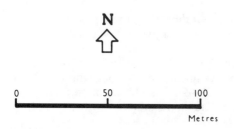

N

0	50	100

Metres

ADDRESS Finedon Dolben Cricket Club, Dolben Cricket Ground, Avenue Road, Finedon, Northamptonshire NN9 5JJ.
TELEPHONE NUMBER PROSPECTS OF PLAY   0933 681117

DESCRIPTION OF GROUND AND FACILITIES

The ground is entered off Avenue Road, some 360 car parking spaces are available in the ground through this entrance with additional car parking available in an adjoining field at the Pavilion End. An area is set a side for invalid cars which can be parked in a position to view the cricket.

The only permanent building is the pavilion, which is in the north-east corner. To one side provision is made in temporary accommodation for the press and scorers. The area in front of the pavilion is reserved for members, whilst the rest of the ground is available to the public. In total, some 2,000 seats are provided, which is about one-third of the ground capacity. The ground being in a natural bowl or saucer surrounded by trees on three sides, it provides excellent views of the cricket from all sides. The playing area is oval shaped and about 130 metres by 119 metres and defined by a rope with advertising boards. The scoreboard is on the south side of the ground. The north side provides the best view of the cricket as here the ground is banked higher than on the other three sides.

Refreshment tents, sponsors' areas and other temporary accommodation are disposed around the ground, mainly on the north side. The surrounding lime trees help to give the ground its individual character.

GROUND RECORDS AND SCORES

LIMITED-OVERS MATCHES
Highest innings total for County: 242 for 6 v. Derbyshire (JPL) 1986
Highest innings total against County: 149 by Nottinghamshire (RAL) 1989
Lowest innings total for County: 170 for 8 v. Gloucestershire (RAL) 1987
Lowest innings total against County: 145 by Derbyshire (JPL) 1986
Highest individual innings for County: 97 A.J. Lamb v. Derbyshire (JPL) 1986
Highest individual innings against County: 53 D.J.R. Martindale for Nottinghamshire (RAL) 1989
Best bowling performance for County: 5 for 7 D.J. Wild v. Derbyshire (JPL) 1986
Best bowling performance against County: 5 for 45 K. Saxelby for Nottinghamshire (RAL) 1989
Best attendance: 4,400 v. Derbyshire (JPL) 1986

HOW TO GET THERE

Rail Wellingborough (BR), 3 miles.

Bus   United Counties 45/7 from Church Street, Wellingborough (0.75 mile from Wellingborough BR Station) (Telephone: 0604 36681).

Car   From north: A6 or A510 signposted Finedon, ground situated off Avenue Road on north-western outskirts of village. Finedon is 2 miles north-east of Wellingborough. From east: as north. From west: A510 signposted Finedon, then as north. From south: A6 or A510 signposted Finedon, then as north.

WHERE TO STAY AND OTHER INFORMATION

Tudor Gate Hotel, High Street, Finedon (0933 680408) or stay in Wellingborough or Northampton.

Disabled Areas   Arrangements can be requested in advance, otherwise an area is available near the Pavilion End sightscreen.
Local Radio Station(s)   BBC Radio Northampton (104.2 MHz FM/ 1107 KHz MW), Hereward Radio (96.6 MHz FM/1557 KHz MW), Chiltern Radio (96.9 MHz FM/792 KHz MW).
Local Newspaper(s)   The Evening Telegraph, The Chronicle and Echo.

Tring

Cricket may well have been played in Tring prior to the Tring Park Cricket Club's foundation in 1836. The players of that time consisted of ten farmers and workers on the Rothschild's Tring Park Estate. Before the move to the present ground, previously known as Knuckle Stile Close in 1873, two other grounds were used in the town at Tring Grove Park and in the area of Tring Park to the west of Hastoe Park. A footpath to Pendley was closed when the new road to Tring Railway Station was made.

Northamptonshire C C C association with Tring Park C C began in 1955 when a benefit match was staged for the Australian left-hander Jock Livingston. Since 1956 a number of benefit matches have been staged for county players including George Tribe, Dennis Brookes, Frank Tyson, Keith Andrew and Geoff Cook.

In 1974 when Ken Turner, the former county secretary decided to take cricket outside the county after the success of the previous season's visit to Wardown Park, Luton, Tring Park C C was fortunate to be asked to participate in the venture. The first limited-overs match was a John Player Sunday League match staged with Middlesex.

Crowds of 4,000 are quite usual for the county club's one match in Hertfordshire, the largest attendance was for a visit by Kent in 1977 which attracted 5,500 spectators plus the BBC TV cameras. The club ground is owned by the Tring Park C C and it fields four XIs during the

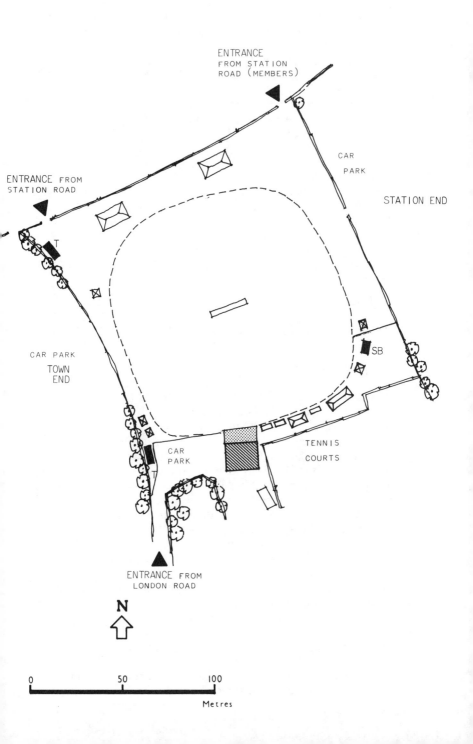

ENTRANCE
FROM STATION
ROAD (MEMBERS)

CAR
PARK

STATION END

ENTRANCE FROM
STATION ROAD

T

CAR PARK
TOWN
END

SB

CAR
PARK

TENNIS
COURTS

ENTRANCE FROM
LONDON ROAD

N

0   50   100

Metres

season. The club participates in the Bryan-Grasshopper Hertfordshire Cricket League and the Thames Valley Cricket League. Much of the organisation of county matches is handled by Peter Haynes of Tring Park C C. The Hertfordshire-Buckinghamshire county boundary is less than a mile from the ground and over the years club members have represented both Hertfordshire and Buckinghamshire. Three players have represented Buckinghamshire since 1989: R.M. Baigent, S.M. Sherman and F.S. Stanway.

The Tring Park club have hosted Minor County Championship and knock-out trophy matches for Hertfordshire C C C for some years. Other friendly matches staged at the Station Road ground include fixtures with MCC and Tannon's XI, which was captained by H.P. H. 'Harry' Sharp the former Middlesex C C C player and official county scorer from 1964 to 1982.

Ground records have included fine hundreds from Wayne Larkins and Peter Willey who scored the first century on the ground in 1976 against Hampshire. Five-wicket bowling hauls have been achieved by the Pakistan Test player Sarfraz Nawaz for the home county and by Norman Graham for the visitors. After eighteen games no visiting batsman has yet recorded a century against Northamptonshire on this ground.

ADDRESS Tring Park Cricket Club, The Pavilion, Station Road, Tring, Hertfordshire.
TELEPHONE NUMBER PROSPECTS OF PLAY 0442 823080

DESCRIPTION OF GROUND AND FACILITIES

Access can be gained either from London Road (A41), adjoining the pavilion by players and officials, pedestrians and disabled spectators or from entrances on Station Road to the north of the ground for members and the public. Car parking is available in the fields adjoining either side of the ground to the west and east for members and the public. Street parking is also available in the town centre market car park a short walk away. The only permanent buildings are the pavilion, scoreboard and groundsman's store. There is no permanent seating and you will be advised to bring your own seats as the club only provide seats for about 35 per cent of the 8,000 capacity.

The small scoreboard is in the south-east corner, and the members' enclosure extends from the pavilion on the south side to the sightscreen at the Station End and around to the sightscreen at the Town End. All other facilities are provided in temporary tents or stalls, including refreshments and a Northants C C C souvenir shop. An area for sponsers' tents is situated close to the scoreboard with press box, scorers' room and the club office
located in temporary buildings between this area and the pavilion backing onto the tennis courts.

The ground is used for hockey during the winter months and a strong tennis club section is also apparent. The playing area is about 124 metres by 125 metres and is defined by a rope and advertising boards. Toilets, except those in the pavilion are in temporary accommodation on the west side of the ground. The TV commentary position is usually sited on a gantry high above the sightscreen at the Town End.

This is a pleasant park-like venue enclosed by hedges and trees and close to Tring centre and some 2 miles from the Tring Railway Station on the Euston-Northampton line.

GROUND RECORDS AND SCORES

LIMITED-OVERS MATCHES

Highest innings total for County: 290 for 6 *v.* Lancashire (RAL) 1987
Highest innings total against County: 236 by Lancashire (RAL) 1987
Lowest innings total for County: 59 *v.* Middlesex (JPL) 1974
Lowest innings total against County: 119 for 4 by Middlesex (JPL) 1974
Highest individual innings for County: 107 n.o. W. Larkins *v.* Surrey (JPL) 1978
Highest individual innings against County: 88 M.R. Benson for Kent (JPL) 1984
Best bowling performance for County: 5 for 31 Sarfraz Nawaz *v.* Middlesex (JPL) 1981
Best bowling performance against County: 5 for 7 J.N. Graham for Kent (JPL) 1975
Best attendance: 5,500 *v.* Kent (JPL) 1977

HOW TO GET THERE

Rail   Tring (BR), 2 miles.
Bus   Luton & District 27 links Tring BR Station with town centre and ground; also London Country Aylesbury–Luton 61 links with town centre and ground (Telephone: 0296 84919); London Country (NW) 501, 768 Aylesbury–Hemel Hempstead pass ground (Telephone: 0923 673121).
Car   10 miles north-west of Hemel Hempstead on (A41) to Aylesbury. From north: M1 junction 11, then follow A505, B489 and B488 to Tring, then follow A41 Tring town centre, ground situated off main High Street at eastern end in Station Road. From east: M1 junction 8 then follow A41 to Tring, ground situated off A41 on southern outskirts of town centre. From west: A41, A4011, A413 signposted Tring, then as north. From south: A41 signposted Tring, then as east.

WHERE TO STAY AND OTHER INFORMATION

Royal Hotel, Tring Station (0442 827616), Pendley Manor Hotel, Tring (0442 891891), Hamblings Hotel, Northchurch, Hemel Hempstead Moat House, Bourne End (0442 871241), Forte Crest Hotel, Aston Clinton Road (0296 393388).

Disabled Areas Special area in front of players' car park close to the pavilion.

Local Radio Station(s) BBC Radio Bedfordshire (95.5 MHz FM/792 KHz MW), Chiltern Radio (96.9 MHz FM/792 KHz MW), Greater London Radio (94.9 MHz FM/1458 KHz MW).

Local Newspaper(s) Bucks Herald, Bucks Advertiser, Aylesbury News, Berkhamsted and Tring Gazette.

NOTTINGHAMSHIRE

CHURCHMAN'S CIGARETTES.

NOTTS.

NOTTINGHAM – TRENT BRIDGE

CLEETHORPES

WORKSOP

Nottinghamshire

Founded March/April 1841
Colours Green and gold
Crest Coat of arms of the City of Nottingham
President R.T. Simpson
Chairman C.W. Gillott
Chairman cricket committee A. Wheelhouse
Secretary/General Manager B. Robson
Cricket manager J.D. Birch
Coach K. Higgs
Cricket office manager J.H.C. Cope
Commercial & PR executive C.S. Slater
Commercial manager B. Hasson
Captain R.T. Robinson
Groundsman R. Allsopp
Scorer 1st XI L. Beaumont
Scorer 2nd XI G. Stringfellow
Statistician P. Wynne-Thomas
Sponsors Homes Bitter
Newsletter *Trent Bridge Monthly*
Address County Cricket Ground, Trent Bridge, West Bridgford, Nottingham, Nottinghamshire NG2 6AG
Telephone 0602 821525
Facsimile 0602 455730
Nottinghamshire Rapid Cricketline 0891 567512
Test Match Commentaries Rapid Cricketline 0891 567567
Test Match Updates Rapid Cricketline 0891 567500

ACHIEVEMENTS

County Championship Champions (14) 1865, 1868, 1871, 1872, 1875, 1880, 1883, 1884, 1885, 1886, 1907, 1929, 1981 and 1987; joint champions (5) 1869, 1873, 1879, 1882 and 1889
Gillette Cup Semi-finalists (1) 1969
National Westminster Bank Trophy Winners (1) 1987; finalists (1) 1985
Benson & Hedges Cup Winners (1) 1989; finalists (1) 1982
John Player Sunday League 2nd 1984
Refuge Assurance Sunday League Champions (1) 1991
Refuge Assurance Cup Finalists (1) 1989; semi-finalists (1) 1991
Tilcon Trophy Winners (1) 1977; finalists (2) 1984 and 1985

GROUNDS

Nottingham (Trent Bridge, West Bridgford); Cleethorpes (Cleethorpes C C, Chichester Road) and Worksop (Town Ground, Central Avenue).

Other grounds that have been used since 1969 are: Nottingham (John Player & Sons Sports Ground, Aspley Lane) and Newark-on-Trent (RHP Limited Sports Ground, Elm Avenue).

SECOND XI GROUNDS
In addition to the above mentioned grounds the following are used for second XI matches: Caythorpe C C, Sports Ground, Caythorpe, Nottingham. Telephone: 0602 663132; Farnsfield C C, Station Road, Farnsfield, Mansfield, Notts. Telephone: 0623 882986; Steetley Ironworks C C, Sports Ground, Shireoaks, Near Worksop, Notts. Telephone: 0909 480682; Worksop College, Worksop, Notts. Telephone: 0909 472286; Worthington Simpson Sports Ground, Lowfield Lane, Balderton, Newark-on-Trent, Notts. Telephone: 0636 702672; Clipstone Welfare C C, Seventh Avenue, Mansfield, Notts. Telephone: 0623 636590; Collingham C C, Dale Field, Collingham, Notts. Telephone: 0636 892921; John Player's Athletic Club, Sports Ground, Aspley Lane, Nottingham. Telephone: 0602 294244.

By happy chance, Nottinghamshire began 1988 celebrating the 150th anniversary of Trent Bridge as the reigning champions and holders of the NatWest Trophy. A hat-trick was missed by 2 points in the Sunday League. With timely opportunism a £150,000 appeal was launched to spend on ground improvements, including a plan for a stand named after William Clarke, founder of Trent Bridge.

Inter-city contests with Sheffield and other neighbours, which stimulated interest, commenced as early as 1771, and it was William Clarke who first spotted the commercial possibilities of cricket by founding and captaining the All-England Eleven in 1846. The cream of the professionals toured the country in what was realistically a money-making enterprise, but it served to widen cricket's appeal. Clarke was astute but tight-fisted, and a group broke away called the United All-England Eleven. Once the novelty of the touring sides faded, and the clubs became better organized, county cricket came into its own. Opinions on Clarke are mixed, but he left his county a magnificent centre, which has staged Test matches since 1899, and a quality of players more than ready to accept any new challenge. Nottinghamshire were the first of the northern sides to end southern supremacy and, starting from 1865 to 1889, they were champions ten times, and co-champions in five other seasons.

Famous names live on – Richard Daft, Alfred Shaw, often seen as the bowler of the century, and George Parr, whose leg sweep battered a tall elm tree. 'Parr's tree' became a Trent Bridge landmark. When Parr was asked why he played cricket for a living he replied: 'Because I don't like work!'

Arthur Shrewsbury was a master of back play and Grace's favourite. 'Give me, Arthur,' said the Doctor to the selectors, 'and you pick the rest.'

Trent Bridge

T. Wass.
Nottinghamshire.

The Gunns, William, and his two nephews, and the Hardstaffs, Joe Snr and Joe Jr are celebrated names. William Gunn refused to tour Australia because of the unattractive terms offered to the pros, putting his time to the benefit of his growing sports business of Gunn and Moore. He left £60,000. After providing for his widow and daughter the rest went to employees who had helped to build up the enterprise.

George lightened the scene for thirty years with a whimsical, almost eccentric outlook, batting according to the mood of the moment. One innings would be the last word in classical execution, the next would produce dazzling shots off the best ball and a dead bat to the worst. He had the scorn of the truly gifted for the second rate. Going to Australia for health reasons in 1907–08 he was pressed into service when the captain, Arthur Jones, fell ill, and he scored 119 and 74 in the opening Test at Sydney. In the later stages of his century he complained his concentration was affected by a flat cornet playing in a band. Gunn's series average of 51 was above Hobbs and his county team-mate Joe Hardstaff.

On his 50th birthday he scored a memorable 164 not out against Worcestershire, and the records have the statistic – G. Gunn (183) and G.V. Gunn (100 not out) at Birmingham in 1931. It is the only instance of father and son each scoring a century in the same innings of a first-class match. Gunn was over 50 when he toured the West Indies, and not only scored well in all four Tests, but baited the fast bowler Learie Constantine by going down the pitch and putting his tongue out at him. This extraordinary by-play was all very well but his batting partner, Sandham, remarked: 'George didn't stay all that long and I was left to deal with some very irate bowlers!'

Gunn would have found a soul-mate in Randall, who delighted crowds – particularly in India – with his enthusiasm and sheer brilliance at cover point. Though his fidgety movements at the crease worried the purists and enraged Lillee and Co, he scored 2,470 runs in 47 Tests with

GUNN, G.

NOTTINGHAMSHIRE

WILLS'S Cigarettes

A. SHREWSBURY. NOTTINGHAMSHIRE

PLAYER'S CIGARETTES

W. W. KEETON (NOTTINGHAMSHIRE)

7 centuries, including 174 brave and skilful runs in the Melbourne centenary Test.

The bowling of Wass and Hallam played a significant part in the championship success of 1907, and the captaincy of A.W. Carr, who was a considerable batsman, produced a high level of consistency from 1919 to 1934 – the title in 1929, three 2nd places and always in single-figures.

Harold Larwood and Bill Voce, who started as a left arm spinner, formed as menacing a fast bowling partnership as county cricket has seen. They were the instruments of Jardine's leg theory, or bodyline, which caused so much trouble and was rightly outlawed. The last match of 1932 was used by Larwood and Voce as a rehearsal for the theory and holds a coveted niche in Glamorgan's folklore. Far from being intimidated Turnbull (205) and Dai Davies feasted on the short-pitched attack and added 220 for the 3rd wicket, a county record to stand until Emrys Davies and Willie Jones took 310 off Essex in 1946.

That night at Cardiff the Notts players left the pavilion after quaffing some beer and walked across the ground towards their hotel. On the way they relieved their frustrations on the pitch, much to the outrage of groundsman Trevor Preece when he made the discovery of the tainted wicket the next morning. Lord's decided it was a matter for the captains, Turnbull and Carr, and Turnbull unsurprisingly said it was no concern of his as Notts were due to bat. The match was drawn.

After the bodyline tour Larwood was left with an injury to his left foot, and the mental scars of an affronted scapegoat. The only solace for him was to settle happily in Sydney on the sponsorship of Jack Fingleton, Australia's opening bat in the ill-fated 1932–33 series. Larwood deserves to be chiefly remembered for the poetry of his co-ordinated movements, his speed and accuracy and the perfect follow-through which had his knuckles brushing the turf.

Nottinghamshire spent too many of the post-war years in the

discouraging exercise of evading the wooden spoon – they were bottom five times between 1958 and 1966 – and the lack of in-depth strength was even too much for such eminent performers as Simpson, Hardstaff, who retired with 83 centuries in 1955, and Sir Gary Sobers, who joined in 1968 and was engaged in the teeth of fierce competition.

Simpson was the pride of post-war Nottinghamshire scoring four centuries for England and showing how fast bowling should be played and bumpers avoided. The Australian Dooland took 770 wickets for Nottinghamshire with his leg breaks and scored 4,782 runs for the county in five years.

Sobers was captain of the West Indies when he accepted a contract worth around £5,000 a season in 1968. He worked wonders for South Australia, and in his first season at Trent Bridge there was a rise from 15th to 4th, and his 6 sixes in an over at Swansea was a sensation. Unfortunately for his county Sobers was lost for half the next season on Test call, and in his third came an unexpected duty to lead the Rest of the World in a hastily-arranged rubber to replace the cancelled visit by South Africa. The fates seemed to conspire against him, and the sheer grind of county cricket was really not to his taste. He was the man for the big occasion.

The long-awaited revival came with the Springbok Clive Rice and the Kiwi Richard Hadlee. The championship was won under Rice in 1981 with Hadlee taking 105 wickets. The batting of Randall and the experienced bowling of Hemmings also played a substantial part. Rice's initial triumph broke a 52-year barren spell, and in 1987 came the double of the championship and the NatWest Trophy.

Hadlee emerged as one of the world's foremost all-rounders. In eight years he headed the national bowling averages five times, and was twice 2nd. In 1984 he was the first to complete the double since the championship programme was reduced in 1969, and as Rice and Hadlee passed into the legends Franklyn Stephenson, from Barbados, also completed the double in 1988.

Since the departure of Rice and Hadlee, it has taken a little time to achieve another trophy at Trent Bridge, but in 1991 under the captaincy of Robinson the Refuge Assurance Sunday League was won. Stephenson did not renew his contract at the end of the 1991 season and signed to play for Sussex in 1992. Chris Cairns the New Zealander will be his replacement. Randall topped both the batting and bowling averages in 1991.

Nottingham – Trent Bridge

Truly the definitive home of cricket in Nottinghamshire, Trent Bridge became a cricket ground due to the enterprise of William Clarke. He moved from the Bell Inn, still to be found in the main city square, to the Trent Bridge Inn and laid out a cricket ground at the back of his new home. By trade a bricklayer, William Clarke was also the organizer of

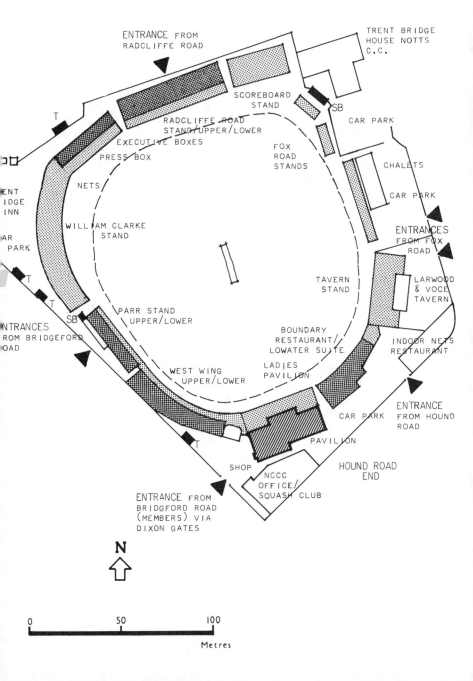

RADCLIFFE ROAD END

ENTRANCE FROM
RADCLIFFE ROAD

TRENT BRIDGE
HOUSE NOTTS
C.C.

SCOREBOARD
STAND

SB

CAR PARK

RADCLIFFE ROAD
STAND/UPPER/LOWER

EXECUTIVE BOXES

FOX
ROAD
STANDS

CHALETS

PRESS BOX

CAR PARK

NETS

WILLIAM CLARKE
STAND

ENTRANCES
FROM FOX
ROAD

TAVERN
STAND

LARWOOD
& VOCE
TAVERN

PARR STAND
UPPER/LOWER

ENTRANCES
FROM BRIDGFORD
ROAD

SB

BOUNDARY
RESTAURANT/
LOWATER SUITE

INDOOR NETS
RESTAURANT

WEST WING
UPPER/LOWER

LADIES
PAVILION

TRENT
BRIDGE
INN

CAR
PARK

T

T

T

ENTRANCE
FROM HOUND
ROAD

CAR PARK

PAVILION

HOUND ROAD
END

SHOP

NCCC
OFFICE/
SQUASH CLUB

ENTRANCE FROM
BRIDGFORD ROAD
(MEMBERS) VIA
DIXON GATES

N

0   50   100

Metres

the Nottingham first XI in the 1830s. In late 1837 he married Mrs Chapman, the landlady and lessee of the Trent Bridge Inn known today to locals as the 'TBI', and the open ground behind the building.

On 10 July 1838 he organized the first cricket match on the ground behind the Inn between T. Baker's XI and W. Clarke's XI. In July 1840 the first county match was staged with Sussex the visitors.

William Clarke left Nottingham to move to London in 1846 and was succeeded by his stepson John Chapman. It was not until 1881 that the owners, the Chaworth-Musters family, signed a 99-year lease for both the inn and ground with Nottinghamshire C C C. In 1919 Nottinghamshire C C C purchased both the inn, which they later sold, and the ground which has been in their sole ownership since that date.

The present members' pavilion was built in 1886 and designed by H.M. Townsend of Peterborough. It has since been altered and extended but much of its original character remains. Developments have continued to take place at the ground over the intervening years so that Trent Bridge is one of the best grounds in the country. Recent additions have seen in 1985 the Larwood and Voce Stand and at the rear the Tavern public house entered from the ground at Fox Road to the side of the ground. During the winter of 1989–90 part of the Bridgford Road Stand was demolished and replaced by the William Clarke Stand with additional open seating for 2,000 and a further area with a new press box. To the rear of the stand in 1990 the car park and TBI beer garden were reconstructed thanks to a donation by Ansells Brewery.

The ground has been used for association football by both Nottingham Forest F C and Notts County F C, both of whose grounds are within walking distance of Trent Bridge on either side of the nearby River Trent. In 1988 the Nottinghamshire C C C celebrated '150 years of Trent Bridge'. The proceeds some £151,000, went towards the reconstruction of the Bridgford Road Stand and the new press lounge. A further £600,000 was provided by Rushcliffe Borough Council and £60,000 by a local midlands businessman Mr Nat Puri.

The first Test Match at Trent Bridge was played in 1899 when England played Australia. In recent years the ground has seen many limited-overs international matches including Prudential Cup, Prudential Trophy and Texaco Trophy matches. In 1978–79 the new squash courts and Nottinghamshire C C C offices were built by the Dixon Gates, which form the members' entrance.

Much has been written and spoken of Parr's Tree, which stood close to the Bridgford Road side of the ground behind the Parr Stand and was blown down during a gale in January 1976. It was an elm tree which gained its name in the last century from the frequency with which George Parr (1826–91, Nottinghamshire 1845–70) managed to hit balls into its branches. Mini cricket bats have been made from the tree and indeed, close to the ground is the home of bat making: the Gunn and Moore bat factory is only five minutes away by car in Haslam Street off Castle Boulevard.

Over 1,250 Nottinghamshire C C C matches have been staged on the ground and all Test Match nations have played on the hallowed turf.

Nottinghamshire C C C have played on four other grounds in the city; the most recent journey from headquarters was to the John Player & Sons Sports and Social Club Ground at Aspley Lane in 1973 for a John Player Sunday League match with Gloucestershire. Others include The Forest, now an area bounded by Mansfield Road and Gregory Boulevard, and King's Meadow, known as The Meadows, between Castle Boulevard and the River Trent.

Crowds at Trent Bridge tend to be 5,000–6,000 these days with one-day limited-overs and Test Matches attracting the greatest number of spectators. One of the largest crowds was 35,000 against Surrey in 1948 for a single day's play and 35,000 in 1938 during the England v. Australia Test Match. The present ground capacity is 15,000.

Ground records have included scores of over 200 from Charlie Macartney, A.O. Jones, Denis Compton and Frank Worrell. Tom Graveney took 258 off the West Indies during the 1950s. In recent years, a 232 from Vivian Richards against England in 1976 graced this historic venue. During the 1989 Cornhill Test match between England and Australia, the Australian openers Geoff Marsh (138) and Mark Taylor (219) added 329 for the 1st wicket. At the close of play on the first day the total was 301 for 0. The Australians' first innings total of 602 for 6 dec. was a ground record against England in a Test Match. In the same season Nottinghamshire scored 296 for 6 against Kent in the Benson & Hedges Cup, beating the previous highest innings total recorded in 1968. The Nottingham public has seen some great players in action including William Clarke, George Parr, Alfred Shaw, Bill Voce, Harold Larwood, Reg Simpson, Gary Sobers, Clive Rice, Derek Randall, Richard Hadlee and Franklyn Stephenson.

ADDRESS County Cricket Ground, Trent Bridge, Bridgford Road, Nottingham, Nottinghamshire NG2 6AG.
TELEPHONE NUMBER PROSPECTS OF PLAY 0602 822753

DESCRIPTION OF GROUND AND FACILITIES

Entry to the ground for members and the public is made from Bridgford Road, but there are further entrances in Hound Road
and Fox Road. Some car parking, available within the ground on normal county match days, is situated on the Fox Road side of the ground. But for Test Matches this space is allocated for temporary seating and hospitality facilities. Car parking is available in the park off Bridgford Road, Nottingham Forest F C car park and in adjoining streets. All seating is permanent and located within permanent structures. Additionally, for Test Matches and one-day international matches, temporary seating is provided in front of the main scoreboard and adjoining the temporary hospitality suites erected on the car park next to the office tower.

The areas restricted to members include not only the pavilion and the west wing stand on the Bridgford Road side, but also the Larwood and Voce Tavern Stand and the area in front of the Lowater Suite which includes a Ladies' Stand as well as the Boundary Restaurant. These areas together extend to the whole of the southern half of the ground. However, there is still more than adequate accommodation for the public in the Parr Stand, new William Clarke Stand, lower part of the press box stand, Scoreboard Stand and the Radcliffe Road Stand upper and lower (covered) enclosure. There is ample space for disabled spectators and they should request a suitable position. As is to be expected of a Test Match venue, there are ample refreshment and bar facilities as well as toilets. This is a large ground with a playing area extending to 160 metres by 150 metres, but this is restricted on match days to approximately 141 metres by 144 metres.

A small Nottinghamshire C C C souvenir shop is situated in the reception to the squash club near the main members' entrance through the Dixon Gates. There are additional souvenir kiosks available around the ground at the rear of the William Clarke Stand during Test Matches only and at the bottom of the main scoreboard. The Association of Cricket Statisticians headquarters shop can be found a few minutes walk from the ground in Radcliffe Road.

The pavilion houses a fine library with a splendid collection of cricket memorabilia which can be inspected on request. The bar area includes the display of many old cricket bats and photographs. The TV camera/commentary position is situated on the pavilion balcony. The scorers' and radio commentary box is also situated in the pavilion complex. Executive boxes are available for sponsor's use at the Radcliffe Road End and in temporary chalets for Test Matches.

Trent Bridge is an excellent ground which provides a good view of cricket from every position. The most recent buildings, the William Clarke Stand and the Larwood and Voce Tavern Stand are both excellent structures providing good seating and the latter includes a tavern in keeping with the traditions of the area. The Trent Bridge Inn remains open to cricket spectators for refreshment, with direct access from the ground.

GROUND RECORDS

TEST MATCHES

Highest innings total for England: 658 for 8 dec. *v.* Australia 1938
Highest innings total against England: 602 for 6 dec. by Australia 1989
Lowest innings total for England: 112 *v.* Australia 1921
Lowest innings total against England: 88 by South Africa 1960
Highest individual innings for England: 278 D.C.S. Compton *v.* Pakistan 1954
Highest individual innings against England: 261 F.M.M. Worrell for West Indies 1950
Best bowling performance in an innings for England: 8 for 107 B.J.T. Bosanquet *v.* Australia 1905
Best bowling performance in an innings against England: 7 for 54 W.J. O'Reilly for Australia 1931

Best bowling performance in a match for England: 14 for 99 A.V. Bedser *v*. Australia 1953
Best bowling performance in a match against England: 11 for 129 W.J. O'Reilly for Australia 1934

LIMITED-OVERS INTERNATIONALS
Highest innings total: 330 for 6 by Pakistan *v*. Sri Lanka (PC) 1975
Lowest innings total: 138 by Sri Lanka *v*. Pakistan (PC) 1975
Highest individual innings: 118 A.J. Lamb for England *v*. Pakistan (PT) 1982
Best bowling performance: 6 for 39 K.H. MacLeay for Australia *v*. India (PC) 1983

FIRST-CLASS MATCHES
Highest innings total for County: 739 for 7 dec. *v*. Leicestershire 1903
Highest innings total against County: 706 for 4 dec. by Surrey 1947
Lowest innings total for County: 13 *v*. Yorkshire 1901
Lowest innings total against County: 16 by Derbyshire 1879
Highest individual innings for County: 296 A.O. Jones *v*. Gloucestershire 1903
Highest individual innings against County: 345 C.G. Macartney for Australians 1921
Best bowling performance in an innings for County: 9 for 19 J. Grundy *v*. Kent 1864
Best bowling performance in an innings against County: 9 for 32 J.T. Hearne for Middlesex 1891/M.S. Nichols for Essex 1936
Best bowling performance in a match for County: 17 for 89 F.C. Matthews *v*. Northamptonshire 1923
Best bowling performance in a match against County: 16 for 122 C.L Townsend for Gloucestershire 1895
Best attendance: 35,000 *v*. Surrey 1948

LIMITED-OVERS MATCHES
Highest innings total for County: 296 for 6 *v*. Kent (BHC) 1989
Highest innings total against County: 306 for 2 by Essex (JPL) 1983
Lowest innings total for County: 81 *v*. Derbyshire (JPL) 1972
Lowest innings total against County: 84 by Surrey (JPL) 1974
Highest individual innings for County: 123 D.W. Randall *v*. Yorkshire (RAL) 1987
Highest individual innings against County: 171 G.A. Gooch for Essex (JPL) 1983
Best bowling performance for County: 6 for 12 R.J. Hadlee *v*. Lancashire (JPL) 1980
Best bowling performance against County: 7 for 41 A.N. Jones for Sussex (JPL) 1986
Best attendance: 8,500 *v*. Somerset (JPL) 1979

HOW TO GET THERE

Rail   Nottingham Midland (BR), 1 mile.
Bus   Nottingham City 12, 69, 85, 90–97 and Trent Buses link BR Nottingham Station with ground and city centre (Telephone: 0602 503665).
Car   From north: M1 junction 26, follow signs Nottingham A610, then follow signs to Melton Mowbray, Trent Bridge A606, across River Trent and the ground is ahead of you behind TBI. From east: A52 signposted Nottingham, into West Bridgford, then follow Bridgford Road for ground. From south: M1 junction 24, then follow signs Nottingham (South) for Trent Bridge, then right into Bridgford Road for Trent Bridge. From west: A52 follow signposts Nottingham, then follow signs Melton Mowbray, then Trent Bridge, then as north.

WHERE TO STAY AND OTHER INFORMATION

Albany Hotel (0602 470131), Victoria Hotel (0602 419561), Royal Moat House International Hotel (0602 414444), Talbot House Hotel (0602 811123).

Disabled Areas   Ample room on boundary edge, request suitable position. Car parking off Fox Road.
Local Radio Station(s)   BBC Radio Nottingham (95.5 MHz FM/ 1584 KHz MW), Radio Trent (96.2 MHz FM/999 KHz MW).
Local Newspaper(s)   Nottingham Evening Post, Nottingham Trader, Football Post (Saturday Only).

Cleethorpes

The Chichester Road ground is the home of the Cleethorpes Cricket Club and is located about 150 yards from Cleethorpes boating lake which forms part of the seafront. Cleethorpes is the only ground used for first-class cricket by Nottinghamshire C C C outside the county and has brought first-class cricket to the doorstep of cricket-lovers in Grimsby, Cleethorpes and North Lincolnshire.

Cricket has been played at this ground since 1930. The first club match on the ground was staged on 13 June 1931 against Scunthorpe C C in a Grimsby and District League match. The Cleethorpes Cricket Club first XI play in the Websters Yorkshire League, the second XI play in the Ridings League and the third XI play in the Lincolnshire League. Fixtures are staged at weekends throughout the season and some midweek matches take place in August. Club captains since 1957 have included Ray Mawer, Martin Maslin, John Sunley and Bob Leafe. During the winter months the playing area is used by Winteringham Ladies Hockey Club, who have two pitches.

The first match of importance played at Chichester Road was in 1968 when Lincolnshire C C C staged a home match with the touring USA

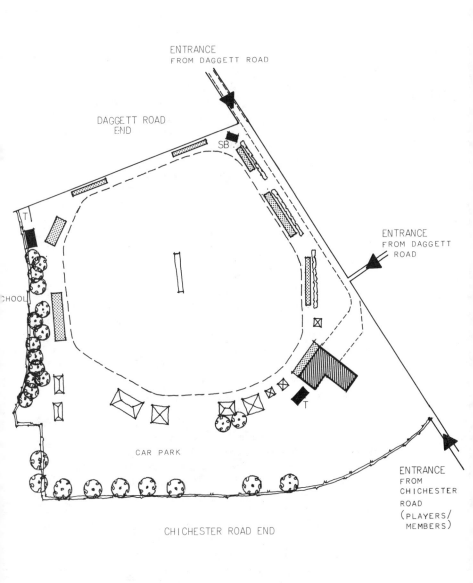

ENTRANCE
FROM DAGGETT ROAD

DAGGETT ROAD
END

SB

ENTRANCE
FROM DAGGETT
ROAD

CHOOL

T

CAR PARK

ENTRANCE
FROM
CHICHESTER
ROAD
(PLAYERS/
MEMBERS)

CHICHESTER ROAD END

N

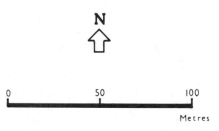

0   50   100

Metres

team. Since then Lincolnshire C C C have staged home Minor County Championship matches on the ground with, amongst others, Staffordshire, Yorkshire 2nd XI, Norfolk, Cambridgeshire, Cumberland, Northumberland and, in 1969, a match with the touring Canadians. On 9 August 1970 a Lincolnshire County League Team played the International Cavaliers XI which comprised the following players: Bob Barber, Eddie Barlow, Graeme Pollock who scored 105, Ted Dexter, Brian Davison, Derek Murray, John Mitchell, Freddie Trueman (4 for 32), Neil Hawke and Godfrey Evans. The International Cavaliers won by 116 runs. In 1974 a benefit match was staged for Jack Birkenshaw of Leicestershire C C C who brought a full county side plus one outsider Bob Taylor the Derbyshire and England wicketkeeper.

The Test Match Umpire Don Oslear hails from the Cleethorpes club and his brother Roy is the club chairman and second XI captain. Don Oslear played for the club first XI during the 1964 season. Martin Maslim who represented Lincolnshire C C C and Minor Counties C A against the tourists for some years still plays for the club. Martin Maslim won the man of the match award for scoring 62 n.o. for Lincolnshire C C C when they beat Glamorgan by 4 wickets at Swansea in the Gillette Cup 1st round in 1974.

The former pavilion since demolished was situated near the sightscreen at the Chichester Road End with the wicket at 90 degrees, and, until purchased, the ground was leased from Sydney Sussex College, Cambridge. A new pavilion was constructed in 1963 and an extension with a couple of squash courts was added in 1978. The pavilion houses a table tennis and pool lounge together with kitchen, bar area and on the upper level, players' dressing rooms and a small balcony from which to view the cricket. The ground was approximately 7.3 acres until 1960 when an area was sold for housing and a school. The current ground is some 4 acres.

Nottinghamshire C C C first staged a first-class match at Cleethorpes in 1980 against Worcestershire with subsequent visits in 1982 against Northamptonshire and twice against the touring Sri Lankans in 1984 and 1990. A single limited-overs John Player Sunday League match was staged against Middlesex in 1983, with Nottinghamshire winning by 4 wickets. In 1981 the club celebrated its Golden Jubilee Anniversary of the Ground (1931–1981).

Other matches have included games staged by the Minor Counties C A for a Benson & Hedges Cup zonal match between Minor Counties (North) and Nottinghamshire in 1972 with Nottinghamshire winning by 55 runs thanks to 97 n.o. by Gary Sobers and 3 for 37 by Bob White. For the home side, Alan Burridge scored 37 and G. Hardstaff took 3 for 39. A Minor Counties C A fixture was staged with the touring Zimbabweans in 1985 with the game finishing as a draw. The tourists' captain Andy Pycroft scored 110 n.o. in the second innings. Graeme Hick only managed 19 and 38 in his two knocks.

Crowds at Cleethorpes are usually around 2,000 per day. The best was 5,000 for the first County Championship match with Worcestershire in 1980. Ground records include batting records by Mike Newell for Nottinghamshire and Roshan Mahanama for the visitors. Bowling performances have been achieved by Richard Hadlee and Norman Gifford.

ADDRESS Cleethorpes Cricket Club, The Pavilion and Squash Club, Chichester Road, Cleethorpes, South Humberside.
TELEPHONE NUMBER PROSPECTS OF PLAY 0472 691271

DESCRIPTION OF GROUND AND FACILITIES

The Chichester Road ground is situated to the south of the town centre and the main ground entrance is from Chichester Road to the south of the playing area. There are also pedestrian and vehicle entrances from two access points in Daggett Road to the north and east. Car parking is available to the rear of the pavilion and to the south of the playing area for approximately 300 cars. Additional car parking is available at the nearby Sportscentre and in adjoining streets. The only permanent buildings on the ground are the pavilion and squash club, scoreboard, groundsman's store and several areas of raised timber seating and some benches.

The ground is enclosed by housing to the north, east and south of the playing area and by a school and treed area to the west. For Nottinghamshire C C C matches temporary seating is installed for use by members and the public, together with temporary refreshment and bars located in tents. The ground capacity is 3,500 and seating is available for 80 per cent so spectators are only advised to bring their own seats to popular matches. There are no special facilities for disabled spectators although vehicles can be positioned to enable watching from cars. Two temporary toilets are located in the ground together with the facilities in the pavilion available to players/officials and members. At the Chichester Road End are three large marquees for sponsors, together with a committee/members' dining tent, press tent and Radio commentary position. The scorers are located in the scoreboard to the north-east of the playing area. To the south-west of the playing area is the Nottinghamshire C C C office and club souvenir tent. The members' enclosure extends from the sightscreen at the Chichester Road End, in front of the pavilion and at least a third of the way towards the scoreboard.

If required, the TV camera/commentary box would be positioned on a gantry facility directly above and behind the sightscreen at the southern end of the ground. The playing area is circular in shape with dimensions of 121 metres by 128 metres and slopes from the Daggett Road End towards the Chichester Road End. The playing area is defined by a rope and some advertising boards.

GROUND RECORDS AND SCORES

FIRST-CLASS MATCHES
Highest innings total for County: 319 *v*. Northamptonshire 1981
Highest innings total against County: 308 for 8 by Worcestershire 1980
Lowest innings total for County: 227 for 8 dec. *v*. Worcestershire 1980
Lowest innings total against County: 85 by Northamptonshire 1981
Highest individual innings for County: 112 M. Newell *v*. Sri Lankans 1990
Highest individual innings against County: 114 R.S. Mahanama for Sri Lankans 1990
Best bowling performance in an innings for County: 5 for 34 R.J. Hadlee *v*. Northamptonshire 1981
Best bowling performance in an innings against County: 4 for 39 N. Gifford for Worcestershire 1980
Best bowling performance in a match for County: 8 for 69 R.J. Hadlee *v*. Northamptonshire 1981
Best bowling performance in a match against County: 5 for 124 N. Gifford for Worcestershire 1980
Best attendance: 5,000 *v*. Worcestershire 1980

LIMITED-OVERS MATCH (JPL)
Highest innings total for County: 186 for 6 *v*. Middlesex 1983
Highest innings total against County: 181 for 8 by Middlesex 1983
Highest individual innings for County: 48 C.E.B. Rice *v*. Middlesex 1983
Highest individual innings against County: 33 G.D. Rose for Middlesex 1983
Best bowling performance for County: 3 for 29 K. Saxelby *v*. Middlesex 1983
Best bowling performance against County: 2 for 25 K.D. James for Middlesex 1983
Best attendance: 2,500 *v*. Middlesex 1983

HOW TO GET THERE

Rail Cleethorpes (BR), 1.5 miles.
Bus From BR Cleethorpes take Grimsby–Cleethorpes Transport Company hopper bus 8, 8X or 9X for Chichester Road or Daggett Road bus passes Chichester Road; ground entrance (Telephone 0472 358646).
Car From north: Use A1 then follow A16 signposted Grimsby, then follow signs to Cleethorpes A1098 and seafront, then follow signs old Cleethorpes and County Cricket for Chichester Road Ground close to seafront at southern end. From west: as north. From south: Use A1 then follow A16 signposted Cleethorpes and seafront, then as north or west.

WHERE TO STAY AND OTHER INFORMATION

Hotel Kingsway (0472 601122), The Grimsby Crest Hotel (0472 359771), plus many other small hotels and guesthouses.

Disabled Areas   No special area, request suitable position.
Local Radio Station(s)   BBC Radio Humberside (95.9 MHz FM/ 1485 KHz MW), Viking Radio (96.9 MHz FM/1161 KHz MW).
Local Newspaper(s)   Grimsby Evening Telegraph, Grimsby Gazette, Grimsby Target.

Worksop

The first match staged at Worksop was in 1880 when Nottingham played against the Twenty-two of Sheffield, but the initial first-class Nottinghamshire C C C match at the present Central Avenue ground was in 1921 when neighbours Derbyshire were the visitors. The ground which is situated only minutes from the town centre, is the home of Worksop Town Cricket Club which play in the Bassetlaw Cricket League. The land for the cricket ground was given to the club in 1900 by William Allen, a director of a local brewery, who also financed the building of the original pavilion. The previous ground was situated south of the River Ryton, which bounds the ground at the Central Avenue End, in Bridge Street where the main Bus Station is now located.

The present ground, a valuable piece of land close to the town centre, was previously agricultural land and before cricket could be played levelling of the ground had to take place. Some locals said at the time that an error was made as the pitch now lies four to five feet below the water level of the nearby Chesterfield Canal. The ground tends to hold the dampness, and as it is shared with the Worksop Town Football Club the outfield on the east side of the playing area tends to be quite rough.

The original pavilion was opened in 1901 prior to a match between Worksop Town C C and a Nottinghamshire Club and Ground XI but the match was washed out due to heavy rain. The pavilion was demolished and replaced in 1972 by a new structure which includes squash facilities as well as changing room for cricketers. In 1986–87 the cricket club decided to have its own pavilion. The extension is neat, has ample facilities and includes a players' area in front over-looking the playing area. The pavilion and the scoreboard are the only permanent buildings for cricket but on the football ground side are stands and terrace facilities. These are sufficiently distant from the playing area not to be used much by cricket spectators, except during poor weather. Other facilities are limited compared with the county's headquarters but despite this the County Club visit Worksop for one County Championship match usually in July. This is invariably with Yorkshire as the ground is only a few miles from the county boundary. However, the visitors in 1992 will be Gloucestershire in early August.

The number of Yorkshire visits is significant in that a careful look at

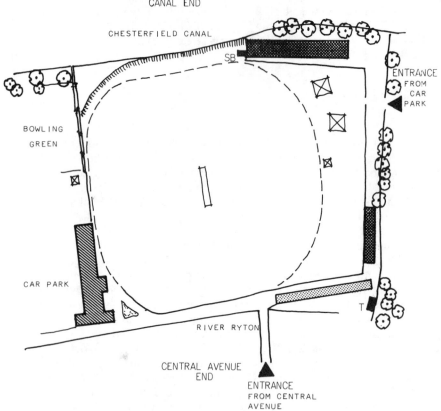

CANAL END

CHESTERFIELD CANAL

SB

ENTRANCE FROM CAR PARK

BOWLING GREEN

CAR PARK

RIVER RYTON

T

CENTRAL AVENUE END

ENTRANCE FROM CENTRAL AVENUE

N

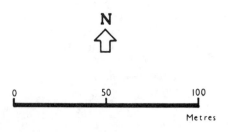

0   50   100

Metres

the ground records show that no less than three belong to Yorkshire, including a double century from Geoffrey Boycott and 8 wickets from Freddie Trueman. For Nottinghamshire, W.W. Keeton, H.J. Butler and F. Barratt hold ground records. Crowds at Central Avenue are usually around 4,000–4,500. The largest was in 1966 when some 7,000 saw the Yorkshire championship match. Two limited-overs matches have been staged at the ground, in 1970 and 1971, both in the John Player Sunday League.

Geoffrey Boycott will have fond memories of Central Avenue for he has scored over 900 runs on this ground, averaging well over 100. In 1986 three Nottinghamshire batsmen scored centuries against Yorkshire: Chris Broad (122), Tim Robinson (105) and Paul Johnson (105 n.o.). In 1988 Philip de Freitas then of Leicestershire scored a quick fire 113 in just 82 minutes. In a high scoring match in 1990 Glamorgan beat Nottinghamshire by 238 runs with centuries being recorded by Alan Butcher (121 n.o.), Hugh Morris (110 and 102 n.o.), Matthew Maynard (115) and Vivian Richards (127). The only limited-overs century was recorded by Mike Buss (121) for Sussex in 1971.

Over the years many famous players have represented Worksop Town C C, including Les Jackson the Derbyshire bowler, Ken Farnes of Essex who taught at Worksop College, Bill Voce and Wilfred Rhodes before he joined Yorkshire C C C.

This ground is the only other venue in the county other than Trent Bridge which is used regularly for County Championship matches. The ground is also used for second XI matches by Nottinghamshire C C C. Since 1980 Cleethorpes C C in Lincolnshire has also staged matches.

ADDRESS Worksop Town Cricket Club, The Pavilion, Central Avenue, Worksop, Nottinghamshire.
TELEPHONE PROSPECTS OF PLAY 0909 472681

DESCRIPTION OF GROUND AND FACILITIES

Entry to the ground for members, players and officials is from Central Avenue and adjoining the rear of the football stand near the car park of the Netherholme Shopping Centre for the public. The ground is within minutes of Worksop's main shopping street and is bounded to the north by the now disused Chesterfield Canal and to the south by the River Ryton. The pavilion and sports building is west of the playing area and close to the bowling greens. The northern Canal End has a steep bank where temporary seating can be found for members and on which the scoreboard is situated. To the north and west the stands and dressing rooms of the Worksop Town Football Club are located. Much of the seating is temporary and spectators are advised to bring their own seating to all matches as only 2,500 seats are provided for a ground capacity of 7,000. The east side of the ground houses facilities for the press and scorers and is where refreshments are located.

Near to the pavilion on the opposite side of the playing area is the Nottinghamshire C C C office and souvenir tent. The members' enclosure is in front of the pavilion and on the north side of the ground. The playing area is 126 metres by 123 metres and is quite flat. The playing area outfield to the east is on the football pitch and it is on this side of the ground that the only covered accommodation can be found which is a fair distance from the play! Car parking is available within the ground to the rear of the pavilion for 100 cars but ample parking can be found in nearby car parks close to the town centre shopping area. There is no special area for disabled spectators.

The playing area is defined by a rope with a number of advertising boards transported from Trent Bridge for the match. The TV camera/ commentary box position, if required, would be positioned at the Central Avenue End. A Radio commentary position is situated near the pavilion.

GROUND RECORDS AND SCORES

FIRST-CLASS MATCHES
Highest innings total for County: 540 *v*. Worcestershire 1934
Highest innings total against County: 434 by Yorkshire 1983
Lowest innings total for County: 67 *v*. Northamptonshire 1975
Lowest innings total against County: 54 by Derbyshire 1980
Highest individual innings for County: 223 W.W. Keeton *v*. Worcestershire 1934
Highest individual innings against County: 214 n.o. G. Boycott for Yorkshire 1983
Best bowling performance in an innings for County: 7 for 66 H.J. Butler *v*. Glamorgan 1935
Best bowling performance in an innings against County: 8 for 84 F.S. Trueman for Yorkshire 1962
Best bowling performance in a match for County: 12 for 130 F. Barratt *v*. Worcestershire 1923
Best bowling performance in a match against County: 11 for 174 D.S. Steele for Derbyshire 1980
Best attendance: 7,000 *v*. Yorkshire 1966

LIMITED-OVERS MATCHES
Highest innings total for County: 161 for 6 *v*. Sussex (JPL) 1971
Highest innings total against County: 273 for 4 by Sussex (JPL) 1971
Lowest innings total for County: 125 for 8 *v*. Derbyshire (JPL) 1970
Lowest innings total against County: 162 for 7 by Derbyshire 1970
Highest individual innings for County: 39 S.B. Hasson *v*. Derbyshire (JPL) 1970
Highest individual innings against County: 121 M.A. Buss for Sussex (JPL) 1971
Best bowling performance for County: 4 for 39 D.J. Halfyard *v*. Derbyshire (JPL) 1970
Best bowling performance against County: 3 for 33 J. Denmon for Sussex (JPL) 1971
Best attendance: 3,000 *v*. Derbyshire 1970

HOW TO GET THERE

Rail Worksop (BR), 0.75 mile.
Bus Numerous local bus services link BR Worksop and surrounding areas with town centre shopping area close to ground.
Car From north: M1 junction 31, then follow A57 signposted Worksop; ground is situated close to town centre off Central Avenue. From east: A57 or B6089 from A1 signposted Worksop, then as north. From west: A619 follow signs Worksop, then as north. From south: M1 junction 30, then follow A619 signposted Worksop, then as north, or A60 or B6005, then as north.

WHERE TO STAY AND OTHER INFORMATION

The Lion Hotel (0909 2179), Ye Olde Bell, Barnby Moor/Retford (0777 705121).

Disabled Areas No special area, request suitable position.
Local Radio Station(s) BBC Radio Nottingham (95.5 MHz FM/ 1584 KHz MW), Radio Trent (96.2 MHz FM/999 KHz MW).
Local Newspaper(s) Nottingham Evening Post, Worksop Guardian, Sheffield Star.

SOMERSET

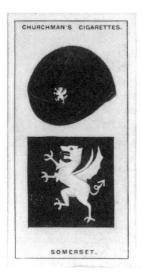

TAUNTON

BATH

WESTON-SUPER-MARE

Somerset

Founded 18 August 1875
Colours Black, white and maroon
Crest Wessex Wyvern
President J. Luff
Chairman R. Parsons
Chairman cricket committee B.C. Rose
Chief executive P.W. Anderson
Manager R.M.H. Cottam
Marketing manager Miss G. Caiger
Senior coach P.J. Robinson
Assistant coach D. Breakwell
Captain C.J. Tavaré
Groundsman P. Frost
Scorer 1st XI D.A. Oldham
Scorer 2nd XI D.A. Cooke
Statisticians N. Johns and M.F. Hill
Sponsors Taunton Cider
Newsletter *Somerset News*
Address The County Ground, St. James's Street, Taunton, Somerset TA1 1JT.
Telephone 0823 272946/253666/254287
Facsimile 0823 332395
Somerset Rapid Cricketline 0891 567513

ACHIEVEMENTS

County Championship 3rd (5) 1892, 1958, 1963, 1966 and 1981
Gillette Cup Winners (1) 1979; finalists (2) 1967 and 1978
National Westminster Bank Trophy Winners (1) 1983
Benson & Hedges Cup Winners (2) 1981 and 1982
John Player Sunday League Champions (1) 1979
Refuge Assurance Sunday League 4th 1987
Tilcon Trophy Finalists (1) 1976
Seeboard Trophy Semi-finalists (1) 1991

GROUNDS

Taunton (The County Ground, St James's Street) Bath (Recreation Ground, William Street) and Weston-super-Mare (Clarence Park, Walliscote Road).

Other grounds that have been used since 1969 are: Bristol (Imperial Ground, West Town Lanes); Yeovil (Westland Sports Ground, Westbourne Close); Yeovil (Johnson Park, Boundary Close); Glastonbury (Morlands Athletic Sports Ground, Street Road); Torquay (Recreation Ground); Weston-super-Mare (Devonshire Road Park Ground); Brislington (Ironmold Lane); Street (Millfield School) and Frome (Agricultural Showgrounds).

SECOND XI GROUNDS

In addition to the above mentioned grounds the following are used for Second XI matches: North Perrott C C, Cricket Ground, North Perrott, Near Crewkerne. (No Telephone); Glastonbury C C, Tor Leisure Centre, 7 Street Road, Glastonbury. Telephone: 0458 32393; Clevedon C C, Esmond Grove, Clevedon. Telephone: 0272 877585; King's College, Taunton. (No Telephone); Weston-super-Mare C C, Devonshire Park Road, Weston-super-Mare, Somerset. (No Telephone); Winscombe C C, Recreation Ground, Winscombe. Telephone: 093484 2720; Westland's Sports C C, Westbourne Close, Preston Grove, Yeovil. Telephone: 0935 703619; Bristol Imperial Ground, West Town Lanes, Bristol, Avon. Telephone: 0272 776659.

At one time the image of Somerset was of Jack ('Farmer') White wheeling down his deceptive left arm slows, and Harold Gimblett smiting one of his career's 265 sixes – an astonishing number for an opening bat. The picture changed with a business-like restructuring of county finances and the instant registration of overseas stars.

Taunton, Bath and Weston-super-Mare might have been regarded as charming backwaters of the game, but not when they became the stage for Vivian Richards, the most fluent West Indies batsman since Sir Gary Sobers, Joel ('Big Bird') Garner, the fast bowler, and England's own Ian Botham.

Once the dressing room was full of amateurs – the club couldn't run to many pros – and there was always the chance of laughter when R.C. ('Crusoe') Robertson-Glasgow, a man of letters and good swing bowler, was in the team. It was noticed in one match only ten of Somerset took the field, but 'Crusoe' suddenly emerged from behind a sightscreen with an ice cream cone in each hand.

Bill Andrews, new ball partner of Wellard the mighty hitter, camped out at Maidstone and Clacton to save expenses – carefully selecting a site next to the beer tents – and persuaded the police at Warrington to let him pass a night in a cell.

Only Somerset could found their club in Devon in 1875, the Gentlemen of Somerset being on tour at the time, and only Somerset could have had the nerve to pluck Australian Bill Alley from League club Colne at the age of 38, and chortle four years' later when his season's haul was 3,019 runs and 62 wickets. Alley gathered 19,612 runs, 31 centuries, and 768 wickets after most players have retired.

No cricketer has made a more startling début than Gimblett, a 20-year-old from Bicknoller, a tiny village near Watchet where he was a farmer's boy. Going in at 107 for 6 he hit 123 out of 175 in 79 minutes at Frome, and won the Lawrence Trophy for the fastest century of 1935. *Punch* was not lost for a suitable rhyme:

> How comes it that this agricultural youth
> Can meet the wiliest ball and freely scotch it?
> Simple and elementary is the truth,
> His Gimblett eye enables him to Watchet.

TAUNTON

S. J. COOK

Though Gimblett totalled 21,142 runs in fourteen seasons he gained only three pre-war caps, a disappointment which might have contributed to the self-doubts later to assail him. He was perhaps a victim of his sensational start, and the war robbed him of his prime years, but he had better claims than many selected for post-war teams and tours. Even Gimblett never matched Botham's 80 sixes in 1985, nor Wellard's 66 in 1935. Wellard, discarded by Kent, was one of the old school of bowlers who delighted in a tail-end slog, and he hit 50 or more sixes in a season four times. He was one of the best opening bowlers in the country.

Somerset, awarded first-class ranking in 1891, creditably justified their status and have invariably had compulsive crowd pullers. Vivian Richards had peak years with Somerset, who have made good use of their overseas registrations with such notables as Greg Chappell, McCool, O'Keefe, Garner, Stephen Waugh, Martin Crowe, and Jimmy Cook. One of their first major personalities, S.M.J. (Sammy) Woods, was born in Sydney, and played for both Australia and England. But for an injury he would have been in the 1902 England side against Australia. An old-style Cambridge Corinthian games player – he was an outstanding rugby forward – Woods steered Somerset through the difficult transition from second- to first-class cricket with aggressive inclinations. Once, when it was suggested Somerset's only hope was to play for a draw, he snorted: 'Draws, draws – they're only fit for bathing in.' He was secretary from 1894 to 1923 and captain from 1894 to 1906.

His successor as captain was the graceful bat, L.C.H. Palairet, and one of the county's best-known pros was Len Braund, an attractive stroke-maker, leg spinner and superb slip catcher. Unwanted by Surrey he played in twenty Tests against Australia and in three against South Africa.

Somerset's most famous bowler until the advent of the all-rounder Botham was White, who, over 28 summers, divided his hours between

W. E. ALLEY

J. C. WHITE.

PLAYER'S CIGARETTES

H. GIMBLETT

his farm at Combe Florey and the cricket field where he found 2,356 victims. His success was founded on flight and length and, if some eminent wicket-keepers who stood up to him are to be believed, he never consciously spun the ball in his career. His flight played a large part in England's victory in Australia in 1928–29, and when he returned jubilant supporters pulled his car with ropes all the way from Taunton station to his home. He was also accepted as a shrewd and wise tactical captain.

Tremlett, who suffered from a surfeit of praise early in his career through no fault of his own, was Somerset's first pro captain. Ken Palmer could hardly have been a more consistent bowler, and Stephenson carried the dual responsibility of wicket-keeper and captain for five years with much credit. Another top-ranking wicket-keeper was Taylor. In recent years batsman Roebuck and all-rounder Marks made splendid contributions. Marks' tight bowling in single-innings competitions was often a feature of Somerset's success.

After leading Yorkshire to 4 championships and the Gillette Cup in seven seasons, and serving England as captain, Brian Close accepted a new challenge at Somerset at the age of 40 in 1971, becoming captain in 1972, and in 1978 handed on to Brian Rose a strong side able to cope with the demands of the various competitions. To Somerset's satisfaction Close was recalled by England at the age of 45 – twenty-seven years after his first cap – to face the West Indies battery of speed.

In his second term Rose took Somerset to their first-ever success, a double in two days. The Gillette Cup was the first prize in 104 years with Richards scoring 117 and Garner taking 6 for 29. The Sunday League was won the next day.

The year of their double triumph, however, was marred by Somerset's expulsion from the Benson & Hedges Cup for the 'shame' (*Wisden's* word) of declaring at Worcester after one over with the score at one, a no-ball. The home side took 2 singles to win, and the farcical proceedings ended after 17 balls. Somerset already had 9 points in their Group against 6 by Glamorgan and Worcestershire. They also had the advantage of a faster wicket-taking rate than either of the other two teams, but, by declaring, Worcestershire were not given the chance to improve their wicket-taking rate.

Somerset were within the laws of the competition – hastily amended – but the Test and County Cricket Board were not prepared to allow its spirit to be so fragrantly breached and by a majority of 17 to 1 replaced Somerset with Glamorgan. Two years later Somerset won the same competition, Richards overwhelming Surrey with 132 not out, and retained the Cup by 9 wickets against Nottinghamshire.

In 1985 Somerset enhanced their reputation for the unexpected by finishing bottom of the championship, despite Botham's staggering average of 100 (5 centuries) and Richards' 76.50 (9 centuries) and 3,047 runs between them.

Botham resigned the captaincy that autumn, giving as his reason his many outside interests, and was replaced by Roebuck, and in late August 1986 the contracts of Richards and Garner, who had been at the core of Somerset's surge of success, were not renewed. There were cricketing reasons, as the West Indies were due to tour England the following summer but, despite protests, the committee survived a no-confidence vote at a Special General Meeting. Botham resigned and left for Worcestershire. A sad ending to Somerset's proudest years.

Since 1989 Somerset supporters have had little to shout about other than the signing of Jimmy Cook the prolific Transvaal and South African batsman. In 1989 his first season in county cricket Cook scored 2,173 first-class runs with eight centuries and seven fifties. In his second season Cook achieved 2,432 runs with eight centuries and eleven fifties with a top score of 313 n.o. against Glamorgan at Cardiff. In his last season in 1991 Cook scored 2,370 runs with nine centuries and eight fifties. Vic Marks retired in 1989 and Jon Hardy and Adrian Jones both moved counties in 1990. During the 1991 season Roebuck retired to become a full-time cricket writer like Marks, and Graveney after one season moved to Durham to become the captain. Roland Lefebvre the Dutchman scored his maiden century in 1991 and was the first Dutch player to score a championship century in county cricket.

Taunton

The County Ground, St James's Street has been the headquarters of Somerset cricket since 1882, although admission to the County Championship was not granted until 1891. The county club acquired the ground from the Taunton Athletic Company and secured a lease for the ground in 1885. The club has shown an interest in improving facilities at the ground by the River Tone ever since 1891 when a running track was built around the perimeter of the cricket pitch. The track was

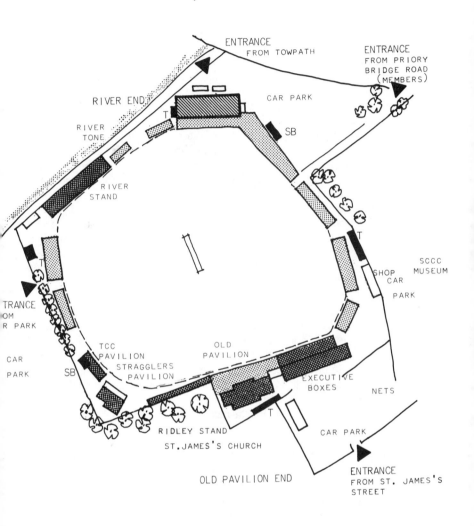

ENTRANCE
FROM TOWPATH

ENTRANCE
FROM PRIORY
BRIDGE ROAD
(MEMBERS)

RIVER END

CAR PARK

RIVER
TONE

SB

T

RIVER
STAND

T

SCCC
MUSEUM

SHOP

TRANCE
OM
R PARK

CAR
PARK

CAR
PARK

TCC
PAVILION

SB

STRAGGLERS
PAVILION

OLD
PAVILION

EXECUTIVE
BOXES

NETS

T

RIDLEY STAND

CAR PARK

ST. JAMES'S CHURCH

OLD PAVILION END

ENTRANCE
FROM ST. JAMES'S
STREET

N

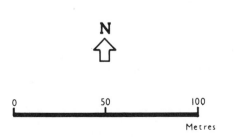

0   50   100

Metres

later used for greyhound racing. The Old Pavilion was erected together with the Ridley Stand which is situated under the shadow of St James's Church. The River Stand was built thanks to funds generated from the Somerset Supporters' Club in 1955.

The ground is used by Taunton C C and the Somerset Stragglers C C who both have small separate pavilion facilities on the ground. The past decade has produced a major advance for the club as a result of the achievements in limited-overs competitions and money has been spent to build a new pavilion, executive boxes, a scoreboard which was presented by Saab UK in 1981 and more recently the Somerset Cricket Museum. In 1990 the pavilion was named the Colin Atkinson Pavilion. Since 1989 the club have refurbished a number of small barns on the Priory Bridge Road side of the ground and these redevelopments now offer stores, offices, refreshment facilities and the Somerset Cricket Museum and Library, which is well worth a visit during an interval in play or out of season. Additional members' car parking has also been provided.

The initial first-class match was staged on the ground in 1882 against Hampshire with the first championship match being against Lancashire in 1891. Crowds of over 8,500 have been known for popular limited-overs matches in the early 1980s. The ground record was 10,000 established in 1948 when the Australians visited the most westerly county ground on the county circuit.

Taunton will certainly be remembered as the stage on which in 1925 Jack Hobbs scored with 126th and 127th centuries to surpass W.G. Grace's record. Grace completed his century of centuries on this ground too, in 1895, and went onto score 288 for the visitors. Two more recent innings will be remembered by spectators: Vivian Richards' 322 taken off Warwickshire in 1985 in double-quick time and Graeme Hick's, the Worcestershire and England batsman scored a mammoth 405 n.o. in 1988 and so nearly reached the record 424 scored by A.C. MacLaren of Lancashire in 1895.

In 1991 Somerset C C C celebrated 100 years of championship cricket. Somerset play the majority of matches at Taunton, though two cricket weeks are spent at Bath and Weston-super-Mare. It is often said by local followers, 'If you can see the Quantock Hills it is going to rain and if you can't see them it is already raining'. However the new pavilion has its back to the hills and the members can no longer see them! The ground was used for international cricket in 1983 when the Prudential Cup match between England and Sri Lanka was staged. Taunton has also seen several single wicket competitions and a floodlit match between Somerset and West Indies in 1980.

ADDRESS County Cricket Ground, St James's Street, Taunton, Somerset TA1 1JT.
TELEPHONE NUMBER PROSPECTS OF PLAY 0823 70007

DESCRIPTION OF GROUND AND FACILITIES

The past thirteen years has seen so many improvements that the visiting spectator will find few familiar sights. Entry to the ground is gained from Priory Bridge Road as well as from the old entrance in St James's Street. During matches access is still available through the adjoining car park and mower shed off Coal Orchard in the south-west corner of the ground. There is limited car parking available in the ground for members only. Town centre car parks are close by, as are the railway station car park and cattle market. The main permanent building is now the Colin Atkinson Pavilion on the north side of the ground but all the former buildings on the south side of the ground remain and are restricted to members. There are now therefore two separate members areas on the ground. Seating for the public is available on the east and west sides of the ground as well as the covered stand to the north side. A large proportion of the 8,000 capacity can be accommodated on the permanent plastic tip-up seating, although there is space available for those who may wish to bring their own seats. There are ample facilities for refreshments and all other facilities are now much improved. The Somerset Club Shop is situated close to the refurbished barns on Priory Bridge Road overlooking the playing area and is much improved. Some hospitality suites are available at the old pavilion end above the indoor cricket nets. The playing area is approximately 127 metres by 140 metres and is an uneven oval shape. The shorter dimension is in the direction of the wicket so that a straight hit over the bowler's head will frequently fall in the River Tone, barely 90 metres from the batsman.

GROUND RECORDS AND SCORES

FIRST-CLASS MATCHES
Highest innings total for County: 592 *v.* Yorkshire 1892
Highest innings total against County: 801 by Lancashire 1895
Lowest innings total for County: 48 *v.* Yorkshire 1954
Lowest innings total against County: 37 by Gloucestershire 1907
Highest individual innings for County: 322 I.V.A. Richards *v.* Warwickshire 1985
Highest individual innings against County: 424 A.C. MacLaren for Lancashire 1895
Best bowling performance in an innings for County: 10 for 49 E.J. Tyler *v.* Surrey 1895
Best bowling performance in an innings against County: 10 for 42 A.E. Trott for Middlesex 1900
Best bowling performance in a match for County: 15 for 95 E.J. Tyler *v.* Sussex 1895
Best bowling performance in a match against County: 15 for 131 A.W. Mold for Lancashire 1891
Best attendance: 10,000 *v.* Australians 1948

LIMITED-OVERS MATCHES

Highest innings total for County: 310 for 3 *v*. Derbyshire (BHC) 1990

Highest innings total against County: 303 for 7 by Derbyshire (BHC) 1990

Lowest innings total for County: 63 *v*. Yorkshire (GC) 1965

Lowest innings total against County: 68 by Combined Universities (BHC) 1978

Highest individual innings for County: 139 n.o. I.V.A. Richards *v*. Warwickshire (GC) 1978

Highest individual innings against County: 154 n.o. M.J. Proctor for Gloucestershire (BHC) 1972

Best bowling performance for County: 5 for 11 J. Garner *v*. Kent (GC) 1979

Best bowling performance against County: 6 for 15 F.S. Trueman for Yorkshire (GC) 1965

Best attendance: 8,500 *v*. Kent (GC) 1979

HOW TO GET THERE

Rail   Taunton (BR), 0.5 mile.

Bus   From surrounding areas to Bus Station, thence 500m; also shuttle from town centre 5 minutes.

Car   From north and east: M5 junction 25, then follow A358 from Creech Castle roundabout to town centre; at next roundabout take exit signposted County Ground for county cricket; County Ground is situated close to main shopping street in St James's Street and Priory Bridge Road. From west: M5 junction 26, then follow A38 Taunton and town centre, then follow signs County Ground for county cricket. From South: A358 or B3170 then as north.

WHERE TO STAY AND OTHER INFORMATION

Castle Hotel (0823 72671), County Hotel (0823 87651).

Disabled Areas   Special enclosure in front of the Old Pavilion.
Local Radio Station(s)   BBC Radio Bristol (95.5 MHz FM/1548 KHz MW), BBC Radio Devon (103.4 MHz FM/801 KHz MW).
Local Newspaper(s)   Somerset County Gazette, West Somerset Free Press, Western Daily Press.

Bath

The Recreation Ground is situated almost in the middle of the Roman city; it lies in the very bottom of the hollow in which Bath nestles, next to the River Avon and close to Bath Abbey. The ground is shared with the Bath Rugby Football Club who play in the national Courage Club League Division 1. The Bath Sportscentre, located at the North Parade

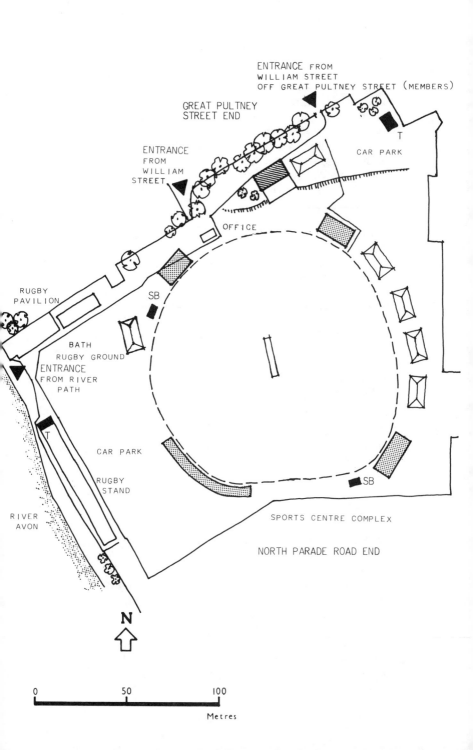

ENTRANCE FROM
WILLIAM STREET
OFF GREAT PULTNEY STREET (MEMBERS)

GREAT PULTNEY
STREET END

CAR PARK

ENTRANCE
FROM
WILLIAM
STREET

T

OFFICE

RUGBY
PAVILION

SB

BATH
RUGBY GROUND

ENTRANCE
FROM RIVER
PATH

CAR PARK

T

RUGBY
STAND

SB

RIVER
AVON

SPORTS CENTRE COMPLEX

NORTH PARADE ROAD END

N

| 0 | 50 | 100 |

Metres

Road End of the ground, once caused the players to be called from the field on a sunny day when the batsman were blinded by rays of sunlight reflected from the glass roof. The ground can be approached by William Street from Great Pultney Street through a fine architectural turnstile or via the rugby entrance by the river. The players' pavilion is the only permanent feature on the ground. There are ample facilities for lawn tennis, croquet and bowls on the Pultney Street side. In 1977 when Somerset hosted the touring Australians at Bath, two silver birch trees were planted to the west of the pavilion by captains Brian Close and Greg Chappell, who himself played for Somerset in the early 1970s.

The first match was with Sussex in 1880 with the initial first-class match being with Hampshire in 1884. In 1897 a match was staged with the touring Philadelphians and 1898 saw the county match with Yorkshire. The ground is maintained by the City of Bath Leisure Services Department.

During the winter, hockey and rugby are played but cricket provides the Recreation Ground's history. Two ground records stand out for Somerset here: the highest innings total ever for the county against Hampshire in 1924 and the bowling performances of J.C. White in 1919 and 1932. Warwick Armstrong, the Australian Captain, in 1905 scored his career best innings of 303 n.o. in an innings total of 609 for 4 declared. In recent years Mike Gatting of Middlesex has shown a liking for the Bath wicket with scores of 258 in 1986 and 196 a year later.

The Bath Cricket Festival always attracts good crowds, usually around 5,000 plus each day, and attendances are boosted for limited-overs matches. The ground is not to be confused with those of Bath C C who play on the other side of North Parade Road or Lansdown C C who have used the ground but only play a small number of matches these days. The Recreation Ground is only used for cricket by Somerset C C C.

ADDRESS   The Pavilion, The Recreation Ground, William Street, off Great Pultney Street, Bath, Avon.
TELEPHONE NUMBER PROSPECTS OF PLAY   0225 25180

DESCRIPTION OF GROUND AND FACILITIES

The main entrance into the ground is from William Street although there is also an entrance via the rugby field from Spring Gardens Road, adjoining the River Avon. The only permanent buildings are the small players' cricket pavilion close to the main entrance in William Street and a block of toilets in the north-west corner of the ground. The rugby stands are some 70 metres from the cricket playing area and provide little benefit other than as a shelter in bad weather. Car parking is available within the ground for members on the rugby ground, whilst the public must seek parking in the city centre car parks a short distance away. All facilities are temporary and include a tiered seating stand for members and two tiered stands for the public at the southern end of the ground, adjoining the sight screen. The members' enclosure is to the north side of the ground and facilities are provided for disabled spectators. Refreshments can also be taken in the Bath R F C clubhouse. The ground capacity is 8,000 and seats are provided for approximately 80 per cent. Spectators may therefore need to bring their own seats to popular matches. The playing area is approximately 133 metres by 131 metres and has a near circular boundary defined by advertising boards.

The ground is now somewhat overshadowed by the new sportscentre to the south and has lost some of its charm, as an urban sports ground within sight of Bath Abbey and the buildings of the city centre. Being a local authority ground the small cricket square is wedged between the hockey, football and rugby pitches, a part of each serving as the cricket outfield in summer.

GROUND RECORDS AND SCORES

FIRST-CLASS MATCHES
Highest innings total for County: 675 for 9 dec. *v.* Hampshire 1924
Highest innings total against County: 609 for 4 dec. by Australians 1905
Lowest innings total for County: 35 *v.* Yorkshire 1898
Lowest innings total against County: 37 by Derbyshire 1919
Highest individual innings for County: 198 A. Young *v.* Hampshire 1924
Highest individual innings against County: 303 n.o. W.W. Armstrong for Australians 1905
Best bowling performance in an innings for County: 9 for 51 J.C. White *v.* Glamorgan 1932
Best bowling performance in an innings against County: 9 for 77 H. Dean for Lancashire 1910
Best bowling performance in a match for County: 16 for 83 J.C. White *v.* Worcestershire 1919
Best bowling performance in a match against County: 16 for 80 D.V.P. Wright for Kent 1939
Best attendance: 6,500 *v.* Australians 1905

LIMITED-OVERS MATCHES
Highest innings total for County: 262 for 5 *v.* Lancashire (JPL) 1978
Highest innings total against County: 241 for 7 by Nottinghamshire (JPL) 1986
Lowest innings total for County: 61 *v.* Hampshire (JPL) 1973
Lowest innings total against County: 72 by Nottinghamshire (JPL) 1982
Highest individual innings for County: 131 D.B. Close *v.* Yorkshire (JPL) 1974
Highest individual innings against County: 130 n.o. J. Hopkins for Glamorgan (JPL) 1983
Best bowling performance for County: 5 for 27 J. Garner *v.* Yorkshire (JPL) 1985
Best bowling performance against County: 5 for 44 E.E. Hemmings for Nottinghamshire (JPL) 1982
Best attendance: 5,000 *v.* Lancashire (JPL) 1978

HOW TO GET THERE

Rail Bath Spa (BR), 0.5 mile.
Bus Badgerline 4, 18 link Bath Spa BR Station with ground (Telephone: 0225 64446); also from surrounding areas to Bus Station, thence 0.5 mile.
Car From north: M4 junction 18, then follow A46 signposted Bath; the ground is situated off Great Pultney Street A36 to the east of the city centre by the River Avon and adjoining Bath R F C. From east: M4 junction 18, then as north; or M4 junction 17 then A429 and A4 to Bath, then as north. From west: A4, A431, A36 to Bath, then as north. From south: A367 or A36 to Bath, then as north.

WHERE TO STAY AND OTHER INFORMATION

Royal Crescent Hotel (0225 319090), Fernley Hotel (0225 61603), The Francis Hotel (0225 24257).

Disabled Areas Special area in front of members' enclosure. Car parking on rugby field.
Local Radio Station(s) BBC Radio Bristol (95.5 MHz FM/1548 KHz MW), GWR Radio (96.3 MHz FM/1260 KHz MW).
Local Newspaper(s) Bath Chronicle, Evening Post and Echo.

Weston-super-Mare

Clarence Park is located very close to the coast of Somerset's popular family holiday resort. The county travel there during the holiday season in August, usually playing two championship and one limited-overs fixture. The park was given to the town in 1882 as a gift from Rebecca Davies, the landowner in memory of her husband Henry. The pavilion, which is a single storey and painted white and green, dates from 1882 and is the only permanent building on the ground. The county made its first visits to Clarence Park in 1914 when the consideration of facilities failed to include the pitch, for Yorkshire won by 140 runs and Essex by 10 wickets. The third match, with Northamptonshire, was cancelled due to the outbreak of World War One and not until 1919 did county cricket return to Clarence Park. The county have made annual visits ever since. The county played several limited-overs matches at Weston-super-Mare C C at Devonshire Park Road during the 1970s.

Clarence Park is a public park and is only used for the Somerset festival cricket weeks; no other cricket matches are played on the square. If you visit the ground when the festival is not in full swing, you will find the square fenced off, to protect it from ball games or holiday makers in the summer months and from the hockey pitches flanking it on two sides in the winter months. Weston Hockey Club use the ground and pavilion facilities for matches. The wicket is prepared by the county groundsman

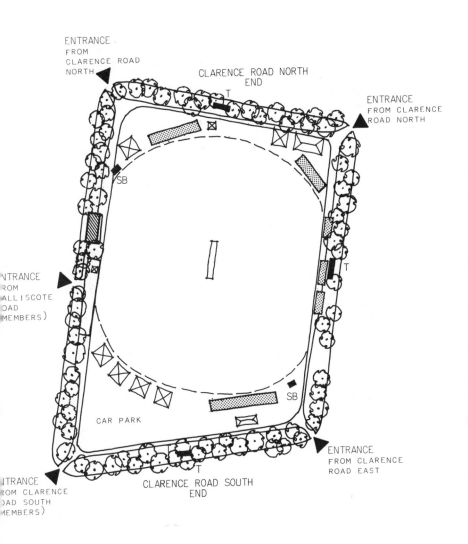

ENTRANCE
FROM
CLARENCE ROAD
NORTH

CLARENCE ROAD NORTH
END

ENTRANCE
FROM CLARENCE
ROAD NORTH

T

SB

NTRANCE
ROM
ALLISCOTE
OAD
MEMBERS)

T

CAR PARK

SB

ENTRANCE
FROM CLARENCE
ROAD EAST

NTRANCE
ROM CLARENCE
OAD SOUTH
MEMBERS)

T

CLARENCE ROAD SOUTH
END

N

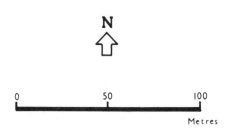

0   50   100

Metres

from Taunton and the park grounds are maintained by Woodspring District Council.

The ground has had its fair share of records, including the county's ninth and tenth wicket record partnerships. Individual record performances are plentiful: M.M. Walford's 264 was the highest innings on the ground. In recent years Ian Botham's 134 against Northamptonshire in 1985 included ten sixes. Clarence Park was where former captain and cricket writer Vic Marks scored his maiden century. In his first season for Somerset, the prolific South African Jimmy Cook notched up his 2,000th run on the ground. Batting records cannot be concluded without mention of A. Hyman, playing for a scratch team against Thornbury C C in 1902 (Graces included) who scored 359, of which 192 came in sixes off the bowling of 62 year old E.M. Grace.

No doubt holiday makers enjoy watching cricket at Clarence Park each annual holiday in the hope of seeing a repetition of that innings! Bowling records don't come much greater than that of cricketer/footballer visitor to the ground Alonzo Drake of Yorkshire and Sheffield United F C, who took all ten Somerset wickets for 35 in the first festival match. On a sad note, however, this is the ground where Vivian Richards jumped over an advertising hoarding, prompted by racial abuse from the visiting crowd.

ADDRESS The Pavilion, Clarence Park East, Walliscote Road, Weston-super-Mare, Somerset.
TELEPHONE NUMBER PROSPECTS OF PLAY 0934 642345

DESCRIPTION OF GROUND AND FACILITIES

This is a public park and entry is gained from each corner of the rectangular space. The only permanent buildings are the pavilion on the west side, which is used by players and officials only, and a block of toilets on each of the other sides of the ground. All other facilities are temporary. Car parking is only available for players, officials, sponsors and disabled persons. Seating areas are allocated to members on the west and north sides of the ground, while temporary seating for the public is provided on the other two sides. Areas are allocated for disabled spectators in both the members' enclosure near the pavilion and in the public area. Refreshment facilities are numerous and may vary from year to year as one would expect from a seaside resort! The ground capacity is 6,000 of which 80 per cent can be accommodated on the seats provided. The county also brings a temporary Somerset Souvenir shop which is situated in a temporary building near the secretary's office at the north end of the ground. Two temporary scoreboards are installed, together with open raised plastic seating stands and a number of sponsors' marquees. The press box and scorers' room is situated on a gantry high above the sightscreen at the north end, the Somerset C C C office can be found below.

The playing area is approximately 118 metres by 134 metres and therefore has relatively short, square boundaries. The ground provides what must be a good representation of the atmosphere of a match held in the early years of the century.

GROUND RECORDS AND SCORES

FIRST-CLASS MATCHES
Highest innings total for County: 507 for 6 dec. *v.* Surrey 1946
Highest innings total against County: 514 by Middlesex 1937
Lowest innings total for County: 36 *v.* Surrey 1955
Lowest innings total against County: 47 by Sussex 1936
Highest individual innings for County: 264 M.M. Walford *v.* Hampshire 1947
Highest individual innings against County: 222 n.o. Nawab of Pataudi (Senior) for Worcestershire 1933
Best bowling performance in an innings for County: 9 for 26 B.A. Langford *v.* Lancashire 1958
Best bowling performance in an innings against County: 10 for 35 A. Drake for Yorkshire 1914
Best bowling performance in a match for County: 15 for 54 B.A. Langford *v.* Lancashire 1958
Best bowling performance in a match against County: 16 for 88 J.A. Newman for Hampshire 1927
Best attendance: 6,000 *v.* Hampshire 1947

LIMITED-OVERS MATCHES
Highest innings total for County: 271 for 3 *v.* Warwickshire (RAL) 1990
Highest innings total against County: 288 for 5 by Hampshire (JPL) 1975
Lowest innings total for County: 109 *v.* Lancashire (JPL) 1976
Lowest innings total against County: 99 by Surrey (JPL) 1984
Highest individual innings for County: 112 n.o. S.J. Cook *v.* Warwickshire (RAL) 1990
Highest individual innings against County: 113 Asif Din for Warwickshire (RAL) 1990
Best bowling performance for County: 4 for 11 V.J. Marks *v.* Surrey (JPL) 1984
Best bowling performance against County: 4 for 22 B.J. Griffiths for Northamptonshire (JPL) 1977
Best attendance: 5,000 *v.* Warwickshire (RAL) 1990

HOW TO GET THERE

Rail   Weston-super-Mare (BR), 0.5 mile.
Bus   Badgerline 5 links Weston-super-Mare BR Station with ground (Telephone: 0934 621201); also from surrounding areas to town centre, thence 0.5 mile.
Car   From north: M5 junction 21, then follow A370 signposted

Weston-super-Mare and seafront; ground situated at Clarence Park East in Walliscote Road signposted County Cricket from seafront. From east: A370 or A368 signposted Weston-super-Mare, then as north. From south: M5 junction 22 then A370 to Weston-super-Mare, then as north.

WHERE TO STAY AND OTHER INFORMATION

Berni Royal Hotel (0934 23601), Albert Hotel (0934 21363), and many small hotels and guest houses.

Disabled Areas   Special area in south-west corner of ground on concrete hardstanding.
Local Radio Station(s)   BBC Radio Bristol (95.5 MHz FM/1548 MW), GWR Radio (96.3 MHz FM/1260 KHz MW).
Local Newspaper(s)   Western Mercury, Weston Daily Press.

SURREY

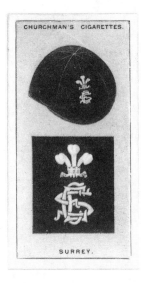

LONDON – THE FOSTER'S OVAL

GUILDFORD

Surrey

Founded 22 August 1845
Colours Chocolate and silver
Crest Prince of Wales' Feathers
Patron HM The Queen
President W.D. Wickson
Chairman D.H. Newton
Chairman cricket committee J.A. Fulford
Secretary D.G. Seward
County coach G.G. Arnold
Assistant county coach G.S. Clinton
Marketing manager M. Newton
Cricket development officer M. Edwards
Captain A.J. Stewart
Groundsman H. Brind
Scorer 1st XI/statistician M.L.W.R. Ayres
Scorer 2nd XI K.J. Smith
Sponsors Austin Reed
Newsletter *Around The Foster's Oval*
Address The Foster's Oval, Kennington, London SE11 5SS.
Telephone 071 582 6660
Surrey Rapid Cricketline 0891 567514
Test Match Commentaries Rapid Cricketline 0891 567567
Test Match Updates Rapid Cricketline 0891 567555

ACHIEVEMENTS

County Championship Champions (18) 1864, 1887, 1888, 1890, 1891, 1892, 1894, 1895, 1899, 1914, 1952, 1953, 1954, 1955, 1956, 1957, 1958 and 1971; joint champions (2) 1889 and 1950
Gillette Cup Finalists (2) 1969 and 1980
National Westminster Bank Trophy Winners (1) 1982; finalists (1) 1991
Benson & Hedges Cup Winners (1) 1974; finalists (2) 1979 and 1981
John Player Sunday League 5th 1969 and 1980
Refuge Assurance Sunday League 5th 1988 and 1989
Tilcon Trophy Winners (1) 1991; finalists (2) 1978 and 1989
Seeboard Trophy Finalists (1) 1990; semi-finalists (1) 1989

GROUNDS

London (The Foster's Oval, Kennington) and Guildford (Guildford C C, Woodbridge Road).

Other grounds that have been used since 1969 are: Byfleet (BAC Ground, Byfleet); Sunbury-on-Thames (Kenton Court Meadow, Lower Hampton Road); Leatherhead (St John's School); Sutton (Cheam Road); Godalming (Charterhouse School); Tolworth (Decca

Sports Ground); East Molesey (Metropolitan Police Sports Ground, Imber Court); Croydon (Old Whitgiftians C C, Croham Road) and Banstead (Banstead C C, Avenue Road).

SECOND XI GROUNDS
In addition to the above mentioned grounds the following are used for second XI matches: Banstead C C, Avenue Road, Banstead, Surrey. Telephone: 0737 358838; National Westminster Bank Sports Ground, Turle Road, Norbury, Surrey. Telephone: (Pavilion) 081 764 1170 (Office) 081 679 5638; Oxted C C, Master Park, Oxted, Surrey. Telephone: 0883 712792; Wimbledon C C, Church Road, Wimbledon, London SW19. Telephone: 081 946 7403; Bank of England Sports Ground, Priory Lane, Roehampton, London SW15. Telephone: 081 876 8417; Purley C C, The Ridge, off Foxley Lane, Purley, Surrey. Telephone: 081 660 0608.

If the convivial meeting at 'The Horns' tavern, Kennington, in October 1845 had been granted the power to see the outcome of their decision to provide Surrey cricket with a 'local habitation and a name' there would have been both awe and satisfaction. The sight of a packed house at The Oval on a great occasion, a Jack Hobbs-Tom Hayward first-wicket stand, Peter May in full attacking flight, a bowling burst from Tom Richardson, overs from Alec Bedser, Jim Laker and Co and the fielding during those incredible seven championship seasons, would have exceeded all expectations.

No county can boast a longer or richer history – mention of the game at Guildford goes back to 1550 – and The Oval, once a 10-acre market garden, has an honoured place ever since it staged the first home Test against Australia in 1880.

The first county fixture was on 25 and 26 June 1846, when Kent were defeated, and the vision of Harrovian Charles Alcock, the county's first paid secretary, put the ground firmly on the sporting map. Not only did he have the initiative to arrange the first Test match in England, but in his joint role as secretary of the Football Association, he dreamed up the FA Challenge Cup. Its first final, and the first home soccer internationals with Scotland and Wales, were played at The Oval, and, for good measure, the first rugby internationals against Scotland and Ireland Packer had nothing on Alcock.

A century on and it was imperative to embark on big-scale developments on the west side, and to undertake general improvements. After much negotiation and disappointment involving even government departments, Elders IXL, the brewery group, in the name of their Foster's brand lager, offered and agreed a sponsorship package by which the famous old ground became 'The Foster's Oval' for the 15-year duration of the sponsorship from October 1988. This sponsorship, together with donations raised through the Ken Barrington Appeal and Save The Oval Appeal, has enabled the south-west corner of the ground

THE FOSTER'S OVAL

WILLS'S
Cigarettes.

R. ABEL,
SURREY

to be redeveloped. This includes a sports centre/indoor cricket school, new changing rooms, press box, bars, executive boxes and groundstaff headquarters as well as some 1,700 terraced seats for members and public. The only alternative to sponsorship would have been the unthinkable loss of The Oval as a Test centre, or, at worst, the ground itself. It remains, of course, part of the lands of the Duchy of Cornwall. Edward, then Prince of Wales, jokingly made that plain when he saw a note pinned to the door of the Australian dressing room in 1930 forbidding entry without the manager's permission. 'You can't keep me out,' was his response. 'I'm your landlord!'

Surrey have often been the pacemakers. H.H. Stephenson captained the first side to Australia, and in the late 'eighties and 'nineties they were seldom off the top. Shuter was one of many outstanding captains of Surrey – general agreement is that Percy Fender was the finest of all and a length in front of Jardine – and was the first to declare an innings closed.

The roll of honour of distinguished players and their deeds for England and Surrey could fill a fat volume, but the pride of place belongs to John Berry Hobbs, the first professional cricketer to be knighted. 'The Master' enobled the art of batting, conquered all forms of newly-invented bowling from swing to the googly, and left a string of records which could stand for all time. He scored 197 centuries, 98 coming after the age of 40, and 61,760 runs, and as a natural No. 1, shared in 166 first-wicket stands of 100 or more, including 66 with Andy Sandham and 40 with Hayward. Twenty-eight of the stands passed 200, and in 13 days he shared opening partnerships of 428, 182, 106 and 123 before a wicket fell.

In 61 Tests he had 15 centuries, 12 of which were against Australia, and 23 opening stands of 100 or more, 15 with Herbert Sutcliffe, 8 with Wilfred Rhodes. At Melbourne in 1991–12 Hobbs and Rhodes realized 323. In the words of Fender, Hobbs was simply the best in all conditions of all time; indeed he made runs on old-style Australian gluepots and

J. B. HOBBS. SURREY

P. B. H. MAY

TONY LOCK

had to an astonishing degree, that quality which separates the great from the very good, of being able to score off the good ball.

Hobbs came from Cambridge where his idol Tom Hayward lived. Hayward was the first to follow Grace with 100 centuries, and was one of the elite scoring 1,000 runs in twenty seasons – before the end of May in 1990 – and totalled 3,170 in 1904 and 3,518 two years later. A classical batsman he came from a family of cricketing perfectionists, who played for Surrey XIs. The young Hobbs could have had no better mentor, and no better tribute can be imagined than to say he was even better than Hayward.

Only Surrey can boast of four batsmen with over 100 centuries. After Hobbs, comes Sandham with 107, Hayward 104 and John Edrich 103. To find Edrich, the efficient left hander in such company is perhaps surprising, but he had all the merits and determination of his Norfolk clan and was effective for both Surrey and England. No doubt May, the one genuinely great batsman of England since 1946, and Barrington, a high-ranker with 20 Test centuries and an average of almost 60 from 76 hundreds would have joined the elite club if they had played longer. May's dual responsibilities as leading batsman and captain in 41 Tests eventually took its toll, and Barrington, without an enemy in the world, suffered a second and fatal heart attack while serving as assistant manager to England at Barbados in 1981.

Way back in the 'eighties The Oval took little Bobby ('The Gov'nor') Abel to its heart – no-one has overtaken his 357 not out in 1899 – and Tom Richardson, who used to walk to his home at Mitcham carrying his bag after a day's fast bowling, was one of the game's greatest fast bowlers. Herbert Strudwick, the famed wicket-keeper, recommended to The Oval by a Sunday School mistress, always said Richardson never wittingly bowled a short pitcher in his life. The Richardson-Lockwood partnership was much feared, and George Lohmann and J.N. Crawford, who quarelled with the club and went to Australia, were outstanding.

For all Fender's ingenuity Surrey, handicapped by the quality of home pitches and sometimes by the inability to take the catches off the potent fast bowling of Alf Gover, could not manage a championship between the wars. The first tangible success after the 1914 victory was to share the title in 1950, but it was then very clear that Surrey were on the brink of high achievement. Before he started his captaincy in 1952 Stuart Surridge wrote in his diary: 'Surrey will be champions for the next five years.' How right he proved to be.

Surridge was born within two miles of The Oval, and one important reason for Surrey's success was that he had grown up with many of his team; the Bedser twins, McIntyre, a superb wicket-keeper, Constable and the hitter Whittaker. His attack of Alec Bedser, an all-time great, Loader, and the spinners Laker and Lock was virtually England's, and as a back-up all-rounder Eric Bedser was close to that class as an off spinner. The fielding was dramatic, and Surrey played with such fire and purpose that they expected to take a wicket with every ball. Some of Surridge's declarations were so audacious that they seemed to be acts of folly, but they invariably came off, and the psychological pressure alone with often too much for the opposition.

Surrey raced to championships with bowlers who stood out at Test level, let alone at county. Laker was arguably the best off spinner of all time with 19 wickets against Australia at Old Trafford, a record never likely to be beaten. When Surridge retired in triumph May extended the run to seven championships and in 1971 Micky Stewart, later England's team manager, completed Surrey's 18th outright success.

In recent seasons Surrey have finished 5th, 6th and 7th in the Refuge Assurance Sunday League and were finalists in the 1991 National Westminster Bank Trophy. Much of the fine team spirit has been built around the captaincy of Ian Greig who returned from grade cricket in Australia to assist with bringing the youngsters along. Both Bicknell brothers, Thorpe, Stewart and Medlycott have toured with England teams abroad. Alec Stewart was appointed captain for 1992 and without the explosive Waqar Younis, who will be on Test duty for Pakistan in 1992, it will be interesting to see how Surrey will fare.

The Foster's Oval

The formation of Surrey County Cricket Club was precipitated by the removal of the Montpelier Club, one of the strongest clubs in South London, from their ground at Walworth. The Walworth ground was bought in 1844 and left the club without a ground, but a member, Mr William Baker, came to the club's assistance. He suggested that Kennington Oval, a market garden and the property of the Duchy of Cornwall, might be used for cricket. The Duchy was willing to let it for the purpose of a cricket ground and a lease of thirty-one years was granted at £120 per year, with taxes which amounted to a further £20.

At the time of its conversion to a cricket ground, Kennington Oval

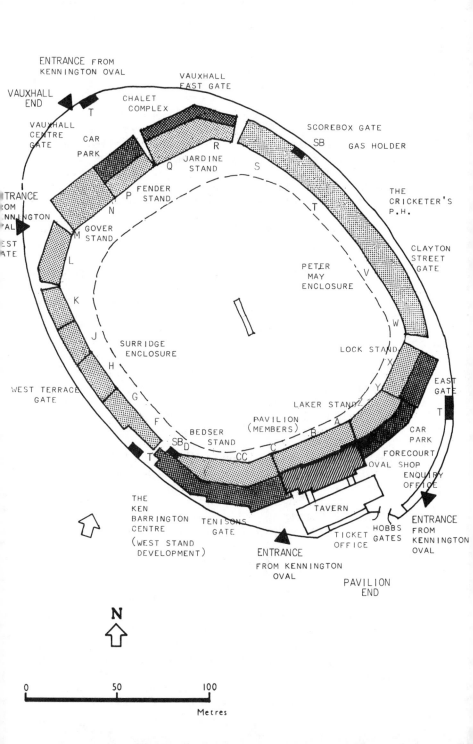

ENTRANCE FROM KENNINGTON OVAL

VAUXHALL
EAST GATE

VAUXHALL
END

T

CHALET
COMPLEX

VAUXHALL
CENTRE
GATE

CAR
PARK

R

SCOREBOX GATE

SB

GAS HOLDER

Q

JARDINE
STAND

S

ENTRANCE
FROM
KENNINGTON
OVAL

P

FENDER STAND

N

T

THE
CRICKETER'S
P.H.

M

GOVER
STAND

EST
ATE

L

PETER
MAY
ENCLOSURE

V

CLAYTON
STREET
GATE

K

J

SURRIDGE
ENCLOSURE

W

LOCK STAND

H

X

WEST TERRACE
GATE

G

Y

EAST
GATE

F

LAKER STAND Z

PAVILION
(MEMBERS)

B   A

T

SB D

BEDSER
STAND

CC   C

CAR
PARK

T

THE
KEN
BARRINGTON
CENTRE

(WEST STAND
DEVELOPMENT)

TENISONS
GATE

ENTRANCE
FROM KENNINGTON
OVAL

TAVERN

TICKET
OFFICE

HOBBS
GATES

FORECOURT
OVAL SHOP
ENQUIRY
OFFICE

ENTRANCE
FROM
KENNINGTON
OVAL

PAVILION
END

N

0   50   100

Metres

was mainly an open space with a small hedge surrounding it and it takes its name from the surrounding streets rather than the shape of the playing area itself. The original turf came from Tooting Common and was laid in March 1845 by Mr M. Turtle of Clapham Road for £300.

The first match on the ground is recorded as having been played on 13 May 1845 between Mr Fould's XI and Mr Houghton's XI. The first Surrey match was on 21 and 22 August 1845 between the Gentlemen of Surrey and the Players of Surrey. Following the meeting of the Montpelier Club on 22 August 1845 at the Horns Tavern, Kennington, more than a hundred members of different clubs in the county proposed the formation of the Club for the County of Surrey. The resolution was carried amidst cheering and the formal inauguration took place at the Horns Tavern on 18 October 1845. The first Surrey C C C home match was staged with neighbours Kent in 1846, while the first County Championship fixture was staged in 1873 against Sussex; the first Test Match took place in 1880 between England and Australia.

During that first Test Match Dr W.G. Grace scored 152 for England and W.L. Murdoch replied for the Australians with 153 n.o. The ground was used for association football in the nineteenth century and was the venue for the FA Cup Final in 1872 and again from 1874 to 1892. The pavilion was built in 1896 and was designed by the architect Mr A.T. Muirhead who was also responsible for the Old Trafford pavilion. Although much altered in subsequent years it still retains much of its original character.

The Mound Stand including a number of fine executive boxes was rebuilt during the 1980s. The nets and the West Stand were demolished after the 1988 season to make way for the new Bedser Stand Development which includes the Ken Barrington Cricket Centre. The majority of this work was paid for by funds raised by the 'Save the Oval Fund' with assistance from Foster's Australian brewery. (The ground is today known as The Foster's Oval and as well as cricket during summer months a highlight of the autumn sporting calender in recent years has been Australian Rules Football, which has been staged between the two top Australian sides for the Foster's Challenge Cup. Other tournaments staged at the Oval have included an International Batsman of the Year competition staged in 1979.) Construction was carried out by Eve Construction PLC at a cost of £3m. The complex was fully completed in 1991 and was opened by HM The Queen on 31 July 1991 during the Surrey *v*. Essex National Westminster Bank Trophy Quarter-final match. The West Stand Development includes open seating for members, together with bar, restaurant and refreshment areas. The building includes facilities for players and officials with changing areas and indoor nets within The Ken Barrington Centre to the rear and in the basement of the development. The upper levels include two storeys of executive boxes and on the very top floor a new press room and media centre. The Ken Barrington Centre includes facilities for a number of sports other than cricket nets including: martial arts, circuit training, five-a-side football, six-a-side hockey, badminton, volleyball, aerobics, netball, short tennis, table tennis, golf practice and yoga. The centre offers probably the best such facilities in the Surrey and South London area and a centre of cricketing excellence.

In 1990 Surrey C C C named the stands at the Foster's Oval after a number of famous players to have represented the county club as follows The Laker Stand (formerly the Taverners Stand), The Lock Stand (formerly the Mound Stand), The Jardine Stand (formerly the Vauxhall East Stand), The Fender Stand (formerly the Vauxhall Centre Stand), The Gover Stand (formerly the Vauxhall West Stand), The Surridge Enclosure (formerly the West Terrace) and The Bedser Stand (formerly the West Stand and Nets Stand). The Peter May Enclosure remains as previously named.

There are many famous paintings and items of cricketana in the various parts of the pavilion as well as in the Surrey C C C Centenary Library in the basement. The world famous Hobbs Gates form the main entrance to the ground at the rear of the pavilion. Like most Test Match grounds, the facilities for members are good and except for the Peter May Enclosure and the West Terrace, other parts of the ground are covered. In 1988 a new executive box area was constructed at the Vauxhall End of the ground. A large TV screen was installed high above the Vauxhall Stand to view action replays of the cricket during the England v. New Zealand Test Match in 1983. This facility did not return until 1991 for the fifth Cornhill Insurance Test Match between England and the West Indies and during this match was situated on the Harleyford Road side of the ground and was sponsored by Toyota.

One of the main cricket records at the Oval is of course Sir Len Hutton's 364 against Australia in 1938. Well remembered also is the occasion in 1948 when Don Bradman was bowled for a duck on his last appearance in Test cricket by Eric Hollies of Warwickshire, so finishing with a Test match average of 99.94. Surrey C C C records have included their highest innings total of 811 against Somerset which included 357 n.o. from Bobby Abel. In 1990 Lancashire scored 863 the highest innings total on the ground against Surrey and this included the highest individual innings on the ground in any competition: 366 by Neil Fairbrother. In the same season Surrey recorded their highest limited-overs total against Hampshire and the late 1980s saw highest individual innings by Darren Bicknell and Neil Taylor.

The Oval has staged matches in all major competitions for Surrey C C C and England as well as international matches (not including England) in the Prudential Cup competitions of 1975, 1979 and 1983. Middlesex C C C have staged two matches at the Oval; firstly in 1870 when the home match with Surrey due to have been played at Lille Bridge in West Brompton was transferred as the playing area was unfit; secondly in 1939 the home County Championship match with Nottinghamshire was staged at the Oval as Lord's was being used for the annual Eton v. Harrow match.

Crowds at the Oval are restricted to the present ground capacity of 16,000, increased thanks to the West Stand Development, but the largest attendance over three days was 80,000 for the visit of Yorkshire in 1906, when many spectators were required to stand all day.

ADDRESS The Foster's Oval, Kennington, London SE11 5SS.
TELEPHONE NUMBER PROSPECTS OF PLAY 071 582 6660

DESCRIPTION OF GROUND AND FACILITIES

The members' entrances are in Kennington Oval, turnstiles 1–18 next to the enquiry office with additional public entrances at turnstiles 19–22, 23–26 and 27–30 in Harleyford Road. All buildings on the ground are permanent and the main structures are to be found at the southern end adjoining the pavilion and Bedser Stand with the Ken Barrington Sportscentre.

The centre piece is the pavilion, little changed since it was built and still a credit to the ground that first provided a venue for Test Cricket in England. All members' accommodation and facilities are in the buildings which span the south-east side of the ground, the Lock Stand, Laker Stand, pavilion and Bedser Stand. All the remaining areas are available to the public with the exception of the executive chalets at the Vauxhall End and on the upper levels of the Bedser Stand. The only covered area available to the public is the Fender Stand. All the seats in the ground are plastic in a number of colours: white, blue, buff, pink, and green. Refreshments are available in several locations around the ground including the bar at the rear of the Lock Stand, the Banqueting Suite and the Tavern itself just outside the Hobbs Gates.

An enlarged and improved Surrey C C C Oval souvenir and book shop is also available at the rear of the Laker Stand. Additional souvenir stalls are situated elsewhere in the ground for popular matches. The playing area is very large, extending to 170 metres by 150 metres, within which the actual playing area is defined by a rope stretched to the appropriate dimensions depending on the position of the playing strip being used, but usually about 137 metres by 140 metres.

There is only a very limited amount of car parking in the ground for members on a strictly first come first served basis at £2 per day at the Vauxhall End. This facility is not available for popular matches. Car owners must seek to park in neighbouring streets where permitted or the car parks (NCP) closer to Central London. There are facilities for disabled spectators both in the pavilion and in the public stands. The current ground capacity is 16,000 and all can be accommodated on permanent modern plastic seating so spectators will not be required to bring their own seating to matches at all.

This is very much an urban situation, overshadowed as it has been for so many years by the gas holders and blocks of flats, but still retaining from the upper part of the pavilion a fine view of the tower of the Palace of Westminster and Central London.

GROUND RECORDS AND SCORES

TEST MATCHES
Highest innings total for England: 903 for 7 dec. *v.* Australia 1938
Highest innings total against England: 708 by Pakistan 1987
Lowest innings total for England: 52 *v.* Australia 1948
Lowest innings total against England: 44 by Australia 1896
Highest individual innings for England: 364 L. Hutton *v.* Australia 1938

Highest individual innings against England: 291 I.V.A. Richards for West Indies 1976

Best bowling performance in an innings for England: 8 for 29 S.F. Barnes *v*. South Africa 1912

Best bowling performance in an innings against England: 8 for 65 A. Trumble for Australia 1902

Best bowling performance in a match for England: 13 for 57 S.F. Barnes *v*. South Africa 1912

Best bowling performance in a match against England: 14 for 90 F.R. Spofforth for Australia 1882

LIMITED-OVERS INTERNATIONALS

Highest innings total: 328 for 5 by Australia *v*. Sri Lanka (PC) 1975

Lowest innings total: 154 by Pakistan *v*. England (PT) 1978

Highest individual innings: 125 n.o. G.S. Chappell for Australia *v*. England (PT) 1977

Best bowling performance: 5 for 31 M. Hendrick for England *v*. Australia (PT) 1980

FIRST CLASS MATCHES

Highest innings total for County: 811 *v*. Somerset 1899

Highest innings total against County: 863 by Lancashire 1990

Lowest innings total for County: 16 *v*. Nottinghamshire 1880

Lowest innings total against County: 20 by Kent 1870 (1 man absent)

Highest individual innings for County: 357 n.o. R. Abel *v*. Somerset 1899

Highest individual innings against County: 366 N.H. Fairbrother for Lancashire 1990

Best bowling performance in an innings for County: 10 for 45 T. Richardson *v*. Essex 1894

Best bowling performance in an innings against County: 10 for 28 W.P. Howell for Australians 1899

Best bowling performance in a match for County: 15 for 83 T. Richardson *v*. Warwickshire 1898

Best bowling performance in a match against County: 15 for 57 W.P. Howell for Australians 1899

Best attendance: 80,000 *v*. Yorkshire 1906

LIMITED-OVERS MATCHES

Highest innings total for County: 331 for 5 *v*. Hampshire (BHC) 1990

Highest innings total against County: 300 for 9 by Warwickshire (JPL) 1985

Lowest innings total for County: 86 *v*. Gloucestershire (JPL) 1969

Lowest innings total against County: 65 by Glamorgan (JPL) 1969

Highest individual innings for County: 135 n.o. D.J. Bicknell *v*. Yorkshire (NWBT) 1989

Highest individual innings against County: 137 N.R. Taylor for Kent (BHC) 1988

Best bowling performance for County: 6 for 25 Intikhab Alam *v.*
Derbyshire (JPL) 1974
Best bowling performance against County: 7 for 15 A.L. Dixon for
Kent (GC) 1967
Best attendance: 12,000 *v.* Lancashire (NWBT) 1988

HOW TO GET THERE

Rail   Oval Underground (Northern Line) 200m; Vauxhall (BR) and
Underground (Victoria Line) 600m.
Bus   LRT 3, 36, 36A, 36B, 59, 95, 109, 133, 155–159, 185, 196
(Telephone: 071 222 1234).
Car   From north: from Edgware Road A5 follow signs Marble Arch,
then take A202 Park lane to Grosvenor Place, then follow signs
Vauxhall Bridge using Vauxhall Bridge Road, after passing over the
River Thames go under the railway bridge and turn right down
Harleyford Road for Kennington and The Foster's Oval. The ground
is located south of the River Thames at Kennington close to the A3,
A23 and A202 trunk roads from Central London. From east: follow
A202 to Kennington district, take Harleyford Road and follow signs
for The Oval and county cricket for Kennington and The Foster's
Oval. From west: M4/M3 or A23, A24 follow signs Central London,
then signs Kennington, or as north. From south: from M25 junctions
6, 7, 8 or 9, then take A22, A23, A24 or A243 signposted London,
then follow signs Kennington for county cricket and The Foster's
Oval.

WHERE TO STAY AND OTHER INFORMATION

London Park Hotel, London SE1 (071 735 9191) or stay in any
Central London Hotel.

Disabled Areas   Pavilion area for members or in two special areas
for the public. Car parking by arrangement in advance.
Local Radio Station(s)   Greater London Radio (94.9 MHz FM/1458
KHz MW), Capital Radio (95.8 MHz FM/1548 KHz MW), LBC
(97.3 MHz FM/1152 KHz MW).
Local Newspaper(s)   The Evening Standard, South London Press,
Surrey Advertiser.

Guildford

The earliest known reference to the playing of cricket within the borders
of Surrey is in a document of 1598 relating to a dispute over a plot of
land at Guildford. The document speaks of a John Derrick, a scholar in
the Free School of Guildford and states that 'he and several of his fellows
did run and play there at cricket'.

The Guildford Cricket Club was founded in 1862 by two brothers W.

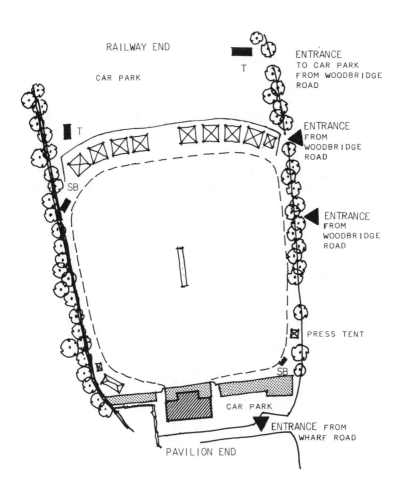

RAILWAY END

CAR PARK

T

ENTRANCE
TO CAR PARK
FROM WOODBRIDGE
ROAD

T

ENTRANCE
FROM
WOODBRIDGE
ROAD

ENTRANCE
FROM
WOODBRIDGE
ROAD

SB

PRESS TENT

SB

CAR PARK

ENTRANCE FROM
WHARF ROAD

PAVILION END

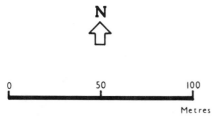

N

0	50	100

Metres

and J. Stevens in 1886 and the first mention of cricket at Guildford was in the James Lillywhite Cricket Annual of 1873. Mr J. Stevens scored 191 for the club during the 1874 season. At that time the ground was located on the cattle market which is now close to the law courts and car parks at the rear of the Guildford Sportscentre. Two famous players scored heavily in club matches at Guildford: C.T. Studd made 222 n.o. for Horsham C C against Guildford C C in 1881 and in the same season W.W. Read scored 263 for Reigate Priory C C.

The present Woodbridge Road Ground was given to the town by Sir Harry Waechter-Bart in 1911 for cricket, cycling, military parades and charitable purposes. Guildford Cricket Club disbanded between 1914 and 1922, though after 1918 the club's players played under the name of Guildford Wanderers Cricket Club. In May 1922 the cricket players donned the club colours of claret, pink and black again when Guildford played its first home match since 1914 against Woking. The famous amateur football club the Guildford Pinks had the same colours and shared the Woodbridge Road Sports Ground until their demise in the early 1950s.

Covering some eight acres, the ground is lush and green with trees around most of the perimeter. The busy Woodbridge Road runs along the east side of the tree-lined area. At the far end from the pavilion brief glimpses of the Thameslink trains linking Bedford, London and Guildford can be seen through the poplars and beeches. The only permanent buildings on the ground are the pavilion, the groundsman's stores and the scoreboard, which was built along the lines of the original famous Sydney Cricket Ground scoreboard in Australia. Woodbridge Road is reputed to be one of the few level playing areas in the city.

The first visit to Guildford by Surrey C C C was in 1938 when Hampshire were the visitors; the first two days attracted a total of 10,000 spectators. Except for occasional breaks, since the inaugural match fifty-five years ago the ground has been regularly used for County Championship and in recent years limited-overs Sunday League matches. In 1988 Guildford C C celebrated a jubilee of county cricket in the county town. Other matches staged have included a one-day match between the Club Cricket Conference and the touring South Africans in 1947 when a total of 715 runs were scored in a single day's play by the two sides. In 1957 HM The Queen and Duke of Edinburgh attended a match with Hampshire and met both teams.

Guildford C C play in the Surrey Championship sponsored by Eve Construction Group PLC. The former president was David Frith (the editor of Wisden Cricket Monthly). The present club chairman who is responsible for the Guildford Cricket Festival is Mr Charles Woodhouse.

Crowds at Woodbridge Road are usually around 4,000–5,000, the best for a single day was 7,000 against Hampshire in 1938. Ground records include a double hundred by Gordon Greenidge for Hampshire and fine bowling performances from Tony Lock and Derek Shackleton. In 1989 Nottinghamshire made 475 for 8 to record the highest innings total on the ground against Surrey. In the limited-overs game Allan

Lamb hit the highest individual score of 132 n.o. on the ground, with Tony Pigott taking the most wickets 5 for 28.

The majority of matches on the ground have been staged with neighbouring counties Sussex and Hampshire. In recent seasons, rather than just four days' cricket over a weekend, the Guildford Festival has been extended to six days, starting mid-week and including two County Championship matches. In 1992 the visitors to Woodbridge Road will be Kent and Warwickshire.

ADDRESS Guildford Cricket Club, The Pavilion, Woodbridge Road, Guildford, Surrey.
TELEPHONE NUMBER PROSPECTS OF PLAY 0483 572181

DESCRIPTION OF GROUND AND FACILITIES

Entry to the ground is from Woodbridge Road, with the members' entrance at the junction of Wharf Road. Car parking is available to the north of the cricket field towards the railway embankment. Other car parking is available in the city centre a short walk away and in adjoining streets. The only permanent buildings are the two-storey cricket pavilion and some terrace seating on either side of it. This area of the ground is restricted to members only. The main scoreboard is in the north-west corner of the cricket field with a smaller secondary scoreboard close to the Surrey C C C Executive Club marquees in the south-east corner of the ground. All seating is temporary and the northern side of the ground is allocated to sponsors' tents and refreshment tents for the public. Members' refreshments and bar facilities are provided in the pavilion and in a tent to the west of the pavilion adjoining the Surrey C C C (The Oval Shop) souvenir tent. A press room/radio commentary box is available in the pavilion and tent on the ground. Provision is made for disabled spectators and a toilet is provided at the rear of the pavilion. Temporary toilets are provided around the ground although there are permanent toilets to the north of the car park area near the railway bridge.

The ground capacity is 7,500 and seats for 50 per cent are provided, however, it is appropriate to bring your own seats to popular matches. The playing area is approximately 113 metres by 119 metres. If required, the TV camera/commentary box position would be located on the balcony of the pavilion at the southern end of the ground.

GROUND RECORDS AND SCORES

FIRST-CLASS MATCHES
Highest innings total for County: 504 v. Hampshire 1948
Highest innings total against County: 475 for 8 by Nottinghamshire 1989
Lowest innings total for County: 77 v. Derbyshire 1939
Lowest innings total against County: 48 by Hampshire 1946
Highest individual innings for County: 172 H.T. Barling v. Hampshire 1946
Highest individual innings against County: 200 n.o. C.G. Greenidge for Hampshire 1977

Best bowling performance in an innings for County: 9 for 77 G.A.R. Lock *v*. Oxford University 1960

Best bowling performance in an innings against County: 7 for 34 D. Shackleton for Hampshire 1958

Best bowling performance in a match for County: 12 for 148 G.A.R. Lock *v*. Oxford University 1960

Best bowling performance in a match against County: 9 for 125 A.C.S. Pigott for Sussex 1987

Best attendance: 7,000 *v*. Hampshire 1938

LIMITED-OVERS MATCHES

Highest innings total for County: 270 for 6 *v*. Worcestershire (JPL) 1983

Highest innings total against County: 306 for 2 by Northamptonshire (JPL) 1985

Lowest innings total for County: 89 *v*. Gloucestershire (JPL) 1978

Lowest innings total against County: 133 by Gloucestershire (JPL) 1980

Highest individual innings for County: 87 R.D.V. Knight *v*. Worcestershire (JPL) 1983

Highest individual innings against County: 132 n.o. A.J. Lamb for Northamptonshire (JPL) 1985

Best bowling performance for County: 4 for 31 I.R. Payne *v*. Northamptonshire (JPL) 1977

Best bowling performance against County: 5 for 28 A.C.S. Pigott for Sussex (JPL) 1982

Best attendance: 5,000 *v*. Northamptonshire (JPL) 1985

HOW TO GET THERE

Rail   Guildford (BR) or Guildford London Road (BR), both 0.75 miles.

Bus   Green Line buses from surrounding areas to Bus Station, thence 0.5 mile.

Car   From north: A320 follow signs Guildford and city centre, ground situated north of city centre off A320 Woodbridge Road. From east: M25 junction 10, then follow A3 signposted Guildford and city centre, then as north, or A25 signposted Guildford, then as north. From south: A281 or A3100 follow signs Guildford and city centre, then take A320 for Woodbridge Road, north of city centre. From west: A3 or A31 follow signs Guildford and city centre, then as north.

WHERE TO STAY AND OTHER INFORMATION

Angel Hotel (0483 64555), White Horse Hotel (0483 64511).

Disabled Areas   No special area, request suitable position.

Local Radio Station(s)   County Sound (96.4 MHz FM/1476 KHz MW), Radio 210 (102.9 MHz FM/1431 KHz MW).

Local Newspaper(s)   Surrey Advertiser, Surrey Times.

SUSSEX

HOVE

ARUNDEL CASTLE

EASTBOURNE

HASTINGS

HORSHAM

Sussex

Founded   1 March 1839
Colours   Dark blue, light blue and gold
Crest   County arms of six martlets (in shape of inverted pyramid)
President   The Duke of Richmond and Gordon
Chairman   A.M. Caffyn
Secretary   N. Bett
County coach   N. Gifford
Assistant coaches   C.E. Waller and I.C. Waring
Marketing manager   J.M. Parks
Captain   A.P. Wells
Groundsman   P.J. Eaton
Physiotherapist   Miss B.K. Turner MCSP, SRP
Scorer 1st XI   L.V. Chandler
Scorer 2nd XI   F.T. Ketley
Statistician/Librarian   H.O. Osborne
Sponsors   Ruddles County
Newsletter   *Sussex C.C.C. Newsletter*
Address   County Ground, Eaton Road, Hove, East Sussex BN3 3AN.
Telephone 0273 732161
Sussex Rapid Cricketline   0891 567515

ACHIEVEMENTS

County Championship   2nd (7) 1902, 1903, 1932, 1933, 1934, 1953 and 1981
Gillette Cup   Winners (3) 1963, 1964 and 1978; finalists (3) 1968, 1970 and 1973
National Westminster Bank Trophy   Winners (1) 1986
Benson & Hedges Cup   Semi-finalists (1) 1982
John Player Sunday League   Champions (1) 1982
Refuge Assurance Sunday League   13th 1989, 1990 and 1991
Tilcon Trophy   Winners (1) 1979
Seeboard Trophy   Winners (2) 1989 and 1991; semi-finalists (1) 1990

GROUNDS

Hove (County Ground, Eaton Road); Arundel Castle (The Friends of Arundel Castle C C, Arundel Castle, Castle Park); Eastbourne (Eastbourne Saffrons Sports Club, The Saffrons) and Horsham (Horsham C C, Cricket Field Road).

Other grounds that have been used since 1969 are: Pagham (Pagham C C, Nyetimber Lane, Pagham) and Hastings (Central Cricket Ground, Priory Meadow).

The Pavilion at Hove Cricket Ground.

SECOND XI GROUNDS

In addition to the above mentioned grounds the following are used for second XI matches: Hastings and St Leonards Priory C C, Central Cricket and Recreation Ground, Priory Meadow, Queens Road, Hastings, East Sussex. Telephone: 0424 424546; Hurstpierpoint College, College Grounds, Hurstpierpoint. Telephone: 0273 833636; Chichester Priory Park C C, Priory Park, Priory Lane, Chichester, West Sussex. Telephone: Directory Enquiries; Eastbourne College, College Grounds, Eastbourne. Telephone: 0323 37411; Brighton College, College Grounds, Brighton. Telephone: 0273 697136; Lewes Priory C C, Cricket Ground. Telephone: 0273 473732; Sidley C C, Cricket Ground, Sidley. Telephone: 0424 217078.

In 1903, a year after playing full back for Southampton in an FA Cup final and scoring 82 on the following Monday against Surrey, C.B. Fry touted his idea of a cricket knock-out competition. Believing the counties needed a new impetus and would benefit financially from pooled gate receipts he wrote to W.G. Grace, m'Lords Hawke and Harris among others. All agreed in principle, but when it came to the crunch the traditionalists prevailed.

Fry would have been well gratified if sixty years on he had seen not only the adoption of his plan – and broadly for the same reasons – but his own county of Sussex take the Gillette Cup in the first two years of its

ROBIN MARLAR

PRINCE RANJITSINHJI.
SUSSEX.

inception, and led by another Corinthian spirit, Ted Dexter.

Sussex also won the competition in 1978 and 1986, and were beaten finalists on three other occasions, but seven Lord's finals in twenty-three years, and the Sunday League in 1982 by a record margin, is something to shout about. In contrast, though belonging to the original nine counties in 1873, Sussex have failed to land the championship. There have been seven near-misses in 2nd place, including three in succession from 1932 to 1934 under Kumar Shri Duleepsinhji, nephew of the batting magician Ranji, hard-hitting Robert Scott and Alan Melville, who later captained South Africa in England.

At the turn of the century Ranjitsinhji, HH the Maharajah Jam Sahib of Nawanagar, finished runner-up in successive seasons, but powerful as he was in batting he did not have the balance enjoyed in the other two near-misses by David Sheppard, who became the Anglican Bishop of Liverpool and the first priest to play in Test cricket, and the Etonian John Barclay.

As a general rule Sussex captains have shared the common problem of batting outshining bowling, but it is an oddity that the championship has proved so elusive for, since the foundation in 1839 – making Sussex the oldest first-class club – no county can assemble a gallery of such notable captains. Going back to C. Aubrey Smith, who tramped the New York streets flat broke in his sixties, and went on to earn £17,000 a year in Hollywood and a knighthood, Sussex can boast of a team of Test captains.

W.L. Murdoch, Australia's captain in the original Test at The Oval and later an England wicket-keeper in South Africa, preceded Ranji and Fry, and there has been the ever-popular A.E.R. Gilligan and his brother A.H.H., Duleep (dubbed Smith at Cambridge), Melville, Sheppard, the Nawab of Pataudi, a second generation captain of India, Dexter and Greig, whose association with Packer cost him the England captaincy.

For all that he was an outstanding leader and all-rounder. S.C. Griffith, an accomplished wicket-keeper, is the only England player to have scored his maiden first-class century in his first Test in 1947–48 at Port of Spain – some years before he became secretary of MCC.

Imran Khan divided his brilliant all-rounder talents between captaining Pakistan and lifting Sussex. His pretensions to the crown worn by the top world all-rounder were genuine.

Sussex were awash with runs with Ranji and Fry, two of the jewels of the Golden Age of amateur batting. As the Australians said of Ranji after his first innings against them: 'He's no cricketer. He's a conjurer, an Eastern juggler.' Ranji's natural gifts of an eagle eye, nimble feet, supple wrists and instant judgement, were assiduously cultivated by day-long sessions in the nets, and not only was he glorious to watch but he vastly extended the techniques of batting. Fry, the Oxford classicist who applied his academic mind to all his sporting activities – he held the world record long jump for twenty-one years and was a soccer international – admitted he did not become a true England batsman until he learned from Ranji during their eight years at Hove.

In 1899 Ranji totalled 3,159 runs and 3,065 the next season with 5 double centuries, and such was the faith of the Sussex pros in him that after a hard day against Somerset they told him he must reply with a triple century. His response was 285 not out though he spent the whole night fishing!

Fry hit 94 centuries, including 6 in succession in 1901, and his aggregate of 30,886 averaged 50 an innings. He was particularly strong on the on side.

Sussex have always been a family club. There were four generations of Lillywhites, and the Tates, Gilligans, Langridges, Coxes, Parkes, Griffiths, Busses, Lenhams, Oakeses have made telling contributions. Duleep, as Ranji's nephew, also qualifies, and he positively dazzled until felled by ill health. Between 1929 and 1931 he scored 7,791 runs, more than any other batsman, and how he scored them! He murdered slow bowling, and 'christened' a new scoreboard at Hove with an even time innings of 333 against Northamptonshire.

Sheppard was a record-breaking batsman at Cambridge, and took Sussex from 13th to 2nd in 1953. He scored a century in 'Laker's match' against Australia. Inevitably David was the subject of good-natured leg pulling. On his second Australian tour he had a rash of dropped catches, which prompted Freddie Trueman to growl: 'If the reverend gentleman cannot put his hands together, what hope is there for the rest of us?' In another Test at Manchester Sheppard was dismissed as the light deteriorated. Soon play was suspended and as umpire Frank Lee came off he was confronted by the batsman. 'I would like you to know the light had nothing to do with my getting out,' said David.

The Arthur Gilligan-Maurice Tate fast-bowling partnership was formidable. Together they dismissed South Africa for 30 at Birmingham. Gilligan, who was really fast, took 6 for 7 and after a couple of wickets he turned to Maurice and pointed to the visitors balcony. There were seven batsmen with their pads on.

Tate, like his father, Fred started as an off spinner, and his progress was so moderate that there were elements within the club who wanted him to abandon bowling in favour of his aggressive batting – he scored 23 centuries on top of his 2,784 wickets. Fortunately for England, for whom he took 155 wickets in 39 Tests, there were opposing batsmen –notably Ernest Tyldesley – who were victims of his faster ball and advised him to change his methods. He became the best fast-medium bowler of his age.

John Snow had 202 wickets from 49 Tests, and was Illingworth's key fast bowler in the 1970–71 campaign. A poet and self-confessed rebel Snow had several clashes with the club, but, in the mood, he was high in post-war international rankings.

The Langridges and the Parkses were of more placid nature. James Langridge would have been followed in the England team by brother John but for the Second World War – a first-class slip he scored 1,000 over seventeen times – and Jim Parks, whose father and uncle gave sterling service, had a spell as captain. He appeared in 46 Tests and hit 51 centuries. The family tradition is maintained by his son, Bobby, the Hampshire wicket-keeper.

After finishing bottom of the championship in 1990 Sussex rose to 11th in 1991. In 1990 Sussex won the Second XI Rapid Cricketline Championship and with the introduction of several young players the future looks bright. Franklyn Stephenson has signed as the overseas player for 1992 and Alan Wells has been appointed captain with the departure of Paul Parker to Durham.

Hove

The Sussex cricket headquarters has been at Eaton Road, Hove since 1872. Previously the club played on the Royal Brunswick cricket ground, which opened in 1848 and was sited where Fourth Avenue now

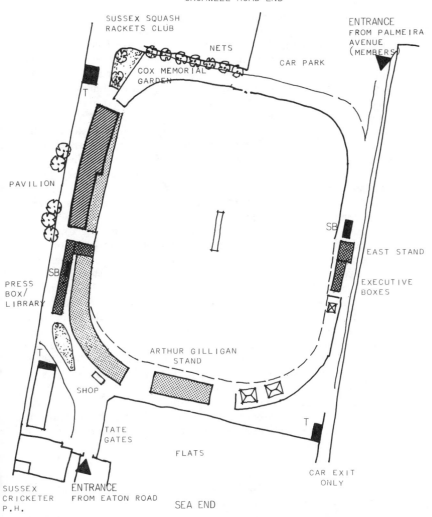

CROMWELL ROAD END

SUSSEX SQUASH
RACKETS CLUB

NETS

COX MEMORIAL
GARDEN

CAR PARK

ENTRANCE
FROM PALMEIRA
AVENUE
(MEMBERS)

T

PAVILION

PRESS
BOX/
LIBRARY

SB

SB

EAST STAND

EXECUTIVE
BOXES

T

ARTHUR GILLIGAN
STAND

SHOP

TATE
GATES

T

FLATS

CAR EXIT
ONLY

SUSSEX
CRICKETER
P.H.

ENTRANCE
FROM EATON ROAD

SEA END

N

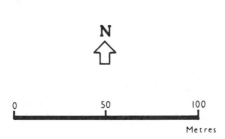

0   50   100

Metres

lies. The land was leased in 1858 to Tom Box, the wicket-keeper, who also managed the local hotel, but in 1863 the lease was transferred to Sussex C C C, providing it with its own ground for the first time. The last important match was played there in August 1871. When the club moved to Eaton Road, the Brunswick turf was removed, transported and re-laid there.

The initial first-class match staged by Sussex was against Gloucestershire in June 1872 and county matches have been played at Eaton Road ever since. Today Sussex play most of their matches at Hove, but games are also staged at Eastbourne, Horsham and, since 1990, at Arundel Castle. The last first-class match staged at the Central Cricket and Recreation Ground, Hastings was in 1989 when Middlesex were the visitors.

The pavilion was built in the 1880s, with extensions in 1921, and the major refurbishment and extension in 1933; the upper pavilion was reconstructed in 1961. The Gilligan Stand was opened in 1971 and houses cricket nets for indoor practice by youngsters. The Sussex club are confident that 1992 will see the start of a new pavilion and significant ground alterations and improvements to the buildings. Sussex is the oldest county cricket club and many historic items of cricketana can be viewed in the pavilion and club library.

The ball can be lost against the stands or flats which surround the ground on two sides and the sea mist or 'fret' at Hove can provide differing conditions, for the seafront is only a short walk away. The ground is entered from Eaton Road through the Tate Memorial Gates. A plaque marking the centenary of cricket at Hove can be found in the ground. Hove was the home of William Lillywhite, James Dean and John Wisden, founder of the *Wisden Cricketers' Almanack*. The main scoreboard which dates from the 1930s was paid for by the Harmsworth family. Visitors will also notice large eggs around the ground: these are sponsored by Stonegate County Eggs Company, which offers £3,000 to players who hit an egg while batting. Paul Parker the former club captain now with Durham hit one in 1986 when they were located at the Saffrons Ground but no one has hit one at the County Cricket Ground. A new East Stand was built in 1988 and has taken the place of the 'cowshed', which was demolished the previous year to the displeasure of locals. A squash rackets club exists to the north-west of the playing area near the Cox Memorial Garden and this is managed by Tony Pigott, the club's fast bowler.

Crowds at Hove are usually about 4,000–5,000 with more for popular limited-overs games. The largest was 14,500 for the Australians in 1948. Many great players have played at Hove including Prince Ranjitsinhji, C.B. Fry, K.S. Duleepsinhji, M.W. Tate, the Gilligans and the Langridges. No one will forget Ted Alletson who, playing for Nottinghamshire in 1911 threatened the ground with demolition with 189 in 90 minutes, the last 142 coming in 40 minutes after lunch. Alletson hit Killick for 34 in one over and this record was not beaten until Gary Sobers scored 36 off Malcolm Nash at Swansea in 1968.

Ground Records have included scores of over 300 by K.S. Duleepsinhji for the county and against the county by Eddie Paynter.

J.E.B.B.P.Q.C. Dwyer and A.P. 'Tich' Freeman hold the bowling records. In the limited-overs game Graham Gooch holds the competition record of 198 n.o. scored for Essex in the Benson & Hedges Cup. While playing for Derbyshire in 1988, Michael Holding took 8 Sussex wickets for just 21 in the National Westminster Bank Trophy, the best bowling figures in the competition.

ADDRESS County Cricket Ground, Eaton Road, Hove, East Sussex BN3 3AN.
TELEPHONE PROSPECTS OF PLAY 0273 772766

DESCRIPTION OF GROUND AND FACILITIES

There are two entrances to the County Ground, the main one from Eaton Road by the Sussex Cricketer public house, through the Tate Gates for members' at the Sea End. A second entrance for members, the public and cars is from Palmeira Avenue.

The pavilion, Wilbury Stand, press box, library, secretary's office and general club offices are situated to the west of the playing area and at right angles to the wicket. To the south at the Sea End, are the Arthur Gilligan Stand and the indoor cricket school together with the Sussex C C C souvenir shop and sometimes a number of marquees for sponsors. To the east is the main scoreboard, East Stand, sponsors' executive boxes and a disabled car park and viewing area. To the north at the Cromwell Road End are the outdoor cricket nets, members' car park, the George Cox Memorial Garden and the Sussex County Squash Rackets Club. The Sussex Cricket Society have a small office/shed adjoining the memorial garden which is open on match days. Much of the seating to the north is deckchairs and benches and to the west in the pavilion and terrace enclosures are some benches together with plastic tip-up seats in the colours of blue and white. The TV camera/ commentary position and radio commentary boxes are located in the Arthur Gilligan Stand behind the bowler's arm. Ample refreshment facilities, bars and permanent toilet facilities are available around the ground for both members and other spectators. The playing dimensions are 130 metres by 150 metres and are defined by a rope and advertising boards. The pitch slopes towards the Sea End and there is also a plastic wicket within the square for practice use. A second scoreboard is situated near the library and scorers'/press box in the Wilbury Stand. The ground capacity is 6,000 and 4,500 seats are provided. Spectators are therefore advised only to bring their own seats to popular limited-overs matches. The ground is surrounded by houses and multi-storey flats in the Hove district to the west of the centre of Brighton.

There is a good, comprehensive history of the ground for members, a little cricketana and some pictures in the pavilion despite much having been sold by the club in the early 1980s to raise funds. Hove is a pleasant county ground to view cricket and enjoy the local surroundings.

GROUND RECORDS AND SCORES

FIRST-CLASS MATCHES

Highest innings total for County: 670 for 9 dec. *v.* Northamptonshire 1921

Highest innings total against County: 703 for 9 dec. by Cambridge University 1890

Lowest innings total for County: 19 *v.* Nottinghamshire 1873

Lowest innings total against County: 23 by Kent 1859

Highest individual innings for County: 333 K.S. Duleepsinhji *v.* Northamptonshire 1930

Highest individual innings against County: 322 E. Paynter for Lancashire 1937

Best bowling performance in an innings for County: 9 for 35 J.E.B.B.P.Q.C. Dwyer *v.* Derbyshire 1906

Best bowling performance in an innings against County: 9 for 11 A.P. Freeman for Kent 1922

Best bowling performance in a match for County: 16 for 100 J.E.B.B.P.Q.C. Dwyer *v.* Derbyshire 1906

Best bowling performance in a match against County: 17 for 67 A.P. Freeman for Kent 1922

Best attendance: 14,500 *v.* Australians 1948

LIMITED-OVERS MATCHES

Highest innings total for County: 305 for 6 *v.* Kent (BHC) 1982

Highest innings total against County: 327 for 2 by Essex (BHC) 1982

Lowest innings total for County: 61 *v.* Middlesex (BHC) 1978

Lowest innings total against County: 86 by Gloucestershire (GC) 1969

Highest individual innings for County: 141 n.o. G.D. Mendis *v.* Warwickshire (GC) 1980

Highest individual innings against County: 198 n.o. G.A. Gooch for Essex (BHC) 1982

Best bowling performance for County: 6 for 14 M.A. Buss *v.* Lancashire (JPL) 1983

Best bowling performance against County: 8 for 21 M.A. Holding for Derbyshire (NWBT) 1988

Best attendance: 6,000 *v.* Middlesex (GC) 1980

SEEBOARD TROPHY COMPETITION

Highest innings total: 338 for 6 by Kent *v.* Sussex (ST) 1990

Lowest innings total: 117 by Kent *v.* Sussex (ST) 1991

Highest individual innings: 128 N.J. Lenham for Sussex *v.* Kent (ST) 1989

Best bowling performance: 8 for 49 M.A. Ealham for Kent *v.* Surrey (ST) 1990

HOW TO GET THERE

Rail   Hove (BR), 0.5 mile Brighton, Thameslink (BR), 1 mile.

Bus   Brighton & Hove 7 from Brighton BR Station and Hove BR Station to Cromwell Road for ground (Telephone: 0273 206666); also 1, 2, 3, 5, 5B, 6, 19, 26, 33, 37, 43, 43A, 46, 49 and 59 pass close to the ground.

Car   From north: M25 junction 7, then follow M23 and A23 signposted Brighton, follow signs Pyecombe and Hove after entering Brighton, then follow signs County Ground for county cricket. From east: A27 follow signs Brighton and town centre, then Worthing, for Hove and County Ground, or take seafront (Kingsway) to Second Avenue, Hove, then cross the A277 into Wilbury Road and Eaton Road is then the first turning on the right for County Ground. From west: A27 follow signs Hove for County Ground or A259 seafront (Kingsway) to Second Avenue, then as east.

WHERE TO STAY AND OTHER INFORMATION

Alexandra Hotel (0273 202722), Imperial Hotel (0273 731121), The Dudley Hotel (0273 736266), and many other small hotels and guest houses.

Disabled Areas   Special area plus car parking spaces opposite main pavilion, north of main scoreboard with entrance from Palmeira Avenue.

Local Radio Station(s)   BBC Radio Sussex (104.5 MHz FM/1161 KHz MW), Southern Sound (103.4 MHz FM/1332 KHz MW).

Local Newspaper(s)   Evening Argus, Brighton & Hove Leader.

Arundel Castle

For history and description of ground and facilities, see Friends of Arundel Castle section.

GROUND RECORDS AND SCORES

FIRST-CLASS MATCHES

Highest innings total for County: 383 for 9 dec. v Hampshire 1990
Highest innings against County: 393 for 7 dec. by Surrey 1991
Lowest innings total for County: 144 for 7 dec. v Hampshire 1990
Lowest innings total against County: 220 for 6 by Hampshire 1990
Highest individual innings for County: 107 C.M. Wells v Hampshire 1990
Highest individual innings against County: 132 n.o. C.L. Smith for Hampshire 1990
Best bowling performance in an innings for County: 3 for 79 B.T.P. Donelan v Hampshire 1990
Best bowling performance in an innings against County: 4 for 56 K.T. Medlycott for Surrey 1991

Best bowling performance in a match for County: 4 for 177 I.D.K. Salisbury v Hampshire 1990
Best bowling performance in a match against County: 6 for 156 S. D. Udal for Hampshire 1990
Best attendance: 3,500 v Hampshire 1990

LIMITED-OVERS MATCHES
The only limited-overs match at Castle Park was the proposed John Player Sunday League match between Sussex and Derbyshire on 17 August 1975 which was abandoned without a ball being bowled.

Eastbourne

The Saffrons ground is the home of the Eastbourne Cricket Club which was founded in 1855 and plays in the Sussex County Cricket League. The outfield is shared with Eastbourne Town Football Club. The sports complex is known today as the Eastbourne Saffrons Sports Club and Saffrons celebrated its centenary in 1986. Cricket has been played in Eastbourne for about 248 years, a fact which may surprise many followers of the game, but the Saffrons has not always been the venue. The earliest ground was at Paradise, now the Royal Eastbourne Golf Club. The Dental Estimates Board offices now stand on the second ground and the third ground at Ashford Road was on the site now occupied by the multi-storey car park near the Eastbourne Railway Station.

The Aboriginals played on this ground in 1868. In 1870 Dr W.G. Grace visited with a United South of England XI and played an Eastbourne team of XVII. The club moved in 1874 to Devonshire Park, given to the town by the Duke of Devonshire, and cricket was played there until the turn of the century. A move to the Saffrons was made in 1884 but Sussex C C C did not play on the ground until 1897 when Middlesex were the visitors.

The main pavilion was destroyed by fire in 1947 and was replaced by the existing building, which was itself damaged by fire in 1977. Plans are in hand for the refurbishment of the pavilion and car parking area to the rear. A number of squash courts have already been constructed. On the Old White Pavilion known as the War Memorial Pavilion, and squash courts is a plaque bearing the name of the illustrious D.R. Jardine. The other pavilion on the ground is the Harry Bartlett Pavilion, which is also at the Meads Road End.

The name 'the Saffrons' originates from the use to which the land was put over a century ago, when saffron was grown for dyeing and medicinal purposes. The part of the ground known as Larkin's Field dates from the 1700s when a saddler named Larkin rented the ground there to graze the cattle he raised for their hides.

Most of the famous players appeared at the Saffrons: the Hide brothers, both Eastbourne men, M.W. Tate when a Sussex colt and Dr

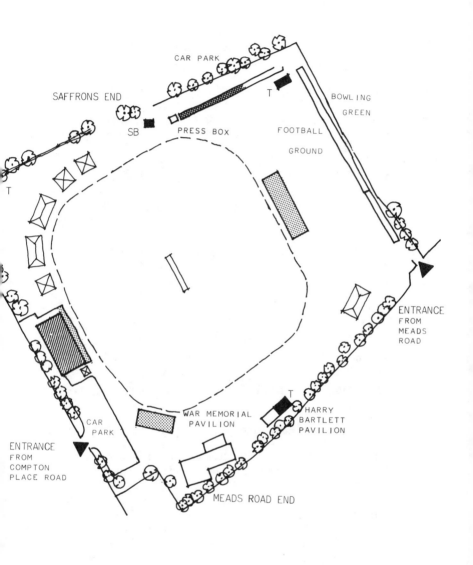

CAR PARK

SAFFRONS END

BOWLING

GREEN

SB

PRESS BOX

FOOTBALL

GROUND

T

T

ENTRANCE
FROM
MEADS
ROAD

WAR MEMORIAL
PAVILION

T

HARRY
BARTLETT
PAVILION

CAR
PARK

ENTRANCE
FROM
COMPTON
PLACE ROAD

MEADS ROAD END

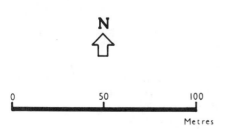

N

| 0 | 50 | 100 |

Metres

W.G. Grace; but Jack Hobbs only played once in a Festival match. Archie MacLaren's Young Amateurs defeated the formidable Australians in 1921 at the Saffrons; this is possibly the most famous match to have taken place on this ground. Sussex C C C have, in addition to championship matches, staged limited-overs matches on the ground, with the first being in 1969. The ground has also been used for tourists matches by Sussex, Derek Robin's XI, H.D.G. Leveson-Gower's XI and Col. H.C. Steven's XI.

Ground records have included 272 n.o. by R.R. Relf for the home county and 310 by H. Gimblett for the visitors. In 1972 Pat Pocock of Surrey captured 7 wickets for 4 runs in two overs. His earlier figures were 14–1–67–0 but twelve balls later his innings figures were 16–1–71–7.

The Eastbourne club has been served well by groundsmen notably Wilf Wooller for 54 years (1922–76) and his father for 50 years (1884–1934). Between them they prepared over 5,000 wickets. The most recent men to have played for the Saffrons club and then played first-class cricket are former Sussex Captain J.R.T. Barclay and R.J. Parks the Hampshire wicket-keeper.

Crowds at the Saffrons have been in the region of 4,000–5,000. The largest was 8,000 for a John Player Sunday League match with Kent in 1978. Some 25,000 watched cricket during the 1981 Festival Week when some exciting cricket was played. Sussex C C C take two championship and one limited-overs match to the Saffrons Ground each season, usually in early August to attract the seaside holiday makers to the Eastbourne Festival Cricket Week.

ADDRESS Eastbourne Cricket Club, Eastbourne Saffrons Sports Club, The Saffrons, Compton Place Road, Eastbourne, East Sussex.
TELEPHONE NUMBER PROSPECTS OF PLAY 0323 24328

DESCRIPTION OF GROUND AND FACILITIES

There are two entrances to the ground: for members in Compton Place Road to the rear of the main pavilion and for the public and disabled persons in Meads Road. There is a large car park available at the rear of the football stands which is entered from Old Orchard Road and Saffrons Road close to the bowling greens. The only permanent buildings on the ground are the main pavilion, to the west of the playing area, which comprises the changing facilities for players, members' bar, refreshments and, in front of the pavilion, a members' enclosure. Refreshments are available in a number of tents for the public disposed around the ground. To the south of the playing area is the War Memorial Pavilion, where refreshments can be obtained, and the Harry Bartlett Pavilion which houses the Sussex C C C souvenir shop. A scoreboard is situated on the north football ground side with a groundsman's store and a press box below. The football stands and terraces are too far away from the cricket field and only provide shelter during poor weather. The seating is all temporary and is made up of large, raised timber open seats, semi-raised areas and plastic seats as well as a number of deckchairs. The west side of the ground is the members' enclosure and includes an area for sponsors' marquees, the Sussex C C C committee tent, the secretary's office in a caravan, and car parking for players and officials together with a small temporary members' stand enclosure.

On the east football ground side, directly behind the sightscreen, is the TV camera/commentary position, radio commentary box and first aid tent; also temporary seating for the public and an area for disabled spectators and vehicles, together with an area of public deck chair seating. The ground capacity is 8,000 and usually 3,000 seats are provided for all matches so spectators would be advised to bring their own seats only to very popular matches. There are both permanent and temporary toilet facilities. The playing area is 120 metres by 130 metres and defined by a rope on one side and on the other by some advertising boards.

The ground is enclosed and a view of Eastbourne Town Hall, with its fine clock tower and dome can be seen from the members' enclosure adjoining the main pavilion.

GROUND RECORDS AND SCORES

FIRST-CLASS MATCHES

Highest innings total for County: 540 for 6 dec. *v.* Glamorgan 1938
Highest innings total against County: 586 by Gloucestershire 1936
Lowest innings total for County: 38 *v.* Hampshire 1950
Lowest innings total against County: 57 by Nottinghamshire 1962
Highest individual innings for County: 272 n.o. R.R. Relf *v.* Worcestershire 1909
Highest individual innings against County: 310 H. Gimblett for Somerset 1948
Best bowling performance in an innings for County: 8 for 41 A.F. Wensley *v.* Leicestershire 1933
Best bowling performance in an innings against County: 9 for 62 A.G. Nicholson for Yorkshire 1967
Best bowling performance in a match for County: 12 for 86 J. Langridge *v.* Hampshire 1950
Best bowling performance in a match against County: 14 for 106 R.C. Robertson-Glasgow for Somerset 1923
Best attendance: 5,000 *v.* Somerset 1948

LIMITED-OVERS MATCHES

Highest innings total for County: 227 for 8 *v.* Gloucestershire (JPL) 1975
Highest innings total against County: 206 for 7 by Nottinghamshire (JPL) 1980
Lowest innings total for County: 146 *v.* Nottinghamshire (JPL) 1980
Lowest innings total against County: 63 by Minor Counties (East) (BHC) 1978

Highest individual innings for County: 109 R.D.V. Knight *v.* Leicestershire (JPL) 1976
Highest individual innings against County: 93 n.o. C.E.B. Rice for Nottinghamshire (JPL) 1980
Best bowling performance for County: 5 for 28 A.N. Jones *v.* Essex (JPL) 1984
Best bowling performance against County: 4 for 21 S. Oldham for Derbyshire (JPL) 1983
Best attendance: 8,000 *v.* Kent (JPL) 1978

HOW TO GET THERE

Rail   Eastbourne (BR), 0.5 mile.
Bus   From surrounding areas to within 0.5 mile of ground; also Eastbourne Bus 8B from town centre passes ground.
Car   From north: A22 follow signs Eastbourne and town centre, then take A259 to Grove Road and then Saffrons Road; Meads Road is then the first turning on the right for the Saffrons Ground; the ground is situated 0.5 mile from the town centre and town hall. From east: A259 follow signs Eastbourne and town centre, then as north. From west: A259 follow signs Eastbourne and town centre, then as north.

WHERE TO STAY AND OTHER INFORMATION

Grand Hotel (0323 22611), Chatsworth Hotel (0323 30327), The Wish Tower (0323 22676), and many other small hotels and guest houses.

Disabled Areas   Special area available on football ground side of ground.
Local Radio Station(s)   BBC Radio Sussex (104.5 MHz FM/1161 KHz MW), Southern Sound (103.5 MHz FM/1323 KHz MW).
Local Newspaper(s)   Eastbourne News, Eastbourne Gazette and Herald.

Hastings

Cricket at Hastings Priory Meadow started in 1864. The Central Cricket and Recreation Ground, as it is known today, is the home of Hastings and St Leonards Priory Cricket Club. The club was established in 1957 and plays in the Sussex Cricket League. The first Hastings cricket festival took place in 1887 and the first county match was in 1865 against Kent. The ground is nominally owned and managed by a group of trustees for the benefit of the townspeople. It is occasionally used for activities other than cricket, but because the ground is at sea level and subject to flooding, it cannot be used for sport during the winter months. Until the last match with Middlesex in 1989, Sussex played one County

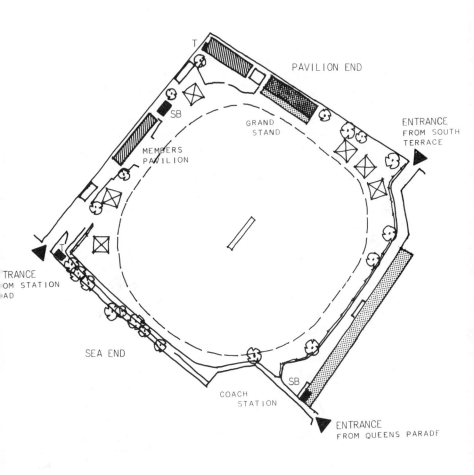

PAVILION END

T

GRAND
STAND

ENTRANCE
FROM SOUTH
TERRACE

SB

MEMBERS
PAVILION

TRANCE
OM STATION
AD

T

SEA END

COACH
STATION

SB

ENTRANCE
FROM QUEENS PARADE

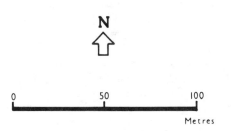

N

0   50   100

Metres

Championship and one Sunday League limited-overs match here in late June, July or early August. The Sussex second XI also staged matches on the ground until 1989. The last match took place on 1 October 1989 when a Sussex XI played a Kent XI.

The players' pavilion suffered fire damage in September 1985, the bar being destroyed along with many historic photographs. Part of the roof of the visitors' dressing room was also severely damaged. In 1986 Hastings Council announced that the ground would be developed into a major shopping centre development and work was due to start in 1989 after the last match. In 1991 the development company ceased to be involved with the proposed project and hence no construction has taken place yet. This will be of extreme pleasure to cricket followers and it is hoped that Sussex C C C will make a return to Priory Meadow rather than the new ground which was constructed at Bohemia Road, St Leonards next to the fire station. This ground has been developed since 1986 but Sussex have yet to stage a match of any type here. Sussex are once again to stage a second XI match at Hastings in 1992 with Nottinghamshire.

The ground, which is steeped in cricket history, was laid out in 1864 by the estate of the Cornwallis family. Situated close to the seafront and the town's main shopping streets the ground is sited in a bowl-like depression. It is surrounded by houses of every description and to the east high on the hill is Hastings castle. The pavilion and much of the older stands date back to the 1880s but have had extensions and improvements in recent years.

Ground records have been numerous and include, for Sussex their highest ever total in first-class cricket of 705 for 8 declared against Surrey, and a score of 246 by K.S. Duleepsinhji against Kent in 1929. Traditionally, the Hastings Festival always took place in September and many records have been made during these fixtures. The first name that comes to mind is Gilbert Jessop who scored seven centuries on the ground, six during festivals. In 1947 Denis Compton scored 101 for the South of England against the touring South Africans, his seventeenth century of the season, passing the previous record held by Jack Hobbs since 1925. C.T.B. Turner took 17 wickets for 50 on the ground (8 for 13 and 9 for 37) for the Australians against an England XI during the second festival. This is still the best bowling feat achieved on the ground. Recent records include 203 by Ted Dexter in 1968 against Kent, his only double century for Sussex, and, in 1975, Tony Greig scored 226 against Warwickshire. The traditional visitors to Hastings have been Kent and in 1972 and 1973 each side had a large victory, Sussex by 10 wickets and Kent by an innings and 161 runs. Derek Underwood will have fond memories of Hastings for in 1964 he took 9 for 28 and in 1984 scored his maiden first-class century of 111.

Crowds have been as many as 20,000 for festival matches. Against Kent in 1932 the crowd was 6,889 for the first day; in all, 20,000 watched the match over the three days. In recent years crowds of 4,500–5,000 have been usual.

ADDRESS Hastings and St Leonards Priory Cricket Club, The Pavilion, Central Cricket and Recreation Ground, Priory Meadow, Queens Road, Hastings, East Sussex TN34 1RP.
TELEPHONE NUMBER PROSPECTS OF PLAY   0424 424546

DESCRIPTION OF GROUND AND FACILITIES

The ground can be entered from Station Road where there is limited car parking for players/officials and members, via Queens Parade, through the Coach Station which is used for car parking and for pedestrian access only from South Terrace. The members' pavilion houses refreshment facilities, a bar, the secretary's office and a press box. Next to this is the main scoreboard, groundsman's equipment store and, fenced off, the players' pavilion and enclosure.

Also adjoining this is the grandstand which is situated directly behind the sightscreen at the South Terrace End. Situated on the Queens Parade side of the ground is the Cantilever Stand which provides open seating high above the playing area, at the rear of the houses and shops. A secondary scoreboard is also situated at the southern end of this enclosure which is only available to members. The TV camera/ commentary box position is at the Station Road End and sponsors' marquees can be found at the opposite end of the ground, on the Queens Parade side.

The ground capacity is 7,000 and about 3,500 seats are provided so spectators are advised to bring their own seats to popular matches. The playing area is 122 metres by 127 metres and is defined by a rope and advertising boards. The Sussex club provides a souvenir caravan and ample temporary refreshment facilities. Toilets are available within the pavilion and in out buildings around the ground. The members' pavilion has a good collection of cricket photographs and a small library which can be viewed by appointment.

GROUND RECORDS AND SCORES

FIRST-CLASS MATCHES
Highest innings total for County: 705 for 8 dec. *v.* Surrey 1902
Highest innings total against County: 552 for 8 by Surrey 1923
Lowest innings total for County: 56 *v.* Derbyshire 1963
Lowest innings total against County: 66 by Kent 1955
Highest individual innings for County: 246 K.S. Duleepsinhji *v.* Kent 1929
Highest individual innings against County: 228 n.o. K.W.R. Fletcher for Essex 1968
Best bowling performance in an innings for County: 8 for 40 G.R. Cox *v.* Warwickshire 1912
Best bowling performance in an innings against County: 9 for 28 D.L. Underwood for Kent 1964
Best bowling performance in a match for County: 13 for 194 M.W. Tate *v.* Kent 1929

Best bowling performance in a match against County: 15 for 173 D.V.P. Wright for Kent 1947
Best attendance: 6,889 *v*. Kent 1932

LIMITED-OVERS MATCHES
Highest innings total for County: 267 for 5 *v*. Essex (JPL) 1980
Highest innings total against County: 259 for 8 by Essex (JPL) 1980
Lowest innings total for County: 100 *v*. Northamptonshire (JPL) 1986
Lowest innings total against County: 113 by Warwickshire (JPL) 1974
Highest individual innings for County: 121 n.o. P.W.G. Parker *v*. Northamptonshire (JPL) 1983
Highest individual innings against County: 136 K.S. McEwan for Essex (JPL) 1980
Best bowling performance for County: 4 for 25 M.A. Buss *v*. Worcestershire (JPL) 1974
Best bowling performance against County: 6 for 12 D.L. Underwood for Kent (JPL) 1984
Best attendance: 5,500 *v*. Kent (JPL) 1984

HOW TO GET THERE

Rail Hastings (BR), 0.25 mile.
Bus Hastings and District Bus Company from surrounding areas to town centre Bus Station adjoining ground.
Car From north: A21 and A2101, follow signs Hastings and seafront, then take Station Road or Queens Road for Central Cricket Ground; the ground is situated close to the Bus/Coach Station and Town Hall. From east: A259 follow signs Hastings and town centre, then as north. From west: A259, A269 or A2101 follow signs Hastings and town centre, then as north.

WHERE TO STAY AND OTHER INFORMATION

Burlington Hotel (0424 424303), and many other hotels and guesthouses.

Disabled Areas No special area, request suitable position.
Local Radio Station(s) BBC Radio Sussex (104.5 MHz FM/1161 KHz MW).
Local Newspaper(s) Evening Argus, Hastings Observer and Hastings Citizen.

Horsham

Sussex first appeared at Horsham as a representative side in 1853 but not on the present ground at Cricket Field Road, which is the home of the Horsham Cricket Club founded in 1771, who play in the Sussex County Cricket League and who share facilities with Horsham Caledonians Cricket Club founded in 1949. Horsham C C have played home fixtures at Cricket Field Road since 1851. Four other grounds in the town have been used for cricket: The Artillery Ground (the first site), the Common in North Parade at the south side of the junction with Hurst Road, Denne Park and Stanford's or the 'new' ground. The county have played on the present Cricket Field Road ground since 1908 when the initial first-class match was staged with Essex. Matches have been played during the following periods: 1908–10, 1912–14, 1920–39 and 1946–56. The county visited in 1971 and 1974 against Oxford and Cambridge Universities but not until 1983 did championship cricket return to Horsham. The county have made sixteen visits to this delightful, rural setting since 1974 for limited-overs Sunday League fixtures.

Horsham C C has hosted a Festival Cricket Week over the years but recently this has only been one championship and one limited-overs match, usually over a weekend in June. The Horsham club celebrated its 200th anniversary in 1971 with a match between Sussex and Cambridge University.

The first pavilion was situated close to the footbridge crossing the railway line but was demolished. The present pavilion was built in 1921. There are facilities for tennis with both grass and hard courts. Ample space is available surrounding the playing area. To the north, the ground is bounded by the River Arun which runs close to the ground where willow trees were planted by Ben Warsop the former cricket bat manufacturer. The ball has been hit into the river once, by 'Jacko' Watson the mightiest of Sussex hitters. At the southern end of the ground is the BR Southern Region railway line and trains can often be heard. So can the more pleasing sound of bells ringing from the local St Mary's Church a short walk from the ground. Horsham C C own the ground and there has been talk in recent years of improving the facilities to attract more county matches to Cricket Field Lane.

Ground records at Horsham include 176 by E.H. Bowley against Warwickshire and 224 by C.P. Mead of Hampshire who was John Arlott's favourite batsman. Limited-overs match records include 147 by Glenn Turner for Worcestershire against Sussex and Sussex's highest innings total in the 40 Overs game. 1991 saw the home county's lowest innings total in the Sunday League against Essex. During the 1980s spectators will recall Garth Le Roux's swashbuckling knock against Hampshire to set up victory in a Sunday League match. Vivian Richards kept wicket here for Somerset one Sunday in 1985 after Trevor Gard was injured warming up on the slippery outfield.

Cricket here attracts crowds of 4,500–5,000, probably the largest

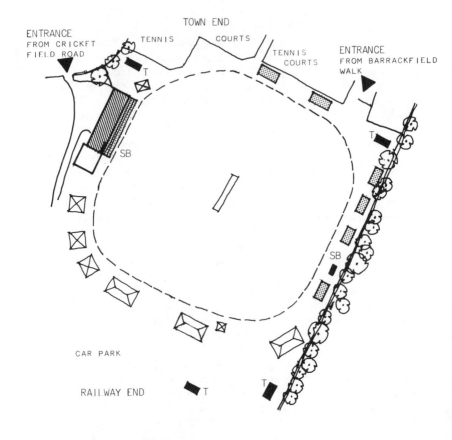

TOWN END

ENTRANCE
FROM CRICKFT
FIELD ROAD

TENNIS   COURTS

T

SB

TENNIS
COURTS

ENTRANCE
FROM BARRACKFIELD
WALK

T

SB

CAR PARK

RAILWAY END   T

T

N

0   50   100

Metres

attendance was 6,500 against Worcestershire for the John Player Sunday League match in 1980. Durham will be visiting Cricket Field Lane in 1992 for a championship and Sunday League match.

ADDRESS   Horsham Cricket Club, The Pavilion, Cricket Field Lane, Worthing Road, Horsham, West Sussex.
TELEPHONE NUMBER PROSPECTS OF PLAY   0403 54628

DESCRIPTION OF GROUND AND FACILITIES

The main entrance to the ground is from Cricket Field Road which is a narrow road off the A24 Worthing Road although there is another pedestrian access off a footpath from St Mary's churchyard at the Town End of the ground. There is a large area for car parking to the south and east of the ground, together with central car parking in the town centre a short walk away. The only permanent building is the large pavilion/club house which has been extended by adding two storeys. It is situated on the west side of the ground, the whole of which is given over to members. All other areas are available to the public and a number of small groups of tiered bench seats are provided. The capacity of the ground is about 5,500 of which about 20 per cent can be accommodated on the seats provided so you are advised to bring your own. Bars and refreshments are available to members in the pavilion and to the public in tents disposed around the ground.

There are no special arrangements for disabled spectators so they should ask for suitable accommodation. The main scoreboard is situated opposite the pavilion. The playing area is approximately 126 metres by 122 metres and is bounded by advertisement boards. A sponsors' enclosure including marquees and a Sussex C C C souvenir tent are situated between the pavilion and sightscreen at the Railway End of the ground. The press box is located within the pavilion as is the radio commentary position. The TV camera/commentary box is located on a gantry high above the sightscreen at the Railway End.

This is a pleasant club ground although the facilities for the public on popular match days are limited.

GROUND RECORDS AND SCORES

FIRST-CLASS MATCHES
Highest innings total for County: 519 *v*. Leicestershire 1921
Highest innings total against County: 438 by Surrey 1938
Lowest innings total for County: 35 *v*. Glamorgan 1946
Lowest innings total against County: 51 by Leicestershire 1924
Highest individual innings for County: 176 E.H. Bowley *v*. Warwickshire 1927
Highest individual innings against County: 224 C.P. Mead for Hampshire 1921
Best bowling performance in an innings for County: 9 for 50 G.R. Cox *v*. Warwickshire 1926

Best bowling performance in an innings against County: 9 for 48 V. Broderick for Northamptonshire 1948

Best bowling performance in a match for County: 17 for 106 G.R. Cox *v.* Warwickshire 1926

Best bowling performance in a match against County: 10 for 154 V. Broderick for Northamptonshire 1948

Best attendance: 6,000 *v.* Northamptonshire 1948

LIMITED-OVERS MATCHES

Highest innings total for County: 293 for 4 *v.* Worcestershire (JPL) 1980

Highest innings total against County: 261 by Worcestershire (JPL) 1980

Lowest innings total for County: 154 for 7 *v.* Essex (RAL) 1989

Lowest innings total against County: 136 for 8 by Somerset (JPL) 1978

Highest individual innings for County: 106 n.o. P.W.G. Parker *v.* Worcestershire (JPL) 1980

Highest individual innings against County: 147 G.M. Turner for Worcestershire (JPL) 1980

Best bowling performance for County: 4 for 32 D.A. Reeve *v.* Nottinghamshire (JPL) 1985

Best bowling performance against County: 4 for 26 A.M. Ferreira for Warwickshire (JPL) 1981

Best attendance: 6,500 *v.* Worcestershire (JPL) 1980

HOW TO GET THERE

Rail   Horsham (BR), 1 mile.

Bus   London Country (SW) H1/2/5 link BR Horsham Station with ground. (Telephone: 081 668 7261).

Car   From north: M25 junction 9, then follow A24 signposted Horsham and town centre, then take Worthing Road and turn into Cricketfield Road for Horsham C C. The ground is situated a short walk from the town centre. From east: A264 follow signs Horsham and town centre, then as north. From west: A281 or A264 follow signs Horsham and town centre, then as north. From south: A24 or A281 follow signs Horsham and town centre, then as north.

WHERE TO STAY AND OTHER INFORMATION

Ye Olde King's Head (0403 53126).

Disabled Areas   No special area, request suitable position.

Local Radio Station(s)   BBC Radio Sussex (104.5 MHz FM/1161 KHz MW), Radio Mercury (102.7 MHz FM/1521 KHz MW).

Local Newspaper(s)   West Sussex County Times, Crawley Observer, West Sussex Gazette.

WARWICKSHIRE

WARWICKSHIRE.

BIRMINGHAM – EDGBASTON

COVENTRY

NUNEATON

Warwickshire

Founded   8 April 1882
Colours   Blue, gold and silver
Crest   Bear and ragged staff
President   The Rt. Hon. The Earl of Aylesford K St J, J P,
   Her Majesty's Lord Lieutenant for the County of West Midlands
Chairman   M.J.K. Smith OBE
Chairman cricket committee   D.L. Amiss
Secretary   D.M.W. Heath
Assistant secretary (cricket)   A.S.M. Oakman
Cricket development officer   R.M. Cox
Director of coaching   R.A. Woolmer
Marketing manager   S. Edwards
Coach/manager Indoor Cricket School   R.N. Abberley
Captain   T.A. Lloyd
Club superintendent   M. White
Groundsman   A. Atkinson
Scorer 1st XI   A.E. Davis (home) S.P. Austin (away)
Scorer 2nd XI   R. Burrows
Statistician   R.W. Brooke
Sponsors   Carling Black Label
Newsletter   *Beyond The Boundary*
Address   County Ground, Edgbaston, Birmingham, West Midlands
B5 7QU.
Telephone 021 446 4422
Facsimile 021 446 4544
Warwickshire Rapid Cricketline   0891 567516
Test Match Commentaries Rapid Cricketline   0891 567567
Test Match Updates Rapid Cricketline   0891 567555

ACHIEVEMENTS

County Championship   Champions (3) 1911, 1951 and 1972
Gillette Cup   Winners (2) 1966 and 1968; finalists (2) 1964 and
1972
National Westminster Bank Trophy   Winners (1) 1989; finalists (1)
1982
Benson & Hedges Cup   Finalists (1) 1984
John Player Sunday League   Champions (1) 1980
Refuge Assurance Sunday League   5th 1991
Fenner Trophy   Finalists (1) 1974
Tilcon Trophy   Winners (2) 1985 and 1990; finalists (2) 1986 and
1988
Seeboard Trophy   Semi-finalists (1) 1990

Edgbaston from the air, reproduced by courtesy of Photo Precision Ltd

GROUNDS

Birmingham (County Ground, Edgbaston) Coventry (Coventry &
North Warwickshire C C, Bulls Head Ground) and Nuneaton (Griff
& Coton Sports Ground, Heath End Road).
  The only other ground that has been used since 1969 is: Coventry
(Courtaulds Sports Ground, Lockhurst Lane).

SECOND XI GROUNDS
In addition to the above mentioned grounds the following are used
for second XI matches: Knowle & Dorridge C C, Knowle, Warwicks.
Telephone: 0564 774338; Leamington Town C C, Arlington Avenue,
Leamington Spa, Warwicks. Telephone: 0926 423854; Mitchells &
Butlers C C, Portland Road, Birmingham, West Midlands. Telephone:
021 429 2467; Moseley C C, Moseley, Birmingham, West Midlands.
Telephone: 021 744 5694; Old Edwardians C C, Solihull,
Birmingham, West Midlands. Telephone: 021 744 6831; Solihull
C C, Solihull, West Midlands. Telephone: 021 705 5271; Stratford-
on-Avon C C, Stratford-on-Avon, Warwicks. Telephone: 0789
297968; Studley C C, Studley, Warwicks. Telephone: 0527 853668;
Walmley C C, Walmley, West Midlands. Telephone: 021 351 1349.

EDGBASTON

W. E. HOLLIES

When Warwickshire outpaced Kent to become the first outside the Big Six to win the championship in 1911, *Punch* celebrated an event, which stunned English cricket by its audacious brilliance, with a full-page cartoon. Frank Foster, the dashing 22-year-old captain from Small Heath, was shown with another with a Warwickshire qualification, William Shakespeare. 'Tell Kent from me she hath lost,' says Foster. The Bard replies, 'Warwick, thou art worthy.'

Warwickshire in post-war years have twice won the championship and the Gillette Cup, and, as a bonus, the Sunday League, and boast of such renowned bowlers as Field, Foster's partner, Hollies, Howells, Willis, Cartwright, Small and the West Indian off spinner Gibbs, but the exploits of Foster and his unfancied side – 14th out of 16 the previous year – is the most vivid page in the annals of the club.

There have also been distinguished captains of the calibre of Calthorpe, Wyatt, Cranmer, Dollery, M.J.K. Smith, A.C. Smith and Brown, yet Foster remains unique, a meteor flashing across the cricket sky in a briefly sad career lasting from 1908 to 1914. It was all over in 1915 when he was crippled for life in a motor cycle crash.

His epic season began with him twice changing his mind before accepting the captaincy – typically his decision came after a two-day innings defeat at The Oval and an announced intention to retire from first-class cricket – and ended in triumph after a nerve-wracking night spent playing cards. *Wisden* described him as the best young captain since W.G. Grace, and H.S. Altham, the cricket historian, wrote: 'There was about all his cricket an atmosphere of supreme confidence and inexhaustible vitality that acted as a wonderful inspiration to his side.'

Foster, whose first two victims in London were Hobbs and Hayward, was established as the country's leading all-rounder taking 116 wickets with his fast-medium left arm attack directed at the leg stump, and 1,383 runs from his aggressive batting. Field was his perfect foil, and together they dismissed Yorkshire, beaten twice that year, for 58 at Scarborough. Decades passed before the estimable Cartwright emulated Foster's 'double', and with

Septimus Kinneir and wicket-keeper Jim ('Tiger') Smith adding to Foster's automatic selection Warwickshire had three representatives in one of the most powerful sides to visit Australia.

Australia, beaten 4–1, declared Barnes, who had one unremarkable outing for Warwickshire, and Foster to be the finest opening bowling pair ever sent there, a view endorsed by the captain Warner. Barnes had 34 wickets at 22.88, and Foster 32 at 21.62. Foster had the extra recommendation of a batting place among Hobbs, Woolley, Gunn, J.W. Hearne, Mead and Douglas. Unrelated to the Fosters of Worcestershire he was indeed some cricketer.

There were so many variations and paces of his bowling that Smith, who had just succeeded the outstanding Test wicket-keeper Lilley at Edgbaston, now found himself ahead of Strudwick because his knowledge of Foster's methods and signals was essential. 'Tiger', who had a 75-year love affair with Edgbaston, used to say that the only Australian able to detect a signal was an observant Sydney tram conductor who rightly interpreted a foot shuffle to warn a slower ball was coming up!

One of Foster's batting stalwarts was the model stylist Willy Quaife, the smallest man ever to play for England. If he lacked inches he was not short of staying power for he was 56 when he made the last of his 72 centuries. Warwickshire also had J.H. Parsons, a future Canon who played for both Gentlemen and Players, and Percy Jeeves, whose name was adopted by P.G. Wodehouse as his fictional butler after watching the county at Cheltenham.

A shortage of penetrative bowling found success hard to come by in the Calthorpe and Wyatt years, but Wyatt's 4th position in 1934 was the highest since 1911. Wyatt, with 85 centuries and 40 Test appearances, including 16 as captain, was as good a batsman, and possibly the best technically equipped, as Warwickshire have produced, an opinion Amiss would be entitled to challenge.

Cranmer, the rugby international, had his problems in the seasons straddling the Second World War, but he was never deterred and put Warwickshire on to the road of the title in 1951 by Dollery's all-pro side.

The strength was built around Dollery the batsman and Hollies, the spin bowler, reinforced by New Zealander Pritchard and Grove with the new ball, Spooner a batsman–wicket-keeper, Ord, Gardner and Townsend. The superb left hander, Donnelly, was also briefly available but left before the championship year.

The most famous of Hollies' 2,323 dismissals (2,201 for Warwickshire) deprived Sir Don Bradman of a Test average of 100, and he extended his services to the county by taking the captaincy for a year while M.J.K. Smith, from Leicestershire, qualified. Smith had an uncanny knack of leadership, both for England and Warwickshire, and his eleven years were marked by his own run-getting, superb close-in catching and near-misses in the championship, a losing final and the taking of the Gillette Cup in 1966.

After Smith came another Smith, Alan, the winner of the Man of the Match award in the 1968 Gillette Cup final. Lord's was a fitting place for the future chief executive of the TCCB to shine. Warwickshire, nourished by the hugely successful Supporters' Association, by now had the brilliant West Indians, Gibbs and Kanhai, and backed to the hilt Smith's determination to go for the championship. He almost did it in 1971 when Surrey, with the same number of points, took the title by virtue of more victories. Another West Indian, Kallicharran, as run-hungry as Kanhai, was secured and in 1972 Warwickshire ended undefeated and 36 points in front of Kent. They were also beaten finalists in the Gillette Cup. Willis, from Surrey, came in mid-way through the season as the main support to Brown.

Willis was captain when the Sunday League was won in 1980 and the eight home games were watched by 46,000 spectators – a proper response to a magnificent Test-ranking ground which stands as a compliment to the initative of former secretary Leslie Deakins and the husband and wife team of David Blakemore and Winnie Crook of the Supporters' Association.

Brown, as fast bowler and captain and subsequently team manager, and Amiss, who ended with 43,423 runs and in the company of the greats with 102 centuries in twenty-eight seasons, could hardly have given better service. From 1972 to 1974 Amiss was England's most prolific batsman averaging 71 over 20 Tests. His rearguard action scoring 262 not out at Kingston in 1973–74 was an epic innings of skill and concentration. Other equally masterful scores were 174 and 118. He ended the series with an average of 83.87, and added to his high reputation with a double century against the West Indies at The Oval in 1976. Like Hollies, who broke all the county's bowling records, Amiss, 11th in the list of all-time batsmen, set new batting standards for Warwickshire. He was the first local-born player to hit a century for England.

In 1989 Warwickshire won the National Westminster Bank Trophy final and in 1991 came 2nd in the championship only 13 points behind Essex. 1990 saw the retirement of Humpage and Kallicharran, Moody moved to Worcestershire as the county decided to retain the South African Allan Donald, one of the fastest bowlers in county cricket. In 1991 Reeve was selected for England and finished the season with 1,260 runs at 48.46 and 45 wickets at 21.26 a piece. Other run scorers were Ostler, Moles and the skipper Lloyd. Donald took 83 wickets and Munton 71. The future looks bright with Bob Woolmer as coach at the helm.

Birmingham – Edgbaston

Edgbaston is the third ground in Birmingham to be used by Warwick-shire County Cricket Club. The other grounds were at Aston Lower Grounds, Trinity Road, close to Aston Villa Football Club, where just one match was staged in 1884, and the Mitchell and Butlers' Ground at Portland and City Road where thirteen matches were staged from 1931 until the last match in 1961 against Cambridge University.

Mitchell and Butlers' one of the club's main sponsors allow their ground to be used for second XI matches by Warwickshire C C C. The first Warwickshire C C C match at Edgbaston was played against Kent in 1894. However, the initial match was between an England XI and the Australians of 1886. MCC also played in that year but not until 1895 when the club was admitted to the County Championship did matches take place frequently.

The main part of the ground was acquired by the reorganized Warwickshire County Cricket Club in 1886 and the freehold land has been added to, piecemeal, at intervals since then. It has now been developed into one of the best equipped cricket grounds in the country. In 1902 the ground was recognized as suitable for staging Test Matches when England met Australia in the first Test of that series. Test Matches continued to be played until 1929, but there was a gap until the England v. West Indies Test in 1957, since when it has remained one of six regular test venues in the country.

The ground was originally a 'meadow of rough grazing land' and belonged to Lord Calthorpe until he allowed the club to lease it for cricket purposes. The original pavilion still remains but so much alteration has taken place that, except for the distinctive, red-tiled roof, it is difficult to recognize it among all the new additions at the Pavilion End. The William Ansell Stand was built during the 1950s from funds raised by the Warwickshire C C S A and the stand was named after the first key figure in Warwickshire and Edgbaston's history. In 1975 an executive suite was added to the William Ansell Stand and in recent seasons more sponsors' suites and plastic tip-up seats have been installed to improve the facilities for members. The majority of building took place in 1946 and thereafter various additions were made and con-structed in the 1950s and 1960s. The Thwaite Memorial Scoreboard was constructed in 1950 and was moved and rebuilt in replica during 1988–89 because of the reconstruction and improvements made to the Stanley Barnes Stand and seating accommodation at the City End.

Edgbaston is still one of the few grounds where the press box is immediately behind the sightscreen at the opposite end of the ground to the pavilion. All the bars around the ground are named after fielding positions and together with a number of refreshment kiosks there are many outlets for food at popular matches. Within the pavilion is the Warwickshire C C C museum room where many items of Warwickshire cricket memorabilia can be viewed. The club is at present considering the possibility of building a separate building within the ground to house

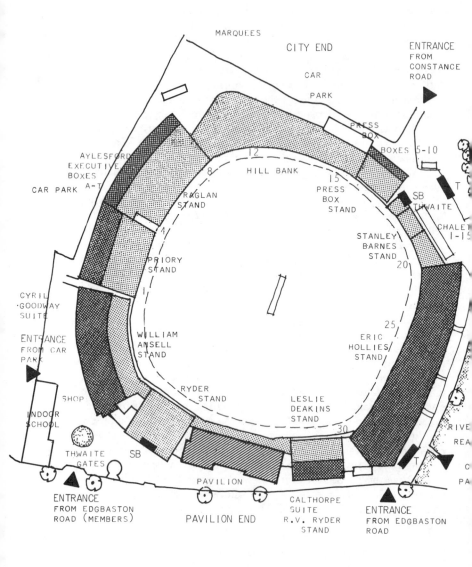

MARQUEES

CITY END

ENTRANCE
FROM
CONSTANCE
ROAD

CAR

PARK

PRESS
BOX

BOXES 5-10

AYLESFORD
EXECUTIVE
BOXES
A-T

CAR PARK

12

8

HILL BANK

15

PRESS
BOX
STAND

SB
THWAITE

RAGLAN
STAND

STANLEY
BARNES
STAND

CHALET
1-15

4

PRIORY
STAND

20

CYRIL
GOODWAY
SUITE

25

ENTRANCE
FROM CAR
PARK

WILLIAM
ANSELL
STAND

ERIC
HOLLIES/
STAND

SHOP

RYDER
STAND

LESLIE
DEAKINS
STAND

RIVE
REA

INDOOR
SCHOOL

30

THWAITE
GATES

SB

PAVILION

C
PA

ENTRANCE
FROM EDGBASTON
ROAD (MEMBERS)

PAVILION END

CALTHORPE
SUITE
R.V. RYDER
STAND

ENTRANCE
FROM EDGBASTON
ROAD

N

0   50   100

Metres

a Warwickshire Cricket Museum. On the Edgbaston Road frontage of the ground the observant visitor will note the site of the Sydney Barnes Wicket Gate. The Warwickshire Indoor Cricket School, built in 1955, is located on the ground and the most interesting innovation at Edgbaston has been the installation of a large mechanically operated pitch cover known as the 'Brumbreller'.

In 1989 as part of the ground development scheme at Edgbaston some key county names were perpetuated; the executive club is now known as the Cyril Goodway Suite, the members' bar/lounge as the Tom Dollery Lounge, the Rea Bank Stand as the Eric Hollies Stand, the West Wing Stand as the R.V. Ryder Stand and the East Wing Stand as the Leslie Deakins Stand, acknowledging the service to the county club of two secretaries during the years 1889–1976.

Recent additions since 1989 have seen the construction of the Aylesford Executive Boxes A to T, situated above the Priory and Raglan Stands. It is proposed to construct executive boxes to the rear of the Hill Bank in years to come.

On 19 July 1989, HRH The Prince of Wales visited Edgbaston for a match between The Prince's Trust XI captained by Imran Khan, and A Rest of the World XI captained by Michael Holding.

Crowds at Edgbaston have always been good; the record was 28,000 in 1951 for a County Championship match against Lancashire. The record for a single day of a Test Match was 32,000 for the first day of the England *v*. West Indies Test Match of 1957. A record 60,000 spectators attended the 1991 Cornhill Test Match between the same two teams, including our cricket-loving Prime Minister, John Major. The current ground capacity is 17,500 and this gate is achieved regularly for Test Matches, one-day internationals and county knock-out limited-overs matches.

During the period 1988–90 Edgbaston hosted the final of the Refuge Assurance Cup competition with the following counties winning the trophy in Birmingham: Lancashire, Essex and Middlesex. The last final in 1991 was staged at Old Trafford and won by Worcestershire.

Ground records at Edgbaston with the bat include double centuries from Percy Holmes, S.P. Kinneir, Alvan Kallicharran, Peter May and Zaheer Abbas in various competitions. With the ball, achievements have been obtained by Wilfred Rhodes, Sonny Ramadhin, Freddie Trueman, Joel Garner, Eric Hollies and Bob Willis, to name a few. In addition to staging county matches, Edgbaston has been used for all limited-overs matches by the county and international matches including Prudential Trophy, Prudential Cup and Texaco Trophy matches.

Edgbaston is certainly a most welcoming ground to enter after a journey of some distance, with its fine facilities, covered accommodation and permanent plastic seating, and Lord's is really its only superior in the United Kingdom.

ADDRESS County Cricket Ground, Edgbaston Road, Edgbaston, Birmingham, West Midlands B5 7QU.
TELEPHONE NUMBER PROSPECTS OF PLAY 021 440 3624

DESCRIPTION OF GROUND AND FACILITIES

This is one of the premier cricket grounds in the country, perhaps it is now more of a stadium, being surrounded on all sides by tiers of raised plastic seating. Nevertheless, a backcloth of trees is still visible in many areas. Edgbaston Park is only five minutes walk away to the south of the ground.

The main access to the ground is gained from Edgbaston Road for members through the Thwaite Gates and for the public through turnstiles at the opposite end. There are also entrances for the spectators from Pershore and Constance Roads. There are substantial areas for car parking, adjoining the ground, mainly for members' cars. For important matches additional car parking is available south of Edgbaston Road adjoining Edgbaston Park. Car parking is available also in surrounding streets and in multi-storey car parks closer to the city centre.

The ground capacity is 17,500 and all seating is in permanent stands providing excellent views of the playing area. The members' enclosure includes the William Ansell Stand, the Pavilion Centre, East and West Wings above the pavilion dining room and County Suite. On occasions the Pavilion Centre is sometimes restricted to Warwickshire members only and these seats are reserved during Test Matches whereas seating in all other members' areas is unreserved. The remainder of the ground is open to the public but on Test Match days and other popular matches all seats are allocated numbers thereby reducing crowd movements. An area is available for disabled spectators in front of the Thwaite scoreboard and Sydney Barnes Stand. Car parking is available within the ground for disabled drivers and vehicles.

Ample toilets are available at the rear of most stands, including facilities for disabled spectators. Excellent provisions for obtaining refreshments, meals and snacks exist in all parts of the ground. Members are well served by the bar and fast food restaurant in the William Ansell Stand, the County Suite and several other bars in the members' area. The general public is well catered for below the Press Box Stand and in the Long On (south-east corner) and Third Man (north-west corner) bars.

The TV camera/commentary box position is at the Pavilion End above the members' enclosure and scorers'/public address boxes. The radio commentary box is situated on the first floor of the pavilion overlooking the playing area. The members' club room/museum houses many items of Warwickshire cricket memorabilia and is situated on the ground floor of the pavilion to the western end.

Edgbaston is a large ground with plenty of space surrounding the playing area and stands for car parking and practice areas. The playing area is 148 metres by 145 metres. The actual playing area for a particular match will depend on the position of the playing strip selected and boundaries defined by ropes may vary, though for Test Matches boundaries will only vary between 68 metres and 70 metres. Substantial entertainment facilities are available in executive boxes. On Test Match days a virtual tented city is developed at the City End to the rear of the Hill Bank and Press Box Stands.

The Warwickshire C C C souvenir shop is situated to the rear of the William Ansell Stand and has been enlarged and improved in recent seasons. During Test Matches two further outlets are set up near the Third Man bar and to the rear of the hospitality chalets near the Stanley Barnes Stand. A secondhand bookstall and newspaper kiosk is situated close to the members' Thwaite Gate entrance at the Pavilion End.

GROUND RECORDS AND SCORES

TEST MATCHES
Highest innings total for England: 633 for 5 dec. *v*. India 1979
Highest innings total against England: 608 for 7 dec. by Pakistan 1971
Lowest innings total for England: 101 *v*. Australia 1975
Lowest innings total against England: 30 by South Africa 1924
Highest individual innings for England: 285 n.o. P.B.H. May *v*. West Indies 1957
Highest individual innings against England: 274 Zaheer Abbas for Pakistan 1971
Best bowling performance in an innings for England: 7 for 17 W. Rhodes *v*. Australia 1902
Best bowling performance in an innings against England: 7 for 49 S. Ramadhin for West Indies 1957
Best bowling performance in a match for England: 12 for 119 F.S. Trueman *v*. West Indies 1963
Best bowling performance in a match against England: 9 for 108 J. Garner for West Indies 1984

LIMITED-OVERS INTERNATIONALS
Highest innings total: 320 for 8 by Australia *v*. England (PT) 1980
Lowest innings total: 70 by Australia *v*. England (PT) 1977
Highest individual innings: 171 n.o. G.M. Turner for New Zealand *v*. East Africa (PC) 1975
Best bowling performance: 5 for 18 G.J. Cosier for Australia *v*. England (PT) 1977

FIRST-CLASS MATCHES
Highest innings total for County: 657 for 6 dec. *v*. Hampshire 1899
Highest innings total against County: 887 by Yorkshire 1896
Lowest innings total for County: 35 *v*. Yorkshire 1963
Lowest innings total against County: 15 by Hampshire 1922
Highest individual innings for County: 268 n.o. S.Kinneir *v*. Hampshire 1911
Highest individual innings against County: 250 P. Holmes for Yorkshire 1931
Best bowling performance in an innings for County: 10 for 49 W.E. Hollies *v*. Nottinghamshire 1946
Best bowling performance in an innings against County: 10 for 67 E.A. Watts for Surrey 1939

Best bowling performance in a match for County: 14 for 93 T.L. Pritchard *v*. Glamorgan 1951
Best bowling performance in a match against County: 15 for 154 H. Young for Essex 1899
Best attendance: 28,000 *v*. Lancashire 1951

LIMITED-OVERS MATCHES
Highest innings total for County: 392 for 5 *v*. Oxfordshire (NWBT) 1984
Highest innings total against County: 283 for 3 by Glamorgan (GC) 1976
Lowest innings total for County: 86 *v*. Surrey (JPL) 1979
Lowest innings total against County: 74 by Yorkshire (JPL) 1972
Highest individual innings for County: 206 A.I. Kallicharran *v*. Oxfordshire (NWBT) 1984
Highest individual innings against County: 163 n.o. C.G. Greenidge for Hampshire (JPL) 1979
Best bowling performance for County: 7 for 32 R.G.D. Willis *v*. Yorkshire (BHC) 1981
Best bowling performance against County: 5 for 18 J.K. Lever for Essex (JPL) 1972
Best attendance: 12,000 *v*. Yorkshire (NWBT) 1982

REFUGE ASSURANCE CUP FINALS (RAC)
Highest innings total: 201 for 5 by Lancashire *v*. Worcestershire 1988/Middlesex *v*. Derbyshire 1990
Lowest innings total: 149 by Worcestershire *v*. Lancashire 1988
Highest individual innings: 59 T.E. Jesty for Lancashire *v*. Worcestershire 1988
Best bowling performance: 4 for 20 D.R. Pringle for Essex *v*. Nottinghamshire 1989

HOW TO GET THERE

Rail   Birmingham New Street (BR), 1.75 miles.
Bus   West Midlands Travel 45/7 link BR Birmingham New Street with ground. Also 41 from John Bright Street to Pershore Road, 61, 52 and 63 from Navigation Street to Bristol Road and 1 from city centre to Edgbaston Road (Telephone: 021 200 2601).
Car   From north: M6 junction 6, follow A38 city centre and pass through city centre and tunnels, 1.5 miles south of city centre, take left at traffic lights into Priory Road, across Pershore Road traffic lights and the entrance to the ground is then on the left off Edgbaston Road. Follow signs Edgbaston and County Cricket once south of city centre area for ground. From east: A45, A41 or A34, follow signs Birmingham and city centre, then Edgbaston for County Cricket, or as north. From west: M5 junction 4, follow A38 Birmingham and city centre, pass through Selly Oak and then follow signs Edgbaston and County Cricket for ground in Edgbaston Road. From south: A441,

A435, A34, M41, A41 or A45, follow signs Birmingham and city centre, then follow signs Edgbaston and County Cricket for ground, or as north.

WHERE TO STAY AND OTHER INFORMATION

Beech House Hotel (021 373 0620), Wentsbury Hotel, Selly Oak (021 472 1258), The Albany (021 631 2528), Forte Post House Hotel (021 357 7444).

Disabled Areas In front of Thwaite Scoreboard and by special arrangement in advance in other areas.
Local Radio Station(s) BBC Radio WM (95.6 MHz FM/1468 KHz MW), BRMB (96.4 MHz FM/1152 KHz MW).
Local Newspaper(s) Birmingham Post, Birmingham Evening Mail, Birmingham Despatch, Daily News, Sports Argus (Weekends only).

Coventry

The Bull's Head Cricket Ground, situated at the rear of the Bull's Head Inn in Binley Road, Coventry is the home of the Coventry and North Warwickshire Cricket Club, founded in 1900. The first ever Warwickshire match staged in Coventry was against Leicestershire in 1843 at the Craven Ground.

The Coventry and North Warwickshire C C formerly played home matches at The Butts Ground, now known as the Butts Stadium which is used as a local community recreation area. Warwickshire C C C staged ten County Championship matches at this venue between 1925 and 1930.

The land at Binley Road was, until the clubs move from the Butts Ground, being used as a meadow by the Fellowship of Drapers who were an ancient Coventry established company, and close to this land stood The Old Bull's Head Inn where the landlord was at that time Mr G.E. Wharmby, who played cricket, making his debut for Nottinghamshire C C C in 1891, and later played for Bedfordshire C C C, and also acted as groundsman and cricket professional for the Coventry and North Warwicks C C. The ground is situated one mile east of the city centre.

The Bull's Head Ground was opened on 5 May 1900 when a match was staged between H.W. Bainbridge's XI, the then Warwickshire C C C captain, and the Coventry and North Warwicks C C. Three years later in 1903 Warwickshire C C C staged their initial first-class match on the ground against the touring Philadelphians. During the period 1903–19 Warwickshire C C C staged thirteen matches at the ground before they moved home matches in the city to the Butts Ground during the seasons 1925–30 and later to the Courtaulds during the seasons 1946–82. Warwickshire C C C did not return to the city for a home first-class County Championship match until some eight years later and,

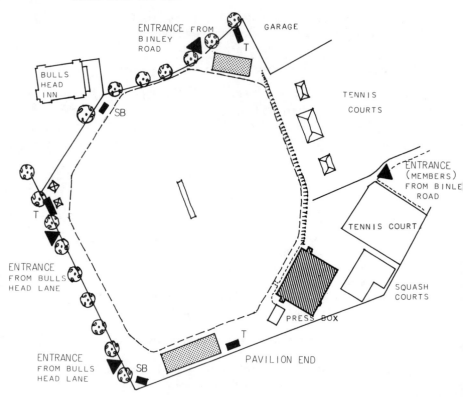

BULLS HEAD INN END

ENTRANCE FROM BINLEY ROAD

GARAGE

BULLS HEAD INN

SB

TENNIS COURTS

T

ENTRANCE (MEMBERS) FROM BINLE ROAD

ENTRANCE FROM BULLS HEAD LANE

TENNIS COURT

SQUASH COURTS

ENTRANCE FROM BULLS HEAD LANE

PRESS BOX

T

SB

PAVILION END

N

0   50   100

Metres

in fact, seventy-one years since the last county match on the Bull's Head ground, in 1990 when a match was arranged with Lancashire for 18–20 July at the Bull's Head Ground.

The drawn match was interesting and high-scoring, which must have given great pleasure to the Coventry and North Warwickshire Club for its fine batting wicket. For the home side, scores of fifty or more were recorded by Andy Moles (100 n.o.), Tom Moody (96), Paul Smith (82) and Dermot Reeve (78). For the visitors, Lancashire, Neil Fairbrother recorded the highest individual innings on the ground of 203 n.o. and in his second knock scored 50. His first innings double century beat the previous highest score of 198 by J. Chapman for Derbyshire in 1909. In 1991 a match was staged with Sussex and in June 1992 the visitors to the Bull's Head Ground will be Middlesex.

Coventry City Football Club played at Binley Road between 1883 and 1887 until their move to Stoke Road in 1887–89, and thence to Highfield Road in 1899, where they remain to date. Coventry Rugby Football Club played home matches at the Bull's Head Ground during 1919 before their move to their new ground at Coundon Road. The present ground is used for hockey by Coventry Hockey Club during the winter months. There are also facilities for tennis, with both grass and hard courts, squash and cricket nets.

Probably the most famous cricketer to have played for the Coventry and North Warwickshire C C and Warwickshire C C C is R.E.S. 'Bob' Wyatt (1923–39, captain 1930–37), who was born in the city and attended King Henry VIII School. He later played for and captained Worcestershire C C C and England and is the oldest surviving captain of England. Other players include Freddie Gardner, Jim Stewart and Tom Cartwright.

In 1935 a cricket pavilion and clubhouse was constructed and this was partly financed by a club life membership scheme. The only permanent buildings on the ground are the pavilion and clubhouse, scoreboard, groundsman's store, toilets and squash courts. The majority of facilities for Warwickshire C C C matches staged at the ground are of a temporary nature.

During May 1941 a Hampden bomber returning to base crashed onto the ground, killing its crew, and it was not until after the war that the damage to the cricket square was properly repaired. After the war had ended the club purchased the ground from the Fellowship of Drapers. The club has staged Warwickshire C C C second XI matches since 1961, and increased development within the other sections of the club has put the club on a good footing for the future. A benefit match was staged for Andy Lloyd in 1990.

After sixty-six years of resistance owing to the travel distance from Birmingham for matches by the established league club organizations, the Coventry and North Warwickshire C C was elected in 1986 to the Birmingham League for the first time.

The Coventry City F C goalkeeper Steve Ogrizovic has represented the club and played Minor County cricket for Shropshire C C C and the MCCA during the 1980s.

The ground capacity is 6,500 and the largest recorded crowd to date was 4,000 for the Lancashire match in 1990. Ground records include performances with the bat by C.S. Baker and N.H. Fairbrother and with the ball by S. Santall, E.M. Cregar and A.R. Warren.

ADDRESS   Coventry and North Warwickshire Cricket Club, The Pavilion, The Bull's Head Ground, Binley Road, Stoke, Coventry, Warwickshire.
TELEPHONE NUMBER PROSPECTS OF PLAY   0203 466281

DESCRIPTION OF GROUND AND FACILITIES

The ground is entered by players, officials and members from Binley Road via the rear of the tennis courts to the pavilion and clubhouse area. There are three other entrances for members and the public from Binley Road and Bull's Head Lane. Car parking is only available for players, officials, sponsors and a few members to the rear of the pavilion and on the tennis courts. Car parking is available within the surrounding streets and in an area between the Walsgrave Road to the north and The Barley Lea Road to the south, although this is subject to the normal traffic regulations.

The only permanent buildings are the pavilion, scoreboard, squash courts and toilets, with the majority of seating and facilities being temporary. There are two open raised plastic seating areas together with a number of plastic seats and chairs. Facilities for sponsors are situated on the lawn tennis courts and there are several refreshment facilities and bars located in small tents around the playing area. A Warwickshire C C C supporters souvenir table and bookstall/newspaper shop is situated at the Bull's Head Inn End. The main scoreboard is situated in the south-west corner of the ground and a secondary scoreboard is situated in front of the fence nearest the Inn. Toilets are available within the pavilion and in three separate buildings around the ground. The wicket lies in a north-south disposition and the playing area is defined by a rope and some advertising boards. The playing area is smooth and 132 metres by 123 metres.

A press tent and scorers' tent are to be found within the members' enclosure at the Pavilion End. A radio commentary position is situated next to the pavilion and, if required, a TV camera/commentary box would be located on a gantry directly above and behind the sightscreen at the Pavilion End.

This is a traditional out ground by county standards and it is quite a pleasant location to watch a day's cricket, subject to having fine weather, as there are no covered stands, just marquees, to shelter under.

GROUND RECORDS AND SCORES

FIRST-CLASS MATCHES
Highest innings total for County: 482 for 9 dec. *v.* Hampshire 1912
Highest innings total against County: 436 by Derbyshire 1909
Lowest innings total for County: 48 *v.* Leicestershire 1919

Lowest innings total against County: 86 by Leicestershire 1907
Highest individual innings for County: 151 C.S. Baker *v.* Sussex 1913
Highest individual innings against County: 203 n.o. N.H. Fairbrother for Lancashire 1990
Best bowling performance in an innings for County: 7 for 38 S. Santall *v.* Leicestershire 1907
Best bowling performance in an innings against County: 8 for 35 E.M. Cregar for Philadelphians 1903
Best bowling performance in a match for County: 11 for 91 S. Santall *v.* Leicestershire 1907
Best bowling performance in a match against County: 10 for 195 A.R. Warren for Derbyshire 1909
Best attendance: 4,000 *v.* Lancashire 1990

453 WARWICKSHIRE COVENTRY

HOW TO GET THERE

Rail   Coventry (BR), 1.5 miles.
Bus   Coventry Centro Buses 12, 13, 13A, 22, 86, 87 and X86 operated by Midland Red (South) and West Midland Travel pass ground on Binley Road from BR Coventry Station, city centre and surrounding districts (Telephone: 0203 559559).
Car   From north: M6 junction 3 or 2, then follow signs Coventry and city centre, follow signs County Cricket, then A46 to Comet warehouse at junction of Ansty Road and Walsgrave Road, then take Burns Road for Binley Road A427 and ground is situated off this road to the rear of the Bull's Head Inn public house. From east: A427 or A45 signposted Coventry and city centre then follows signs Binley and Stoke Aldermoor districts for Binley Road, then as north. From west: A45 or A427 signposted Coventry and city centre then follow signs Binley, then as north. From south: A45 or A46 or M45 then A45, follow signs Coventry and city centre then at London Road junction with Allard Way take right and then left for Binley Road, follow signs County Cricket.

WHERE TO STAY AND OTHER INFORMATION

Longshoot Hotel (0203 329711), Forte Crest (0203 613261), Forte Post House Coventry (0203 402151).

Disabled Areas   No special area, request suitable position. Disabled toilet near sightscreen at Pavilion End.
Local Radio Station(s)   Mercia Sound (97.0 MHz FM/1359 KHz MW), BBC Radio WM (95.6 MHz FM/1468 KHz MW).
Local Newspaper(s)   Coventry Evening Telegraph.

Nuneaton

Within the geographical triangle defined by Birmingham, Coventry and Nuneaton lie the former Warwickshire coalfields and just 1.5 miles from the Nuneaton town centre was the village of Chilvers Coton, where Griff Colliery was located. The first Chilvers Coton Cricket Club ground was situated at the rear of the Hare and Hounds public house in the village. The land which also included the Griff and Coton Cricket Club, established in 1901, was owned by Sir Francis Newdegate, the Governor of Tasmania and Western Australia between 1917 and 1924. The ground at Heath End Road has been used for cricket since 1906 and was known to locals as the Chilvers Coton Ground. When the land came under the ownership of Griff Colliery, sheep were allowed to graze on the outfield during weekdays.

The Chilvers Coton C C played in the Nuneaton Cricket League until 1912 when it moved to the Coventry and District Cricket League. The club changed its name to the Griff and Coton C C in August 1929 and later that year under the guidance of Mr F. Whiting an application was made for a county match, the following season saw Griff and Coton C C receive preference over Nuneaton Town C C to stage a match during the 1930 season.

The ground was and still is a miners' social welfare club and has changed very little since Warwickshire C C C made their initial first-class visit in 1930 when neighbours Leicestershire were the visitors. After 1933 the ground was not used again by the Warwickshire C C C until 1960 when thanks to Mr F.G. Watson, a local building contractor who loved his cricket, and a donation of £1,000 from the Warwickshire C C S A, improvements and development took place. The effort to attract county matches again was successful, cricket returned and a year later in 1961 the colliery closed down, as it had become uneconomic to continue mining. Today there is little to remind the visitor that this was once a colliery ground. Nuneaton is one of two Warwickshire C C C venues away from Edgbaston. Although the Courtaulds Ground, Coventry ceased to be used after 56 home matches had been staged at the ground between 1946 and 1982, since 1990 Warwickshire C C C have staged home matches at the Coventry and North Warwickshire Cricket Club at The Bull's Head Ground in Coventry. Championship matches have not been arranged at Nuneaton since 1989, when the twenty-seventh home match on the Griff and Coton ground was staged with visitors Derbyshire.

Warwickshire C C C have played matches in the town at Nuneaton Cricket Club located in Weddington Road during the period 1912–14 when three matches were played with Gloucestershire, Leicestershire and Sussex.

The colliery bandstand is still situated on the ground and a football pitch can still be viewed from the pavilion. There are facilities for bowling and tennis behind the main scoreboard. The only permanent buildings are the players' pavilion, a members' pavilion and social club,

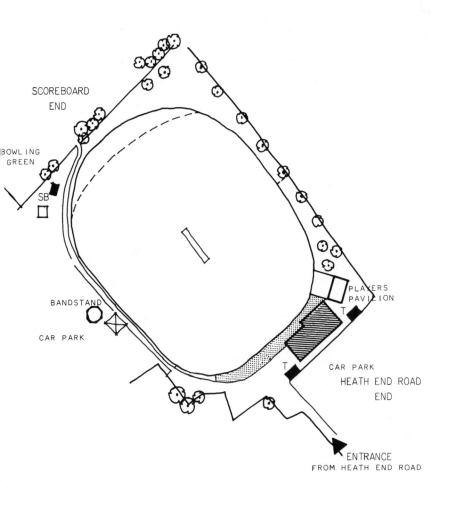

SCOREBOARD
END

BOWLING
GREEN

SB

BANDSTAND

CAR PARK

PLAYERS
PAVILION

T

T

CAR PARK
HEATH END ROAD
END

ENTRANCE
FROM HEATH END ROAD

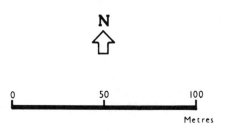

N

0   50   100

Metres

the scoreboard and the groundsman's store. In 1979 major improvements to the pavilion were made to create more space and a further bar area. Today the ground remains one of the best appointed for staging first-class cricket in the county away from the county club's central headquarters in Birmingham. Seating of a temporary nature is provided for county matches and the record crowd was 6,000 for a John Player Sunday League match with Lancashire in 1970. Crowds are usually around 2,500–3,500 for County Championship matches.

Ground records at Griff and Coton have included two double centuries: Tom Cartwright (210) and, for the visitors, Bill Alley the Australian while playing for Somerset (221 n.o.) in 1961 – a career best in his record breaking summer with the bat. With the ball Tom Cartwright, R.L. Savage and A. Brown have all achieved fine bowling performances.

Alan Smith and Tom Cartwright shared a partnership of 244 for the seventh wicket in just under three hours against Middlesex in 1962. This is still a record partnership for any wicket on the ground for or against the county. In limited-overs matches between 1969 and 1980 the highest individual innings was scored by Dennis Amiss and the best bowling performance was by Tom Cartwright. In recent seasons Alvin Kallicharran has always enjoyed scoring heavily on this ground and in 1982 Bob Willis hit 62 n.o. against Gloucestershire, which was his career best innings with the bat.

ADDRESS Griff and Coton Cricket Club, The Pavilion, Griff and Coton Sports Club Ground, Heath End Road, Nuneaton, Warwickshire.
TELEPHONE NUMBER PROSPECTS OF PLAY 0203 386798

DESCRIPTION OF GROUND AND FACILITIES

The ground is entered from Heath End Road to the south. A car park immediately adjoins the road and there is an additional area for car parking on the football field to the west of the playing area. The playing area, which is a small oval shape and quite narrow, is 108 metres by 130 metres and is enclosed by a two-railed white timber fence. The pavilion to the south is a substantial single-storey building with dormers but provides no raised seating.

The players' dressing room is a small pavilion in the south-east corner surmounted by a clock and weathervane. The scoreboard is on the opposite side of the ground and affixed to it is a plaque to the memory of Jack Smart, Warwickshire 1919–36 and subsequently a first-class umpire and later groundsman at Griff and Coton C C. The members' enclosure adjoins the pavilion to the south and east of the playing area. The remainder of the ground is for the public, who are advised to bring their own seats as only 2,500 are available on the ground.

Nuneaton is a somewhat featureless ground now, rather dominated by the backs of semi-detached houses to the east, but attempts are being made to provide a tree screen on this boundary. Perhaps the most interesting feature is the bandstand just to the west of the playing area, which is usually within the area set aside for a sponsors' marquee. A press tent is available near the scoreboard in which the scorers are also sited. Toilets are available at the south end and refreshment and bar facilities are available in the pavilion for members and in temporary tents for the public. A newspaper stall and supporters souvenir table is located near to the pavilion. A radio commentary position is situated within the members' enclosure and, if required, a TV camera/commentary box would be located at the Scoreboard End.

GROUND RECORDS AND SCORES

FIRST-CLASS MATCHES
Highest innings total for County: 446 *v*. Gloucestershire 1982
Highest innings total against County: 434 for 5 dec. by Gloucestershire 1982
Lowest innings total for County: 70 *v*. Hampshire 1979
Lowest innings total against County: 34 by Nottinghamshire 1964
Highest individual innings for County: 210 T.W. Cartwright *v*. Middlesex 1962
Highest individual innings against County: 221 n.o. W.E. Alley for Somerset 1961
Best bowling performance in an innings for County: 7 for 50 R.L. Savage *v*. Glamorgan 1977
Best bowling performance in an innings against County: 8 for 47 A. Brown for Kent 1963
Best bowling performance in a match for County: 9 for 40 T.W. Cartwright *v*. Nottinghamshire 1964
Best bowling performance in a match against County: 10 for 97 A. Brown for Kent 1963
Best attendance: 3,500 *v*. Leicestershire 1930

LIMITED-OVERS MATCHES
Highest innings total for County: 234 for 5 *v*. Northamptonshire (JPL) 1980
Highest innings total against County: 208 for 7 by Northamptonshire (JPL) 1980
Lowest innings total for County: 153 *v*. Lancashire (JPL) 1969
Lowest innings total against County: 204 for 5 by Lancashire (JPL) 1969
Highest individual innings for County: 81 D.L. Amiss *v*. Northamptonshire (JPL) 1980
Highest individual innings against County: 69 R.G. Williams for Northamptonshire (JPL) 1980
Best bowling performance for County: 3 for 31 T.W. Cartwright *v*. Lancashire (JPL) 1969
Best bowling performance against County: 2 for 17 J. Sullivan for Lancashire (JPL) 1969
Best attendance: 6,000 *v*. Lancashire (JPL) 1969

HOW TO GET THERE

Rail   Nuneaton (BR), 1.5 miles.
Bus   Midland Red (South) N1 links BR Nuneaton Station with ground (Telephone: 0203 553737).
Car   From north: M6 junction 3, follow A444 signposted Nuneaton, at first roundabout take left into Bridge Street, which leads into Heath End Road for Griff and Coton Sports Ground; or A44, A47 or M69 junction 1, then A5 and A47 signposted Nuneaton and town centre for Griff and Coton Sports Ground. From east, west and south: M6 junction 3, follow A444 signposted Nuneaton, then as north.

WHERE TO STAY AND OTHER INFORMATION

Longshoot Hotel (0203 329711).

Disabled Areas   No special area, request suitable position.
Local Radio Station(s)   BBC Radio WM (95.6 MHz FM/1468 KHz MW), Mercia Sound (97.0 MHz FM/1359 KHz MW).
Local Newspaper(s)   Nuneaton Evening Tribune, Coventry Evening Telegraph.

WORCESTERSHIRE

CHURCHMAN'S CIGARETTES.

WORCESTERSHIRE.

WORCESTER

KIDDERMINSTER

HEREFORD

Worcestershire

Founded   5 March 1865
Colours   Dark green and black
Crest   Shield argent bearing fess between three pears stable
Patron   His Grace The Duke of Westminster
President   G.H. Chesterton
Chairman   C.D. Fearnley
Chairman cricket committee   M.G. Jones
Secretary   Rev. M.G. Vockins
County coach   K.J. Lyons
Assistant coach   M.S. Scott
Public relations officer   B.L. D'Oliveria
Commercial manager   J. Osborne
Captain   T.S. Curtis
Groundsman   R. McLaren
Scorer 1st XI   J.W. Sewter
Scorer 2nd XI   S.S. Hale
Statistician   L.W. Hatton
Sponsors   MEB Midlands Electricity PLC
Newsletter   *Worcestershire Members Newsletter*
Address   County Cricket Ground, New Road, Worcester,
Worcestershire WR2 4QQ.
Telephone 0905 422694
Facsimile 0905 748005
Worcestershire Rapid Cricketline   0891 567517

ACHIEVEMENTS

County Championship   Champions (5) 1964, 1965, 1974, 1988 and
1989
Gillette Cup   Finalists (2) 1963 and 1966
National Westminster Bank Trophy   Finalists (2) 1988; semi-
finalists (2) 1989 and 1990
Benson & Hedges Cup   Winners (1) 1991; finalists (3) 1973, 1976
and 1990
John Player Sunday League   Champions (1) 1971
Refuge Assurance Sunday League   Champions (2) 1987 and 1988
Refuge Assurance Cup   Winners (1) 1991; finalists (1) 1988
Tilcon Trophy   Winners (2) 1981 and 1989
Ward Four Counties Knockout Competition   Semi-finalists (1) 1989

GROUNDS

Worcester (County Cricket Ground, New Road)   Hereford
(Racecourse Ground, Grandstand Road) and Kidderminster (Offmore
Lane, Chester Road).
   Other grounds that have been used since 1969 are: Dudley (The

County Ground, Tipton Road) Stourbridge (Stourbridge War
Memorial Ground, Amblecote) Stourport-on-Seven (Parsons Controls
Holdings Limited, The Chainwire Club Sports Ground, Minister Road)
and Halesowen (Halesowen C C, Sports Ground, Grange Road).

SECOND XI GROUNDS
In addition to the above mentioned grounds the following are used for
second XI matches: Halesowen C C, Grange Road/Dog Kennel Lane,
Halesowen, West Midlands. Telephone: 021 550 2744; Old Hill C C,
Haden Hill Park, Cradley Heath, West Midlands. Telephone: 0384
66827; Ombersley C C, Cricket Ground, Ombersley, Near
Kidderminster. (No Telephone); Stourbridge C C, Stourbridge War
Memorial Ground, Amblecote, Stourbridge, West Midlands.
Telephone: Directory Enquiries; Royal Grammar School Worcester,
Flagge Meadow, Worcester. (No Telephone); Barnt Green C C, Cherry
Hill Road, Barnt Green, West Midlands. Telephone: 021 445 1684.

Worcestershire are a prime example of the changes brought about by the
up-dating of the format of county cricket. Cinderella's rags have been
well and truly cast aside. After almost winding up in 1914 and years of
amiable failure between the wars – four wooden spoons and ten times
clamped in the bottom four – twenty-eight exciting seasons of transformation from 1963 have brought five championships, the John Player
League in 1971 and the first two years of the Refuge Assurance League,
1987 and 1988, plus seven Lord's finals, albeit all but one ending in
defeat, until 1991 when the Benson & Hedges Cup was won.

Frankly, Worcestershire were not up to first-class strength, but in
1988 Botham's claim that theirs was 'far and away the strongest team'
was not only hard to refute but graphically illustrated the change of
power since the emancipating 'sixties. The achievement of the 'double'
of the championship and the retention of the Sunday League was all the
more meritorious as Botham was absent injured for the best part of the
season. It might well have been a hat-trick with the prize of the NatWest
Trophy if skipper Phil Neale had not made his only error of his
triumphant season by losing the toss which led to Worcestershire being
put in and committed to bat on a damp pitch. Maybe that was Gatting's
one piece of luck in his traumatic year.

As the championship pennant, plus cheque, was parachuted in, Neale
was deservedly re-appointed captain for the 8th time, and, to crown all
the achievements were the deeds of Graeme Hick, a batting nugget to fall
in Worcestershire's lap from Zimbabwe's distant sky. Not since the days
of Hutton, Compton, May and Cowdrey has a young batsman been so
universally praised. He became the 9th, and the youngest since
Bradman, to score 1,000 before the end of May. His 1,019 came from
only 1,343 balls, including 600 in boundaries, and was highlighted by a
mammoth 405 not out against Somerset, the highest innings in county
cricket since McLaren's record 424 in 1895, also at Taunton.

WORCESTER

G. A. HICK

Another of Worcestershire's distinguished imports, Glenn Turner, scored 1,018 before the end of May, but it was on behalf of the touring New Zealanders! Hick also equalled Turner's county record of 10 centuries in a season, and in 1988, when he confirmed his high class, he totalled 2,713 runs in 37 first-class innings. Like Turner, Hick found his way to Worcester because other clubs had their quota of overseas players – Warwickshire recommended Turner and Leicestershire Hick – and within two years he broke Hutton's 49-year-old record as the youngest to reach 2,000 in an English season. Hick was 20, Hutton 21. In 1986 Hick and Curtis scored an undefeated 287 to improve on the previous county record for the second wicket set up 53 years before by the Nawab of Pataudi Snr and Gibbons. In due course Hick, despite some recent shortcomings, might set ambitious eyes on the 287, then an individual record Test score, made by R.E. Foster at Sydney in 1903–04. Foster was one of the leading three or four batsman in the early years of the century, and was the most gifted of the seven brothers. Four appeared in one game, and it was hardly surprising that the county was dubbed 'Fostershire.'

Reginald captained England in the home series with South Africa in 1907, the year Worcestershire were runners-up, a heady position not equalled until 1962 when the modern era of professionalism was already entrenched. In his short life – he died from diabetes at 36 – Foster was also a renowned soccer international.

Arnold, an early all-rounder of note, went to Australia with Foster and was highly successful, and in the run-up to the first war Simpson-Hayward, the last of the famous under-arm bowlers, was captain. As relatively late as 1910–11 he took 6 South African wickets for 42 on the Johannesburg mat. Strudwick kept wicket to him and volunteered to bat early against him for Surrey as he could 'read' him. Struddy used to make the grinned confession that he was immediately out to him – to a full toss! Chester, the finest of all umpires, started at Worcester at the age of

TOM GRAVENEY

PLAYER'S CIGARETTES

R. T. D. PERKS

ROOT

14 and was marked for the highest honours. By 1914 he had hit 4 centuries – one against Essex of 178 not out including 4 sixes off Douglas – and was praised by W.G. Grace. He lost his right hand in Salonika in 1917.

Worcestershire, though never far from the wrong end of the table between the wars, were often indebted to the skills of Bowley, scorer of 276 in a day off Hampshire, Root, the deadly exponent of leg theory swing bowling, the batting of the Nawab of Pataudi, the graceful Test opener and secretary from Glamorgan, Walters, and Nichol and Gibbons. 'Doc' Gibbons – so named because he first appeared on the ground carrying an old-style doctor's bag – was one of the best batsmen never to have been capped by England.

The emergence of fast bowler Perks, 2,233 wickets, the first pro captain and twenty-seven sterling years, and the spinners, Howorth and Jenkins, was important in Worcestershire's next phase in the building-up of the Kenyon-led championship sides. Appointed captain in 1959, some years after he had failed to do himself justice at Test level, Kenyon brilliantly bridged the old and new Worcestershire. In his 39th year he all but took the title finishing 4 points behind Yorkshire, but that 1962 disappointment proved but a rehearsal for Worcestershire's first success in sixty-five years.

Coming in 1964 it was within but a few months of the club's centenary. However, that event was celebrated in style with the retention of the championship in a thrilling dash for the post. Ten wins in the last 11 matches took Kenyon's able side to the top for the first time in the season in the closing overs. As D'Oliveira pointed out, it was the only time it really mattered!

Though Peter Richardson, who had reached, 1,000 Test runs in fewer innings than any previous Englishman, had departed for Kent, Kenyon had exceptional fire power. Graveney was on a high in the second lease of his career, D'Oliveira was collecting his 43 centuries and 44 caps –

and considerable respect for his dignity amid the crisis he innocently provoked over his native South Africa – and Headley, Ormrod and Dick Richardson were consistent run-getters. The bowlers came up trumps led by Flavell, Coldwell, Gifford, Slade, Carter and Brain. The all-rounders, D'Oliveira and Horton, were vital cogs in an impressive side.

The experience of D'Oliveira was influential when Gifford captained Worcestershire to a 3rd victory in 1974. Now assisted by Turner, one of the world's leading batsmen who flowered at Worcester, and fast bowler Holder, Gifford led what *Wisden* described as a triumph of team participation adding, 'there is no reason why this performance should be rated below that of Kenyon's possibly more gifted champions.' Gifford also took the Sunday League in 1971, and extended his own successful career with Warwickshire.

Whether Neale, with Hick, Curtis, the two Test fast bowlers, Dilley and Newport, and even Botham sidelined, had the strongest of the title-winning teams could be an endless argument, but it was all a far cry from the days when Worcestershire managed to dismiss Yorkshire for 99 at Bradford and still lost by an innings!

Worcestershire were county champions in 1989 for the fifth time thanks to runs from Hick, Curtis and Neale. The majority of wickets were shared between Radford, Botham, Dilley and McEwan. In 1990 Worcestershire were again beaten in a one-day final at Lord's by Lancashire in the Benson and Hedges Cup, but in 1991 made amends with two victories against Lancashire. Firstly in July, Worcestershire lifted the Benson and Hedges Cup by 65 runs thanks to 88 from Graeme Hick and 3 for 48 by Neil Radford. Then later in September at Old Trafford, Worcestershire won by 7 runs thanks to 105 by Steve Rhodes and 5 for 42 by Neil Radford to win the last Refuge Assurance Cup Final. Moody had a splendid first season scoring 3,157 in all competitions with 12 centuries and 15 fifties. Curtis was elected captain for 1992 and both Botham and McEwan left for the newcomers Durham.

Worcester

The County Cricket Ground at Worcester is situated in New Road, west of the bridge crossing the River Severn and within walking distance of the city centre. Worcester is probably the most attractive county ground in the country and was the property of Worcester Cathedral until purchased by the club in 1976 for £30,000. The view of the playing area from the pavilion enclosure has as its backcloth the fourteenth-century Cathedral. This scene is illustrated frequently in books on cricket. The county club moved to New Road in 1899 from Boughton Park and the initial first-class match staged on the ground was with Yorkshire in May that year. So urgent were the preparations that the sightscreen was still being painted by ground staff on the morning of the match. The members' pavilion was built in 1898–99 and remains today little different externally, although internal alterations have taken place.

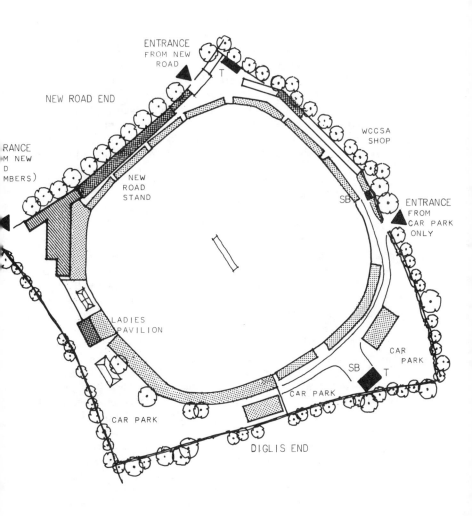

ENTRANCE
FROM NEW
ROAD

T

NEW ROAD END

WCCSA
SHOP

RANCE
M NEW
D
MBERS)

NEW
ROAD
STAND

SB

ENTRANCE
FROM
CAR PARK
ONLY

LADIES
PAVILION

CAR
PARK

SB

T

CAR PARK

CAR PARK

DIGLIS END

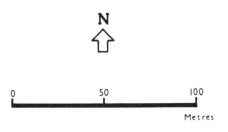

N

0   50   100

Metres

Since 1951 when Worcestershire C C Supporters' Association was founded by the Lord Lieutenant of the County, Admiral Sir William Tennant, much money has been raised to improve the county ground. Changes have included the addition of new seating in 1952 on the popular side of the ground, a scoreboard in 1954 and two years later a Ladies Pavilion. In 1965 the championship year, the Severn Bar on the east side was rebuilt and in the winter 1973–74 major additions were made to the New Road Stand, notably a roof, press box/scorers' room and the secretary's office. In 1984–85 further development was undertaken when an executive suite was built on the site of the old supporters' association offices, scorers' room and press box. The scorers' and press have now been moved to the other end of the New Road Stand, near to the pavilion. The Supporters' Association is now housed in the offices of the club's marketing department. 1989–90 saw the construction of new executive boxes on top of the existing New Road Stand and since that winter almost all seats within the ground are of the plastic tip-up variety in the club colours of green and white.

Regular floods from the nearby River Severn have on occasions introduced fishing, boating, swimming and even ice skating to the County Ground! In the members' pavilion there is a brass plate showing the highest water level in 1947 – some 3.5 feet above the floor and several feet above the playing area outside. The flooding usually occurs around Christmas but as recent as 1987 flooding took place only a few weeks before the start of the season in March.

The ground has staged Test trial and international matches, including the 1983 Prudential Cup match between West Indies and Zimbabwe, a Young England against Young Australia Test Match, the 1979 ICC Trophy final between Sri Lanka and Canada and, more recently, a Ladies' Test Match in 1984 between England and New Zealand. This was the third Ladies' Test Match staged at Worcester. After the restructuring of the Minor Counties Cricket Association in 1983 the winners of the two divisions, East and West, met at New Road to decide the Champions until in 1989 the final was transferred to Lord's, with subsequent finals in 1990 and 1991 being staged at Wardown Park, Luton. The 1992 Final will again be staged at New Road. For many years Worcester was traditionally the first county match for the touring side, but this has altered in recent years with many tourists commencing tours at Arundel Castle.

Ground records include Glenn Turner's 311 n.o. against Warwickshire, which was his 100th hundred. Another favourite local who achieved this feat at New Road in 1964 was Tom Graveney who scored 132, his 100th hundred, against Northamptonshire. Graeme Hick and Tom Moody have scored important centuries in limited-overs matches in recent seasons for the home county. Crowds at Worcester have been good and in recent years limited-overs matches have attracted large attendances. The largest crowd for a match was probably 14,000 against the Australians in 1948. Recent limited-overs matches have attracted full houses of 8,500 for popular matches.

ADDRESS County Cricket Ground, New Road, Worcester, Worcestershire WR2 4QQ.
TELEPHONE NUMBER PROSPECTS OF PLAY 0905 422011

DESCRIPTION OF GROUND AND FACILITIES

There are two entrances in New Road, one for members and their cars at the rear of the pavilion and a second, adjoining the club offices and marketing offices. Car parking is available in the ground and in the field adjoining the Diglis End, close to the river and cricket nets. Street parking and nearby car parks are within a short walk over the bridge and into the city centre or within the park opposite the entrance in New Road. Much of the members' covered accommodation is at the New Road End of the ground and in addition to the New Road Stand, the members' pavilion and Ladies Pavilion, the remainder of the ground is uncovered. All the terracing of plastic seats and benches are available to the public on the Severn side of the ground. For popular matches large banks of temporary, raised plastic seating are erected at the Diglis End and these provide attractive views of the playing area.

There is no need to bring your own seats to matches as seating is provided for the capacity of 8,500. The main radio commentary point is in the New Road Stand and the TV camera position is at the Diglis End on a gantry directly above and behind the sightscreen. The members' enclosure stretches from the Diglis End sightscreen westwards to the sponsors' balcony area adjoining the New Road Stand – at least half the ground. There is a Worcestershire C C C souvenir shop situated on the Severn side adjoining the bar and refreshment area. Other refreshments can be obtained from under the main scoreboard and in the portacabin or tent between the members' pavilion and the Ladies pavilion as well as in the New Road Stand.

The press and scorers sit in the New Road Stand, close to the secretary's office and the players' dining room. The playing area falls slightly towards the west side and is defined by a rope and advertising boards. The playing area is 145 metres by 136 metres and is roughly circular in shape. Possibly the finest view of the cricket and Cathedral can be seen across the beautiful county ground from a vantage point sitting in the members' pavilion enclosure.

GROUND RECORDS AND SCORES

FIRST-CLASS MATCHES
Highest innings total for County: 633 *v*. Warwickshire 1906
Highest innings total against County: 701 for 4 dec. by Leicestershire 1906
Lowest innings total for County: 40 *v*. Leicestershire 1971 (only 8 wickets fell, two batsmen absent hurt); 47 *v*. Derbyshire 1936/ Cambridge University 1955
Lowest innings total against County: 30 by Hampshire 1903
Highest individual innings for County: 311 n.o. G.M. Turner *v*. Warwickshire 1982

Highest individual innings against County: 331 n.o. J.D.B. Robertson for Middlesex 1949
Best bowling performance in an innings for County: 9 for 23 C.F. Root *v.* Lancashire 1931
Best bowling performance in an innings against County: 10 for 51 J. Mercer for Glamorgan 1936
Best bowling performance in a match for County: 15 for 106 R.T.D. Perks *v.* Essex 1937
Best bowling performance in a match against County: 15 for 175 J.C. White for Somerset 1921
Best attendance: 14,000 *v.* Australians 1948

LIMITED-OVERS MATCHES
Highest innings total for County: 404 for 3 *v.* Devon (NWBT) 1987
Highest innings total against County: 284 for 6 by Derbyshire (BHC) 1982
Lowest innings total for County: 81 *v.* Leicestershire (BHC) 1983
Lowest innings total against County: 59 by Lancashire (GC) 1963
Highest individual innings for County: 172 n.o. G.A. Hick *v.* Devon (NWBT) 1987
Highest individual innings against County: 142 G. Boycott for Yorkshire (BHC) 1980
Best bowling performance for County: 6 for 14 J.A. Flavell *v.* Lancashire (GC) 1963
Best bowling performance against County: 6 for 14 H.P. Cooper for Yorkshire (JPL) 1975
Best attendance: 8,500 *v.* Lancashire (NWBT) 1989

HOW TO GET THERE

Rail   Worcester Foregate Street (BR), 0.5 mile; Worcester Shrub Hill (BR), 1 mile.
Bus   Midland Red West Nos 23–6, 33 link Angel Place (200m from BR Foregate Street Station) with ground (Telephone: 0345 212555)
Car   From north: M5 junction 5, then follow A38 signposted Worcester and city centre, then take A44 for New Road and County Cricket; the ground is situated south of the city centre and south of the River Severn close to Bridge Street; or A443, A449 to city centre then as above. From east: A422 or A44, follow signs Worcester and city centre, then as north. From west: A44, A4103 or A419, follow signs Worcester and city centre, then as north. From South: M5 junction 7, follow A44 signposted Worcester and city centre, then as north.

WHERE TO STAY AND OTHER INFORMATION

Giffard Hotel (0905 27155), Star Hotel (0905 24308), Bredon Manor Hotel (0684 72293).

Disabled Areas Two viewing points on the ground accessible to wheelchairs. Toilet facilities for disabled. Unfortunately, owing to danger of flooding, most buildings are 6–8 feet above ground and are accessible only by steps.
Local Radio Station(s) Radio Wyvern (102 MHz FM/1530 KHz MW), BBC Radio WM (95.6 MHz FM/1468 KHz MW).
Local Newspaper(s) Worcester Evening News, Birmingham Post, Birmingham Mail, Express and Star, Berrow's Worcester Journal.

Kidderminster

The Chester Road ground was established in 1870 but cricket has been played in the town since 1850. The present Kidderminster Cricket Club was formed in 1890 and its ground is located close to the main Chester Road. The club played previously at Worcester Road, Kidderminster until the land was purchased for a steeplechasing racecourse. For two years the club played at Comberton Road, on a field provided by the Kidderminster Grammar School, but then the club had to move again. This time the club was more fortunate and rented some land close to Offmore Farm, which was part of the Earl of Dudley's estate. The ground opened on 20 August 1870 and is still the home of the club today. By 1896 the club had secured the lease direct from the Earl of Dudley and this was renewed annually until 1918 when the Dudley property was sold by auction. A local carpet manufacturer Mr Michael Tomkinson, the then President of the club, purchased the freehold for £1,287 10s on 31 December 1918 with a view to taking over when finances permitted. Still owned by the club, the old pavilion was brought from the Worcester Road ground and rebuilt on its present site. The new pavilion was built in 1925 at a cost of £886, subscribed by members to commemorate winning the Birmingham League in 1924. Close to this is a recreation and tea room with ample bar facilities for members, known as the Long Room.

The first Worcestershire C C C match staged at Kidderminster was in 1921 when Glamorgan were the visitors. After some 46 consecutive seasons in 1973, after a game against Northamptonshire, the run ended – possibly because Worcestershire were bowled out for 63. In 1987, however, first-class cricket returned, with Nottinghamshire the visitors and one championship match has been staged each season since.

Kidderminster C C is a member of the Birmingham Cricket League which it joined in 1895. The club won the league for the first time in 1899 and on eleven occasions since, the last being in 1991. The ground has been used by the county for Second XI Championship fixtures. ICC Trophy matches have been staged at Chester Road since 1979, with Denmark, Malaysia (twice) and Bangladesh taking part. Only one limited-overs match has been staged at Kidderminster – in 1969 when the visitors Middlesex were bowled out for only 56. In 1984 the association between Kidderminster C C, the Kidderminster Hockey

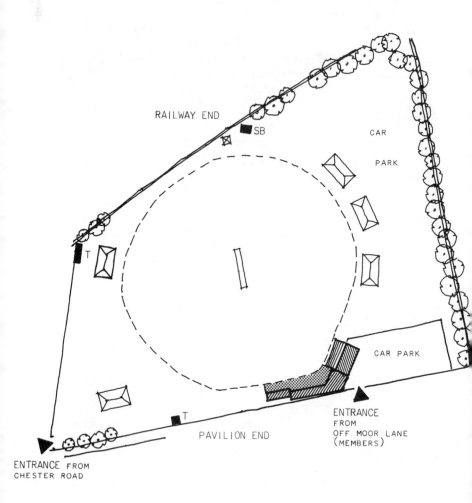

RAILWAY END

SB

CAR PARK

T

CAR PARK

ENTRANCE FROM OFF MOOR LANE (MEMBERS)

T

PAVILION END

ENTRANCE FROM CHESTER ROAD

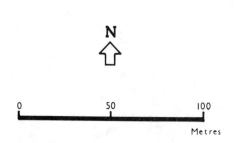

N

| 0 | 50 | 100 |

Metres

Club, who use the ground during the winter months, and the Old Carolians was formalized with the creation of the Chester Road Sporting Club, in which the land and buildings are now vested.

Crowds have been in the region of 4,500–5,500. The largest attendance was 7,000 for the visit of Yorkshire in 1956. Ground records have included 259 from Don Kenyon against Yorkshire in 1956 and fine bowling performances for and against the county by Jack Flavell and Alf Gover. Duncan Fearnley the Worcestershire Chairman, former player and cricket bat manufacturer will no doubt have fond memories of Chester Road, for he scored his only first-class century here against Derbyshire (112) in 1966.

The association between Kidderminster C C and the Worcestershire C C C has meant that players of the calibre of Laddie Outschoorn, Fred Rumsey, Basil D'Oliveira and latterly Graeme Hick have represented the club.

ADDRESS Kidderminster Cricket Club, Chester Road Sports Club, Offmore Lane, Chester Road, Kidderminster, Worcestershire DY10 1TH.
TELEPHONE PROSPECTS OF PLAY 0562 4175

DESCRIPTION OF GROUND AND FACILITIES

Entrance to the ground is from Chester Road where the main entrance is situated. The entrance in Offmore Lane adjoining the car park is for members and sponsors only. The pavilion, the Long Room, where refreshment facilities for members are provided, and the old pavilion are situated at the Offmore Lane End south of the playing area. The members' enclosure is in front of the pavilion and on the terracing adjoining the building, and in front of the Long Room. The scoreboard is at the Lyndholm Road End close to the railway cutting. Sponsors' tents and refreshment facilities can be found to the east side and temporary seating for the public is on the west side of the playing area. There are ample refreshment tents and temporary toilets on the west side of the ground.

The playing area is 131 metres by 121 metres and defined by a rope and advertising boards. The Chester Road side of the ground is bounded by housing on the main A449 trunk road, whilst to the north and east are plenty of trees. The ground is very flat with a slight fall towards the Chester Road in the direction of the main entrance gates. There is no fixed seating except near the pavilion. The ground capacity is 5,500 but seating is provided for only about one-third of that number. Spectators are therefore advised to bring their own seats. Several old photographs and prints in the pavilion and Long Room bar relate to Kidderminster cricket and the history of the Chester Road ground.

GROUND RECORDS AND SCORES

FIRST-CLASS MATCHES

Highest innings total for County: 477 *v*. Northamptonshire 1946
Highest innings total against County: 551 for 7 by Leicestershire 1929
Lowest innings total for County: 63 *v*. Northamptonshire 1973
Lowest innings total against County: 71 by Leicestershire 1933
Highest individual innings for County: 259 D. Kenyon *v*. Yorkshire 1956
Highest individual innings against County: 200 n.o. W.E. Bates for Warwickshire 1927
Best bowling performance in an innings for County: 9 for 56 J.A. Flavell *v*. Middlesex 1964
Best bowling performance in an innings against County: 7 for 35 A.R. Gover for Surrey 1938
Best bowling performance in a match for County: 13 for 96 J.A. Flavell *v*. Somerset 1965
Best bowling performance in a match against County: 14 for 85 A.R. Gover for Surrey 1938
Best attendance: 7,000 *v*. Yorkshire 1956

LIMITED-OVERS MATCH (JPL)

Highest innings total for County: 116 for 9 *v*. Middlesex 1969
Highest innings total against County: 56 by Middlesex 1969
Highest individual innings for County: 45 B.L. D'Oliveira *v*. Middlesex 1969
Highest individual innings against County: 11 C.T. Radley for Middlesex 1969
Best bowling performance for County: 3 for 8 N. Gifford *v*. Middlesex 1969
Best bowling performance against County: 3 for 14 J.S.E. Price for Middlesex 1969
Best attendance: 3,500 *v*. Middlesex 1969

HOW TO GET THERE

Rail Kidderminster (BR), 0.5 mile.
Bus Midland Red from surrounding areas to Bus Station, thence 0.75 mile; Midland Red No. 7 passes ground.
Car From north: M5 junction 3, then follow A456 signposted Kidderminster, then take junction with A449 bypass for Offmore Lane and County Cricket close to railway line; or A449, A442 to Kidderminster, then as above. From east: A456 or A448 signposted Kidderminster, then as north. From west: A456 or A451 signposted Kidderminster, then as north. From south: M5 junction 6, then follow A449 signposted Kidderminster, then as north.

Gainsborough House Hotel (0562 754041), Cedars Hotel (0562 745869).

Disabled Areas   No special area, request suitable position.
Local Radio Station(s)   BBC Radio WM (95.6 MHz FM/1468 KHz MW), Beacon Radio (97.2 MHz FM/990 KHz MW), Radio Wyvern (102 MHz FM/1530 KHz MW) BRMB (96.4 MHz FM/1152 KHz MW).
Local Newspaper(s)   Berrows's Worcester Journal, Kidderminster Shuttle, Kidderminster Chronicle.

Hereford

The Hereford Cricket Club ground is part of the Hereford racecourse complex and has been the home of the town cricket club since 1909. The club was founded in 1836 and played at Widemarsh Common until the move to the present ground. The club notched up 150 years in 1986. Celebrations included a tour of Barbados and a visit from Worcestershire C C C for a John Player Sunday League match with neighbours Gloucestershire. The ground was, until 1989, when the last match was staged, the only one in Britain used for first-class cricket which is within a racecourse, now that the County Cricket Ground, Derby, formerly the Racecourse Ground, no longer shares that distinction.

Widemarsh Common and the Westfield racecourse were the same area until separated by a new road. The original pavilion was built at the common in 1889 and is still in use today. The initial first-class match staged was in 1919 when Worcestershire played H.K. Foster's XI and the game was part of the county's programme after they decided not to re-enter the County Championship after World War One. Hereford hosted later matches for H.K. Foster's XI, including a match with the Australian Imperial Forces touring side. In another friendly first-class match in 1947, Worcestershire played the Combined Services XI. With the formation of the County of Hereford and Worcestershire, first-class cricket returned to the Racecourse Ground after 34 years with the visit of Glamorgan. Subsequent games included visits from Kent and Leicestershire. In 1983 the first limited-overs match was staged with Nottinghamshire in the John Player Sunday League and later years have seen Sunday League matches with Gloucestershire and Surrey in the Refuge Assurance Sunday League. Middlesex were due to visit in 1984 but the fixture was transferred to Worcester.

Hereford C C play in the Three Counties League which was formed in 1968 and includes club sides from Hereford, Gloucestershire and the South Wales region. The club has won the First XI League nine times since 1972 and the Second XI on three occasions. Reg Perks and Peter Richardson both played for Hereford C C and represented Worcestershire C C C and England during their careers. Ground records have

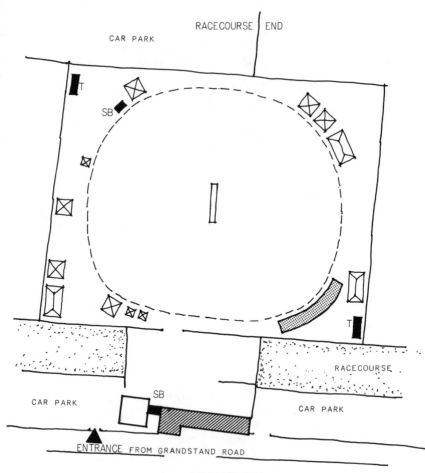

RACECOURSE END

CAR PARK

T

SB

RACECOURSE

T

CAR PARK

SB

CAR PARK

ENTRANCE FROM GRANDSTAND ROAD

PAVILION END

N

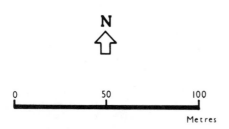

0   50   100

Metres

included hundreds from Glenn Turner and Mark Benson, both in the same match together, with a Sunday League career best from the England wicket-keeper Jack Russell for Gloucestershire in 1986. Crowds are quite good: 4,000 can be expected. In 1987 a crowd of over 7,500 witnessed the Refuge Assurance Sunday League match with Surrey in which Tim Curtis and Ian Botham took the home side to a 9-wicket victory and the top of the Refuge Sunday League, which the club was later to win that season for the first time. From 1992 the venue will be used for home Minor County Championship matches by Herefordshire C C C during the inaugural Minor County season in the Western Division.

ADDRESS Hereford Cricket Club, Hereford City Sports Club, Racecourse Cricket Ground, Grandstand Road, Hereford.
TELEPHONE NUMBER PROSPECTS OF PLAY 0432 273098

DESCRIPTION OF GROUND AND FACILITIES

Situated within the Racecourse Grounds, the playing area is some way from the pavilion. Players therefore view the match from a tent adjoining the press and scorers' tents in the south-west corner of the ground. All the seating is open and some for members is on raised timber platforms to the south and west of the ground. The north-west and west side of the ground is for the public. The north-east side, which is for sponsors, includes tents and a double-decker bus. A scoreboard adjoins the pavilion and a temporary scoreboard is sited close to the playing area on the west side. The playing area is 140 metres by 120 metres and is defined by a rope and advertisement boards.

The members' enclosure includes refreshment tents and temporary toilet facilities. Similar facilities are found on the west side of the ground together with a Worcestershire C C S C souvenir tent. Car parking is available off Grandstand Road and in the overflow car park at the northern Racecourse End of the ground, where there is an entrance to the ground through the temporary white canvas fencing. The main entrance is from Grandstand Road adjoining the pavilion. The radio commentary and TV camera/commentary box positions are at the Grandstand Road End. A fine view of the ground, playing area and racecourse can be seen from the first floor of the pavilion, although at some distance. There are no trees near the ground, which is possibly one of the most open locations on the county circuit, with no covered accommodation whatsoever for spectators other than some tents to shelter in.

The ground capacity is 7,500 and as only 60 per cent of seating is provided, spectators are advised to bring their own seats to popular matches.

GROUND RECORDS AND SCORES

FIRST-CLASS MATCHES

Highest innings total for County: 321 *v*. Kent 1982
Highest innings total against County: 321 for 7 dec. by Kent 1982
Lowest innings total for County: 84 *v*. Combined Services 1947
Lowest innings total against County: 87 by Combined Services 1947
Highest individual innings for County: 118 G.M. Turner *v*. Kent 1982
Highest individual innings against County: 107 M.R. Benson for Kent 1982
Best bowling performance in an innings for County: 5 for 13 R. Howorth *v*. Combined Services 1947
Best bowling performance in an innings against County: 6 for 50 H.A. Gilbert for H.K. Foster's XI 1919
Best bowling performance in a match for County: 8 for 70 R. Howorth *v*. Combined Services 1947
Best bowling performance in a match against County: 12 for 122 H.A. Gilbert for H.K. Foster's XI 1919
Best attendance: 4,000 *v*. Kent 1982

LIMITED-OVERS MATCHES

Highest innings total for County: 233 for 6 *v*. Gloucestershire (JPL) 1986
Highest innings total against County: 230 by Gloucestershire (JPL) 1986
Lowest innings total for County: 195 for 9 *v*. Nottinghamshire (JPL) 1983
Lowest innings total against County: 154 by Surrey (RAL) 1987
Highest individual innings for County: 86 P.A. Neale *v*. Nottinghamshire (JPL) 1983
Highest individual innings against County: 108 R.C. Russell for Gloucestershire (JPL) 1986
Best bowling performance for County: 3 for 23 A.P. Pridgeon *v*. Gloucestershire (JPL) 1986
Best bowling performance against County: 2 for 39 M. Hendrick for Nottinghamshire (JPL) 1983
Best attendance: 7,500 *v*. Surrey (RAL) 1987

HOW TO GET THERE

Rail   Hereford (BR), 1.5 miles.
Bus   Midland Red West Nos 102, 112 from city centre; 104/5, 115 link BR Hereford Station with city centre (Telephone: 0345 212555 – local rate from anywhere in Britain).
Car   From north: A49 or A4110 signposted Hereford and city centre, follow signs Racecourse and Grandstand Road for Hereford Sports Club. From east: A465 or A438 signposted Hereford and city centre, then follow signs Leominster A49 into Grandstand Road.

From west: A438 or A465 signposted Hereford and city centre, then as east. From south: A49 or B4224 or B4399 signposted Hereford and city centre, then as east.

WHERE TO STAY AND OTHER INFORMATION

Green Dragon Hotel (0432 272506), Hereford Moat House Hotel (0432 54301).

Disabled Areas   All areas except pavilion which is up stairs are accessible, although if the weather is poor wheelchairs maybe a problem.
Local Radio Station(s)   Radio Wyvern (102 MHz FM/1530 KHz MW), Severn Sound (95.0 MHz FM/774 KHz MW).
Local Newspaper(s)   Hereford Times.

YORKSHIRE

CHURCHMAN'S CIGARETTES.

YORKSHIRE.

LEEDS – BASS HEADINGLEY

BRADFORD

HARROGATE

MIDDLESBROUGH

SCARBOROUGH

SHEFFIELD

HULL

Yorkshire

Founded   8 January 1863
Colours   Oxford blue, Cambridge blue and gold
Crest   White rose of Yorkshire
Patron   HRH The Duchess of Kent
President   Sir Lawrence Byford CBE, QPM, LLB, DL
Chairman   B. Walsh QC
Chairman cricket committee   D.B. Close CBE
Chief executive   C.D. Hassell
Secretary   D.M. Ryder
Director of cricket   S. Oldham
Club coach   D.E.V. Padgett
Academy coach   M.K. Bore
Captain   M.D. Moxon
Groundsman   K. Boyce
Scorer 1st XI   J.T. Potter
Scorer 2nd XI   W. Petherbridge
Statistician   R.D. Wilkinson
Sponsors   Tetley Bitter
Newsletter   *The White Rose*
Address   Headingley Cricket Ground, St Michael's Lane,
Headingley, Leeds, West Yorkshire LS6 3BU
Telephone 0532 787394
Facsimile 0532 784099
Yorkshire Rapid Cricketline   0891 567518
Test Match Commentaries Rapid Cricketline   0891 567567
Test Match Updates Rapid Cricketline   0891 567555

ACHIEVEMENTS

County Championship   Champions (31) 1867, 1870, 1893, 1896,
1898, 1900, 1901, 1902, 1905, 1908, 1912, 1919, 1922, 1923, 1924,
1925, 1931, 1932, 1933, 1935, 1937, 1938, 1939, 1946, 1959, 1960,
1962, 1963, 1966, 1967 and 1968; joint Champions (2) 1869 and
1949
Gillette Cup   Winners (2) 1965 and 1969
National Westminster Bank Trophy   Semi-finalists (1) 1982
Benson & Hedges Cup   Winners (1) 1987; finalists (1) 1972
John Player Sunday League   Champions (1) 1983
Refuge Assurance Sunday League   6th 1990
Fenner Trophy   Winners (3) 1972, 1974 and 1981; finalists (5)
1973, 1975, 1976, 1978 and 1979
Asda Trophy   Winners (1) 1987; finalists (1) 1984
Ward Four Counties Knockout Competition   Winners (1) 1989;
finalists (1) 1988 Semi-Finalists (1) 1990
Tilcon Trophy   Winners (2) 1978 and 1988 Finalists (2) 1983 and 1990
Joshua Tetley Festival Trophy   Winners (1) 1991

Scarborough C C from the air, reproduced by courtesy of Valentine and Son Ltd

GROUNDS

Leeds (Headingley Cricket Ground, St Michael's Lane); Bradford (Yorkshire Cricket Academy, Park Avenue); Harrogate (Harrogate C C, St George's Road); Middlesbrough (Acklam Park, Green Lane); Scarborough (Scarborough C C, North Marine Road); Sheffield (Abbeydale Park, Abbeydale Park Road South, Dore); Hull (The Circle, Anlaby Road).

Other grounds that have been used since 1969 are: Huddersfield (Fartown); Sheffield (Bramall Lane) and Barnsley (Shaw Lane).

SECOND XI GROUNDS

In addition to the grounds mentioned above the following are used for second XI matches: Bingley and Bingley C C, Wagon Lane, Cottingley Bridge, Bingley. Telephone: 0274 563480; Sheffield United C C, Bawtry Road Ground, Sheffield. Telephone: 0742 431099; Todmordon C C, Centre Vale, Burnley Road, Todmordon. Telephone: 0706 813140; York C C, Clifton Park, Shipton Road, York. Telephone: 0904 623602; Marske-by-Sea C C, Windy Hill Lane, Marske-by-Sea. Telephone: 0642 484361; Elland Cricket Athletic and Bowling Club, Hullen Edge, Elland, Leeds. Telephone: 0422 372682.

BASS HEADINGLEY

M. LEYLAND, YORKSHIRE

Great teams and great players elevated Yorkshire to a place of special eminence in English cricket. To beat Yorkshire was the aim of every county and touring team, and it is a remarkable fact that they did not drop into a double-figure position in the table until 1953 when Hutton was excusably absent, winning the Ashes with the help of Watson, Wardle and Trueman. By far the biggest of the Big Six they won 29 outright championships before a staunchly conservative and principled club was engulfed by internal strife.

In 1983 the unthinkable (at least to older generations) happened with Yorkshire at the bottom, a calamity not offset by the winning of the John Player League. There were also painful defeats in Cup matches by Durham and Shropshire of the Minor Counties. How the mighty had fallen.

For years the white rose was in perennial bloom. Team work, based on principles laid down long ago by the father figure, Lord Hawke, was Yorkshire's hallmark. The powerful Leagues supplied the county with their finest talent, and a loyal public helped to set a pace and standard others toiled to emulate.

All-Yorkshire talent flowed in a never ending stream from decade to decade ... from Emmett, Freeman, Ulyett, Peel, to Hirst, Rhodes, Haigh, the Hon F.S. Jackson, to Sutcliffe, Leyland, Verity, Bowes, to Hutton, Boycott, Illingworth, Trueman. On three occasions Yorkshire had five representatives in a Test team, and it was no idle boast that a strong Yorkshire meant a strong England.

Sheffield was the original starting point, and the rugged individualism of the early times was made into one cohesive force by the guiding hand of Lord Hawke, who, paradoxically, was born in Lincolnshire and broke the unwritten law of 'no outsiders'. 'In the 1880s when I became captain of Yorkshire they were a fine lot,' Hawke once said. 'There were ten drunks and a chapel parson – and he wasn't ordained!'

The 7th Lord Hawke undoubtedly had some of the faults of the

H. SUTCLIFFE, YORKSHIRE

PLAYER'S CIGARETTES

H. VERITY

HOLMES, P.

YORKSHIRE

autocrat, but the disciplinary codes and values he promoted far outlived the twenty-eight years of his captaincy, which produced 8 championships and marked a rise in the standing of his professionals. He introduced winter pay, started a policy whereby the club retained two-thirds of a benefit for investment, and insisted on a more presentable appearance than had been the custom. He was strong enough to sack the England all-rounder Peel, an act which gave the legendary Wilfred Rhodes an early chance to launch a career which brought him 4,187 wickets at 16.71, 39,802 runs and 58 centuries. The last of his home Tests was at the age of 48 when he was recalled for the final Test at The Oval in 1926, and with 4 for 44 in 20 overs played a significant part in the recovery of the Ashes. Three years later he played in four Tests in the West Indies!

Rhodes' partner George Hirst – 'my Georgie' as Hawke called him – is credited with inventing swing bowling, an innovation to raise him to a loftier class. Incredibly in 1906 he scored 2,385 runs and took 208 wickets (2,180 and 203 for Yorkshire), and his career record was 2,739 wickets at 18.72, and 36,323 runs with 60 hundreds. His 14 doubles is surpassed only by Rhodes' 16.

Four all-rounders of the calibre of Rhodes, Hirst, Haigh and Jackson and all the property of one club is something to contemplate, even if 'Jackers' could make only erratic appearances. Jackson, standing as a municipal candidate in Leeds, asked Hirst to speak on his behalf, and when he rose he urged the audience not to vote for him as it would be a bad thing for Yorkshire and England if he got on the council!

Jackson, later an MP and Governor of Bengal, had only one full season for Yorkshire, but he managed to have 33 innings in home Tests and hit 5 centuries. As fine an example for Sutcliffe as Sutcliffe was in the course of time for Hutton. Sutcliffe and Holmes had first-wicket partnerships of 100 or more sixty-nine times, and broke the record of 554 set up by their predecessors, Brown and Tunnicliffe, by one run. Or did they? Sutcliffe unwisely gave his wicket away when the Leyton scoreboard showed 555, but the scorers declared the total to be 554. Amid the ensuing panic a no-ball, not recorded, was conveniently discovered and the new record was accepted.

Immaculate and assured, Sutcliffe epitomized Yorkshire power which reached its zenith between 1931, the first of two successive seasons in which he exceeded 3,000 runs, and 1939. In all but two of those seasons Yorkshire were champions, and many of the 153 victories were achieved inside two days. The batting of Sutcliffe, Leyland, Holmes, Mitchell, the magnificent catcher, and Barber, and the bowling of Bowes, Verity, Macaulay and all-rounder Smailes was supreme. Hutton was schooled in an academy of cricket wisdom. Its teachings were never forgotten.

During the fateful September weekend of 1939, Hutton and Yardley scored centuries, and Verity, to die from battle wounds in an Italian PoW camp, took 7 for 9 as Sussex were dismissed for 33. As the world plunged into war Yorkshire confirmed their third successive title, and on the way home a last supper was held at Leicester. Time was to show how much of Yorkshire's pride and spirit – so often accepted as their most precious ingredients – disappeared with the break-up of a celebrated team.

Hutton returned in 1946 with an injured left arm and a 50 per cent disability pension, but overcame his handicap to remain a supreme batsman and be knighted and appointed the first pro captain of England, in the twentieth century. Not the least of his triumphs was to rise above the ritual snobbery of the diehards unable to come to terms with a new order.

Sellers took Yorkshire to the top again in the first post-war season, and Burnet, installed as a disciplinarian, did the same in 1959. Vic Wilson, the county's first pro captain, retained the title, and the reign of the combative Close was like old times with four championships and the Gillette Cup twice, but he left for Somerset after an avoidable clash with authority, and Illingworth went to Leicestershire when he was refused more than a one-year contract. Clearly both still had much to offer, and some trace their departure as the starting point of Yorkshire's internal bust-up.

The complex Boycott, with 48,426 runs and 151 centuries was unarguably the champion batsman of his time, but he spent eight years as captain without winning anything, and, with Botham, was the most discussed figure in thirty years of English cricket. His finest hour was to complete his 100th century in a Test with Australia on his home ground of Leeds following three years of self-imposed exile from Test cricket.

Not even the return of Illingworth as manager produced results or harmony in the dressing room, and public frustration concentrated around Boycott, seen as an idol and a symbol of a glorious past. Emotions erupted when Yorkshire finished bottom in 1983 and, with the decision to concentrate on a youth policy, Boycott was sacked. Morale was rock bottom, and the pro-Boycott lobby conducted a campaign against the club officials which the *Sunday Telegraph* observed would not have shamed a by-election. After a long and bitter wrangle a special meeting ousted the general and cricket committees and backed Boycott's reinstatement. By a majority vote his contract was finally ended at the end of the 1986 season. His record in the championship was 29,485 runs, averaging 58.27.

The desperation of Yorkshire's uncertainty was reflected in the turnover of captains – Carrick providing the best hope of a brighter future with the Benson & Hedges Cup 1987 – but there was no tangible improvement in the championship.

Basically Yorkshire's decline is due to their cherished policy – massively endorsed in opinion polls – of fielding a genuine Yorkshire team. The other sixteen clubs have the pick of the world. The local Leagues have also gone over to limited-over cricket to the detriment of spin. Once Yorkshire spin was a source of immense strength, but a shortage over the past decades is a significant cause of their problems.

The Yorkshire Academy of Cricket at Bradford Park Avenue has produced a number of young players who have been introduced into the county team including Batty, Kellett, Gough, White, Chapman, Grayson and Broadhurst. The departure of Bairstow and Love at the end of the 1990 season has allowed for the younger players to take centre stage under the captaincy of Martin Moxon. The Yorkshire team will be welcoming the county's first overseas player in 1992, thereby breaking a club tradition.

Leeds – Bass Headingley

Leeds is not the original headquarters of Yorkshire cricket; its first centre was at Bramall Lane, Sheffield from 1863 to 1888, when a group of wealthy developers who were also sportsmen joined together to buy lot 17a, a plot of land in the north-west of the City of Leeds, at an auction of land by the Cardigan Estate. The gentlemen formed the Leeds Cricket, Football and Athletic Company Limited. Their chairman was Lord Hawke who himself captained Yorkshire C C C from 1883 to 1910. The purchase was the first major step towards the establishment of the County's headquarters at Headingley Cricket Ground.

Cricket and rugby football have been played at Headingley since 1890 when the first important match here was staged between the North and the touring Australians. The next year saw Yorkshire's initial first-class match on the ground against Kent and in 1899 Headingley staged its first Test Match between England and Australia. The majority of Yorkshire C C C matches are staged at Headingley and the ground is still owned by the Leeds Cricket, Football and Athletic Company Limited. Yorkshire C C C moved its headquarters to the City of Leeds in 1903; the county club previously leased offices in Park Road and now leases its administration offices and changing facilities, built in 1962 in the north-east corner of the ground, from the Leeds club at Headingley.

Much of the development at Headingley was undertaken by Sir Edwin Airey, a local building contractor who in 1932 undertook improvements

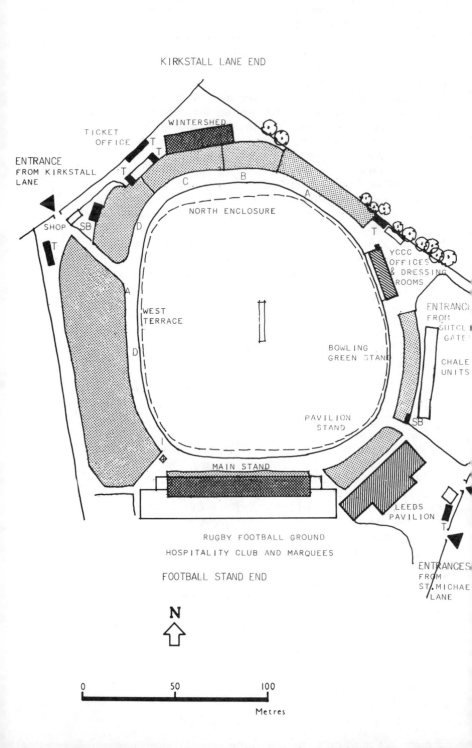

KIRKSTALL LANE END

TICKET
OFFICE

WINTERSHED

ENTRANCE
FROM KIRKSTALL
LANE

SHOP   SB

T

C   B

A

D

NORTH ENCLOSURE

YCCC
OFFICES
& DRESSING
ROOMS

A

D

WEST
TERRACE

ENTRANCE
FROM
SUTCLIFFE
GATE

CHALET
UNITS

BOWLING
GREEN STAND

PAVILION
STAND

SB

MAIN STAND

LEEDS
PAVILION

RUGBY FOOTBALL GROUND

HOSPITALITY CLUB AND MARQUEES

FOOTBALL STAND END

ENTRANCES
FROM
ST. MICHAEL
LANE

N

0   50   100

Metres

designed to establish Headingley as a major cricketing venue. The dual-purpose Football or Main Stand stretches along the southern boundary of the field and from it one can view the cricket to the north or rugby league football to the south, for Headingley is also the home of the Leeds Rugby League Football Club. The Leeds pavilion is the oldest building on the ground and houses the Leeds office, the scorers' room and the computerized scoreboard operators equipment. There is also a number of hospitality areas, restaurants and bars for use by members and sponsors. Other additions have included the Kirkstall Lane End and the Winter Shed Stand which contains executive boxes and ample seating. All seating is of the plastic tip-up variety throughout the ground, in the vast West Terrace and North Enclosure areas. In recent years the computerized scoreboard has been installed, sponsored by the Scottish and Newcastle Brewery and it is operated by members of the York University staff throughout the season. The Sutcliffe Gates in St Michael's Lane form the main entrance to the ground; just opposite is the newly constructed Yorkshire Indoor Cricket School and county library. There are many historic photographs in the old Leeds pavilion and in the bars and the new indoor cricket school. Yorkshire C C C are planning to build a museum at the ground to house the cricketing history of the white rose county in the near future.

Headingley is to be refurbished by a £2.5m improvement programme announced in 1989 and this is hoped to improve all facilities and make Headingley the 'Wembley' of the north. A large executive and hospitality complex is planned for the top level of a restructed Main Stand with additional new seating. Since 1989 only seating of the plastic tip-up variety has been installed and in 1991 the Kilburn Press Gallery opened, located on the ground floor of the main stand behind the bowlers arm at the Football Stand End. The new press box was opened on the morning of the Test Match between England and the West Indies by former Yorkshire Post cricket writer Jim Kilburn. The ground was renamed Bass Headingley in 1990 after the brewery had put money into sponsoring the ground improvements.

Crowds at Headingley are usually 8,000–10,000 for popular county matches. The present ground capacity is set at 20,000 and this is achieved for most Test Matches and one-day internationals. The record attendance for a county match over three days was 44,507 against Lancashire in 1948 and for a single day 30,000 for the England and Australia Test Match of 1948. The ground has been used for all the major county cricket competitions together with Prudential Trophy, Prudential World Cup and Texaco Trophy one-day international matches. Achievements on the field at Headingley include Geoffrey Boycott's 100th hundred scored in a Test Match against Australia in 1977 in front of his home public. Big scores have included innings from Don Bradman, Herbert Sutcliffe, Allan Lamb and John Edrich. Spectators will recall a day of pure genius from Ian Botham who put England on the way to regaining the Ashes in 1981 under the captaincy of Mike Brearley at Leeds. Significant bowling performances over the years have been achieved by Colin Blythe, Hedley Verity, Richard Peel,

Richard Hutton and Bob Willis. Headingley spectators have also seen some strange sights on the ground including the George Davis protests in 1975, the burst pipe episode with Curtley Ambrose and Dickie Bird in 1988, and the usual occurrence of streakers and eccentric crowd behaviour 'Mexican Wave' Yorkshire style.

ADDRESS The Pavilion, Headingley Cricket Ground, St Michael's Lane, Leeds, West Yorkshire LS6 3BR.

TELEPHONE NUMBER PROSPECTS OF PLAY 0532 787394

DESCRIPTION OF GROUND AND FACILITIES

Entry to the ground for members is from St Michael's Lane through the Main Gates or the Sutcliffe Gates, while the public gains access from Kirkstall Lane. All buildings are permanent with the exception of the hospitality boxes erected on the east side of the ground for Test Matches and other international matches. The members' pavilion is in the south-east corner of the ground and is separated from the players' pavilion and club offices which are situated on the north-east side of the ground. On the south side of the ground is the Main Stand which provides the only covered seating area on the ground and from where you can view rugby football during the winter months. The members' enclosure includes part of the Main Stand, the pavilion and seating around the ground to the Winter Shed stand to the north of the playing area. The western terraces and part of the north enclosure and main stand are available to the public. Some car parking is available in the south stand car park, but this is limited on international match days, and car parking must be found in the adjoining streets, or the local authority parking areas at Beckett Park and Woodhouse Moor. Members' car parking is available off St Michael's Lane on the practice area of the Leeds RFC although for international matches tickets have to be obtained in advance to gain entry. Bar service and refreshments are available in various parts of the ground, for members in the pavilion and for the public in small kiosks and facilities in the Winter Shed Stand and the Grandstand bar in the Main Stand. Facilities are available for disabled spectators and they should request a suitable position either adjoining the players' pavilion or a place close to the ringside seats on the walkway which surrounds the playing area. The playing area is oval in shape and measures 137 metres by 140 metres and is defined by advertising boards. However the actual playing area for a match is defined by a rope within the boards and this provides an area of approximately 130 metres by 134 metres subject to the location of the wicket. The covers are kept in the space available on the north side of the ground. Although most of the ground provides two rows of seats immediately outside the boundary boards (ringside seats), the ground has a 5-metre walkway round it, behind these two rows of seats and in front of the terraces of white plastic tip-up seating. This can be very distracting to those who choose to sit in the front rows of the tiered seating with spectators always walking in front of you and these should therefore be avoided.

The main scoreboard which is electronic is sited on the north-west side of the ground and to the rear is the new White Rose Yorkshire C C C souvenir shop. There is an additional smaller shop next to the players' pavilion in a small van and a secondary smaller traditional scoreboard close to the pavilion. The Yorkshire C C C Supporters' Club caravan is sited near the betting tent. The present ground capacity is 20,000 and seats are available for all. As a Test match venue, Headingley has all the facilities one would expect.

GROUND RECORDS AND SCORES

TEST MATCHES

Highest innings total for England: 550 for 4 v. India 1967
Highest innings total against England: 601 for 7 dec. by Australia 1989
Lowest innings total for England: 76 v. South Africa 1907
Lowest innings total against England: 67 by New Zealand 1958
Highest individual innings for England: 310 n.o. J.H. Edrich v. New Zealand 1965
Highest individual innings against England: 334 D.G. Bradman for Australia 1930
Best bowling performance in an innings for England: 8 for 43 R.G.D. Willis v. Australia 1981
Best bowling performance in an innings against England: 7 for 40 Imran Khan for Pakistan 1987
Best bowling performance in a match for England: 15 for 99 C. Blythe v. South Africa 1907
Best bowling performance in a match against England: 11 for 87 C.G. Macartney for Australia 1909
Record attendance: 30,000 v. Australia 1948

LIMITED-OVERS INTERNATIONALS

Highest innings total: 298 for 9 by New Zealand v. England (TT) 1990
Lowest innings total: 93 by England v. Australia (PC) 1975
Highest individual innings: 128 R.A. Smith for England v. New Zealand (TT) 1990
Best bowling performance: 7 for 51 W.W. Davis for West Indies v. Australia (PC) 1983

FIRST-CLASS MATCHES

Highest innings total for County: 560 for 6 dec. v. Leicestershire 1921
Highest innings total against County: 630 by Somerset 1901
Lowest innings total for County: 33 v. Lancashire 1924
Lowest innings total against County: 23 by Australians 1902
Highest individual innings for County: 270 H. Sutcliffe v. Sussex 1932
Highest individual innings against County: 235 A.J. Lamb for Northamptonshire 1990

Best bowling performance in an innings for County: 10 for 10 H. Verity *v*. Nottinghamshire 1932
Best bowling performance in an innings against County: 9 for 57 F.A. Tarrant for Middlesex 1906
Best bowling performance in a match for County: 15 for 50 R. Peel *v*. Somerset 1895
Best bowling performance in a match against County: 15 for 154 T. Richardson for Surrey 1897
Best attendance: 44,507 *v*. Lancashire 1948

LIMITED-OVERS MATCHES
Highest innings total for County: 317 for 5 *v*. Scotland (BHC) 1986
Highest innings total against County: 297 for 3 by Australians (Tour) 1989
Lowest innings total for County: 109 *v*. Leicestershire (GC) 1975
Lowest innings total against County: 23 by Middlesex (JPL) 1974
Highest individual innings for County: 127 n.o. A.A. Metcalfe *v*. Warwickshire (NWBT) 1990
Highest individual innings against County: 172 D.C. Boon for Australians (Tour) 1989
Best bowling performance for County: 7 for 15 R.A. Hutton *v*. Worcestershire (JPL) 1969
Best bowling performance against County: 5 for 33 B.J. Griffiths for Northamptonshire (NWBT) 1983
Best attendance: 9,500 *v*. Warwickshire (BHC) 1987

HOW TO GET THERE

Rail   Headingley (BR), 0.5 mile; Leeds Central (BR), 2.5 miles.
Bus   Yorkshire Rider 74–77 link BR Leeds Central with ground; also 1, 4, 56, 93 and 96 from city centre pass ground and 38, 39, 93 and 96 from city suburbs pass ground (Telephone: 0532 457676).
Car   From north: A660, A61 or A58, follow signs Leeds and city centre, then follow signs Kirkstall district and Headingley for County Cricket and Headingley Cricket Ground; turning off A660, the ground is situated to the north-west of the city centre about 1.5 miles and west of the A660. From east: A64, A63 or M62 and M1 follow signs Leeds and city centre, then follow signs Kirkstall district and Headingley on A660 for Headingley Cricket Ground. From west: A58, A62, A647 or M62 and M621 follow signs Leeds and city centre, then follow signs Kirkstall district and Headingley on A660 for Headingley Cricket Ground. From south: A653, A61 or M1 to junction 43, then follow A61 Leeds and city centre, then follow signs Kirkstall district and Headingley on A660, 1.5 miles north-west of city centre for Headingley Cricket Ground.

WHERE TO STAY AND OTHER INFORMATION

Queen's Hotel (0532 431323), Golden Lion Hotel (0532 436454),

Forte Post House Leeds/Bramhope (0532 842911), The Metropole (0532 45081).

Disabled Areas   In special designated areas or by arrangement in advance.
Local Radio Station(s)   BBC Radio Leeds (95.3 MHz FM/774 KHz MW), Radio Aire (96.3 MHz FM/828 KHz MW).
Local Newspaper(s)   Yorkshire Post, Yorkshire Evening Press, Leeds Weekly News, Bradford Telegraph & News.

Bradford

Yorkshire C C C have played at two venues in Bradford, the first ground was at Great Horton Road (also known as Easby Road) between 1863 and 1874. The first match was on 22–24 June 1863 against Notting-hamshire with the last match being staged on 10–12 August 1874 with Lancashire. Seven years later in 1881 Yorkshire C C C played their first match at Horton Park Avenue, known today as Bradford Park Avenue on 13–15 June 1881 against Kent, and after 104 years the link with this venue situated to the south of the city centre ceased after the last match on 31 July, 1–2 August 1985 against Derbyshire. This was due to the burden of ground maintenance and the improvements required to the ground and facilities in light of the Taylor Report after the Bradford Fire at Bradford City's Valley Parade football ground. The last match staged by Yorkshire C C C on the ground was a limited-overs match with Surrey on 14 July 1985 in the John Player Sunday League which produced a few records for the ground. Yorkshire C C C will play their first match at Bradford for seven years when Surrey will again be the visitors in August 1992 for a Britannic Assurance County Champion-ship match. The Yorkshire Cricket historian Tony Woodhouse hoped 'that Park Avenue will continue to be the scene of exciting cricket in the old traditions of the game', and it certainly looks that this may be the case with Yorkshire making a return in 1992.

Just as soon as cricket ceased being played at Bradford a Society was formed, named The Friends of Park Avenue, to win back first-class status to this historic Yorkshire venue. The Society has staged many fund raising events. The president of the Society is Brian Close, and thanks to support from this Society and the Yorkshire C C C the Yorkshire Academy of Cricket (YAC) was founded on 15 May 1989. The ground is owned by Bradford Metropolitan Council and they offered considerable support to this venture with a 999-year lease at nominal rent, £15,000 per annum for five years towards upkeep of the grounds and £40,000 towards ground improvements. A further £60,000 has been obtained from sponsorship, donations and other fund raising activities. On 7 June 1989 the chairman of the England Test selectors Ted Dexter named an Intercity 125 Power Car locomotive 'Yorkshire Academy of Cricket' at Leeds Central Station. The Director of YAC is

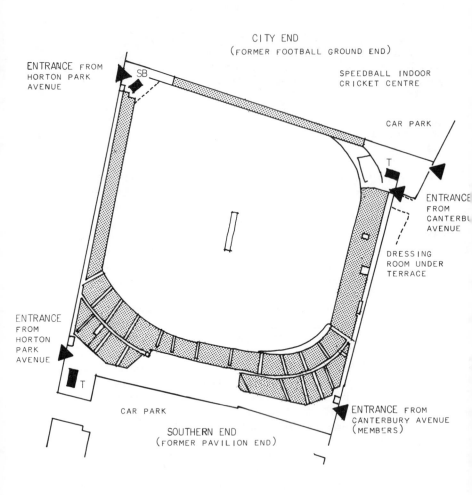

CITY END
(FORMER FOOTBALL GROUND END)

ENTRANCE FROM
HORTON PARK
AVENUE

SB

SPEEDBALL INDOOR
CRICKET CENTRE

CAR PARK

T

ENTRANCE
FROM
CANTERBU
AVENUE

DRESSING
ROOM UNDER
TERRACE

ENTRANCE
FROM
HORTON
PARK
AVENUE

T

CAR PARK

ENTRANCE FROM
CANTERBURY AVENUE
(MEMBERS)

SOUTHERN END
(FORMER PAVILION END)

N

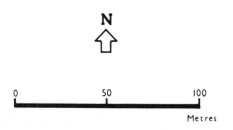

0   50   100

Metres

Mike Bore the former Yorkshire and Nottinghamshire player.

YAC play a number of matches against local universities, cricket clubs, league XIs, club touring Teams, colleges and county second XIs throughout the season from April to September at Bradford Park Avenue. In the winter of 1990–91 new changing rooms and refreshment facilities were built, together with six new pitches. Six more pitches have been laid, during the winter of 1991–92 ready for the 1992 season. Players who have represented the YAC include: Jeremy Batty, Matthew Doidge, Darren Gough, Paul Grayson and Stuart Milburn, amongst others.

To many supporters, Bradford Park Avenue was the ideal Yorkshire home venue, with its splendid old Victorian pavilion together with ample bench seating on raised concrete whitewashed terracing. The ground was previously adjoining the football ground of Bradford Park Avenue F C, which has since been demolished, and at one end is the privately owned Speedball Indoor Cricket Centre, in a large industrial unit/warehouse. The pavilion, football stand and most of the outbuildings were demolished during the winter of 1987–88. The only permanent structures which remain are the concrete terraces, scoreboard and groundsman's stores. Any visitor who has memories of Park Avenue in the last 10–15 years, will be rather surprised by the nature of the present ground, which has lost all of its past charm. The ground capacity was 20,000 although the largest crowd was 30,790 when the county played Gloucestershire in 1947. The playing area is rather small and over the years some spinners have always found it difficult to contain a batsman in full flow on this ground. The old Pavilion End of the ground has been cleared and levelled to create ample car parking space for members.

Three centuries were scored in an innings against Middlesex in 1899: F.S. Jackson (155), D. Denton (113) and F. Mitchell (121). The Yorkshire ninth-wicket record partnership of 192 was recorded on the ground in 1898 by G.H. Hirst (130 n.o.) and S. Haigh (85) against Surrey. Ground records at Bradford include performances by some famous players of the past: Percy Holmes, C.B. Fry, E.Robinson, Hedley Verity, A.E. Thomas and George Tribe. In the limited-overs game records belong to Jim Love, Monte Lynch, Tony Nicholson, and Ray Illingworth against his former county. Bradford Park Avenue was Sir Leonard Hutton's favourite ground.

ADDRESS   The Yorkshire Academy of Cricket, Bradford Park Avenue Cricket Ground, Canterbury Avenue, Bradford, West Yorkshire.
TELEPHONE NUMBER PROSPECTS OF PLAY   0274 391564

DESCRIPTION OF GROUND AND FACILITIES

The ground is entered from Canterbury Avenue where there are two entrances. Two further pedestrian entrances are available in Horton Park Avenue. Car parking is available at the southern end and in the car park of the Yorkshire Cricket Academy to the north-east of the playing area. The former pavilion has since been demolished and this area is now used for members' car parking and sponsors' marquees. The only remaining structure is the scoreboard and groundsman's store which is located in the northern corner of the ground. The concrete terracing which has been whitewashed remains and this is where the majority of the temporary seating is positioned for matches. Some refreshment tents are available at the former Football Stand End (City End). The TV camera/commentary box and radio commentary positions are located at the former Pavilion End. There are new changing facilities, a members' bar and refreshment facilities available beneath the east terrace, together with ample toilet facilities around the ground. At the City End there are a number of temporary buildings which include a tea room and store; the Yorkshire C C C souvenir shop is located here in a small van. The members' enclosure is likely to comprise the east and south-east terrace with the rest of the ground available to the public.

The playing area at the southern end is approximately six feet higher than that at the northern end so there is a gentle fall towards the Speedball Indoor Cricket Centre building and former Bradford Park Avenue Football Ground which is now derelict. The playing area is 124 metres by 130 metres and is defined by a rope, whitewashed wall and some advertising boards.

GROUND RECORDS AND SCORES

FIRST-CLASS MATCHES
Highest innings total for County: 590 v. Lancashire 1887
Highest innings total against County: 558 for 8 dec. by Sussex 1903
Lowest innings total for County: 40 v. Lancashire 1932/Kent 1967
Lowest innings total against County: 43 by Somerset 1930
Highest individual innings for County: 275 P. Holmes v. Warwickshire 1928
Highest individual innings against County: 234 C.B. Fry for Sussex 1903
Best bowling performance in an innings for County: 9 for 36 E. Robinson v. Lancashire 1920
Best bowling performance in an innings against County: 9 for 30 A.E. Thomas for Northamptonshire 1920
Best bowling performance in a match for County: 14 for 68 H. Verity v. Glamorgan 1939
Best bowling performance in a match against County: 15 for 75 G.E. Tribe for Northamptonshire 1955
Best attendance: 30,790 v. Gloucestershire 1947.

LIMITED-OVERS MATCHES
Highest innings total for County: 263 for 8 v. Surrey (JPL) 1985
Highest innings total against County: 262 for 6 by Surrey (JPL) 1985
Lowest innings total for County: 122 for 9 v. Surrey (BHC) 1976
Lowest innings total against County: 66 by Nottinghamshire (JPL) 1969
Highest individual innings for County: 118 n.o. J.D. Love v. Scotland (BHC) 1981

Highest individual innings against County: 136 M.A. Lynch for Surrey (JPL) 1985
Best bowling performance for County: 5 for 24 A.G. Nicholson *v.* Derbyshire (BHC) 1975
Best bowling performance against County: 5 for 31 R. Illingworth for Leicestershire (JPL) 1977
Best attendance: 8,000 *v.* Nottinghamshire (GC) 1969

HOW TO GET THERE

Rail Bradford (BR), 1.25 mile.
Bus Yorkshire Rider Buses from surrounding areas to Bradford Bus Station, thence approximately 0.75 miles to ground (Telephone: 0532 457676).
Car From north: A650, A6038 or A658 signposted Bradford and city centre then follow signs for Halifax; the ground is situated to the south-west of the city centre and is located off Great Horton Road A647 to Halifax. From west: A647, B6145, A6025 or M62 junction 26, then M606, then follow signs Bradford and city centre, then A647 for ground. From east: A647, A650, A6120 or M62 junction 26 then M606, then follow signs Bradford and city centre, then as north. From south: M1 junction 42, then follow M62 junction 26, then M606, then follow signs Bradford and city centre, then as north or A650, A641, A638 or A6036 signposted Bradford and city centre, then as north.

WHERE TO STAY AND OTHER INFORMATION

Norfolk Gardens Hotel (0274 734734), Victoria Hotel (0274 728706).

Disabled Areas No special area, request suitable position at City End adjoining scoreboard.
Local Radio Station(s) BBC Radio Leeds (95.3 MHz FM/774 KHz MW), Radio Aire (96.3 MHz FM/828 KHz MW).
Local Newspaper(s) Yorkshire Post, Yorkshire Evening Press, Bradford Telegraph and Argus.

Harrogate

The St. George's Road Ground has been the home of Harrogate Cricket Club since its foundation in 1877. The initial first-class match staged here was in 1882 when an England XI played the touring Australians. The match was the first in England to be started on a Saturday. The first County Championship fixture at Harrogate was staged in 1894 when Yorkshire C C C's opponents were Leicestershire.

The main pavilion for players and members was built in 1896, the Mound Stand in 1956 and the Tavern bar and restaurant in 1965. The ground was for many years owned by Harrogate Cricket Club but in 1936, during a difficult period in the club's history, the ground was purchased by the Harrogate Corporation, which still owns it.

Harrogate's pride and joy was of course Maurice Leyland, who represented his home town club Harrogate C C, Yorkshire C C C and England and was undoubtedly the finest local player ever produced. Appropriately, the Leyland Gates welcome you at one of the ground's entrances, which is approached from St Marks Avenue. The gates were erected in 1965, two years before Leyland's death. The Centenary Gates, erected in 1977, form the main entrance to the ground from St George's Road.

Attempts were made to establish an annual cricket festival at Harrogate in 1913, 1925 and 1947, but this was discontinued each time after one year due to poor support. It was not until 1974 that a regular Harrogate Cricket Festival was successfully launched; since then it has consisted of a Yorkshire C C C County Championship match together with a three-day knockout competition for the Tilcon Trophy. This is played under identical rules to that of the Benson & Hedges Cup, by four counties invited by Tilcon from those counties not involved in the Benson & Hedges Cup semi-final round. The Harrogate festival week is usually in mid-June and daily crowds of 4,000–5,000 can be expected. The ground is used for private company matches, and for Harrogate C C engagements; the club play in the Yorkshire Cricket League fielding three XIs and the ladies' matches played during mid-week.

The best crowd for a single day was 15,000 when India played Pakistan in 1986 for the charity Help the Aged. The best attendance for a Yorkshire C C C match was 13,630 in 1962 for the County Championship match with Glamorgan. In addition to championship matches, Yorkshire C C C have staged tour matches and other friendly matches with the 1901 South Africans, 1906, 1933 and 1939 West Indians, 1932 Indians and 1931 New Zealanders. Limited-overs matches have been staged in the John Player Sunday League 1969–71 and the Gillette Cup in 1970 and 1973. Durham, then a minor county, beat Yorkshire by 5 wickets in the 1973 Gillette Cup match staged at St George's Road Ground and became the first minor county to beat a first-class county in this particular competition. On 14 June 1991 a royal visit to St George's Cricket Ground was made by HRH The Duchess of Kent – 25 years as Patroness of Yorkshire C C C – when the County Championship match in progress was with Kent. Percy Holmes and Vivian Richards have both hit double centuries here and wickets have been taken to great effect by G.G. Macaulay and Ray Illingworth for the home county and F.E. Field and E.G. Dennett for the visitors.

Ground records in the Tilcon Trophy competition belong to Darren Bicknell with the bat and, with the ball, Phil Bainbridge while playing for Gloucestershire, his former county. Robin Jackman took 7 wickets for 33 for Surrey in the first Gillette Cup match staged on the ground in 1970.

Many Harrogate C C players besides Maurice Leyland have represented Yorkshire C C C; they include: A. Booth, J.H. Hampshire (now

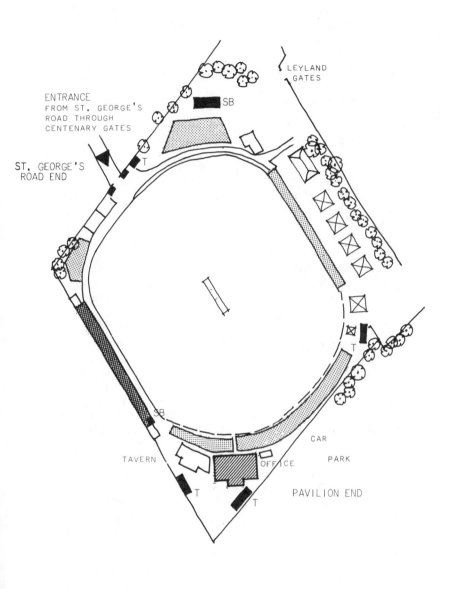

ENTRANCE
FROM ST. GEORGE'S
ROAD THROUGH
CENTENARY GATES

ST. GEORGE'S
ROAD END

LEYLAND
GATES

SB

T

SB

TAVERN

OFFICE

CAR

PARK

PAVILION END

T

T

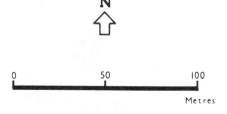

N

0   50   100

Metres

first-class umpire), R. Kilner, G.G. Macaulay, T.F. Smailes, H. Wilkinson and J.D. Love (now captain of minor county Lincolnshire C C C). County cricketers to have represented Harrogate C C after retiring from the first-class game have included: W.E. Bates, B.S. Boshier, J.T. Brown, G.R. Cass, Lord Hawke, W.B. Stott, W.H.H. Sutcliffe, F.S. Trueman and N.W.D. Yardley.

ADDRESS   Harrogate Cricket Club, The Pavilion, St George's Cricket Ground, St George's Road, Harrogate, North Yorkshire.
TELEPHONE NUMBER PROSPECTS OF PLAY   0423 561301

DESCRIPTION OF GROUND AND FACILITIES

The main access to the ground is from St George's Road at its junction with West End Avenue, through the Centenary Gates.

The playing area is bounded by permanent terraces on three sides. The western side is a partly covered stand. The two storey pavilion, hospitality suite, scorers' room and press room, which is in the roof of the pavilion, and Tavern bar and restaurant buildings are in the south corner of the ground and, with the adjoining terraces, provide the accommodation for members. The main scoreboard is in the north corner of the ground directly opposite the pavilion. The east side of the ground has only a few rows of bench seats and there is adequate space for the provision of hospitality tents. Refreshment facilities are available for the public by the covered stand and near the scoreboard. Limited car parking is available at the ground and one should therefore try to park in the adjoining streets.

The playing area is approximately 118 metres by 140 metres and is open except at the north and west sides of the ground, where, similar to Headingley, there is a walkway between the playing area and the spectators. Some bench seating is situated at ground level around the perimeter of the playing area. The ground capacity is 8,000 and seating is provided for 65 per cent of this number. There is no special provision for disabled spectators but access is unencumbered and they should ask for an appropriate position at the northern end close to the sightscreen. The Yorkshire C C C White Rose souvenir shop is located close to the main entrance and Centenary Gates. This is a ground which encourages the watching of cricket and for an out ground the facilities are good.

GROUND RECORDS AND SCORES

FIRST-CLASS MATCHES
Highest innings total for County: 548 for 4 *v*. Northamptonshire 1921
Highest innings total against County: 439 by Derbyshire 1984
Lowest innings total for County: 50 *v*. West Indians 1906
Lowest innings total against County: 42 by Worcestershire 1923
Highest individual innings for County: 277 n.o. P. Holmes *v*. Northamptonshire 1921

Highest individual innings against County: 217 n.o. I.V.A. Richards for Somerset 1975
Best bowling performance in an innings for County: 8 for 21 G.G. Macaulay *v*. Indians 1932
Best bowling performance in an innings against County: 7 for 20 F.E. Field for Warwickshire 1911
Best bowling performance in a match for County: 14 for 64 R. Illingworth *v*. Gloucestershire 1967
Best bowling performance in a match against County: 12 for 176 E.G. Dennett for Gloucestershire 1907
Best attendance: 13,630 *v*. Glamorgan 1962

LIMITED-OVERS MATCHES
Highest innings total for County: 174 for 4 *v*. Derbyshire (JPL) 1971
Highest innings total against County: 177 for 9 by Derbyshire (JPL) 1971
Lowest innings total for County: 76 *v*. Surrey (GC) 1970
Lowest innings total against County: 134 for 8 by Surrey (GC) 1970
Highest individual innings for County: 55 A.J. Dalton *v*. Derbyshire (JPL) 1971
Highest individual innings against County: 47 R. Inglis for Durham (GC) 1973
Best bowling performance for County: 4 for 38 C.M. Old *v*. Derbyshire (JPL) 1971
Best bowling performance against County: 7 for 33 R.D. Jackman for Surrey (GC) 1970
Best attendance: 15,000 India *v*. Pakistan (Help the Aged Charity Match) 1986

TILCON TROPHY COMPETITION (TTC)
Highest innings total: 336 by Northamptonshire *v*. Glamorgan 1981
Lowest innings total: 58 by Nottinghamshire *v*. Surrey 1978
Highest individual innings: 149 n.o. D.J. Bicknell for Surrey *v*. Durham 1991
Best bowling performance: 6 for 38 P. Bainbridge for Gloucestershire *v*. Leicestershire 1986

HOW TO GET THERE

Rail   Harrogate (BR), 1.25 mile.
Bus   Harrogate & District 36, 653 from BR Harrogate Station–Leeds/Bradford pass end of St George's Road (Telephone: 0423 66061).
Car   From north: A1 and A6055 signposted Harrogate or A61 to town centre; the St George's Cricket Ground is situated about 0.5 mile south of the town centre, off the A61 to Leeds. From east: A59 follow signs Harrogate and town centre, then follow A61 south for St George's Cricket Ground off the Leeds road, signpost for ground located in centre of roundabout. From west: A59 or B6162 follow signs Harrogate and town centre, then as east. From south: A1 and A661 signposted Harrogate or A61 then as north or east.

WHERE TO STAY AND OTHER INFORMATION

Crown Hotel (0423 67755), Prospect Hotel (0423 65071), Majestic (0423 68972).

Disabled Areas   No special area, request suitable position on walkway at northern end of ground.
Local Radio Station(s)   BBC Radio York (95.5 MHz FM/1260 KHz MW).
Local Newspaper(s)   Yorkshire Post, Yorkshire Evening Press, Harrogate Herald.

Middlesbrough

Acklam Park in Green Lane is the home of Middlesbrough Cricket Club, founded in 1875 and has been the club's home ground since 1932. The third ground to be used by Yorkshire C CC in Middlesbrough, Cleveland, it is situated in the pleasant suburb of Acklam on the southern outskirts of the town. The ground is one of two situated outside Yorkshire used for first-class cricket, the other is Hull in Humberside. Middlesbrough until the entry of Durham C C C in 1992 was the most northerly venue used for County Championship cricket in the country. Middlesbrough Cricket Club play in the North Yorkshire and South Durham Cricket League and field three XIs throughout the summer.

The ground of 12 acres comprises not only the main cricket ground but two full size rugby football pitches, 12 grass practice wickets and two all-weather practice wickets. The whole ground is in excellent condition and the pavilion, which is at right angles to the wicket, includes changing rooms, baths and a large dining room over-looking the playing area. The rear of the pavilion is the clubhouse which has two attractively furnished bars. The scorebox is modern and fully automatic; it is built on two levels, the lower being a garage store area for the groundsman's equipment.

The first-class County Championship Yorkshire C C C match at Acklam Park was in 1956 against Glamorgan when some 9,423 people attended the first two days of the match; the third day was abandoned due to poor weather. The groundsman in 1956 said of Middlesbrough, 'You won't find a better pitch in Yorkshire', but the County Club would probably not fully agree with this statement as a few years later, in 1965, Hampshire, the visitors bowled Yorkshire all out for just 23, the lowest ever completed innings by the county. Yorkshire C C C usually play four days' cricket at Middlesbrough in the early part of the season comprising one County Championship and one limited-overs Sunday League match.

The first organized cricket match in Middlesbrough was in 1844, promoted by William Taylor for members of the Mechanics Institute. From this was established the nucleus of Middlesbrough C C The first

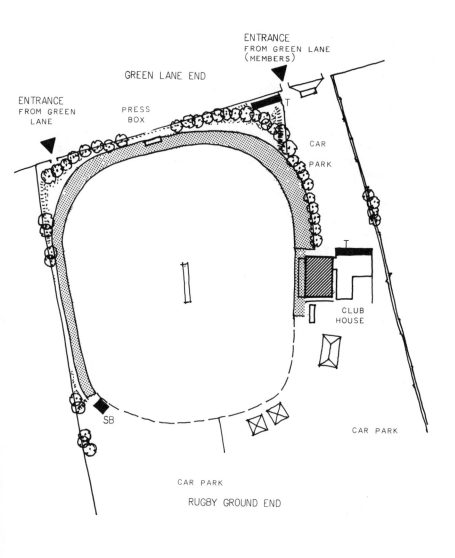

ENTRANCE
FROM GREEN LANE
(MEMBERS)

GREEN LANE END

ENTRANCE
FROM GREEN
LANE

PRESS
BOX

T

CAR
PARK

CLUB
HOUSE

SB

CAR PARK

CAR PARK

RUGBY GROUND END

N

0   50   100

Metres

ground was at Albert Road, where Yorkshire C C C staged matches between 1864 and 1867; this ground is now the site of the Royal Exchange. In 1871 the club moved to Swatters Carr or Kipling's Farm, known today as Linthorpe Road, where it stayed until its move to Breckon Hill in 1900. Yorkshire C C C played one match at Linthorpe Road against the touring Australians in 1882; soon after the ground was occupied by Middlesbrough Football Club until their move to their present home Ayresome Park. The ground is now the site of St George's Church. The club only played at Breckon Hill until 1911 when it moved once again, this time to North Ormesby. After twenty-one years they moved to their present ground when Middlesbrough C C joined forces with the town's rugby football club. They continue to share the same facilities and ground. The pavilion and the majority of the banks surrounding the playing area were built in 1953 thanks to the organization of J. Eric Thomas, the chairman, and H.E. Thomas the club secretary. In 1989 a match between a Local League XI was staged with the touring Australian Aboriginal XI at Acklam Park.

Crowds at Acklam Park are usually 6,500–7,000. The best was 13,100 for the visit of Warwickshire in 1967. Ground performances have included scores of the highest order with the bat from Geoffrey Boycott, Allan Wells (253 n.o. for Sussex in 1991) and Mark Waugh (207 n.o. for Essex in 1990). With the ball Freddie Trueman, Don Wilson, Chris Old and for the visitors Fred Titmus have found the wicket lively. Despite this, Geoffrey Boycott scored many runs at Acklam Park including in 1986 his 150th century in first-class cricket, which made him Yorkshire's leading century-maker, ahead of Herbert Sutcliffe. In 1991 Martin Moxon the Yorkshire captain recorded the highest individual innings for the county in a limited-overs match on the ground.

ADDRESS   Middlesbrough Cricket Club, The Clubhouse, Acklam Park, Green Lane, Acklam, Middlesbrough, Cleveland.
TELEPHONE NUMBER PROSPECTS OF PLAY   0642 818567

DESCRIPTION OF GROUND AND FACILITIES

Acklam Park is entered from Green Lane to the north of the ground. There is ample car parking on the south side of the ground, on the rugby field. The main buildings are the pavilion and clubhouse on the east side of the ground and the scorebox in the south-west corner of the cricket field. On the west, north and east sides of the ground there are permanent tiered mounds of bench seating, mainly for the public, and north of the pavilion and enclosure for members. The members' enclosure also extends south of the pavilion and round to the sight-screen; also to be found in this area are additional refreshment kiosks and the Yorkshire C C C White Rose souvenir shop located in a van. A separate area is provided for disabled spectators close to the sightscreen at the Rugby Ground End.

There are adequate toilets for both members and the public. The playing area is approximately 144 metres by 124 metres and is defined by a rope and advertising boards and the existing change of levels. The press box is sited at the Green Lane End adjoining the scorers' room and when required the TV camera/commentary box is also sited at this end of the ground.

Although bounded on three sides by the backs of residential housing the fenced sides are planted with trees in most places and this is a pleasant ground at which to watch cricket in fine weather.

GROUND RECORDS AND SCORES

FIRST-CLASS MATCHES
Highest innings total for County: 408 for 4 dec. *v*. Glamorgan 1983
Highest innings total against County: 436 by Sussex 1991
Lowest innings total for County: 23 *v*. Hampshire 1965
Lowest innings total against County: 41 by Gloucestershire 1969
Highest individual innings for County: 180 n.o. G. Boycott *v*. Warwickshire 1968
Highest individual innings against County: 253 n.o. A.P. Wells for Sussex 1991
Best bowling performance in an innings for County: 8 for 72 A. Sidebottom *v*. Leicestershire 1986
Best bowling performance in an innings against County: 7 for 39 F.J. Titmus for Middlesex 1974
Best bowling performance in a match for County: 10 for 81 F.S. Trueman *v*. West Indians 1963
Best bowling performance in a match against County: 14 for 114 F.J. Titmus for Middlesex 1974
Best attendance: 13,100 *v*. Warwickshire 1967

LIMITED-OVERS MATCHES
Highest innings total for County: 274 for 8 *v*. Sussex (RAL) 1991
Highest innings total against County: 282 for 4 by Northamptonshire (JPL) 1982
Lowest innings total for County: 151 for 8 *v*. Sussex (RAL) 1989
Lowest innings total against County: 124 by Warwickshire (JPL) 1983
Highest individual innings for County: 112 M.D. Moxon *v*. Sussex (RAL) 1991
Highest individual innings against County: 100 n.o. J.B. Bolus for Nottinghamshire (GC) 1963
Best bowling performance for County: 6 for 27 A.G. Nicholson *v*. Minor Counties (North) (BHC) 1972
Best bowling performance against County: 4 for 30 D.J. Capel for Northamptonshire (JPL) 1982
Best attendance: 6,000 *v*. Nottinghamshire (GC) 1963

HOW TO GET THERE

Rail Middlesbrough (BR), 1.25 mile.
Bus Cleveland Transit 14, 15, 16, 24 link Bus Station – 400m from

BR Middlesbrough Station – with ground (Telephone: 0642 607124).
Car From north: A1(M), then follow A177 signposted
Middlesbrough or take A19 or A178 to town centre; the ground is
situated south of the town centre in the Acklam district in Green
Lane. From west: A66 follow signs Middlesbrough and town centre,
then A19 to Acklam turn off using A174 or A1130. From south: A1,
then follow A168 and A19 signposted Middlesbrough, follow signs
Acklam for Green Lane and county cricket, or A172 then as above.

WHERE TO STAY AND OTHER INFORMATION

Blue Bell Hotel (0642 593939), Dragonara Hotel (0642 248133).

Disabled Areas Special railed-off area provided at Rugby Ground
End adjoining sightscreen.
Local Radio Station(s) BBC Radio Cleveland (95.0 MHz FM/1548
KHz MW), TFM (96.6 MHz/1170 KHz MW).
Local Newspaper(s) Northern Echo, Evening Gazette, Hartlepool
Mail, Yorkshire Post, Journal, Sunday Sun.

Scarborough

The North Marine Road cricket ground was leased by Scarborough
Cricket Club for £15 a year from 1863 until it was purchased in 1878.
Cricket has been played in Scarborough since 1849 when Scarborough
Cricket Club was established.

It's first matches were staged at Castle Hill, also known as the Queen's
Cricket Ground, which has long since been built on. Yorkshire C C C
staged matches at Castle Hill from 1874 to 1877 and has visited the
seaside resort on the North Yorkshire coast ever since. The first match
staged by Yorkshire C C C at the present North Marine Road Ground
was against I Zingari in 1878. The first cricket festival was staged in
1876, the first teams to play in the festival being New Forest Rangers
C C, Yorkshire C C C, MCC and Scarborough C C.

The original pavilion erected in 1874 was replaced at a cost of £2,150
in 1895 by a new pavilion which still stands in the north-west corner of
the ground. Before the first County Championship match staged by
Yorkshire C C C on the ground in 1896 against Leicestershire, the
pavilion clock was presented as a gift from Mr and Mrs J. Compton-
Rickett and Mr J.H. Morton. In 1902, thanks to funds generated from a
most successful festival, a new seating enclosure was erected, this was
added to in 1903 and 1907. In 1903 a press box/scorers' room was
constructed at a cost of £250. A concrete stand was built in the north-east
corner in 1926. The West Stand built in 1956 is the most recent addition
to the ground. Scarborough C C has remained one of the best in the
county, thanks to Robert Baker, the Secretary at the time of its
formation and the later presidents Rt. Hon. Lord Hawke, The Earl of

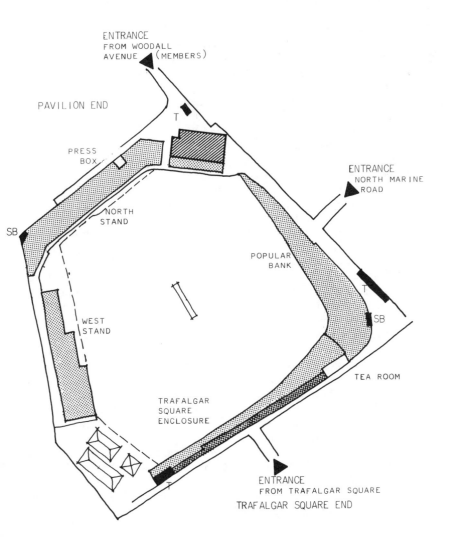

ENTRANCE
FROM WOODALL
AVENUE (MEMBERS)

PAVILION END

PRESS
BOX

NORTH
STAND

SB

WEST
STAND

ENTRANCE
NORTH MARINE
ROAD

POPULAR
BANK

T

SB

TEA ROOM

TRAFALGAR
SQUARE
ENCLOSURE

ENTRANCE
FROM TRAFALGAR SQUARE

TRAFALGAR SQUARE END

N

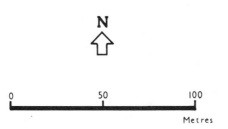

0   50   100

Metres

Londesborough and H.D.G. Leveson Gower. Yorkshire C C C play two championship and three limited-overs matches in Scarborough each season, usually one in June followed by the others in August, as well as the later festival matches. The Scarborough Cricket Festival takes place in late August–early September. Yorkshire C C C competes with three other invited counties for the Festival Trophy. The limited-overs competition was established in 1971 by J.H. Fenner Limited, the Hull-based engineering firm. It consists of two 50-over matches involving four first-class counties, the winners of the two matches meeting to decide the outright winner in the final. In 1982 sponsorship of the competition was taken over by Asda Stores, the rules remaining unaltered. After six seasons, in 1988 Ward Building Components took over as sponsor and the competition became the Ward Four-County Knockout Competition. In 1990 there was no sponsor and in 1991 the new sponsor was Joshua Tetley.

Games have been staged at Scarborough between the Gentlemen and the Players and with various touring teams. In 1988 MCC staged a match with a Michael Parkinson's XI and this is now an annual feature of the festival, as is the Yorkshire C C C versus The Yorkshiremen XI. Other visiting teams have included C.I. Thornton's, H.D.G. Leveson Gower's, Lord Londensborough's, T.N. Pearce's and D.B. Close's XIs. In 1976 a Prudential Trophy match was staged at North Marine Road between England and the West Indies. The most significant recent event on the ground involving tourists was in 1986 when Ken Rutherford scored 317 against D.B. Close's XI, which included eight test players. Crowds at Scarborough are usually 8,000–10,000 and the present ground capacity is 15,000. The largest attendance was 22,946 for the championship match with Derbyshire in 1947. Some 12,000 watched the Worcestershire Refuge Assurance Sunday League match in 1989 and 8,000 the Ward Knockout Trophy Final in the same year. Scarborough C C play in the Yorkshire League and Websters Cricket League and field three XIs throughout the season. They also enter the Cockspur Cup and have reached the final at Lord's.

Many great cricketers have played at Scarborough; G.J. Bonnor the 'Colonial Hercules', Sir Jack Hobbs, Sir Donald Bradman, Denis Compton and Richie Benaud have all notched up many notable achievements on this ground. Sir Donald Bradman still considers his innings of 132 against H.D.G. Leveson Gower's XI in 1934 as one of his best, if not his best innings ever played in England! Sir Jack Hobbs scored 266 n.o. for the Players in 1925 which remains the record highest individual innings for a Gentlemen versus Players match. In 1921 at the Scarborough Festival, one of Yorkshire's finest cricketers retired from first-class cricket George Hirst. Dennis Amiss of Warwickshire played his last innings for Warwickshire here in 1986.

ADDRESS   Scarborough Cricket Club, The Pavilion, North Marine Road, Scarborough, North Yorkshire YO12 7TJ.
TELEPHONE NUMBER PROSPECTS OF PLAY   0723 365625

DESCRIPTION OF GROUND AND FACILITIES

The main access to the ground for members is from North Marine Road but there is also an entrance in Woodall Avenue at the rear of the pavilion and another in Trafalgar Square to the rear of the Trafalgar Square enclosure. The pavilion and club office is located to the north of the ground together with the press/scorers' box which is situated at the top of the North Stand terrace. To the east of the playing area is the large Popular Bank and to the rear is the Yorkshire C C C White Rose Souvenir van, Scarborough C C souvenir stall and ample refreshment facilities. To the south at the Trafalgar Road end is the famous 'tea room' bar and refreshment area and the covered Trafalgar Road Stand and open terrace. The west side includes the huge West Stand terrace as well as the 'Dropped Catch Bar', an open area for sponsors' marquees, and an area for the storage of the groundsman's equipment. There are two scoreboards on the ground, the main one to the north-west corner and another smaller secondary scoreboard in the south-east corner. Permanent toilet facilities are available. All the seating is permanent and includes benches, backless seats, plastic tip-up seats and of course a number of deckchairs, just to remind spectators that the sea is just across the road!

The ground is surrounded by houses on all four sides and therefore car parking is not possible within the ground, even for players, so spectators are advised to park in one of the numerous town centre car parks. The playing area is 132 metres by 128 metres and is defined by a rope and some advertising boards. The ground capacity is 15,000 and 90 per cent of this is provided with permanent seats so spectators are advised only to bring seats to very popular matches. The TV camera/commentary box position is at the Trafalgar Square end with the Radio commentary box adjoining the press room.

Scarborough is one of the best club grounds where county cricket is played and the annual festivals are always a successful venture.

GROUND RECORDS AND SCORES

FIRST-CLASS MATCHES
Highest innings total for County: 562 *v.* Leicestershire 1901
Highest innings total against County: 478 for 8 by MCC 1904
Lowest innings total for County: 46 *v.* MCC 1876/MCC 1877
Lowest innings total against County: 31 by MCC 1877
Highest individual innings for County: 223 n.o. J.V. Wilson *v.* Scotland 1951
Highest individual innings against County: 208 n.o. M.P. Donnelly for MCC 1948
Best bowling performance in an innings for County: 9 for 28 J.M. Preston *v.* MCC 1888
Best bowling performance in an innings against County: 8 for 37 A. Shaw for MCC 1876
Best bowling performance in a match for County: 13 for 63 J.M. Preston *v.* MCC 1888

Best bowling performance in a match against County: 13 for 145 R. Henderson for I Zingari 1877
Best attendance: 22,946 *v.* Derbyshire 1947

LIMITED-OVERS MATCHES

Highest innings total for County: 271 for 7 *v.* Middlesex (RAL) 1990
Highest innings total against County: 263 for 5 by Lancashire (RAL) 1990
Lowest innings total for County: 91 *v.* Surrey (JPL) 1970
Lowest innings total against County: 87 by Derbyshire (JPL) 1973
Highest individual innings for County: 115 n.o. A.A. Metcalfe *v.* Gloucestershire (JPL) 1984
Highest individual innings against County: 129 A.W. Greig for Sussex (JPL) 1976
Best bowling performance for County: 4 for 24 A. Sidebottom *v.* Surrey (JPL) 1975
Best bowling performance against County: 4 for 10 I.T. Botham for Somerset (JPL) 1979
Best attendance: 12,000 *v.* Worcestershire (RAL) 1989

FESTIVAL MATCHES

Highest innings total: 323 for 5 by Essex *v.* Durham (JTFT) 1991
Lowest innings total: 53 by Sussex *v.* Leicestershire (FT) 1980
Highest individual innings: 158 K.J. Barnett for Derbyshire *v.* Lancashire (Asda) 1987
Best bowling performance: 5 for 13 P. Carrick for Yorkshire *v.* Derbyshire (Asda) 1984

HOW TO GET THERE

Rail   Scarborough Central (BR), 0.75 mile.
Bus   United Automobile Services from Whitby and Middlesbrough, East Yorkshire Motor Services from Bridlington and Hull, West Yorkshire Road Car Company from Malton, York and Leeds to town centre Bus Station.
Car   From north: A171 or A165, follow signs Scarborough and seafront; the ground is situated north of the town centre off the B1364 North Marine Road adjoining Trafalgar Square. From west: A170 follow signs Scarborough and seafront, then follow A165 and B1364 for North Marine Road and Trafalgar Square. From south: A64 or A165 follow signs Scarborough and seafront, then as west.

WHERE TO STAY AND OTHER INFORMATION

Crown Hotel (0723 373491), Reads Hotel (0723 361071), Holbeck Hall (0723 374374), and many other small hotels and guest houses.

Disabled Areas   Special area situated within the Trafalgar Square enclosure.

Local Radio Station(s)   BBC Radio York (95.5 MHz FM/1260 KHz MW).
Local Newspaper(s)   Scarborough Evening News, The Mercury, Whitby Gazette, Ryedale Shopper, Yorkshire Post, Northern Echo.

Sheffield

Abbeydale Park is located on the south-western outskirts of the City of Sheffield in a village called Dore on the Yorkshire–Derbyshire border and closer to the Peak District National Park than to the Yorkshire Dales. Until boundary changes, the ground was in Derbyshire and was used by Derbyshire C C C in 1946–47.

From 1855–1973 cricket in Sheffield, including a single Test Match with the 1902 Australians, was staged at Bramall Lane on the ground shared with Sheffield United Football Club. But the encroachment of association football finally put an end to first-class cricket there, the last County Championship match being with Lancashire. The historic turf was sold to Sheffield cricket-lovers, whilst bulldozers moved in within a week to prepare for the major construction and erection of a new football stand for Sheffield United. This stand is known today by the opposing Wednesday supporters as the White Elephant Stand! Alternative grounds for Sheffield Collegiate Cricket Club were the Hadfields Ground or the Old Firth Vickers Ground but finance was not forthcoming and decisions not made at the right time and so Yorkshire C C C finally made the commitment to stage its first-class cricket in the City at Abbeydale Park. Yorkshire C C C's first match there was in May 1974 against Warwickshire; nowadays at least two County Championship matches are staged on the ground each season. A limited-overs match has been added to the fixture list since 1985.

Abbeydale Park is the home both of Sheffield Collegiate Cricket Club which was established in 1881 and the Sheffield Amateur Sports Club (SASC) which hosts the following sports: football, badminton, squash, archery, bowls, tennis, hockey, rugby football, table tennis and snooker. There is also a resident sports doctor and a sports injury clinic on the premises. Yorkshire C C C were restricted to mid-week matches until 1980 when the SASC changed its policy to permit county matches to be played at weekends. Sheffield Collegiate C C first played league cricket in 1892 when they were members of the old Hallamshire League and the Rotherham and District League; it was during the Victorian era that their rivalry with the Sheffield United C C began. In 1962 the club joined the Yorkshire County League.

Abbeydale Park is surely one of the more attractive out grounds in the county, in an open, idyllic setting in sharp contrast to the traditional stadium-like grounds of Yorkshire. Both players and spectators enjoy their visits for the excellent facilities offered in the pavilion and conference rooms. Much of the success of Abbeydale is thanks to the good work of David Fleetwood who has played a key role in the club's

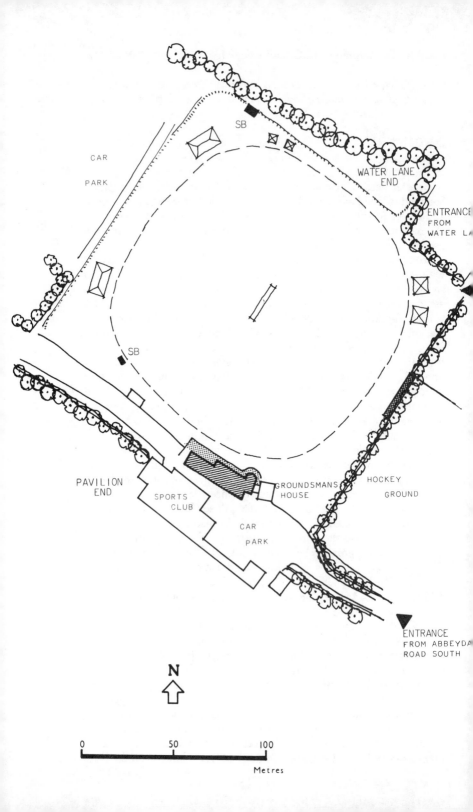

rise since his move from Sheffield United C C in 1970. Many Sheffield people have developed an affection for Abbeydale even though deep nostalgia for Bramall Lane still remains, as most of the great games staged in the City have been at that venue.

Many improvements have been made since the first match in 1974, but naturally it has not been the SASC's aim to convert Abbeydale into another Bramall Lane. SASC believes it has one of the premier grounds of its kind in the country and the success achieved so far suggests this is the kind of venue that modern cricket supporters want and enjoy visiting. Abbeydale has maintained Sheffield's reputation of attracting good crowds: 5,500–6,000 on average. The best attendance was 8,000 for the tourist match with the West Indians in 1976.

Most spectators enjoy cricket at Abbeydale and a number of local companies sponsor cricket here because of the fine sponsorship facilities available which they are thus able to offer to their clients and customers. The ground is located on a slope, but the square is flat and well maintained by the SASC groundsmen. During the winter of 1991–92 much of the playing area has been re-levelled and visitors will notice that the slope towards the hockey ground is now not so severe. The ground is owned by the SASC and during the winter months Sheffield Rugby Football Club play matches on the ground; they are members of the Courage League Division 3. In August 1991 a number of floodlit international matches were staged between Yorkshire C C C and a World XI at the Don Valley Stadium in the north of the City, which was constructed for the World Student Games earlier in the summer. For history and description of ground and facilities, see Don Valley Stadium section.

Ground records at Abbeydale include batting achievements by Geoffrey Boycott, Alan Fordham, Ashley Metcalfe and Tim Boon. Other large championship centuries have been recorded by Alan Hill (172 n.o. for Derbyshire) and Graeme Hick (150 n.o. for Worcestershire). Fine spells of bowling have also been achieved by Stuart Fletcher, Phil Carrick, Tony Gray, Chris Old, Ole Mortensen and Imran Khan. While batting against Leicestershire in 1990 Martin Moxon killed a pigeon.

ADDRESS   Sheffield Amateur Sports Club, The Pavilion, Abbeydale Park, Abbeydale Park Road South, Dore, Sheffield, South Yorkshire S17 3LJ.
TELEPHONE NUMBER PROSPECTS OF PLAY   0742 362040/ 367011

DESCRIPTION OF GROUND AND FACILITIES

Entry to Abbeydale Park sports complex is from two access points along Abbeydale Park Road South and there is ample car parking within the ground for cricket matches. The main, permanent building used for cricket matches is the substantial two-storey pavilion which is on the south side of the ground and on the main entrance from the drive. The scoreboard is on the north-east side of the ground. The members' enclosure is the pavilion and the temporary stands on the south and west side of the ground. All other areas are available to the public and various marquees are provided for refreshment facilities and bars. The Yorkshire C C C White Rose Shop van is located close to the pavilion near the secondary scoreboard. Temporary toilets are provided for the public and in the pavilion for members.

The TV camera/commentary box position is at the Pavilion End directly above and behind the sightscreen. The press and scorers are located in separate tents. The rugby field side of the playing area is used for sponsors' marquees. The ground capacity is 8,000, and as only 3,500 seats are provided spectators are therefore strongly advised to take their own seats to all popular matches. The playing area is approximately 150 metres by 148 metres and is defined by a rope and advertising boards.

GROUND RECORDS AND SCORES

FIRST-CLASS MATCHES
Highest innings total for County: 424 *v.* Worcestershire 1982
Highest innings total against County: 480 by Derbyshire 1981
Lowest innings total for County: 90 *v.* West Indians 1976
Lowest innings total against County: 35 by Warwickshire 1979
Highest individual innings for County: 159 n.o. G. Boycott *v.* Worcestershire 1982
Highest individual innings against County: 199 A. Fordham for Northamptonshire 1989
Best bowling performance in an innings for County: 8 for 58 S.D. Fletcher *v.* Essex 1988
Best bowling performance in an innings against County: 8 for 40 A.H. Gray for Surrey 1985
Best bowling performance in a match for County: 12 for 89 P. Carrick *v.* Derbyshire 1983
Best bowling performance in a match against County: 11 for 49 O.H. Mortensen for Derbyshire 1983
Best attendance: 8,000 *v.* West Indians 1976

LIMITED-OVERS MATCHES
Highest innings total for County: 208 for 2 *v.* Leicestershire (RAL) 1990
Highest innings total against County: 207 for 6 by Leicestershire (RAL) 1990
Lowest innings total for County: 164 for 8 *v.* Essex (JPL) 1986
Lowest innings total against County: 162 by Essex (JPL) 1986
Highest individual innings for County: 79 A.A. Metcalfe *v.* Essex (RAL) 1988
Highest individual innings against County: 88 T. Boon for Leicestershire (RAL) 1990
Best bowling performance for County: 4 for 28 S.D. Fletcher *v.* Essex (RAL) 1988
Best bowling performance against County: 4 for 15 Imran Khan for Sussex (JPL) 1985
Best attendance: 4,500 *v.* Essex (JPL) 1986

HOW TO GET THERE

Rail   Dore and Totley (BR), 100m (link from Sheffield Midland BR).
Bus   South Yorkshire Traction 17, 24 from Pinstone Street – 700m
from BR Sheffield Midland Station – to Abbeydale Park Road South
(Telephone: 0742 755655).
Car   From north: M1 junction 34, follow signs Sheffield and city
centre, then A621 signposted Bakewell and Baslow; Abbeydale Park
is situated off the A621 at Dore adjoining Totley off Abbeydale Park
Road South, or A6102, A61, A6135 or A618 signposted Sheffield and
city centre, then follow A621 to Dore, then as above. From east: M1
junction 33, follow A630 signposted Sheffield and city centre, then as
north, or A57 then as north. From west: A625 or A621 follow signs
Dore and Totley for Abbeydale Park off A621 at Abbeydale Park
Road South, 6.5 miles south-west of Sheffield city centre. From south:
M1 junction 29, follow A617 Chesterfield, then A61 Sheffield after
passing Dronfield, take Greenhill roundabout on southern outskirts of
Sheffield and follow signs Dore and Totley on B6054 for Abbeydale
Park Road South and SASC ground, or A616, A621, then as north.

WHERE TO STAY AND OTHER INFORMATION

Grosvenor House Hotel (0742 20041), Hallam Tower Forte Post
House (0742 686031), Hotel St George (0742 583811).

Disabled Areas   No special area, request suitable position. A
disabled toilet is available in the pavilion.
Local Radio Station(s)   BBC Radio Sheffield (104.1 MHz FM/1035
KHz MW) Radio Hallam (103.4 MHz FM/1548 KHz MW).
Local Newspaper(s)   Sheffield Star, Yorkshire Post, The Morning
Telegraph.

Hull

Anlaby Road cricket ground is known as The Circle, a name of course
taken from its shape. It is the second ground in Humberside that has
been used by Yorkshire C C C The original venue for county matches
was Argyle Street near Anlaby Road, where matches were staged in
1879 by Yorkshire C C C and in 1875 by the North. The Circle is the
home of Hull Cricket Club formerly Hull Town Cricket Club, which
moved to its present ground from Argyle Street in 1894. The ground is
shared with Hull and East Riding Rugby Football Club.
    The first Yorkshire C C C visit to The Circle was in 1892 when
Staffordshire were the visitors; the initial County Championship match
was staged in 1899 against Somerset. The last County Championship
match was staged in 1974 against Worcestershire, but Yorkshire C C C
still travel once each season to the East Coast to stage a limited-overs
Sunday League fixture. The last occasion was a Refuge Assurance

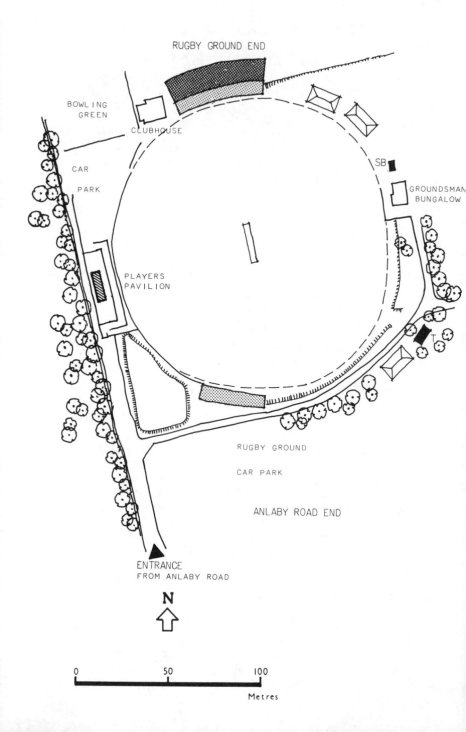

RUGBY GROUND END

BOWLING
GREEN

CLUBHOUSE

CAR
PARK

SB

GROUNDSMAN
BUNGALOW

PLAYERS
PAVILION

T

RUGBY GROUND

CAR PARK

ANLABY ROAD END

ENTRANCE
FROM ANLABY ROAD

N

0   50   100

Metres

Sunday League match with Surrey in 1990. No match was staged in 1991, the first season in which no limited-overs match has been played at Hull. In 1983 the West Indians were to have played Lancashire at Hull in the Wilberforce Commemoration international cricket match, which marked the 150th anniversary of the abolition of slavery and the death of William Wilberforce, a distinguished citizen of Hull, but the match was abandoned.

Association football has also been staged on the ground, opposite the old pavilion which was demolished in 1987. In 1904 negotiations took place in an endeavour to stage an FA Cup tie between Hull City and Stockton on the cricket ground, but this was not allowed and eventually the match was staged at Ayresome Park, Middlesbrough.

Hull Cricket Club play in the Yorkshire County Cricket League and the Ridings League. In recent years there have been significant changes at the ground. In 1986 Humberside County Council took over the leasehold of the ground in order to make the ground into a large sports complex. The ground has a large playing area and plenty of seating accommodation although little is covered. In 1987 the old pavilion, which had stood on the ground for a hundred years or more, was demolished to make way for the sports complex development, which is designed to cope with multi-sports demands of the next decade and beyond. Expansion plans at The Circle ground include a floodlit artificial pitch for hockey, major improvements to the existing rugby stand and the provision of further permanent seating to attract more Yorkshire C C C county matches. The £500,000 facelift will restore the ground to its original former glory as one of Yorkshire's major venues.

The Circle usually attracts crowds of 5,000–6,000, the best in recent years was 6,500 for the match against Nottinghamshire in the 1986 John Player Sunday League, but the ground record is 21,394 for the visit of Northamptonshire in 1946. Historical events at The Circle have been numerous; one of Yorkshire's most stupendous efforts was achieved here in 1922 when they bowled out Sussex for just 20. Other achievements have included high scores from Maurice Leyland against Essex in 1936 and Basil D'Oliveria (227 n.o. for Worcestershire in 1974). In 1954 there was some fine bowling by Johnny Wardle against Sussex. In limited-overs matches Barry Richards scored 155 n.o. for Hampshire in 1970 and a year earlier Ray East, the Essex spinner took 6 for 18.

No mention of Hull Cricket Club would be complete without reference to Charles Ullathorne, the first Yorkshire player to hail from the East Coast club. After his playing career he coached and later became groundsman at Eccles C C across the Pennines in Manchester. It is expected that Yorkshire C C C will return to The Circle just as soon as the improvements have been completed.

ADDRESS Hull Cricket Club, The Circle, Anlaby Road, Anlaby, Kingston-Upon-Hull, North Humberside HU3 6RR.
TELEPHONE NUMBER PROSPECTS OF PLAY 0482 507098

DESCRIPTION OF GROUND AND FACILITIES

The Circle ground is entered from Anlaby Road, to the south of the playing area. This is the main entrance for members, players and officials and the public, together with all cars. Car parking is available on the rugby pitch or in the main car park near to the clubhouse for players and officials. The only permanent buildings on the ground, now that the old pavilion has been demolished and replaced by a two-storey portacabin for players' changing facilities are the clubhouse, rugby stand and press box/scorers' room and radio commentary position to the north, and the scoreboard, groundsman's bungalow and equipment stores to the west.

The playing area is circular in shape despite a rugby pitch being positioned to the north of the square, is 150 metres by 152 metres and is defined by a rope and advertising boards. A number of tents and temporary, open seating areas are available together with temporary toilets, refreshment facilities and a Yorkshire C C C White Rose souvenir shop van. The members' enclosure is in front of the players' temporary changing facilities and the main rugby stand. A temporary refreshment area and a bar are available to members in the clubhouse on matchdays. The ground capacity is 8,000 and seating of approximately only 10 per cent is available so spectators are strongly advised to bring their own seating to all matches in order to view the cricket from the grass banking which surrounds the greater part of the playing area.

GROUND RECORDS AND SCORES

FIRST-CLASS MATCHES
Highest innings total for County: 523 for 3 dec. *v.* Leicestershire 1937
Highest innings total against County: 458 by Leicestershire 1937
Lowest innings total for County: 77 *v.* Kent 1905
Lowest innings total against County: 20 by Sussex 1922
Highest individual innings for County: 263 M. Leyland *v.* Essex 1936
Highest individual innings against County: 227 B.L. D'Oliveria for Worcestershire 1974
Best bowling performance in an innings for County: 9 for 48 J.H. Wardle *v.* Sussex 1954
Best bowling performance in an innings against County: 8 for 40 W.W. O'Dell for Leicestershire 1907
Best bowling performance in a match for County: 16 for 112 J.H. Wardle *v.* Sussex 1954
Best bowling performance in a match against County: 12 for 86 F. Ridgway for Kent 1947
Best attendance: 21,394 *v.* Northamptonshire 1946

LIMITED-OVERS MATCHES
Highest innings total for County: 255 for 6 *v.* Nottinghamshire (JPL) 1986
Highest innings total against County: 232 for 4 by Gloucestershire (JPL) 1980

Lowest innings total for County: 74 for 9 *v*. Hampshire (JPL) 1970
Lowest innings total against County: 120 by Essex (JPL) 1973
Highest individual innings for County: 119 J.H. Hampshire *v*.
Leicestershire (JPL) 1971
Highest individual innings against County: 155 n.o. B.A. Richards for
Hampshire (JPL) 1970
Best bowling performance for County: 5 for 17 A.G. Nicholson *v*.
Nottinghamshire (JPL) 1972
Best bowling performance against County: 6 for 18 R.E. East for Essex
(JPL) 1969
Best attendance: 6,500 *v*. Nottinghamshire (JPL) 1986

HOW TO GET THERE

Rail Hull Paragon (BR), 1 mile.
Bus Kingston upon Hull Buses 2, 15, 23, 24 link east end of Anlaby
Road, adjacent BR Hull Paragon Station, with ground (Telephone:
0482 222222).
Car From north: A164, A1079, A165 or A1034 follow signs
Kingston-Upon-Hull, from A1 or A19 follow A1079 signposted
Kingston-Upon-Hull and town centre, follow signs Anlaby for Anlaby
Road and The Circle cricket ground, the ground is situated off Anlaby
Road off the A63. From east: A1033 follow signs Kingston-Upon-Hull,
then as north. From west: M62 junction 38, then follow A63 signposted
Kingston-Upon-Hull for Anlaby district and Anlaby Road for The
Circle cricket ground. From south: M1 junction 32, follow M18 and
M62 to junction 38, then as west, or A15 from M180 junction 5, across
the Humber Bridge, then follow signs Anlaby and A63 for The Circle
cricket ground.

WHERE TO STAY AND OTHER INFORMATION

West Park Hotel, Anlaby Road (0482 571888), The Marina Forte Post
House (0482 225221).

Disabled Areas No special area request suitable position.
Local Radio Station(s) BBC Radio Humberside (95.9 MHz FM/1485
KHz MW), Viking Radio (96.9 MHz FM/1161 KHz MW).
Local Newspaper(s) Hull Daily Mail, Hull Star.

CAMBRIDGE UNIVERSITY

CAMBRIDGE – FENNER'S

Cambridge University

Founded 1820
Colours Pale blue
Crest University crest
President Professor A.D. Buckingham (Pembroke)
Hon. secretary (elected annually) J.P. Arscott (1992) (Tonbridge and Magdalene)
Fixture secretary J.G.W. Davies MA, OBE, 31 Wingate Way, Cambridge, CB2 2HD
Cricket Coach G.J. Saville
Captain J. Crawley (1992) (Manchester G.S. and Downing)
Groundsman A. Pocock
Scorer/Statistician A.R. May
Sponsors Boots Company PLC
Address Cambridge University Cricket Club, Fenner's University Cricket Ground, Wollaston Road, off Mortimer Road, Cambridge, Cambridgeshire.
Telephone 0223 353552
County Scores Rapid Cricketline 0891 567500

ACHIEVEMENTS

Varsity Match: Winners of the University Match on 53 occasions
Benson & Hedges Cup Quarter-finalists (1) 1990 as Combined Universities

GROUND

Cambridge (Fenner's University Cricket Ground)
 No other grounds have been used for matches.

Cambridge – Fenner's

There is reference to Cambridge University playing a match against Cambridge Town in 1710, presumably on Parker's Piece, but the first recorded match against the town was in 1821. The Cambridge University Cricket Club was founded in 1820 and the first match against Oxford University was played at Lord's in 1827. Since 1848 all home matches have been played at Fenner's University Cricket Ground in the centre of the city.

 The development of cricket at the University was such that by the latter part of the century Cambridge could give any side in England a good game. Regular fixtures were arranged with the first-class counties and these have continued to the present day. The present fixtures now normally comprise, in addition to the annual encounter with Oxford

University at Lord's, about ten matches with counties plus a number of other games. Like Oxford University C C, Cambridge University C C is afforded first-class status although there have been those who have thought to question this status in recent years. The universities no longer play the tourists individually but play as Combined Universities (Oxford and Cambridge) and the fixtures alternate yearly between the two university grounds. Similarly, the Combined Universities play in the Benson & Hedges Cup zonal competition, and in recent years these teams have included students from Durham and Loughborough Universities in addition to those from Oxford and Cambridge. In 1989 Combined Universities reached the quarter-Finals of the Benson & Hedges Cup and were defeated by Somerset at Taunton. Victories were achieved against Surrey at Fenner's and Worcestershire at New Road in earlier rounds.

Sixty-seven Cambridge men have played for England and thirteen of these have captained, ranging from the Hon. Ivo Bligh in 1882 to Mike Brearley in the period 1977–81. Many fine players represented Cambridge during the golden years of cricket prior to 1914 and these included Lord Hawke and Prince Ranjitsinhji.

Since World War Two captains have included Doug Insole, Ted Dexter, Peter May, Tony Lewis and Michael Atherton, while among those who have played are Trevor Bailey, Raman Subba Row, Richard Hutton, Peter Roebuck and Derek Pringle.

DESCRIPTION OF GROUND AND FACILITIES

In 1846 Mr. F.P. Fenner leased from Gonville and Caius College a field to the east of Parker's Piece and opened a cricket ground. Two years later he sub-let it to Cambridge University Cricket Club, and while the ground has continued to retain the name Fenner's, it has been the home of University cricket since then.

The freehold of the ground was acquired from the College in 1894 and assigned to a company which held it in trust, until in 1976 the University assumed full financial responsibility for the ground.

Until the 1950s the ground was shared with the University Athletes and contained a running track surrounding the playing area, this has now been removed. The ground is still used for tennis in summer and hockey and soccer in the winter.

The ground, which is renowned for its true pitches and even outfield, is partly enclosed by walls and adjoining buildings. The earlier pavilions were on the south-west side backing onto Gresham Road, but in 1972 a new pavilion, designed by architect Colin Stansfield-Smith RIBA (Cricket Blue 1954–57), was built on the Wollaston Road side to the north-east. It provides infinitely better facilities but there remain those who still prefer the character of the old building. The site of the old pavilion and adjoining land have since been developed into three-storey flats with a direct view of the cricket.

The ground is entered at the junction of Mortimer Road and Wollaston Road and the nearest car parking is in the multi-storey car

FENNER'S CAMBRIDGE

MR S.M.J. WOODS
*Cambridge University/
Somerset*

park entered from Gonville Place adjoining the indoor swimming pool. A small number of cars are allowed into the ground.

The members' enclosure is in front of the pavilion, but groups still congregate on the south side on benches in the shade of the trees. You are advised to take your own seats as few are available for spectators. The still rudimentary scoreboard and press box/scorers' room are sited on the west side of the ground. The general impression is still that of a quiet backwater in the city centre, surrounded by brick buildings and mature trees. Tennis courts to the east are separated from the ground by a wooden fence and tree planting. Regrettably, the north-west corner of the ground is now overshadowed by a multi-storey car park. The pitch is disposed in a north-south direction. The playing area is 147 metres by 148 metres.

The match against the tourists has always been a great attraction and, until the advent of the Benson & Hedges Cup, was the only game for which admission was charged. The tourists' match is now undertaken by a Combined Universities team and held at Fenner's and the Parks in alternate years. The record attendance is said to be 9,000, achieved when the University played the touring West Indians in 1950 in a drawn match which produced 1,324 runs in 3 days. Some 4,500 attended the Combined Universities match with the Australians in 1985. Ground records include highest scores by Duleepsinhji and Everton Weekes together with fine spells of bowling by Sammy Woods and F.P. Fenner on his own ground.

The ground is also used by Cambridgeshire C C C for home Minor Counties Championship matches and has staged the Minor Counties English Estates Knockout Trophy Final during the 1980s.

A. P. F. CHAPMAN

RAMAN SUBBA ROW

WILLS'S CIGARETTES

K. S. DULEEPSINHJI

ADDRESS Cambridge University Cricket Club, Fenner's University Cricket Ground, Wollaston Road, off Mortimer Road, Cambridge, Cambridgeshire.
TELEPHONE NUMBER PROSPECTS OF PLAY 0223 353552

GROUND RECORDS AND SCORES

FIRST-CLASS MATCHES

Highest innings total for University: 594 for 4 *v.* West Indians 1950
Highest innings total against University: 730 for 3 by West Indians 1950
Lowest innings total for University: 30 *v.* Yorkshire 1928
Lowest innings total against University: 43 by Warwickshire 1936
Highest individual innings for University: 254 n.o. K.S. Duleepsinhji *v.* Middlesex 1927
Highest individual innings against University: 304 n.o. E. de C. Weekes for West Indians 1950
Best bowling performance in an innings for University: 10 for 69 S.M.J. Woods *v.* C.I. Thornton's XI 1890
Best bowling performance in an innings against University: 9 for 17 H.L. Jackson for Derbyshire 1959/9 for ?? F.P. Fenner for Cambridge Town 1844
Best bowling performance in a match for University: 15 for 88 S.M.J. Woods *v.* C.I. Thornton's XI 1890
Best bowling performance in a match against University: 17 for ?? F.P. Fenner for Cambridge Town 1844
Best attendance: 9,000 *v.* West Indians 1950

LIMITED-OVERS MATCHES

Highest innings total for Combined Universities: 212 *v.* Kent (BHC) 1983

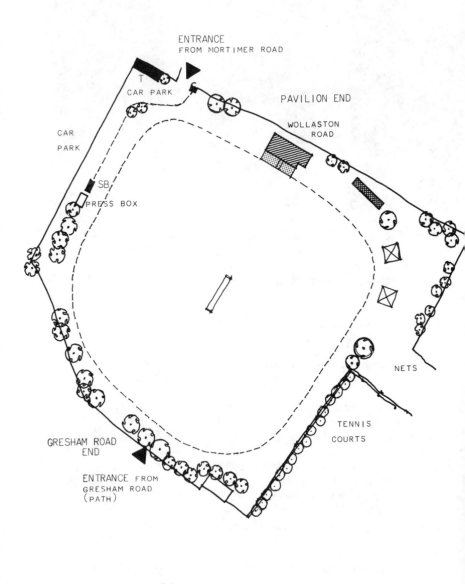

ENTRANCE
FROM MORTIMER ROAD

T
CAR PARK

PAVILION END

WOLLASTON
ROAD

CAR
PARK

SB
PRESS BOX

NETS

GRESHAM ROAD
END

TENNIS
COURTS

ENTRANCE FROM
GRESHAM ROAD
(PATH)

N

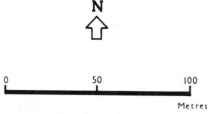

0   50   100
          Metres

Highest innings total against Combined Universities: 276 for 9 by Kent (BHC) 1983

Lowest innings total for Combined Universities: 59 *v.* Glamorgan (BHC) 1983

Lowest innings total against Combined Universities: 92 by Worcestershire (BHC) 1975

Highest individual innings for Combined Universities: 82 S.P. Henderson *v.* Kent (BHC) 1983

Highest individual innings against Combined Universities: 108 D.C. Boon for Australians (Tour) 1985

Best bowling performance for Combined Universities: 4 for 14 Imran Khan *v.* Worcestershire (BHC) 1975

Best bowling performance against Combined Universities: 5 for 28 M.A. Feltham for Surrey (BHC) 1989

Best attendance: 4,500 *v.* Australians (Tour) 1985

HOW TO GET THERE

Rail Cambridge (BR), 0.75 mile.
Bus Cambus 142 or 143 from Bus Station to ground.
Car From north: A1 and A604 signposted Cambridge and city centre, then A1309 for Mortimer Road and Fenner's University Cricket Ground situated close to Parker's Piece and at rear of multi-storey car park, or A10 to city centre, then as above.

From east: A1303 or A45 signposted Cambridge and city centre, then as north. From west: A45, A1303 or A603 follow signs Cambridge and city centre, then as north. From south: M11 junction 11, then follow signs Cambridge and city centre, then as north, or A1301, A1307 to city centre, then as north.

WHERE TO STAY AND OTHER INFORMATION

Gonville Hotel (0223 66611), Forte Post House (0223 237000), University Arms (0223 351241).

Disabled Areas No special area, request suitable position.
Local Radio Station(s) BBC Radio Cambridgeshire (95.7 MHz FM/1026 KHz MW), Hereward Radio (96.6 MHz FM/1557 KHz MW).
Local Newspaper(s) Cambridge Evening News.

OXFORD UNIVERSITY

OXFORD – THE PARKS

Oxford University

Founded 1800
Colours Dark blue
Crest Two crowns above OUCC
President C.A. Fry
Hon. Secretary (elected annually) R. Montgomerie (1992) (Rugby and Worcester)
Senior Treasurer and Fixture Secretary Dr S.R. Porter MA, DPhil, Nuffield College, Oxford OX1 1NF
Assistant Secretary P.G.B. James
Cricket Coach L.J. Lenham
Captain G.B.T. Lovell (1992) (Sydney C. of E.G.S., University of Sydney and Exeter)
Groundsman R. Sula
Scorer/statistician P. Gordon
Newsletter: OUCC Bulletin
Address Oxford University Cricket Club, The Pavilion, The University Parks, Oxford, Oxfordshire
Telephone 0865 57106
Rapid Cricketline County Scores 0891 567500

ACHIEVEMENTS

Varsity Match Winners of the University Match on 45 occasions
Benson & Hedges Cup quarter-finalists (1) 1990 as Combined Universities

GROUND

Oxford (The University Parks).

In addition to the above mentioned ground the following venue has also been used occasionally for matches:

Christchurch Cricket Ground, Iffley Road, Oxford. Telephone: 0865 243992

Oxford – The Parks

The first mention of cricket in Oxford appears to have been in 1727, but the first known match was in 1795 when Bullingdon Club played the MCC. However the direct forerunner of Oxford University Cricket Club was Magdalen Club, which was established in about 1800, although the reference to Oxford University Cricket Club did not appear in a match until 1827. The early matches were played on Cowley Marsh until in 1881 Dr Evans, Master of Pembroke College, succeeded in obtaining a lease on 10 acres of land in the University Parks. This venue has remained the club's ground for all home matches and many consider it to be one of the most attractive venues in the country. Occasionally, the ground at Christchurch College has been used for matches against the tourists, in part owing to the need to charge admission to the game. At the Parks charges cannot be levied, since the ground is not enclosed.

As early as 1884 Oxford University defeated the touring Australians by seven wickets, no mean feat as the Australian team differed little from that which had won the Ashes in 1882.

Many fine cricketers played at Oxford in the years before 1914, including P.F. 'Plum' Warner, R.E. Foster and C.B. Fry. Later personalities who experienced their early first-class cricket at the Parks were D.R. Jardine, England captain in the bodyline series of 1932–33, Colin Cowdrey and M.J.K. Smith, who has the unique achievement of a century in each of his three University matches against Cambridge in the Varsity match at Lord's. Alan C. Smith led the club to six victories against first-class counties in 1959 and is now the Chief Executive of the Test & County Cricket Board.

DESCRIPTION OF GROUND AND FACILITIES

The University Parks cover about 65 acres and are freely open to the public. The cricket ground lies within the Parks but it is not in any way separated from them. Thus apart from the small pavilion complex, no part of the ground is in any way enclosed, except by trees on the north, east and south sides. Entrance therefore cannot be charged and no crowd numbers established.

The first match was played in 1881 by which time the pavilion had been constructed to the designs of Sir Thomas G. Jackson, architect of many nineteenth and early twentieth-century Oxford buildings. The pavilion is the main focus of the ground, it is a most impressive building with three striking gables in its steeply pitched roof surmounted by an impressive cupola. A part of the veranda has been enclosed to provide a press box. The Long Room is reminiscent of a University Hall with its great roof trusses. The walls are in panelled oak, on which the names of all Blues are recorded in gold lettering. A small scoreboard is situated to the side of the pavilion, while on the other side a single-storey modern building houses the assistant secretary's office and refreshment facilities.

A few benches are dispersed around the boundary, which is marked by a rope. The playing area is 132 metres by 140 metres and the pitch is positioned approximately north-south with the pavilion to the south. The pavilion area provides bench seating for about 300 spectators. Members of the public are advised to bring their own seats to matches. There are no car parking facilities for the general public or members except in the city centre car parks or in those streets to the north which are free from parking restrictions.

The character of the Parks is unique and the ground has seen many outstanding performances, beginning in 1886 when W.G. Grace took all 10 Oxford wickets for 49 runs when playing for MCC. This followed his 104 runs earlier in the same match.

THE PARKS OXFORD

WILL'S CIGARETTES.

E. R. T. HOLMES

ADDRESS   Oxford University Cricket Club, The Pavilion, University Parks, Parks Road, Oxford, Oxfordshire.
TELEPHONE NUMBER PROSPECTS OF PLAY   0865 57106

GROUND RECORDS AND SCORES

FIRST-CLASS MATCHES
Highest innings total for University: 589 *v.* Gents of England 1908
Highest innings total against University: 627 for 2 dec. by Gloucestershire 1930
Lowest innings total for University: 12 *v.* MCC 1877
Lowest innings total against University: 24 by MCC 1846
Highest individual innings for University: 236 E.R.T. Holmes *v.* Free Foresters 1927
Highest individual innings against University: 266 n.o. W. Place for Lancashire 1927
Best bowling performance in an innings for University: 9 for 38 T.B. Raikes *v.* Army 1924
Best bowling performance in an innings against University: 10 for 49 W.G. Grace for MCC 1886
Best bowling performance in a match for University: 15 for 65 B.J.T. Bosanquet *v.* Sussex 1900
Best bowling performance in a match against University: 16 for 225 J.E. Walsh for Leicestershire 1953
Best attendance: No crowd figures established.

LIMITED-OVERS MATCHES
Highest innings total for Combined Universities: 228 for 8 *v.* Surrey (BHC) 1990

MR L.C.H. PALAIRET
Oxford University/
Somerset

D. R. Jardine. 71

WILLS'S CIGARETTES.

MR. C. B. FRY (SUSSEX).

Highest innings total against Combined Universities: 366 for 4 by Derbyshire (BHC) 1991
Lowest innings total for Combined Universities: 122 *v.* Kent (BHC) 1976
Lowest innings total against Combined Universities: 127 for 2 by Warwickshire (BHC) 1973
Highest individual innings for Combined Universities: 91 A.J.T. Miller *v.* Surrey (BHC) 1984
Highest individual innings against Combined Universities: 133 C.G. Greenidge for Hampshire (BHC) 1987
Best bowling performance for Combined Universities: 3 for 31 P.L. Garlick *v.* Surrey (BHC) 1984
Best bowling performance against Combined Universities: 5 for 28 R.W. Hills for Kent (BHC) 1976
Best attendance: No crowd figures established.

HOW TO GET THERE

Rail Oxford (BR), 1 mile.
Bus Oxford 2/A, 10/A from Cornmarket Street; 52 links BR Oxford Station with Cornmarket Street (Telephone: 0865 711312).
Car From north: M40/A34, A423 or A43 signposted Oxford and city centre, then follow A4165 for University Parks signposted Parks Road for pedestrian access only to the Parks and cricket ground. From east: M40/A40 signposted Oxford and city centre, then follow A4165 for University Parks, situated 0.5 mile north-east of city centre in Parks Road. From west: A40, A420 or A34 signposted Oxford and city centre, then as east. From south: M40 junction 7 then follow A423 to city centre, then as north.

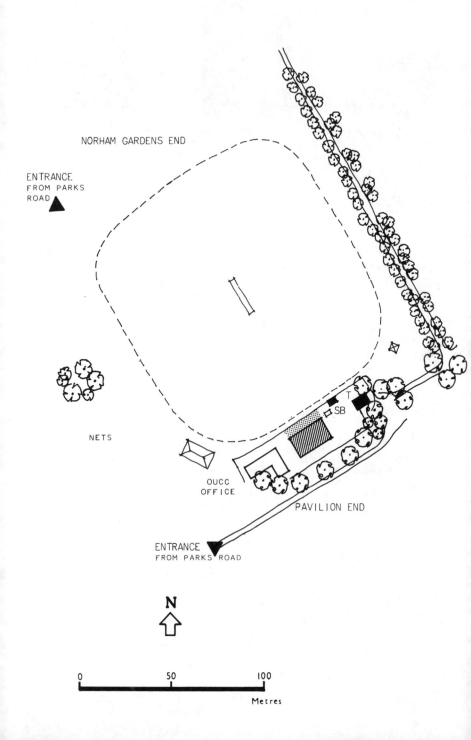

NORHAM GARDENS END

ENTRANCE
FROM PARKS
ROAD

NETS

OUCC
OFFICE

T

SB

PAVILION END

ENTRANCE
FROM PARKS ROAD

N

0   50   100

Metres

WHERE TO STAY AND OTHER INFORMATION

Cotswold Lodge (0865 512121), The Randolph (0865 247481), Eastgate (0865 248244) and many other smaller hotels and guest houses.

Disabled Areas   The ground is in a public park and there is ample access, but no car parks. Special arrangements in advance to Assistant Secretary's office.

Local Radio Station(s)   BBC Radio Oxford (95.2 MHz FM/1485 KHz MW), Radio 210 (102.9 MHz FM/1431 KHz MW).

Local Newspaper(s)   Oxford Mail, Oxford Times.

FRIENDS OF
ARUNDEL CASTLE

ARUNDEL – CASTLE PARK

Friends of Arundel Castle

Founded 1975
Colours Dark blue
Crest Red Baskerville 'N'
Secretary Miss D. Osborne, Friends of Arundel Castle C C, The
  Cricket Office, Arundel Park, Arundel, West Sussex BN18 9LH
  Telephone 0903 882462
Scorer Mrs K. Cohen
Groundsmen P. Eaton/Arundel Castle C C
Rapid Cricketline County Scores 0891 567500

GROUND

Arundel (Arundel Castle Park)
  No other grounds have been used for matches.

Arundel – Castle Park

While it is possible to establish that an Arundel Cricket Club existed as long ago as 1774, it was not until the work undertaken by the fifteenth Duke of Norfolk in 1894–95 that the present ground and pavilion to the north of Arundel Castle were constructed. All will agree that this was quite a perfect setting for a cricket arena, and the work commenced in 1894 was continued by Bernard, the sixteenth Duke of Norfolk, at one time president of M.C.C. and in 1962–63 manager of the MCC Tour of Australia. The team always played as the Duke of Norfolk's XI.

In 1975 Lavinia, Duchess of Norfolk, decided that, as a memorial to her late husband, cricket should continue at Arundel Park with the object of sustaining its unique character and to aid 'the promotion, encouragement and maintenance of the playing of cricket'.

With the assistance of two former secretaries of the MCC, Ronnie Aird and Billy Griffith, and Eddie Harrison of Sussex Martlets and Colin Cowdrey, she set about the task which led to the establishment of the Friends of Arundel Castle Cricket Club. Since that time, some forty-five matches have been played each year by teams assembled from various sources. For the more important matches the team is defined as Lavinia, Duchess of Norfolk's XI and of these the major fixture is always the annual match against the touring team. The first match with a touring team was in 1977 against the Australians when a crowd of some 6,000 attended.

In recent years the Friends of Arundel Castle Cricket Foundation has been established, assisted by a generous donation from Mr. J. Paul Getty Jr, with the aim of providing cricket and cricket coaching for youngsters. The former captain of Sussex John Barclay was appointed director of

COLIN COWDREY

A. I. C. DODEMAIDE

cricket and coaching, and in 1989 a new indoor cricket school was opened at the rear of the present pavilion. The pavilion is 22 yards long, the length of a cricket pitch.

DESCRIPTION OF GROUND AND FACILITIES

The cricket ground is to the north of Arundel Castle and set in idyllic surroundings. Access is obtained from London Road through the stable area to the south-west. There is ample car parking in the entrance area and to the south of the cricket ground. Cars can also be positioned close to the playing area if space is available. It is from this higher area that many sit to view the cricket. A new scoreboard has been erected on the north-west side and this also houses the scorers. Refreshment tents and other facilities are disposed in various parts of the ground, and there are ample toilet facilities. Members of the public are advised to bring their own seats (as are club members) to the special matches, particularly those against the tourists.

The ground slopes naturally from north-west to south-east but the cricket area has been levelled and is approximately circular, 152 metres by 140 metres. The pitch is aligned in a north–south direction. The area is enclosed within a surround of mature landscaped trees which provide a green backcloth to all activities on the field. Regrettably, the hurricane in October 1987 was responsible for removing many of the trees in the south and south-east areas but this has given a better view of the castle from the Park End. In 1990, championship cricket made a welcome first appearance at Castle Park when Sussex entertained neighbours Hampshire. Surrey were the visitors in 1991 and Hampshire will be the opponents in 1992. The only three first-class centuries scored on the ground have been by Darren Bicknell of Surrey, Chris Smith, formerly of

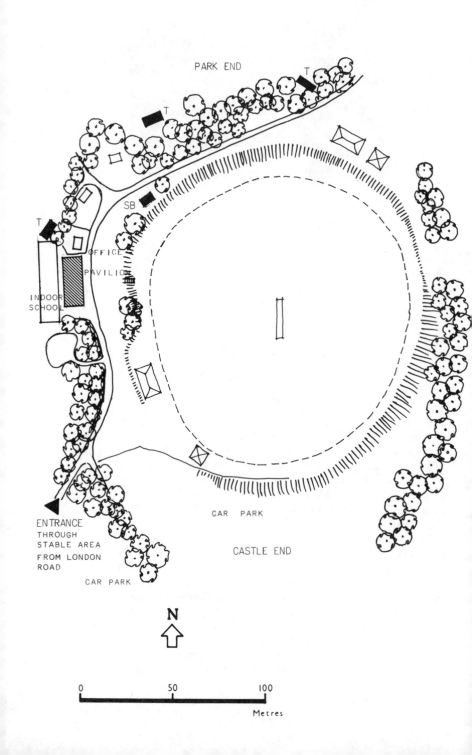

PARK END

T

T

T

SB

OFFICE

PAVILION

INDOOR
SCHOOL

ENTRANCE
THROUGH
STABLE AREA
FROM LONDON
ROAD

CAR PARK

CAR PARK

CASTLE END

N

0   50   100

Metres

Hampshire and Colin Wells for the hosts. Sussex had previously proposed using Castle Park in 1975 for a John Player League match with Derbyshire but the match was abandoned owing to heavy rain.

ADDRESS   Friends of Arundel Castle Cricket Club, The Pavilion, Arundel Park, Arundel, West Sussex BN18 9LH.
TELEPHONE NUMBER PROSPECTS OF PLAY   0903 882462

GROUND RECORDS AND SCORES

FIRST-CLASS MATCHES
For ground records and scores of first-class matches staged on the ground, see Sussex C C C section.

LIMITED-OVERS MATCHES (Lavinia Duchess of Norfolk's XI)

Highest innings total for Lavinia Duchess of Norfolk's XI: 277 for 6 v. New Zealanders 1990
Highest innings total against Lavinia Duchess of Norfolk's XI: 314 for 6 by Australians 1989
Lowest innings total for Lavinia Duchess of Norfolk's XI: 122 for 9 v. West Indians 1980
Lowest innings total against Lavinia Duchess of Norfolk's XI: 106 by Australians 1981
Highest individual innings for Lavinia Duchess of Norfolk's XI: 131 A.I.C. Dodemaide v. New Zealanders 1990
Highest individual innings against Lavinia Duchess of Norfolk's XI: 114 D.C. Boon for Australians 1989
Best bowling performance for Lavinia Duchess of Norfolk's XI: 3 for 17 R.A. Woolmer v. Australians 1977
Best bowling performance against Lavinia Duchess of Norfolk's XI: 4 for 18 G.J. Cosier for Australians 1977
Best attendance: 10,000 Lavinia Duchess of Norfolk's XI v. Australians 1989.

HOW TO GET THERE

Rail   Arundel (BR), 1 mile.
Bus   Southdown 212, 230 Worthing–Arundel Castle (Tel: 0903 37661).
Car   From north: A29 and A284 signposted Arundel, entrance to Arundel Park off Arundel bypass in London Road, north of town centre, enter park through stables and parkland, follow signs cricket. From east: A27 signposted Arundel and town centre, then follow signs Arundel Park and London Road for cricket ground, situated within Castle Park grounds. From west: A27 signposted Arundel and town centre, then as east. From south: A284 signposted Arundel and town centre, then as east.

WHERE TO STAY AND OTHER INFORMATION

Norfolk Arms (0903 882101), Bridge Hotel (0903 882242).

Disabled Areas No special area, request suitable position on path near pavilion.

Local Radio Station(s) BBC Radio Sussex (104.5 MHz FM/1161 KHz MW), Southern Sound (103.5 MHz FM/1323 KHz MW).

Local Newspaper(s) West Sussex Gazette.

SCOTLAND

DUNDEE – BROUGHTY FERRY

FORFAR

GLASGOW (CLYDESDALE C C)

GLASGOW (WEST OF SCOTLAND CRGP C C)

Scotland

Founded   1909 (Present Cricket Union)
Colours   Blue and white
Crest   Thistle
President   J.R. Laing
Chairman   C.H. Carruthers
Secretary   R.W. Barclay
General manager   A.J. Ritchie
Captain   O. Henry
Scorer/statistician   N.J. Leitch
Address   Caledonia House, South Gyle, Edinburgh, Scotland EH12 9DQ.
Telephone 031 317 7247 (SCU Office) 031 552 0828 (Home) 031 225 1516 (Office)
Facsimile 031 317 7103 (SCU Office)
Rapid Cricketline County Scores   0891 567500

ACHIEVEMENTS

Benson & Hedges Cup   Zonal rounds (12) 1980, 1981, 1982, 1983, 1984, 1985, 1986, 1987, 1988, 1989, 1990 and 1991.
National Westminster Bank Trophy   1st round (9) 1983, 1984, 1985, 1986, 1987, 1988, 1989, 1990 and 1991.

GROUNDS

 Forfarshire C C (Forthill, Broughty Ferry, Dundee)   Strathmore County C C (Lochside Park, Forfar)   Teacher's Clydesdale C C (Titwood, Pollokshields, Glasgow) and West of Scotland CRGP C C (Hamilton Cresent, Partick, Glasgow).

Other Grounds that have been used since 1969 are: Aberdeenshire C C, Mannofield, Morningside Road, Aberdeen AB1 7NB. Telephone: 0224 317888; Ayr C C, Cambusdoon, Alloway, Ayr. Telephone: 0292 42296; Drumpellier C C, Langloan, Coatbridge. Telephone: 0236 23713; Dumfries C C, Nunholm, Nunholm Road, Dumfries DG1 1JW. Telephone: 0387 52527; Grange C C, Raeburn Place, Edinburgh EH4 1HQ. Telephone: 031 332 2148; Greenock C C, Glenpark, Brisbane Street, Greenock. Telephone: 0475 24037; Kelburne C C, Whitehaugh, Paisley, Glasgow. Telephone: 041 889 4844; Perth County C C, Gannochy Sports Pavilion, The North Inch, Perth. Telephone: 0738 23852; Stenhousemuir C C, The Tryst, Stenhousemuir, Larber. Telephone: 0324 562448; Watsonians C C, Myreside, Myreside Road, Edinburgh. Telephone: 031 447 5200/ 1395.

Dundee – Broughty Ferry
(Forfarshire C C)

The Broughty Ferry ground will be used for the Scotland versus Ireland three day first-class match on 20–22 June 1992.

The ground is owned by Forthill Sports Club and the ground capacity is 5,000, and this figure was achieved for the local derby Forfarshire *v.* Perthshire on 6 June 1957. The formation of the Forfarshire Cricket Club was in the 1880s when the club was established at a meeting at the Royal British Hotel. Forfarshire C C's first match was with Glenalmond College and later games were staged with near neighbours Perthshire C C The club fields four XIs throughout the season with a number of junior teams. The club plays in the Scottish Championship, Shish Mahal Trophy, Beneagles Quaich Trophy and Haig National club knockout competition.

In 1882 a prominent member of the club first appeared and his name appears throughout the annals of Forfarshire cricket – W.R. Sharp, a prolific batsman and indeed a genuine all-rounder who kept wicket and bowled occasionally. In 1885 'W.R.' was elected club captain and he held this office for 40 years. He holds the highest score on the ground for the club and the main entrance gates to the ground were erected in his memory.

The Broughty Ferry ground is regarded as one of the best in Scotland and has been used for over 110 seasons. The club has long been regarded as one of the major teams in Scotland and a number of its cricketers have represented their country, including Alex Steele and Peter Rhind. The ground has a fine playing surface and many high-scoring matches have been staged here at Forthill. Scotland have staged a number of international matches on the ground and a whole variety of county teams have made visits. Tourists have included the Australians, Indians, New Zealanders and West Indians.

The Forfarshire club have engaged a professional for many years and the following have acted in this capacity since the Second World War; Frank Smailes, Dickie Fuller, Clairmonte Depeiza and Alf Pope. In 1970 the Forthill Sports Club was established and in 1972 the new pavilion was built. A match was staged between Forfarshire C C and The Lord's Taverners in 1972 to celebrate the opening of the pavilion.

Ground records for Forfarshire C C include a total of 422 against Fifeshire in 1907, and highest individual innings for the club of 198 n.o. by W.R. Sharp against Edinburgh Academicals in 1898. Kim Hughes the former Australian Test Captain, has the highest score on the ground of 218 n.o. while acting as professional for Watsonians in 1978. With the ball, J.H. Melville took 10 for 21 against the Grange in 1935.

ADDRESS Forfarshire C C, The Pavilion, Forthill, Fintry Place, Broughty Ferry, Dundee, Scotland.
TELEPHONE NUMBER PROSPECTS OF PLAY 0382 75550

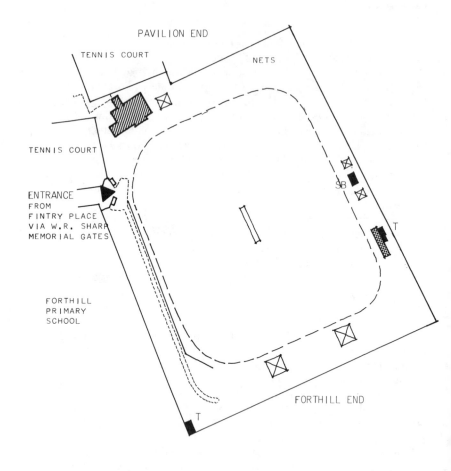

PAVILION END

TENNIS COURT

NETS

TENNIS COURT

SB

T

ENTRANCE
FROM
FINTRY PLACE
VIA W.R. SHARP
MEMORIAL GATES

FORTHILL
PRIMARY
SCHOOL

FORTHILL END

T

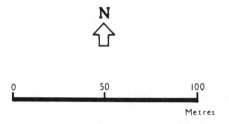

N

0	50	100

Metres

DESCRIPTION OF GROUND AND FACILITIES

The ground is entered from Fintry Place through the W.R. Sharp Memorial gates near the Forthill Primary School. The only permanent buildings are the pavilion/clubhouse, a small covered stand, the scoreboard and the groundsman's store and the toilets. Car parking is available within the ground and street parking is also available in the surrounding neighbourhood.

The members' enclosure is restricted to the main bar and clubroom within the clubhouse and all other areas are available to all spectators. Spectators are advised to bring their own seats to matches as only a few benches are provided. Refreshments are available in the main clubroom for members and in temporary tents for all other spectators. The pavilion/clubhouse is situated to the north-west of the playing area with a scoreboard and small covered stand sited to the east of the ground. The wicket is sited in a north–south disposition. Car parking within the ground is sited to the south and east of the playing area. Some cricket nets are sited to the north of the playing area. All the facilities are temporary and of the usual nature for out ground matches. The playing area is 130 metres by 108 metres and is defined by a rope and some advertising boards. The TV camera/commentary box and radio commentary point are positioned in the elevated viewing area of the pavilion.

GROUND RECORDS AND SCORES

FIRST-CLASS MATCHES
Highest innings total for Country: 190 v. New Zealanders 1978
Highest innings total against Country: 472 for 8 dec. by New Zealanders (Tour) 1978
Lowest innings total for Country: 81 v. Indians 1932
Lowest innings total against Country: 134 by Ireland 1924
Highest individual innings for Country: 64 J. Aitchison v. Worcestershire 1951
Highest individual innings against Country: 200 n.o. L. Outschoorn for Worcestershire 1951
Best bowling performance for Country in an innings: 5 for 32 J.H. Melville v. Indians (Tour) 1932
Best bowling performance against Country in an innings: 5 for 41 R. Jenkins for Worcestershire 1951
Best bowling performance for Country in a match: 8 for 67 J.H. Melville v. Indians 1932
Best bowling performance against Country in a match: 10 for 110 R. Jenkins for Worcestershire 1951
Best attendance: 3,000 v. Indians 1932

HOW TO GET THERE

Rail Dundee (BR), 2 miles; Broughty Ferry (BR), 0.25 mile (peak times only).

Bus   Tayside Buses 7/8 from Dundee, Seagate Bus Station and Dundee city centre to Forthill; 9/10/11 and 12 from Dundee city centre to Nursery Road, thence 5 minute walk for ground; also some buses from surrounding areas; Strathtay Scottish Stagecoach from Dundee city centre to Broughty Ferry Post Office, thence 10 minute walk.

Car   The ground is situated in Forthill Road adjoining Forthill Primary School, follow Kingsway and Balgillo Road for ground. From north: A929 or A92, signposted Dundee, then follow signs Broughty Ferry for Forthill Cricket Ground. From east: A930 or A92 signposted Dundee, then follow signs Broughty Ferry on eastern outskirts of Dundee. From west: A972 and A92 or A85 and A930, follow signs Dundee, then follow signs Broughty Ferry for Forthill Cricket Ground. From south: A92 taking Tay Road Bridge or M90 junction 10, then M85 junction 1, then A85 and A972 signposted Dundee, then as west.

WHERE TO STAY AND OTHER INFORMATION

Numerous hotels and guesthouses in Dundee and surrounding towns.

Disabled Areas   No special area, request suitable position.
Local Radio Station(s)   Radio Tay (102.8 MHz FM/1161 KHz MW).
Local Newspaper(s)   Dundee Courier, Evening Telegraph, The Scotsman, Scotland on Sunday.

Forfar (Strathmore County C C)

CLUB HISTORY AND DESCRIPTION OF GROUND AND FACILITIES

Strathmore County C C was established in 1868 and played at Zoar until the move to their present home in 1873. The first match was with Brechin and it was not until 1923 that the pavilion was built, with a further extension in 1926. Mr. J.A. Grant gifted the tea pavilion in 1935 and the scorebox was built in 1937. After a fire following a break-in during 1971 the pavilion was rebuilt and opened by the Earl of Strathmore. Recent years have seen the introduction of a new scoreboard, ground equipment, an artificial wicket and an improved square. The ground is located near to Forfar Loch to the north-west of the town centre. The permanent buildings include a pavilion with bar, 50 seats and changing facilities, tea room veranda, store and scoreboard together with nets. For Scotland matches the majority of the facilities are temporary and these include 200 seats, toilets, hospitality marquees and refreshment tents. The ground capacity is 3,000 and 100 cars can be parked within the ground itself. The playing area is defined by a rope and

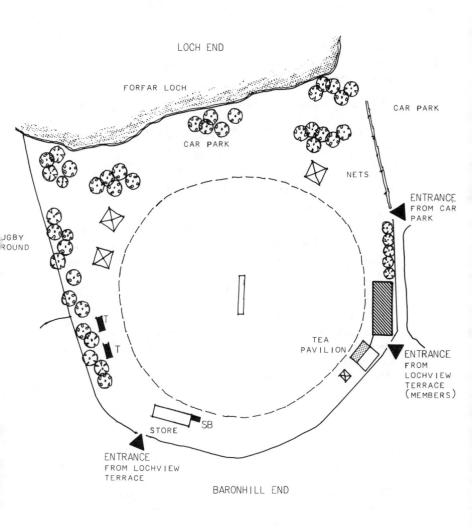

LOCH END

FORFAR LOCH

CAR PARK

CAR PARK

NETS

RUGBY GROUND

ENTRANCE FROM CAR PARK

T

T

TEA PAVILION

ENTRANCE FROM LOCHVIEW TERRACE (MEMBERS)

STORE

SB

ENTRANCE FROM LOCHVIEW TERRACE

BARONHILL END

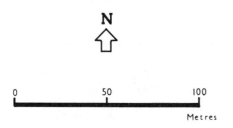

N

| 0 | 50 | 100 |

Metres

some advertising boards with dimensions of 126 metres by 134 metres. Car parking is also available on the football pitch for 200 cars. A press box is sited in a caravan from where radio commentary is also undertaken. The only Scotland Benson and Hedges Cup zonal group match to have been staged here was in 1990 against Lancashire. Northamptonshire are due to visit Lochside on 21 April 1992. The snow capped Grampian mountains and the nearby loch provide this venue with a special appeal.

ADDRESS Strathmore County Cricket Club., The Pavilion, Lochside Park, Forfar, Scotland.
TELEPHONE PROSPECTS OF PLAY 0307 64289

GROUND RECORDS AND SCORES

LIMITED-OVERS MATCH (BHC)
Highest innings total for Country: 163 for 8 *v*. Lancashire 1991
Highest innings total against Country: 164 for 3 by Lancashire 1991
Highest individual innings for Country: 31 A.B. Russell *v*. Lancashire 1991
Highest individual innings against Country: 63 G.D. Mendis for Lancashire 1991
Best bowling performance for Country: 2 for 47 D. Cowan *v*. Lancashire 1991
Best bowling performance against Country: 4 for 21 P.A.J. DeFreitas for Lancashire 1991
Best attendance: 2,500 *v*. Lancashire 1991

HOW TO GET THERE

Rail Dundee (BR), 12 miles.
Bus City Link buses serve Dundee, then take local Scottish Buses from Dundee and surrounding areas to Forfar town centre.
Car From north: A94 and B9128, signposted Forfar and town centre, then follow signs for Lochside Park for Strathmore County C C ground. From east: B9134, B9133 or A932, signposted Forfar and town centre, then as north or as north. From west: A929 and A932 or A94 or A928, signposted Forfar and town centre, then as north. From south: A929 and A932 or B9128 signposted Forfar and town centre, then as north.

WHERE TO STAY AND OTHER INFORMATION

Royal Hotel or smaller guesthouses, or stay in Dundee.

Disabled Areas No special area request suitable position surrounding playing area.

Local Radio Station(s) Radio Tay (102.8 MHz FM/1161 KHz MW).
Local Newspaper(s) Dundee Courier and Advertiser, Forfar Dispatch (Weekly).

Glasgow (Clydesdale C C)

The Clydesdale Cricket Club was established in 1848 and its founder and guiding light for the first twenty-five years was Mr Archie Campbell from Hawick. A cricket ball presented to Mr Campbell while club president in 1873 can be found in the pavilion trophy cabinet today. Around that time the Clydesdale C C players passed their winters playing association football and became founder members of the Scottish Football Association with Mr Campbell as the first president. Clydesdale was one of the big four football teams of its time, the others were Renton, Third Lanark and Queen's Park. In 1874 Clydesdale were finalists in the first ever Scottish Cup Final, they lost to Queen's Park at Hampden Park.

Clydesdale C C moved from their first ground in Kinning Park to their present location though the original Titwood Ground was where the adjacent Hutchenson's Grammar School is now situated. The Kinning Park ground was sold to a little-known, up and coming young football club established in 1873 called Glasgow Rangers! Clydesdale has always had a tradition of Rangers support since then. Clydesdale C C is one of the oldest clubs in Scotland and were founder members of Scotland's top cricket league, the Western District Cricket Union, founded in 1903. The club has won the league on twelve occasions and has won the Scottish Knockout Cup six times in the last twenty-six years and made six appearances in the final in the last seven seasons.

In 1977 the Titwood Athletic Grounds were chosen by the Scottish Sports Council as the National Sports Facility for cricket. The club therefore hosts the majority of international and tourists matches. In 1986 the ground was purchased from the feu superiors and vested its ownership in a charitable trust, the Titwood Sports Ground Trust. In 1989 the club embarked on a five year programme to develop the ground with improved wickets and three new hockey pitches.

The club's proudest moment was reaching the quarter-finals of the NCA Cup in 1978 by beating Northumberland County at Jesmond with a team of twelve players all home grown who started their cricket as junior members at Titwood. Clydesdale C C has contributed numerous international players to Scotland C U teams, and probably the most famous were Dan Mackay, between the wars, and Terry Racionzer who played for Sussex C C C winner of over fifty Scottish caps during the period 1963–88. In 1992 the matches to be staged at Titwood will include two tourists one-day internationals with the Pakistanis. Clydesdale C C will celebrate its 150th anniversary in 1998.

ADDRESS   Clydesdale Cricket Club, The Pavilion, Titwood Athletic Grounds, Beaton Road, Pollokshields, Glasgow, Scotland G41 4LA.
TELEPHONE PROSPECTS OF PLAY   041 423 1463

DESCRIPTION OF GROUND AND FACILITIES

The ground is enclosed and is overlooked by flatted housing to the north and south, with traditional housing to the west, and the Hutcheson's Grammar School to the east. Car parking is available within the ground for members and there is ample space in the adjoining school grounds and local street parking. Entry to the Titwood Athletic Grounds is from Beaton Road via the car park at the rear of the members' pavilion and through the vehicle gate from Dolphin Road. A further pedestrian entrance is available in Meldrum Gardens.

Facilities for cricket include an enormous cricket square over 100 metres long with an integral non-turf pitch at the western end. There are also two non-turf practice nets and some grass nets to the north-west of the playing area. During the cricket season the club expects to stage cricket seven days a week and frequently two matches are being played at the same time, one at each end of the square. The 7.5 acre ground is picturesque and very flat with the wicket sited in a north–south disposition. There is a slight slope away from the cricket table at the south-western corner. There is a two-level covered concrete stand along the boundary at the Kirkcaldy End of the ground with a 200-seat mobile aluminium stand available near to the boundary. The original pavilion, built early this century has been much added to, but the cluster of permanent buildings in the north-east corner of the ground also includes a separate junior cricket pavilion.

The pavilion and pavilion terrace are available to members and players only. The rest of the ground is available to all spectators. Members of the general public are advised to bring their own collapsible seats to all matches as only 1,500 seats are available in a ground with a capacity of 5,000. Refreshment and bar facilities are available for members in the main pavilion and for the public in tented accommodation and the junior pavilion. Toilets are available in the main pavilion, junior pavilion and temporary buildings. A SCU souvenir shop is available near the pavilion area. The press tent is situated adjacent to the scoreboard and the TV camera/commentary box is sited in the North Stand. An area for hospitality marquees is situated to the east of the playing area. The dimensions of the playing area are 131 metres by 137 metres and the field is almost circular in shape and is defined by a rope and some advertising boards.

KIRKCALDY ROAD END

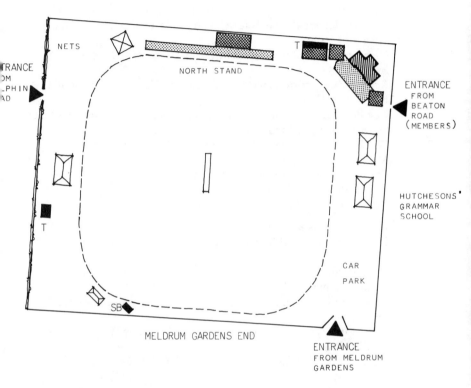

NETS

NORTH STAND

ENTRANCE
FROM
DOLPHIN
ROAD

ENTRANCE
FROM
BEATON
ROAD
(MEMBERS)

HUTCHESONS'
GRAMMAR
SCHOOL

CAR

PARK

T

SB

MELDRUM GARDENS END

ENTRANCE
FROM MELDRUM
GARDENS

N

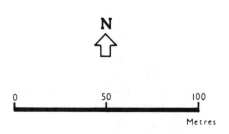

0   50   100

Metres

GROUND RECORDS AND SCORES

FIRST-CLASS MATCHES

Highest innings total for Country: 396 for 7 dec. *v.* Ireland 1986
Highest innings total against Country: 356 by Ireland 1984
Lowest innings total for Country: 193 *v.* MCC 1963
Lowest innings total against Country: 186 by Ireland 1986
Highest individual innings for Country: 145 I.L. Philip *v.* Ireland 1986
Highest individual innings against Country: 95 J.D. Monteith for Ireland 1984
Best bowling performance in an innings for Country: 5 for 48 C.R. Hogan *v.* MCC. 1963
Best bowling performance in an innings against Country: 4 for 113 S.C. Corlett for Ireland 1986
Best bowling performance in a match for Country: 7 for 117 D.G. Moir *v.* Ireland 1986
Best bowling performance in a match against Country: 5 for 98 S.C. Corlett for Ireland 1984
Best attendance: 3,000 *v.* Ireland 1986

LIMITED-OVERS MATCHES

Highest innings total for Country: 208 for 6 *v.* Nottinghamshire (BHC) 1990
Highest innings total against Country: 259 for 5 by Northamptonshire (BHC) 1982
Lowest innings total for Country: 82 *v.* Northamptonshire (BHC) 1982
Lowest innings total against Country: 110 for 8 by Worcestershire (BHC) 1986
Highest individual innings for Country: 74 O. Henry *v.* Indians (Tour) 1990
Highest individual innings against Country: 130 n.o. C.E.B. Rice for Nottinghamshire (BHC) 1982
Best bowling performance for Country: 4 for 16 C.L. Parfitt *v.* Nottinghamshire (BHC) 1990
Best bowling performance against Country: 4 for 21 Sarfraz Nawaz for Northamptonshire (BHC) 1982
Best attendance: 3,500 *v.* Indians (Tour) 1990

HOW TO GET THERE

Rail Crossmyloof (BR), 100m; Maxwell Park (BR), 100m from Glasgow Central (BR).
Bus Various buses from City Centre to Shawlands Cross, thence 5 minute walk to Crossmyloof for Titwood Athletic Grounds.
Car M8 to M77 Spur then take left at roundabout following signs to Kilmarnock, go straight ahead at first traffic lights and then take

left into Dolphin Road at second traffic lights for Titwood Athletic
Ground and Clydesdale C C. From north: A81, A879, A803 or A80,
follow signs Glasgow city centre, then follow signs Pollokshields for
Titwood Athletic Ground in Kirkcaldy Road. From east: M8 junction
20, then follow signs Pollokshields for Titwood Athletic Ground; or
A8, A89, A74 or A724 to Glasgow city centre then as north. From
west: M8 junction 20, then as east; or A737, A736, A8, A814 or A77
to Glasgow city centre, then as north. From south: M74, M73 then
M8 junction 20, then as east or west; or A749, A724 or A77 to
Glasgow city centre then as north.

WHERE TO STAY AND OTHER INFORMATION

Various hotels and guesthouses in Greater Glasgow and surrounding
areas. For details contact Glasgow Tourist Board (041 204 4400).

Disabled Areas   No special area exists so request suitable position.
Access to the pavilion is difficult. Car parking is available in Beaton
Road to the rear of the pavilion.
Local Radio Station(s)   BBC Radio Scotland (92.5 MHz FM/810
KHz MW), Radio Clyde (102.5 MHz FM/1152 KHz MW).
Local Newspaper(s)   Glasgow Herald, The Scotsman, Scotland on
Sunday, Daily Record.

Glasgow (West of Scotland CGRP C C)

The West of Scotland Cricket Club was founded in 1862 in the suburban
village of Partick to the north-west of central Glasgow by a group of
local businessmen under the presidency of Col Buchanan, later Sir David
Carrick Buchanan. In the early days, because of the facilities and
support, the ground was much in use for more events than just cricket. In
the years 1870–72 Scotland played England in association football
international matches at Hamilton Cresent, and the 1876 Scottish Cup
Final played between Queen's Park and Third Lanark was staged at the
Partick Ground. Hockey internationals were staged by Scotland during
the period from 1914 to the late 1960s. From 1870 to 1939 Partick was
home of the West of Scotland Rugby Football Club and four Scottish
rugby internationals were staged on the ground rather than at Murray-
field in Edinburgh.
    The first note of cricket at Hamilton Cresent dates from 1878 when
the club became famous for organizing matches against famous England
XIs which included W.G. Grace, J.T. Tyldesley and C.B. Fry. The
Australian tourists were frequent visitors and have played several times
in the last 110 years, the last was in 1989 when the attendance was some
3,500. The West of Scotland C C plays in the Western District Cricket
Union, formed in 1893, including nine other clubs within the wider
district. Until recently (1989 and 1991) the West of Scotland C C were

PAVILION END

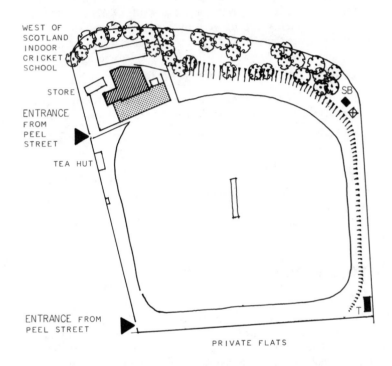

WEST OF
SCOTLAND
INDOOR
CRICKET
SCHOOL

STORE

ENTRANCE
FROM
PEEL
STREET

TEA HUT

SB

ENTRANCE FROM
PEEL STREET

T

PRIVATE FLATS

BURGH HALL STREET END

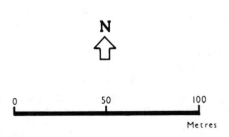

N

0   50   100

Metres

champions only once in this century. Before and after the Second World War the club has nearly always engaged a club professional for his playing and coaching ability and these have included; Harry Preston, Bert Wensley, Charlie Harris, Frank Vigar and Tom Atkinson. In later years the club relied on overseas professionals, including Intikhab Alam, Salahuddin, Trevor Bayliss, Clive Rice and in 1991, Mark Harper. In 1962 the club celebrated its centenary with a cricket week and dinner in a major hotel with Harry Altham, President of MCC as guest of honour. The club stage many fund raising events and thanks to the sponsorship of Colin Robertson Graham and Partners CRGP-Bute UK, a firm of Surveyors and Architects, the club has managed to secure overseas professionals for the last two seasons. The West of Scotland C C field three XIs during the season named The Eleven, Partick XI and Hamilton Cresent XI. There are also under-18, under-15 and under-12 colts teams.

In 1992 the Hamilton Cresent Ground will again be used for a Benson & Hedges Cup zonal group match, with the visitors being Hampshire. The ground has particularly good drying conditions. The Scottish Knockout Cup Final, Divisional Games and Scotland 'B' matches are staged on the ground each season. During the winter months the ground is used for hockey by two local clubs and is the training ground for Glasgow Rangers F C.

ADDRESS   West of Scotland Cricket Club, The Pavilion, Hamilton Cresent, Peel Street, Partick, Glasgow, Scotland G11 5LU.
TELEPHONE NUMBER PROSPECTS OF PLAY   041 339 0688

DESCRIPTION OF GROUND AND FACILITIES

The West of Scotland C C ground is owned by the club and is self-contained with permanent facilities including a pavilion, Tea room, scoreboard, indoor cricket school and some seating. Entry to the ground is from Peel Street and car parking is only available within the ground for players and officials. Street parking is available within the neighbouring streets; Peel Street, Fortrose Street and Burgh Hall Street for the public. The cricket square has approximately 36 wickets and the playing area is well drained with ample groundsman's equipment. The pavilion sited in the north-west corner of the ground and this is available to members' only. Bar and refreshment facilities are also provided in this building.

To the north and west of the playing area is the raised grass bank where spectators can view the play from a level above the playing area. A scoreboard sited in the north-east corner of the ground houses the scorers and adjacent is a press tent. Refreshment facilities are available in the tea room for all spectators and also in temporary facilities around the playing area. Close to the pavilion is the groundsman's stores and to the rear of the pavilion is the West of Scotland Indoor Cricket School, which is used during big matches as an area for hospitality suites. The southern end of the ground is used by sponsors and temporary seating is installed there for the public.

The majority of seating consists of temporary chairs and these can be moved around the ground by spectators. The best views are available from the banks and pavilion enclosure. The ground capacity is 3,500 and seating for 1,500 is provided, so spectators are advised to bring their own collapsible seating to all important matches. Toilets are available in the pavilion, extension hut and in temporary buildings around the ground. The SCU have a small souvenir tent on the ground near the main entrance. The TV camera/commentary box is positioned on a gantry at the southern end of the ground when required. The playing area is rectangular in shape and the dimensions are 112 metres by 123 metres and is defined by a rope and white fence which surrounds the perimeter of the playing area.

GROUND RECORDS AND SCORES

LIMITED-OVERS MATCHES
Highest innings total for Country: 226 for 9 *v.* Essex (BHC) 1990
Highest innings total against Country: 319 for 8 by Kent (BHC) 1991
Lowest innings total for Country: 90 *v.* Gloucestershire (BHC) 1983
Lowest innings total against Country: 91 for 7 by Gloucestershire (BHC) 1983
Highest individual innings for Country: 70 B.M.W. Patterson *v.* Australians (Tour) 1989
Highest individual innings against Country: 110 N.R. Taylor for Kent (BHC) 1991
Best bowling performance for Country: 5 for 33 D.G. Moir *v.* Australians (Tour) 1989
Best bowling performance against Country: 4 for 34 S.D. Fletcher for Yorkshire (BHC) 1987
Best attendance: 3,500 *v.* Australians (Tour) 1989

HOW TO GET THERE

Rail   Partick (BR), 100m from Glasgow Queen's Street Station.
Bus   Strathclyde Buses 6, 16, 62 and 64, and Kelvin Bus 5 link ground with Glasgow city centre and Partick.
Car   Hamilton Cresent is situated in Peel Street off Dumbarton Road to the north-west of central Glasgow. From north: A81, A879, A803 or A80, follow signs Partick and Partickhill for Hamilton Cresent cricket ground which is entered from Peel Street close to Partick Railway Station. From east: M8 junction 17, then follow A82 and Dumbarton for Partick and Peel Street; or A80, A8, A74 or A724 to Glasgow city centre, then follow A82 for Partick. From west: M8 junction 25 then follow A739 signposted Partick for Hamilton Cresent; or A82, A8 or A737 to Glasgow city centre, then follow A82 for Partick. From south: M74, M73 then M8 junction 17, then as east or A749, A726, A77 or A736 to Glasgow city centre, then follow A82 for Partick.

WHERE TO STAY AND OTHER INFORMATION

Nearby hotels include The Wickets beside the ground, or stay in Central Glasgow at the Central, Albany, Hospitality or Holiday Inn. Contact Glasgow Tourist Board for details (Telephone: 041 204 4400).

Disabled Areas   An enclosure is available around the perimeter of the ground on the level area near the tea room.

Local Radio Station(s)   Radio Clyde (102.5 MHz FM/1152 KHz MW), BBC Radio Scotland (92.5 MHz FM/810 KHz MW).

Local Newspaper(s)   Glasgow Herald, Daily Record, The Scotsman, Glasgow Guardian, Glasgow Glaswegian.

IRELAND

DUBLIN (CLONTARF C C)

Ireland

Founded 1859
Colours Green
Crest Shamrock
President K.F. O'Riordan
Chairman F.A. Malin
Secretary D. Scott
Manager J. Boyce
Director of coaching V.F. Savino
Captain P.B. Jackson
Scorer E.M. Power
Statistician D. Scott
Address 45 Foxrock Park, Foxrock, Dublin, Republic of Ireland 18.
Telephone 010 3531 2893943 (Home) 010 3531 6793661 (Office)
Facsimile 010 3531 6798837
Rapid Cricketline County Scores 0891 567500

ACHIEVEMENTS

Gillette Cup 1st round (1) 1980
National Westminster Bank Trophy 1st Round (11) 1981, 1982,
1983, 1984, 1985, 1986, 1987, 1988, 1989, 1990 and 1991.

GROUNDS

Clontarf C C (Castle Avenue, Dublin).
Other grounds that have been used since 1969 are: Carlisle C C,
Kimmage, Dublin. Telephone: (010) 3531 555490; Coleraine C C,
Lodge Road, Coleraine, Co. Derry. Telephone: 0265 3972;
Downpatrick C C, Stangford Road, Downpatrick. Telephone: (010)
3531 612869; Leinster C C, Observatory Lane, Rathmines, Dublin 6.
Telephone: (010) 3531 972428; Londonderry C C, Beechgrove,
Londonderry. Telephone: Directory Enquiries; Malahide C C,
Malahide Cricket Ground, Malahide, Co. Dublin. Telephone: (010)
3531 450607; North of Ireland C C, Ormeau Cricket Ground,
Ormeau Road, Belfast 7. Telephone: 0232 221096.

Dublin (Clontarf C C)

Castle Avenue is the home of Clontarf Cricket Club in Dublin. The Club
fields three XI's throughout the season and plays in the Belvedere Bon
League within the Leinster section. Clontarf C C plays league matches
against thirteen teams including; Leinster, Carlisle, North County,
Phoenix, Malahide, Merrion and Dublin University Cricket Clubs.
Clontarf won the Wiggins Teape League Final in 1990 by 10 wickets

against Old Belvedere at Malahide. The only current Ireland players who represent Clontarf C C are Michael Rea and Deryck Vincent.

The Castle Avenue ground has been used for three previous National Westminster Bank Trophy – matches against Gloucestershire (1981), Sussex (1983) and Middlesex (1991). The new eighteenth county, Durham, are due to play a 1st round National Westminster Bank Trophy tie at Castle Avenue against Ireland in 1992.

On 8–9 June 1990 Worcestershire visited Castle Avenue and staged two one-day matches against Ireland. During the first match Graeme Hick scored 101 n.o. and Ian Botham 40 n.o. in a Worcestershire total of 224 for 4 in 34 overs. Ireland replied with 89 for 8 in 34 overs. In the second match Worcestershire recorded 304 all out with David Leatherdale scoring 76 and Ian Botham 61. A. Nelson took 4 for 81 including the wickets of Curtis and Hick. Ireland scored 158 for 8 with S. Smythe scoring 59. The matches were sponsored by James Martin Associates and the Allied Irish Bank.

Many tourists' matches have been staged at Castle Avenue when the Irish Cricket Union has hosted Test nations to Ireland for one-day and two-day visits. In recent years matches have been spread between Northern Ireland and the Republic.

Ground records for National Westminster Bank Trophy matches include innings of 69 from M.A. Masood against Sussex and 70 by Andy Stovold for Gloucestershire. The best bowling performances have been achieved by D.A. Lewis and D.A. Graveney, while captain of Gloucestershire. Ground attendances have been in the region of 2,500–3,500; the best was 4,000 for the visit of Middlesex in 1991.

ADDRESS   Clontarf Cricket Club, The Pavilion, Castle Avenue, Clontarf, Dublin, Republic of Ireland 3.
TELEPHONE NUMBER PROSPECTS OF PLAY   010 3531 336214

DESCRIPTION OF GROUND AND FACILITIES

The only entrance to the Clontarf Cricket Ground is from Castle Avenue to the south-east of the playing area. Car parking is available within the ground to the rear of the pavilion and near the groundsman's stores where play can be viewed from some positions. Car parking is also available outside the ground within the neighbouring streets.

The only permanent buildings are the pavilion, changing rooms, members' bar/lounge and press box, which is situated at right angles to the wicket. The scoreboard and groundsman's stores are situated to the north of the pavilion at the Northern End of the ground. To the south of the pavilion are temporary marquees where refreshments can be obtained. Members' refreshments can be obtained in the clubhouse area where Guinness is on tap!

The majority of tents at the Castle End are for sponsors. Only 20 per cent of the seating which is provided is permanent so all spectators are advised to bring their own collapsible seating to all matches. Seating is temporary for all spectators. There is no special members' enclosure for matches and the entire ground is open to all spectators. The playing area

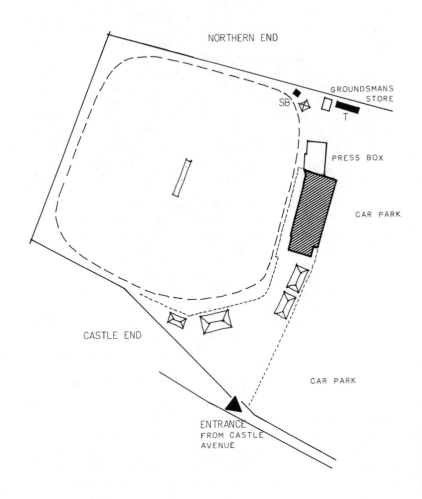

NORTHERN END

GROUNDSMANS
STORE

SB

T

PRESS BOX

CAR PARK

CASTLE END

CAR PARK

ENTRANCE
FROM CASTLE
AVENUE

N

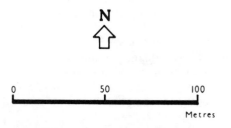

0   50   100

Metres

is smooth and flat and is defined by a rope and some advertising boards. The dimensions are 122 metres by 118 metres. Toilets are available in the pavilion and in temporary buildings around the ground.

A small Irish Cricket Union stall sells programmes, ties and souvenirs but there is little cricketana in the pavilion other than some Clontarf C C team photographs.

If required, the TV camera/commentary box is sited at the Castle End directly above the sightscreen.

GROUND RECORDS AND SCORES

LIMITED-OVERS MATCHES
Highest innings total for Country: 171 for 9 *v*. Middlesex (NWBT) 1991
Highest innings total against Country: 267 for 7 by Sussex (NWBT) 1983
Lowest innings total for Country: 75 *v*. Gloucestershire (NWBT) 1981
Lowest innings total against Country: 216 for 9 by Middlesex (NWBT) 1991
Highest individual innings for Country: 69 M.A. Masood *v*. Sussex (NWBT) 1983
Highest individual innings against Country: 70 A.W. Stovold for Gloucestershire (NWBT) 1981
Best bowling performance for Country: 4 for 47 D.A. Lewis *v*. Middlesex (NWBT) 1991
Best bowling performance against Country: 5 for 11 D.A. Graveney for Gloucestershire (NWBT) 1981
Best attendance: 4,000 *v*. Middlesex (NWBT) 1991

HOW TO GET THERE

Rail Dart service from Dublin City Station to Killester Station.
Bus Dublin Buses 32, 44A and 54A from Dublin city centre to Castle Avenue.
Car The Clontarf C C ground is situated off Castle Avenue close to the junction with Kincora Grove, to the east of the city centre. From north: M1, N1, N2 or N3, follow signs Dublin and city centre, then Howth for Clontarf and cricket ground. From west: N4 or N7, follow signs Dublin and city centre, then as north. From south: N7 or N11 follow signs Dublin and city centre, then as north.

WHERE TO STAY AND OTHER INFORMATION

Forte Crest Hotel, Dublin Airport (010 353 1379211)

Disabled Areas No special area, request suitable position.
Local Radio Station(s) Radio Ulster (93.0 MHz FM/1341 KHz MW).
Local Newspaper(s) Irish Post, Dublin Mail.

LEAGUE CRICKET CONFERENCE

HASLINGDEN

League Cricket Conference

Founded 1962
Colours Green
Crest Daffodil and red rose above 'LCC'
President T.W. Graveney OBE
Vice-president J.D. Scholfield FCIS
Chairman R. Cherry
Secretary N. Edwards ACII
Team manager M. Regan
Captain (chosen on a match basis)
Scorer (chosen on a match basis)
Statistician N. Edwards ACII
Address 1 Longfield, Freshfield, Formby, Merseyside L37 3LD.
Telephone 07048 77103 (Home)
Rapid Cricketline County Scores 0891 567500

GROUNDS

Haslingden C C (Bentgate, Haslingden).

Other grounds that have been used since 1969 are: Oxton C C, Townfield Lane, Birkenhead, Wirral. Telephone: 051 652 1331; Colwyn Bay C C 77 Penrhyn Avenue, Rhos-on-Sea, Colwyn Bay. Telephone: 0492 44103; West Bromwich Dartmouth C C, Sandwell Park, West Bromwich, West Midlands. Telephone: Directory Enquiries; Chester-le-Street C C, Ropery Lane, Chester-le-Street. Telephone: 091 388 3684; Sunderland C C, Ashbrooke Cricket Ground, Ashbrooke, Sunderland. Telephone: 091 528 4536; Middleton C C, Cricket Ground, Middleton, Manchester. Telephone: Directory Enquiries; Nantwich C C, Whitehouse Lane, Nantwich. Telephone: 0270 626155; Wolverhampton Town C C, Cricket Ground, Wolverhampton. Telephone: Directory Enquiries.

Haslingden C C

The Haslingden Cricket Club was founded in 1853 and the ground at Bentgate has been used since that date. Haslingden C C have been members of the Matthew Brown Lancashire League since its formation in 1892 and have won the league on ten occasions: in 1892, 1900, 1920, 1953, 1983, 1985, 1987, 1988, 1989 and 1991.

Club professionals have mainly been overseas imports, which have included many Test players including: West Indians – George Headley, Clive Lloyd and Andy Roberts, Australians – Dennis Lillee, Mick Malone, Geoff Lawson, Simon O'Donnell and Mike Whitney; and Indian Vinoo Mankad. The 1992 professional will be Phil Simmons, the West Indian Test opening batsman. Other Test players who played for

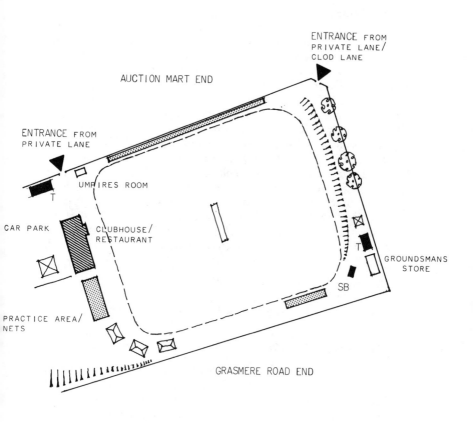

ENTRANCE FROM PRIVATE LANE/ CLOD LANE

AUCTION MART END

ENTRANCE FROM PRIVATE LANE

T

UMPIRES ROOM

CAR PARK

CLUBHOUSE/ RESTAURANT

T

GROUNDSMANS STORE

SB

PRACTICE AREA/ NETS

GRASMERE ROAD END

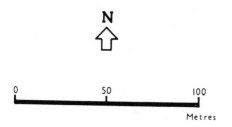

N

0   50   100

Metres

Lancashire League clubs in 1991 included; Roger Harper (Bacup), Peter Sleep (Rishton), Mudassar Nazar (Burnley) and Hartley Alleyne (Nelson).

The Bentgate Ground is owned by Haslingden C C and is pleasantly situated on the southern outskirts of the town; it is easily reached by car and public transport although the nearest railway station is some miles away. The pavilion has been extended several times in recent years and has a members' lounge room and a large ballroom.

In 1992 the ground will be used for the first time by the League Cricket Conference for a one-day match with the tourists from Pakistan to celebrate the centenary of the Lancashire League. Haslingden as hosts by virtue of their current status as League Champions and as owners of a ground with ample facilities to accommodate a crowd of approximately 4,000. The match will be played for the first time for the Boddingtons Bitter International Cricket Challenge. This will be the eighth match staged by the League Cricket Conference with the tourists and the first with Pakistan; the previous matches have been staged with West Indians (Colwyn Bay) 1984, Zimbabweans (Middleton C C, Manchester) 1985, Indians (Chester-le-Street) 1986, Sri Lankans (Oxton C C, Birkenhead) 1988, Australians (West Bromwich Dartmouth) 1989, Indians (Sunderland) 1990 and West Indians (Trowbridge) 1991.

ADDRESS Haslingden Cricket Club, The Pavilion, Private Lane, Bentgate, Haslingden, Rossendale, Lancashire.
TELEPHONE NUMBER PROSPECTS OF PLAY 0706 215365

DESCRIPTION OF GROUND AND FACILITIES

The main entrance to the ground is from Private Lane to the north-west of the pavilion and clubhouse. A further entrance is available at the junction of Private Lane and Clod Lane opposite the Sykeside County House Hotel. Once inside the ground, the only permanent buildings are the pavilion, which includes a bar, restaurant, members lounge, ballroom and two toilet areas, scorebox and groundsmans store. The majority of the seating is temporary and a further quantity of 2,000 seats will be provided for the League Cricket Conference match. Refreshments and bar facilities will be available in temporary marquees and a number of small kiosks around the ground. A press tent will be located next to the scoreboard in the south-east corner of the ground. Car parking will not be available within the ground, other than for players and officials, so spectators should park on the practice ground or car parks situated off Private Lane near the former Cattle Market and Auction Mart. Hospitality marquees will be available at the rear and to the side of the pavilion and spectators would be advised to bring their own seats to this match. The playing area is 97 metres by 121 metres, approximately circular in shape, and is defined by a rope and some advertising boards.

LEAGUE CRICKET CONFERENCE versus TOURISTS: RECORDS AND SCORES

NON-FIRST-CLASS/LIMITED-OVERS MATCHES

Highest innings total for Conference: 264 for 7 *v*. Zimbabweans at Middleton 1985

Highest innings total against Conference: 401 by West Indians at Colwyn Bay 1984

Lowest innings total for Conference: 120 for 4 dec. *v*. Sri Lankans at Oxton 1988

Lowest innings total against Conference: 138 for 3 dec. by Sri Lankans at Oxton 1988

Highest individual innings for Conference: 75 C.L. Hooper *v*. Indians at Chester-le-Street 1986

Highest individual innings against Conference: 170 D.M. Jones for Australians at West Bromwich Dartmouth 1989

Best bowling performance for Conference: 6 for 37 A. Merrick *v*. Zimbabweans at Middleton 1985

Best bowling performance against Conference: 6 for 26 C.A. Walsh for West Indians at Colwyn Bay 1984

Best attendance: 3,500 *v*. West Indians at Colwyn Bay 1984

HOW TO GET THERE

Rail Rawtenstall (BR), 3 miles; Accrington (BR) 5 miles.

Bus Blackburn Corporation buses pass ground and link between Blackburn Bus Station and Manchester Central Bus Station.

Car Haslingden is situated to the south-east of Blackburn and south-west of Burnley in Lancashire. From north: A680 or A56, signposted Haslingden, then follow signs for cricket and entrance to Haslingden C C near the large Auction Mart Car Centre off Clod Lane. From east: A682 or A681, signposted Haslingden, then as north. From west: A677 or B6232, signposted Haslingden, then as north. From south: M66 then A56 or A56, signposted Haslingden, then as north.

WHERE TO STAY AND OTHER INFORMATION

Sykeside Country House Hotel (0706 831163), Bank House Hotel (0706 217641).

Disabled Areas No special area, request suitable position.

Local Radio Station(s) Radio Lancashire (104.5 MHz FM/1557 KHz MW), Red Rose Radio (97.3 MHz FM/999 KHz MW).

Local Newspaper(s) Lancashire Evening Telegraph, Rossendale Free Press, Rossendale Citizen.

MINOR COUNTIES CRICKET ASSOCIATION

MARLOW

STONE

Minor Counties Cricket Association

Founded 1895
Colours Red, silver and black
Crest White horse
President V.M.E. Holt DL
Chairman J.E.O. Smith MBE
Secretary/team secretary/statistician D.J.M. Armstrong
Captain S. Greensword
Scorer A.J. Pearce
Address Thorpe Cottage, Mill Common, Ridlington, North
 Walsham, Norfolk NR28 9TY.
Telephone 0692 650563 (Home)
Minor Counties Rapid Cricketline 0891 567519

ACHIEVEMENTS

Benson & Hedges Cup Zonal group stage
Minor Counties (North) (5) 1972, 1973, 1974, 1975 and 1979
Minor Counties (South) (5) 1972, 1973, 1974, 1975 and 1979
Minor Counties (East) (3) 1976, 1977 and 1978
Minor Counties (West) (3) 1976, 1977 and 1978
Minor Counties C.A. (12) 1980, 1981, 1982, 1983, 1984, 1985,
1986, 1987, 1988, 1989, 1990 and 1991.

GROUNDS

Marlow C C (Pound Lane, Marlow), and Stone C C (Priory Road,
Stone).

Other grounds that have been used for staging home matches against
the tourists and in the Benson & Hedges Cup zonal rounds since 1969
are listed below, for full address details please refer to Minor County
sections.

Trowbridge C C, Newcastle-Upon-Tyne (Jesmond Cricket Ground).,
Darlington C C, Old Hill C C, (Cradley Heath), Oxford.,
(Christchurch College Cricket Ground). Slough C C, Walsall C C,
Shrewsbury C C, Reading C C, Bowdon C C, Wellington C C,
Watford Town C C, Chippenham C C, High Wycombe C C, Lincoln
C C, Ipswich C C, Chesham C C, Amersham C C, Norwich C C
(Lakenham), Longton C C, Stoke-on-Trent, Bedford Town C C,
Scunthorpe & Appleby Frodingham Works C C, Torquay C C,
Macclesfield C C, Swindon C C, Chester-le-Street C C, Cheadle C C,
Plymouth C C, (Peverell Park). Cleethorpes C C, Chester C C,
(Boughton Hall). and Birkenhead Oxton C C.

Marlow

CLUB HISTORY AND DESCRIPTION OF GROUND AND FACILITIES

The ground is located in Pound Lane off the main High Street in the town centre and is the home of Marlow Cricket Club who were established in 1829 and are one of the strongest club teams in the county. The only permanent buildings on the ground are the pavilion, tea room and scoreboard. The majority of facilities are temporary and include: seating, refreshment/bars, marquees for sponsors and tents. The original pavilion (tea room) was built in the 1890's and the new pavilion which houses changing facilities and a bar was built during the early 1960's. Car parking is available near the Municipal Offices sited in the Court Garden and space is available for 300 cars on the ground to the west of the playing area. Facilities are available for tennis and hockey within the ground and for bowling and putting nearby. To the east of the playing area is the River Thames where rowing takes place frequently. The playing area is smooth and is defined by a rope and some advertising boards. The playing area is 116 metres by 128 metres.

The ground has been used by Buckinghamshire C C C for Minor County Championship and National Westminster Bank Trophy matches and has also been used previously by the Minor Counties Cricket Association for a Benson and Hedges Cup Zonal Group match in 1990. In 1990 Nottinghamshire scored 312 for 9 with Chris Broad scoring 115, Buckinghamshire replied with 120 all out, the visitors winning by a margin of 192 runs. In 1992 the club will host three days cricket with a Benson and Hedges Zonal Group match again with Sussex and the two-day MCCA *v*. Pakistanis tour match in July 1992.

ADDRESS   Marlow Cricket Club, The Pavilion, Pound Lane, off High Street, Marlow, Buckinghamshire.

TELEPHONE NUMBER PROSPECTS OF PLAY   0628 43638

GROUND RECORDS AND SCORES

LIMITED-OVERS MATCH (BHC)
Highest innings total for Minor Counties: 273 for 2 *v*. Sussex 1990
Highest innings total against Minor Counties: 274 for 5 by Sussex 1990
Highest individual innings for Minor Counties: 121 M.J. Roberts *v*. Sussex 1990
Highest individual innings against Minor Counties: 85 n.o. P.W.G. Parker for Sussex 1990
Best bowling performance for Minor Counties: 2 for 36 A.J. Mack *v*. Sussex 1990
Best bowling performance against Minor Counties: 1 for 3 N.J. Lenham for Sussex 1990
Best attendance: 2,000 *v*. Sussex 1990

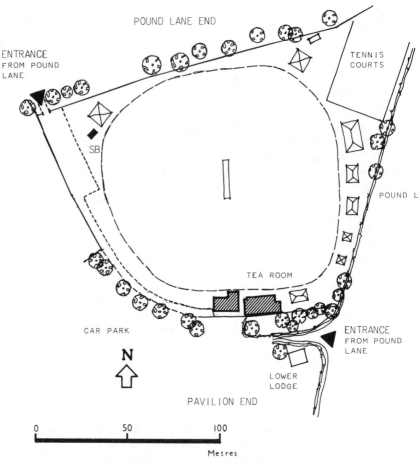

POUND LANE END

ENTRANCE
FROM POUND
LANE

TENNIS
COURTS

SB

POUND L

TEA ROOM

ENTRANCE
FROM POUND
LANE

CAR PARK

N

LOWER
LODGE

PAVILION END

| 0 | 50 | 100 |

Metres

C. H. TITCHMARSH

220-C   HERTS

WILLS'S CIGARETTES.

S. F. BARNES (STAFFORDSHIRE)

HOW TO GET THERE

Rail Marlow (BR), 1.5 miles.
Bus From surrounding areas to town centre, thence 0.25 mile to ground.
Car From north: B482 or M40 junction 4, then follow A404 signposted Marlow and town centre, from High Street take Pound Lane for Marlow C C From west: A4155 or M4 junction 8/9, then follow A423(M), A423 and A404 signposted Marlow and town centre, then as north. From east: A4155 or M4 junction 8/9, then as west. From south: as west or as east.

WHERE TO STAY AND OTHER INFORMATION

The Compleat Angler (0628 484444).

Disabled Areas No special area, request suitable position.
Local Radio Station(s) Chiltern Radio (97.6 MHz FM/828 KHz MW).
Local Newspaper(s) Bucks Herald.

Stone

CLUB HISTORY AND DESCRIPTION OF GROUND AND FACILITIES

The ground is entered from Priory Road, where there is an entrance at the side of the pavilion. Other permanent buildings include a smaller club pavilion, groundsman's store, tea pavilion and scorebox.

The ground is bounded by Lichfield Road, Willow Walk and Priory Road within a residential area not far from the Trent and Mersey Canal. The wicket is sited in an east–west disposition and the ends are named the Pavilion End and Lichfield Road End. The playing area is defined by a rope and some advertising boards. The dimensions are 124 metres by 106 metres. Facilities for county matches are temporary and include seating, refreshment/bars in tents and sponsors' marquees. This venue has been used for Gillette Cup and National Westminster Bank Trophy matches since the first match in 1973 with Dorset. Other matches have been staged with Essex, Northamptonshire and Sussex.

The ground will be used by Minor Counties C.A. for the first time against Leicestershire in the Benson & Hedges Cup zonal group match and by Staffordshire C C C for a possible National Westminster Bank Trophy 2nd round match with either Buckinghamshire or Sussex if Warwickshire are defeated at Edgbaston in the 1st round. Staffordshire will play Bedfordshire in a Minor Counties Championship here on 16–17 August 1992. Ground records include performances from Nasim-ul-Ghani and Rob Bailey with the bat and Jack Ikin and Derek Shackleton with the ball.

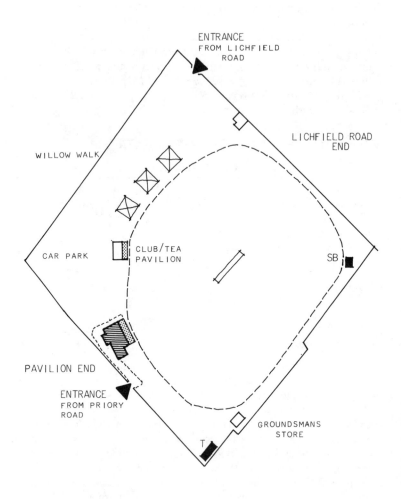

ENTRANCE
FROM LICHFIELD
ROAD

LICHFIELD ROAD
END

WILLOW WALK

CAR PARK

CLUB/TEA
PAVILION

SB

PAVILION END

ENTRANCE
FROM PRIORY
ROAD

GROUNDSMANS
STORE

T

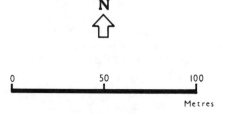

N

| 0 | 50 | 100 |

Metres

ADDRESS   Stone Cricket Club, The Pavilion, Priory Road, Stone, Staffordshire.
TELEPHONE PROSPECTS OF PLAY   0785 813068

GROUND RECORDS AND SCORES

LIMITED-OVERS MATCHES
Highest innings total for County: 219 for 9 *v.* Sussex (GC) 1978
Highest innings total against County: 316 for 6 by Essex (GC) 1976
Lowest innings total for County: 108 *v.* Northamptonshire (NWBT) 1991
Lowest innings total against County: 84 by Dorset (GC) 1973
Highest individual innings for County: 85 Nasim-ul-Ghani *v.* Sussex (GC) 1978
Highest individual innings against County: 145 R.J. Bailey for Northamptonshire (NWBT) 1991
Best bowling performance for County: 3 for 13 J. Ikin *v.* Dorset (GC) 1973
Best bowling performance against County: 4 for 11 D. Shackleton for Dorset (GC) 1973
Best attendance: 3,500 *v.* Essex (GC) 1976

HOW TO GET THERE

Rail   Stone (BR), 1 mile.
Bus PMT Buses pass close to ground and link BR Stone Station with Bus Station in town centre (Telephone: 0782 747000).
Car   From north: A34, A520 or M6 junction 15 signposted Stone and town centre, then follow A51 Lichfield Road for ground with entrance off Priory Road. From east: A51, B5027 or A520, signposted Stone and town centre, then as north. From west: A51 or B5026 signposted Stone and town centre, then as north. From south: A51, A34 or M6 junction 14, then follow A34 signposted Stone and town centre, then as north.

WHERE TO STAY AND OTHER INFORMATION

Forte Post House Hotel (0782 717171), or stay in Stafford or Stoke-on-Trent.

Disabled Areas   No special area, request suitable position. Car parking available within ground.
Local Radio Station   BBC Radio Stoke-on-Trent (94.6 MHz FM/1503 KHz MW), Radio Signal (102.6 MHz FM/1170 KHz MW).
Local Newspaper(s)   Evening Sentinel.

MINOR COUNTIES

BEDFORDSHIRE

BERKSHIRE (Finchampstead C C)

BUCKINGHAMSHIRE (Beaconsfield C C)

CAMBRIDGESHIRE (March Town C C)

CHESHIRE

CORNWALL

CUMBERLAND (Netherfield C C)

DEVON

DORSET (Bournemouth Sports Club)

HEREFORDSHIRE

HERTFORDSHIRE

LINCOLNSHIRE

NORFOLK

NORTHUMBERLAND

OXFORDSHIRE (Cowley St John C C)

SHROPSHIRE (St George's C C)

STAFFORDSHIRE

SUFFOLK

WALES

WILTSHIRE

Bedfordshire

Founded   3 November 1899
Colours   Purple and black
Crest   Rampant lion with three shells
(taken from Duke of Bedford's insignia)
President   J. Oliver
Secretary   D.J.F. Hoare
Team manager   H. Hayhurst
Captain   J.R. Wake
Scorer   P. Finlay
Statistician   A.J. Pearce
Address   5 Brecon Way, Bedford, Bedfordshire MK41 8DF.
Telephone 0234 266648 (Home) 0462 815888 (Office)
Minor Counties Rapid Cricketline   0891 567519

ACHIEVEMENTS

Minor County Championship   Champions (2) 1970 and 1972
Minor County Holt Knockout Competition   Finalists 1983
Gillette Cup   2nd Round (1) 1968
National Westminster Bank Trophy   1st Round 1982, 1985 and
1991

GROUNDS

Bedford School, Burnaby Road, Bedford. Telephone: 0234 53435
(School hours only); Bedford Town C C, Goldington Bury, Church
Lane, Goldington, Bedford. Telephone: 0234 52458; Cople C C,
Cricket Ground, Cople. Telephone: Directory Enquiries; Dunstable
Town C C, Bull Pond Lane, Dunstable. Telephone: 0582 63735;
Henlow C C, (Henlow Sports Association), Park Lane, Henlow.
Telephone: 0462 811218; Leighton Buzzard C C, Bell Close, Lake
Street, Leighton Buzzard. Telephone: 0582 372736; Luton Town
C C, Wardown Park, Old Bedford Road, Luton. Telephone: 0582
27855; Southill Park C C, Southill Park, Near Biggleswade.
Telephone: Directory Enquiries; Vauxhall Motors C C, Brache Estate,
Osborne Road, Luton. Telephone: 0582 23061.

Berkshire

Founded   17 March 1858
Colours   Narrow old gold stripe between broad stripes of purple and green
Crest   A white hart passing under a polled oak with a dark green background
President   J.J. Warr
Chairman   A. Sears
Secretary   C.M.S. Crombie
Team manager   F. Orton
Captain   M.L. Simmons
Scorer   L. Cross
Statistician   T. Bampton
Address   Orchard Cottage, Waltham St Lawrence, Reading, Berkshire RG10 OJH.
Telephone 0491 578555 (Home) 0734 343387 (Office)
Minor Counties Rapid Cricketline   0891 567519

ACHIEVEMENTS

Minor County Championship   Champions (3) 1924, 1928 and 1953
Minor Counties Championship Final   Finalists (1) 1990
Minor County Holt Knockout Competition   Quarter-finalists (1) 1987
Gillette Cup   2nd Round (1) 1966
National Westminster Bank Trophy   1st Round (8) 1983, 1984, 1985, 1986, 1988, 1989, 1990 and 1991.

GROUNDS

Finchampstead (Memorial Park, The Village)
   Other grounds that have been used since 1969 are: Bracknell C C, Large's Lane, Bracknell. Telephone: 0344 423492; Bradfield College, Bradfield, Theale, Near Reading. Telephone: 0734 744429; Courage (Reading) C C, Courages Cricket Ground, Ashley Road, Berkeley Avenue, Reading. Telephone: 0734 52725; Falkland C C, Washcommon, Essex Street, off Andover Road, Near Newbury. Telephone: 0635 47658; Hurst C C, Wokingham Road, Hurst, Reading. Telephone: 0734 340088; Kidmore End C C, Gallows Tree Common, Kidmore End Village, Near Reading. Telephone: 0734 724143; Reading C C, Sonning Lane, off London Road, Reading. Telephone: 0734 699049; Reading School, Erleigh Road, Reading. Telephone: 0734 61815; Reading University, Elmhurst Road, Reading. Telephone: 0734 83775; Wellington College, Derby Field, Crowthorne, Near Wokingham. Telephone: 0344 772261.

Finchampstead C C

CLUB HISTORY AND DESCRIPTION OF GROUND AND FACILITIES

Memorial Park is the home of Finchampstead Cricket Club, who play in the Berkshire Cricket League. There are four current Finchampstead C C players who represent Berkshire C C C: G.T. Headley, P.J. Lewington, who also played for Warwickshire C C C between 1970–76 and 1982, M.G. Lickley and P.J. Oxley. The ground has been used by Berkshire C C C for Minor County Championship matches and was last used for a National Westminster Bank Trophy 1st round match with Yorkshire in 1988. The ground may be used on 9 July 1992 for a National Westminster Bank Trophy 2nd round tie between Berkshire and Leicestershire/Norfolk if Derbyshire are defeated at Derby in the 1st round. Derbyshire lost at the first hurdle against Hertfordshire at Bishop's Stortford last year in a bowl-out at an unguarded wicket.

The permanent buildings on the ground include a pavilion and scoreboard/groundsman's store. There are also several tennis courts adjoining the Village Hall which is sited to the south-west of the playing area. Car parking is available to the east of the playing area in a separate field. The ground is enclosed by bushes and hedges with some trees at the pavilion end. The ground capacity is 3,500 and 3,000 attended the Yorkshire match in 1988. The playing area is 146 metres by 110 metres and is a small ground by club standards; it is defined by a rope and advertising boards.

ADDRESS Finchampstead Cricket Club, The Pavilion, Memorial Park, The Village, Finchampstead, Berkshire.
TELEPHONE NUMBER PROSPECTS OF PLAY   0734 732890

GROUND RECORDS AND SCORES

LIMITED-OVERS MATCH (NWBT)
Highest innings total for County: 105 *v*. Yorkshire 1988
Highest innings total against County: 109 for 0 by Yorkshire 1988
Highest individual innings for County: 23 M.G. Stear *v*. Yorkshire 1988
Highest individual innings against County: 74 n.o. A.A. Metcalfe for Yorkshire 1988
Best bowling performance for County: 0 for 9 T.P.J. Dodd *v*. Yorkshire 1988
Best bowling performance against County: 3 for 20 S.D. Fletcher for Yorkshire 1988
Best attendance: 3,500 *v*. Yorkshire 1988 ·

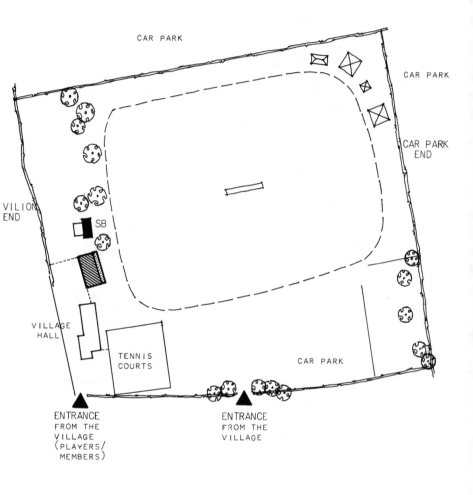

CAR PARK

CAR PARK

CAR PARK
END

VILION
END

SB

CAR PARK

VILLAGE
HALL

TENNIS
COURTS

ENTRANCE
FROM THE
VILLAGE
(PLAYERS/
MEMBERS)

ENTRANCE
FROM THE
VILLAGE

N

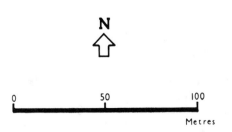

0   50   100

Metres

HOW TO GET THERE

Rail   Wokingham (BR), 3 miles; Crowthorne (BR), 2 miles.
Bus   Local buses connect Finchampstead village with Reading, Wokingham, Camberley and Frimley.
Car   From north: B3016 from Wokingham, follow signs Finchampstead; the ground is situated in Memorial Park to the south-west of the village off the B3348. From east: B3430 from Bracknell or B3348 from Crowthorne, follow signs Finchampstead, then as north. From west: B3348 from Eversley and Hartfordbridge, follow signs Finchampstead, then as north. From south: B3016 from Hartfordbridge or A327 and B3016 from Frimley, follow signs Finchampstead, then as north.

WHERE TO STAY AND OTHER INFORMATION

The Waterloo Hotel, Crowthorne (0344 777711).

Disabled Areas   No special area, request suitable position.
Local Radio Station(s)   Radio 210 (97.0 MHz FM/1431 KHz MW).
Local Newspaper(s)   Reading Evening News, Evening Echo.

Buckinghamshire

Founded   15 January 1891
Colours   Green, silver and white
Crest   Chained swan
President   T. Orford
Chairman   K. Drucquer
Secretary   S.J. Tomlin
Team secretary   E. Thompson
Captain   N.G. Hames
Scorer   Mrs Lesley Hawkins
Statistician   G. Anscomb
Address   Orchardleigh Cottage, Bigfrith Lane, Cookam Dean, Berkshire SL5 9PH.
Telephone 06284 2202 (Home) 06285 24922 (Office)
Minor Counties Rapid Cricketline   0891 567519

ACHIEVEMENTS

Minor County Championship   Champions (8) 1922, 1923, 1925, 1932, 1938, 1952, 1968 and 1987; joint champions (1) 1899
Minor Counties Championship Final   Winners (1) 1987
Minor County Holt Knockout Cup Competition   Winners (1) 1990
Gillette Cup   2nd Round (2) 1970 and 1972
National Westminster Bank Trophy   2nd Round (1) 1987

Beaconsfield C C (Wilton Park).

Other grounds that have been used since 1969 are: Amersham C C, Shardeloes, London Road, Amersham Old Town. Amersham. Telephone: 0494 433020; Aylesbury Town C C, Aylesbury Sports Club, Wendover Road, Aylesbury. Telephone: 0296 5187; Bletchley Town C C, Manor Fields, Bletchley, Milton Keynes. Telephone: 0908 72298; Buckingham Town C C, Bourton Road, off Bletchley Road, Buckingham. Telephone: 0280 22546; Chesham C C, Amy Lane, New Road, Chesham. Telephone: 0240 53635; High Wycombe C C, London Road, High Wycombe. Telephone: 0494 22611; Marlow C C, Pound Lane, off High Street, Marlow. Telephone: 0628 43638; Monks Risborough, Molins Sports Club, Monks Risborough, Princes Risborough. Telephone: 0844 43959; Slough C C, Chalvey Road, Slough. Telephone: 0753 20982; Stowe School, Stowe, Near Buckingham. Telephone: 0280 23164.

Beaconsfield C C

The Beaconsfield Cricket Club was founded in 1825 and the club celebrated 150 Years in 1975. Beaconsfield field four XIs throughout the season and have been members of the Thames Valley Cricket League since 1975; they last won the league in 1991. Early records of the club have either disappeared or never existed, therefore it is was not until 24 August 1849 that the first match was recorded with Eton and Windsor Star Club at Brocas, Eton. Early club matches included fixtures with Gerrards Cross, Slough, Chalfont Park and Chalfont St Peter cricket clubs. In May 1896 the club celebrated the occasion of the coming of age of Mr W. Baring Du Pre and his accession to the Wilton Park Estates, in which the ground is sited. In 1898 a match was staged with Chalfont St Giles C C who included within their team the Hearne brothers J.T. (Middlesex) and Walter (Kent).

The early 1900s proved a successful period for the club with matches against West Herts, Stoke Green, Chelsea (not the football club), High Wycombe, Marlow and an Oxford University XI. After the First World War an appeal was set up to generate funds for the club to improve the ground and facilities. 1924 saw the first Buckinghamshire C C C match staged on the ground, with the last visit in 1989 against Berkshire. In 1925 Patsy Hendren played in a charity match on the ground. The club president Colonel Du Pre offered the club additional land for cricket in 1929.

The Tea Pavilion was built in 1930 at a cost of £150 and in 1931 the A40 Oxford Road was enlarged and took a small piece of land at the southern end of the ground, hence the playing area today is tight against the fence and trees. In 1932 six regular Beaconsfield players represented the County Club which won all ten matches and finished the season with

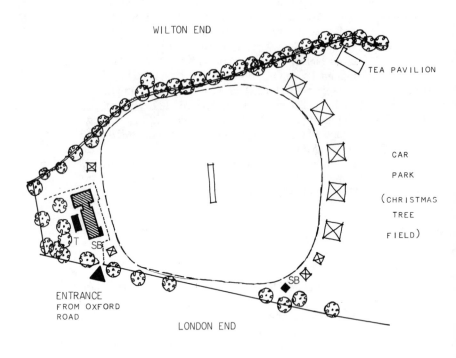

WILTON END

TEA PAVILION

CAR

PARK

(CHRISTMAS

TREE

FIELD)

T SB

SB

ENTRANCE
FROM OXFORD
ROAD

LONDON END

N

0   50   100

Metres

a 100 per cent record. The new pavilion, constructed in 1933 at a cost of £300, was financed by Colonel Du Pre. The architect was Mr L. Taylor and the builder was Mr J. Strickland. The pavilion was opened on 12 May 1937 by Mrs Du Pre. The majority of the timber seats were made from an oak tree which was felled by Mr Rissik and presented to the club.

On Sunday 24 May 1942 a match was staged between Capt. Alan Parker's XII and the Beaconsfield and District XII. Many first-class players were on view including; J.D. Robertson, S.M. Brown, D.C.S. Compton, M. Leyland, E.D.R. Eagar, M.S. Nichols, P. Smith, H.M. Garland Wells, T.N. Pearce, W.H.V. Levett, C. Emmett, T.G. Evans, E.J. Unwin, J.W.A. Stephenson and A.V. Gover.

In 1958 the ownership of the Wilton Park ground changed from the Du Pre family to the club. In 1965 a match was staged between the club and Worcestershire C C C, who included Tom Graveney, Martin Horton, Duncan Fearnley, Ron Headley, Basil D'Oliveira, Alan Ormrod, Ted Hemsley and Norman Gifford in their side. A second fixture was staged with Worcestershire in 1966 when a crowd of 2,000 were present. Basil D'Oliveira scored 100 on the day it was announced he would play for England in the Second Test at Lord's against the West Indies. Several players have represented the county club including: R.E. Bond, R.H.J. Brooke, C.A. Pickett, C.V. Raffety and R.H. Rutter.

On 24 June 1992 Buckinghamshire C C C will hold their National Westminster Bank Trophy 1st round tie with Sussex at Wilton Park and this will be the first time that a match of this nature has been staged on the ground. Buckinghamshire C C C have previously used venues at Amersham, Chesham, Marlow and High Wycombe.

ADDRESS Beaconsfield Cricket Club, The Pavilion, Wilton Park, Oxford Road, Beaconsfield, Buckinghamshire.
TELEPHONE NUMBER PROSPECTS OF PLAY 0494 674134

DESCRIPTION OF GROUND AND FACILITIES

The ground is entered from Oxford Road close to Old Beaconsfield and to the south of the pavilion. Car parking for 1,000 cars is available within Christmas Tree Field to the east of the playing area off Oxford Road where there is a pedestrian entrance through the trees. The members' enclosure is sited in front of the pavilion and Long Room to the west of the playing area. The east side of the playing area comprises of marquees, temporary seating and the Tea Pavilion. The new Gordon Scott Scoreboard is sited to the south-east of the playing area and was constructed in 1991–92. A smaller secondary scoreboard is sited at one end of the pavilion. Some permanent bench seating is available at the Oxford Road End of the ground and near the pavilion enclosure. Temporary facilities include seating, press tent, sponsors' marquees and refreshment/beer tents. The boundary at the north Wilton End of the ground is rather tight against the fence and tree landscape.

The wicket is sited in a north–south disposition and the dimensions of the playing area are 100 metres by 120 metres. If required, the TV camera/commentary box and radio commentary point would be positioned at the southern end of the ground.

GROUND RECORDS AND SCORES

LIMITED-OVERS MATCHES
No previous Buckinghamshire C C C Gillette Cup or National Westminster Bank Trophy matches have been staged at this venue.

HOW TO GET THERE

Rail   Beaconsfield (BR), 1.5 miles.
Bus   From surrounding areas to Beaconsfield Bus Station, thence 1.5 miles.
Car   From north: A355 or B474 signposted Beaconsfield and town centre, then follow signs for Old Beaconsfield and Winton Park for ground off Oxford Road. From west: M40 junction 2, then follow signs Beaconsfield, before reaching Old Beaconsfield take Oxford Road for ground in Winton Park. From east: A40 or M40 junction 2, then as west. From south: A355 or M40 junction 2, then as west.

WHERE TO STAY AND OTHER INFORMATION

Old New George Hotel (0494 674134), The Crown, Amersham (0494 721541), Forte Posthouse, High Wycombe (0494 442100).

Disabled Areas   No special area, request suitable position. Car parking available in Christmas Field.
Local Radio Station(s)   Chiltern Radio (97.6 MHz FM/828 KHz MW).
Local Newspaper(s)   Bucks Herald.

Cambridgeshire

Founded   6 June 1891
Colours   Blue, maroon and straw
Crest   A pair of bustards
President   M. Crouch
Chairman   D. Fairey
Secretary   P.W. Gooden
Captain   N.T. Gadsby
Scorer   A.R. May/R. Skilbeck
Statistician   A.R. May
Address   The Redlands, Oakington Road, Cottenham, Cambridge, Cambridgeshire CB4 4TW.
Telephone 0954 50429 (Home)
Minor Counties Rapid Cricketline   0891 567519

ACHIEVEMENTS

Minor County Championship   Champions (1) 1963
Minor Counties Championship Final   Finalists (1) 1988
Minor County Holt Knockout Cup Competition   Finalists (1) 1988
Gillette Cup   2nd Round (1) 1967
National Westminster Bank Trophy   (7) 1982, 1983, 1986, 1987, 1988, 1989 and 1991

GROUNDS

March Town C C (Burrowmoor Road, March).
   Other grounds that have been used since 1969 are: Cambridge University C C, Fenner's University Cricket Ground, Cambridge. Telephone: 0223 353552; Ley's School, School Grounds, Cambridge. (No Telephone); Papworth C C, Chequer's Lane, Papworth Everard. Telephone: 0480 830331; Peterborough Town C C, Bretton Gate, Westwood, Peterborough. Telephone: 0733 262202; Royston C C, Royston Heath, Royston, Herts. Telephone: 0763 43613; Wisbech Town C C, Harecroft Road, Wisbech. Telephone: 0945 585429.

March Town C C

CLUB HISTORY AND DESCRIPTION OF GROUND AND FACILITIES

The Sports Ground situated off Burrowmoor Road to the south-east of the North Cambridgeshire market town of March is the home of March Town Cricket Club.

The ground is used by Cambridgeshire C C C for Minor County Championship matches and the only National Westminster Bank Trophy match to be staged on the ground was the 1st round tie in 1989 when Worcestershire were the visitors. Worcestershire won by 9 wickets thanks to 91 n.o. from Tim Curtis, who will be the new county captain in 1992. Ian Lawrence top scored for Cambridgeshire with 74.

The ground is enclosed and permanent facilities include a pavilion, clubhouse, groundsman's store, toilets, scoreboard and a bowling green pavilion. The south of the ground is surrounded by trees and to the south-east of the playing area is a car park. The only entrance to the ground is from Burrowmoor Road; an observant visitor will notice that the nearby housing estate is called Cricketers' Close. Car parking is available for some members' cars at the Bowling Green End of the ground with space for players and officials at the rear of the pavilion. The playing area is 127 metres by 106 metres and is defined by a rope with some advertising boards.

ADDRESS March Town Cricket Club, The Pavilion, Sports Ground, Burrowmoor Road, March, Cambridgeshire.
TELEPHONE NUMBER PROSPECTS OF PLAY 0354 52029

GROUND RECORDS AND SCORES

LIMITED-OVERS MATCH (NWBT)
Highest innings total for County: 202 for 4 v. Worcestershire 1989
Highest innings total against County: 206 for 1 by Worcestershire 1989
Highest individual innings for County: 74 I.S. Lawrence v. Worcestershire 1989
Highest individual innings against County: 91 n.o. T.S. Curtis for Worcestershire 1989
Best bowling performance for County: 1 for 29 D.C. Collard v. Worcestershire 1989
Best bowling performance against County: 2 for 44 I.T. Botham for Worcestershire 1989
Best attendance: 2,500 v. Worcestershire 1989

HOW TO GET THERE

Rail March (BR), 1 mile.
Bus From surrounding areas to March with links to Peterborough, Wisbech and Ely.

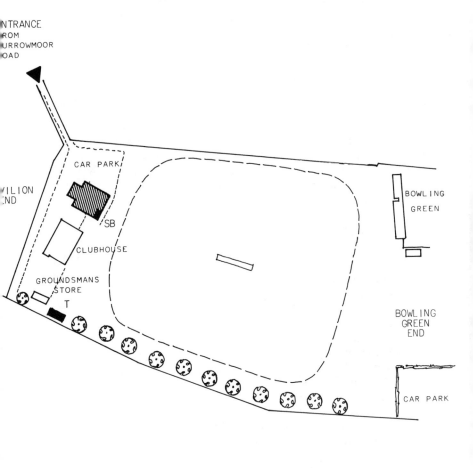

ENTRANCE
FROM
BURROWMOOR
ROAD

CAR PARK

PAVILION
END

SB

CLUBHOUSE

GROUNDSMANS
STORE

T

BOWLING

GREEN

BOWLING
GREEN
END

CAR PARK

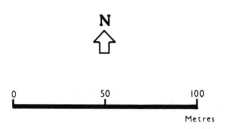

N

0   50   100

Metres

Car From north: A141 or B1101 signposted March and town centre, then follow signs County Cricket for sports ground off Burrowmoor Road to the south-east of the town centre. From east: B1099 signposted March and town centre, then as north. From west: B1093 and A605 and A141, signposted March and town centre, then as north. From south: A141 and B1101, signposted March and town centre, then as north.

WHERE TO STAY AND OTHER INFORMATION

Forte Post House, Peterborough (0733 240209), or stay in March or Ely.

Disabled Areas No special area, request suitable position.
Local Radio Station(s) BBC Radio Cambridgeshire (95.7 MHz FM/ 1026 KHz MW), Hereward Radio (96.6 MHz FM/1557 KHz MW).
Local Newspaper(s) Cambridge Evening News.

Cheshire

Founded 29 September 1908
Colours Purple, black and silver
Crest Wheatsheaf
President B. Lowe
Chairman R. Richardson
Secretary J.B. Pickup
Team manager K. Holding
Captain I. Cockbain
Scorer/statistician H. Smith
Address 2 Castle Street, Northwich, Cheshire CW8 1AB.
Telephone 0606 74970 (Home) 0606 74301 (Office)
Minor Counties Rapid Cricketline 0891 567519

ACHIEVEMENTS

Minor County Championship Champions (3) 1967, 1985 and 1988
Minor Counties Championship Final Winners (2) 1985 and 1988; finalists (1) 1984
Minor County Holt Knockout Cup Competition Winners (1) 1983
Gillette Cup 2nd Round (1) 1968
National Westminster Bank Trophy 2nd Round (1) 1988

GROUNDS

Bowden C C, South Downs Road, Bowden, Altrincham. Telephone: 061 928 1358; Chester C C, Boughton Hall, Boughton Hall Avenue, Filkins Lane, Chester. Telephone: 0244 326072; Nantwich C C,

Whitehouse Lane, Nantwich. Telephone: 0270 626155; Oxton C C, Townfield Lane, Birkenhead, Wirral. Telephone: 051 652 1331; Toft C C, Chelford Road, Knutsford. Telephone: 0565 2734; Stalybridge Cricket and Athletic Club., Gorse Hall Road, Dukinfield. Telephone: 061 338 2094; Neston C C, Parkgate, South Wirral. Telephone: 051 336 4199; Warrington C C, Walton Lea Road, Higher Walton, Warrington. Telephone: 0925 63210; Cheadle Hulme C C, Meadway Road, Cheadle Hulme. Telephone: Directory Enquiries; Heaton Mersey C C, Sibley Road, Heaton Mersey, Near Stockport. Telephone: Directory Enquiries.

Cornwall

Founded   12 November 1894
Colours   Red, yellow and black
Crest   White chough
President   J. Williams
Chairman   Col. R. Potts
Secretary   T.D. Meneer
Team manager   J. Angove
Captain   G.G. Watts
Scorer   B. Holder/E. Brewer
Statistician   B. Holder
Address   Falbridge, Penvale Cross, Penryn, Cornwall TR10 9AN
Telephone 0326 72389 (Home) 0326 312405 (Office)
Minor Counties Rapid Cricketline   0891 567519

ACHIEVEMENTS

Minor County Championship   2nd 1974 and 1976
Minor County Holt Knockout Cup Competition   Quarter-finalists (1) 1988; 2nd round proper (1) 1990
Gillette Cup   1st Round (4) 1970, 1975, 1977 and 1980
National Westminster Bank Trophy   1st Round (1) 1986

GROUNDS

Camborne C C, Roskear, Camborne. Telephone: 0209 25478; Falmouth C C, Trescobeas, Falmouth. Telephone: 0326 74000; Helston C C, Clodgey Lane, Helston. Telephone: 0326 53423; Liskeard C C, New Pavilion, Lux Park, Liskeard. Telephone: 0579 42665; Penzance C C, St. Clare, Penzance. Telephone: 0736 2960; Redruth C C, Cricket Ground, Redruth. Telephone: Directory Enquiries; St Austell C C, Wheal Eliza, Bethel, St Austell. Telephone: 0726 2588; Troon C C, Treslothnan Road, Troon. Telephone: 0209 715923; Truro C C, Boscawen Park, Truro. Telephone: 0872 77468; Wadebridge C C, Egloshayle Road, Wadebridge. (No Telephone).

Cumberland

Founded   10 April 1948
Colours   Bottle green, gold and red
Crest   Original Cumberland county crest
Patron   R. Bowan
President   W. Hirst
Chairman   J.H. Millican
Secretary   M. Beaty
Team managers   A. Wilson, D. Spruce and A. Pemberton
Captain   J.R. Moyes
Scorer   Mrs S. Twentyman/C. Bland
Statistician   Mrs S. Twentyman
Address   Wetheriggs, 9 Abbey Drive, Natland, Near Kendal,
Cumberland LA9 7QN
Telephone 05395 60470 (Home) 0539 24146 (a.m.) 0539 21601
(p.m.) (Office)
Minor Counties Rapid Cricketline 0891 567519

ACHIEVEMENTS

Minor County Championship   Champions (1) 1986
Minor Counties Championship Final   Winners (1) 1986
Minor County Holt Knockout Cup Competition   Winners (1) 1989
National Westminster Bank Trophy   1st Round (6) 1984, 1985,
1986, 1987, 1988 and 1989.

GROUNDS

Netherfield C C (Parkside Road, Kendal)
   Other grounds that have been used since 1969 are: Appleby C C,
Cricket Ground, Appleby. Telephone: Directory Enquiries; Barrow
C C, Abbey Road, Barrow. Telephone: 0229 25201; Carlisle C C,
Edenside, Carlisle. Telephone: 0228 28593; Kendal C C, Shap Road,
Burneside, Kendal. Telephone: 0539 22910; Millom C C, St George's
Road, Millom. Telephone: 0657 2839; Penrith C C, Tynefield Park,
Penrith. Telephone: 0768 63087; Workington C C, Ernest Valentine
Ground, The Cloffochs, Workington. Telephone: 0900 5515.

Kendal (Netherfield C C)

CLUB HISTORY AND DESCRIPTION OF
GROUND AND FACILITIES

No members of the cricketing press seem to know exactly where Netherfield Cricket Club is, for it is in a suburb of Kendal, an old market town of Cumberland, the now defunct County of Westmorland. Kendal, the Auld Grey Town, lies peacefully in the valley of the meandering River Kent. The remains of the Norman castle locate one of the original Roman camps that guarded the route to the Scottish Border, with a superb view over the market town and cricket ground. The Castle was the birthplace and childhood home of Katherine Parr, the sixth wife of Henry VIII, but it was in good order until Bernard Reidy set about the Netherfield bowlers in 1977 when he established an individual ground record of 184 n.o.

Parkside Road is the home of Netherfield C C who were established in the 1890s and are members of the powerful Northern Cricket League. The original ground was situated opposite the current ground. The ground is owned by 'K' Shoes to provide recreation for the employees from the factory. However, as the workforce dwindled, non-employees were allowed to join and now represent 90 per cent of the current cricket membership. The ground is situated half a mile from a junction with the A65, which itself is only 70 metres from the start of Kendal town centre. The five acre ground provides facilities for two cricket fields, bowls, hockey, soccer and tennis. The playing dimensions are 140 metres by 138 metres. The current pavilion was built in 1960 and was extended and improved on three occasions during the last ten years. The Netherfield club field four XIs throughout the season and three junior teams.

Cumberland C C C have used the ground as one of many in the County, on alternate years until 1982, since when the improved ground, wicket and facilities have encouraged the County Club to use it each season. Two players who have played for Netherfield C C and Cumberland C C C during the last ten years have been Alan Wilson and John Moyes. Other players to have represented the County Club in recent seasons include M. Burns, G.J. Clarke, R. Ellwood, S. Wall and D.M. Wheatman. Only two Cumberland C C C home National Westminster Bank Trophy 1st round matches have been staged at Netherfield: in 1984 against Derbyshire who won by 9 wickets, and in 1989 against Lancashire who won by 4 wickets. Crowds of 2,000 watched the first match and 1,700 the last match in 1989. There is ample car parking available and the ground capacity is set at 4,500. Should Cumberland surprise Essex at Chelmsford in the National Westminster Bank Trophy 1st round tie in 1992, they will be granted a home 2nd round tie with either Lancashire or Oxfordshire at Parkside Road.

Many past and present Test players have graced the ground and none better than the 1989 club professional Carlisle Best, the Barbadian and West Indian batsman. Others have included: Rohan Kanhai, Cammie

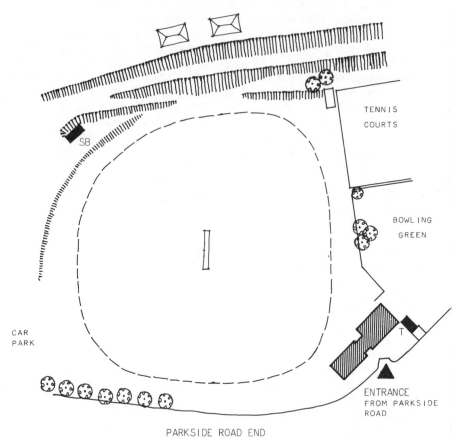

HOCKEY FIELD END

SB

TENNIS
COURTS

BOWLING
GREEN

CAR
PARK

T

ENTRANCE
FROM PARKSIDE
ROAD

PARKSIDE ROAD END

N

| 0 | 50 | 100 |

Metres

View of Netherfield C C, reproduced by courtesy of Steven Taylor

Smith, Mushtaq Mohammad, Collis King, Trevor Franklin, Karsen Ghavri, Brendon Kuruppu, Ravi Shastri, Chetan Sharma, Franklyn Stephenson and Mark Greatbatch.

ADDRESS   Netherfield Cricket Club, The Pavilion, Netherfield Sports Ground, Parkside Road, Kendal, Cumberland.
TELEPHONE NUMBER PROSPECTS OF PLAY   0539 724051

GROUND RECORDS AND SCORES

LIMITED-OVERS MATCHES
Highest innings total for County: 121 *v.* Derbyshire (NWBT) 1984
Highest innings total against County: 124 for 1 by Derbyshire (NWBT) 1984
Lowest innings total for County: 84 *v.* Lancashire (NWBT) 1989
Lowest innings total against County: 86 for 6 by Lancashire (NWBT) 1989
Highest individual innings for County: 36 M.D. Woods *v.* Derbyshire (NWBT) 1984
Highest individual innings against County: 73 n.o. J.G. Wright for Derbyshire (NWBT) 1984
Best bowling performance for County: 3 for 24 S. Wall *v.* Lancashire (NWBT) 1989
Best bowling performance against County: 6 for 24 K.J. Barnett for Derbyshire (NWBT) 1984
Best attendance: 2,000 *v.* Derbyshire (NWBT) 1984

HOW TO GET THERE

Rail   Kendal (BR), 1 mile; Oxenholme (BR), 1 mile.
Bus   National Express Coaches link Kendal with major cities and towns, and local buses link Kendal with the Lake District.
Car   From north: M6 junction 37, then follow A684, signposted Kendal and town centre for Netherfield Sports Ground situated off Parkside Road; or A6 signposted Kendal and town centre. From east: A684 or B6254, signposted Kendal and town centre, then follow north. From west: B5284, A591 and A6, signposted Kendal and town centre, then follow north. From south: M6 junction 36, then follow A590, A591 and A6, signposted Kendal and town centre; or A65, signposted Natland and Kendal and town centre, then as north.

WHERE TO STAY AND OTHER INFORMATION

Woolpack Hotel (0539 723852), Riverside Hotel (0539 724707), County Hotel (0539 722461), Grey Gables, Grayrigg (053984 345).

Disabled Areas   No special area, request suitable position.
Local Radio Station(s)   BBC Radio Cumbria (95.6 MHz FM/756 KHz MW).
Local Newspaper(s)   Barrow Evening Mail, Lancashire Evening Post, Westmorland Gazette.

Devon

Founded   26 November 1899
Colours   Navy blue/Black, gold and sky-blue
Crest   Rampant lion or quartered shield
   in gold depicting crest of
   Courtenay family (Earl of Devon)
President   A.L. Goodrich OBE
Chairman   D.H. Cole
Secretary   G.R. Evans
Team manager   J. Davey
Captain   J.H. Edwards
Scorer/statistician   D. Planton
Address   Blueberry Haven, 20 Boucher Road, Budleigh Salterton, South Devon EX9 6JF
Telephone 03954 5216 (Home) 0392 58406 (Office)
Minor Counties Rapid Cricketline   0891 567519

ACHIEVEMENTS

Minor County Championship   Champions (1) 1978
Minor County Holt Knockout Cup Competition   Finalists (1) 1991
Gillette Cup   2nd Round (1) 1980

National Westminster Bank Trophy   1st Round (8) 1983, 1984, 1985, 1986, 1987, 1988, 1990 and 1991

GROUNDS

Bovey Tracey C C, The Recreation Ground, Newton Road, Bovey Tracey. Telephone: 0626 832780; Chudleigh C C, Kate Brook, Chudleigh. Telephone: 0626 852645; Exeter C C, County Ground, Prince of Wales Road, Exeter. Telephone: 0392 72773; Exmouth C C, The Maer Ground, Seafront, Exmouth. Telephone: 0395 272771; North Devon C C, Instow. Telephone: 0271 860633; Sidmouth C C, The Fortfield, Sidmouth. Telephone: 0395 53229; South Devon C C, Recreation Ground, Marsh Road, Newton Abbot. Telephone: 0626 65343; Torquay C C, Recreation Ground, Torquay. Telephone: 0803 22001.

Dorset

Founded   5 February 1896
Colours   Green
Crest   Three leopards
President/secretary   D.J.W. Bridge TD
Chairman   A.M.R. Lumby
Captain   V.B. Lewis
Scorer/statistician   B. Newbery
Address   Long Acre, Tinneys Lane, Sherborne, Dorset DY9 3DY
Telephone 0935 814318 (Home)
Minor Counties Rapid Cricketline   0891 567519

ACHIEVEMENTS

Minor County Championship   3rd (3) 1923, 1959 and 1982
Minor County Holt Knockout Cup Competition   Finalists (1) 1985
Gillette Cup   1st Round (2) 1968 and 1973
National Westminster Bank Trophy   1st Round (6) 1983, 1986, 1987, 1989, 1990 and 1991

GROUNDS

Bournemouth Sports Club (Dean Park, Cavendish Road)
   Other grounds that have been used since 1969 are: Dorchester C C, The Recreation Ground, Weymouth Road, Dorchester. Telephone: 0305 63641; Kinsor C C, Kinsor Park Road, Northborne, Bournemouth. Telephone: 0202 573089; Sherborne School, School Grounds, Sherborne. (No Telephone); Weymouth C C, Redlands

Sports Ground, Dorchester Road, Upney, Weymouth. Telephone: 0305 813113.

Bournemouth

CLUB HISTORY AND DESCRIPTION OF GROUND AND FACILITIES

The ground is used by Dorset C C C for Minor County Championship matches and NatWest Bank Trophy matches have been staged with Essex in 1983 and Lancashire in 1991.

For full details of ground history and facilities please refer to Bournemouth within the Hampshire C C C section.

ADDRESS Bournemouth Sports Club, The Pavilion, Dean Park, Cavendish Road, Bournemouth, Dorset.
TELEPHONE NUMBER PROSPECTS OF PLAY 0202 25872

GROUND RECORDS AND SCORES

LIMITED-OVERS MATCHES
Highest innings total for County: 147 v. Lancashire (NWBT) 1991
Highest innings total against County: 151 for 5 by Lancashire (NWBT) 1991
Lowest innings total for County: 111 v. Essex (NWBT) 1983
Lowest innings total against County: 117 for 3 by Essex (NWBT) 1983
Highest individual innings for County: 34 M.C. Wagstaffe v. Essex (NWBT) 1983
Highest individual innings against County: 73 n.o. K.S. McEwan for Essex (NWBT) 1983
Best bowling performance for County: 3 for 18 D.R. Hayward v. Essex (NWBT) 1983
Best bowling performance against County: 3 for 19 N.A. Foster for Essex (NWBT)1983
Best attendance: 2,500 v. Lancashire (NWBT) 1991

HOW TO GET THERE AND WHERE TO STAY AND OTHER INFORMATION

Details as for Bournemouth within Hampshire C C C section.

Herefordshire

Founded   9 January 1991
Colours   Red and Azure
Crest   Lion with three lines and bull
President   J.E. Chadd
Chairman   T.J. Goodwin
Secretary   P. Sykes
Team secretary   E. Jenkins
Captain   R. Skyrme
Scorer/statistician   G. Wood
Address   The Mews House, Mordiford, Herefordshire HR1 4LN
Telephone 0432 870491 (Home) 0432 276461 (Office)
Minor Counties Rapid Cricketline   0891 567519

ACHIEVEMENTS

Minor County Championship   Initial Season 1992
Minor County Holt Knockout Cup Competition   Initial Season 1992

GROUNDS

Brockhampton C C, The Parks, Near Brockhampton Court Hotel,
Brockhampton. (No Telephone); Dales C C, F.H. Dale and Company
Sports Ground, Leominster. (No Telephone); Hereford C C, Hereford
City Sports Club, Racecourse Cricket Ground, Grandstand Road,
Hereford. Telephone: 0432 273098.

Hertfordshire

Founded 8 March 1876
Colours Blue, green and yellow
Crest White hart
President C.V.L. Marques
Chairman R.G. Simons
Secretary D.S. Dredge
Assistant secretary (Minor Counties)
Match manager J. Hind
Captain D.S. Surridge
Scorer/statistician Mrs J. Hind
Address 'Trevellis', 38 Santers Lane, Potters Bar, Hertfordshire EN6 2BX
Telephone 0707 58377 (Home) 071 359 3579 (Office)
Minor Counties Rapid Cricketline 0891 567519

ACHIEVEMENTS

Minor County Championship Champions (4) 1936, 1975, 1983 and 1990
Minor Counties Championship Final Winners (1) 1990; finalists (1) 1989
Minor County Holt Knockout Cup Competition Winners (1) 1984; finalists (2) 1986 and 1989
Gillette Cup Quarter-finalists (1) 1976
National Westminster Bank Trophy 2nd Round (1) 1991

GROUNDS

Bishop's Stortford C C, Cricketfield Lane, Bishop's Stortford. Telephone: 0279 654463; Cheshunt C C, Albury Ride, Cheshunt, Waltham Cross. Telephone: 0992 23920; Hertford C C, Balls Park, Mangrove Road, Hertford. Telephone: 0992 51983; Hitchin Town C C, Lucas Lane, Hitchin. Telephone: 0462 4468; Letchworth C C, Letchworth Corner, Letchworth. Telephone: 0462 64530; Old Merchant Taylors C C, Durrants, Croxley Green, Rickmansworth. Telephone: 0923 773014; Potters Bar C C, The Walk, Potters Bar. Telephone: 0707 54801; St Albans C C, Clarence Park, Clarence Road, St Albans. Telephone: 0727 50388; Shenley C C, Shenley Park, Shenley. (No Telephone); Stevenage C C, London Road, Stevenage. Telephone: 0438 51075; Tring Park C C, Pound Meadow, Station Road, Tring. Telephone: 0442 823080; Watford Town C C, Woodside, Horseshoe Lane, Garston, Watford. Telephone: 0923 672283; West Herts C C, 8 Park Avenue, Watford. Telephone: 0923 29239.

Lincolnshire

Founded 28 September 1906
Colours Gold and green
Crest A Lincoln imp
President W.H.L. Brown
Chairman E.N. Hamilton
Secretary D.H. Wright
Team secretary T.F. Bates
Captain J.D. Love
Scorers K.S.C. Trushell and A.D. Shorter
Statistician K.S.C. Trushell
Address 18 Spencers Road, Ketton, Stamford, Lincolnshire PE9 3SE
Telephone 0780 720326 (Home)
Minor Counties Rapid Cricketline 0891 567519

ACHIEVEMENTS

Minor County Championship Champions (1) 1966
Minor County Holt Knockout Cup Competition Finalists (1) 1990
Gillette Cup 2nd Round (2) 1971 and 1974
National Westminster Bank Trophy 1st Round (4) 1983, 1988, 1990 and 1991

GROUNDS

Bourne C C, Abbey Lawn, Bourne. Telephone: 077842 3641; Cleethorpes C C, Chichester Road, Cleethorpes. Telephone: 0472 61271; Grimsby (Ross Sports) C C, Weelsby Road, Grimsby. Telephone: 0472 56952; Grimsby Town C C, Augusta Street, Grimsby. (No Telephone); Lincoln (Lindum Sports Association) C C, St Giles Avenue, Wragby Road, Lincoln. Telephone: 0522 26592; Long Sutton C C, Paradise Field, Park Road, Long Sutton. Telephone: 0406 362943; Market Rasen C C, Rasen Park, Gallomore Lane, Market Rasen. Telephone: 0673 842171; Scunthorpe and Appleby Frodingham Works C C, Brumby Hall, Ashby Road, Scunthorpe. Telephone: 0724 843024; Sleaford C C, London Road, Sleaford. Telephone: 0529 303368; Stamford and Burghley Park C C, Burghley Park, Stamford. Telephone: 0780 62484.

Norfolk

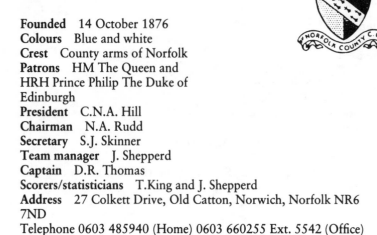

Founded 14 October 1876
Colours Blue and white
Crest County arms of Norfolk
Patrons HM The Queen and
HRH Prince Philip The Duke of
Edinburgh
President C.N.A. Hill
Chairman N.A. Rudd
Secretary S.J. Skinner
Team manager J. Shepperd
Captain D.R. Thomas
Scorers/statisticians T.King and J. Shepperd
Address 27 Colkett Drive, Old Catton, Norwich, Norfolk NR6
7ND
Telephone 0603 485940 (Home) 0603 660255 Ext. 5542 (Office)
Minor Counties Rapid Cricketline 0891 567519

ACHIEVEMENTS

Minor County Championship Champions (3) 1905, 1910 and
1913; joint champions (1) 1895
Minor County Holt Knockout Cup Competition Winners (1) 1986
Gillette Cup 1st Round (4) 1965, 1968, 1969 and 1970
National Westminster Bank Trophy 1st Round (6) 1982, 1983,
1984, 1985, 1990 and 1991

GROUNDS

Norwich C C, Lakenham Cricket Ground, Lakenham, Norwich.
Telephone: 0603 624754; North Runcton C C, The Green, 5 New
Road, North Runcton, King's Lynn. Telephone: 0533 840281 (call
box at edge of ground); Postwick C C, Cricket Ground, Postwick.
(No Telephone); Swardeston C C, The Common, Swardeston.
Telephone: 0508 70010.

Northumberland

Founded   December 1895
Colours   Red, green and gold
Crest   County shield of Northumberland
President   R.B. Caller
Chairman   R.W. Smithson
Secretary   A.B. Stephenson
Assistant secretary   F.J. Farmer
Team secretary   J.T. Hounsome
Captain   M.E. Younger
Groundsman   B. Marshall
Scorers   J.H. Jude and P. Lough
Statistician   J.H. Jude
Address   County Cricket Ground, Osborne Avenue, Jesmond,
Newcastle-Upon-Tyne NE2 1JS
Telephone 091 281 2738 (Club Office)
Minor Counties Rapid Cricketline   0891 567519

ACHIEVEMENTS

Minor County Championship   Champions (2) 1924 and 1925
Minor County Holt Knockout Cup Competition   Semi-finalists (1)
1984
Gillette Cup   2nd Round (1) 1977
National Westminster Bank Trophy   1st Round (4) 1984,

GROUNDS

Newcastle-upon-Tyne (Jesmond), County Cricket Ground, Osborne
Avenue, Jesmond, Newcastle-upon-Tyne. Telephone: 091 281 0775;
Ashington C C, Cricket Ground, Ashington, Northumberland.
Telephone: Directory Enquiries.

Oxfordshire

Founded   14 December 1921
Colours   Blue, gold and magenta
Crest   An ox crossing a ford
President   J.E.O. Smith MBE
Chairman   D. Banton
Secretary   J.E.O. Smith MBE
Assistant secretary   A.W. Moss
Team manager   A. Crossley
Captain   P.J. Garner
Scorer   K. Brighton
Statistician   J. Lawton-Smith
Address   2 The Green, Horton-cum-Studley, Oxford, Oxfordshire
OX9 1AE
Telephone 0867 35687 (Home)
Minor Counties Rapid Cricketline   0891 567519

ACHIEVEMENTS

Minor County Championship   Champions (4) 1929, 1974, 1982 and
1989
Minor Counties Championship Final   Winners (1) 1989; finalists (1)
1986
Minor County Holt Knockout Cup Competition   Semi-finalists (1)
1990
Gillette Cup   2nd Round (1) 1975
National Westminster Bank Trophy   1st Round (9) 1981, 1983,
1984, 1985, 1986, 1987, 1989, 1990 and 1991

GROUNDS

Cowley St John C C (Christchurch Cricket Ground, Iffley Road).
   Other grounds that have been used since 1969 are: Aston Rowant
C C, The Butts Way, Kingston Blount, Aston Rowant. (No
Telephone); Banbury Twenty Club, Daventry Road, Banbury.
Telephone: 0295 3757; Oxford, Morris Motors C C, Morris Motors
Sports Ground, Cresent Road, Cowley, Oxford. Telephone: 0865
77777; Oxford, Pressed Steel Fisher C C, Pressed Steel Fisher Sports
Ground, Horspath Road, Cowley, Oxford. Telephone: 0865 78493;
Oxford, St. Edward's School, Woodstock Road, Oxford. Telephone:
0865 54411; Shipton-under-Wychwood C C, Burford Road,
Shipton-under-Wychwood. Telephone: 0993 831337.

Oxford – Christchurch (Cowley St John C C)

Christchurch Cricket ground is the home of Cowley St John Cricket
Club who were founded in 1887. The first club match was on 9 June

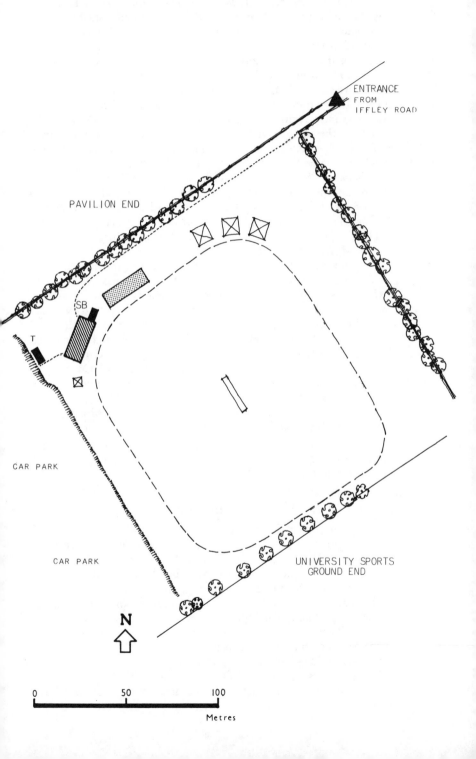

ENTRANCE
FROM
IFFLEY ROAD

PAVILION END

SB

T

CAR PARK

CAR PARK

UNIVERSITY SPORTS
GROUND END

N

0   50   100

Metres

1888 when a match was staged with Headington Quarry C C. Later that season the club was amalgamated with Cowley Road United C C.

The club moved in 1889 to the ground of Magdalen College sited near Magdalen Road and Howard Street. After the 1902 season the clubs tenancy of the Magdalen ground ceased and a move was made to the Oriel College ground. In 1904 Cowley St John were founder members of the Oxford Cricket League and the club won the league for the first time in 1909. Later grounds used included the University College and Lincoln College grounds, prior to the move to Christchurch in Iffley Road.

In 1959 the Minor Counties C A staged a fixture with the touring Indians on the ground. Cowley St John C C entered the National Club knockout competition for the first time in 1970. In 1974 the club joined the Cherwell Cricket League which was renamed the Bucknell and Ballard League in 1979. The club usually have annual fixtures with Aston Rowant, Oxford Nondescripts, Oxford University Authentics, Banbury Twenty, Swindon Town, Horton House, Leighton Buzzard and Headington. The present county club matches are organized off the field by Morris Honey and Andrew Moss.

Of recent years 1984 and 1986 proved to be the most successful for the club with league and cup victories. The ground has been used by Oxfordshire C C C for Minor County Championship matches and for knockout fixtures with counties in the Gillette Cup and National Westminster Bank Trophy. The Minor Counties C A have also staged fixtures in the Benson & Hedges Cup against Surrey and Glamorgan during the 1980s. Over forty-five players have represented the club and county including: R.A. Evans, P.J. Garner, T.A. Lester, I.J. Curtis, P.M. Jobson and S.N.V. Waterton, who also represented Kent, Northamptonshire and Lancashire.

On 24 June 1992 Oxfordshire C C C will host Lancashire in the 1st round of the National Westminster Bank Trophy competition.

ADDRESS   Cowley Saint John Cricket Club, The Pavilion, Christchurch Cricket Ground, Iffley Road, Oxford, Oxfordshire.
TELEPHONE PROSPECTS OF PLAY   0865 43992

DESCRIPTION OF GROUND AND FACILITIES

The only entrance to the ground is from Iffley Road and car parking is available within the ground for 250 cars. Street parking is also available within easy walking distance in the neighbouring area to the south of central Oxford. The only permanent buildings are the pavilion/clubhouse, scorebox and groundsman's store.

The majority of facilities for matches are temporary and include raised seating, loose chairs, sponsors' marquees, refreshment/beer tents and a small club shop sited in a tent. The members' enclosure is in front of the pavilion and toilets are available in the clubhouse and in some temporary buildings around the playing area.

The ground is flat and is defined by a rope with some advertising boards. The dimensions of the playing area are 144 metres by 126 metres.

When required, the TV camera/commentary box is positioned at the southern end of the ground. The radio commentary point is sited near the pavilion.

GROUND RECORDS AND SCORES

LIMITED-OVERS MATCHES
Highest innings total for County: 226 *v*. Gloucestershire (NWBT) 1989
Highest innings total against County: 269 for 3 by Gloucestershire (NWBT) 1989
Lowest innings total for County: 132 *v*. Kent (NWBT) 1990
Lowest innings total against County: 154 for 2 by Glamorgan (NWBT) 1981
Highest individual innings for County: 92 S.N.V. Waterton *v*. Gloucestershire (NWBT) 1989
Highest individual innings against County: 100 n.o. V.J. Wells for Kent (NWBT) 1990
Best bowling performance for County: 2 for 39 D.A. Gallop *v*. Glamorgan (NWBT) 1981
Best bowling performance against County: 5 for 31 M.A. Nash for Glamorgan (NWBT) 1981
Best attendance: 2,750 *v*. Gloucestershire (NWBT) 1989

HOW TO GET THERE

Rail Oxford (BR), 2 miles.
Bus Oxford Buses from Cornmarket Street; Oxford Bus 52 links BR Oxford Station with Cornmarket Street; take bus to Headington via Iffley Road for ground (Telephone: 0865 711312).
Car From north: A34, A423 or A43, signposted Oxford city centre, then follow signs for Cowley, take Cowley Road, then follow Iffley Road from roundabout at south side of Magdalen Bridge for Christchurch Cricket Ground. From east: A40, signposted Oxford and city centre, then follow A4165 for Christchurch Cricket Ground situated 0.5 mile south of the city centre in Iffley Road. From west: A40, A420 or A34, signposted Oxford and city centre, then as north. From south: M40 junction 7, then follow A40 signposted Oxford and city centre, at roundabout, before Magdalen Bridge, take second exit for Iffley Road, signposted Cowley for Christchurch Cricket Ground.

WHERE TO STAY AND OTHER INFORMATION

Cotswold Lodge (0865 512121), The Randolph (0865 247481), Eastgate Hotel (0865 248244), plus many others in Oxford.

Disabled Areas No special area, request suitable position. Car parking available within the ground.
Local Radio Station(s) BBC Radio Oxford (95.2 MHz FM/1485 KHz MW), Radio 210 (102.9 MHz FM/1431 KHz MW).
Local Newspaper(s) Oxford Mail, Oxford Times.

Shropshire

Founded   28 June 1956
Colours   Blue and gold
Crest   Loggerhead (county crest)
President   V.M.E. Holt
Chairman   M.P.T.W. Jones
Secretary   N.H. Birch
Team manager   R.G. Hamar
Captain   J. Foster
Scorer/statistician   J.A. Jones
Address   8 Port Hill Close, Shrewsbury, Shropshire SY3 8RR
Telephone 0743 3650 (Home) 0743 212314 (Office)
Minor Counties Rapid Cricketline   0891 567519

ACHIEVEMENTS

Minor County Championship   Champions (1) 1973
Minor County Holt Knockout Cup Competition   Semi-finalists (1) 1986
Gillette Cup   1st Round (3) 1974, 1976 and 1978
National Westminster Bank Trophy   2nd Round (1) 1984

GROUNDS

St George's C C (St George's Cricket Ground, Church Road).

Other grounds that have been used since 1969 are: Bridgnorth C C, High Town, Bridgnorth. Telephone: 0746 24919; Ludlow C C, The Burway, Ludlow. Telephone: 0584 3244; Market Drayton C C, Cricket Ground, Market Drayton. Telephone: 0995 2786; Newport C C, Audley Avenue, Newport. Telephone: 0952 810403; Oswestry C C, Cricket Ground, Oswestry. Telephone: 0691 3006; Perkins C C, Albert Road, Shrewsbury. Telephone: 0743 52135; Shrewsbury C C, London Road, Shrewsbury. Telephone: 0743 63655; Shifnal C C, Shrewsbury Road, Shifnal. (No Telephone); Wellington C C, Orleton Park, Wellington. Telephone: 0952 51539; Wem C C, Soulton Road, Wem. Telephone: 0939 34680; Wroxeter C C, Cricket Ground, Uppington. Telephone: 0952 86214.

Telford (St George's C C)

CLUB HISTORY AND DESCRIPTION OF
GROUND AND FACILITIES

The St George's Cricket Club was found on 9 March 1922. The initial ground was the football ground which is now again the cricket field. The St George's Recreation committee purchased the field close to the Vicarage Drive in 1924 and four years later in 1928 the club lost some of

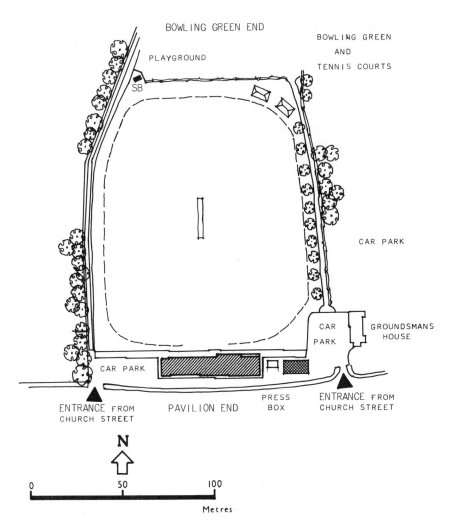

BOWLING GREEN END

PLAYGROUND

BOWLING GREEN
AND
TENNIS COURTS

SB

CAR PARK

CAR
PARK

GROUNDSMANS
HOUSE

CAR PARK

PRESS
BOX

ENTRANCE FROM
CHURCH STREET

PAVILION END

ENTRANCE FROM
CHURCH STREET

N

0   50   100

Metres

its best cricketers due to the Lilleshall Company closing down its new works yard. During the first season after the Second World War the St George's C C were unbeaten throughout the season. In 1948 the club entered a National Cricket Competition organized by the News Chronicle and the club were runners-up. During the same season a new pavilion was constructed and was opened by the Earl of Granville who was at that time the Governor of Northern Ireland. In 1949 Wolverhampton Wanderers Football Club the FA Cup winners staged a friendly match with the cricket club and the cup was on view to locals during the match.

Thanks to proceeds from this match, the club was able to install electricity into the pavilion and make other ground improvements, including a new scoreboard and re-laying of some of the square.

The playing dimensions are 132 metres by 109 metres. St George's

Cricket Club play in the Furrows Shropshire Cricket League and field three XIs throughout the season. A new clubhouse was constructed in 1964 thanks to fund-raising schemes, and during the same year the club moved to the new ground at St George's Cricket Ground, where the playing and club facilities are something to be admired by everybody who visits this ground, whether player or spectator.

Since 1984 the ground has been used by Shropshire C C C for National Westminster Bank Trophy 1st round matches, with the highlight being the defeat of Yorkshire, thanks to a splendid performance from the former Pakistani Test captain Mushtaq Mohammad. Other matches have been staged with Hampshire, Leicestershire and Northamptonshire. Middlesex will be the visitors for the National Westminster Bank Trophy 1st round tie in 1992 and if defeated, Shropshire will host Ireland or Durham in the 2nd round several weeks later. St George's C C had a disappointing period during the 1980s but it is hoped that better times are only around the corner.

ADDRESS St George's Cricket Club., The Pavilion, St George's Cricket Ground, Church Road, St George's, Telford, Shropshire.
TELEPHONE NUMBER PROSPECTS OF PLAY 0952 612911

GROUND RECORDS AND SCORES

LIMITED-OVERS MATCHES
Highest innings total for County: 229 for 5 v. Yorkshire (NWBT) 1984
Highest innings total against County: 294 for 5 by Hampshire (NWBT) 1988
Lowest innings total for County: 170 v. Northamptonshire (NWBT) 1985
Lowest innings total against County: 192 by Yorkshire (NWBT) 1984
Highest individual innings for County: 89 M.R. Davies v. Leicestershire (NWBT) 1989
Highest individual innings against County: 130 G. Cook for Northamptonshire (NWBT) 1985
Best bowling performance for County: 4 for 47 A.S. Barnard v. Northamptonshire (NWBT) 1985
Best bowling performance against County: 2 for 24 C.L. Smith for Hampshire (NWBT) 1988
Best attendance: 5,000 v. Yorkshire 1984

HOW TO GET THERE

Rail Telford (BR), 2 miles.
Bus From surrounding areas including Shrewsbury, Newport, Bridgnorth and Wolverhampton to Telford.
Car From north: A442 or A518, signposted Telford, then follow signs for County Cricket at St George's for Church Road and cricket ground. From east: M54 junction 5, signposted Telford A442, then

follow signs for County Cricket at St George's, then as north. From west: A5 then M54 junction 5, signposted Telford A442, then as east and north. From south: A442, A464 or A4169, signposted Telford, then follow signs for County Cricket at St George's, then as north.

WHERE TO STAY AND OTHER INFORMATION

Prince Rupert Hotel (0743 236000), Madeley Court Hotel (0952 680068), The Shrewsbury Hotel (0743 231246).

Disabled Areas   No special area, request suitable position.
Local Radio Station(s)   BBC Radio Shropshire (756 KHz FM/397 MHz MW).
Local Newspaper(s)   Shropshire Star, Shrewsbury Chronicle.

Staffordshire

Founded   24 November 1871
Colours   Green and gold
Crest   Stafford knot
President   H. Leigh
Chairman   W. Jolley
Secretary   W.S. Bourne
Captain   N.J. Archer
Scorer/statistician   R. McDuell
Address   10 The Pavement, Brewood, Stafford, Staffordshire ST19 9BZ
Telephone 0902 850325 (Home) 0902 23038 (Office)
Minor Counties Rapid Cricketline   0891 567519

ACHIEVEMENTS

Minor County Championship   Champions (7) 1906, 1908, 1911, 1920, 1921, 1927 and 1991
Minor Counties Championship Final   Winners (1) 1991
Minor County Holt Knockout Cup Competition   Winners (1) 1991
Gillette Cup   2nd Round (2) 1973 and 1978
National Westminster Bank Trophy   1st Round (8) 1984, 1985, 1986, 1987, 1988, 1989, 1990 and 1991

GROUNDS

Stone C C (Priory Road, Stone). Refer to Minor Counties Cricket Association section for history of ground and details of facilities.

Other grounds that have been used since 1969 are: Bignall End C C, Boon Hill Road, Bignall End, Stoke-On-Trent. Telephone: 0782 720514; Brewood C C, Deansfield, Four Ashes Road, Brewood, Stafford. Telephone: 0902 850395; Burton-on-Trent, Ind-Coope Brewery, Sports and Social Club Ground, Belvedere Road,

Burton-on-Trent. Telephone: 0283 45320 Ext. 2957; Knypersley
C C, Tunstall Road, Knypersley. Telephone: 0782 513304; Leek C C,
Highfield, Macclesfield Road, Leek. Telephone: 0538 383693;
Longton C C, Trentham Road, Blurton, Stoke-on-Trent. Telephone:
0782 312278; Meir Heath C C, Willow Lane, Meir Heath,
Stoke-on-Trent. Telephone: 0782 394502; Norton C C, Newford,
Smallthorne, Near Burslem, Stoke-on-Trent. Telephone: 0782
882290; Old Hill C C, Cradley Heath, West Midlands. Telephone:
0384 66827; Walsall C C, Cricket Ground, Walsall, West Midlands.
Telephone: Directory Enquiries.

Suffolk

Founded   August 1932
Colours   Maroon and old gold
Crest   Rampant lion
President   J.N. Stevens
Chairman   M.D. Corke
Secretary   T. Pound
Team manager   C. Rutterford
Captain   R.E. East
Scorer/statistician   G. Hirst
Address   94 Henley Road, Ipswich, Suffolk IP1 4NJ
Telephone 0473 213288 (Home) 0473 232121 (Office)
Minor Counties Rapid Cricketline   0891 567519

ACHIEVEMENTS

Minor County Championship   Champions (3) 1946, 1977 and 1979
Minor Counties Championship Final   Finalists (1) 1985
Minor County Holt Knockout Cup Competition   Quarter-finalists
(1) 1986
Gillette Cup   2nd Round (1) 1979
National Westminster Bank Trophy   1st Round (9) 1981, 1983,
1984, 1985, 1986, 1987, 1988, 1989 and 1990

GROUNDS

Bury St Edmunds C C, The Victory Ground, Nowton Road, Bury St
Edmunds. Telephone: 0284 754592; Copdock C C, Old London
Road, Copdock, Ipswich. Telephone: 0473 86752; Framlingham
College, Woodbridge, Framlingham. Telephone: 0728 773436;
Ipswich School, Ivry Street, Ipswich. Telephone: 0473 215455;
Mildenhall C C, Wamil Way, Mildenhall. Telephone: 0638 712018;
Ransomes/Reavell Sports Club, Sidegate Avenue, Ipswich. Telephone:
0473 76134.

Wales

Founded 1969
Colours Green, red and yellow
Crest Duke of Edinburgh's crown above
three dragons
Patron HRH The Prince Philip Earl
of Merioneth
President The Rt. Hon. Lord Gibson-Watt
MC, DL, PC, BA
Chairman S. York
Secretary Bill Edwards
Team manager L. Roberts
Captain A.C. Puddle
Scorers M. Williams/H.S. Evans
Statistician H.S. Evans
Address 59a King Edward Road, Swansea, Wales SA1 4LN
Telephone 0792 462233 (Home) and (Office)
Minor Counties Rapid Cricketline 0891 567519

ACHIEVEMENTS

Minor County Championship 8th 1990
Minor County Holt Knockout Cup Competition 1st Round (1)
1989

GROUNDS

Ammanford C C, Ammanford Park, Ammanford. Telephone: 0269
4988; Barry C C, Cricket Ground, Barry. Telephone: Directory
Enquiries; Brecon College, Christ College Sports Ground, Brecon.
Telephone: Directory Enquiries; Cardiff C C, Sophia Gardens,
Cardiff. Telephone: 0222 43478; Colwyn Bay C C, Penrhyn Avenue,
Rhos-on-Sea, Colwyn Bay. Telephone: 0492 44103; Ebbw Vale C C,
Eugene Cross Park, Ebbw Vale. Telephone: 0495 512157; Llanelli
C C, Stradey Park, Denham Avenue, Sandy, Llanelli. Telephone:
0554 773721; Neath C C, The Gnoll, Dyfed Road, Neath.
Telephone: 0639 3719; Northop Hall C C, Northop Hall Cricket
Ground, Near Mold. Telephone: 0244 810461; Penarth C C, Cricket
Ground, Penarth. Telephone: 0222 708402; Pontarddulais C C,
Pontarddulais Park, Pontarddulais. No Telephone; Swansea C C, The
Pavilion, St Helen's Cricket Ground, Bryn Road, Swansea.
Telephone: 0792 466321; Usk C C, Cricket Ground, Usk. Telephone:
0291 33274; Welshpool C C, Cricket Ground, Welshpool.
Telephone: 0938 3274; Wrexham C C, Cricket Ground, Wrexham.
Telephone: Directory Enquiries.

Wiltshire

Founded   January 1893
Colours   Green
Crest   White horse
President   A. Cooper
Chairman   N.A. Peters
Secretary   C.R. Sheppard
Team/commercial manager   E.G. Burston
Captain   B.H. White
Scorer/statistician   Mrs S. Pitman
Address   45 Ipswich Street, Swindon, Wiltshire SN2 1DB
Telephone 0793 511811 (Home) 0793 484598 (Office)
Minor Counties Rapid Cricketline   0891 567519

ACHIEVEMENTS

Minor County Championship   Champions (2) 1902 and 1909
Minor County Holt Knockout Cup Competition   Semi-finalists (1)
1983
Gillette Cup   1st Round (5) 1964, 1965, 1969, 1972, and 1973
National Westminster Bank Trophy   1st Round (6) 1983, 1984,
1987, 1988, 1989 and 1990

GROUNDS

British Rail (Swindon) C C, British Rail Sports Ground, Shrivenham,
Swindon. Telephone: 0793 523019; Chippenham C C, Hardenhuish
Park, Chippenham. Telephone: 0249 657867; Devizes C C, Devizes
Sports Club Ground, London Road, Devizes. Telephone: 0380
723763; Malmesbury C C, Cricket Ground, Malmesbury. Telephone:
0666 824275; Marlborough School, School Grounds, Marlborough.
No Telephone; South Wiltshire C C, Bemerton Sports Ground,
Wilton Road, Salisbury. Telephone: 0722 20806; Swindon C C,
County Ground, County Road, Swindon. Telephone: 0793 523088;
Trowbridge C C, County Ground, Timbrell Street, Trowbridge.
Telephone: 0225 752538.

OTHER GROUNDS

COMBINED SERVICES CRICKET ASSOCIATION

NATIONAL CRICKET ASSOCIATION
(Young England and England Amateur XI)

FLOODLIT CRICKET
(Sheffield)

Combined Services Cricket Association

Founded   1945
Colours   Blue
Crest   Royal Navy, Army and RAF badges
Secretary   Lt. Col. R. Hitchcock
Captain   Flt. Lt. A.W.J. Spiller (RAF)
Scorer   WO1 D. Smith
Address   c/o Army Sport Control Board, 'M' Block, Clayton
Barracks, Aldershot, Hampshire
Telephone 0252 24431 Ext. 3570 (Office)

GROUNDS

Aldershot, Army Sports Cricket Ground, Aldershot. Telephone 0252
24431; United Services Portsmouth, United Services Officers Sports
Ground, Burnaby Road, Portsmouth, Hampshire. Telephone: 0705
22351.

National Cricket Association
(Young England and England Amateur XI)

Founded   1977
Colours   Blue and yellow
Crest   Lion beneath 'NCA'
Chairman   J.D. Robson
Chief executive   K.V. Andrew
Secretary   T. Bates
Team manager (Young England)   G.J. Saville
Captain   (chosen on a match basis)
Scorer   (chosen on a match basis)
Address   Lord's Cricket Ground, St John's Wood Road, London
NW8 8QZ.
Telephone 071 289 6098 (Office) 071 289 4766 (Competitions
Office)
Facsimile 071 266 4022
Rapid Cricketline County Scores 0891 567500

GROUNDS

Lord's Cricket Ground (St John's Wood Road, London) for matches
against MCC, Combined Services, MCC Young Cricketers and
matches against Young Touring Teams. Luton Town C C (Wardown
Park) will be used to stage the England Amateur XI *v*. Pakistan match
in 1992. Please refer to Marylebone C C and Northamptonshire
chapters for details. In addition a number of the other county grounds
and club venues are used for matches throughout the country.

Floodlit Cricket
Sheffield (Don Valley Stadium)

Don Valley Stadium is located on the north-eastern outskirts of the City of Sheffield close to the Meadowhall Shopping Development and the Sheffield Arena near to junction 34 of the M1 Motorway.

Don Valley is without doubt the most modern British Stadium constructed since Wembley in the 1920's and in accordance with the latest Government Safety at Sports Ground Act. On 14–15 August 1991 floodlit cricket was staged for the first time at the Don Valley Stadium thanks to the Sheffield City Council and a Yorkshire businessman from Scarborough, Mr Don Robinson. Under the bright lights Australian style in South Yorkshire, two matches were staged by Yorkshire C C C wearing all sky blue and a World XI and an International XI wearing yellow and red.

The site of the Stadium was previously occupied by the Brown Bayleys Steel Works and initial works involved grouting shallow mine workings, bell pits and drifts dating back over 200 years.

The construction of the purpose built Don Valley complex was completed in 1990 by Management Contractors, R.M. Douglas Construction at a cost of £30m and the Architects were the Sheffield City Council Design and Building Services Department. Predominately a steel supported structure, the stadium was designed to reflect Sheffield's tradition for manufacturing steel.

In 1990 Don Valley hosted the McVities Challenge meeting when some 23,000 spectators attended the athletics meeting (which was the biggest crowd for a UK athletics meeting in 30 years) to watch Peter Elliot set a new UK all-comers record for the 1,500m in a time of 3:32:69. A similar event was staged in the autumn of 1991. In July 1991 the World Student Games (Universaide) was staged at Don Valley Stadium with some 6,000 competitors from 130 countries taking part.

Stadium facilities include a full-Olympic Standard Athletic 10 lane running track, 10 straight sprint lanes and an infield suitable for first-class team sports (i.e. football, rugby and cricket). An all seater ground capacity of 25,000 includes a covered Grandstand (10,000) and open seating of (15,000). Training facilities are also available for warm-up. The wicket is artificial and is sited in the centre of the outfield with some further artificial turf around the edge of the playing area which is laid on the running tack, so as to make a circular cricket oval. There are four different levels of floodlighting which provide excellent lighting for television coverage of events.

Mr Don Robinson, one of the organisers of the inaugural event, stated that floodlit Day/Night cricket competition will be staged at the Sheffield venue for the next five years. On 10–13 August 1992 a knock-out tournament will be staged with four counties including semi-finals of Nottinghamshire *v.* Durham and Yorkshire *v.* Lancashire with a Final and a Rest of the World XI versus An England XI under lights.

Ground records at Don Valley Stadium include batting achievements by Richard Blakey and Kapil Dev. Fine spells of bowling have been

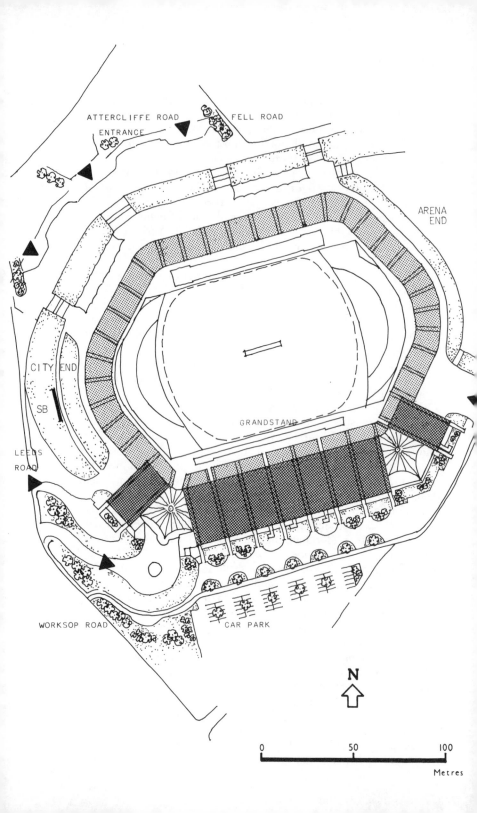

ATTERCLIFFE ROAD
FELL ROAD
ENTRANCE

ARENA
END

CITY END

SB

LEEDS
ROAD

GRANDSTAND

WORKSOP ROAD
CAR PARK

N

0   50   100

Metres

achieved by Chris Pickles, Sachin Tendulkar and Maninder Singh. The record crowd was 15,983 for the first floodlit match with a crowd of 8,763 attending the second match.

ADDRESS Don Valley Stadium, Sheffield International Stadium, Worksop Road, Sheffield, South Yorkshire S9 3TL.
TELEPHONE NUMBER PROSPECTS OF PLAY 0742 560607

DESCRIPTION OF GROUND AND FACILITIES

Entry to the Don Valley Stadium Complex is from Worksop Road and there is ample car parking surrounding the stadium for cricket matches. The main, permanent building used for cricket matches is the substantial grandstand which is on the south side of the ground. A good view of play can be obtained from all seating areas. All seating is permanent and of the plastic tip-up variety in different colours. The scoreboard is electronic and is the same that is used for athletics meetings and is sited at the City End. A number of facilities are provided for refreshments and bars. A souvenir shop is located close to the main entrance. There are 134 toilets in the Grandstand area and 42 toilets in the concrete terracing area.

The TV camera/commentary box position is at the City End directly above and behind the sightscreen, although a secondary camera is also sited at the Arena End of the ground. The press and scorers are located in separate rooms on the 4th floor of the Grandstand close to the hospitality boxes. VIP Lounges and Executive Boxes are available for sponsors on the 3rd floor of the Grandstand and facilities include bars and catering areas. The ground capacity is 25,000 which is all-seated. The playing area is 100 metres by 100 metres and is defined by a rope and advertising boards.

The players' changing rooms are situated within the athletes' changing facilities and entry to the stadium is gained next to the marathon gate.

GROUND RECORDS AND SCORES

LIMITED-OVERS MATCHES
Highest innings total for County: 215 for 7 v. World XI 1991
Highest innings total against County: 214 by World XI 1991
Lowest innings total for County: 150 v. International XI 1991
Lowest innings total against County: 152 for 2 by International XI 1991
Highest individual innings for County: 73 R. Blakey v. World XI 1991
Highest individual innings against County: 76 Kapil Dev for World XI 1991
Best bowling performance for County: 4 for 44 C. Pickles v. World XI 1991

Best bowling performance against County: 3 for 11 Maninder Singh
for International XI 1991
Best attendance: 15,938 Yorkshire *v.* World XI 1991

HOW TO GET THERE

Rail   Sheffield Midland (BR) 2 miles, Meadowhall (BR) 0.5 miles.
Bus   South Yorkshire Traction and South Yorkshire Transport 17
from High Street (Sheffield to Hillsborough), 69 Flat Street (Sheffield
to Rotherham), 130 from High Street (Sheffield to Rotherham via
Brinsworth), 208/209/287 from Central Exchange Platform K1
(Sheffield to Maltby and Dinnington), 44 from Church Street
(Sheffield to Greasborough), 2/59 from Meadowhall (City Centre via
Ecclesall/Crosspool) and 72 from Meadowhall (to Chesterfield).
(Telephone: 0742 755655/768688.)
Car   From north: M1 junction 34, follow signs Sheffield and
Meadowhall Shopping Centre for Don Valley Stadium Complex, take
second turn off at roundabout and at end of the viaduct take the fifth
turn off the roundabout, then follow Attercliffe Common which
becomes Attercliffe Road for approximately 1.5 miles. Don Valley
Stadium is situated on your left hand side after the Broughton Lane
traffic lights with the main entrance off Worksop Road. From east:
M1 junction 33, follow A630 signposted Sheffield and city centre,
then as north. From west: A57 follow signs Sheffield and city centre,
then follow A61 signposted Barnsley to Wicker Arches. Proceed
under the Wicker Arches, along Saville Street, stay in right hand lane,
then take left in Attercliffe Road, which becomes Attercliffe
Common, Don Valley Stadium is situated on the right hand side after
the Stainforth Road traffic lights with the main entrance off Worksop
Road. From south: M1 junction 34, follow signs Sheffield, take
second turn off the roundabout, then follow Attercliffe Common
which becomes Attercliffe Road for approximately 1.5 miles. Don
Valley Stadium is situated on your left hand side after the Broughton
Lane traffic lights with the main entrance off Worksop Road.

WHERE TO STAY AND OTHER INFORMATION

Grosvenor House Hotel (0742 20041), Hallam Tower Forte Post
House (0742 686031), Hotel St George (0742 583811).

Disabled Areas   Special area available, request suitable position. A
number of disabled toilets are available within the stadium and some
special car parking zones.
Local Radio Station(s)   BBC Radio Sheffield (104.1 MHz FM/1035
KHz MW), Radio Hallam (103.4 MHz FM/1548 KHz MW).
Local Newspaper(s)   Sheffield Star, Yorkshire Post, The Morning
Telegraph.

Bibliography

Homes of Sport: Cricket, N. Yardley and J. M. Kilburn, 1952
The Watney Book of Test Match Grounds, I. Peebles, 1967
Famous Cricket Grounds, L. W. Meynell, 1951
Grounds of Appeal, A. Sampson, 1980
Homes of Cricket, G. Plumtree, 1987
Wisden Cricketers' Almanack 1864–1991
The Wisden Book of Cricket Records
The Wisden Book of County Cricket
The Wisden Book of Test Cricket 1877–1989
The Wisden Book of One Day International Cricket 1971–1985
Various histories of Cricket Grounds
Various histories of County Cricket Clubs
Various histories of Cricket Clubs
Various County Annuals, Yearbooks and Brochures
Various Minor Counties' Yearbooks and Brochures
Various Irish, Scottish and League Cricket Conference Yearbooks and Brochures
Various Association of Cricket Statisticians and LOCIG Publications
Wisden Cricket Monthly
The Cricketer and *The Cricketer Quarterly*
Cricket News
Cricket Extra
Playfair Cricket Monthly
Cricket International
Cricket World and The Club Cricketer
Minor Counties Cricket Quarterly

About the Author

William Powell was born in Lahore in 1964 and has had a life-long interest in cricket. He has represented King's Langley C C, where he was a committee member at 16, Watford Town C C, The Cricket Society XI and the Gentlemen of Hertfordshire. During family holidays he has also represented Budleigh Salterton C C and Rye C C.

He has been an avid collector of cricket books and memorabilia since the age of 13. In 1987 he was the Official Scorer to the Pakistan Test team and in 1988 was appointed by the Test & County Cricket Board to act as Official Scorer to the Sri Lankan tourists.

He is a member of Glamorgan, Hertfordshire, Lancashire, Middlesex, Surrey, Warwickshire and Yorkshire CCCs, Minor Counties CA, The Cricket Society, The Cricket Writers' Club, The Association of Cricket Statisticians and the Cricket Memorabilia Society.

William Powell has undertaken studies in Building Management at the Polytechnic of the South Bank, London and Trent Polytechnic, Nottingham. He is a corporate member of The Chartered Institute of Building and is a member of the Hertfordshire Centre and Eastern Region of the Institute.

The author is currently working on a Guide To International Cricket Grounds. Other Books by the author include *The Wisden Guide To Cricket Grounds* (1989) and Association of Cricket Statisticians' *Cricket Grounds of Middlesex* (1990).